Flyfisher's Guide to™

Wisconsin & Iowa

Fishing Titles Available from Wilderness Adventures Press, Inc.™

Flyfishers Guide to™

Flyfisher's Guide to Alaska
Flyfisher's Guide to Arizona
Flyfisher's Guide to the Big Apple
Flyfisher's Guide to Chesapeake Bay
Flyfisher's Guide to Colorado
Flyfisher's Guide to Connecticut
Flyfisher's Guide to the Florida Keys
Flyfisher's Guide to Freshwater Florida
Flyfisher's Guide to Idaho
Flyfisher's Guide to Mexico
Flyfisher's Guide to Montana
Flyfisher's Guide to Michigan
Flyfisher's Guide to Minnesota
Flyfisher's Guide to Missouri & Arkansas
Flyfisher's Guide to Nevada
Flyfisher's Guide to the New England Coast
Flyfisher's Guide to New Mexico
Flyfisher's Guide to New York
Flyfisher's Guide to the Northeast Coast
Flyfisher's Guide to Northern California
Flyfisher's Guide to Northern New England
Flyfisher's Guide to Oregon
Flyfisher's Guide to Saltwater Florida
Flyfisher's Guide to Tennessee
Flyfisher's Guide to Texas
Flyfisher's Guide to the Texas Gulf Coast
Flyfisher's Guide to Utah
Flyfisher's Guide to Virginia
Flyfisher's Guide to Washington
Flyfisher's Guide to Western Washington Lakes
Flyfisher's Guide to Wisconsin & Iowa
Flyfisher's Guide to Wyoming
Flyfisher's Guide to Yellowstone National Park

On the Fly Guide to™

On the Fly Guide to the Northwest
On the Fly Guide to the Northern Rockies

Best Fishing Waters™ Books

California's Best Fishing Waters
Colorado's Best Fishing Waters
Idaho's Best Fishing Waters
Montana's Best Fishing Waters
Oregon's Best Fishing Waters
Washington's Best Fishing Waters

Micro SD Cards with GPS Waypoints

Montana's Best Fishing
Colorado's Best Fishing
Washington's Best Fishing

Anglers Guide to™

Complete Anglers Guide to Oregon
Angler's Guide to the West Coast
Saltwater Angler's Guide to Southern California

Field Guide to™

Field Guide to Fishing Knots

Fly Tying

Go-To Flies™

Flyfishing Adventures™

Montana

Trout Adventures™

North America

Flyfisher's Guide to™

Wisconsin & Iowa

John Motoviloff

Flyfisher's Guide to™ Series

Belgrade, Montana

Also by this author, Driftless Stories: Outdoors in Southwest Wisconsin; Wisconsin Wildfoods

Published by Wilderness Adventures Press, Inc.™
45 Buckskin Road
Belgrade, MT 59714
866-400-2012
Website: www.wildadvpress.com
email: books@wildadvpress.com

Third Edition 2012

Printed in South Korea

ISBN 978-1-932098-87-7 (8-09206-98877-4)

Table of Contents

Acknowledgments xv
Introduction 1
Fly Fisher Guide to Wisconsin and Northeast Iowa 1
Wisconsin 5
Wisconsin 7
Wisconsin Fishing Licenses and DNR Offices 10
License Fees 10
DNR Offices 11
Important Flies for Wisconsin 14
Nymphs and Wet Flies 15
Dry Flies 15
Streamers 16
Terrestrials 16
A Short List of Important Fly Patterns 17
Southwest Wisconsin: Driftless Country Streams 19
Black Earth Creek 25
Mount Vernon Creek 29
Story Creek 33
Allen Creek 36
Token Creek 36
The Madison Chain of Lakes 37
Lake Mendota 38
Lake Monona 39
Lake Waubesa 39
Lake Wingra 39
Capital City Bluegills 42
The Yahara River 43
Hub City: Madison 48
Otter Creek 51
Trout Creek 55
The Blue River 57
Castle Rock Creek 61
Big Spring Creek 65
Galena River 65
The Little Platte 67
Other Rivers of Southwest Wisconsin 67
Twin Valley Lake 68
Hub City: Dodgeville 69
Bear Creek 71
Willow Creek 74
West Branch of the Pine River 77
West Branch of Mill Creek 79
Fancy Creek 83
Hub City: Richland Center 85

- Crooked Creek ... 87
- Richland Creek ... 89
- Borah Creek ... 89
- Big Green River ... 93
- Wisconsin River: Prairie du Sac to Prairie du Chien ... 95
- Hub City: Boscobel ... 100
- The Kickapoo River ... 103
  - Main Stem ... 103
  - Fishing the Main Stem: Headwaters to Gays Mills ... 104
  - The Middle Stretch ... 109
  - Gays Mills to Wauzeka: Primitive Bottomlands ... 109
- West Fork of the Kickapoo River ... 113
- Big Guide, Little Water: A Streamside Profile of Guide Bob Blumreich ... 116
- Tainter Creek ... 119
- Hub City: La Farge ... 119
- Timber Coulee ... 123
- Rullands Coulee ... 127
- Bohemian Valley Creek ... 129
- The Mississippi River ... 131
  - La Crosse to Dubuque ... 131
- Hub Cities: Westby and Coon Valley ... 133
- Hub Cities: La Crosse and Onalaska ... 135
- Hey, There's a Mouse in My Trout! ... 137

West-Central Wisconsin: The Western Upland ... 139
- The Rush River ... 142
- Trimbelle River ... 147
- The Willow River ... 148
- Kinnickinnic River ... 153
- The Red Cedar River ... 157
- Eau Galle River ... 161
- Knapp Creek and Seven Pines Lodge ... 162
- Hub City: Hudson ... 163
- Hub City: River Falls ... 165
- Eau Claire/Chippewa Falls Area Brook Trout Streams ... 167
  - Elk Creek ... 167
  - Duncan Creek ... 169
  - McCann Creek ... 169
- Chippewa River ... 171
  - Flambeau River to Chippewa Falls ... 171
  - Eau Claire to the Juncture with the Mississippi River ... 174
- Buffalo River ... 177
- Hub City: Eau Claire ... 180
- Trempealeau River and Branches ... 183
- Beaver Creek ... 184
- Lake Pepin ... 185
- Mississippi River ... 189
  - Trempealeau to Lake Pepin ... 189

Hub City: Trempealeau . . . 191
The Black River . . . 193
The La Crosse River . . . 194
Fishing the Cranberry Flowages . . . 195
Potters Flowage . . . 196
Hub City: Black River Falls . . . 198
Central Wisconsin: The Sand Counties . . . 201
Lawrence Creek . . . 204
Neenah Creek . . . 208
Caves Creek . . . 209
Mecan River . . . 209
Tagatz Creek . . . 214
Chaffee Creek . . . 214
Big Roche a Cri Creek . . . 215
Dell Creek . . . 218
Devil's Lake . . . 219
Mason Lake . . . 221
Wolf Lake . . . 222
Parker Lake . . . 222
Deep Lake . . . 224
Crooked Lake . . . 224
Buffalo Lake . . . 225
Lake Puckaway . . . 225
Columbia Lake . . . 226
Rocky Run Creek . . . 226
Rowan Creek . . . 228
Hub City: Westfield . . . 231
Pine River . . . 233
Willow Creek (Waushara) . . . 236
West Branch of the White River . . . 238
Main Branch of the White River . . . 241
Soules Creek . . . 241
Wisconsin Rapids Area Ditches . . . 242
A Profile of Wisconsin Rod Maker Don Schroeder . . . 243
Petenwell Flowage . . . 247
Castle Rock Flowage . . . 248
Wisconsin River . . . 251
Castle Rock Lake Dam to Prairie du Sac Dam . . . 251
Twin Lake . . . 251
Hub City: Wild Rose . . . 254
The Tomorrow River . . . 257
The Upper Tomorrow River . . . 257
The Middle Tomorrow River . . . 258
The Lower Tomorrow (Waupaca) River . . . 259
Whitcomb Creek . . . 262
Flume Creek . . . 262

- Hub City: Waupaca 263
- Northwest Wisconsin: Indianhead Country 267
  - Streams of the Bayfield Peninsula 271
    - Sioux River 273
    - Pikes Creek 273
    - Cranberry River 273
    - Flag River 273
  - Chequamegon Bay 275
  - Trout Lakes of the Chequamegon National Forest 279
    - Wanoka Lake 279
    - Perch Lake 279
    - Beaver Lake 280
    - Perch Lake 280
    - Pole Lake 280
    - Patterson Lake 280
    - Twin Lake 280
  - The White River 281
  - Hub City: Bayfield 285
  - Hub City: Ashland 286
  - The Bois Brule River 289
  - Blueberry Creek 295
  - Nebagamon Creek 295
  - Iron River 297
  - The Namekagon River 299
    - Lake Namekagon 299
    - The Namekagon River—Cable to Hayward 302
    - The Namekagon River—Hayward to St. Croix River 304
  - Lake Owen 306
  - Hub City: Brule 307
  - Chippewa Flowage and Upper Chippewa River System 309
    - The Making of the Flowage 309
    - The Chippewa Flowage 312
    - East and West Forks of the Chippewa River 313
    - Main Branch of the Chippewa River 313
  - Ghost, Teal, and Lost Land Lakes 315
  - Lac Courte Oreilles and Little Lac Courte Oreilles 316
  - Grindstone Lake 316
  - Windigo Lake 316
  - Sand Lake 316
  - The Flambeau River 316
    - Turtle-Flambeau Flowage and the North Fork 317
    - South Fork of the Flambeau River 320
    - Flambeau River to Confluence with Chippewa River 320
  - St. Croix River 321
  - Lakes of Burnett County 325
    - Round Lake 325
    - Spirit Lake 325

Mud Hen Lake 325
Wood Lake....325
Devils Lake 325
Conners Lake 326
Webb Lake....326
Small Lakes of Washburn County....326
Little Devil Lake and Big Devil Lake 326
Pavlas Lake 326
Ripley Lake 326
Potato Lake 326
Bean Lake 328
Cable Lake....328
Dunn Lake....328
Casey Lake....328
Balsam Lake 328
Red Cedar Lake 328
Bear Lake....329
Chetek Chain of Lakes....329
Hub City: Hayward....330
Northeast Wisconsin: The Northern Highland 333
Plover River 337
Prairie River....341
The Little Wolf River....345
Hub City: Wausau....348
East Branch of the Eau Claire River 351
Spring Ponds of Langlade County 352
Lakes of Langlade County 352
McGee Lake 352
Rollingstone Lake 352
Enterprise Lake 354
Moccasin Lake 354
Upper Post Lake and Lower Post Lake 354
Wolf River....355
Oconto River 361
North and South Branches of the Oconto River....361
Mainstem Oconto River....364
The Lower Oconto River....365
Pike River 367
Lakes and Streams of the Nicolet National Forest Area....369
Spectacle Lake 369
Stevens Lake 370
Lost Lake 370
Keyes Lake....370
Sea Lion Lake 370
Sand Lake 370
Anvil Lake 370
Julia Lake 371

Pine Lake 371
Little Rice Lake 371
Lake Lucerne 371
Richardson Lake 371
Roberts Lake 375
Townsend Flowage 375
Archibald Lake 375
Boot Lake 375
Boulder Lake 375
Middle Inlet Creek 375
Beaver Creek 375
The Wausaukee River 376
Shawano Lake 376
Lake Noquebay 377
Hub City: Antigo 378
Lakes of the Northern Highlands American Legion State Forest 381
Anne Lake 382
Crystal Lake 382
Firefly Lake 382
Wildwood Lake 382
Fallison Lake 383
Plum and West Plum Lakes 383
Shannon Lake 383
Muskellunge and Snipe Lakes 383
Allequash Springs 383
Escanaba and Nebish Lakes 383
Pallette Lake 384
Starrett Lake 384
Frank Lake 384
Nixon Lake 384
Razorback Lake 384
Lonetree Lake 384
Partridge Lake 385
Stormy Lake 385
Lac du Lune 385
Carol and Madeleine Lakes 385
Wildcat Lake 385
Manitowish River 386
Presque Isle Lake 386
Larger Area Lakes 386
Wisconsin River 389
Butternut Lake 392
Spread Eagle Chain of Lakes 393
Deerskin River 393
Boundary Brule River 396
Menominee River 397
South Branch of the Pemebonwon River 400

North Branch of the Pemebonwon 400
Popple, Pine, and Peshtigo Rivers 403
Popple River 403
Pine River 404
Peshtigo River 405
Oneida County Lakes 407
Perch, Squash, Crescent, and Emma Lakes 407
Indian and Jennie Weber Lakes 407
Birch, Bearskin, and Little Bearskin Lakes 407
Hub City: Boulder Junction 408
Eastern Wisconsin and Lake Michigan Coast 411
Root River 415
Pike River 421
Oak Creek 422
Milwaukee River 423
The Menomonee River 427
Fox River 427
Kettle Moraine State Forest–Southern Unit 428
Paradise Springs 428
South Branch of the Scuppernong River 430
Ottawa Lake 430
Rice Lake 430
Bluff Creek 430
Kettle Moraine State Forest—Northern Unit 432
Mauthe Lake 432
Auburn Lake 432
Forest Lake 432
Butler Lake 432
Long Lake 432
Crooked lake 433
Lake 15 Creek 433
The Crawfish River 433
Rock Lake 434
Hub City: Milwaukee 435
Port Washington Harbor 437
Pigeon River 439
Sheboygan River 441
Hub City: Sheboygan 446
The Manitowoc River 449
East Twin River and West Twin River 451
Hub City: Two Rivers 455
Kewaunee River 457
Ahnapee River 461
Spring-Run Steelhead Streams 465
Fischer Creek 465
Silver Creek 465

Stony Creek 465
Hibbards Creek 467
Heins Creek 467
Hub City: Algoma 468
Fox River 470
De Pere to Green Bay 470
Neenah to De Pere 470
Door County Smallmouth Bass 471
Fishing Facts: 473
Door County Smallmouth Bass 473
Door County Inland Lakes 474
Forestville Flowage 474
Clark's Lake 474
Kangaroo Lake 474
Europe Lake 475
Mink River 476
Hub City: Bailey's Harbor 478
Northeast Iowa 481
Northeast Iowa: Trout on the Edge of the Prairie 483
The Law 484
Hot, Cold, and Dusty 485
Season and Regulations 485
Fishing Licenses 486
Bloody Run 487
Sny Magill 491
Paint Creek 493
Little Paint Creek 496
Hickory Creek 496
Hub City: Marquette/McGregor, IA & Prairie du Chien, WI 497
Yellow River 499
Clear Creek 503
Silver Creek 504
French Creek 504
Hub City: Lansing 508
Waterloo Creek 511
Trout Unlimited Efforts in the Driftless Area 514
Bear Creek 517
South Pine Creek 519
Pine Creek 521
Trout River 521
Trout Run 523
Upper Iowa River 525
Hub City: Decorah 526
Bohemian Creek 529
Turtle Creek, Spring Creek, and Cedar River 529
Otter Creek 530

Glovers Creek 531
Grannis Creek 531
Richmond Springs 535
Joy Spring 535
Maquoketa River 535
Ensign Creek 537
Spring Branch 539
Bailey's Ford 541
Fountain Spring 541
Little Turkey River 543
Turkey River 543
Hub City: Elkader 545
Bankston Creek 547
Upper Swiss Valley and Lower Swiss Valley of Catfish Creek 547
Big Mill Creek and Little Mill Creek 548
LAKES OF NORTHEAST IOWA 551
- Lake Hendricks 551
- Lake Meyer 551
- Frog Hollow Lake 551
- Lake Delhi 551

Iowa's Urban Trout Ponds 552
Put and Grow Streams 553
Mississippi River: Lansing to Dubuque 557
Hub City: Dubuque 558
Color Fly Plates 561
Top Wisconsin Flies 563
Fish of Wisconsin and Northeast Iowa 566
Fisheries Management and Catch-and-Release 583
Equipment Checklist 585
Resources 586
- Reservations for campgrounds in state parks and forests: 888-947-2757 586
- Internet Resources 586
- Conservation Organizations 587

Fly Shops & Sporting Goods Stores 588

The author plies the waters of a driftless area spring creek.

Acknowledgments

Thanks to all who helped with the Iowa material—DNR staff, anglers, and the kind chambers of commerce of Decorah and Elkader. Maybe this will help spread the word about Iowa's fine streams and rivers.

My wife Kerry kept the home fire burning. My daughter, Anne, provided more joy than I can ever repay. Without this support, nothing else would have worked.

As there's goodwill on the home front, so there is among anglers—guides and fly shop owners alike. Craig Amacker of Fontana Sports and Planet Trout Guide Service provided quality advice and photos; Todd Polacek of Madison Outfitters gave good advice on waters close to home and far away. Pat Ehlers of The Fly Fishers in Milwaukee is a fount of wisdom on Lake Michigan and warm waters throughout the state. Tim Landwehr of Tight Lines Fly Shop in De Pere gave excellent advice on Central Wisconsin flies and hatches, as well as copious photo support. Thanks to Bill Sherer of We Tie Fly Shop and Northern Adventure Guide Service, and to his brother Joe, for bringing me up to speed on Northern Wisconsin hatches and lakes. John Koch of Western Wisconsin Fly Fishing, Mike Alwin of Bob Mitchell's Fly Shop, and Andy Roth of Bentley Outfitters helped me understand western Wisconsin streams. Roger La Penter of Anglers All in Ashland told me all I need to know about catching everything that swims in Chequamegon Bay. Among the guides who gave advice are Bob Blumreich, Tom Ehlert, Drake Williams, Steve Cervenka, and David Barron. Thanks to Northwoods guides Steve Cervenka and Drake Williams who gave me good counsel on how to go after muskies and smallmouth with a fly rod. Thanks also to local sportsman's clubs and Trout Unlimited for good work on streams and for answering questions.

Thanks to the resident Irishman, Colm McCarthy, for good photos and for patience during car breakdowns. I only wish that smell would have been chicken curry cooking under the hood.

Thanks to Julie and Liz of Star Photo for their knowledge and help.

Chuck Johnson, Wilderness Adventures Press, Inc., deserves thanks for his guidance and work on this project.

Without the Wisconsin Department of Natural Resources, we'd have no fish to pursue and complain about. Special thanks to Dave Vetrano, Gene Van Dyck, Frank Pratt, Scott Ironside, Matt Coffaro, Cordell Manz, Rick Cornelius, Greg Kornely, and all the good fisheries people who answered my questions. Now that this book is finished, you won't have to hear my rambling messages on Monday morning. And thanks to Elward Engle for sage advice on Sand County streams.

Finally, thanks to my brother, Robert Pallitto, who converts feathers into flies and confused questions into succinct advice. And to Steve Miller and Matt Rogge, fine companions both on and off the stream. Thanks to Lee Strasheim for computer help. If I've forgotten anyone, it's only because so many have helped.

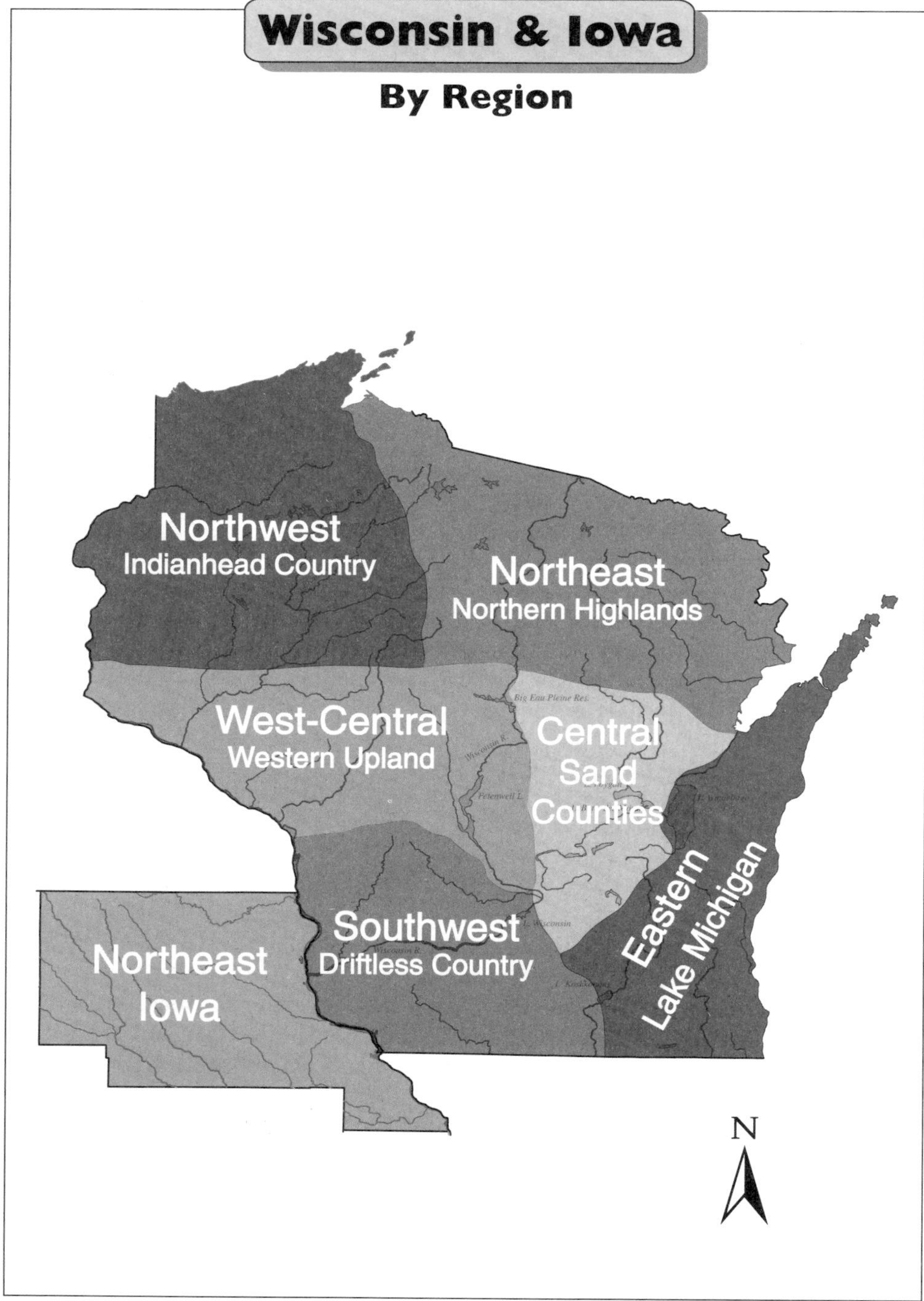
Wisconsin & Iowa
By Region
Northwest
Indianhead Country
Northeast
Northern Highlands
West-Central
Western Upland
Central
Sand
Counties
Southwest
Driftless Country
Northeast
Iowa
Eastern
Lake Michigan
Big Eau Pleine Res.
Wisconsin R.
Petenwell L.
N

Introduction

FLY FISHER GUIDE TO WISCONSIN AND NORTHEAST IOWA

At first glance, Wisconsin and Iowa—other than being neighbors—seem to have little in common. One is a verdant Great Lakes state flush with forest and stream, the other high-and-dry prairie and cornfield. In the former, a tavern adorns most every small-town corner; in the latter, watering holes are few and far between. And from a fisheries perspective, the one has 15,000 lakes—and a river around every bend—while the other has just a handful of lakes, mostly manmade, and a smattering of north-south rivers.

The reasons for fishing Wisconsin are obvious. Just about any kind of fishing experience can be had—casting a deer hair bug among lotus beds for fat largemouth, taking dark-backed brook trout from North Woods streams on a Pass Lake, stalking spring creek trout in the state's western Driftless area, even tussling with tackle-busting salmon and steelhead on Great Lakes tributaries.

While Iowa's border and interior rivers offer some important warmwater fishing for hardworking Iowans, the critical mass of quality waters is lacking to write a flyfisher's guide to the entire Hawkeye state. The state's hilly northeast corner is a different story.

This 120-mile swath of Hawkeye real estate between Dubuque and Decorah—extending about 40 miles to the west—forms the western edge of the trout-stream-rich Driftless or unglaciated area. Fifty streams are open to public fishing here. And Iowa's trout season runs year-round! That means you can enjoy golden autumn days streamside—watching waterfowl migrate along the Great River corridor—and warm (if you call 30 degrees warm) January days when wild turkeys are out scratching acorns in the snow and midges are just starting to come off. A handful of two-story fisheries on bluff-flanked rivers like the Turkey, Upper Iowa, and Yellow offer float trips full of possibilities—where a trout may grab your fly on one bend and a walleye at the next.

Things are only getting better on Iowa trout streams. It's part of Trout Unlimited's high-priority Driftless Area Restoration Effort (also known as D.A.R.E.), which brings with it needed funds and stream improvements. And the Iowa DNR, via habitat improvement and stocking of wild-strain fish, has quadrupled the number of wild-trout-supporting streams from a half dozen to nearly forty over the last 25 years.

So whether you choose to take your longrod to the Badger state for variety or the Hawkeye state for its unique year-round trout season, you can't go wrong.

Tight lines—I'll see you out on the stream!

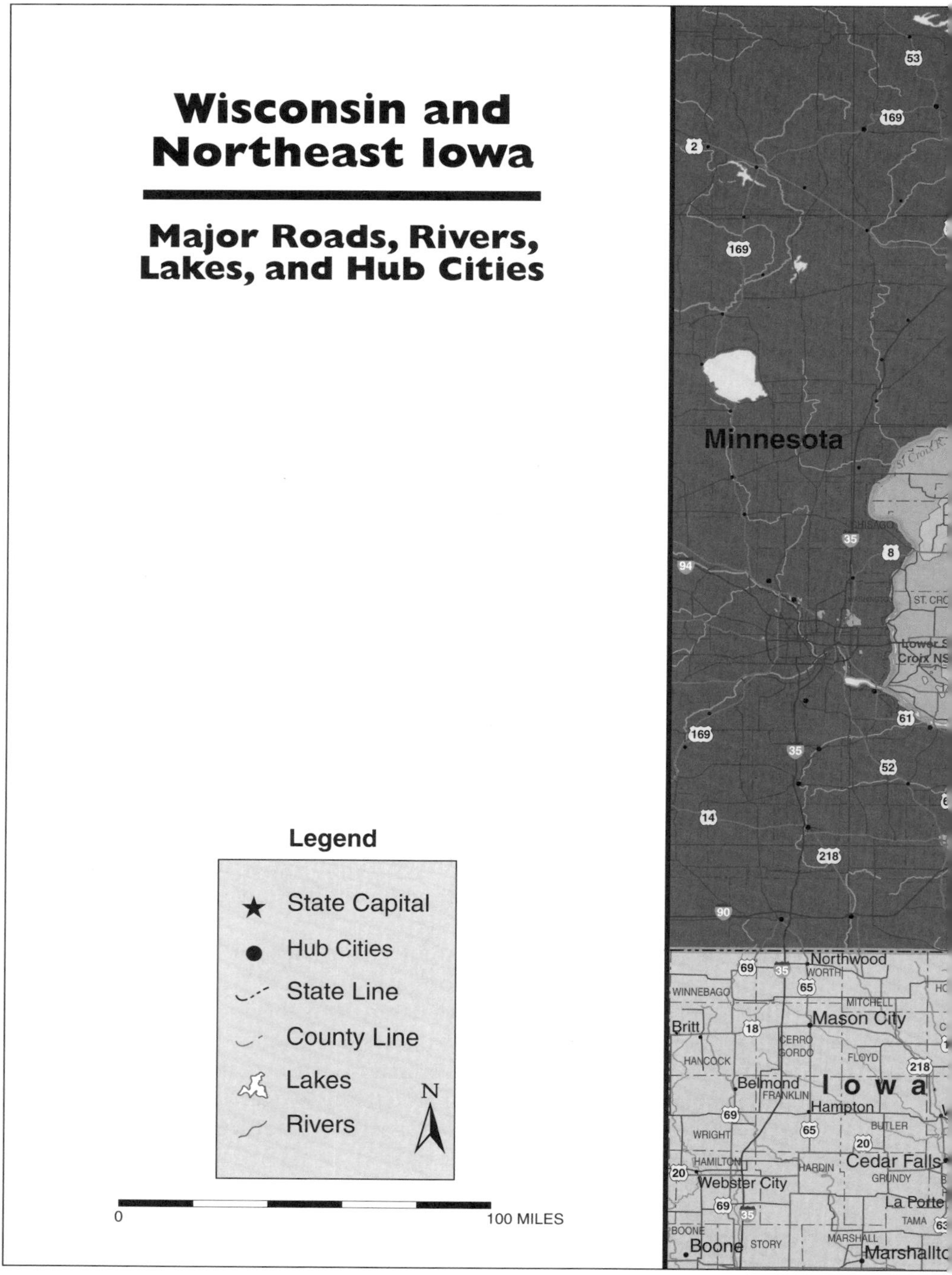

Wisconsin and Northeast Iowa

Major Roads, Rivers, Lakes, and Hub Cities

Legend

- State Capital
- Hub Cities
- State Line
- County Line
- Lakes
- Rivers

N

0 100 MILES

Minnesota

Iowa

Northwood

Mason City

Britt

Belmond

Hampton

Cedar Falls

Webster City

La Porte

Boone

Marshalltown

Lake Superior
Michigan
Wisconsin
Illinois
L. Michigan
Poplar
BAYFIELD
Ashland
Mason
Cable
ASHLAND
IRON
WASHBURN
Hayward
Park Falls
SAWYER
PRICE
RUSK
Rice Lake
Ladysmith
VILAS
Eagle River
ONEIDA
Rhinelander
Tomahawk
FLORENCE
FOREST
MARINETTE
LINCOLN
Merrill
LANGLADE
Antigo
Menominee
MENOMINEE
OCONTO
TAYLOR
CHIPPEWA
Bloomer
Eau Claire
CLARK
MARATHON
SHAWANO
Big Eau Pleine Res.
Clintonville
Green Bay
DOOR
KEWAUNEE
Kewaunee
PEPIN
EAU CLAIRE
Mondovi
Neillsville
WOOD
PORTAGE
WAUPACA
OUTAGAMIE
BROWN
BUFFALO
JACKSON
Black River Falls
TREMPEALEAU
Waupaca
Appleton
WAUSHARA
L. Poygan
WINNEBAGO
CALUMET
MANITOWOC
L. Winnebago
Petenwell L.
Holmen
Tomah
JUNEAU
ADAMS
MARQUETTE
MONROE
LACROSSE
Mauston
GREEN LAKE
FOND DU LAC
SHEBOYGAN
Wisconsin Dells
Waupun
VERNON
Viroqua
RICHLAND
Baraboo
SAUK
DODGE
Kewaskum
OZAUKEE
COLUMBIA
Richland Center
Columbus
Port Washington
WASHINGTON
WINNESHIEK
Decorah
ALLAMAKEE
CRAWFORD
Madison
DANE
Wauwatosa
Milwaukee
JEFFERSON
IOWA
Effigy Mounds NM
Prairie Du Chien
GRANT
Dodgeville
Oregon
Waukesha
West Allis
WAUKESHA
MILWAUKEE
Lancaster
CLAYTON
Guttenberg
Platteville
Evansville
GREEN
Janesville
ROCK
WALWORTH
Racine
RACINE
KENOSHA
Kenosha
LAFAYETTE
Dubuque
DELAWARE
DUBUQUE
Monticello
JONES
LINN
JACKSON
Marion

Wisconsin

Wisconsin

By anyone's definition, Wisconsin has a lot of water. It's sometimes referred to as having three coasts—Lake Michigan to the east, Lake Superior to the north, and the Mississippi to the west. In addition, there are over 10,000 miles of trout streams and some 15,000 inland lakes. For decades, fly fishing was synonymous with trout fishing. While there's a wonderful tradition of going after trout with a fly rod, this is a limited definition, especially with the variety of warmwater species available here in Wisconsin. I've done my best to cast a net around the best of the state's fly fishing waters—trout streams and all the others.

There are smallmouth streams in the southwest corner of the state that are perfectly suited to fly fishing. There are thousands of lily pad and lotus backwaters statewide waiting to be cast over with a rubber spider or deerhair bass bug, where the only sound is the swish of your backcast and the sound of your paddle. The rich coastlines and bays of Lakes Michigan and Superior and their tributaries see runs of anadromous trout and salmon as well as alewife-fatted smallmouths.

Then there are the anonymous rivers, those that lie off the beaten track and are perhaps visited only a few times a year by chugging downstream in a beat-up old jonboat. You won't find stupendous hatches (or trout, for that matter) on most of them, but you will find hackberry and willow trees concealing a wilderness right beneath your nose. The names of these waters provide a poetical tribute to the tribes and creatures of the region: Chippewa, Kickapoo, Crawfish, Yahara, Fox. Drop your streamer next to that deadfall and who knows what will grab it. It may be a smallmouth, northern pike, walleye, channel catfish, or any of a number of other rough fish that make their home here.

Did I mention trout streams? There's a bewildering array of these as well. Spring creeks seep up through the limestone bed of southwestern Wisconsin's unglaciated Driftless Country and rattle through tight hollows called coulees. There are some amazingly large trout in these small, fertile waters. I contracted a spontaneous case of "buck fever" on one such fish when I went to net a 5-pound specimen and found my arm unable to move. The Sand County region, made famous in Aldo Leopold's *Sand County Almanac,* is underlain by a giant aquifer called the Central Sands, from which cold, clean water seeps up and forms many fine trout streams like the Mecan, White, and Willow (all favorites for the Hex hatch) as well as countless tangled little brook and brown trout rivulets. To the west of these are the streams of the Western Upland, an area that experienced early glacial drift yet retains many of the features of the Driftless area to the south—big trout, century-old dairy farms, and water seeping up over limestone. The Rush and Kinnickinnic are standouts here.

Then there is the great piney Northeast, where the wild Wolf and Pine, Pike, and Popple flow. This is definitive freestone water. Interestingly, these long watersheds, despite brutal winter and northern latitude, heat up precipitously, sending trout scurrying for headwaters and spring seeps come summer. Check your stream thermometer to make sure the water you're fishing is cold enough. Otherwise concentrate your efforts on smaller waters like Pemebonwon and Wausaukee in Marinette County. Department of Natural Resources (DNR) studies have shown trout traveling as much as 40 miles in these large river systems to seek out cold water during summer.

Finally, there's the wild northwest corner of the state where famed waters like the Namekagon and Brule drain into Lake Superior. These are both terrific waters, with the Brule and other Superior streams hosting runs of wild trout and salmon. And don't neglect Lake Michigan's tributaries in eastern Wisconsin for first-rate salmon and steelhead fishing. This book is organized according to these geographic divisions (see map on page xvi): Southwest (Driftless Country), West-Central (Western Upland), Central (Sand County), Northwestern (Indianhead Country), Northeastern (Northern Highland), and Eastern (Lake Michigan coast).

What will you need for your fishing sojourns in the Badger state? This book is a good start—with detailed descriptions of streams and lakes, maps, hatch charts, and hub cities with all the travel information you will need. Part of the fun of fishing in Wisconsin is adjourning to its taverns and supper clubs afterwards to recount the joys and sorrows of days spent streamside. You can't always count on the trout, but you will be able to find a decent Manhattan, good local brews, Friday fish fries, and great steak.

If you're traveling in from the coasts, you'll notice that your dollar goes pretty far in rural Wisconsin. My wife and I bought a cabin outside Gays Mills ten years ago for $10,000—and the locals thought we got ripped off. To find your way around the back roads of the state, a copy of the *Wisconsin Atlas and Gazetteer*, available at most bookstores and gas stations, is indispensable. USGS topographical maps help put a finer point on things.

Hotels and motels in the Hub City sections of this book are rated according to price: $ means under $50; $$ means $50 to $75; and $$$ means over $75. Add another $25 to each category for cabins.

A number of DNR publications are a must for fishing in Wisconsin—and they're free. Ask for a copy of the *Wisconsin Trout Fishing Regulations and Guide* and the *Guide to Wisconsin Hook and Line Fishing Regulations.* The former lists all the managed trout water in the state and the regulations for each. You will want to have a current copy of both documents on hand when fishing. The trout guide is useful because it highlights trout streams in colors corresponding to each regulation category. At a glance you can tell which waters are trout water and what regulations govern them.

Category 1 streams are marked in black; there is no minimum size and 10 trout (only 5 rainbows and browns) may be kept; this category was phased out in the 2003-2004 season. Category 2 streams are marked in yellow; minimum size is 7 inches and 5 trout may be kept. Category 3 streams are marked green; 3 trout may be kept with a minimum size of 9 inches. Category 4 is blue; 3 trout may be kept; browns and rainbows must be at least 12 inches and brook trout must be at least 8 inches. Category 5 streams are marked red; they are special regulations streams and often managed for catch-and-release.

When warmwater fishing, look up the county in which you are fishing in the *Guide to Wisconsin Hook and Line Fishing Regulations.* This will advise you of special regulations that differ from the general state regulations (which are also listed). As rules change from year to year, you should always review a current copy before fishing.

Mercury and PCBs are long-term problems in Wisconsin. Years of almost unregulated industry have allowed them to build up in the food chains in many river and lake systems. PCBs are principally a concern along the Great Lakes. Mercury, the result of airborne dust from power plants and other industries, finds its way into waterways all over the state. Get a copy of *Choose Wisely: A Healthy Guide for Eating Fish in Wisconsin.* Women of childbearing years and children should be especially mindful. Large gamefish, such as walleye, bass, and pike, which feed high up on the food chain, tend to accumulate the largest concentrations of PCBs and mercury. Panfish are a safer bet. Trout from inland streams are generally safe to eat.

There are still lots of magical places left. Let's keep it that way!

Wisconsin Fishing Licenses and DNR Offices

The Wisconsin Department of Natural Resources has a very complete website containing electronic versions of DNR publications, maps of wildlife areas, and all season dates: http://www.dnr.state.wi.us/org/water/fhp/fish.

You can purchase your license online at dnr.wi.gov.

Trout season on most inland waters runs from the first Saturday in May to September 30; an early artificials-only, catch-and-release season runs during March and April (only single, barbless hooks are permitted). Consult page 1 of *Wisconsin Trout Fishing Regulations and Guide* for details and exceptions during this early season. (Certain waters in the Sand Counties and Northeast are closed to angling.) Fishing trout and salmon on Lakes Superior or Michigan or their tributaries requires a Great Lakes Trout and Salmon Stamp; fishing trout on inland waters requires a Trout Stamp and a Wisconsin Fishing License. Fishing for warmwater species requires only a Wisconsin Fishing License.

License Fees

- Wisconsin Resident Fishing License (1 year): $20
- Wisconsin Resident Reduced-Rate Fishing License (for 16 and 17 years olds and those over 65 years of age): $7
- Wisconsin Nonresident Fishing License (1 year): $50
- Wisconsin Nonresident Fishing License (15 day): $28
- Wisconsin Nonresident Fishing License (4 day): $24
- Wisconsin Nonresident Fishing License (1 day): $10
- Wisconsin Inland Trout Stamp (residents and nonresidents): $10
- Great Lakes Trout and Salmon Stamp (residents and nonresidents): $10
- Two-Day Great Lakes Sports Fishing License (residents and nonresidents): $14

DNR Offices

Northern Region

Northern Region Co-Headquarters
Rhinelander DNR
107 Sutliff Avenue
Rhinelander, WI 54501
715-365-8900

Northern Region Co-Headquarters
Spooner DNR
810 W. Maple Street
Spooner, WI 54801
715-635-2101

Antigo DNR
Box 310
1635 Neva Road
Antigo, WI 54409
715-627-4317

Barron DNR
1418 E. LaSalle Street
Barron, WI
715-537-5046

Brule DNR
6250 S. Ranger Road
P.O. Box 125
Brule, WI 54820
715-372-4866

Cumberland DNR
1341 Second Avenue
P.O. Box 397
Cumberland, WI 54829
715-822-3590

Mercer DNR
3291 State House Circle
P.O. Box 588
Mercer, WI
715-456-2240

Park Falls DNR
875 South Fourth Avenue
P.O. Box 220
Park Falls, WI
715-762-3204

Peshtigo DNR
101 N. Ogden Road
P.O. Box 127
Peshtigo, WI
920-582-5000

Superior DNR
1705 Tower Avenue
Superior, WI 54880
715-392-7988

Washburn DNR
203 E. Bayfield
Washburn, WI
715-373-6165

Woodruff DNR
8770 County Highway J
Woodruff, WI 54568
715-356-5211

Natural Resources Center
HC 1; Box 81
Florence, WI 54121
715-528-4400

West-Central Region

West-Central Region Headquarters
1300 West Clairemont
Box 4001
Eau Claire, WI 54702
715-839-3771

Alma DNR
P.O. Box 88, Courthouse
Alma, WI 54610
608-685-6222

Baldwin DNR
Suite 104 990 Hillcrest
Baldwin, WI 54002
715-684-2914

Black River Falls DNR
910 Highway 54
Black River Falls, WI 54615
715-284-1400

Friendship DNR
Highway 13, Box 100
Friendship, WI 53934
608-339-3385

Kickapoo Valley Reserve
505 N. Mill Street
La Farge, WI 54639
608-625-2960

La Crosse DNR
3550 Mormon Coulee Road
La Crosse, WI 54601
608-785-9000

Mead Wildlife Area
S. 2148 Highway S
Milladore, WI 54454
715-457-6771

Menominee DNR
Highway 29 and Brickyard Road
Menominee, WI
715-232-1517

Necedah National Wildlife Refuge
W7996 20th Street West
Necedah, WI
608-565-2551

Neillsville DNR
400 Hewett Street
Neillsville, WI 54456
715-743-5135

Sandhill Wildlife Area
County Highway X
P.O. Box 156
Babcock, WI 54413
715-884-2437

Viroqua DNR
220 Airport Road
Viroqua, WI 54665
608-637-3938

Wisconsin Rapids DNR
473 Griffith Avenue
Wisconsin Rapids, WI 54494
715-421-7800

Northeast Region

Northeast Region Headquarters
1125 N. Military Avenue
P.O. Box 10448
Green Bay, WI 54307
920-492-5800

Appleton DNR
Agricultural Services Center
3369 W. Brewster Street
Appleton, WI 54914
920-832-1804

Berlin DNR
Box 343
Berlin, WI 54914
920-361-3149

Horicon DNR
1210 N. Palmatory Street
Horicon, WI 53032
920-485-3012

Manitowoc DNR
1314 Highway 310
Manitowoc, WI 54220
920-683-4926

Oshkosh DNR
905 Bay Shore Drive
Oshkosh, WI 54903
920-424-3050

Plymouth DNR
W5750 Woodchuck Lane
Plymouth, WI 53073
920-892-8756

Shawano DNR
647 Lakeland Drive
Shawano, WI 54166
715-524-2183

Wausaukee DNR
Highway C
Wausaukee, WI 54177
715-856-5146

Wautoma DNR
Highway 22
Wautoma, WI 54982
715-787-4686

South-Central Region

South-Central Region Headquarters
3911 Fish Hatchery Road
Fitchburg, WI 53711
608-275-3266

Madison DNR Information Center
101 S. Webster
Madison, WI 53707
608-266-2621

Dodgeville DNR
3448 Highway 23
Dodgeville, WI 53533
608-935-3368

Poynette DNR
N3344 Stebbins Road
Poynette, WI 53955
608-635-8123

Southeast Region

Southeast Region Headquarters
2300 N. Dr. Martin Luther King, Jr. Drive
Milwaukee, WI 53212
414-263-8500

Kettle Moraine State Forest-
Southern Unit
S91 W39091 Highway 59
Eagle, WI 53110
262-594-6200

Important Flies for Wisconsin

In fly fishing, anglers are often grouped into two camps: those who rely on fly selection and those who rely on fly presentation. Anglers of a certain level of skill will obviously borrow from both sides, but still there are those who will debate long and hard between which of the hundreds of flies to use from their box and those who will carefully move along the shadows of the streambank with a beat up fly box containing just a handful of flies, stalking their quarry as much as trying to entice them. I have always been of the second school. Part of this stems from where I do most of my fishing—the small, brushy coulees of southwest Wisconsin, where a careful approach is a must for taking trout. Mostly, however, I think it's a reflection of personality. Even for activities like woodworking, I prefer a few sturdy hand tools to a well-equipped workshop with lots of machinery. Don't let the fishing overwhelm the fishing, a friend of mine likes to say. Keep it simple. Have fun.

Yes, Wisconsin has 10,000 miles of trout water. Yes, the north is different from the south. Spring creeks are different from freestoners and the clear, sand-bottom waters of central Wisconsin. But trout are trout, after all, and what they eat varies not so much by kind as the degree of what is available. Mayflies, caddis, stoneflies, midges, terrestrials, and forage fish are present in most trout streams. How much of each a trout eats depends on the what's predominant in the stream and the size of the trout. The other important thing to keep in mind is that most of a trout's feeding takes place below the surface, and a mayfly or caddis nymph, passing by at a good clip in fast water, look very much alike.

Thus, I have a strong bias toward fewer flies that can imitate a wide variety of things over hundreds of excruciatingly exact patterns—and a bias for nymphs and wet flies over dry flies. While many, many more fly patterns will work in Wisconsin waters, the ones mentioned below should be in every fly box.

A Blue-Winged Olive pattern next to the real thing. (Tim Landwehr)

Nymphs and Wet Flies

My favorite nymph is the Hare's Ear. I like the Hare's Ear because it can be taken for just about anything a trout eats, particularly in faster water—a mayfly, stonefly, caddisfly, or dragonfly nymph, even a sowbug or scud. In every trout stream in the state, something that looks like a Hare's Ear will be present at all times of the year. Just as all puddle ducks will decoy to mallard decoys, so too all trout will take a Hare's Ear. This nymph pattern is usually tied weighted. If yours is unweighted, just clip micro shot above the fly to reach the desired depth.

The Prince Nymph is a fine all-around dark nymph. I like to fish them on the small side, size 14 or 16. An olive scud is a must for anyone fishing the limestone streams of the Driftless area or western Wisconsin stream like the Rush or Kinnickinnic and to a lesser extent the streams of the Central Sands region. These freshwater shrimp are legion in fertile limestone water and are a year-round source of food for trout. Midge and caddis larvae shouldn't be neglected either; use these in sizes 18 to 22, with red and green good color choices.

Wet flies, for some strange reason, seem to have fallen into relative disuse. One need only scan the color plates in Ray Bergman's 1938 classic, *Trout,* to see that this was not always the case. Of seventeen color plates depicting flies, eleven are devoted to wet flies. Dry flies seem as if they were an aberration in those days. With their swept-back wings, perhaps they were the precursor to modern-day emergers and spinners. A Leadwing Coachman fished with a slow retrieve will still take big trout in the doldrums of summer. Bergman exhorts the reader to let the fly remain at the end of the drift for some time—a minute would be a start—then to gather a loop of fly line between your thumb and index finger. Release that loop and repeat until you have retrieved the fly. Try this retrieve on bluegills first to get the hang of it, then use it on a trout stream. You will be surprised at the strikes it provokes. This is also an exceeding quiet way of fishing, almost like meditation. You'll be amazed at what you see when you do it. Trout swimming at your feet. Swallows making their home along the banks of the stream. A hummingbird perched on a laurel branch. While the Leadwing Coachman resembles a variety of emerging and pupael insects, the red and white Parmechene Bell, which resembles nothing that is natural to a trout stream, is a puzzling but killer fly for brook trout. Perhaps the red connotes blood to hungry brook trout. After all, the Daredevle doesn't look like anything either, but throw it in the lily pads and you'll catch northern pike.

Dry Flies

To the novice, long Latin names and complicated hatch schedules can be off-putting, giving the impression that only the well-schooled expert can catch fish on a dry fly. In fact, nothing could be further from the truth. When a hatch is on, it can often be easy to know exactly where trout are and on what they are feeding. At times, taking trout is just a matter of hitting the right dimple on the water with your cast and letting the fly float by naturally.

Carry a variety of midge patterns, dark and light, in sizes 18 to 22. This is often the first hatch to come off during the March and April trout season in Wisconsin. Blue-Winged Olives (*Baetis*) are another common mayfly, making appearances anytime between March and September. An Adams is a great all-around dry fly in Wisconsin and elsewhere. This will nicely match the Blue-Winged Olive and later the Hendrickson hatches. Sulphur duns will be around any time from late April in the south to mid-July in the north. You will also want Hex patterns in your box for this June and July hatch. A White Wulff does nicely for the *Ephoron leukon*, or White Mayfly, hatch in late summer. Tiny Tricos (size 22 to 26) are good to have in the box come July and August. Caddis hatches can come off anywhere from March to September and it's always a good idea to carry a few Elk Hair Caddis or other caddis dry flies in black and tan.

Streamers

Dave Vetrano, fisheries biologist for Wisconsin's famed coulee country, notes that big trout mostly eat smaller fish and crawfish. I've kept a few large trout in my day and postmortem examinations bear out Vetrano's wisdom. I've found crawfish, minnows, sculpins, baby trout, chubs, and even mice in their stomach—rarely the partially digested insect matter one sees in the stomachs of smaller trout. The implications of this are obvious. If you want to catch big trout, especially browns, fish big flies. Yes, you can take big trout during blanket mayfly hatches, but let's face it, these do not take place on most outings. Your best bet for large trout is fishing the lower ends of trout streams where there are fewer but larger trout—and lots of forage fish and crawfish. Muddler Minnows are a good all-around choice. Woolly Buggers in brown, black, or olive imitate leeches, crawfish, and sculpin.

Woolly Buggers and Muddler Minnows are also good flies for smallmouth, which are often present in the lower ends of trout streams as well in most of the major river systems in the state. The Flambeau, Chippewa, Menominee, and Wisconsin are a few of the best river systems in which to fish smallmouth.

Terrestrials

There is a period of time in summer where mayfly hatches have abated and the cool nights of September have not yet come to kick in trout metabolisms for fall feeding. Wisconsin trout streams are often flanked by stretches of prairie or covered by dense stream canopy, which sets up good conditions for terrestrial fishing. Hopper patterns are a must throughout the entire state—from the pasture streams of the southwest to meadow streams of the north and center of the state. Put on an old pair of tennis shoes and blue jeans and cool your heels in a trout stream. Try to make your casts land like a falling hopper; place them along bankside cover. You might even try twitching your fly back to you on the retrieve. A size 10 Dave's Hopper can be a deadly offering to trout in the doldrums of summer. Beetles and ants will also be in streams this time of year; a black beetle or black ant in size 18 or 20 will do nicely.

A Short List of Important Fly Patterns

Hare's Ear Nymph	size 14 to 18
Scud	size 14 to 18
Leadwing Coachman	size 16 to 18
Pheasant Tail Nymph	size 12 to 18
Midge/Caddis Larvae	size 18 to 22
Griffith's Gnat	size 18 to 22
Adams	size 14 to 20
Blue-Winged Olive	size 14 to 20
Elk Hair Caddis	size 10 to 16
White Wulff	size 8 to 12
Hexagenia dries, emergers, and nymphs	size 4 to 10
Muddler Minnow	size 4 to 10
Woolly Bugger	size 4 to 10
Marabou Leech	size 4 to 10
Dave's Hopper	size 6 to 10
Black Ant	size 12 to 20
Black Beetle	size 10 to 20

A mayfly.

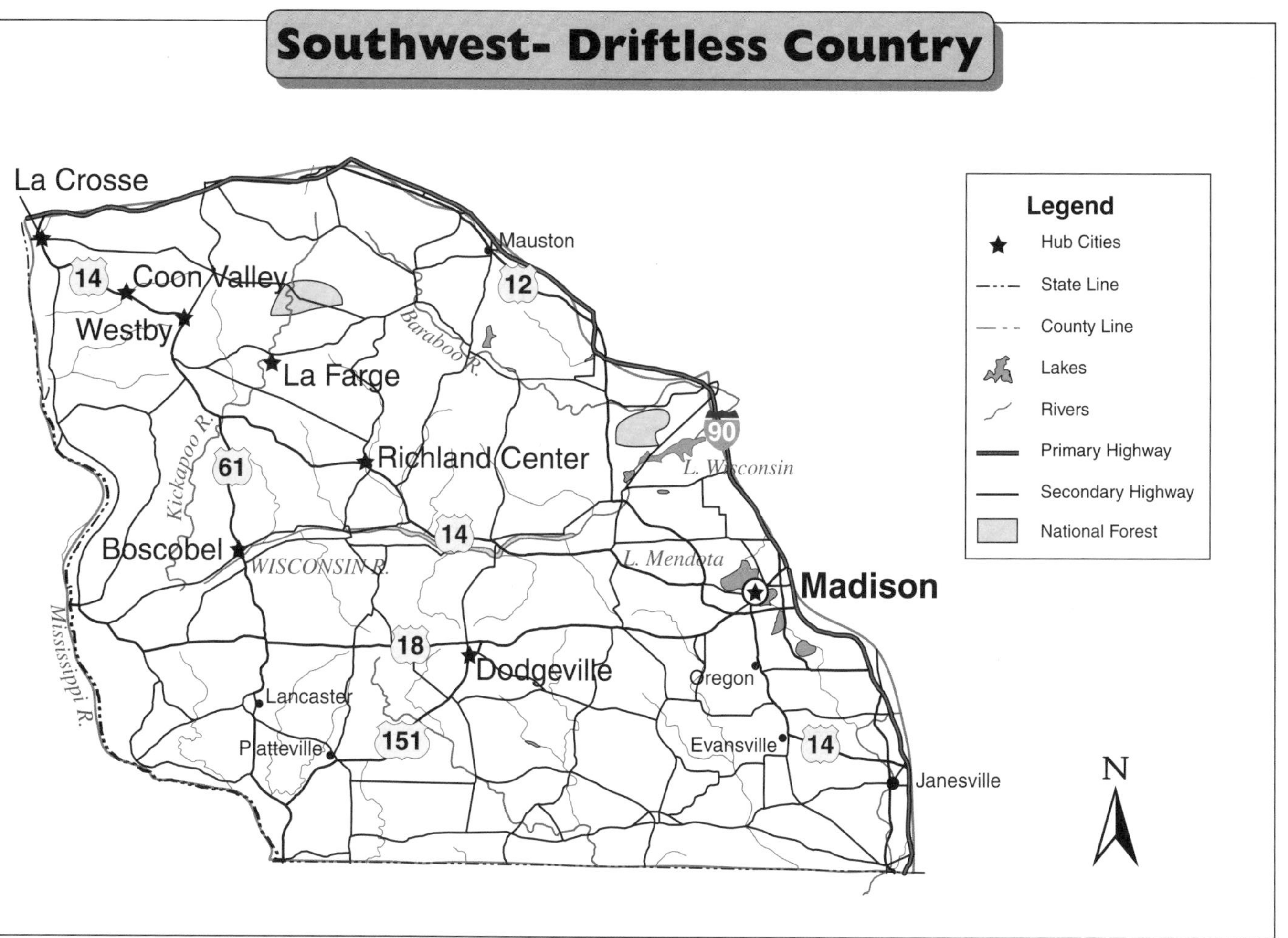
Southwest- Driftless Country
La Crosse
Mauston
14
Coon Valley
12
Westby
Baraboo R.
La Farge
Legend
Hub Cities
State Line
County Line
Lakes
Rivers
Primary Highway
Secondary Highway
National Forest
90
Kickapoo R.
61
Richland Center
L. Wisconsin
14
Boscobel
WISCONSIN R.
L. Mendota
Madison
Mississippi R.
18
Dodgeville
Oregon
Lancaster
151
Platteville
Evansville
14
Janesville
N

Southwest Wisconsin: Driftless Country Streams

I make no pretense at objectivity. This is my favorite section of the state. Perhaps it's because I own a cabin here. Perhaps it's because I wrote a book of essays, *Driftless Stories,* in praise of its beauty. But it's more than convenience and sentiment that draws me. The combination of big trout, lots of trout, little pressure, and unique scenery all contribute to the quality of fishing here. Some ten thousand years ago, when the last glaciers came through Wisconsin, this corner of the state was left unglaciated. Unlike so much of the flat, glaciated Midwest, Driftless Country retains a landscape of steep valleys and gnarled hillsides.

Quoted in *The Physical Geography of Wisconsin,* Wisconsin's first state geologist, Edward Daniels, described it as follows: "About one-third of the surface is prairie, dotted and belted with beautiful groves and oak-surrounded openings. The scenery combines every element of beauty and grandeur—sunlit prairie, with its soft swells, waving grass, and thousands of flowers; the somber depths of primeval forests; and castellated cliffs rising hundreds of feet, with beetling crags that a Titan might have plied for his fortress."

The limestone bluffs of the Driftless area. (Tim Landwehr)

HATCH CHART—Southwest Wisconsin: Driftless Country Streams

Insect/Food Source	J	F	M	A	M	J	J	A	S	O	N	D	Flies
Blue-Winged Olives (*Baetis*) (Peaks mid-March to mid-May)													BWO Thorax, Sparkle Dun #16-22; Pheasant Tail #16-18; Tiny BWO #22-24
Hendricksons													Dark Hendrickson, Adams, Brown Hen Spinners #12-14; Pheasant Tail #12-14
Sulphurs													Sulphur Dun, Light Cahill, Spinner #16; Pheasant Tail, Hare's Ear #16
Hexagenia (Peaks mid to late June/Evening Hatch)													Hex, Olive Drake, Para Drake #4-8; Hex Nymph, Strip Nymph #4-8
Trico													Tiny White Wing Black, CDC Trico, Spent Wing Trico #22
Caddis													Elk Hair Caddis, Peeking Caddis #14-20; Sparkle Pupa, Beadhead Caddis, Caddis Larvae #16
Midges													Midge Pupa, Serendipity, Brassie, RS-2 #16-22; Griffith's Gnat #16-22
Stoneflies													Stimulators #10; Brooks Stonefly Nymph #10

HATCH CHART—Southwest Wisconsin: Driftless Country Streams (cont.)

Insect/Food Source	J	F	M	A	M	J	J	A	S	O	N	D	Flies
Terrestrials							X	X	X				Hoppers and Crickets #10-12; Black Beetles #12-16; Black Ants #14-16
Scuds (Peak use March-September)	X	X	X	X	X	X	X	X	X	X	X	X	Olive, Yellow-Headed, Pink, Tan Scuds #12-16
Leeches, Crawfish, Sculpins, Chubs	X	X	X	X	X	X	X	X	X	X	X	X	Black/Olive Woolly Buggers, Muddler Minnows, Strip Leeches #4-10

A large riseform on a Driftless area spring creek. (Tim Landwehr)

While there are few wetlands here, there are copious streams and springs. Beneath the water there is rock, limestone. Dissolved limestone in the water makes it highly fertile. Beds of watercress and eel grass play host to freshwater shrimp. Pick up any rock and you will see scores of larvae and nymphs clinging to it. Not only are these streams full of food and trout, they do not, as rule, freeze during winter or warm unduly in summer. Holding in the 50s and 60s, they are veritable trout and food incubators. Hatches here are year-round.

On a warm day in December or January you may see clouds of midges or Blue-Winged Olives swarming above the water. Scuds, crawfish, and forage fish are also present year-round. Wild brown and, increasingly, brook trout are becoming common in these cold, narrow creeks. This is thanks to the efforts of DNR fishery managers Dave Vetrano and Gene Van Dyck, Trout Unlimited, and local conservations clubs like the West Fork (of the Kickapoo River) Sportsman's Club. In addition, after 150 years of growing grain, farmers are realizing that these narrow valleys are best suited to dairying. Many plots that were once farmed have reverted to wooded hillsides and are owned by folks who use the land for recreational purposes—hunting, hiking, and mushrooming. Growing numbers of small organic farms are springing up. The upshot of this change in land-use couldn't be better for trout anglers—increased water quality (less fertilizer, more ground water, less erosion) and streams that are reverting to presettlement conditions.

Dane, Iowa, Grant, Crawford, Vernon, Richland, and La Crosse Counties make up the heart of this region, accounting for a third of Wisconsin's trout streams. While the new class of robber barons has taken to building homes on bluff tops, and communities like Cross Plains on Black Earth Creek have begun to swell with subdivisions, the Driftless area in many respects remains as it always has been: ridges and valleys rich in game, short on people and long on beauty.

Base yourself in Richland Center, Viroqua, or Coon Valley, drive in any direction for half an hour, and every stream you come to will be a trout stream. And don't be put off by their diminutive size. These streams, many narrow enough to be vaulted by even the most mediocre athlete, give up browns in the 2-foot range every year. Within a half-hour of the state's capitol building, you'll find legendary Black Earth and Mount Vernon Creeks. The Blue River, Green River, and Castle Rock Creek are standouts in Grant County. Try Copper Creek and Tainter Creek in Crawford County.

The tangle of coulee creeks in Vernon and La Crosse Counties could beguile an angler for a summer or even a lifetime. Fish an olive scud in anything that looks like a trout stream, and you can't go wrong. And if you tire of catching big trout in tight valleys among century-old dairy farms, you can always try the Wisconsin and Mississippi Rivers for bass and panfish.

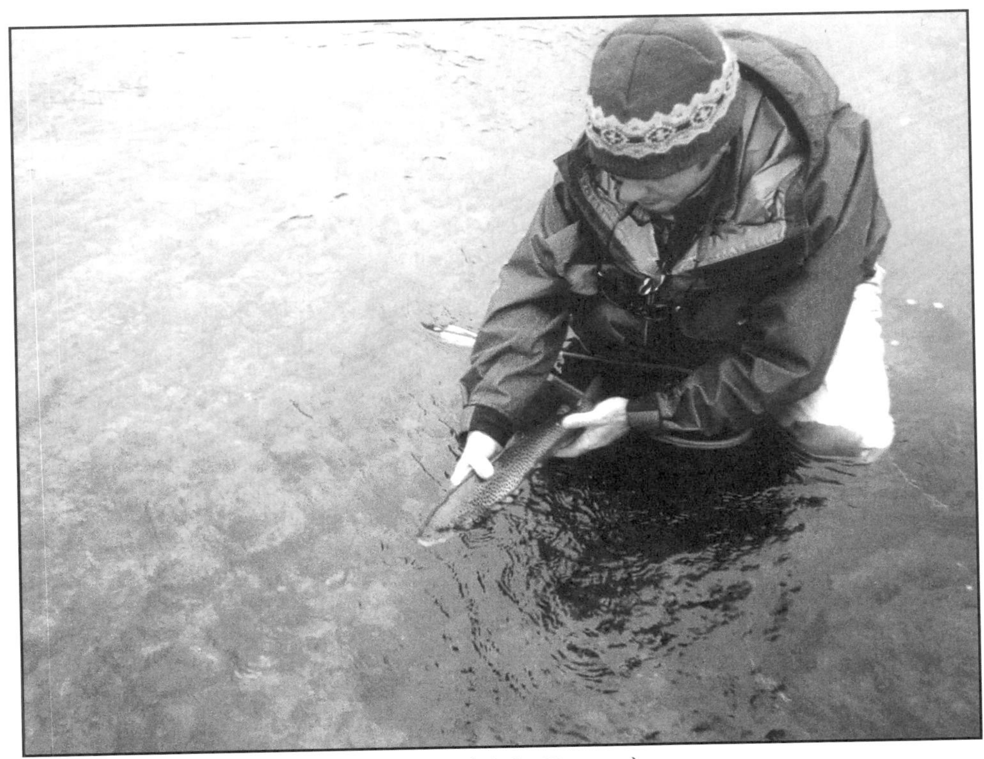

A beautiful brown trout being released. (Blake Hanson)

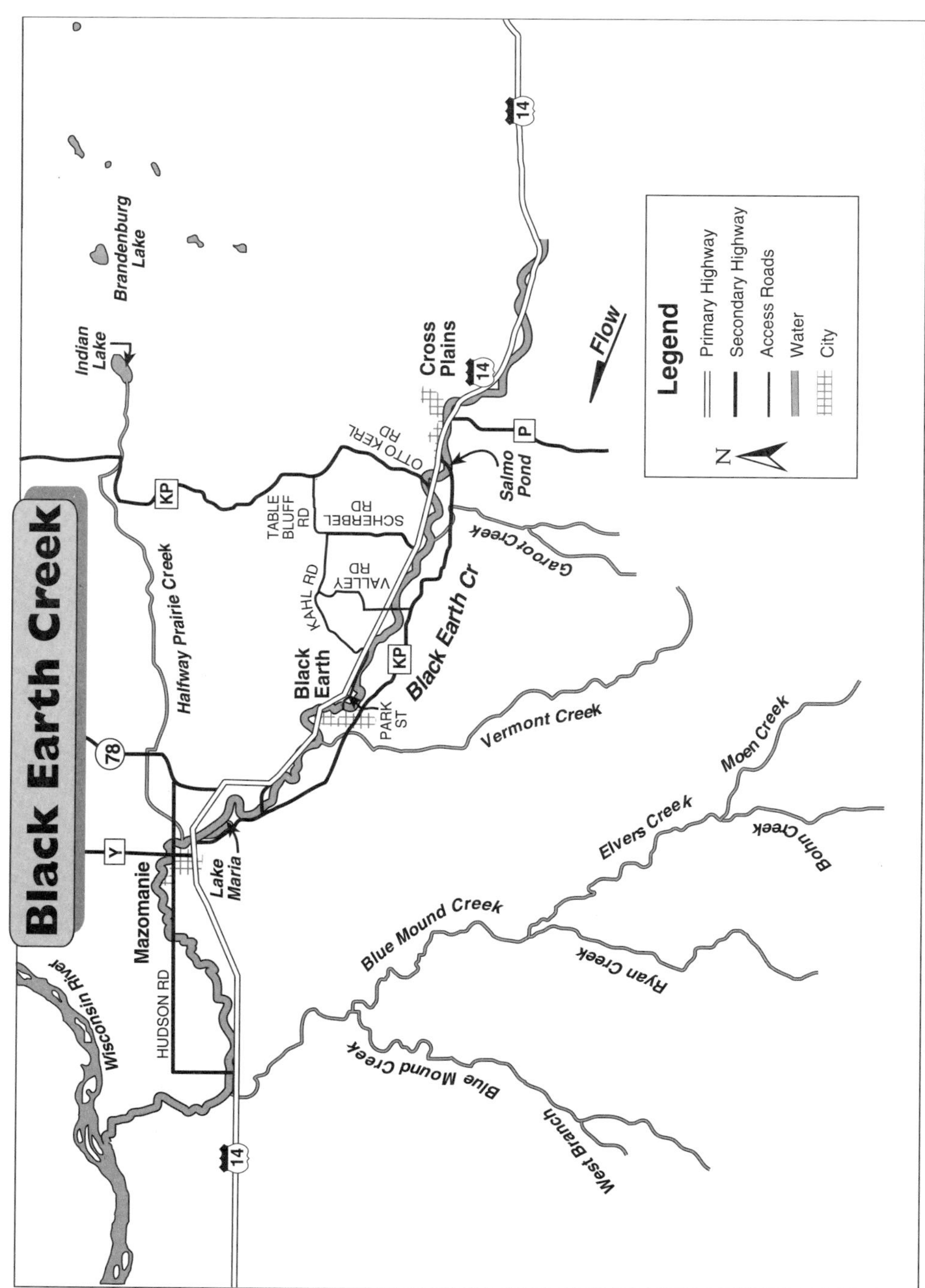

Black Earth Creek
Legend
Primary Highway
Secondary Highway
Access Roads
Water
City
N
Flow
Brandenburg Lake
Indian Lake
Cross Plains
14
P
Salmo Pond
OTTO KERL RD
SCHERBEL RD
TABLE BLUFF RD
KP
Halfway Prairie Creek
Garfoot Creek
VALLEY RD
KAHL RD
Black Earth Cr
Black Earth
PARK ST
Vermont Creek
78
Moen Creek
Elvers Creek
Bohn Creek
Y
Mazomanie
Lake Maria
Blue Mound Creek
Ryan Creek
HUDSON RD
Wisconsin River
West Branch

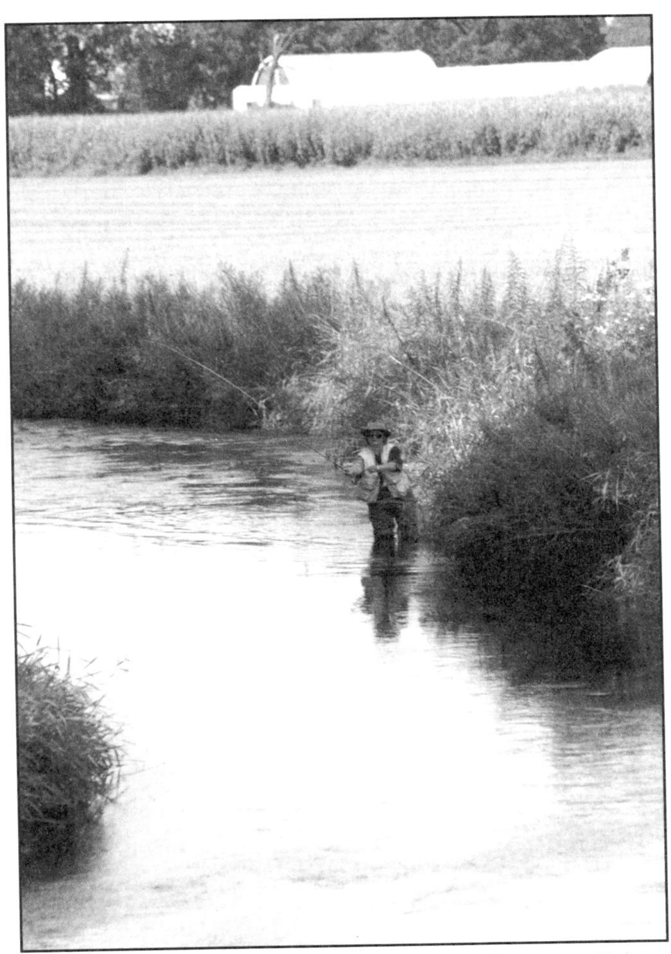

The justifiably famous Black Earth Creek. (Chris Halla)

BLACK EARTH CREEK

Upon hearing that Black Earth Creek harbors upwards of 2,000 trout per mile in its upper reaches, the uninitiated angler may dream of plucking hungry browns from watercress mats amid lush green bluffs. This is a wholly possible daydream, except for the gullible trout. In 20 years of trout fishing—including stints in Scotland and Spain and on Pennsylvania's spring creeks—I've never encountered trout as wary as Black Earth Creek browns.

Rising from springs in the farm (and now suburban) country just 15 miles from Madison's west side, Black Earth Creek flows some 12 miles to Lake Maria just outside Mazomanie. Featured in the L.L. Bean fishing catalog, on ESPN, and consistently rating as one of the top 100 trout streams in the U.S., this stream is not what you'd call a secret. Yet as summer progresses and crowds thin, some remarkable fishing in a picturesque setting can be enjoyed here. It should be pointed out, however, that such a fishery did not just happen. Efforts by Trout Unlimited, the DNR, and other groups have provided crucial habitat. On the other hand, increased development west of Madison, with its accompanying runoff, continue to be a threat to the stream's health. (In fact, June 2001 witnessed a devastating fish kill due to manure runoff.)

The stream becomes visible to the angler immediately upon entering Cross Plains. (There is a Citgo station on your right.) This bend and the water just above and below the snowmobile crossing can be productive, though it gets fished heavily. The stretch running through Cross Plains gives the angler a chance to test his skill in fast riprapped water. The creek opens up a little and begins to meander west of Cross Plains. It broadens and deepens as it nears Salmo Pond, which receives a planting of trout each spring. Some deep bends in this stretch of the creek make for ideal nymphing water.

From South Valley Road to Park Street near the town of Black Earth, the stream is category 5 (artificials only, catch and release); otherwise, the stream is category 3. And from the town of Black Earth to the confluence with Lake Maria there is some deep water holding fewer but larger trout. This downstream area receives less pressure, making it one of my favorite stretches. There are numerous access points and DNR-maintained parking areas along Highway 14. There is also a large lot for parking at Salmo Pond.

Black Earth Creek veteran angler Tom Ehlert describes a full calendar of insect activity. This is due in part, he says, to the mix of habitats on the stream. Thus, rock-dwellers such as caddis, Hendricksons, and Sulphurs find their required habitat, as do vegetation-dwellers such as scuds and cressbugs. The *Hexagenia* mayfly makes itself at home in Black Earth Creek's siltier lower reaches.

As the early season opens in March, anglers can expect a mix of midge and Blue-Winged Olive hatches. Caddis activity heats up in April, as do Sulphurs and Cahills. As for the Hex hatch, expect it to begin in mid-June and continue into early July (a bit earlier than on more northerly waters such as the Wolf). Fish the catch-and-release stretch (downstream from Valley Road) for this hatch, as the Hex larvae thrive in this silty streambed. Consider scouting out the stretch you plan to fish during daylight hours, as the bulk of the hatch occurs from late evening through full dark.

For the dog days, Ehlert likes to fish beetle and cricket imitations. "It's not so much of a hopper stream," he notes. August sees a return of Blue-Winged Olives, plus hatches of Pale Morning Duns, Evening Duns, and midges. I'm never without crawfish and minnow imitations, especially in the lower reaches of Black Earth where browns in the 5-pound range are taken each year. Scuds in olive and tan are good standbys, as are caddis in both black and tan. Ehlert also fishes a western nymph pattern called a Copper John, a cross between a Pheasant Tail Nymph and a Brassie.

Something that is often neglected in fishing (and hunting) literature is the importance of stalking. Perhaps on bigger western and eastern freestone streams this

A nice little brook trout ready to be released.

is not so necessary—the bottom is not as silty and there is plenty of stream to fish if you muddy the waters. However, Black Earth Creek trout won't forgive you casting your shadow or stomping along its banks or wading carelessly. I once watched an old-timer work a heavily fished stretch of Black Earth Creek; I was frustrated by my lack of success and just sat on the banks and observed. It turned out he was fishing night crawlers on a long cane pole, staying out of the water (not casting a shadow, either) and just "dapping" the likely looking water that had been fished several times that day. First a 15-inch brown trout found its way into his wicker creel, then one a little smaller, and finally a fish that looked very close to 20 inches rounded out his hat trick. Now, I'm not suggesting you trade your 5-weight Orvis fly rod for a length of cane, or that you give up dry-fly fishing for night crawlers. But this is about the best one-day catch I've ever seen on this creek—and it was due, I think, to both his natural presentation and his unobtrusive presence.

Stream Facts: Black Earth Creek

Season

- The early season runs from the first Saturday in March to the last Sunday before the first Saturday in May; no-kill, single barbless hooks only. The regular season from first Saturday in May at 5:00 am through September 30.

Regulations

- Park Street upstream to South Valley Road is no-kill, artificials only; otherwise category 3.

Species

- Wild brown trout, stocked rainbows

Miles of Trout Water

- 12

Stream Characteristics

- Spring creek with pools, riffles, undercut banks, extensive habitat work; extremely fertile. Good Hex hatch in late June/early July. Abundant scuds, caddis, forage fish, and mayflies. Middle section suffered fish kill in June 2001.

Access

- DNR holdings along Highway 14; Salmo Pond parking lot on Festge Road.

Fly Shops

- Gander Mountain, Fontana Sports, Madison Orvis, Streamside Outfitters

Map

- *Wisconsin Atlas and Gazetteer*, page 35

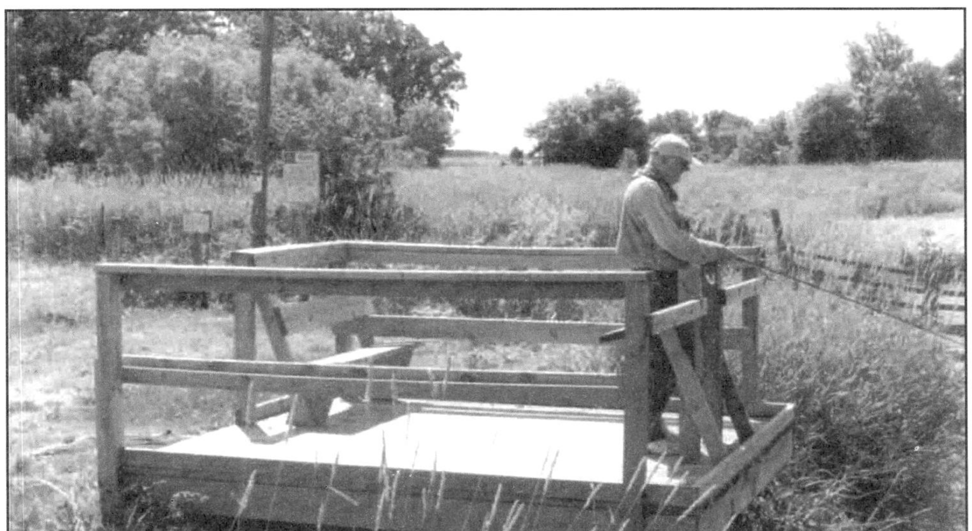

Handicapped fishing platforms, like this one on Mount Vernon Creek, are available on many other Wisconsin streams.

Mount Vernon Creek

Starting as a series of springs and feeder creeks (Deer and Frye) just north of the tiny hamlet of Mount Vernon, this gin-clear stream runs over sand, watercress, and gravel. It is unique not only because it supports self-sustaining populations of brook, brown, and rainbow trout and has not been stocked in years, but also because—and the two are probably related—it is almost completely free of in-stream grazing. The DNR owns or leases much of the land surrounding Mount Vernon Creek. It flows through a lush green valley full of turkey, deer, and pheasant, and amazingly, is less than a half-hour's drive from the state capital. According to Tom Ehlert, Frye Creek has gotten some recent attention from Trout Unlimited in the form of de-brushing and deepening the stream channel. While Frye Creek is probably too narrow for most flyfishers, it pumps much-needed cold water into Mount Vernon.

"Mount Vernon supports a good Hex hatch," says Craig Amacker of Fontana Sporting Goods in Madison. When nothing's happening on top, Amacker recommends beadhead caddis, olive scuds, or an olive Hare's Ear. The hatch progression on Mount Vernon is similar to that of Black Earth and other nearby streams. Midges are dependable throughout the season; Blue-Winged Olives begin to hatch in late March or April, along with caddis. Hendricksons and Sulphurs follow in May, and there's something of a late season Blue-Winged Olive hatch here, too. While terrestrials are present in the summer, I prefer to forgo dog-day fishing on Mount Vernon.

For 2 miles between County Highway U and Highway 92, Mount Vernon is category 5 (artificial only, no-kill). Above Highway U and below Highway 92, it is

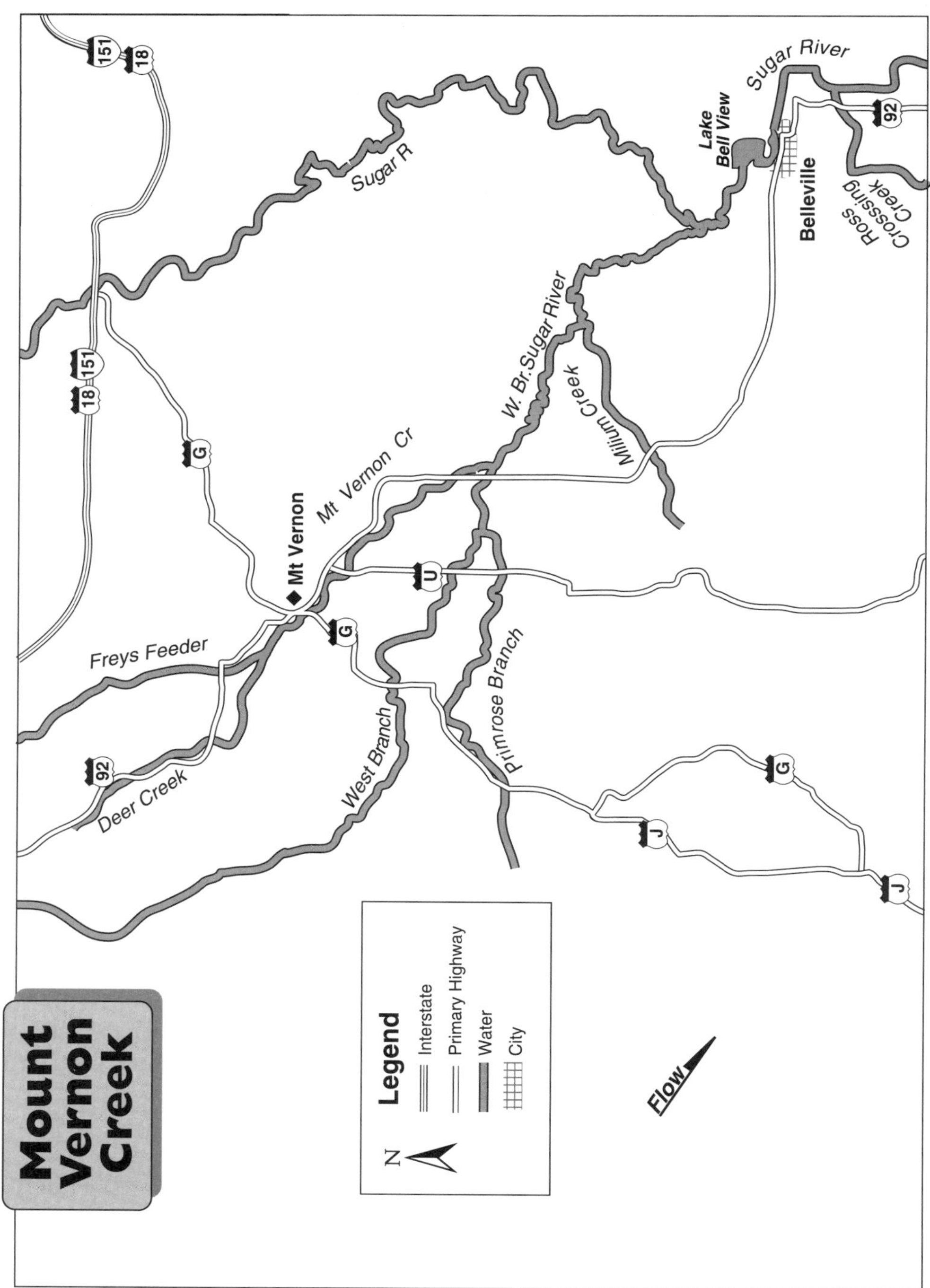
Mount Vernon Creek
Legend
Interstate
Primary Highway
Water
City
N
Flow
Sugar River
Sugar R
Lake Bell View
Belleville
Ross Crosssing Creek
W. Br. Sugar River
Milum Creek
Mt Vernon Cr
Mt Vernon
Freys Feeder
Deer Creek
West Branch
Primrose Branch
151
18
92
G
U
J

category 3. There is another bridge crossing at Highway G, and DNR parking lots north and south of the town of Mount Vernon on Highway 92. No section in my mind is far superior to another, but early season pressure might prompt you to look for a less-crowded area of the stream.

Mount Vernon Creek is no cakewalk to fish, given its combination of clear water and spooky wild browns. My friend Steve Miller spent thirteen years "getting to know" a half-mile stretch of this stream. My experience is that Mount Vernon trout are somewhat less selective than those in Black Earth Creek, but still quite picky. I rarely catch more than one fish from a run. After a good spring rain, I've had luck dragging Woolly Buggers beneath deep, undercut banks, taking fish to 2 pounds. It is a fine creek that supports exclusively wild trout, and it's worth the flyfisher's time, particularly in May and June. It's also just a short jaunt from Madison.

Stream Facts: Mount Vernon Creek

Season

- The early season runs from the first Saturday in March to the last Sunday before the first Saturday in May; no-kill, single barbless hooks only. Regular season runs from the first Saturday in May at 5:00 am through September 30.

Regulations

- Posted area between County U and Highway 92 no-kill, artificials only; otherwise category 3.

Species

- Wild brown trout; some brook and rainbow trout

Miles of Trout Water

- 8

Stream Characteristics

- Spring creek with pools, riffles, undercut banks, extensive habitat work; extremely fertile. Flows through wooded meadow. Abundant scuds, caddis, forage fish, and mayflies.

Access

- Extensive DNR holdings along Highway 92.

Fly Shops

- Gander Mountain, Fontana Sports, Madison Orvis, Streamside Outfitters

Maps

- *Wisconsin Atlas and Gazetteer*, page 27

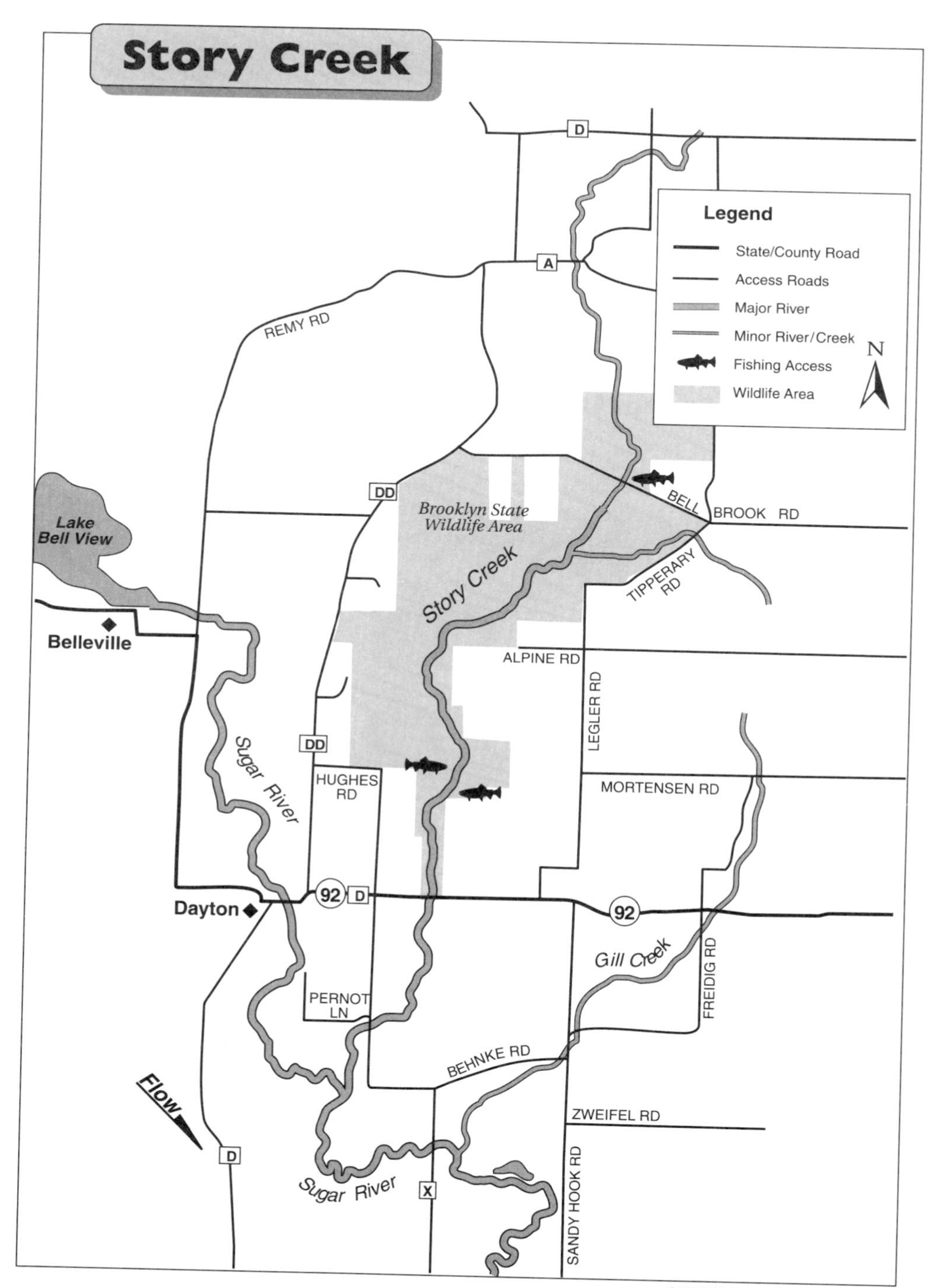
Story Creek
Legend
State/County Road
Access Roads
Major River
Minor River/Creek
Fishing Access
Wildlife Area
N
D
A
REMY RD
DD
Brooklyn State Wildlife Area
BELL
BROOK RD
Lake Bell View
Belleville
Story Creek
TIPPERARY RD
ALPINE RD
LEGLER RD
Sugar River
DD
HUGHES RD
MORTENSEN RD
92
D
Dayton
92
Gill Creek
FREIDIG RD
PERNOT LN
BEHNKE RD
Flow
ZWEIFEL RD
D
Sugar River
X
SANDY HOOK RD

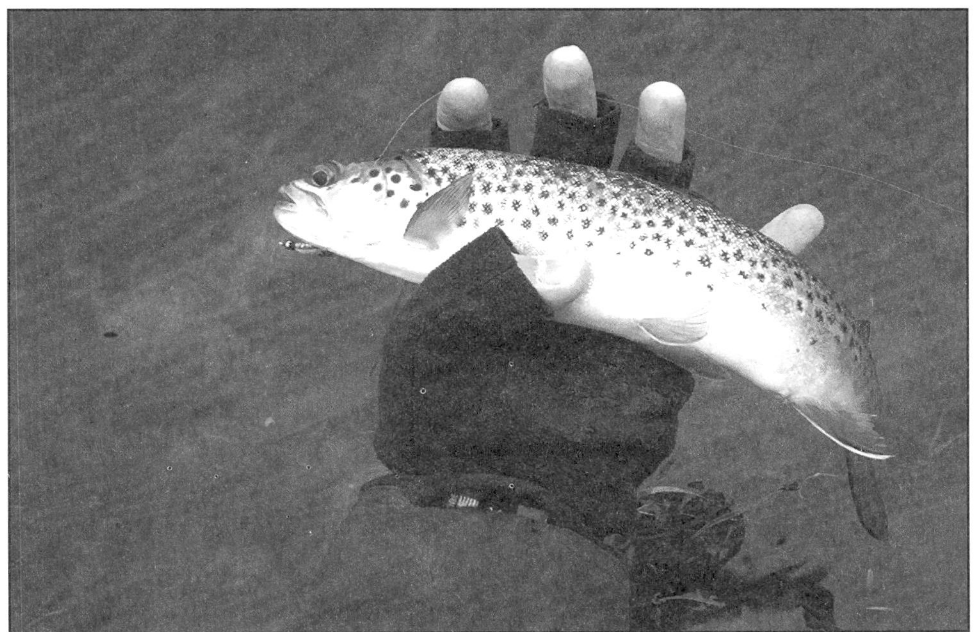

A beautiful brown trout. (Tim Landwehr)

Story Creek

Even considered just for its ecological merits, Story Creek is a gem. It runs through upland and prairie (Brooklyn State Wildlife Area) and hosts many of the fine and noble creatures native to North America. Wild turkey gobble from hillsides, whitetails startle from fencelines, and wood ducks wheel through timber. On summer evenings, as you slip the net beneath a native brook trout, you may hear the call "Bobwhite, bobwhite" in the distance. But it is the proximity to Madison's south-spreading sprawl that makes Story Creek truly remarkable—and vulnerable. The DNR holds some 4,000 surrounding acres through a combination of leased easements and outright ownership. Thank goodness for the DNR, and let's hope the leases stay in place.

Story Creek first becomes fishable where it crosses Bellbrook Road, about 10 miles south of the southwest reaches of Fitchburg and Madison. Before this it is just a spring freshet arising near the town of Story, too small to effectively fish. I have taken small, brilliant-colored brook trout near the Bellbrook Road Bridge, and I have no doubt the bends hold big fish. The problem? The stream's still narrow enough to jump across and the tree canopy gets thick come late May. Your best bet here is dapping the deeper holes in low-light conditions, but go carefully. The marshy margins of this creek are unforgiving of the hurried angler.

While you won't hit another road crossing until Highway 92, there's access via dirt tracks leading to parking areas within the Brooklyn State Wildlife Area. You can find these coming off Legler Road, with one off Alpine Road. This leaves you about 6 miles of stream to fish between bridges. Tree canopy remains thick, so fish during the early season or consider using a shorter rod.

What's the pay-off for fishing this brushy roadless stretch? Brown trout that stretch into the 5-pound range. There are also reports of trout in the ditches that feed the stream, though I've never encountered any. If the beavers have been busy, you may encounter beaver ponds which, oxygen permitting, surely house some nice fish. At Highway 92, the creek is silty and full of deadfalls—a little marginal for fishing. However, at County X, the last bridge crossing above the Sugar River, there has obviously been some habitat work done—a nice deep pool with riprapped sides. A local told me it's his dog's "clean-off spot" after they hunt local marshes and that it's planted heavily with trout.

The same gentleman told me that the Sugar River, just down Highway X, is a good smallmouth stream in its rocky bends. My one visit there produced a redhorse sucker, but it sure looked like good smallmouth water. A July 2001 draining of Lake la Belle in Belleville, just upstream from Highway X, will likely hamper the smallmouth fishery in this stretch for the short term.

There's a nice sulphur hatch in late May on Story Creek. If nothing is happening on top, try the usual suspects—beadhead caddis, olive or pink scuds, and Woolly Buggers in deeper holes. Brook trout are present in the upper reaches. Browns become prevalent as you work downstream. Story Creek is category 3 for its entire length.

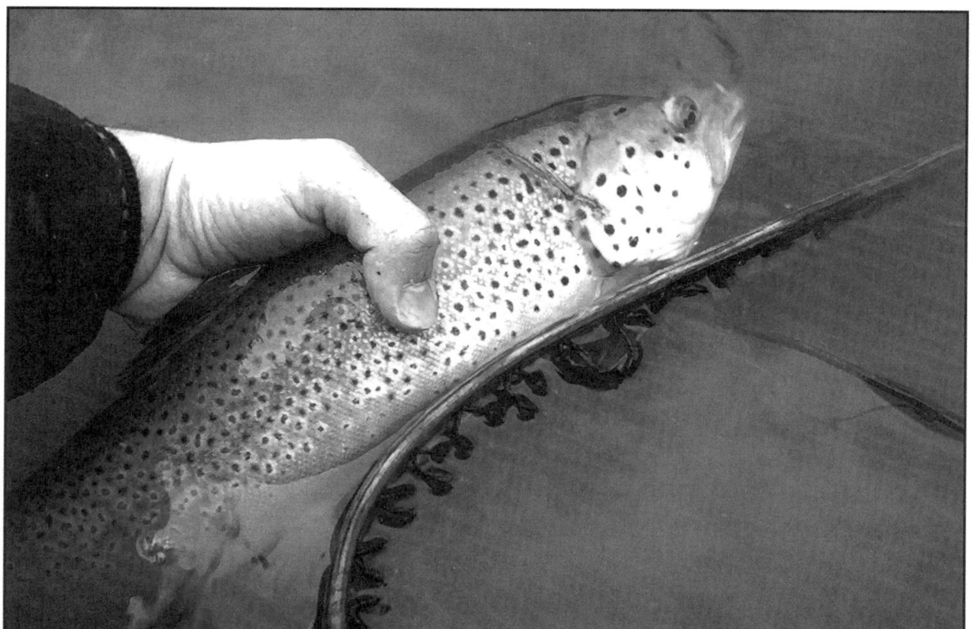

An early season brown trout that fell to a #20 Blue-Winged Olive. (Tim Landwehr)

Stream Facts: Story Creek

Season
- The early season runs from the first Saturday in March to the last Sunday before the first Saturday in May; no-kill, single barbless hooks only. Regular season from the first Saturday in May at 5:00 am through September 30.

Regulations
- Category 3

Species
- Wild brown and brook trout

Miles of Trout Water
- 7

Stream Characteristics
- Spring creek on eastern edge of Driftless area; heavily wooded in places. Almost all surrounding land is DNR land.

Access
- Brooklyn State Wildlife Area along Highway 92 and Highway D/DD.

Fly Shops
- Gander Mountain, Fontana Sports, Madison Orvis, Streamside Outfitters

Maps
- *Wisconsin Atlas and Gazetteer*, page 28

Allen Creek

Located a stone's throw from Rockford, Beloit, and Janesville, Allen Creek receives surprisingly little fishing pressure. Don Bush, fisheries biologist for the Lower Rock River Basin, recommends the stretch of Allen Creek that runs through the Evansville Wildlife Area off Highway 213. There has been some riprapping of stream bends here, and in-stream structures that provide cover have been installed. Two good-sized springs feed Allen Creek in the wildlife area. In addition, since the surrounding land is a public hunting ground, there is no cattle grazing and plenty of public access.

Water temperatures in Allen Creek can reach the upper 70s; still, there is limited natural reproduction and good numbers of holdover fish. Each year, 1,200 legal-sized brown trout and 1,000 fingerlings browns are stocked. Forage fish swim upstream from the Sugar River at Albany and form an important part of the diet of bigger trout. Mayflies and caddis flies are also present.

Allen Creek begins near Brooklyn in northeast Green County. It then runs 2.5 miles to Lake Leota. This stretch is narrow, runs through private land, receives warm water from irrigation ditches, and is of limited interest to the trout fisher. It is best to access Allen Creek where it crosses Highway 213 south of Evansville or from Old 92 Road just above the town of Magnolia. A pair of feeder creeks meets up with Allen Creek between these two points. You might try prospecting between these two bridges and fishing at the mouths of these feeder creeks. A Muddler Minnow wouldn't be a bad choice, given the forage fish that are present. Any standard caddis imitation should do. Streamside vegetation gets pretty thick as the season goes on, so either fish early in the season or expect to do a lot of flipping and/or dapping with your fly.

Allen Creek is no blue ribbon trout stream; however, if you live in the Rock River Basin or are traveling the scenic route to Chicago, stop and give it a try. Located just east of the glaciated/unglaciated line, Allen Creek is something of a curiosity, as southeast Wisconsin has very few trout streams. (Story Creek near Brooklyn is another good bet in this area.)

Token Creek

If you are stranded at the Dane County Regional (Madison) Airport during trout season with a rental car and have a few hours to kill, by all means make the 10-minute drive up Highway 51 to Token Creek. It has received habitat work from the state and county and is stocked with all three species of trout. It is a category 3 stream. A reliable source told me of a 27-inch brown trout taken in the county park section of the creek, though this was no doubt a breeder released from a DNR hatchery.

You'll be able to see where prairie has been replanted and where corners and bends of the stream are reinforced with riprap and the stream channel deepened. A number of spring feeders bring cold clear water into the stream, and there is good access, both via Token Creek County Park off Highway 51, just north of where 51 goes beneath the interstate, and also via the conservation area parking lot on Highway 19. There is a spillway just upstream from Highway 19 that pretty much marks the upper end of trout water. And there's another spillway visible as you enter Token Creek County Park; this marks the lower end of trout water. Below and above the spillways, the stream is too silty and poorly oxygenated for trout.

Token Creek then meanders toward the Cherokee Marsh (Yahara River), which flows into Lake Mendota. Freshwater drum and carp predominate in this lower stretch of Token Creek, and an angler would begin to encounter panfish and some gamefish in Cherokee Marsh. Cherokee Marsh was once known as a destination waterfowling spot, but draining and development have reduced its size, plant, and water quality. Gone are the days when the Madison lakes, come November, were dotted with the white backs of diving ducks.

Fish the bend pools of Token Creek with a nymph. I have not seen much in the way of hatches on this stream in my dozen or so visits. Just ten years ago, this creek was in much worse shape, but it is now showing the ability to hold trout. While the Yahara/Cherokee Marsh portion of this watershed still needs some attention, it's good to see that an important tributary has been improved rather than degraded. In the future, Token may become a self-supporting trout fishery. As for now, it's nice to be able to buzz up there on your lunch hour, or from the airport, and get in a quick hour of fishing.

THE MADISON CHAIN OF LAKES

On any given summer weekend, caravans of vehicles towing fishing boats can be seen heading north on Interstate 90/94, bound for such traditional destinations as Hayward, Minocqua, and Eagle River. Many of these folks from Illinois and southern Wisconsin will drive hundreds of miles roundtrip. If their desire is simply to spend time in the Northwoods, more power to them. Enjoy the pine trees and fresh air. If their goal is topnotch fishing for panfish, northern, musky, bass, and walleye, then they should save their gas money and turn off at the Madison exit, just 50 miles over the Illinois line. Careful management attention from the DNR, including fairly restrictive slot limits for bass, walleye, and northerns, excellent fertility, and efforts by local conservation groups to curb point-source and nonpoint-source runoff into the lakes has turned them into a phenomenal mixed bag fishery.

In this overview, I will be concentrating on fly fishing opportunities and passing over fisheries (like deep-water perch and bottom-feeding catfish) that could technically be pursued with a fly rod but are far better pursued with traditional spinning gear. Fly fishing for shallow water panfish and gamefish is a tried-and-true approach; using a sinking line to catch walleye in 70 feet of water seems to me like trying to turn a Yugo into a race car. That said, there are miles of shoreline and weedbeds just waiting to be fished. Wading is one way to do this. A belly boat is another. I use a duck skiff—a wide-beamed boat somewhere between a kayak and a canoe that comfortably seats two anglers and is much less "tippy" than a canoe. However, any small fishing boat would do here—jonboat, V-hull, canoe, or kayak. I've never been a fan of large, brightly colored motorboats in shallow water, as they spook fish.

Connected by the Yahara (meaning "catfish" in the Winnebago language) River, the Madison Chain of Lakes is situated in south-central Wisconsin. Lake Mendota is the largest, deepest, and northernmost of these lakes. Between Lake Mendota and Lake Monona is the isthmus where the state capitol building and university are located. At the southern end of Lake Monona, the Yahara River widens and meanders toward Lake Waubesa, a smaller, shallower lake. The area between Monona and Waubesa is commonly referred to as Upper Mud Lake. Finally, there is Lake Wingra, the only musky lake in the chain; Murphy's Creek connects this to Monona.

These lakes are urban fisheries to be sure. The state capitol and Madison's downtown are visible from most points on Mendota and Monona. Thus there is much urban runoff—water tinged with oil coming off the miles of paved roads. Lake Mendota's north side and Lake Waubesa's west side are heavily farmed, so there are problems with ag runoff, too. All lakes have something of an algae bloom in midsummer that depletes oxygen and lowers water quality. However, from the Madison schools to the local children's museum, the concept of watershed management is being promoted and taught. And Madison enjoys an active community of paddlers, anglers, and environmentalists, all sharing a deep concern for the lakes. The DNR also recognizes these problems and carefully manages this fishery. So while there are problems there are also advocates.

Let's take a look at the fishing.

Lake Mendota

The weedbeds of Lake Mendota are extremely fertile and full of just about every kind of gamefish you can imagine. And you really don't need much gear to fish here—just a belly boat or canoe. While you will see watercraft fit for hauling barges around the Cape of Good Hope, speedboats, and jet-skis, they should not bother you too much. My favorite areas on Mendota are points and bays; these are good as early as April when the water begins to warm and panfish move in to their spawning beds and as late as November when walleye prowl the shorelines before ice-up. Do exercise caution while boating these waters later in the year. I have seen the weather turn from seasonable to inclement in a matter of hours here during late-season duck hunts. Any day after November 1st can witness severe Canadian cold fronts, with temperatures dropping into the single digits.

Areas on which to concentrate flyfishing efforts are Governor's Island, University Bay/Picnic Point, the Tenney Park Breakwater, Marshall Park, and the Yahara River. You can launch a canoe or skiff at Governor's Island, the Yahara River (Highway 113/Northport Drive), or University Bay (look for a launch pier along the bike path). Maintained launches also can be found at Tenney Park and Marshall Park. Look for bluegills on their spawning beds as early as late April, and fish for them with any bright nymph or even a small Woolly Bugger. What makes this fishery fun is that just when you have set your mind to catching a mess of bluegills for a fish fry, your fly might be grabbed by a smallmouth roving the shallows. I've seen good northerns cruising University Bay and the shallows off Governor's Island. Walleye frequently feed in these shallows at night, too. If you want larger fish, head out in the evening and use a heavy tippet and a larger fly, perhaps a large Muddler Minnow or bucktail streamer. University Bay, along the bike path and behind the dorms, is a good place to wade and cast if you do not have a boat.

One final word of advice: There is an excellent fishing hotline for the Madison lakes. It is updated and maintained by D&S Bait and Tackle on Northport Drive. These folks, while not flyfishers, are a terrific source of information. Call the hotline at 608-244-3474.

Lake Monona

Monona is another known panfish and gamefish producer. It holds the same species as Mendota, but there is some stocking of tiger muskies here. City-maintained launches can be found at Olin Park off John Nolan Drive and at Olbrich Gardens off Atwood Avenue. Both of these are on the western shore of the lake, and this seems to be where most of the action is. Really anywhere between these two points, especially over weeds, should produce panfish from April through August. The dropoff just off the new convention center is popular for walleye, too. (There was some debate about what the construction of the convention center would do to the walleye fishery, but I am not aware of any studies on this.) "The Triangles" between John Nolan Drive and the railroad tracks are popular with early season panfishers. The Yahara River and Upper Mud Lake are also worth a try. There is a launch between Broadway and the Beltline. If the number of ice fishermen in a given area says anything about the fishery, the Yahara/Upper Mud should be first-rate.

Lake Waubesa

Compared to Monona and Mendota, Lake Waubesa is fairy shallow and small. It is known as a good producer of walleyes and northerns as well as perch, crappie, and bluegill. You can launch at Lake Farm Park off Libby Road or Goodland off Goodland Road. Fish weed edges for panfish. Try to locate sandbars and fish them toward evening for walleyes and northerns. There are some nice spring holes in the lower end of Waubesa in the state wetlands area. Try these for northerns during the dog days of summer. The channel between Waubesa and Upper Mud Lake, on either side of the railroad trestle, is popular in spring with panfish anglers and in fall for those seeking walleyes.

Lake Wingra

This is really the only lake in this chain that offers a muskie fishery. And according to fish biologists and sporting goods stores, it offers a superlative one. There is a launch and boat concession off Monroe Street. It weeds up pretty quick, which makes May a popular time to fish it—waters have begun to warm but weed growth is still minimal. It holds both types of bass, northerns, and small panfish. The UW-Arboretum surrounds it on three sides. November is also a good time to fish it, just as the lake is "turning over." Motorboats are not allowed on this lake.

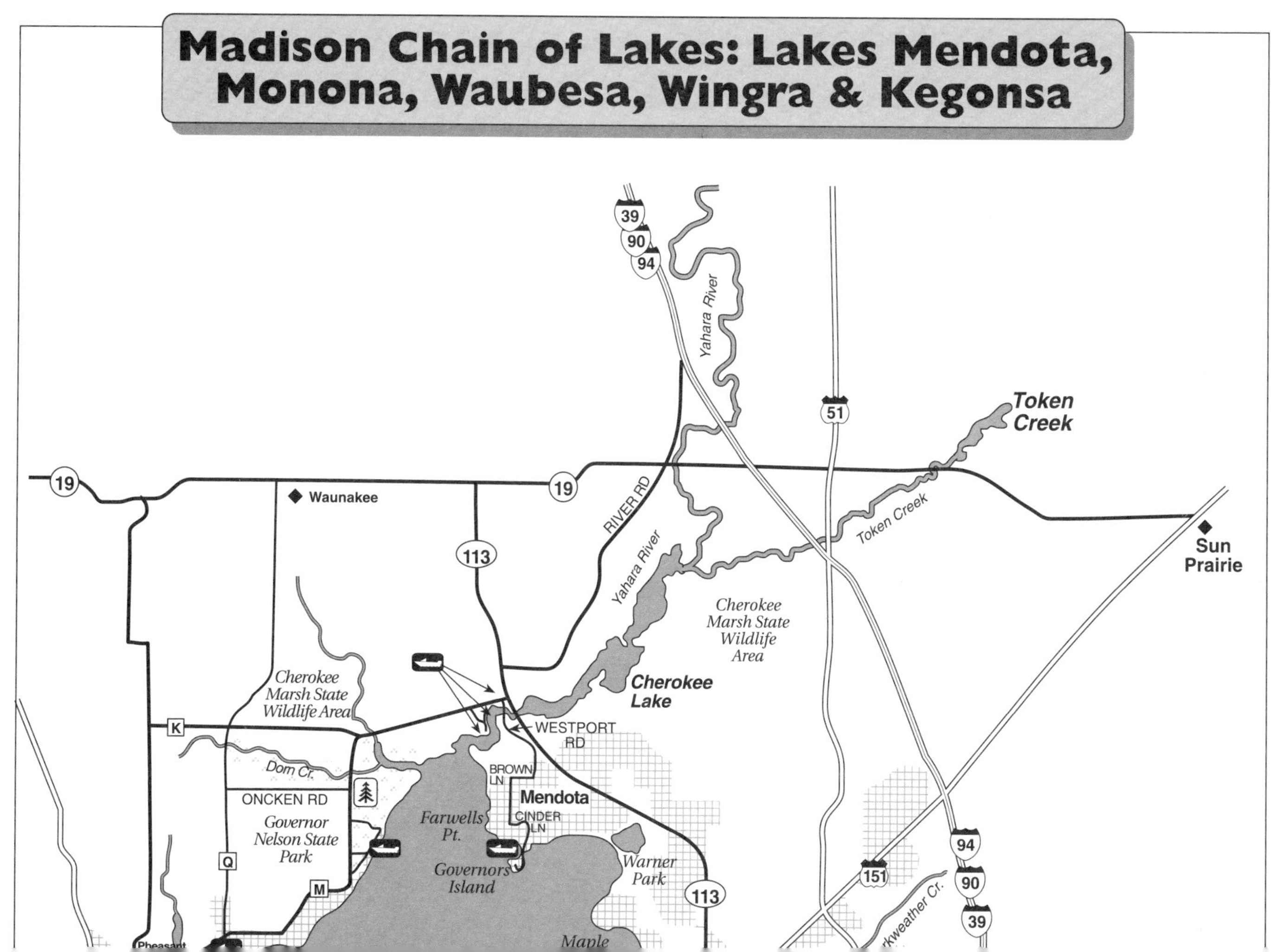
Madison Chain of Lakes: Lakes Mendota, Monona, Waubesa, Wingra & Kegonsa
39
90
94
Yahara River
51
Token Creek
19
Waunakee
19
RIVER RD
Yahara River
Token Creek
Sun Prairie
113
Cherokee Marsh State Wildlife Area
Cherokee Marsh State Wildlife Area
Cherokee Lake
K
WESTPORT RD
Dorn Cr.
BROWN LN
ONCKEN RD
Mendota
Governor Nelson State Park
Farwells Pt.
CINDER LN
Q
Governors Island
Warner Park
M
113
94
151
90
39
Maple

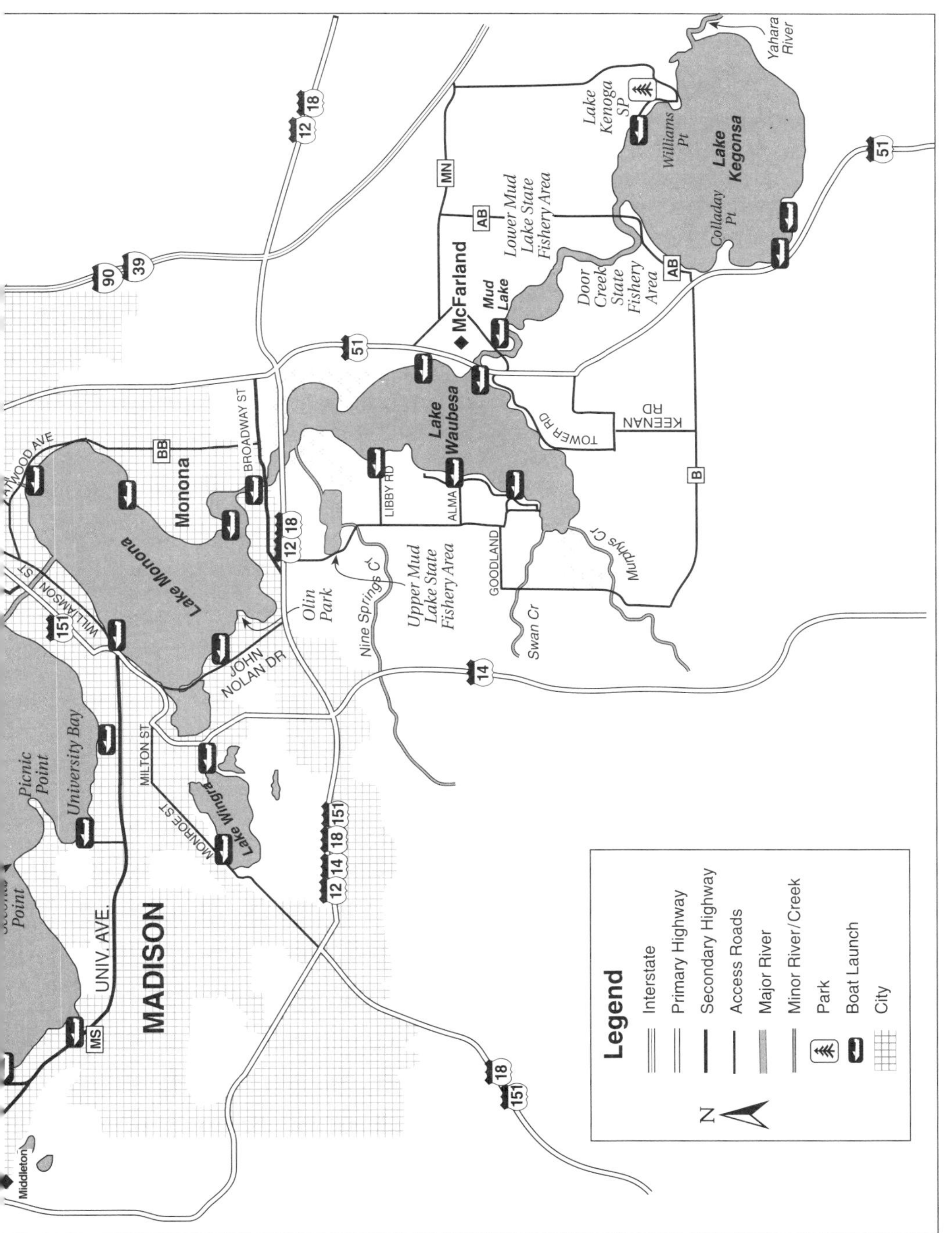

Legend
Interstate
Primary Highway
Secondary Highway
Access Roads
Major River
Minor River/Creek
Park
Boat Launch
City
N
MADISON
McFarland
Middleton
Lake Monona
Monona
Lake Waubesa
Lake Kegonsa
Lake Wingra
Mud Lake
University Bay
Picnic Point
Olin Park
Lake Kenoga SP
Williams Pt
Colladay Pt
Yahara River
Lower Mud Lake State Fishery Area
Door Creek State Fishery Area
Upper Mud Lake State Fishery Area
Nine Springs Cr
Swan Cr
Murphys Cr
UNIV. AVE.
WILLIAMSON ST
JOHN NOLAN DR
BROADWAY ST
ATWOOD AVE
MILTON ST
MONROE ST
LIBBY RD
ALMA
GOODLAND
TOWER RD
KEENAN RD

CAPITAL CITY BLUEGILLS

Come May in southern Wisconsin, you can find bluegills on their spawning beds in just about any lake that has weeds. The Madison Lakes offer some of the best bluegill fishing in the state. Lake Mendota hotspots are Picnic Point, Second Point, and Marshall Park on the northwest side of the lake and the weedbeds off Warner Park and Governor's Island on the northeast side. Squaw Bay on Lake Monona is good, as are the lagoons off John Nolen Drive. Just about any weedy area between the boat launch at Olbrich and the Convention Center should produce fish. Upper Mud Lake and the lower end of Lake Waubesa are worth a try, too. Find weeds and you'll find fish. Fish and Crystal Lakes in northwest Dane County are also known bluegill producers. And by all mean, call the D&S Weekly Fishing Report (608-244-3474) or stop in at 1411 Northrop Drive. These guys know where the fish are.

While I've caught bluegills from shore, I seem to do better from a boat. Small and unobtrusive is the name of the game here. A belly boat would do the trick. I like to fish from my low-draft duck skiff. A canoe, jonboat, or v-hull would also work. I always feel better in a drab-colored craft. I've seen fish taken from big red monster boats, but I can't help but thinking it looks unnatural to the fish. Ditto for dropping anchor and or dropping thermoses in the bottom of your boat—it doesn't send a welcome call. Keep quiet and keep a low profile and you should be good to go. Position your boat just at the edge of the weeds and have at it.

As for tackle, any rod you use for stream trout will work fine for bluegills, with a 4-, 5-, or 6-weight being ideal. In windy conditions you might graduate to a 7- or 8-weight. If you haven't located the fish—or other boats that are furiously hooking and unhooking fish—you can anchor off a likely looking bed and watch through polarized sunglasses to see if there's a pod of bluegills nearby. Vern Lunde of now-closed Lunde's Fly Fishing Chalet in Mount Horeb favors a fly called the Puss Bug in pink or chartreuse. He sight-fishes almost exclusively. Rubber spiders will also work, as will almost any bright-colored nymph. Bluegills have small mouths, so a size 10 or 12 fly should do nicely. Woolly Buggers or other streamers in bright colors are also good choices.

Keep a few fish for the pan; bluegills are prolific breeders. Scale the fish first. Then work your fillet knife from the tail up around the spine and, if you're lucky, around the large rib bones. It took me several fish to get the hang of this—cutting a nice little triangle with no bones.

Keep a low profile, find the weeds, and have fun!

The Yahara River

While the Yahara (meaning "catfish" in the Winnebago language) River is mentioned in passing in the Madison Lakes description above, I'll describe it fully here. Please forgive a bit of overlap in the interest of doing justice to this important fishery. The Yahara River runs the length of Dane County. Catfish, while plentiful, are just one layer of the Yahara's fishery. Northern pike, walleye, bass, panfish and rough fish abound.

The Yahara begins as a small stream near the Columbia County line and the town of Morrisonville and ends at the Stebbinsville Dam, some 30 miles south, on the Rock County line. Between these points it goes through a number of permutations, entering and exiting the Madison Lakes.

From small beginnings, it widens into sprawling Cherokee Marsh, which feeds Lake Mendota at the head of the Madison Lakes. At the outlet of Mendota, it exits a small lock and dam and runs a mile through Madison's isthmus into Lake Monona. Below Monona, it widens, flows beneath Madison's Beltline, and into marshy Upper Mud Lake and Lake Waubesa. Below Waubesa and Highway 51, it goes into Lower Mud Lake, twists and turns a bit before feeding and exiting Lake Kegonsa. Below Kegonsa, it is a serious river, with no more lakes below this point. From here it flows some 15 miles south through the town of Stoughton to Stebbinsville Dam. Within these 30 miles, you can chose between suburban or urban fishing with easy access or an all-day float in its marshy lower reaches where there are only a handful of road crossings. That's the nice thing about the Yahara. Varied habitat and opportunities mean you can fish it to suit your mood.

Cherokee Marsh, a widening of the upper Yahara River just north of Lake Mendota, is a popular spot for early season panfish. Its shallow waters warm faster than large Lake Mendota, and the fish seek spawning sights as early as mid-April here. There's a launch for a cartop boat at the Highway 113 bridge and launches for motorboats in the marinas just downstream from here. Weeds are limited in Cherokee Marsh, but where you find them you will find good-sized bluegills; areas with fallen trees and stumps will hold crappie.

Weed growth is probably best at the upper end of the marsh. However, any little cuts along the cattail shoreline should hold panfish and bass; northern pike frequent its limited lotus beds, best found by exploring with a canoe. Sight-fishing for Cherokee's ubiquitous carp is good. Look for them rooting around in the shallows and cast to them with nymphs. This can provide some exciting fly fishing. If you want to catch channel catfish, try fishing a leech pattern close to the bottom around the Highway 113 bridge, a noted catfish bed.

Fifty years of drainage, siltation, and development runoff have hurt Cherokee's water quality and weed growth. On a hopeful note, though, Dane County's Natural Heritage Land Trust has purchased the headwater springs to Cherokee's largest tributary, Token Creek. With continued restoration of Token Creek, water and weed quality should improve on Cherokee Marsh.

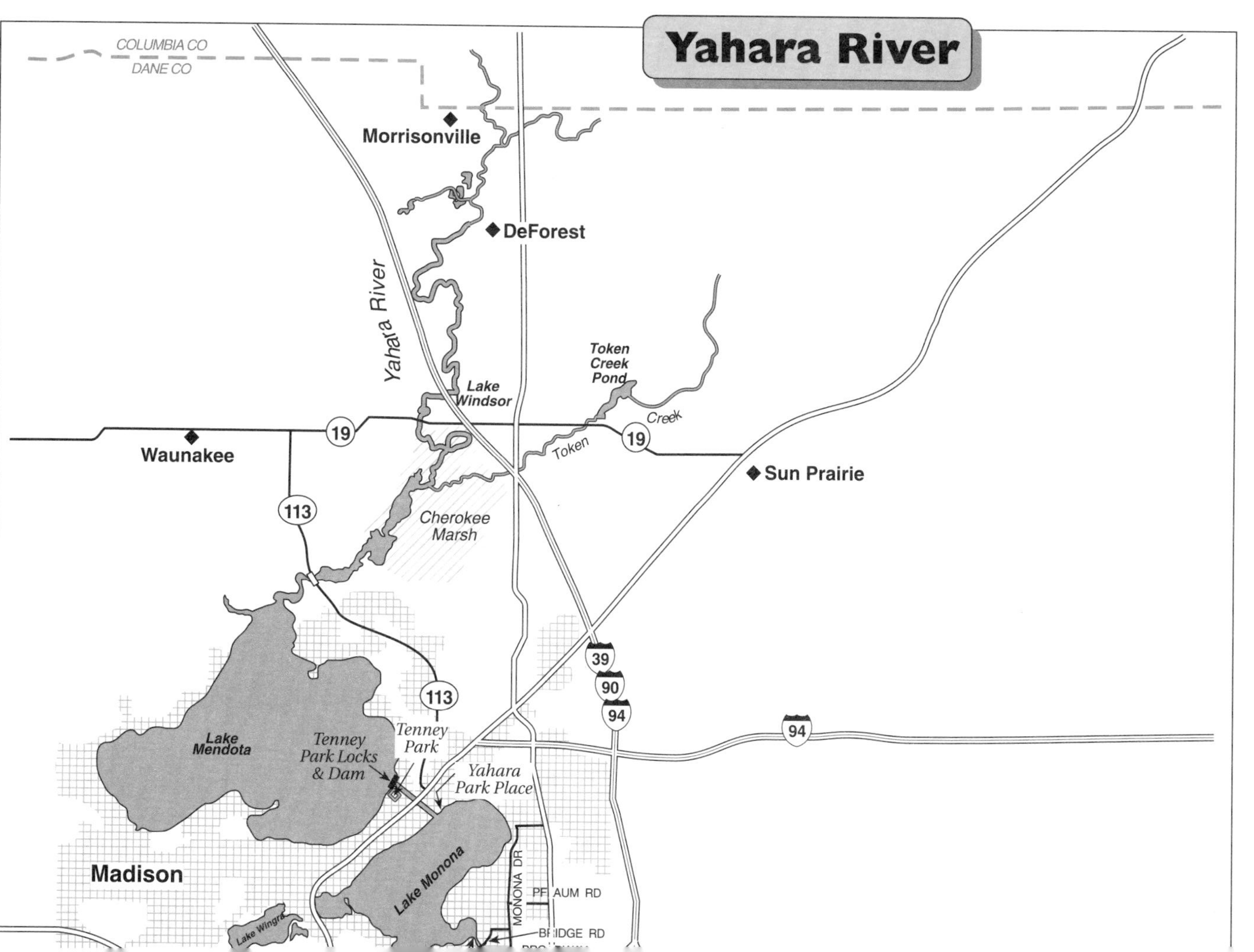
Yahara River
COLUMBIA CO
DANE CO
Morrisonville
DeForest
Yahara River
Token Creek Pond
Lake Windsor
Creek
Token
19
Waunakee
Sun Prairie
113
Cherokee Marsh
39
90
94
Lake Mendota
Tenney Park Locks & Dam
Tenney Park
Yahara Park Place
Madison
Lake Monona
MONONA DR
Lake Wingra

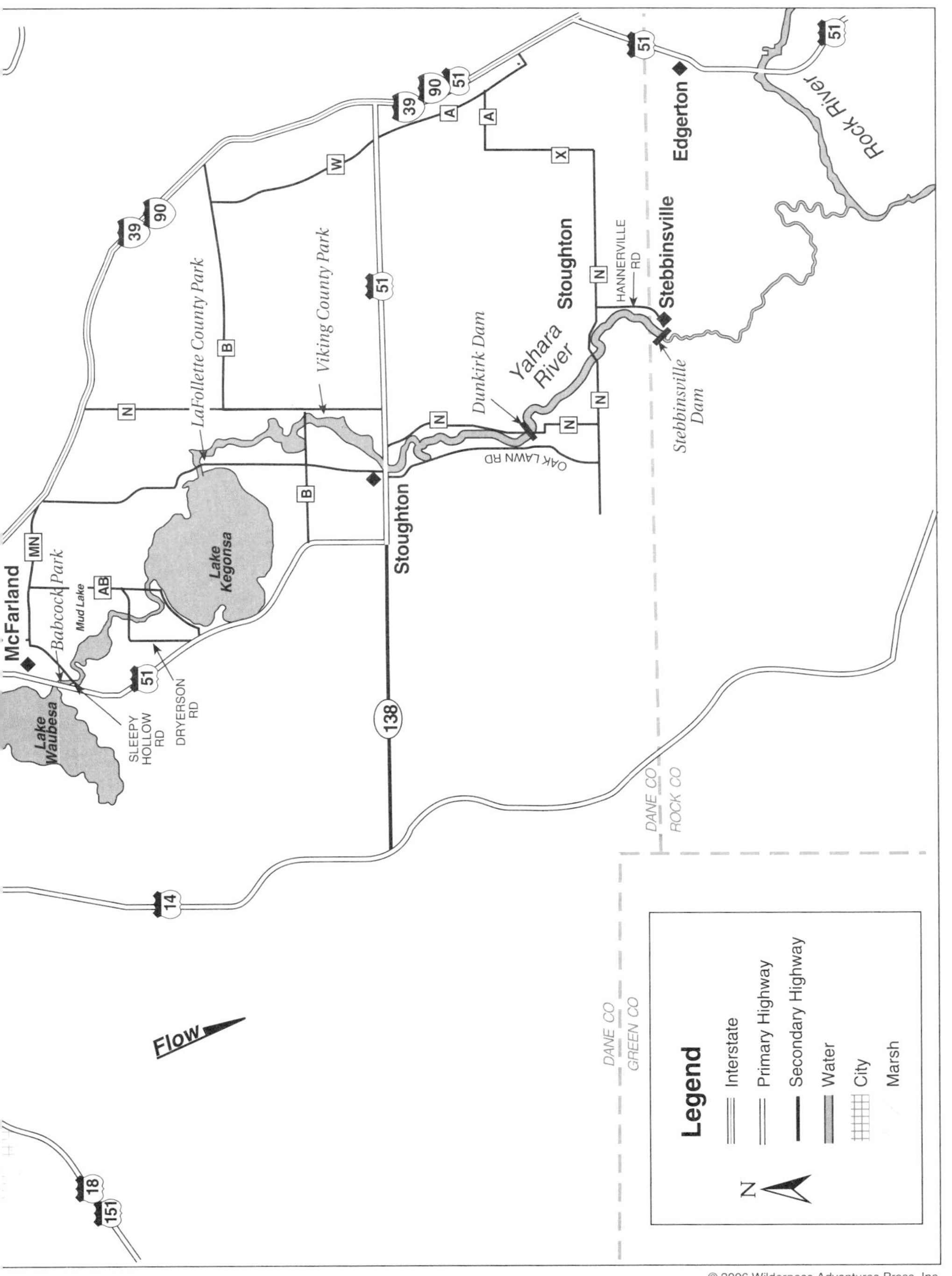

McFarland
Babcock Park
Mud Lake
Lake Waubesa
Lake Kegonsa
SLEEPY HOLLOW RD
DRYERSON RD
LaFollette County Park
Viking County Park
Stoughton
Dunkirk Dam
Yahara River
OAK LAWN RD
HANNERVILLE RD
Stebbinsville
Stebbinsville Dam
Edgerton
Rock River
DANE CO
ROCK CO
GREEN CO
Flow
Legend
Interstate
Primary Highway
Secondary Highway
Water
City
Marsh
N

The next section of interest on the Yahara River is the short stretch that runs between the Tenney Park locks and Lake Monona. More specifically, the mouth of the river at Yahara Place Park on Yahara Place at Lake Monona is probably *the* spot on the Madison Lakes to fish the white bass run. White bass, inveterate minnow eaters, begin to school as early as late April and concentrate in May and June. When you see a hail of minnows coming up to the surface this time of year, you've probably found a white bass school. Fish them with streamer patterns right at the river mouth and along the shoreline.

A bonus along the Monona shoreline is the population of big bluegills. I good day's fishing might leave you with a mixed bag of white bass and bluegill. I've caught white bass to 2 pounds and bluegills to half a pound in this area. It's a great way to pass a summer evening, either fishing from a small boat or casting from shore. If you plan to eat a few white bass, ice them immediately, and they'll be succulent. Leave them in the sun, even briefly, and they become oily and unpalatable.

The Yahara's outflow from Squaw Bay on Lake Monona is another good area for bass and panfish. A friend of mine fishes this area in a float tube, casting streamers along boat moorings and any kind of structure. He routinely catches crappies in the 10- to 12-inch range, big bluegills, and lots of largemouths. It could also be fished effectively from shore or from a small boat. Fish early in the day, around sunup, or you'll be dodging boats. You can access this stretch at Paunack Park off Bridge Road or at Highway BW. The launch at BW is a logical place to put in to fish the river above Upper Mud Lake. Paddle or motor beneath the Beltline Highway and fish the river

The Wisconsin DNR provides stiles that allow anglers access to quality trout water.

anywhere you see weeds. Coontail and pondweed grow here, along with a limited amount of wild celery. For some reason Upper Mud's panfish don't reach the size of Mendota's or Monona's, but they are still a lot of fun on a fly rod. You'll also run into an occasional northern or bass. Carp are numerous, too numerous. Do the lake a favor and keep one to bury in your garden.

Below Lake Waubesa, the Yahara River flows into what is known as Lower Mud Lake. Lower Mud and the Yahara here are good producers of northern pike, panfish, and bass. And while its weeds are not what they were in the 1950s, there's enough coontail and milfoil to provide some spawning cover. To access this stretch, a cartop boat is helpful. Cross the Yahara in McFarland on Highway 51 at Babcock Park; take your first left on Sleepy Hollow Road, which crosses the river. Take a right immediately after the bridge and follow the small road until you see a dirt track on your right leading to the river. You'll find a rough launch for cartop boats (no trailers). Paddle downstream to Lower Mud Lake.

Panfish can be taken here as early as mid-April. Northerns and bass can be caught throughout the year. Since access to Lower Mud is somewhat limited you won't be overrun with powerboats. There's a rocky 2-mile stretch of the Yahara between Lower Mud Lake and Lake Kegonsa in which smallmouth bass, northern pike, and panfish are present. You can wade it or put a boat in on Dryerson Road, which comes off Highway 51. Lake Kegonsa provides a modest fishery for panfish and gamefish; however, it sees a lot of motor traffic, making it of limited interest to the flyfisher.

The quieter waters of the Yahara lie between the outlet of Lake Kegonsa and the Stebbinsville Dam 15 miles to the south. Jason Burnham, fishing manager at Dorn Sporting Goods on Midvale Road in Madison, says you'll find small northern pike, panfish, walleye, and large and smallmouth bass on this undeveloped stretch of river. You can put in immediately below the outlet of Kegonsa and fish the marshy stretch that runs through LaFollette County Park or put in downstream at Highway B above the town of Stoughton. These are launch-from-the-bridge operations, so a trailered boat won't be of much use.

Just above Highway B is the area known as the Widespread. Its islands and weeds make for good bass and panfish habitat. Fish the creek inlet on the east side for northerns. Below Highway B is Viking County Park, a rockier stretch more favorable to smallmouth and walleye. There is good shoreline access in the park. This stretch offers the angler solitude in a pretty setting close to a major city. A 5-weight rod and a fly box with a selection of leech patterns, streamers, bass bugs, and poppers will do nicely. I feel it's almost a duty of any good steward to fish lesser known rivers and marshes. These places need advocates too, and it's only when people get to know places and their inhabitants that they begin to care for them. The Yahara River between Lake Kegonsa and Stoughton is just such a stretch.

Below Stoughton there are two more put-ins on County N and about 8 miles of river to explore. You can put in on County N immediately below the Dunkirk Dam or farther downstream on Highway N closer to Stebbinsville. This stretch has good bass populations, and walleye congregate around the dam in Dunkirk in spring and fall. Below Stebbinsville, the Yahara is a small stream without much to offer the angler.

Hub City: Madison

The eastern edge of the Driftless area begins about 10 miles west of Madison, around Cross Plain. Madison, being the state capital and location of the University of Wisconsin-Madison, which hosts some 40,000 students, has a plethora of accommodations and services, making it a good base to explore streams like Story Creek, Mount Vernon Creek, Black Earth Creek, and Rowan Creek (covered in the Sand County region). In addition, the Madison Chain of Lakes offers some of the best fishing in the state for panfish, smallmouth, northern pike, and muskies.

Madison has a fairly diverse population. Its south side is home to Mexican and southeast Asian restaurants and communities. Downtown houses a good mix of Middle-Eastern, Mediterranean, Asian, and pub-type eateries, catering both to business people and UW students who hail from all over the globe. State Street, which connects the capitol building and the university, is a lively mix of restaurants, coffee shops, record stores and specialty stores. Madison's population is 200,000 and—for better or for worse—growing.

Accommodations

Best Western InnTowner, 2424 University Ave., Madison; 800-258-8321; across the street from Ivy Inn, nice residential neighborhood; $$$

Concourse Hotel, 1 West Dayton Street, Madison; 800-356-8293; elegant hotel off Capitol Square and State Street; $$$

Comfort Inn, 4822 East Washington Ave., Madison; 608-244-6265; located off I-90/94 on Madison's far east side; $$

Campgrounds

Governor Nelson State Park, 5140 County Highway M, Waunakee; 608-831-3005; 5 miles from Madison's north side

Lake Kegonsa State Park, 2405 Door Creek Rd., Stoughton; 608-873-9695; 10 miles from Madison's south side

Token Creek County Park, just north of intersection of Highway 51 and Interstate 90/94 5 miles north of Madison. Fish Token Creek, which runs through the park or Rowan Creek, just 15 miles north.

Restaurants

Husnu's Turkish Restaurant, 547 State St., Madison; 608-256-0900; reasonably priced middle-eastern food on State Street; a sure bet for kabobs, curries, stews and grilled fish.

La Hacienda, 515 Park St., Madison; 608-255-8227; great Mexican food, open till 3 am

Vientiane Palace Restaurant, 151 W. Gorham, Madison; 608-255-2848; good, hot Thai food just off State Street

Famous Dave's Bar-B-Que, 900 S. Park St., Madison; 608-286-9400; a Midwest chain, good smoky meat, heaping portions and good sides; don't miss the drunken apples

Avenue Bar, 1128 E. Washington, Madison; 608-257-6877; great steaks, fish fry, and bloody marys; make reservations for Friday and Saturday nights

Great Dane Pub and Brewery, 123 E. Doty, Madison; 608-284-0000; excellent micro-brewery and pub food in a historic Doty Hotel

Culver's Frozen Custard and Hamburgers, 1325 Northport Drive, Madison; 608-242-7731; local chain on Madison's north side—great burgers, ice cream and malts

Hong Kong Cafe, 2 S. Mills, Madison; 608-259-1668; huge portions, great Chinese food, located just south of the UW campus

The usual chains can be found on all the major commerce thoroughfares. On the east side, East Washington Avenue (also known as Highway 151); on the north side, Northport Drive (also known as Highway 113); on the west side, University Avenue; and on the south side, Park Street (a continuation of Highway 151).

Fly Shops, Outfitters, Sporting Goods, Licenses

Fontana Sports Specialistes, 7948 Tree Lane, Madison; 608-833-9191; www.fontanasports.com; guiding for trout and warmwater species

Streamside Outfitters, 2120 Main Street, Cross Plains; 608 295 6517; streamside-outfitters.com; fly shop and guide service on banks of Black Earth Creek

Cabela's, Highway 35, Prairie du Chien, 608 326 7163; full line of fly fishing gear and good source of information on Driftless streams

Madison Orvis, 1700 Deming Road, Greenway Station, Madison; 608-831-3181; full line of fly fishing gear on Madison's west side

D&S Bait and Tackle, 1411 Northport Dr., Madison; 608-241-4225; good source of information for fishing Madison Lakes, weekly fishing report

Dorn True Value, 1348 S. Midvale Blvd., Madison; 608-274-2511; good selection of flies, right off Beltline Highway

Wisconsin Department of Natural Resources, P.O. Box 7921, Madison; 608-266-2621; downtown DNR office sells licenses during regular business hours

Gander Mountain, 6199 Metra Drive, DeForest; 608-242-9532

Veterinarians

Spring Harbor Veterinary Associates (west), 5129 University Avenue, Madison; 608-238-3461

Spring Harbor Veterinary Associates (east), 5223 Monona Drive, Madison; 608-222-9342

Emergency Clinic for Animals, 229 W. Beltline, Madison; 608-274-7772; 24-hour urgent care if your pet needs it

Medical

University of Wisconsin Hospital and Clinics, 600 Highland Ave., Madison; 608-263-6400

St. Mary's Hospital, 707 S. Mills St., Madison; 608-251-6100

Auto Rental

Enterprise Rent-a-Car, 800-325-8007 (out of town rentals), 800-736-8222 (rentals while in Madison)

National Car Rental, Dane County Regional Airport, 608-249-1614, (800-CAR-RENT)

Automobile Repair

Jensen's Auto Clinic, 1233 Regent St., Madison; 608-257-9201; good garage on Madison's near west side

Tom's Auto Clinic, 2652 E. Washington Avenue, Madison; 608-241-3391; good garage on Madison's east side

Puccio's Towing Service, 813 Stewart, Madison; 608-273-0535; 24-hour towing service

Air Service

Dane County Regional Airport

For More Information

Madison Chamber of Commerce
615 E. Washington Avenue
Madison, WI 53703
800-373-6376 or 608-256-8348
www.visitmadison.com

Otter Creek holds some rainbows. (Chris Halla)

OTTER CREEK

Otter Creek is the source of Blackhawk Lake, north of Cobb and west of Dodgeville. Below Blackhawk Lake, it then runs north for 15 miles to join the Wisconsin River east of Avoca. Fly fishers should concentrate on the 5 miles below the outlet of Blackhawk Lake from Plank Road downstream to County II. This broad, open and fertile stretch fishes well during the March and April season; it is catch and release. Casting is easy here and insect life abundant.

To reach Otter Creek, take Highway 18 to Dodgeville and then follow Highway Q 8 miles to the northwest where it will cross the stream. Follow Highway Q to fish upstream; follow Highway II to fish downstream, where habitat is a bit more open. Access along Highway Q and Highway II is turn-offs and fence-stiles.

Caddis, scuds, and minnow imitations all fish well here.

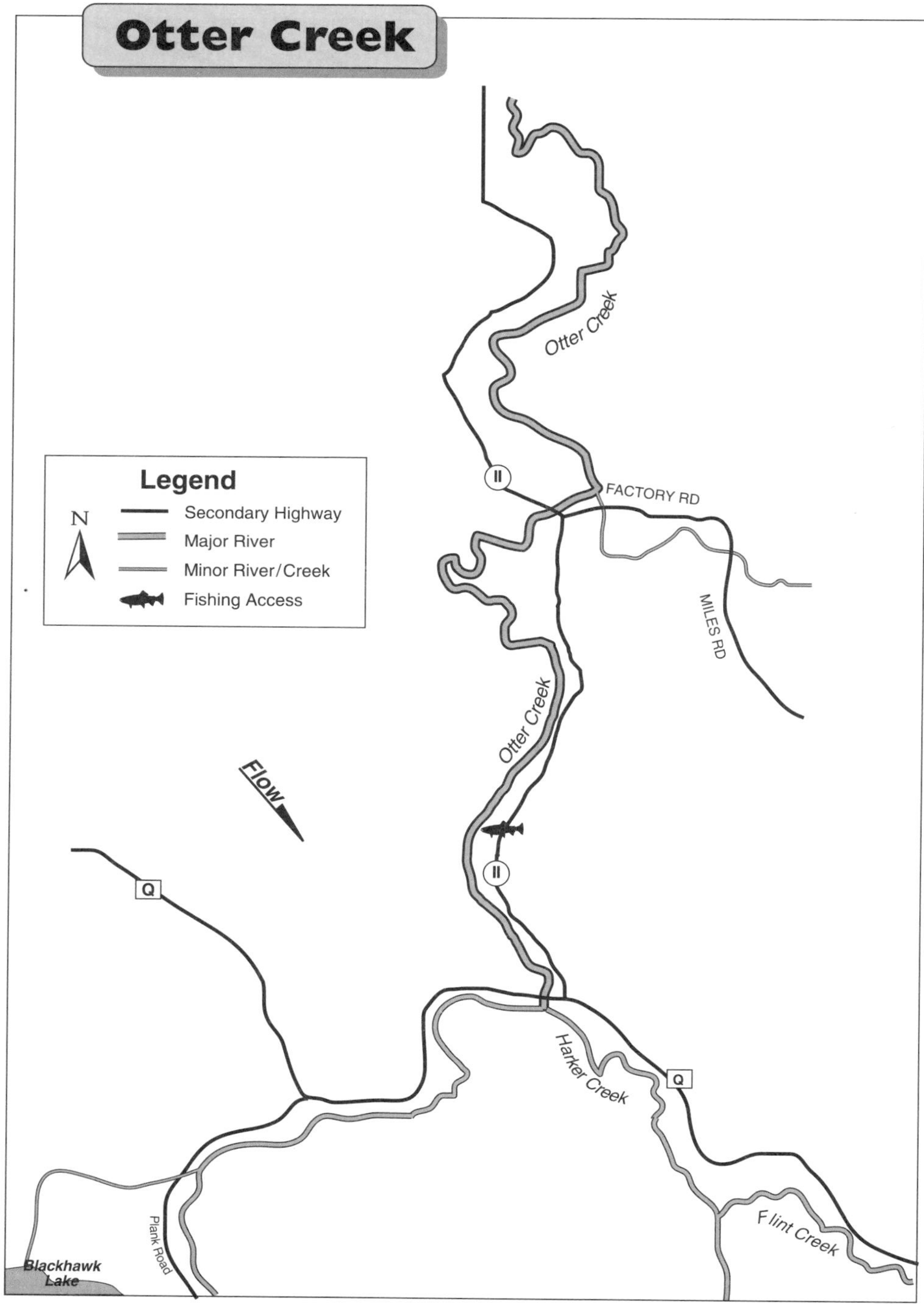
Otter Creek
Legend
N
Secondary Highway
Major River
Minor River/Creek
Fishing Access
Otter Creek
II
FACTORY RD
MILES RD
Otter Creek
Flow
II
Q
Q
Harker Creek
Flint Creek
Plank Road
Blackhawk Lake
© 2006 Wilderness Adventures Press, Inc.

Stream Facts: Otter Creek

Season
- The early season runs from the first Saturday in March to the last Sunday before the first Saturday in May; no-kill, single barbless hooks only. Regular season runs from the first Saturday in May at 5:00 am through September 30.

Regulations
- County Q upstream to Plank Road: no-kill, artificials only. Upstream from Mount Hope Road, category 5 (2 trout limit; size limit, 12 inches).

Species
- Rainbow and brown trout; limited natural reproduction among browns.

Miles of Trout Water
- 8 miles

Stream Characteristics
- Spring creek; flows through open meadow making for easy casting. Abundant scuds, caddis, forage fish, and mayflies. Yields large browns every year.

Access
- DNR holdings along Highway II.

Fly Shops
- Gander Mountain, Fontana Sports, Madison Orvis, Streamside Outfitters

Maps
- *Wisconsin Atlas and Gazetteer*, page 34

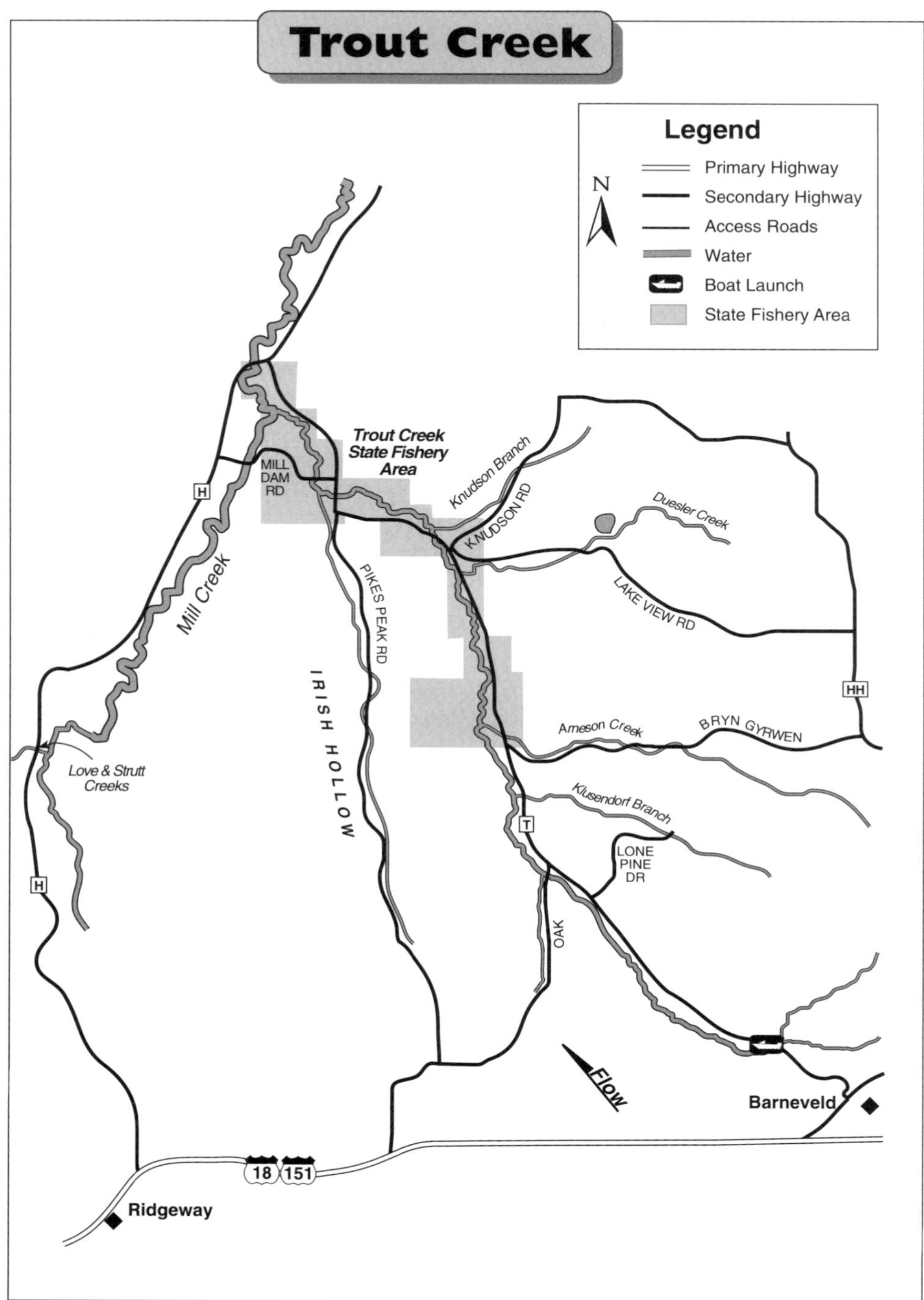
Trout Creek
Legend
Primary Highway
Secondary Highway
Access Roads
Water
Boat Launch
State Fishery Area
N
Trout Creek State Fishery Area
MILL DAM RD
Knudson Branch
KNUDSON RD
Duesler Creek
LAKE VIEW RD
PIKES PEAK RD
IRISH HOLLOW
Mill Creek
H
HH
Arneson Creek
BRYN GYRWEN
Love & Strutt Creeks
Klusendorf Branch
T
LONE PINE DR
OAK
Flow
Barneveld
18
151
Ridgeway
© 2006 Wilderness Adventures Press, Inc.

Trout Creek

According to fisheries biologist Gene Van Dyk, Trout Creek is basically a wild brown trout fishery with a few stocked brookies. It has good per-mile trout densities. Ninety-seven percent of the trout in here are 13 inches or smaller, according to Van Dyk, and they are "extremely wary." This echoes the high densities but relatively small wild fish of other prime southwest Wisconsin streams like Timber Coulee. The large impoundment (called Birch Lake on some maps) on County T in the upper reaches of Trout Creek does not have a positive influence on this stream. It channels silt into the section immediately below the dam, whereas if this silt were allowed to flow freely throughout the stream its effect would be more dispersed and, overall, less harmful. The silt and oxygen depletion caused by the dam have made it all but impossible for brook trout to reproduce.

From its headwaters to the dam, Trout Creek is of little interest to the trout angler. This impoundment is visible from Highway T (which can be reached from downtown Barneveld—rebuilt after a devastating tornado in 1984). Below the dam, and until its confluence with Mill Creek, there is generous public access indicated by DNR signs and parking areas along County T. Mill Creek is category 5 (catch-and-release with no gear restrictions) trout water between Highway H upstream to Mill Road. Downstream from the south line of S30, T17, and R5E, Trout Creek is category 5 (catch-and-release; no gear restriction). Otherwise, it is category 3.

Despite some ag runoff and problems with silt, caddis, scuds, sowbugs, midges, and several varieties of mayflies are present. I heard one story of a UW-Madison professor driving his sweetheart to a Shakespeare performance at American Player's Theatre in Spring Green who caught and released a 20-inch rainbow trout (probably a stocker since rainbows aren't known to reproduce here) from the County Highway T bridge on his first cast and then continued on his way. You might give nearby Strutt and Love Creeks a try if your efforts on Trout Creek are drawing a blank. They are, respectively, a decent-sized tributary of Mill Creek and tiny clear headwater stream holding exceedingly wary trout.

Mill Creek either holds lunker browns or no trout at all depending on whom you talk to. I've caught only suckers here, but it has the feel of water that might hold real lunkers, particularly near its confluence with bona fide trout streams.

Stream Facts: Trout Creek

Season

- The early season runs from the first Saturday in March to the last Sunday before the first Saturday in May; no-kill, single barbless hooks only. Regular season runs from the first Saturday in May at 5:00 am through September 30.

Regulations

- Downstream of south line of S30, T17, R5E category 5 (catch-and-release, no gear restriction); otherwise category 3.

Species

- Wild brown trout; some stocked brook trout.

Miles of Trout Water

- 8 miles

Stream Characteristics

- Spring creek; flows through wooded meadow. Abundant scuds, caddis, forage fish, and mayflies. Impoundments cause silt and oxygen problems.

Access

- DNR holdings along Highway T.

Fly Shops

- Streamside Outfitters

Maps

- *Wisconsin Atlas and Gazetteer*, pages 34-35

The Blue River

While my log results show only modest success at the Blue, reports from the trout cognoscenti indicate that I must be doing something wrong. One DNR employee fishes it almost every weekend during trout season. His routine? Get up at 4 am and leave Madison at 4:30. Arrive 6:30 at stream. Fish until 8:30. Return home. His rationale: that's when it's least crowded, most shadowy, and best for fishing. He's probably right, although I lack his self-discipline. The bit about shadows seems particularly accurate since I've only caught fish here in low-light or rainy conditions.

Bowers Road, below Snow Bottom Road, is a good place to begin. There is a gravel lot there maintained by the DNR and many promising-looking holes both up and

Rigging up for the evening hatch.

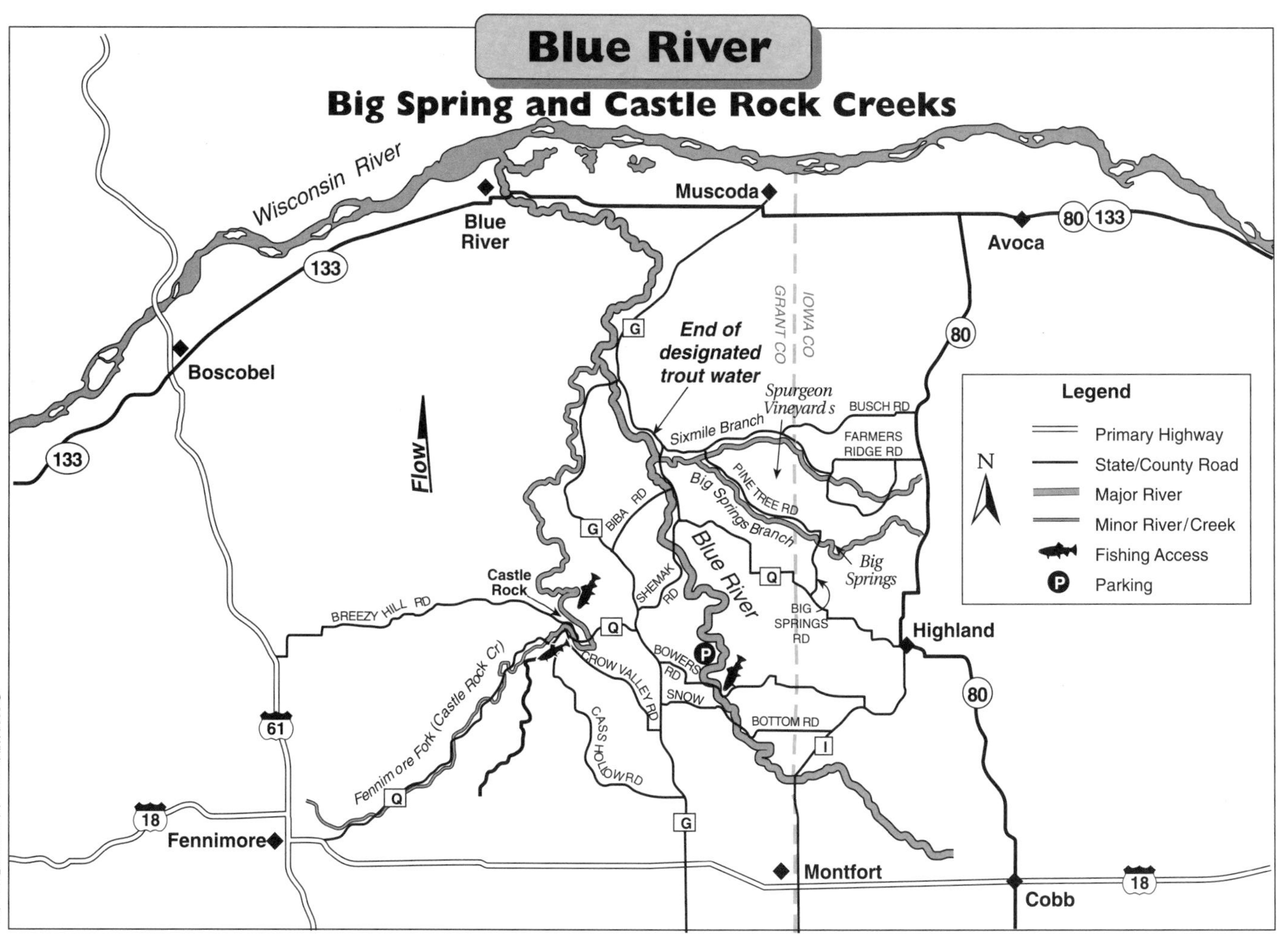
Blue River
Big Spring and Castle Rock Creeks
Wisconsin River
Blue River
Muscoda
Avoca
Boscobel
80
133
End of designated trout water
IOWA CO
GRANT CO
Spurgeon Vineyard s
BUSCH RD
FARMERS RIDGE RD
Sixmile Branch
PINE TREE RD
Big Springs Branch
Big Springs
BIBA RD
SHEMAK RD
Blue River
BIG SPRINGS RD
Castle Rock
BREEZY HILL RD
BOWERS RD
CROW VALLEY RD
SNOW
BOTTOM RD
CASS HOLLOW RD
Fennim ore Fork (Castle Rock Cr)
Flow
Highland
Fennimore
Montfort
Cobb
61
18
G
Q
I
Legend
Primary Highway
State/County Road
Major River
Minor River/Creek
Fishing Access
Parking
N

downstream. I like to fish upstream in a valley that is studded with elms and oaks and rock outcrops, prime morel mushroom habitat. Perhaps this explains my lack of luck on those May outings—I'm thinking about mushrooms instead of trout. These holes are good nymphing water. If you care to fish downstream, you have plenty of access in that direction, too. It is known for having good Blue-Winged Olive hatches and supports good numbers of caddis with its gravel runs and excellent water quality.

The lower end of the Blue, below Shemak, is more heavily posted and begins to take on that "lower watershed look" of siltier, deeper water. Given that the upper reaches of the Blue are reputed to hold very large trout, one shudders to think what lies beneath the fallen willows here. From Snow Bottom Road upstream to the Iowa County line, this stream is category 5 (no-kill, artificials only). From Biba Road upstream to Snow Bottom Road, it is category 5 (2-trout limit, minimum size 12 inches). Big Rock Creek, off County Q outside Highland, is a category 5 (no-kill). Chances are, if the DNR is managing it as category 5, they feel it has some potential.

Stream Facts: Blue River

Season

- The early season runs from the first Saturday in March to the last Sunday before the first Saturday in May; no-kill, single barbless hooks only. Regular season runs from the first Saturday in May at 5:00 am through September 30.

Regulations

- Snow Bottom Road upstream to Iowa County line, category 5—no-kill, artificials only; otherwise, category 5 (2-trout limit; 12-inch minimum size).

Species

- Brown and rainbow trout stocked. Limited natural reproduction among browns; some very large fish present.

Miles of Trout Water

- 14

Stream Characteristics

- Spring creek; flows through open and wooded meadow with rock outcrops—lovely Driftless scenery, especially during green-up in May. Abundant scuds, caddis, forage fish, and mayflies. Yields large browns every year.

Access

- DNR holdings at various road crossings—Bluff Road, Snow Bottom Road, Bower Road.

Fly Shops

- Gander Mountain, Madison Orvis, Fontana Sports, Streamside Outfitters

Maps

- *Wisconsin Atlas and Gazetteer*, pages 25, 33

Brookies on watercress.

Castle Rock Creek. (Chris Halla)

CASTLE ROCK CREEK

Castle Rock Creek is a broad fertile stream regarded by some as the crown jewel of southwest Wisconsin's spring creeks. Beginning northeast of Fennimore in Grant County, Castle Rock is known for good hatches and big trout. Mainly brown are present in the 6.5 miles of designated trout water, with an occasional rainbow or brook trout showing up.

High alkalinity makes it very fertile, and this accounts for rich mats of submerged vegetation and insect life. Despite extensive stocking of wild-strain fish, however, natural reproduction remains poor. The stretch from Church Road downstream to the second County Q bridge is category 5 (catch-and-release, artificials only). From Witek Road upstream to the second County Q bridge, it is category 5 (2-trout limit; minimum size 12 inches). According to Todd Polacek, owner of now-closed Madison Outfitters, Castle Rock's numerous springs help keep it free of ice and at a constant water temperature year-round. As a result, a wide variety of insects (cressbugs, scuds, mayflies, caddis, and midge larvae) are present at all times, offering a constant food source for the trout. Besides poor natural reproduction, turbidity is also a problem on Castle Rock. Anglers should seek other nearby venues (the Blue or Borah and Crooked Creeks come to mind) during Wisconsin's not infrequent gully-washers.

An essential imitation to carry on all Wisconsin spring creeks, midges are present in good numbers throughout the season at Castle Rock. Mid-April to mid-May is the peak of the Blue-Winged Olive hatch, according to Polacek, who also notes that there is an excellent Sulphur hatch in June. Fly-fishing companions of mine report having seen Blue-Winged Olive hatches as early as late January during the early 1990s when there was a winter trout season in certain southwest counties, making BWO patterns another essential group of flies to bring to Castle Rock.

"Caddis hatches can be great here," says Polacek, who favors a size 16 Henryville Special. April and May are good months for this American Grannon hatch. As caddis larvae are present all year, Tom Ehlert fishes a beadhead caddis nymph here well into summer. Of course there are times when there are no visible hatches. During these times, Polacek says, "reach for the nymphing stick." A size 16 olive scud is an excellent choice. Don't neglect "meat" flies such as crawfish imitations, minnow-mimicking streamers, and, of course, Woolly Buggers. Browns in the 20-inch range are common, and there's always the chance of running into a broodstock fish here in the 27-inch range.

I've also enjoyed good terrestrial fishing here in midsummer using beetle and cricket imitations. While the surrounding pasturelands are thick with grasshoppers, I've never had much luck with hopper imitations. Polacek also fishes a two-fly rig with a bushy dry on top and a cressbug or midge larvae deeper in the water column.

To repeat myself a bit: stealth and presentation are more important than fly choice. Much of this stream runs through broad open pasture, and your shadow will ruin your fishing if you don't take care to keep a low profile. Ditto for heavy footsteps along the streambank which, felt in the fishes' lateral line, send them scurrying for the nearest clump of watercress.

Access is good along County Highway Q, which parallels Castle Rock Creek, and the DNR owns many streamside acres along the creek as well. Look for DNR parking areas and/or stiles for access points. Castle Rock's good flow and relatively low water temperatures are due in part to a large spring in the upper reaches that pumps in thousands of gallons of cold water per minute.

Look for deep pasture pools upstream from the first County Q bridge. Trout can be found as far downstream as Witek Road, the end of officially designated trout water. Don't be surprised if there are a few big trout lurking in these margins, growing fat on chubs and crawfish. Much below Witek Road, however, rough fish predominate. Doc Smith Branch is a tributary, the lower 1.4 miles of which are category 5 (artificials only, catch-and-release); it becomes category 4 above Everson Road.

Stream Facts: Castle Rock Creek

Season

- The early season runs from the first Saturday in March to the last Sunday before the first Saturday in May; no-kill, single barbless hooks only. Regular season from the first Saturday in May at 5:00 am through September 30.

Regulations

- Church Road downstream to first Highway Q bridge category 5 (no-kill, artificials only); Witek Road upstream to second County Q bridge, category 5 (2-trout limit; minimum size 12 inches).

Species

- Stocked brown and rainbow trout. Limited natural reproduction among browns; some very large fish present.

Miles of Trout Water

- 6.5 miles

Stream Characteristics

- Spring creek; flows through open and wooded meadow with rock outcrops. Very fertile, with abundant scuds, caddis, forage fish, and mayflies. Holds large browns; tremendous growth rate.

Access

- DNR holdings along Highway Q.

Fly Shops

- Gander Mountain, Madison Orvis, Fontana Sports, Streamside Outfitters

Maps

- *Wisconsin Atlas and Gazetteer*, page 25, 33

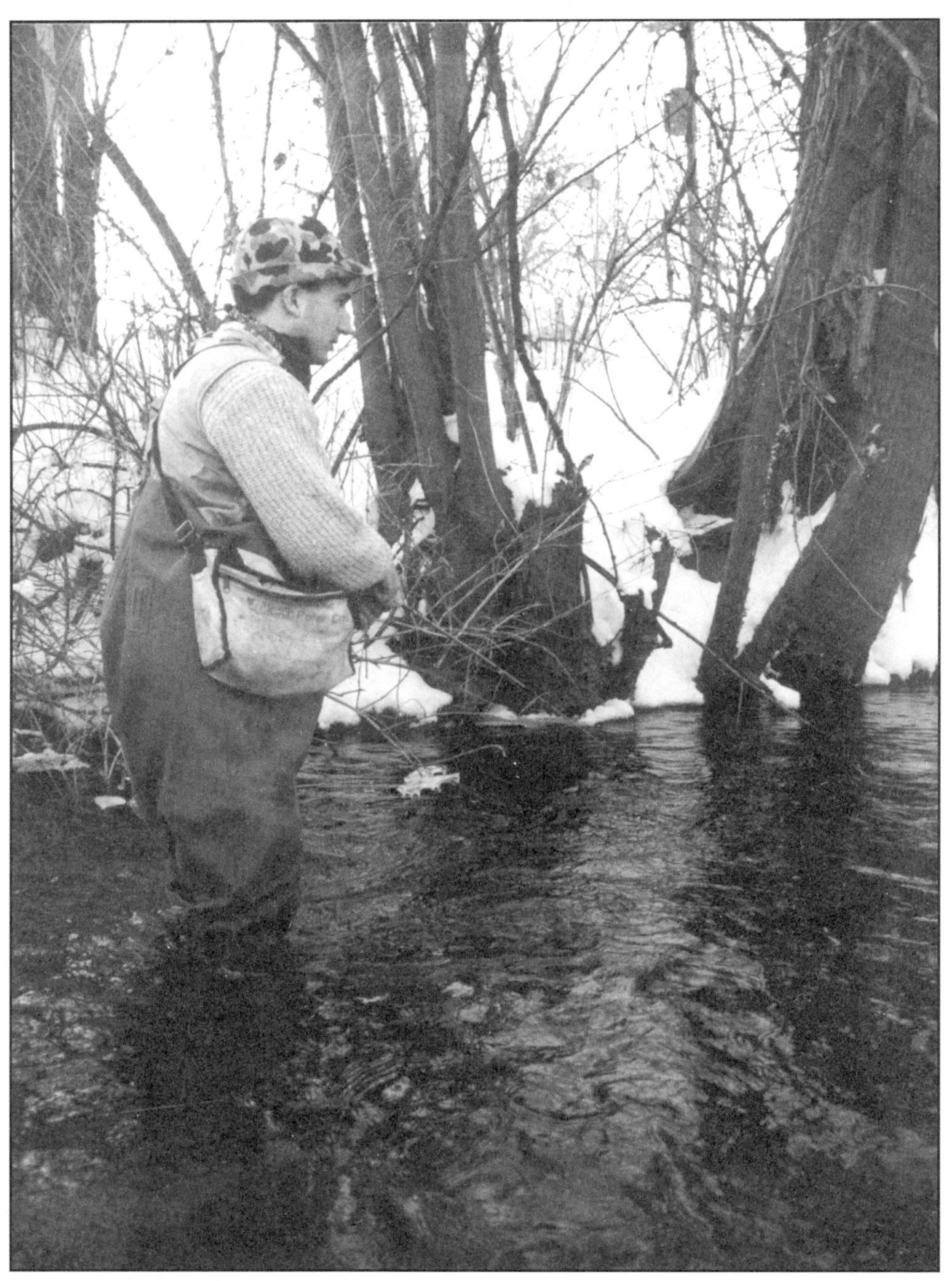

Early season trout fishing in Driftless country can be a chilly but productive proposition.

Big Spring Creek

This tributary joins the Blue River—via Six Mile Branch—just downstream from the end of the Blue's designated trout water. It is called Big Spring Creek (sometimes referred to as Big Spring Branch elsewhere) in the DNR *Trout Fishing Regulations and Guide*. Both names surely derive from Big Spring near the headwaters of this creek.

The creek runs along the Iowa-Grant County border northwest of the town of Highland. Take Highway Q north out of Highland to Pine Tree Road. The water upstream from Pine Tree Road is category 5—no-kill, artificials only. From Pine Tree Road to its confluence with Six Mile Branch, it is category 5 (daily bag limit 2 trout; minimum size 12 inches). You can access the upper reaches via Big Springs Road, the lower two-thirds of the creek via Pine Tree Road. In all, Big Spring Creek is about 6 miles long, all trout water, with the upper reaches supporting wild brookies and browns; the lower reaches are stocked with brown trout.

Ten years after the fact, I still regret not having my rod along when my wife and I visited Spurgeon Vineyard, through which Big Spring Branch runs. It looked very trouty and not heavily fished. While the Blue and Castle Rock hold more trout per mile, you might try Big Spring Branch for a change of pace sometime, especially if you can't find the solitude you're looking for on these popular waters.

If you go on a vineyard tour, bring your fly rod along. That way your spouse won't have to hear you complain for ten years.

Galena River

This is one of the two smallmouth bass rivers that Gene Van Dyk, area fisheries biologist, recommends, the other being the Little Platte. While agricultural runoff and spring floods continue to hamper this fishery, there is still some good fishing to be had by those willing to explore this rugged corner of the state. There is little public land along these streams so you will have to ask permission of the landowner, or make sure to keep your feet wet.

The Galena River begins near the town of Elk Grove in southwestern Lafayette County. It then crosses Highway 81 and flows south for some 20 miles before crossing Highway 11 near the town of Benton and then on to the Illinois line. Between Highways 81 and 11, the Galena picks up tributary flow and becomes a stream of larger size. Fish it below Jenkynsville; Twin Bridges Road might be a good place to begin your efforts.

Smallmouth bass generally eat minnows and crawfish, thus any fly imitating these would be a good choice. A Muddler Minnow, which could pass as a minnow, chub, crawfish, or sculpin, is a good all-around choice. A size 12 would be about right, as most of these fish are in the 9- to 13-inch range. This kind of fishing is akin to trout fishing. Look for gravel-bottom runs or structure such as rocks and trees. Also, look for springs and feeder creeks, since smallmouth are coolwater fish.

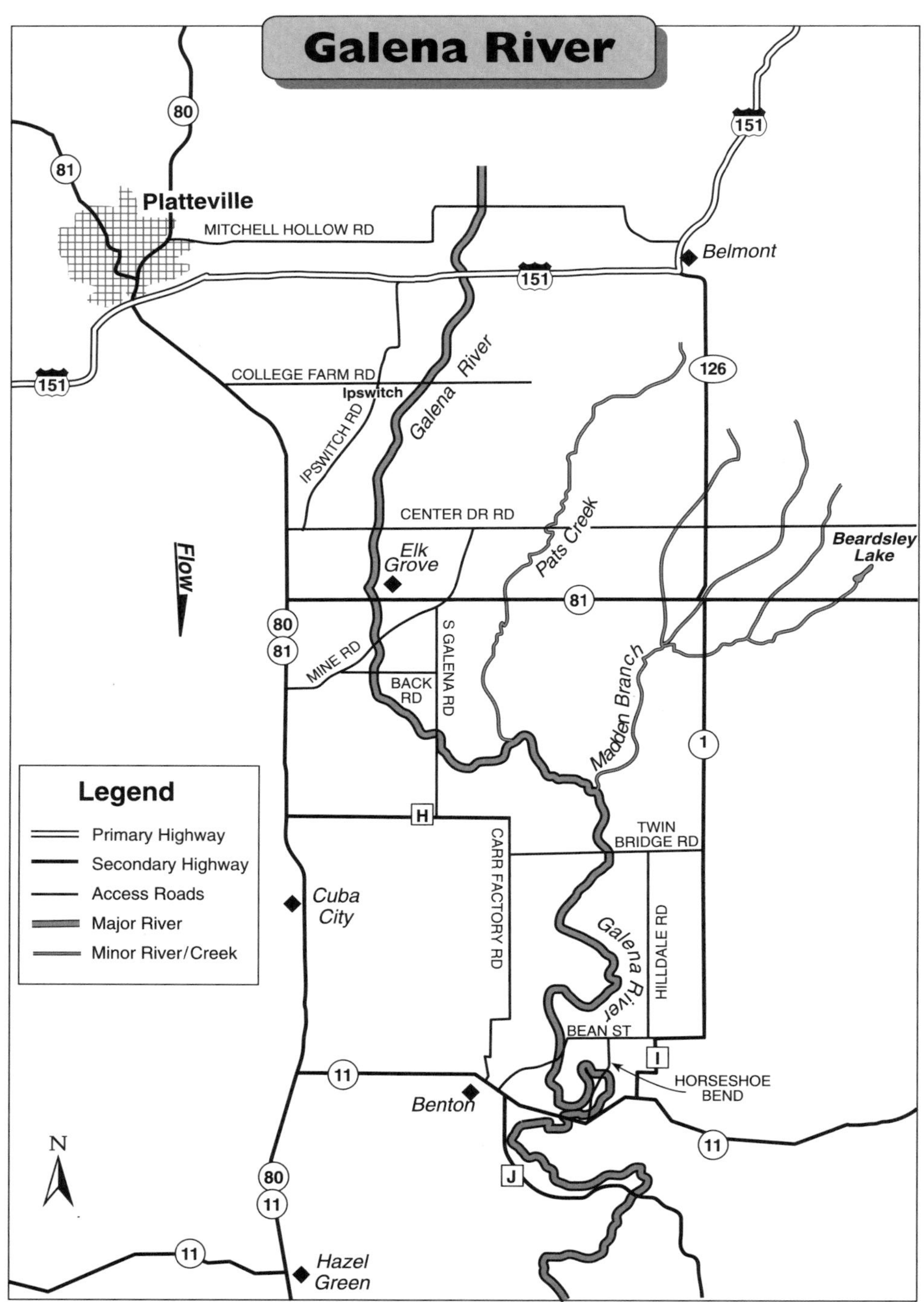
Galena River
80
81
Platteville
MITCHELL HOLLOW RD
151
Belmont
151
COLLEGE FARM RD
Ipswitch
IPSWITCH RD
Galena River
126
CENTER DR RD
Elk Grove
Pats Creek
Beardsley Lake
Flow
81
80
81
MINE RD
BACK RD
S GALENA RD
Madden Branch
1
Legend
Primary Highway
Secondary Highway
Access Roads
Major River
Minor River/Creek
H
CARR FACTORY RD
TWIN BRIDGE RD
Cuba City
Galena River
HILLDALE RD
BEAN ST
I
HORSESHOE BEND
11
Benton
11
N
J
80
11
11
Hazel Green

During recent years, topsoil washing into these streams along with an increase in pesticide use, has hurt the fishery. Van Dyk hopes for drier springs. That would help keep habitat intact, and perhaps help bolster breeding stocks of these hard-fighting fish. Smallmouth bass must be at least 14 inches to be a keeper here, so fish barbless flies (as you will be releasing most or all of your fish).

The Little Platte

The Little Platte River can be described as a two-tier fishery. The headwaters stretch holds trout, and the lower reaches hold smallmouth and an occasional walleye and channel catfish, as well as rough fish such as carp and suckers. Around the town of Arthur, you can enjoy some good trout fishing. There's also a friendly tavern in Arthur with good food if the fishing isn't hot. Between Waterfall Road and Highway 80, there is a catch-and-release, artificials-only stretch holding some good browns. Above Highway 80, the stream is category 3. By far the best habitat is in the catch-and-release area. The upstream section is too small and narrow to bother with. Use your spring-creek stalking techniques here, as the banks don't have much cover. Fish a scud pattern on a long leader and stay back from the bank.

While an occasional trout may show up below Waterfall Road, water temperatures warm quickly. Also, the heavy farming in this area takes its toll on streams—fertilizer, pesticide, topsoil, and manure all wash in during floods and serve to lower water temperature and quality. You can pick up the stream again near Platteville on Highway 81. Below Platteville, Highway 151 more or less parallels the Little Platte. Bridge crossings can be found at Highway B, Stumptown Road, Maple Ridge Road, County O, Church Road, and Oak Road. Below the Highway 61/35 crossing, it becomes a marshy backwater where a few panfish and catfish may be found as it makes its way toward the Mississippi.

Other Rivers of Southwest Wisconsin

While other rivers in this part of the state suffer from the same environmental problems as rivers covered above, there are a handful worth mentioning. As with fishing the coulee streams for trout, there is a sort of art to fishing the far southwest for smallmouths.

This is an area where farm kids once struck out after chores with a minnow bucket to take a few hard-fighting bronzebacks. According to reliable sources, those days are not too far past—this was still happening in the sixties and seventies. The sense of closeness-to-land—like shooting a few squirrels for the stewpot from the back forty or taking the dogs down to the fenceline and kicking up a few roosters—seems important to mention if only for reasons of historical record. But who knows, if streams just 50 miles to the north in Crawford County can be returned to presettlement conditions, then maybe the smallmouth bass fisheries in the southwest streams can also be nursed back to health.

Worthy of mention in this regard are the Pecatonica, the Grant River near Lancaster, the east and main branch of the Pecatonica River in Lafayette County, the

Sinsinawa near Hazel Green, and the Sugar River from Verona in Dane County to the Illinois line. These are medium-sized muddy rivers so don't expect a pristine float. However, they also receive a good amount of tributary and spring flow, which helps lower water temperatures and improve quality. I'm not sure these rivers rank as first-class or even second-class fisheries, but if you want to see a bit of dairy country with a fly rod along in the canoe, then get out and paddle. Probably the best smallmouth fishing is found in the lower Wisconsin River between Spring Green and Prairie du Chien and anywhere on the Mississippi where there are wing dams or riprap and moderately swift current and rocks. Madison's Lake Mendota also offers first-rate smallmouth fishing just about anywhere rocks are present.

Twin Valley Lake

One of three lakes in Governor Dodge State Park just north of Dodgeville, Twin Valley Lake offers good angling for big largemouth bass. Launch a canoe or belly boat and work the weeds and stumps with deerhair bass bugs. May is the best time to fish largemouths at Twin Valley, but fish can be caught all summer, especially toward morning and evening.

Bass fishing in Twin Valley is catch-and-release. This helps the lake grow some very large bucketmouths. Only electric motors are allowed on this 152-acre lake. Cox Hollow and Halverson Lakes, also in the park, hold mostly panfish.

Hub City: Dodgeville

Named after Henry Dodge who became governor of the Wisconsin Territory in 1836, present-day Dodgeville is located where Dodge and others established a lead mine in 1827. Now home to the famed catalog company Lands' End, Dodgeville has a population of about 4,000, with numerous restaurants and motels. Governor Dodge State Park is just north of town on Highway 23. Dodgeville also makes a good base for exploring trout streams—Otter Creek and the Blue River to the west, Trout Creek and Mount Vernon Creek to the east. Bear Creek in Richland County is just a short drive up Highway 130. House on the Rock is a popular Dodgeville attraction, a collection of everything from knight's armor to Clark Gable posters. The Military Ridge Bicycle Trail runs from Verona to Dodgeville, along Highway 18/151, some 39 miles.

Accommodations

Super 8 Motel, 1308 Johns Street, Dodgeville; 608-935-3888, 800-800-8000; $$
Don Q Inn, Highway 23, Dodgeville; 800-666-7848; $$
Best Western, Highway 18, Dodgeville; 608-935-7739; $$
House on the Rock Inn, 3637 State Road 23 North, Dodgeville; 800-348-9310; $$
Pine Ridge Motel, County Highway YZ, Dodgeville; 608-935-3386; $

Campgrounds

Governor Dodge State Park, Route 1, Dodgeville; 608-935-2315; 5,000-acre state park with swimming lakes/beaches and hiking trails
Blackhawk State Recreation Area, 2025 County Highway BH, Highland; 608-623-2707; 20 miles west of Dodgeville off Highway 80
Tower Hill State Park, Route 3, Spring Green; 608-588-2116; 15 miles north of Dodgeville off Highway 23
Blue Mound State Park, P.O. Box 98, Blue Mounds; 608-437-5711; 10 miles east of
Dodgeville Spring Valley Campground, 3318 Spring Valley Road, Dodgeville; 608-935-5725; 12 miles northwest of Dodgeville, Highway 23 north to Highway 130 to Spring Valley Road
Tom's Campground, 2751 County Highway BB, Dodgeville; 608-935-5446

Restaurants

The Cook's Room, 102 N Iowa St., Dodgeville; 608-935-5282; gourmet sandwiches and specialty foods
Dean-o's, 110 Diagonal Street, Dodgeville; 608-935-9380; good tavern eatery
Pizza Hut, 1410 John's Street, Dodgeville; 608-935-2300

Outfitters/Sporting Goods

Jacquish Hollow Angler, 32491 Jaquish So. Rd., Richland Center; 608-585-2239; www.jacquishhollowangler.com
Streamside Outfitters, 2120 Main Street, Cross Plains; 608 295 6517; streamside-

outfitters.com; fly shop and guide service on banks of Black Earth Creek
Cabela's, Highway 35, Prairie du Chien, 608 326 7163; full line of fly fishing gear and good source of information on Driftless streams
Madison Orvis, 1700 Deming Road, Greenway Station, Madison; 608-831-3181; full line of fly fishing gear on Madison's west side
Rockin' K Fly Shop, P.O. Box 6, Coon Valley; 608-452-3678
Bob's Silver Doctor Fly Fishing, P.O. Box 105, Viroqua; 608-637-3417
Fontana Sports Specialists, 7948 Tree Lane, Madison; 608-833-9191; www.fontanasports.com

Veterinarians

Dodgeville Veterinary Service, 105 County Highway YZ, Dodgeville; 608-935-2306

Medical

Memorial Hospital of Iowa County, 825 S. Iowa St., Dodgeville; 608-935-2411

Auto Rental

Enterprise Rent-a-Car, 310 E. Leffler, Dodgeville; 608-935-7878

Automobile Repair

Hallada Motors, 306 Leffler St., Dodgeville; 608-935-2352

Air Service

Iowa County Airport, 3151 Highway 39, Mineral Point; 608-987-9931

For More Information

Dodgeville Chamber of Commerce
877-TO-DODGE
www.dodgeville.com

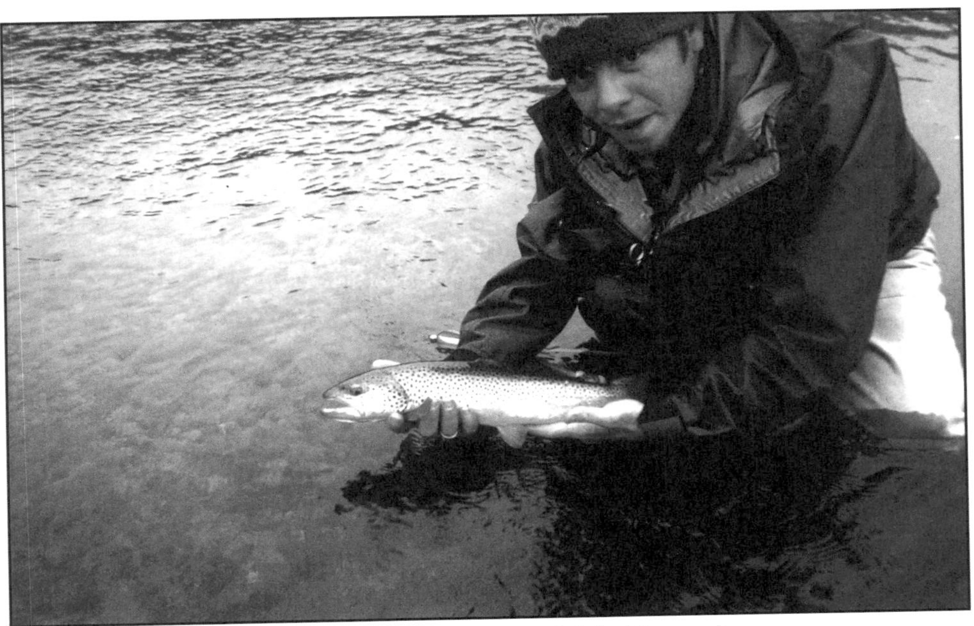

Bart Landwehr with a spring creek brown trout. (Blake Hanson)

Bear Creek

Meandering along the Sauk-Richland County border just west of Willow Creek is Bear Creek, a favorite of Dave Barron, who owns Jacquish Hollow Angler Guide Service. When he is not guiding in Alaska in August and September, Barron fishes the streams of Richland and Vernon County. "I don't carry a lot of flies," says one of the only certified master casters of Wisconsin. He likes to fish a Half-and-Half Emerger tipped with a Z-lon tail during the spring mayfly hatches; this "impressionist" pattern serves to imitate emerging Blue-Winged Olives, Pale Morning Duns, and Sulphurs. Given the good population of caddis in Bear Creek and nearby Willow, Barron often fishes a Yellow Stimulator, which also mimics an immature stonefly. A black beetle imitation is "the" fly for the dog days of summer, better than ants or hoppers, he notes. Barron's forays to Alaska are more than just getting away from the heat: Many if not most streams in the Driftless area become overgrown by weeds this time of year, making access and casting difficult. If you are not fishing in pasture, expect a lot of bugs and weeds this time of year.

Bear Creek begins in western Sauk County near the town of Hillpoint, south of Highway 154. Some 3 miles of upper Bear Creek are no-kill. Highway N and Croal Road bound this section. On the remainder of Bear and its tributaries, two trout may be kept, with a minimum size of 12 inches for all species.

At the tiny hamlet of Wards Corners on Highway 154, find the intersection with Highway 130, which follows Bear to its confluence with the Wisconsin River around

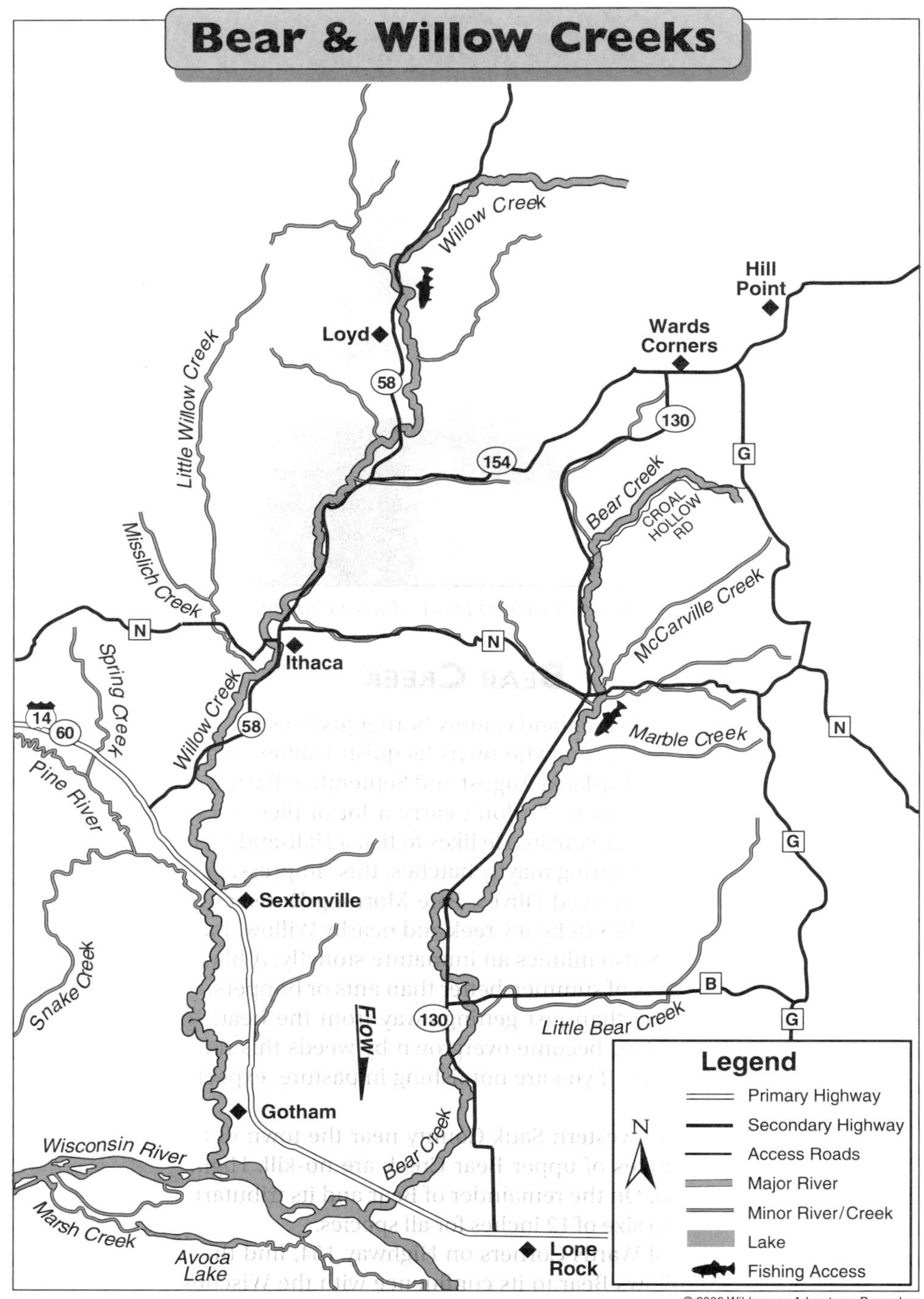
Bear & Willow Creeks
Willow Creek
Hill Point
Loyd
Wards Corners
58
130
G
154
Little Willow Creek
Bear Creek
CROAL HOLLOW RD
Misslich Creek
McCarville Creek
N
Ithaca
Spring Creek
Willow Creek
14
60
58
Marble Creek
Pine River
Sextonville
Snake Creek
Flow
130
B
Little Bear Creek
Legend
Primary Highway
Secondary Highway
Access Roads
Major River
Minor River/Creek
Lake
Fishing Access
Gotham
Wisconsin River
Bear Creek
Marsh Creek
Avoca Lake
Lone Rock

Lone Rock, some 15 miles downstream. Bear's upper 10 miles are designated trout water. Concentrate your efforts above the confluence with Little Bear Creek and the bridges on County B—the lower part of this creek is mainly home to rough fish. Much of the stream along Highway 130 is under DNR lease or ownership, allowing for good access.

Barron mentions the Bear's tendency to muddy after a rain. It is slow to recover to fishable levels of clarity. This is mainly a function of heavy agriculture in Bear Creek Valley. When it's not muddied up, it remains one of Barron's favorite streams.

Stream Facts: Bear Creek

Season

- The early season runs from the first Saturday in March to the last Sunday before the first Saturday in May; no-kill, single barbless hooks only. Regular season runs from the first Saturday in May at 5:00 am through September 30.

Regulations

- Daily bag limit is 2 trout with a minimum size of 12 inches

Species

- Wild and planted brown trout

Miles of Trout Water

- 18 miles

Stream Characteristics

- Spring creek; flows through farmland and silts up badly after heavy rain. Still, very fertile with abundant scuds, caddis, forage fish, and mayflies.

Access

- DNR holdings along Highway 130.

Fly Shops

- Fontana Sports, Cabelas, Rockin' K Fly Shop, Madison Orvis

Maps

- *Wisconsin Atlas and Gazetteer,* page 34

Willow Creek

On opening day 1996, I watched my friend Erik Seeman, an inveterate worm fisherman, take three browns in a row from Willow Creek near the town of Ithaca. This in itself is not unusual. Come May, water temperatures in southwest Wisconsin streams warm to near 60 degrees. A bloom of aquatic life, and thus feeding trout, follows. And who, after all, cannot catch trout on worms? True, perhaps. But each of these football-shaped browns pushed the 2-pound mark. While I can boast no such catch here myself, I have had 3X tippet snapped like nobody's business in the Willow's lower reaches more times than I care to admit.

Guide Dave Barron of Jacquish Hollow Angler also recommends the stretch below Ithaca for big 20-inch-plus browns. Some eavesdropping on a trout website confirms that this lower portion of Willow is lunker territory. However, the Willow, all 18 miles of it, is not simply a "lower watershed" fishery, but a first-class stream (turbidity problems notwithstanding) holding lots of small and medium fish in its upper and middle reaches.

Willow Creek begins from a series of feeder creeks off Highway 58 northeast of Richland Center near the town of Loyd. Given all this spring flow, and some important habitat work by the DNR, a rich aquatic gumbo including caddis, scuds, and mayflies thrive in Willow's upper reaches. Todd Polacek, owner of now-closed Madison Outfitters, calls the Willow "an incredible system." Tom Ehlert who formerly ran Silver Trout Guide Service calls it a "great personal favorite" and says he's found the fish here very cooperative. Both Polacek and Ehlert like the Willow in the vicinity of Loyd. Ehlert notes a lack of aquatic vegetation in this stretch, which makes it fairly easy to fish.

As with most Wisconsin spring creeks, you can find midge hatches off and on throughout the trout season on the Willow. According to my notes, March and September are particularly good for midge hatches on the Willow. Polacek finds good April-May Grannom hatches and May Little Black Caddis hatches in the Willow's upper reaches. For dries, fish an Elk Hair Caddis, size 14; below the surface try a Copper John or beadhead caddis. Ehlert mentions a dependable Brown Drake hatch beginning in May and June Sulphur hatches. I have found a dependable Blue-Winged Olive hatch in the vicinity of Loyd in mid-April, and in late June some years have produced a good Hex hatch on the Willow's lower reaches.

Terrestrial fishing also can be good on the Willow. Dave Barron fishes a black beetle imitation during these hot months. Polacek reports good dog-day hopper fishing. Fish "meat" flies such as Woolly Buggers or Marabou Leeches in the lower stretch between Neptune and Ithaca. Rounding out the hatch schedule in the final month of the season are tiny Blue-Winged Olives, Tricos, and midges. Thirteen of the stream's 18 miles are under DNR control, allowing for good access along Highway 58, which parallels the Willow.

Once, on the way back to Madison after fishing the coulee streams near Westby, smitten by that angling bug that tells you to "fish one more stream," I stopped by Willow Creek. Heavy rains had soaked both the coulees and Willow. While the coulees were silty but fishable the day before, Willow Creek was akin to chocolate milk. Barron, Ehlert, and Polacek all concur that the Willow has serious problems in the way of bank stabilization and erosion control. Polacek attributes this to the lack of buffer-strips along the stream, and to local geography (a wide valley) and intensive agriculture. According to Barron, it can take up to a week for the stream to return to fishable levels after just a quarter-inch of rain.

If the forecast calls for extended rain on your trip to southwest Wisconsin, skip the Willow and nearby Bear and head for the coulees or some of the tributaries running through the Kickapoo Reserve near La Farge.

Stream Facts: Willow Creek

Season

- The early season runs from the first Saturday in March to the last Sunday before the first Saturday in May; no-kill, single barbless hooks only. Regular season runs from the first Saturday in May at 5:00 am through September 30.

Regulations

- Lost Hollow Road upstream to Highway 58 a half-mile north of Loyd, no-kill, artificials only; otherwise, category 5 (2-trout limit, minimum size 12 inches).

Species

- Wild brown trout

Miles of Trout Water

- 18

Stream Characteristics

- Spring creek; flows through farmland and silts up badly after heavy rain. Still, very fertile with abundant scuds, caddis, forage fish, and mayflies. Holds large browns, especially around Ithaca.

Access

- DNR holdings along Highway 58.

Fly Shops

- Rockin' K Fly Shop, Cabelas, Fontana Sports, Madison Orvis, Streamside Outfitters

Maps

- *Wisconsin Atlas and Gazetteer*, page 34

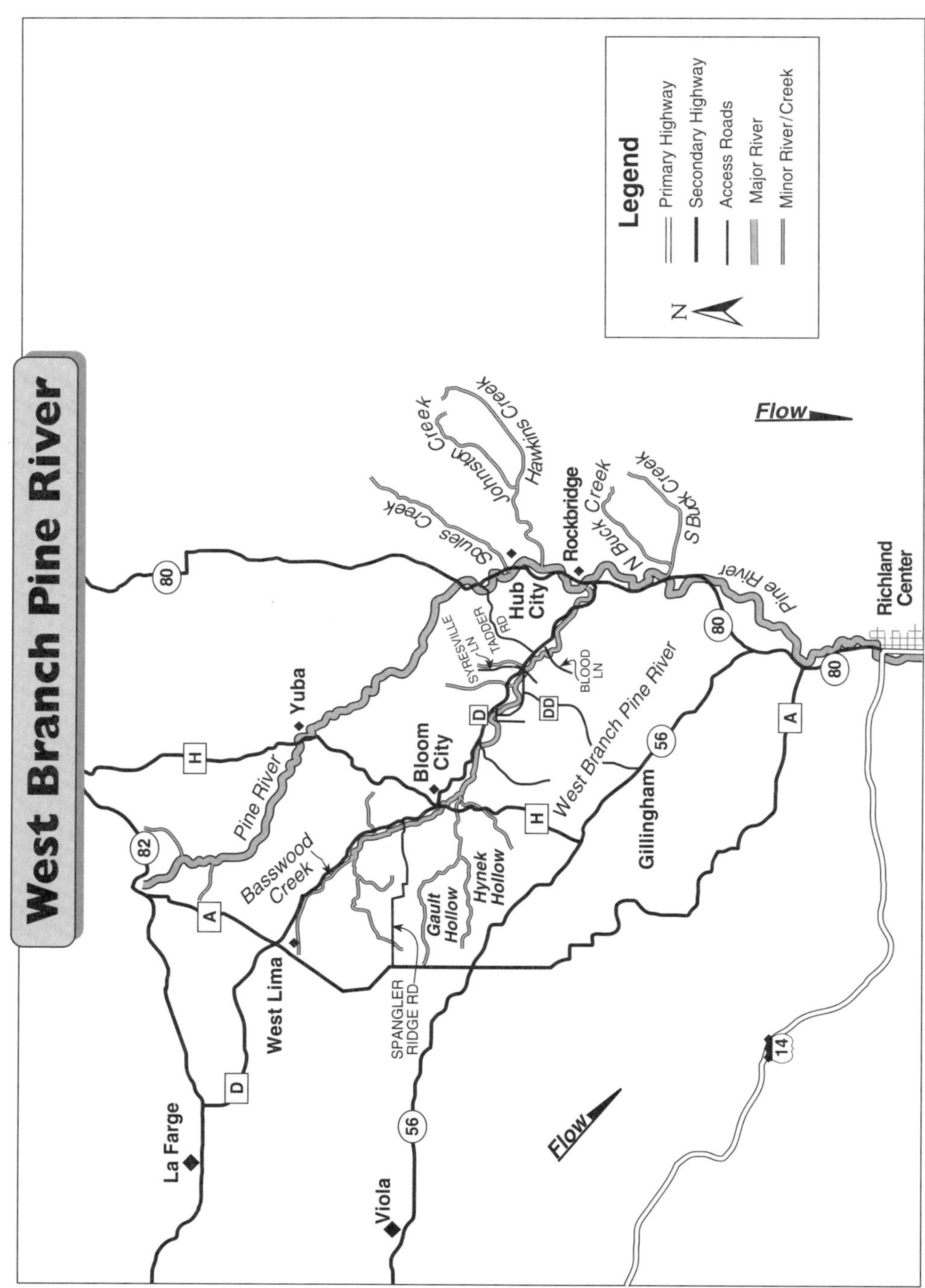
West Branch Pine River
Legend
Primary Highway
Secondary Highway
Access Roads
Major River
Minor River/Creek
N
Flow
Flow
Hawkins Creek
Johnston Creek
Soules Creek
Rockbridge
N Buck Creek
S Buck Creek
Pine River
Richland Center
Hub City
Syresville Ln
Tadder Rd
Blood Ln
Yuba
Bloom City
West Branch Pine River
Pine River
Basswood Creek
Gault Hollow
Hynek Hollow
Gillingham
West Lima
Spangler Ridge Rd
La Farge
Viola
80
82
56
14
A
H
D
DD

WEST BRANCH OF THE PINE RIVER

This might just be the sleeper trout stream of Richland County. At first glance, it looks bigger and siltier than most spring creeks in these parts, and it is often passed over by trout fishermen seeking more familiar-looking water. Still, the DNR manages a good stretch of it as catch-and-release water—a sure sign they think it's something special.

It also gets less fishing pressure than the Fancy Creek, Willow Creek, or Bear Creek systems. And there's plenty of water—11.3 miles to be exact. A friend of mine was repainting his cabin near here with the help of his son one day, and it was raining that particular morning so his son asked to go out fishing. Dad agreed and decided to nod off on the porch. He awoke to a surprise—a 7-pound brown trout in the refrigerator, taken from the West Branch. I've heard similar accounts about the West Branch from house painters, dairy farmers, and all types of anglers. The West Branch of the Pine is a great place for big brown trout.

Its beginnings are just below the town of West Lima in northern Richland County. Follow Highway D southeast out of West Lima and you will see the creek. At this point you are very close to the Kickapoo Valley Reserve, where you will find good trout fishing in Kickapoo tributaries and the chance for big trout in the Kickapoo itself. The small town of La Farge would be a good base from which to explore the Pine River system one day and the Kickapoo the next day. Some maps for Wisconsin show the upper part of the West Branch of the Pine as Basswood Creek, basswood being a common tree in riverine ecosystems in these parts. In presettlement times, oaks predominated because their thick corky bark was able to withstand frequent wildfires. The maple, hackberry, and basswoods now so common along Driftless waterways would never have survived these wildfires.

From its beginnings near West Lima to Spangler Ridge Road, the West Branch is category 3. From Spangler Ridge Road downstream to Old County Farm Drive, the West Branch is managed as a category 5 fishery—catch-and-release, artificials only. Two tributaries feed the West Branch in this section—Hynek Hollow and Gault Hollow; they are both category 5 and home to skittish wild browns and brookies. Below Highway H, Gault Hollow is no-kill, artificials only. The balance of Gault and all of Hynek are category 3. Below County H on the West Branch, category 3 regulations resume. The West Branch joins the main branch of the Pine at Rockbridge. You can access the West Branch from West Lima to Rockbridge via Highway D.

Despite abundant springs and tributaries, the West Branch does have a tendency to silt-up and warm-up during hot or rainy weather. This is typical of streams in this hard-grazed country. Skip the West Branch for a few days after a rain, or try Gault or Hynek Hollow.

The West Branch holds good numbers of forage fish—sculpins, chubs, shiners—that swim up from the Pine. Caddis are present in the upper reaches of the West Branch. Mayfly activity here begins with Blue-Winged Olives in March and continues through June with Sulphurs and Hendricksons. If an angler wanted to endure the jungle-like conditions of Wisconsin trout fishing in summer, he might try grasshopper or beetle imitations in July and August. You'll find classic rolling bluff scenery here, along with some interesting rock formations (hence the name Rockbridge). You might also pick up an occasional brown trout in the main stem around Yuba and Hub City.

Stream Facts: West Branch Pine River

Season
- The early season runs from the first Saturday in March to the last Sunday before the first Saturday in May; no-kill, single barbless hooks only. Regular season runs from the first Saturday in May at 5:00 am through September 30.

Regulations
- Old County Farm Road upstream to Spangler Ridge Road is no-kill and artificials only; uppermost Highway 80 bridge downsream to County AA has a daily bag of 2 trout with a minimum size of 12 inches.

Species
- Wild and planted brown trout

Miles of Trout Water
- 11.3 miles

Stream Characteristics
- Larger than most spring creeks in this area; silts up during rain; interesting rock formations; large brown trout present.

Access
- Along Highway D.

Fly Shops
- Rockin' K Fly Shop, Cabelas, Fontana Sports, Madison Orvis, Streamside Outfitters

Maps
- *Wisconsin Atlas and Gazetteer*, pages 41, 33

West Branch of Mill Creek

Originating near the hamlet of Bosstown and flowing 8 miles southeast along Highway 14 to its confluence with Mill Creek near Boaz, the West Branch of Mill Creek is a fast, clear little stream holding both wild and planted brook and brown trout. Given its small width—you can easily jump across it in many places—it has some surprisingly deep holes, scoured and riprapped corners, and enough spring flow to keep it running in the low to mid-60s, even in summer. Though it runs along Highway 14, the main road between Richland Center and La Crosse, I've never met another angler here. My favorite stretch is adjacent to the Indian Hollow Farms greenhouse and gift shop 10 miles west of Richland Center on Highway 14. There is a little walking trail leading down from Highway 14, opposite Indian Hollow Farms. A Pheasant Tail Nymph presented on a long fine leader fishes well here.

While turning over rocks in the West Branch of Mill Creek I've seen good numbers of caddis cases. Ten miles of Mill Creek's main branch, above Boaz, are rated as trout water. Local lore has it that big trout are caught around the Boaz spillway. I have never cared for the main branch of Mill Creek, which is silty, ditched, and unattractive; however, trout have been taken from stranger places. Below Boaz, Mill Creek holds rough fish, flowing some 20 miles to the Wisconsin River at Orion. The East Branch of Mill Creek, 6 miles in length, looks similar to the West Branch—clear, brushy, and fast. It follows County Highway Z.

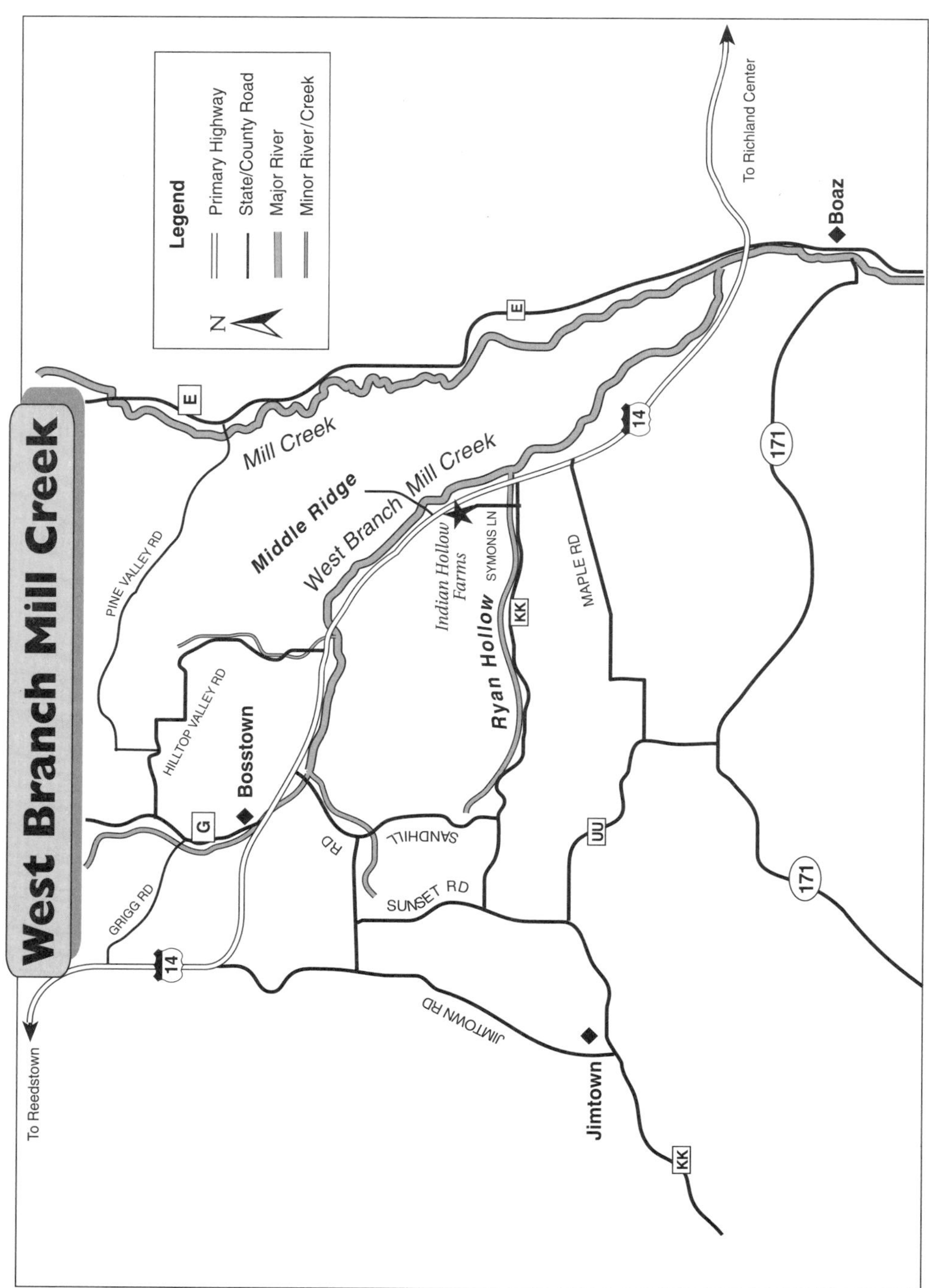
West Branch Mill Creek
Legend
Primary Highway
State/County Road
Major River
Minor River/Creek
N
To Richland Center
Boaz
E
E
Mill Creek
Middle Ridge
West Branch Mill Creek
Indian Hollow Farms
SYMONS LN
Ryan Hollow
KK
MAPLE RD
14
171
171
PINE VALLEY RD
HILLTOP VALLEY RD
Bosstown
G
GRIGG RD
SANDHILL RD
SUNSET RD
UU
14
JIMTOWN RD
Jimtown
KK
To Reedstown

Stream Facts: West Branch Mill Creek

Season

- The early season runs from the first Saturday in March to the last Sunday before the first Saturday in May; no-kill, single barbless hooks only. Regular season runs from the first Saturday in May at 5:00 am through September 30.

Regulations

- Category 3

Species

- Wild browns and brook trout

Miles of Trout Water:

- 8 miles

Stream Characteristics

- Small, cold spring creek with many pockets and riffles.

Access

- Along Highway 14 west of Boaz.

Fly Shops

- Rockin' K Fly Shop, Fontana Sports, Cabelas, Madison Orvis, Streamside Outfitters

Maps

- *Wisconsin Atlas and Gazetteer*, page 33

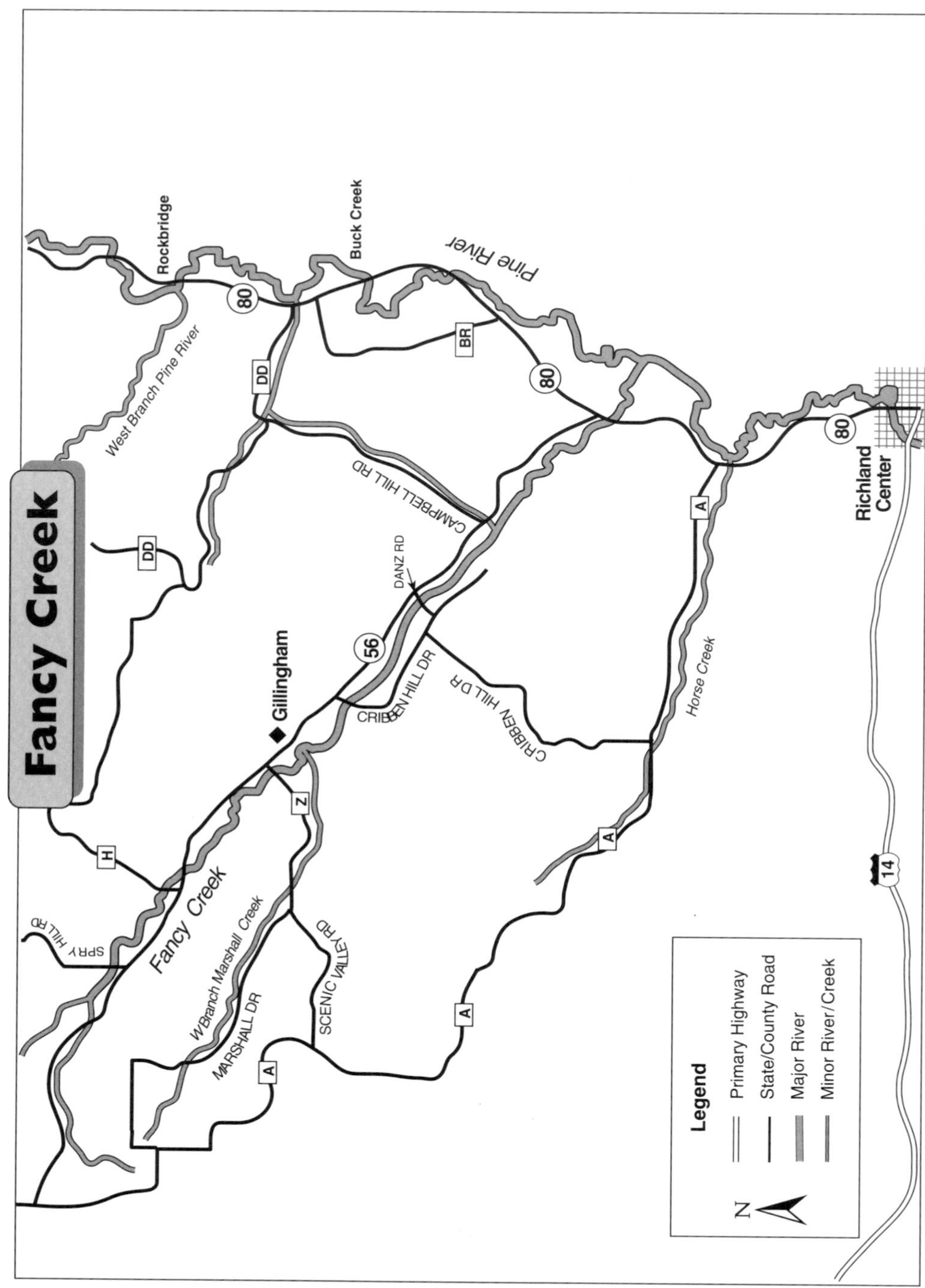
Fancy Creek
Rockbridge
Buck Creek
Pine River
West Branch Pine River
80
DD
BR
CAMPBELL HILL RD
Richland Center
A
DANZ RD
56
Gillingham
CRIBBEN HILL DR
Horse Creek
Z
H
SPRY HILL RD
Fancy Creek
WBranch Marshall Creek
MARSHALL DR
SCENIC VALLEY RD
14
Legend
Primary Highway
State/County Road
Major River
Minor River/Creek
N

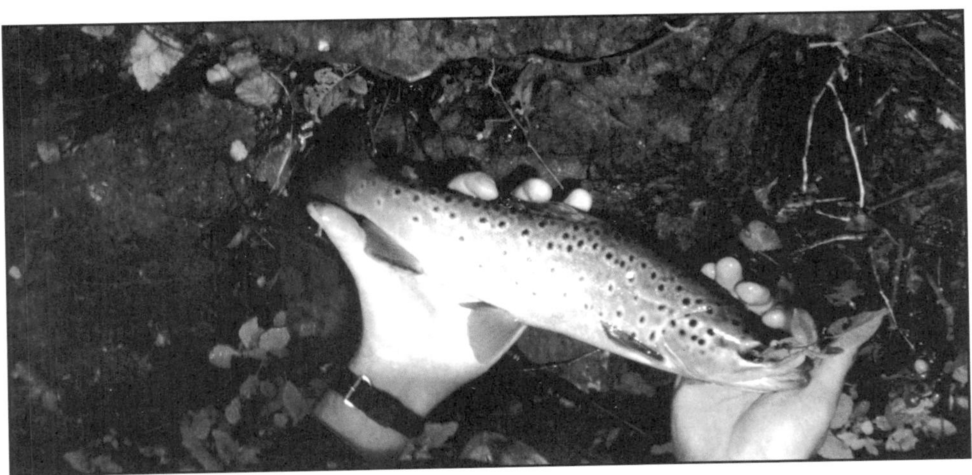

A nice brown trout being released on Fancy Creek

FANCY CREEK

This creek has always remained something of a mystery to me. It is a known producer of trout, often large browns, yet only in its upper third are the conditions for reproducing trout present: gravel spawning beds, good flow, lots of tributary spring flow. Road crossing in this upper stretch are Spry Hill Road, County Highway H, Highway 56 (which parallels the stream from headwaters to mouth), and Highway Z. Much of this land is private. While you are legal to wade or stay within the stream banks without asking permission, this becomes impractical in brushy headwaters. If you wade it, you'll likely spook fish, and if you cross land without asking permission, you are trespassing. So, to fish this section effectively you'll probably need to get permission. If you can find the owner of the land—which is not always the same person as whomever lives in the nearest farm house—you will probably get permission and some good tips. These folks generally aren't flyfishers, but they can be careful observers with valuable fishing knowledge. It may be easiest to fish this stretch of Fancy during the March and April catch-and-release season before the streambanks become jungled in rivergrape, cow parsnip, goldenrod, and willow. As in other headwater stretches of limestone streams, expect good populations of caddis and scuds.

Most of my personal experience with Fancy Creek has been in the section downstream from here. I mentioned earlier that this creek remains something of a mystery. That's because this section does not look all that good—in fact, you might go so far as to say it looks like a ditch—yet I have taken trout of all three species in a size range that indicates good natural reproduction. I fish here because, frankly, I don't know how I'd managed to cast or even dap a fly in the upper reaches; also because there is some DNR access here. What have I seen that has impressed me?

One day I saw an old dairy farmer with a minnow bucket slip into a willow copse on the streambank. I heard a lot of splashing and reel-straining, and then I saw him walk out fairly lugging a stringer of three 20-inch browns.

My wife, on one of her first trout trips, lost a fish in the same size range here. Another friend of mine released a brook trout that went well over a pound and a half. My cohorts and I fish the runs just above and below bridges in this mid-stretch. Look for undercut banks, fallen timber, or little eddies. Bridges in this section are Cribben Hill Road, Danz Road, and Highway 80/56. As to how this stretch can grow trout the way it does, I do not know. It is also prone to flooding and silting-up since it runs through agricultural land and there is little in the way of bank stabilization.

While Fancy Creek is not necessarily known for great hatches, you will encounter scattered Blue-Winged Olives, Hendricksons, and Sulphurs in spring as well as midges throughout the summer. I've generally prospected around fallen timber with a leech fly and have caught good fish this way. Fancy and its tributaries are category 3.

This pasture stream is typical of the smaller trout waters of the Driftless area.

HUB CITY: RICHLAND CENTER

Richland Center is a town of about 5,000 people midway between Madison and La Crosse, founded in the mid-19th century. Early settlers gave the name "Richland" to the area because of the abundance of wild fruit and fertile soil; to date, fruit farms and orchards are plentiful in Richland County. Its downtown boasts a warehouse designed by Frank Lloyd Wright for a local food wholesaler, A. D. German. Chain motels and restaurants can be found on the town's eastern edge, and some local establishments can be found downtown. Willow and Bear Creeks lie to the east of Richland Center; Fancy Creek, Mill Creek, Camp Creek, plus the Kickapoo and its tributaries lie to the north and west. A 15-mile bike trail runs from Richland Center to Lone Rock along the Pine River. Taverns are not as ubiquitous in Richland Center as in the typical small Wisconsin town, as it was a "dry" town until recently. Boscobel, La Farge and Westby are better bases if you like the tavern life.

Accommodations

Super 8 Motel, Highway 14, Richland Center; 608-647-8988, 800-800-8000; $$

Park View Inn, 511 W. Sixth (Hwy. 14), Richland Center; 608-647-6354; $

Candlewood Cabin, 29493 State Hwy 80, Richland Center; 608-647-5720; Norbert & Susan Calnin; $$

Ramada Inn, 1450 Veterans Drive, Richland Center; 608-647-8869; $$

Littledale Bed & Breakfast, 21925 County Highway ZZ, Richland Center; 608-647-7118; Graham and Margaret Phillipson; $$

Jacquish Hollow Bed and Breakfast, 32491 Jacquish Hollow Rd, Richland Center; 608-585 2239; www. jacquishhollowangler.com

Campgrounds

Alana Springs, 22628 Covered Bridge Drive, Richland Center; 608-647-2600

Primitive Camping, Cty Hwy AA, Richland Center, 608-647-8702; Contact: Judy, 647-8702

Manning Farm Retreat, 27321 Manning Lane, Richland Center; 608-647-3869

Pier County Park, Hwy 80 North, Rockbridge; 608-647-4673; register at Natural Bridge Store

Restaurants

Kentucky Fried Chicken, 1140 Sextonville Road, Richland Center; 608-647-3097

Peaches Restaurant, Highway 14, Richland Center; 608-647-8886; supper club fare with good Sunday brunch

Pizza Hut, 719 US Hwy 14, Richland Center; 608-647-3300

Country Kitchen Restaurant and Dewey's Lounge, 1450 Veterans Drive, Richland Center; 608-647-8869; supper club with attached motel

Hennings Fish House, 1885 Allison Park Drive, Richland Center; 608-647-6557; open for dinner Thursday through Saturday; good fish, great prices

Hardees, Hwy 14 East, Richland Center; 608-647-6359

Fly Shops, Outfitters, Sporting Goods

Jacquish Hollow Angler, 32491 Jaquish So. Rd., Richland Center; 608-585-2239

Cabela's, Highway 35, Prairie du Chien, 608 326 7163; full line of fly fishing gear and good source of information on Driftless streams

Madison Orvis, 1700 Deming Road, Greenway Station, Madison; 608-831-3181; full line of fly fishing gear on Madison's west side

Fontana Sports Specialistes, 7948 Tree Lane, Madison; 608-833-9191; www.fontanasports.com; guiding for trout and warmwater species

Rockin' K Fly Shop, P.O. Box 6, Coon Valley; 608-452-3678

Bob's Silver Doctor Fly Fishing, P.O. Box 105, Viroqua; 608-637-3417

Wal-Mart, 2401 Hwy 14 East, Richland Center; 608-647-7141

Veterinarians

Richland Veterinary Service, 378 W Seminary St., Richland Center; 608-647-8944

Medical

Richland Center Hospital, 333 E. 2nd Street, Richland Center; 608-647-6321

Auto Rental

Vetesnik Motors, 27475 US Hwy 14, Richland Center; 608-647-8808

Automobile Repair

Bindl Tire & Auto, 243 E Court Street, Richland Center; 608-647-5851

Air Service

Richland Center Airport, 28694 County Highway B, Richland Center; 608-647-4233

For More Information

Richland Chamber/Main Street Partnership
174 S. Central Ave. Box 128
Richland Center, WI 53581
800-422-1318
www.richlandchamber.com

Crooked Creek

"Buggy, silty. Odd park-like setting. Walked past a pile of burnt garbage. Got stinging nettles in foot when taking off waders." These are my notes from fishing the lower end of Crooked Creek around the Highway 133 bridge, where no recent habitat work has been done. Compare this with my notes of the same evening for the upper part of Crooked Creek, where recent improvements (bank stabilization and riprap) were made by the DNR. "Fished deep pocket pools during a hatch of Sulphur duns. No takers but a lovely end to the evening, set to the sound of running water and the smell of wild mint." Where there is habitat there is food and fish, where there is not, both will be scarce.

My earliest recollection of Crooked Creek is watching from a dirt-road bridge as several 20-inch brown trout finned in the stream's watercress below. Of course I tried to approach them. Of course they scattered like starlings.

Currently managed as a category 5 stream (trout between 10 and 13 inches may be kept, with a 3-fish limit), Crooked Creek starts between Fennimore and Boscobel and winds its way along Highway 61 for some 6 miles until its empties into the Wisconsin River. It first becomes fishable, at least in my estimation, below the first Highway 61 bridge. Between here and Maple Road (where I observed the large browns years ago) it is a clear headwaters stretch running through a bit of tree canopy. Stealth, stealth, and more stealth are required to take trout here.

I recommend fishing between Maple Road and the second Highway 61 bridge. There are DNR stiles here indicating public access and good habitat work. Use a scud, cressbug, or Hare's Ear in this stretch if you don't see rises. Below the second Highway 61 bridge, you'll find a siltier stream flowing through timber—hackberry, elm, and willow. Trout, especially large trout, can be taken in stretches like this, but hacking through jungles of cow parsnip and goldenrod is not everyone's idea of a good time. Your best bet is probably trying these reaches during the early season in March and April when vegetation is less abundant and fly casting is actually possible.

Crooked Creek crosses Highway 61 a third time before heading west toward Highway 133 and the Wisconsin River. It's obviously a stream with good potential since the DNR has invested time and money in it. It's also near Boscobel, a neat river town with good eateries. Try Crooked Creek one morning or evening if your buddies are sleeping in or at the tavern.

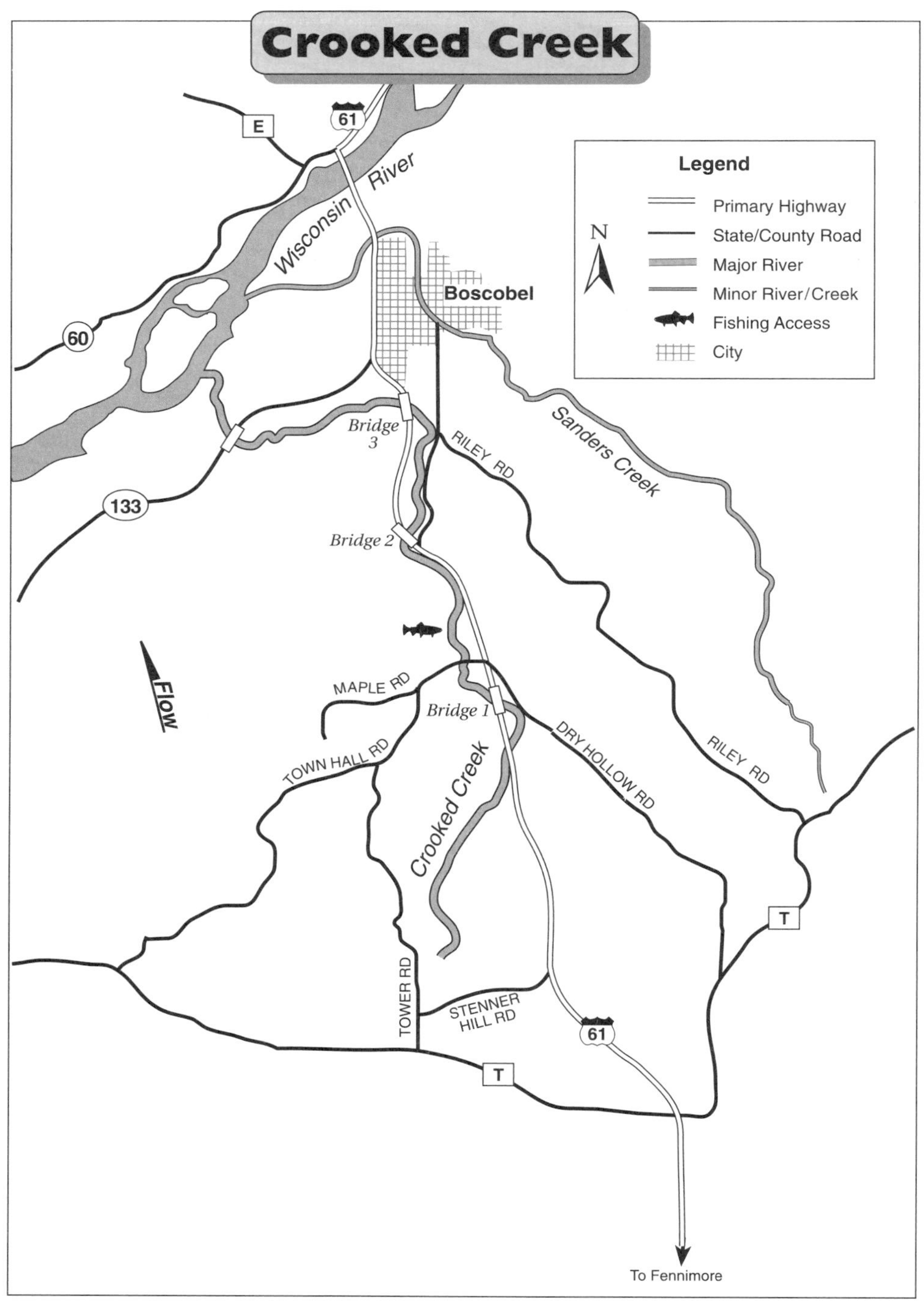
Crooked Creek
Legend
Primary Highway
State/County Road
Major River
Minor River/Creek
Fishing Access
City
N
E
61
60
133
Wisconsin River
Boscobel
Bridge 3
Bridge 2
Bridge 1
RILEY RD
Sanders Creek
Flow
MAPLE RD
TOWN HALL RD
Crooked Creek
DRY HOLLOW RD
RILEY RD
T
TOWER RD
STENNER HILL RD
61
T
To Fennimore
© 2006 Wilderness Adventures Press, Inc.

RICHLAND CREEK

From its headwaters at Mount Zion on Highway 61 to its mouth at the Wisconsin River near Boscobel, Richland Creek runs for 7 miles along Highway 61. It has received a lot of attention from the DNR in the last five years in the form of bank stabilization. It first becomes wide enough to fish at the bridge of Spencer Hill Road. There is a nice pool here, on the downstream side of the bridge. The next bridge crossing is Marietta Valley Road, which loops back around to Highway 61. There are big browns—and a number of cold feeder creeks—in the fallen timber of the Marietta Valley stretch. I've caught and released a good many. Get down on your knees and shoot a quick roll cast into a likely looking lie. Get ready. One of Richland Creek's lunkers might grab your Muddler Minnow.

Wild and planted browns are present. Richland Creek is a category 3 stream.

BORAH CREEK

I've heard it said among outdoorsmen and biologists alike that the road built along the Military Ridge—built in the 19th century for carrying lead and military supplies and people from Green Bay to Prairie du Chien—is a dividing line for species: trout and grouse to the north, smallmouth and pheasant to the south. It also marks a drainage line between north-flowing tributaries of the Wisconsin River and south-flowing tributaries of the Rock and Mississippi Rivers. While this generally holds true, south-flowing Borah Creek seems to be the exception to the rule, occurring below the magic "trout" line. Nonetheless, regional fisheries biologist Gene Van Dyk says it is a fine stream with lots of public access, decent insect populations, and a self-supporting population of wild brown trout. Trout densities may be a bit lower than Barneveld's Trout Creek, Van Dyk notes, but fish are somewhat larger in Borah. Another plus for Borah is that no one I know has fished it, and that's saying something since most of my friends are trout fishermen.

Borah Creek is located north of the town of Lancaster and is crossed at numerous points by Borah Road. Take Highway 61 out of Lancaster and find Highway K; take a left on K and then take your first right on Borah Road. Borah Creek is category 3, with about 6 miles of trout water. You can't go wrong with a size 16 olive scud, Hare's Ear, or beadhead caddis; as for dries carry small midges, Blue-Winged Olives and Sulphur Duns and you should be able to cover most hatch situations.

The Grant River, which is fed by Borah Creek, is managed as trout water downstream from its juncture with Borah. Between County A and County K, the Grant River is catch-and-release water; otherwise it is Category 3. In years past the Grant River was considered a fine smallmouth stream, but it has suffered habitat degradation in the form of flooding and agricultural runoff.

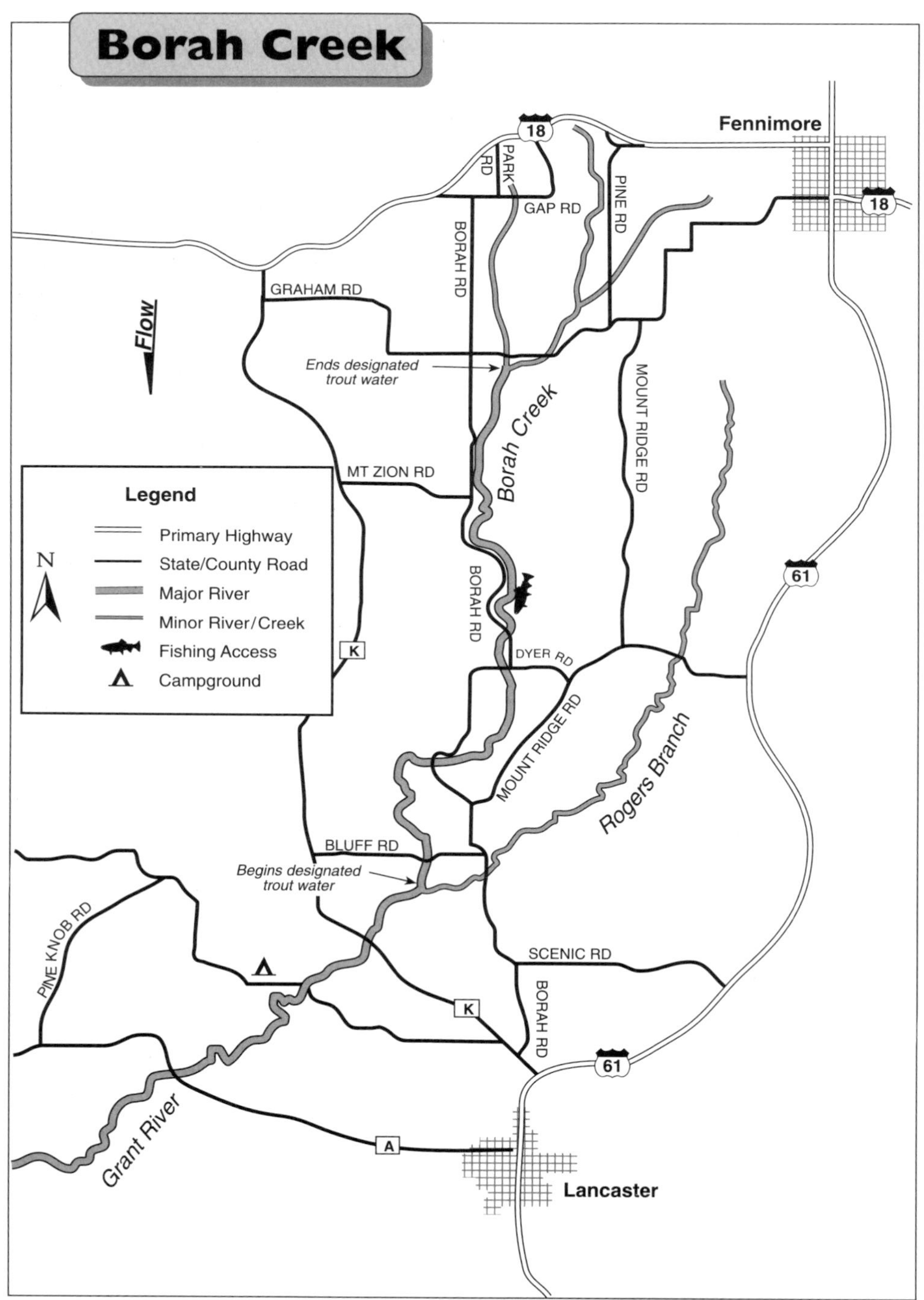

Borah Creek
Fennimore
18
PARK
RD
GAP RD
PINE RD
BORAH RD
GRAHAM RD
Flow
Ends designated
trout water
Borah Creek
MOUNT RIDGE RD
MT ZION RD
Legend
Primary Highway
State/County Road
Major River
Minor River/Creek
Fishing Access
Campground
N
K
61
DYER RD
MOUNT RIDGE RD
Rogers Branch
BLUFF RD
Begins designated
trout water
PINE KNOB RD
SCENIC RD
Grant River
A
Lancaster

Stream Facts: Borah Creek

Season

- The early season runs from the first Saturday in March to the last Sunday before the first Saturday in May; no-kill, single barbless hooks only. Regular season runs from first Saturday in May at 5:00 am through September 30.

Regulations

- Category 3

Species

- Wild browns

Miles of Trout Water

- 3 miles

Stream Characteristics

- Spring creek with abundant scuds, caddis, forage fish, and mayflies and good natural reproduction.

Access

- Bridges on Bluff Road and Borah Road.

Fly Shops

- Fontana Sports, Madison Orvis, Cabelas, Streamside Outfitters

Maps

- *Wisconsin Atlas and Gazetteer*, page 25

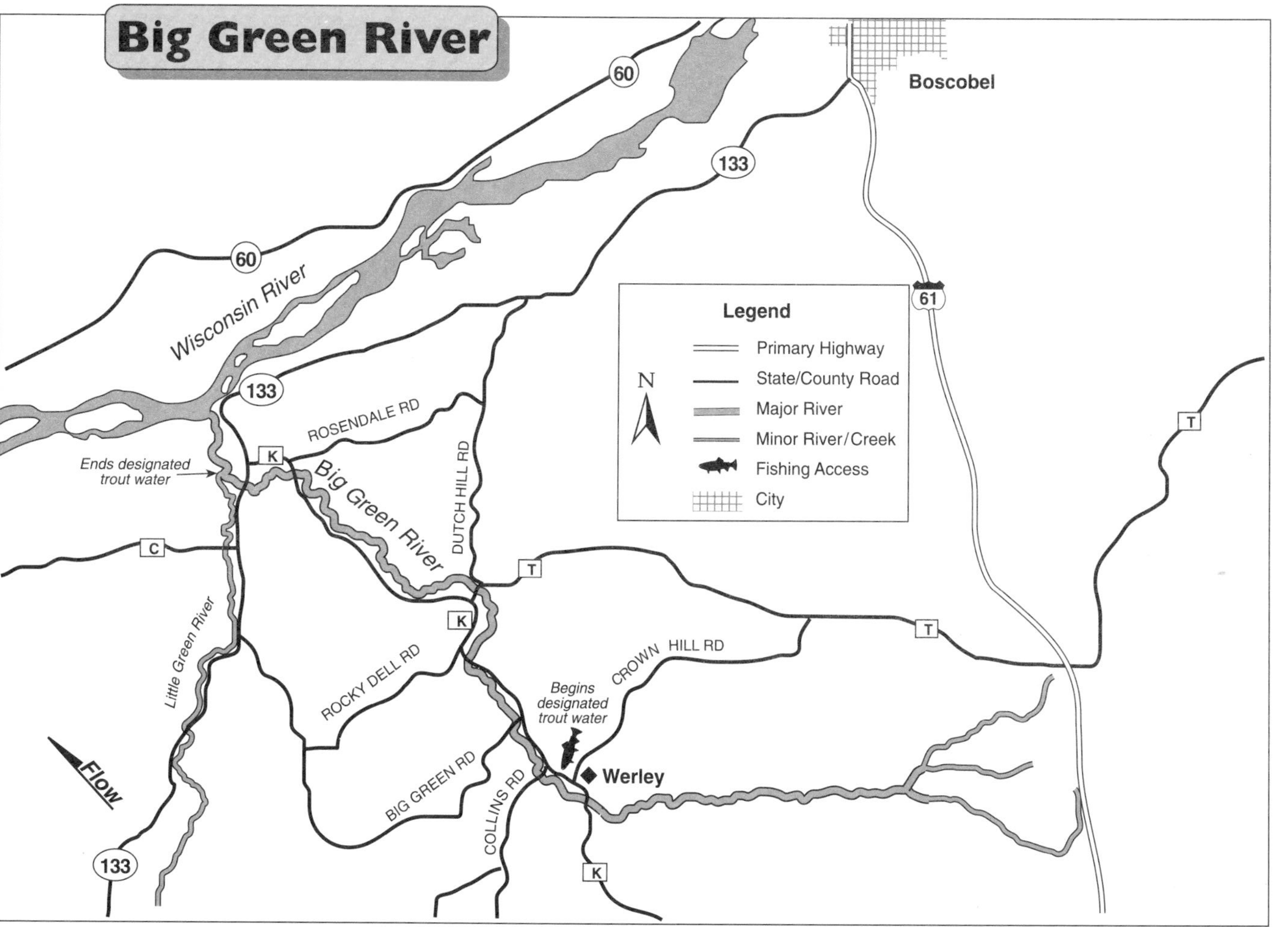
Big Green River
Boscobel
Legend
Primary Highway
State/County Road
Major River
Minor River/Creek
Fishing Access
City
N
61
133
60
T
K
C
CROWN HILL RD
Werley
Begins designated trout water
COLLINS RD
BIG GREEN RD
ROCKY DELL RD
DUTCH HILL RD
ROSENDALE RD
Big Green River
Wisconsin River
Ends designated trout water
Little Green River
Flow

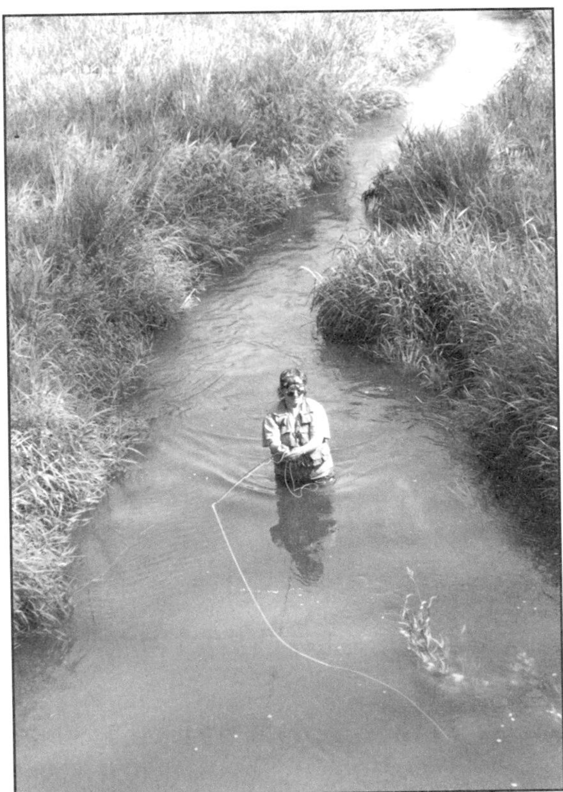

An angler works within the narrow banks of the Big Green River. (Chris Halla)

Big Green River

The Big Green River is among the finest of southwest Wisconsin's spring creeks, holding both good numbers and good-sized trout. Wild-strain brown trout stocked here some ten years ago have taken well to the Big Green, reproducing in numbers comparable to Vernon County's Timber Coulee. Unlike Timber Coulee, however, the Big Green holds a good population of browns in the 18- to 22-inch range. To boot, there is public access on most of the stream, and it supports rich aquatic life.

The Big Green begins east of the town of Werley. Its upper reaches can be accessed via Green River Road. At Werley, Green River Road joins up with County Highway K, which follows the Big Green to its confluence with the Little Green. This confluence marks the end of the Big Green's designated trout water. Between Highway 133 and Highway T, the Big Green is category 5—catch-and-release, no-kill; upstream from Highway T, it is category 5—3 trout between 10 and 13 inches may be kept. Stream access is available at fence stiles or bridges on County K and Green River Road.

Insect activity on the Big Green follows a progression not unlike that of other area spring creeks. Midge and Blue-Winged Olive hatches begin in March. Sulphurs and Hendricksons come off in April and May. Meanwhile, caddis hatches get under way in April and continue into early summer. Freshwater shrimp and snails are present year-round in the stream's eel grass and watercress beds, as are forage fish and crawfish. Terrestrials (crickets, hoppers, beetles) are present in good numbers during the dog days of summer. You might try a size 14 Half-and-Half Emerger for spring mayfly hatches. A size 14 Yellow Stimulator or Elk Hair Caddis would be a good choice for caddis hatches. A beetle or hopper imitation fished on a long leader is the ticket for summer fishing. Scuds are a good bet year-round, and you might fool one of the streams larger fish with a Woolly Bugger.

Like Castle Rock and the Blue, the pasture sections of the Big Green allow actual fly casting instead of the dapping necessitated by the overgrown banks of many area streams. This luxury, along with the lovely green valley scenery and rock outcrops, big fish, and plenty of public access, makes the Big Green a real destination stream.

Stream Facts: Big Green River

Season

- The early season runs from the first Saturday in March to the last Sunday before the first Saturday in May; no-kill, single barbless hooks only. Regular season runs from the first Saturday in May at 5:00 am through September 30.

Regulations

- Between Highway 133 and Highway T, the Big Green is category 5—catch-and-release, no-kill; upstream from Highway T, it is category 5—3 trout between 10 and 13 inches may be kept.

Species

- Wild browns

Miles of Trout Water

- 11 miles

Stream Characteristics

- Spring creek, with abundant scuds, caddis, forage fish, and mayflies. Good natural reproduction, with some large browns present. Wooded valley with rock outcrops, very scenic.

Access

- DNR holdings on Green River Road and Highway K.

Fly Shops

- Fontana Sports, Cabelas, Madison Orvis, Streamside Outfitters

Maps

- *Wisconsin Atlas and Gazetteer*, page 25

The view from a sandbar on the Wisconsin River. (Craig Amacker)

Wisconsin River: Prairie du Sac to Prairie du Chien

Playing host to duck hunters, walleye and catfish anglers, morel mushroom hunters, canoeists, this stretch of the Wisconsin River offers a little something for everyone. The good news, thanks to DNR land acquisition, is that the Lower Wisconsin Riverway (thousand of acres of bottomland, marsh, prairie, and upland) is under public ownership, so hunters, campers, anglers, and nature-lovers can all enjoy it.

Earl Loyster, a deceased game warden and acquaintance of my friend Steve Miller, was responsible for much of this acquisition. Loyster told of driving sand roads from Sauk City all the way to Prairie du Chien, some 150 miles. And if you are wondering about the French names, these are the stamp of voyageurs and explorers who paddled their canoes from the Fox River near Green Bay to the 2-mile portage between the Fox and Wisconsin (hence the city Portage) and then made their way down the Wisconsin, laden with furs and trade goods from Indians, to the Mississippi River at Prairie du Chien.

The river in these 150 miles is unique in that it is undammed from Prairie du Sac all the way to its confluence with the Mississippi at Prairie du Chien. Thus float-trip anglers don't need to worry about their boats being sucked into current vortexes dams often create. There are no other fish barriers in this stretch, so fish may move freely.

The fishery here might be broken down into fishing the main channel of the river—including its sandbar eddies and oxbows—and fishing its abundant backwaters. The main channel holds good numbers of walleye, smallmouth bass, channel catfish,

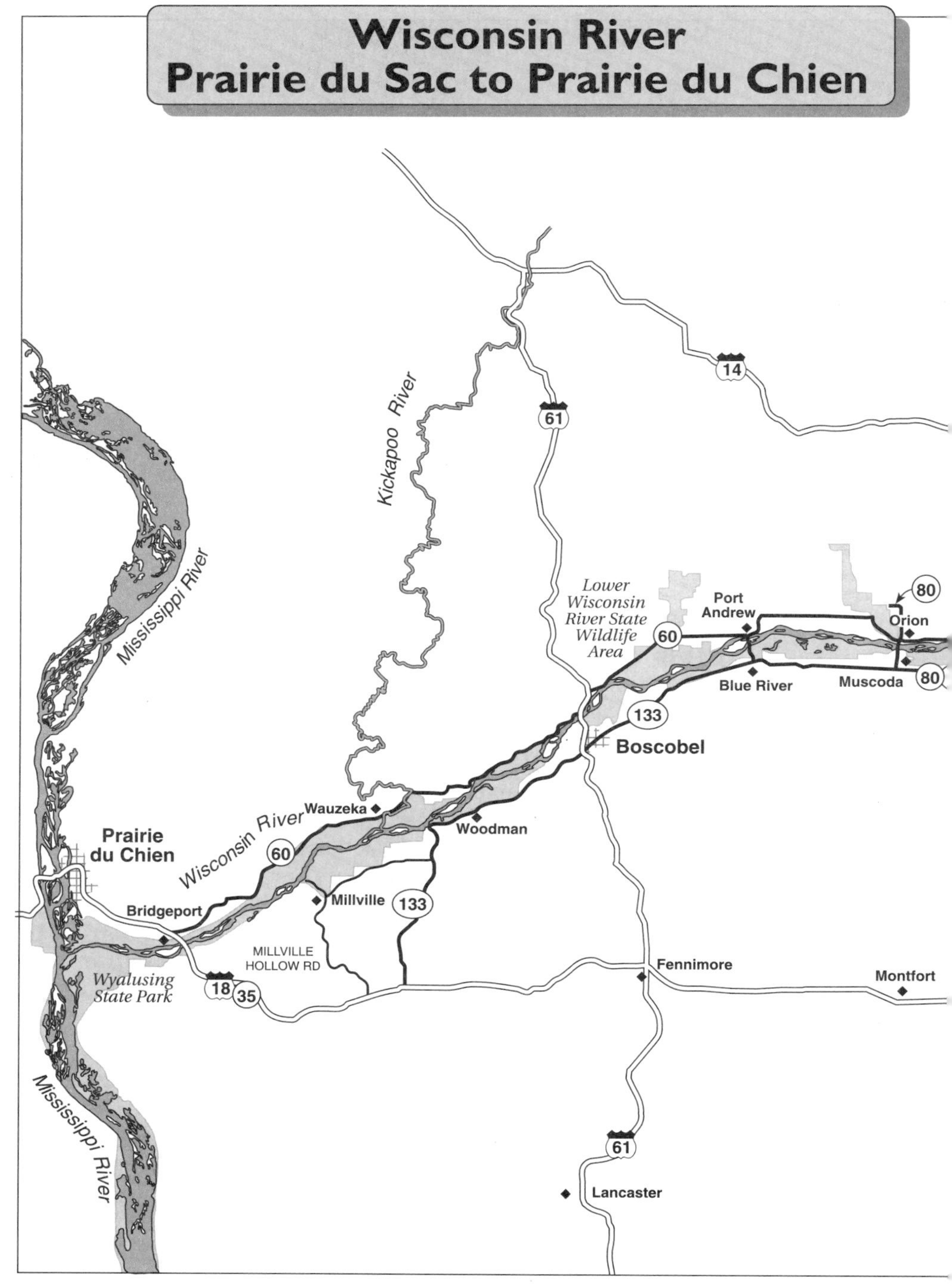
Wisconsin River
Prairie du Sac to Prairie du Chien
Kickapoo River
Mississippi River
14
61
Lower Wisconsin River State Wildlife Area
Port Andrew
80
Orion
60
Blue River
Muscoda
80
133
Boscobel
Wauzeka
Wisconsin River
Woodman
Prairie du Chien
60
Bridgeport
Millville
133
MILLVILLE HOLLOW RD
Fennimore
Montfort
Wyalusing State Park
18
35
Mississippi River
61
Lancaster

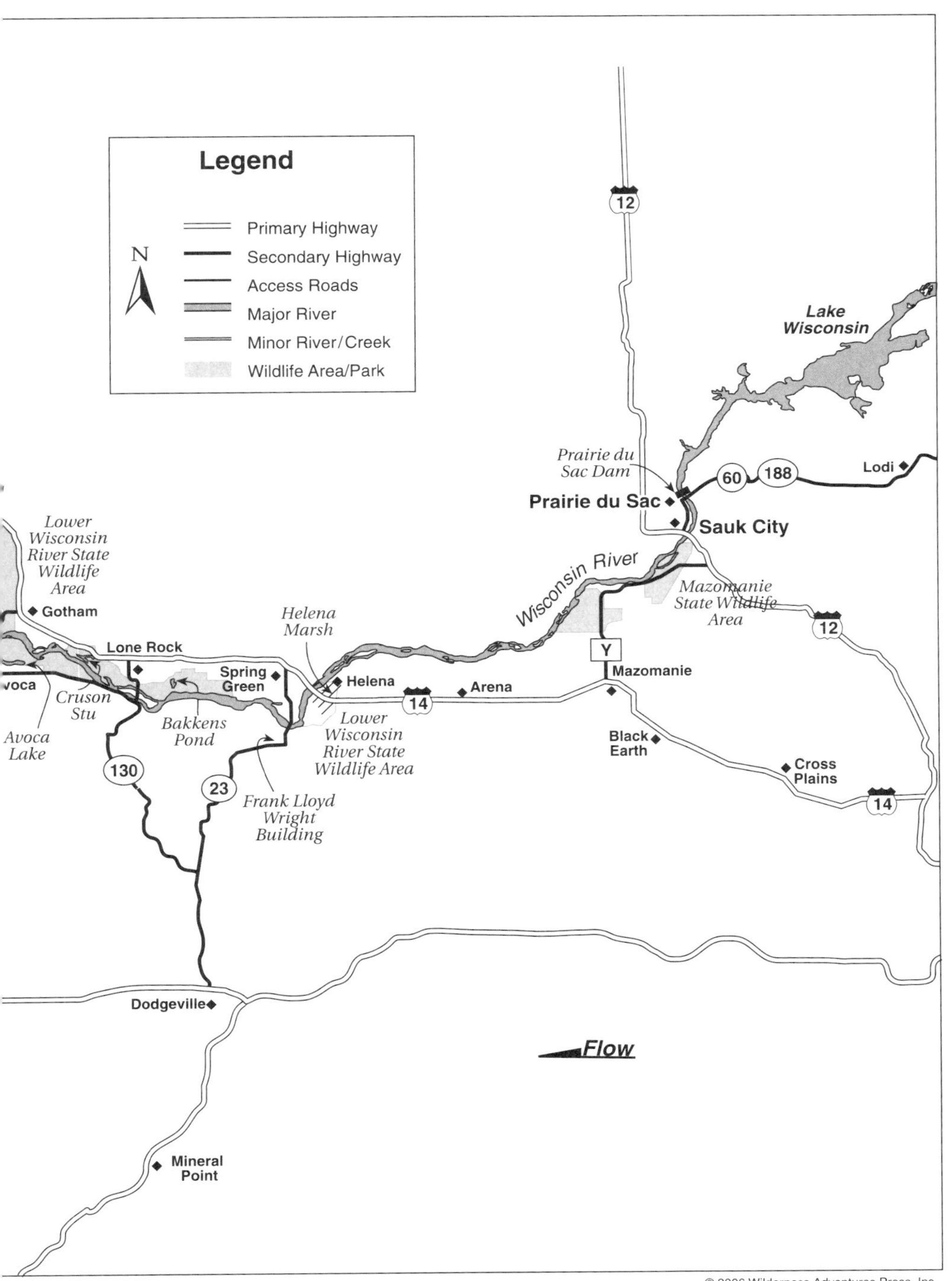

Legend
Primary Highway
Secondary Highway
Access Roads
Major River
Minor River/Creek
Wildlife Area/Park
N
12
Lake Wisconsin
Prairie du Sac Dam
60
188
Lodi
Prairie du Sac
Sauk City
Wisconsin River
Mazomanie State Wildlife Area
12
Lower Wisconsin River State Wildlife Area
Gotham
Helena Marsh
Lone Rock
Spring Green
Helena
14
Arena
Y
Mazomanie
voca
Cruson Stu
Bakkens Pond
Lower Wisconsin River State Wildlife Area
Black Earth
Cross Plains
Avoca Lake
130
23
Frank Lloyd Wright Building
14
Dodgeville
Flow
Mineral Point

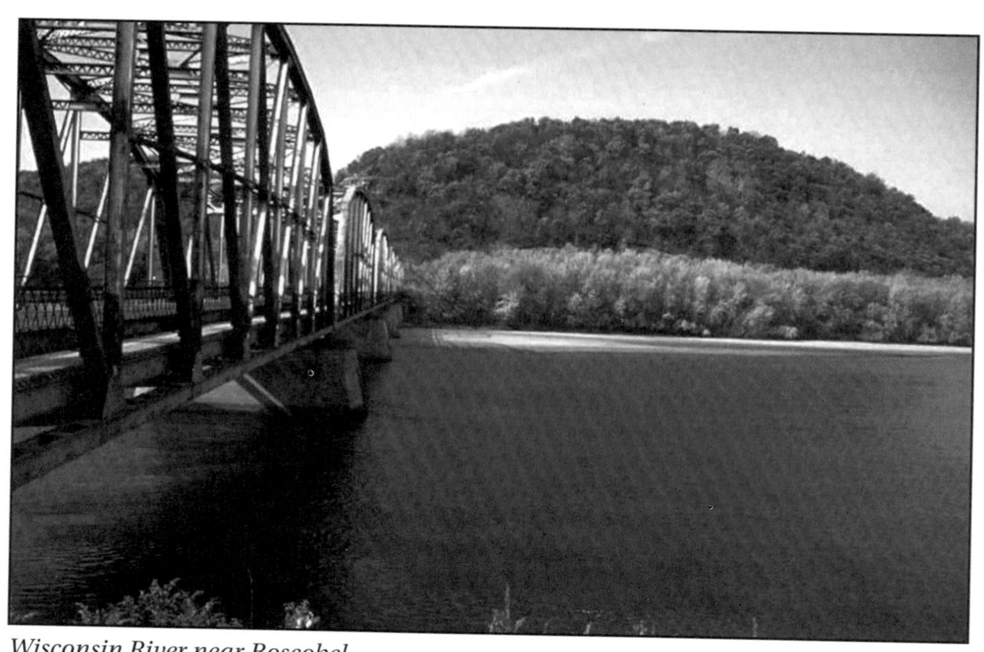

Wisconsin River near Boscobel.

white bass, and northerns. Backwaters are replete with panfish year-round and can provide great early-season northern action; they also hold largemouth bass. The sloughs in the vicinity of Spring Green, Avoca, Muscoda, and Boscobel hold good panfish populations. On the main channel, wet-wading around the Spring Green Bridge can be productive in summer for smallmouth and walleye.

The confluence with the Mississippi, visible from the impressive vistas at Wyalusing State Park, is a maze of islands, backwaters, and braided channels that offer a great variety of fish habitat—from stump-studded backwaters housing largemouth, pike, and panfish to sandy runs thick with walleye and smallmouth. Highway 60 follows this stretch of the Wisconsin from Prairie du Sac to Prairie du Chien. Mixed-bag fishing is popular throughout the entire stretch of river with Spring Green/Helena, Muscoda/Blue River, and the confluence of the Wisconsin and the Mississippi at Prairie du Chien being the most popular areas.

Prairie du Sac Dam marks the beginning of this water. The dam can be found just upstream from where Highway 60/188 crosses the river. In spring and fall, walleye fishermen ply minnows and leeches for the tasty goggle-eye. Most fishing is done from boats, though adventurous souls may be found using belly boats. Landlubbers see their share of action, too. In truth, this section, with its snags and fast water, is probably of interest to only the most diehard fly angler willing to use a sinking line and lots of weight.

There is no heresy in doing a little spin fishing where conditions merit. Walleye are especially abundant—and vulnerable—here in early spring as this dam marks the upper limit of their spawning range. There are walleye upstream, but this dam and others like it farther up separate the lower fish from mid- and upper-river walleyes. Ditto for white bass, channel catfish, sturgeon, and smallmouth populations. Immediately downstream from the Prairie du Sac Dam, there are boat landings at the Highway 12 bridge, off County Y (Mazomanie Unit), and at Highway 14 just east of Spring Green (Helena Unit).

It is important to note that the Wisconsin River claims lives every few years. There is the inevitable sheriff with bloodshot eyes being interviewed by the TV crew in darkness, saying he and his men did all they could, but the fishermen or hunters or bathers are feared dead. Unexpected currents or hypothermia impaired their judgment. Always keep personal floatation devices handy. Wisconsin law requires it, and it may be a life-saver. Be extra careful in late season situations where ice flows and frigid temperatures are common. That said, the river can also be a place of family float trips and camping on willow islands and eating fresh fish beneath the stars. Float trips (overnight canoe-camping trips) are particularly popular from Spring Green down to Prairie du Chien. Pick-ups and drop-offs and canoe rentals can be arranged with one of the many canoe liveries in Mazomanie, Spring Green, Arena, Lone Rock, Gotham, Muscoda, or Blue River.

Around the Spring Green Bridge, wet-wading is popular in summer in the shallow eddies of the river. Currents here can be swift and unexpected; go slowly and remember it's best to not "fight" the river if you do get swept up. Try to stay calm and let the river carry you to the next sandbar. This area is most often frequented by anglers casting Mepps spinners, but there's no reason one couldn't cast a minnow imitation (or any of a variety of streamer patterns) on the longrod with the same results. Smallmouth and walleye are common, along with an occasional northern that might have strayed from a backwater, spring, or the lower end of a feeder stream.

And speaking of backwaters, Helena Marsh (visible just before you cross the Spring Green Bridge) is a favorite haunt of panfishermen. Just after ice-out to early May are popular times, and then again in midsummer. Bakkens Pond and Cruson Slu near Lone Rock are popular backwaters, as are others between Avoca and Boscobel on the southern shore of the river. Depending on the particular slough and how much rain has been received, these may or may not be accessible via motorboat. It's always best to ask in the nearest town if you are unsure. People in this part of the state are friendly if you aren't in too much of a hurry.

Launches can be found on either side of the river at Lone Rock. There are several on the south shore around Muscoda, along Highway 80/133, and at Orion and Port Andrew on the north shore along Highway 60. From here to the confluence with the Kickapoo and then Mississippi, launches are fewer and farther between. Along the south shore, find them at Boscobel, Woodman, Millville, and Bridgeport where Highway 18/35 crosses the Wisconsin.

On the north shore you will find one east of Wauzeka, which is actually on the Kickapoo River some 3 miles upstream from the Wisconsin. This would make for an interesting float and some good mixed-bag fishing in a backwater setting. Bridge crossings include Highway 23 south of Spring Green, Highway 130/133 at Lone Rock, Highway 80 in Muscoda, Highway X in Blue River, Highway 61 in Boscobel, and finally 18/35 just east of Prairie du Chien.

Again, species in this lowest part of the watershed are pretty much what they are around Spring Green. Walleye and smallmouth in running channels, channel catfish in deep fast holes near bridges or riprap, northerns and panfish in backwaters. There are also a host of rough fish, including carp, suckers, sheepshead (freshwater drum), as well as sturgeon and paddlefish. The best bets for fly fishing are backwaters where you can cast from a jonboat, skiff, or canoe or wet-wading in shallow areas. If you are going to fish the main channel, you will likely need a boat with a decent outboard (bigger than a 10-horsepower) or a strong rower so you can get back to the launch ramp. The current, especially during high water, can be difficult to paddle against.

If trout efforts are drawing a blank in this scenic region, or if you want to embark on a river trip, give the Wisconsin River a try. There's plenty of access, hundreds of miles of river and sloughs, and a varied fishery to boot. If you want to do a driftboat trip, call Craig Amacker of Fontana Sports (608-833-9191).

Hub City: Boscobel

Its name a corruption of the French words for "beautiful wood," Boscobel is a small town situated on the banks of the Wisconsin River about 30 miles east of its confluence with the Mississippi River at Prairie du Chien. This moniker, given by French explorers Marquette and Joliet, does indeed describe the area's rolling bluffs and valleys. It is also known as the Wild Turkey Hunting Capital of Wisconsin and home of the Gideon Bible. Of interest to flyfishers are the hundreds of miles of trout streams in Grant and nearby Crawford County. Boscobel has several good eateries and places to sleep.

Accommodations

Hubbell's Motel, 41120 State Highway 60, Boscobel; 608-375-4277; $
Super 8 Motel, 1700 Elm St., Highway 61 South, Boscobel; 608-375-8000; $$
Fennimore Hills Motel, 5814 Highway 18, Fennimore 58309; 608-822-3281; $$
The Sands Motel, 300 N. Elm Street, Highway 61 South; 608-375-4167; $$
River Inn, 1700 Elm St; 608 375 6323; $$

Campgrounds

Wyalusing State Park, 13342 County Highway C, Bagley; 608-996-2261; 25 miles west of Boscobel
Steve & Kim Liss, 4452 Highway 133 East, Boscobel; 608-375-4525

Restaurants

A & W Family Restaurant, 509 Elm Street, Boscobel; 608-375-5171
Boscobel Hotel, 1005 Wisconsin Avenue, Boscobel; 608-375-4714; old-fashioned hotel restaurant with good brunches
Dairy Queen Brazier, 1100 Elm Street Boscobel; 608-375-4252
Unique Café, 1100 Wisconsin Avenue, Boscobel; 608-375-4465; breakfast, lunch, and dinner are all great in this homey cafe

Fly Shops, Outfitters, Sporting Goods

Jacquish Hollow Angler, 32491 Jaquish So. Rd., Richland Center; 608-585-2239
Rockin' K Fly Shop, P.O. Box 6, Coon Valley; 608-452-3678
Bob's Silver Doctor Fly Fishing, P.O. Box 105, Viroqua; 608-637-3417
Cabela's, Highway 35, Prairie du Chien, 608 326 7163; full line of fly fishing gear and good source of information on Driftless streams
Madison Orvis, 1700 Deming Road, Greenway Station, Madison; 608-831-3181; full line of fly fishing gear on Madison's west side
Tall Tales Sports and Spirits, 101 Le Grand Street; 608 375 5540; fishing licenses
Driftless Angler, 106 S. Main St., Viroqua; 608 637 8779; driftlessanglercom;. fly shop and guiding

Veterinarians

Boscobel Veterinary Clinic, 102 LaBelle St., Boscobel; 608-375 4440
Companion Care Animal Hospital, 838 Depot Lane, Boscobel; 608-375-5992

Medical

Boscobel Area Health Center, 205 Parker St., Boscobel; 608-375-4112; hospitals in Richland Center and La Crosse

Auto Rental

Nearest car rentals available in Richland Center and La Crosse.

Automobile Repair

Harwoods Auto Repair, 209 E. LeGrand St., Boscobel; 608-375-2563
Boscobel Tire and Tow, 501 Elm St., Boscobel; 608-375-2350

Air Service

Boscobel Municipal Airport, 5178 Highway 133 East, Boscobel; 608-375-5223

For More Information

Boscobel Chamber of Commerce
800 Wisconsin Avenue
P.O. Box 6
Boscobel, WI 53805
608-375-2672
www.boscobelwisconsin.com

The Kickapoo Restoration Project should improve angling for years to come. (Tim Landwehr)

THE KICKAPOO RIVER

Main Stem

> *In a valley originally inhabited by the Ho-Chunk tribe, the Kickapoo River slowly makes its way though a rich variety of landscapes beginning with narrow stone passages carved by water erosion; to temperate forests held in public trust; and ending with pastoral farmlands in wide open floodplains.*
>
> *Kickapoo River Water Trail*
> September 1999

Even without its unique cultural history, its flora and fauna (including the endangered Lapland Rosebay and Kentucky Warbler), and its varied and stunning topography, the Kickapoo River would be of interest to the angler. In its upper reaches and its pristine tributaries live a growing population of brown trout. Below Gays Mills Dam, a line of demarcation between coolwater and warmwater fisheries, northern pike wallow in spring seeps, channel catfish suspend themselves in deep bends, and walleye make their way up from the Wisconsin River.

Just as an angler may be confounded by where to begin fishing this river—wet-wading an icy tributary in summer with limestone water cool against your thighs, drifting the main stem on a misty morning while trying to sweep a Muddler Minnow along a bluff-shaded pool, or trying your luck with a gaudy Mickey Finn amid thick bottomland forest at the juncture of a milky spring seep and the muddy river—so a writer is confounded by which to pursue first in writing about this storied waterway. As this is a fishing guide and not a cultural history, I'll try to hold myself to only a page or two of history, which in Kickapoo County always seems pretty close to the present moment. When you ask permission of a farmer to fish a certain pool, you may have to listen to tales of how his ancestors came from Bohemia with only a few trunks of possessions and, of course, a gunnysack of dried mushrooms.

Floods of biblical proportions washed over the valley in 1907, 1912, 1917, 1935, 1951, and 1956; all exacted millions of dollars of damage on farm and home and town. In 1935, some Kickapooians, including Congressman Gardner Withrow, lobbied Washington for relief. In the 1950s, both the Corps of Engineers and the Wisconsin Conservation Department had their own plans for flood control. By 1967, the Corps proposed a 1,780-acre reservoir with the primary purpose of flood control and the secondary purpose of drawing in tourist dollars to an area whose economy had stagnated.

But the '60s and '70s saw a change in attitudes about resource-use. The Sierra Club and other conservation agencies, along with local residents, questioned the wisdom of the project. A landmark study by the UW-Madison Institute for Environmental Studies in 1974 found that the dam would in fact hurt water quality and was the economic equivalent of killing the goose that laid the golden egg since it would destroy the very reason for visiting this area. By 1975, even though the Corps had spent $15 million acquiring some 8,500 acres and had half-finished the dam, it agreed to halt its actions.

Twenty years later, in 1995, the Wisconsin Legislature passed a resolution to return ownership of these lands to the state. Now some 10,000 acres, the Kickapoo Reserve is managed by a diverse group of local citizens and the Ho-Chunk nation, which co-owns roughly 1,200 acres of the reserve. While this history may sound top-down, you can never underestimate the will and reserve of this valley's people, be they Ho-Chunks, organic farmers, traditional dairymen, woodcutters, or other independent souls piecing together a living in what *Mother Earth Magazine* called one of the ten best places to live in America.

Fishing the Main Stem: Headwaters to Gays Mills

Rising above the town of Wilton in southern Monroe County, the first 20 miles of the Kickapoo River are nothing more than a spring creek running through pasture and paralleled by Highway 131. At the time of this writing, it has received no plantings of trout from the DNR and, to my knowledge, does not support natural reproduction, making it of little interest to the flyfisher. However, as the Kickapoo has received much restoration help from Trout Unlimited, the DNR, and others, don't be surprised if this stretch is soon managed as a trout fishery. By its appearance, it lacks nothing that would make it a viable trout stream.

The upper Kickapoo begins to take on its quintessential characteristics around the village of Ontario, which is also home to numerous canoe liveries. The river here twists and turns around sandstone bluffs, forming deep grotto-pools among stands of white pine and hemlock. Numerous high-quality tributaries pump in cold, clear water. So why not just dive in and begin fishing? One impediment to fishing is the 10,000-plus canoes a year that visit this stretch. These visitors range from quiet nature lovers to loud partiers leaving a trail of beer cans in their wake. Since these people will be out in force during fishing season—May through September—this means something like 2,000 canoes a month or 500 a week or something like 75 a day.

The good news is that river-use follows predictable patterns, with holidays and weekends getting the heaviest traffic. So it will certainly help anglers to fish during off-times—cloudy or rainy days or weekdays. Aaron Larson of the Kickapoo Reserve Management Office in La Farge, an avid trout fisherman, recommends fishing the Kickapoo in the lower half of the Reserve between Rockton and La Farge. He notes that this stretch holds good trout and gets much less canoeing pressure than the run between Ontario and Rockton.

If the angler puts in at the Highway 131 bridge in Ontario on a weekday he is in the enviable position of having 14,000 acres and ten hours of canoeing and good fishing between the bow of his craft and the village of La Farge. Wildcat Mountain State Park provides some 3,500 acres and the Kickapoo Reserve some 10,000 more. To those accustomed to the vast open spaces of the American west or north, this may not seem like much. But in this patchwork country comprised of 80-acre dairy farms, it is a rare thing to have so much space in front of you. Pick-ups or drop-offs of your canoe or car can be arranged with one of the local canoe outfitters. See the hub city of La Farge for contact information for these services.

While previous fishing guidebooks for Wisconsin don't encourage anglers to fish the main stem of the Kickapoo for trout, the view of Kickapoo locals is somewhat different. The main stem may lack the numbers of trout found in the Kickapoo's West Fork or area tributaries, but Kickapoo locals—mostly baitfishers—do fish the main stem intensively from Ontario to Viola. Most of these folks fish night crawlers or minnows in deep bends or at confluences with tributaries. Terry Anderson, a Viola native, thinks the next state record stream trout will come out of the Kickapoo main stem.

My view is that the main stem of the Kickapoo is definitely worth a float trip during times of light canoe traffic (weekday or rainy weather). This way, you can prospect its deep green grottoes and move on to a tributary if nothing is doing on the main river. Pull your canoe up on a sand or gravel bank to work an area or wet-wade to the most promising holes. Forget about hatches here. Instead, use a streamer pattern that resembles the abundant crawfish or minnows in the stream. Be prepared to catch a sucker or two. But don't be surprised if your sucker has dark spots on a light

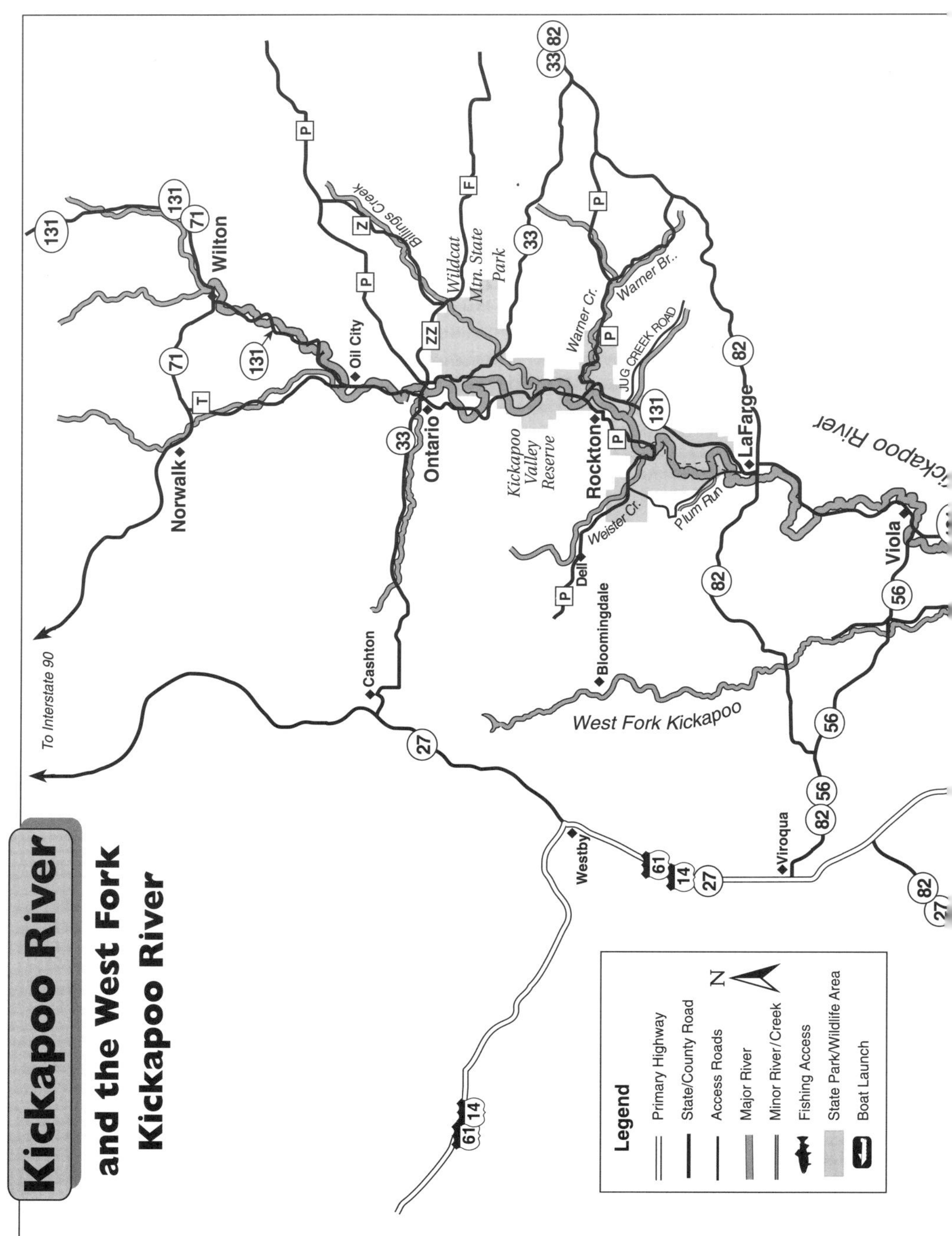
Kickapoo River
and the West Fork
Kickapoo River
Legend
Primary Highway
State/County Road
Access Roads
Major River
Minor River/Creek
Fishing Access
State Park/Wildlife Area
Boat Launch
N
To Interstate 90
Norwalk
Wilton
Oil City
Ontario
Cashton
Westby
Viroqua
Rockton
LaFarge
Viola
Dell
Bloomingdale
Billings Creek
Wildcat Mtn. State Park
Kickapoo Valley Reserve
Warner Cr.
Warner Br.
JUG CREEK ROAD
Weister Cr.
Plum Run
Kickapoo River
West Fork Kickapoo
131
71
33
82
27
56
61
14
P
Z
F
ZZ
T

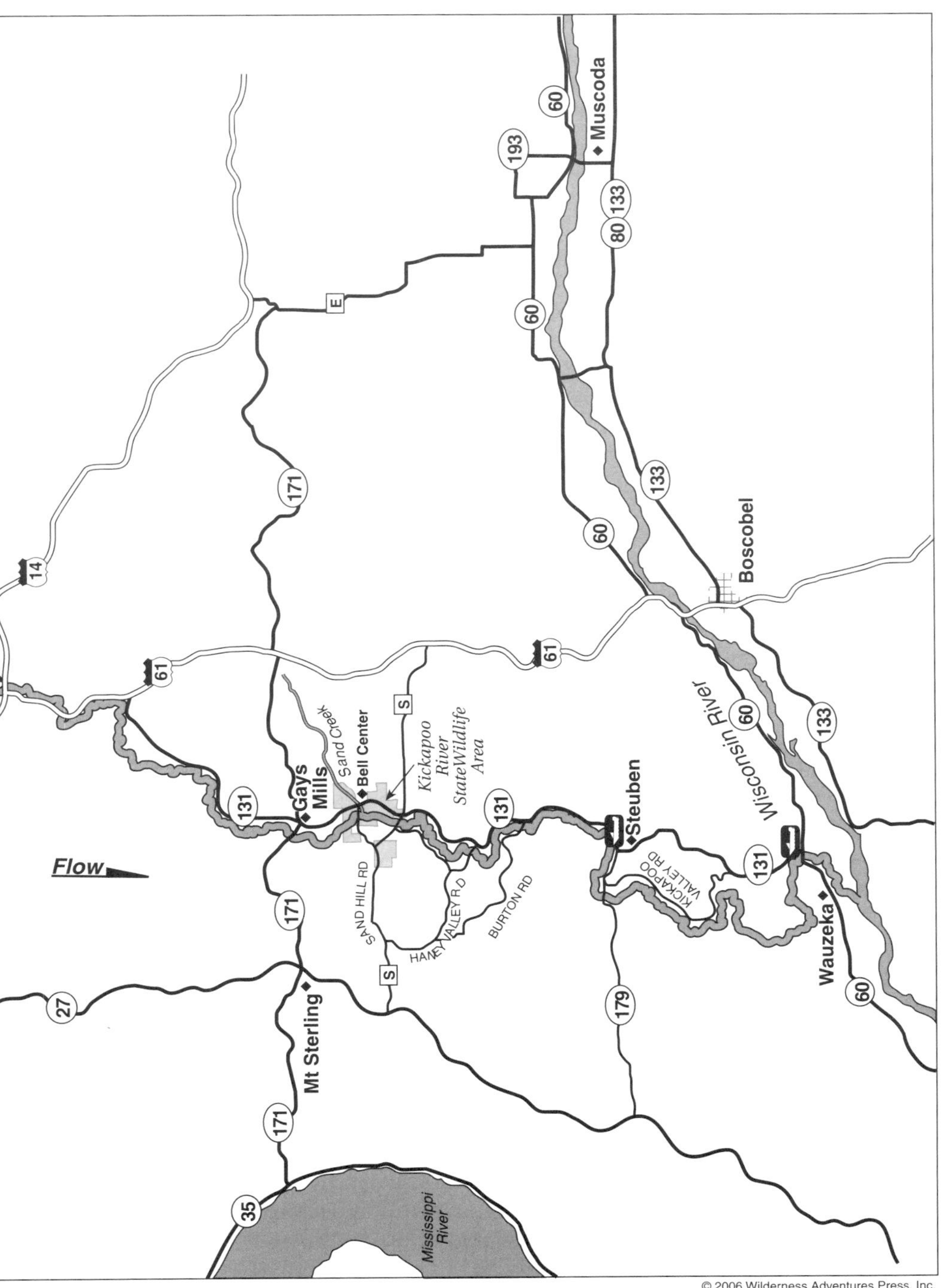

Muscoda
60
193
133
80
E
171
14
61
60
133
Boscobel
Wisconsin River
Sand Creek
Bell Center
S
Kickapoo River State Wildlife Area
Gays Mills
131
Steuben
Flow
SAND HILL RD
HANEY VALLEY RD
BURTON RD
KICKAPOO VALLEY RD
Wauzeka
179
27
Mt Sterling
35
Mississippi River

background and is hell-bent on taking your fly line into the backing. You'll want a reel loaded with a sink-tip line for this stretch.

There is a certain character to the main stem between Ontario and La Farge (basically the stretching running through Wildcat Mountain State Park and the Kickapoo Reserve). It is somewhat silty, fertile, and full of deadfalls that sometimes require the paddler to portage around them. Use your trout-fisher's eye and fish deep. These fish see a lot of canoe traffic. Try deep pools and heads of runs. There are also a few undercut banks in this stretch just begging to have a Woolly Bugger dragged beneath them. There are 16 bridge crossings in this stretch, many of them with gravel pullouts. Just follow Highway 131 South. From north to south there are also crossings on Hay Valley Road, Winchel Valley Road, County P, and Star Valley Road. For a small fee, the canoe outfitters will put your canoe on their trailer and take it back to your vehicle. Or you can rent a canoe from them, or have your buddy wait with the canoe as you get a ride back to your vehicle.

For the serious flyfisher, it may be the tributaries that are of most interest. I'll list the tributaries of this stretch of the Kickapoo from north to south. (Kickapoo tributaries occurring downstream from the reserve are treated as separate waters in this section.)

Billings Creek is a pretty spring creek that rises to the east of Wildcat Mountain State Park in southern Monroe County; it winds some 7 miles before emptying into the Kickapoo. The stretch that runs through Wildcat Mountain has received a lot of habitat attention from the DNR. Shocking surveys reveal good numbers of trout with enough 18- to 20-inchers to keep things lively. Find it along Highway Z. It is a fairly small stream above the Monroe County line. Concentrate your efforts between the Highway Z/ZZ bridge in the park and then in the reserve where it feeds into the Kickapoo. Rich aquatic life makes scud or cressbug patterns natural choices. It is category 3, as are all the tributaries discussed here, along with the Kickapoo main stem.

Next downstream is an unnamed creek that parallels Winchel Valley Road. It is too narrow to fly fish.

Warner Creek is a known trout-producer for its 8-odd miles. Find it and its tributaries along Highway P. Aaron at the Kickapoo Reserve recommends this creek. It holds brook and brown trout and supports some natural reproduction.

Jug Creek, a tributary flowing in from the east, and Indian Creek, to the west, are too small and brushy to bother with.

Weister Creek, flowing in from the west and beginning near the town of Dell, can be found along Highway P. It is a fine stream that has received habitat attention recently, and it is a favorite of local meat anglers and flyfishers alike. One hot buggy morning while researching this book, I picked up 6 trout to 13 inches—browns and brook trout—on a scud fished in deep green holes. Weister receives lots of spring flow.

One morning I came upon a father and son fishing at a bridge. Mourning doves sprang up from the gravel road as I walked from the car to greet them. "My boy just caught an 11-inch brookie, and I know there's bigger in here," said the father. There's a primitive campsite at the juncture of County P and Weister Creek Road. A drinking cup is attached to the pipe with a piece of bailing wire. Drink from it, be renewed, and be grateful that this area was not turned into a giant reservoir.

I have not fished Plum Run, but it is reputed to be fast and holds wild brook and brown trout. Find it along Plum Run Road just north of La Farge.

The Middle Stretch

Like middle children, the middle stretch of a river often falls into a kind of anonymity. We think about the beginning and end of things but less about the middle. The same goes for the Kickapoo from La Farge to the dam in Gays Mills. Below La Farge it becomes too silty to hold trout in large numbers, and warmwater gamefish from the Wisconsin River can't make it above the dam in Gays Mills. These middle 20 miles of river don't offer the fly angler very much, unless he is after rough fish.

Gays Mills to Wauzeka: Primitive Bottomlands

The Gays Mills Dam marks a habitat dividing line on the Kickapoo: 20 miles above it lies some fine trout fishing in the main stem and tributaries; below it, fishing is for warmwater species. The fact that there is a dam in Gays Mills—and has been since the middle part of the 19th century—is probably not a good thing from an ecological viewpoint. It impedes oxygen flow for the water below, and it serves as a habitat barrier to fish like walleye that would probably go farther upriver to spawn if they could. However, quite a lively local fishery has sprung up around it. You can even see Amish fathers and sons fishing there. The species? You name it: channel catfish, freshwater drum, carp, largemouth bass, northern pike, walleye, an occasional trout, and panfish.

From the flyfisher's point of view the dam would be difficult to fish. It is too deep and fast to wade safely, and throwing casts from the cement supports is hardly reminiscent of a classic fly fishing scene. But those willing to boat this stretch will find a *terra incognita* known only to the intrepid angler willing to go through the effort of launching a boat without a launch ramp. One note for those floating this stretch: If it looks like trout water, take a cast. A Gays Mills youngster dragged out a 26-inch rainbow trout at the juncture of Sand Creek and the Kickapoo.

A good way to fish this stretch of river would be to put in at the Gays Mills Dam and fish as far down as Stueben. At the dam, you will find Robb Park, which offers camping and something like a boat launch—a road that comes within 50 yards of the river. This would be a good long day of fishing or perhaps a two-day float—20 miles or so—but a small outboard could speed things up a bit. Bridge crossings from north to south in this stretch are Sand Hill Road, Highway S, Haney Valley Road, and Burton Road. Stueben would be a good place to take out. Both Gays Mills and Steuben offer good old-time taverns with fish fries, steak, and cold beer. Depending on river flow, trees may block passage in certain places here. Bring a pair of hip boots and be prepared to portage.

If you float this stretch, you'll find springs and lots of them. These inflows of water and food are congregation points for a variety of fish. Concentrate your efforts around these springs. Following a local tip, I once went down to the Kickapoo on our neighbor's property (my cabin is the gray ramshackle one on West River Road south of Gays Mills) to catch some dinner. This had absolutely nothing to do with sport or fly fishing. I was trying to get catfish for dinner. Fishing where a good-size spring dumped into the river, I was surprised to see my line move immediately upstream. I set the hook and watched a large brown form bolt into the main river and snap my line like a petty insult. This fish may have been a walleye, a bass, a trout, or even a large rough fish—I never found out. An hour later, after I had suffered all the mosquito bites I could stand, the same thing happened.

I was a step ahead of my piscine opponent this time. I had the drag as loose as it would go. So when the line started to move, I set the hook, letting the fish go into the main river and guiding him away from the fallen trees along the bank. After a half-hour of drag-screaming and cold sweats, I brought to hand a northern pike a few inches shy of 3 feet long. On 4-pound test! After doing some checking around, I found that this is not unusual for the Kickapoo or other little-fished rivers of southern Wisconsin, including the Pecatonica, the Crawfish, the Baraboo, and the Sugar.

River-dwelling northerns like springs and grow big and fat by cooling themselves while waiting for bait to drift by. So fish the springs. A good fly choice would be a Mickey Finn or big Muddler or Clouser Minnow. No subtlety here, and not much competition from other fly anglers, but the reward could test your tackle.

If you are quiet enough in your fly fishing exploration, you may see egrets, sandhill cranes, pileated woodpeckers, the garden-variety furbearers (mink, otter, beaver, muskrat), coyote, deer, and fox. Wood duck, blue-winged teal, mallard, and Canada geese breed in the backwaters along this stretch, and there are often some hooded mergansers nesting in hollow trees. A gaudy scarlet tanager may enliven the riverbottom canopy. Many a dairy farmer claims to have seen or heard cougars in the rugged bluffs of this country.

At Highway 60 just east of Wauzeka there is a fine launch used by duck hunters in fall and all but unvisited the rest of the year. From the launch it is about 5 miles to the confluence with the Wisconsin River. Bottomlands again predominate. The stretch from Highway 60 to the Wisconsin makes a nice summer float. It's uncrowded, hosts a variety of fish (walleye, smallmouth, white bass, and channel catfish are common here), and paddling back up on the Kickapoo is easy here since there's not much current.

In its 125 miles from Wilton to its juncture with the Wisconsin River, the Kickapoo (the name means "he goes here, then there" in Algonquin), a river that I call home, traverses a stunning variety of topography and holds just about every gamefish (except the muskellunge) known to Wisconsin. Its upper reaches in the reserve remind me of very rural parts of northern Spain—Galicia and Asturias. Chickens peck feed beneath the shade of elm trees; bluffs form a dreamy backdrop broken now and again by small towns and churches and farmsteads. And in its lower reaches, you might think you have descended into the deep south—a world of bean fields, trot lines, hackberry trees, and coon hunters.

Naturalists and anglers should thank their lucky stars—as well as local and national conservation groups—that the La Farge Lake dam was stopped. Otherwise, we would be looking at a very different, and less healthy, place. For flyfishers, this river represents a chance to explore interesting, serene waters largely passed over in favor of the more famous spring creeks in the region.

Stream Facts: Kickapoo River

Season

- Kickapoo River currently not managed as a trout stream. Regulation status being reassessed by DNR. Those wishing to fish it for trout should follow seasons and general guidelines for inland trout fishing: The early season runs from the first Saturday in March to the last Sunday before the first Saturday in May; no-kill, single barbless hooks only. Regular season runs from the first Saturday in May at 5:00 am through September 30. Other gamefish follow DNR limits/seasons for Wisconsin's Southern Zone.

Regulations

- Category 3 regulations apply to all Kickapoo tributaries within Kickapoo Reserve and the Kickapoo River.

Species

- Brown trout in main stem in good numbers down to La Farge; brook and brown trout in tributaries; main stem below Gays Mills, northern pike, walleye, channel catfish, rough fish, panfish.

River Miles

- Wilton to Ontario (25), Ontario to La Farge (25), La Farge to Gays Mills (25), Gays Mills to Steuben (20), Steuben to Wauzeka and juncture with Wisconsin River (25)

Characteristics

- Wide, somewhat silty stream flowing through mixed woodlands; Weister, Warner, and Billings Creek all high-quality trout streams.

Access

- Canoes or kayaks can be put in at bridge crossings throughout the Kickapoo Reserve, at Robb Park in Gays Mills, and at Highway 60 in Wauzeka.

Fly Shops

- Rockin' K Fly Shop, Gander Mountain (La Crosse), Cabela's, Driftless Angler

Maps

- *Wisconsin Atlas and Gazetteer*, pages 41, 33, 32

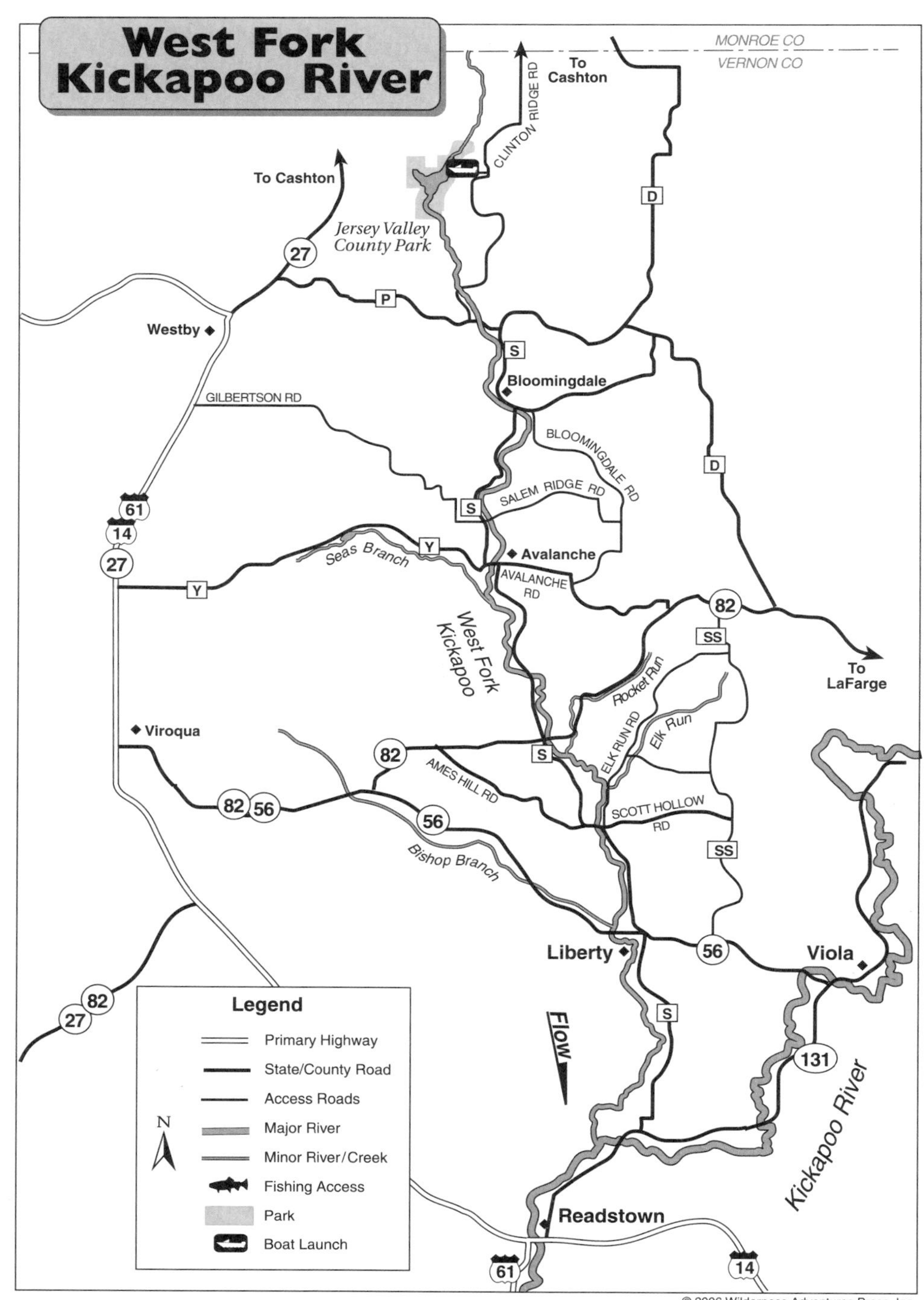

West Fork Kickapoo River
MONROE CO
VERNON CO
To Cashton
CLINTON RIDGE RD
To Cashton
Jersey Valley County Park
Westby
Bloomingdale
GILBERTSON RD
BLOOMINGDALE RD
SALEM RIDGE RD
Avalanche
AVALANCHE RD
Seas Branch
West Fork Kickapoo
Rocket Run
ELK RUN RD
Elk Run
To LaFarge
Viroqua
AMES HILL RD
SCOTT HOLLOW RD
Bishop Branch
Liberty
Viola
Flow
Kickapoo River
Readstown
Legend
Primary Highway
State/County Road
Access Roads
Major River
Minor River/Creek
Fishing Access
Park
Boat Launch
N

West Fork of the Kickapoo River

The West Fork of the Kickapoo River begins just south of Cashton at the Vernon-Monroe County line. It winds for 24 miles (paralleled by Highway S) before emptying into the main stem of the Kickapoo River near Readstown. Thanks to an abundance of feeder streams, where trout can spawn and seek relief from water temperatures that sometimes climb into the mid-70s, and to extensive habitat work from the Westfork Sportsman's Club, parts of the West Fork have developed into a first-class, self-sustaining trout fishery. Just a quarter-century ago the stream was a marginal, put-and-take fishery.

Bishops Branch, near Liberty off Highway 56, and Seas Branch, near Avalanche off Highway Y, are feeder creeks that hold trout. For the West Fork, concentrate your efforts in the 8 miles of catch-and-release water between Bloomingdale and Highway 82. Above Bloomingdale, it is a bit narrow to fish; below Highway 82, it begins to silt up. The stretch below Highway 82 is more popular with locals fishing Rapalas, night crawlers, and chubs for large trout. Above Bloomingdale and below Avalanche, the river is category 3. Brown trout are no longer stocked in the catch-and-release area thanks to excellent natural reproduction.

When I spoke to Bob Blumreich, of Silver Doctor Fly Fishing in Viroqua, about this stream it was Halloween day and he had been out photographing spawning browns on the West Fork. Blue-Winged Olives and midges were hatching, both of

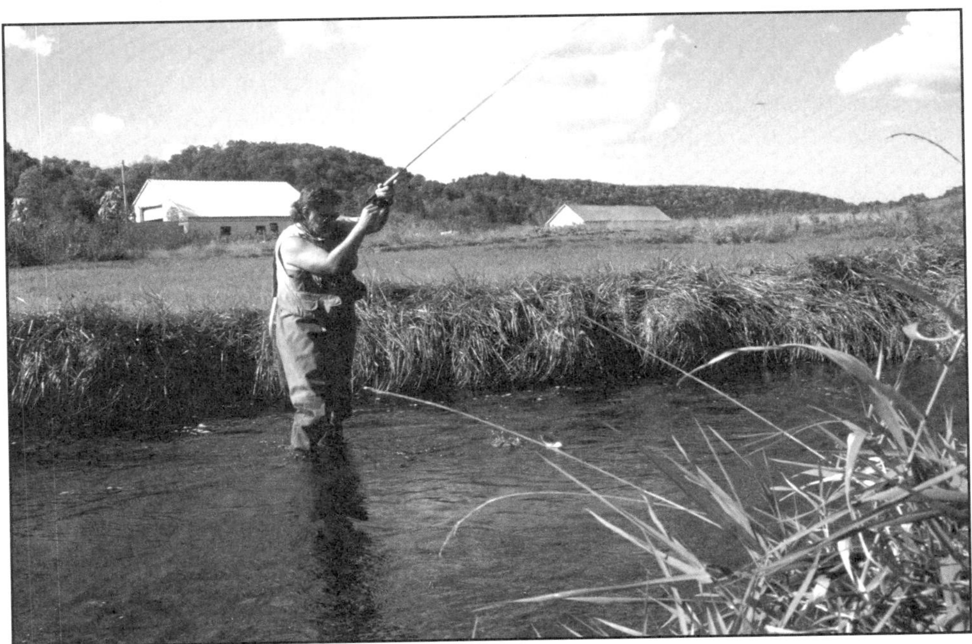

The West Fork of the Kickapoo is a favorite with flyfishers. (Chris Halla)

which are present throughout the trout season (March to September). He notes that hatches tend to occur earlier and last a bit longer on the West Fork because its water temperatures are slightly warmer than surrounding streams. Aside from this slight variation—which makes the West Fork an excellent choice for the March and April season—hatches here pretty much follow the timetable of other area spring creeks, according to Blumreich.

You will encounter Hendricksons beginning in April and into May, and Sulphurs and Cahills from early May into September. The rocky bottom is home to a variety of caddis species, all of which can be profitably fished subsurface all season long with a size 16 beadhead caddis. Look for caddis hatches beginning as early as late March, especially on warm and windy days; fish these with the traditional Elk Hair Caddis. Scuds are present and also can be fished throughout the season. Terrestrial fishing is good in summer. Look for crickets beginning in mid-July and hoppers in August, both of which provide good fishing well into September. Finally, forage fish and crawfish are present in good numbers so don't be afraid to try streamer patterns.

Todd Polacek, owner of the former Madison Outfitters, calls the West Fork a very unique river with qualities of a both a freestone river ("at times you think you're fishing in a canyon," he says) and a classic spring creek. Besides the hairy and scary, Polacek recommends Copper Johns, cressbugs, and Pheasant Tail Nymphs for fishing the West Fork. He also notes exceptional landowner cooperation and stream improvements—as well as big browns—as hallmarks of this fishery. While many of spring creeks in the area are good by default, the West Fork, he says, is good by design, by cultivation.

The thriving fishery now present in the West Fork did not just happen. In the 1960s and '70s it was a put-and-take stream with no natural reproduction. Thanks to thousands of man-hours and dollars from Trout Unlimited chapters, the West Fork Sportsman's Club, and other local conservation clubs, the catch-and-release section no longer requires stocking of brown trout.

Browns are still stocked above and below the catch-and-release water; brook trout are present in feeder streams and sometimes show up in the West Fork. Stream banks have been stabilized to help retard erosion. Fish cribs help protect trout from predators like herons and otters. Local landowners have cooperated by minimizing in-stream grazing and allowing buffer strips. We owe a debt of gratitude to these landowners, to the West Fork Sportsman's Club, and to the DNR for their efforts in establishing wild trout in this stream.

There is public access to the majority of the catch-and-release water along Highway S thanks to the easements negotiated by the West Fork people. Fly fishing above Bloomingdale is probably not worth your time; below Highway 82, you can cross the stream on Ames River Road and Highway SS (a mix of rough fish and big trout amid fallen timber characterizes this stretch).

Stream Facts: West Fork Kickapoo River

Season
- The early season runs from the first Saturday in March to the last Sunday before the first Saturday in May; no-kill, single barbless hooks only. Regular season runs from the first Saturday in May at 5:00 am through September 30.

Regulations
- Highway 82 upstream to Highway S and Bloomingdale Rd is category 5—no-kill, artificials only; remainder is category 3.

Species
- Wild browns

Miles of Trout Water
- 24 miles

Stream Characteristics
- Somewhere between Driftless spring creek and main stem of Kickapoo. Large browns present. Lots of forage fish and crawfish; diverse insect life—scuds, mayflies, caddis. Bishops Branch and Seas Branch (tributaries) are worth a try. Flows past stands of hemlock and white pine.

Access
- Highway S, West Fork Sportsman's Club

Fly Shops
- Cabela's, Rockin' K Fly Shop, Gander Mountain (La Crosse), Driftless Angler

Maps
- *Wisconsin Atlas and Gazetteer*, page 41, 33

Big Guide, Little Water: A Streamside Profile of Guide Bob Blumreich

The week after setting a fishing date with guide Bob Blumreich, who owns and operates Silver Doctor Fly Fishing out of Viroqua, Wisconsin, I was struck with a number of worries. Call it March Anglers' Disorder, a.k.a. MAD, afflicting trout anglers before their first early season outing. A foot of snow had just blanketed southern Wisconsin. Weather Radio called for rain, more snow, then cold for the following week. It looked like we'd be fishing chocolate milk or picking ice from guide-eyes.

What's more, five years ago I had fished the stream Bob suggested without so much as a strike. But, being deferential and deadline-bound, I tried to perk up. I'd be away from the computer and in the pretty Driftless Country west of Madison. I could always shoot photos if not catch fish. Besides, as we all know, a day spent fishing is not ordinarily subtracted from your limited days on earth. And I looked forward to meeting Blumreich in person—"a helluva a fly tier and an odd dude" I'd been told, who also provided critical information for the *Flyfisher's Guide to Wisconsin.*

A person's choice of water says a lot. In sporting literature we hear about the same faces in the same places as if fly fishing were nothing more than the mechanics of showing up at the appointed destination on a certain date with the right fly and the right rod and having lots of photo ops with trophy fish in sparkling Caribbean bonefish flats or idyllic Alaskan wilderness. While Bob Blumreich has fished many of the destination waters in his 50-plus years, he breaks way out of the box, or perhaps goes further inside it.

I descended a steep, wooded valley to the creek where we'd meet and tried to catch a glimpse on the way over it, but it was too damned small! Let me say it again: Too damned small. You don't hear that in sporting books very often. I pulled into the gravel lot and there was Bob sitting on the back of his minivan smoking a cigarette. A blue haze lay over the valley, making its ridges all the more sharp. The temperature had climbed into the 40s. I rigged up and Bob led the way down the stream.

"They're taking little black midges," he said. And sure enough, there was a dimple next to some recent riprapping on the stream. I told Bob to go ahead, that I needed to shoot photos. Framing the picture, I was struck by asymmetry. Easily 6'2" and 250 pounds, Bob cut a strange shape against this stream that could be vaulted, even straddled, in places. He handled a Reddington 3-weight with nothing short of artistry. It's easier to picture Blumreich throwing big loops on a spey rod in a Lake Michigan tributary (that's where he does the other half of his guiding).

Just as I was focusing the camera, I heard the whip of fly line snapped tight. A brook trout grabbed Bob's midge on the second cast. He brought to hand a fat male, orange below, blue on top, and released it into the clear water. Moving upstream, we walked over a stream-hugging grass mat. Scores of brook trout scattered like pellets from a tightly choked shotgun. As we moved farther upstream—which we did slowly and methodically, at Bob's urging—he'd call this piece of water "cute," that one "gorgeous." I liked his phrasing, but it was his attention to detail that really struck me. He'd point out pocketwater no bigger than a shoebox and call it Caddis Heaven. He'd point out a feeding lane, all 6 inches of it, and sure enough fish held there.

The quantity of fish in this trickle was astounding, especially since I'd written it off years earlier. More striking still was the small tableaux, the tiny canvas on which Bob worked. Everyone knows the Blue and Green and Timber Coulee are full of fish. These streams have obvious structure and their milky depths forgive a certain amount of sloppiness. Here on this gin-clear brook trout stream, however, the slightest mis-step meant scurrying trout. Bob occasionally showed himself on purpose to demonstrate the number of trout in a hole or to point out effective (or ineffective) lunker structure, but there was no carelessness.

As we moved upstream, the water got prettier and prettier, or cuter and cuter in Bob's parlance. Plunge pools, riprap, lunker structures, and deep corners made for a smorgasbord of trout habitat. We came upon a pool reminiscent of Crawford County streams I fished over the years—green and grotto-deep. With casting instruction from Bob, I placed a Pheasant Tail Nymph into the throat of the pool and took a fat bright-colored brook trout. Nature gave me other surprises this day as well—an appreciation for the tiny stream and temperatures nearing 50 degrees and a deepened respect for gemütlichkeit limestone streams. My M.A.D. was, apparently, dissipating.

Bob and I pushed up toward the headwaters of this unnamed stream running through the heart of Driftless Country. He saw a pod of feeding fish just below a lunker structure. In fisherman's honesty, I must tell you the water was clear as a fresh-cleaned mirror and no more than 6 inches deep. Bob stood well downstream and cast to them. He hooked a male, again sashed with orange below, and released the fish after I snapped a picture. Next it was my turn. I hooked a big brook trout that rolled like a salmon and spit out the fly. Just as well. Sometimes it's better to be smitten by a pixie than to take one's fill of something common.

If you want to fish with Bob, he guides for trout on southwest Wisconsin coulees and on Lake Michigan's tributaries for salmon and steelhead. He's an FFA-certified casting instructor and can teach you how to cast traditional rods for trout or spey rods for salmon and steelhead. Visit his website at www.silverdoctor.net or call him at 608-637-3417.

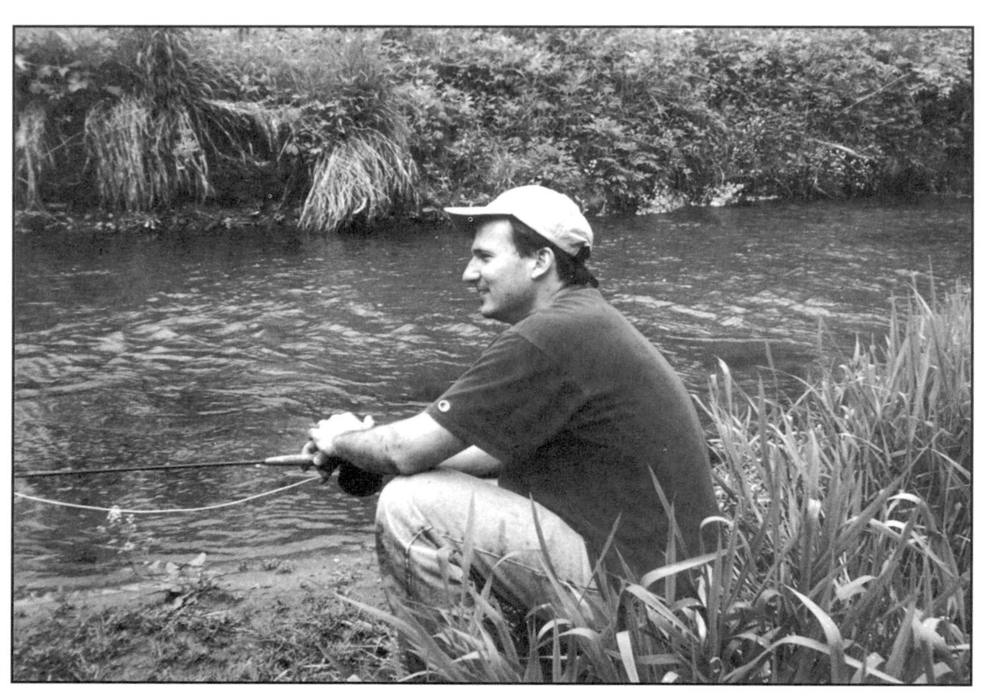

The author taking a break from fishing Tainter Creek

TAINTER CREEK

Tainter Creek deserves to be mentioned in any fishing guide to Wisconsin. Why? Because of the 10-pound brown trout that hangs on the wall of Dregne's Hardware in Westby, Wisconsin, caught in Tainter Creek by a GI just home from World War II. It's a bit faded from 50 years behind glass but still an impressive fish. Perhaps most striking is how puny its companion brown trout (a 5- or 6-pounder) looks by comparison. Will you catch another 10-pounder out of Tainter Creek? Probably not, but fisheries biologist Dave Vetrano says it still coughs up a few 20-inchers every year.

Its clear-running waters rise in a primeval wooded hollow, just over the Vernon County line along Tainter Hollow Road. It then runs through a meadow stretch under DNR control, with good springtime mayfly hatches and summer midge hatches. Below the Vernon County line, County Highway B joins up with Tainter Hollow Road; follow B all the way down to the confluence with the Kickapoo River, some 5 miles. There are public fishing easements along Highway B. Land-use practices have improved on Tainter Creek, and some natural reproduction of brown trout occurs. The best habitat is along County Highway B where the DNR and Gays Mills Sportsmen's Club have worked to stabilize stream banks with boulders and riprap. The upper stretch of meadow water is also good. Tainter is a category 3 stream for its entire length.

HUB CITY: LA FARGE

From pre-European times to the mid-19th century, La Farge was a center for fur trade. Logging was its mainstay in the late 19th century, when its population was double what it is now. Today, it is a center for organic farming and nature-related activities on the 10,000-acre Kickapoo Reserve.

Accommodations

River Valley Motel, 115 S. Bird St., Box 25; 608 606 0922; www.rivervalleymotel.com; $
Driftwood Inn, 305 Garden St., Ontario; 608-337-4660; $
Trillium, Route 2, Box 121; 608-625-4492; $$
End of the Trail Farm, E13722 Cass Valley Rd., Ontario; 608-337-4738; $$
Blakely's Hobbit, RR 1, Viola 54664; 608-627-1461; $
Kickapoo Vacation Rentals, P.O. Box 187; 608-625-4604; $$
Back Door Bed and Breakfast, 1223 Front St., Cashton; 608-654-5950; $$

Campgrounds

Wildcat Mountains State Park, P.O. Box 99, Ontario WI 54651
Kickapoo Valley Reserve, Highway 131, La Farge; 608-625-2960; http://kvr.state.wi.us
Brush Creek Campground, S190 Opal Rd., Ontario; 608-337-4344
West Fork Sports Club Campground, c/o Roger Widner; 608-634-2303

Restaurants

Debbie's Diner, 110 W. Main Street; 608-625-4040; good homestyle food, great prices, pies, breakfasts, hot lunches, and dinners

Phil and Deb's Town Tap, 115 W. Main St.; 608-625-4122; good burgers, lunch and breakfast in tavern atmosphere

Gudgeon's Food Mart, 101 N. Maple; 608-625-4413; small supermarket in downtown La Farge.

Kickapoo Paddle Inn, P.O. Box 86, Ontario; hamburger stand

Back Door Cafe, 1223 Front St., Cashton; 608-654-5950; homestyle lunches, $5-$7; dinner by reservation only, entrees include roast duck, lamb, and beef medallions; good choice for fine dining in Coulee County, prices from $15.95 to $19.95.

Fly Shops, Outfitters, Sporting Goods

Jacquish Hollow Angler, 32491 Jaquish So. Rd., Richland Center; 608-585-2239

Rockin' K Fly Shop, 106 E. Roosevelt St, Coon Valley; 608 452 2142; rockinkflyshop.com; fly shop and guiding

Cabela's, Highway 35, Prairie du Chien, 608 326 7163; full line of fly fishing gear and good source of information on Driftless streams

Madison Orvis, 1700 Deming Road, Greenway Station, Madison; 608-831-3181; full line of fly fishing gear on Madison's west side

Kickapoo Kwikstop & Liquor Store, (license, no flies), Highway 14 West, Readstown 608-629-5717

Bob's Silver Doctor Fly Fishing, P.O. Box 105, Viroqua; 608-637-3417

Fontana Sports Specialists, 7948 Tree Lane Drive; 608-833-9191; guiding for trout and warmwater fly fishing

Streamside Outfitters, 2120 Main Street, Cross Plains; 608 295 6517; streamside-outfitters.com; fly shop and guide service on banks of Black Earth Creek

Driftless Angler, 106 S. Main St., Viroqua; 608 637 8779; driftlessanglercom; fly shop and guiding

Veterinarians

Barcee Veterinary Clinic, 1214 Goose Creek Rd, Viola; 608-627-1442

Coulee Mobile Veterinary; 608-634-MVET

Medical

Nearest hospitals in Richland Center and La Crosse.

Auto Rental

Nearest car rental in Richland Center and La Crosse.

Automobile Repair

Heartland County Co-op, 210 W. Main; 608-623-2324

La Farge Truck Center, 319 W. Main; 608-625-4285

Air Service

Nearest airports Richland Center and La Crosse.

Canoes and/or Canoe Shuttles

Crooked River in Readstown, 608-629-5624
Kickapoo Paddle Inn in Ontario, 800-947-3603
Mr. Duck in Ontario, 608-337-4711
Titanic Canoe Rental in Ontario, 608-337-4551
Fisher's in Wilton, 608-435-6802
Drifty's in Ontario, 608-337-4228

For More Information

Village of La Farge
P.O. Box 37
La Farge WI 54639
608-625-4422
www.lafarge-wisconsin.com

Kickapoo Reserve Office
Highway 131
La Farge WI 54639
http://kvr.state.wi.us

Visit the Kickapoo Reserve office located on the northern edge of La Farge on Highway 131. Read about the history of the failed La Farge Lake, and all of the good conservation initiatives going on today. Visit the reserve's 10,000 acres for a glimpse of pre-glacial scenery.

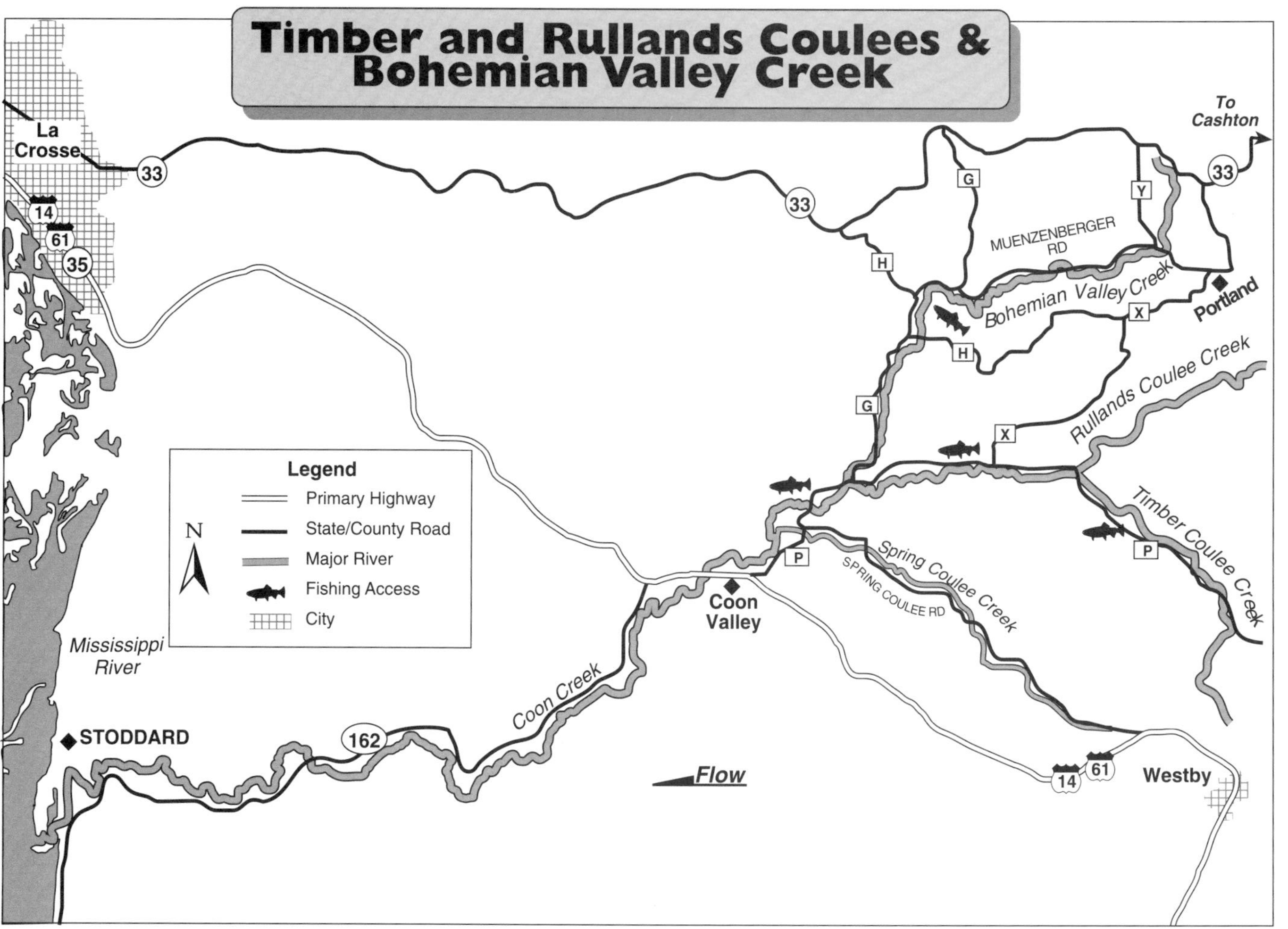

Timber and Rullands Coulees & Bohemian Valley Creek
La Crosse
To Cashton
MUENZENBERGER RD
Bohemian Valley Creek
Portland
Rullands Coulee Creek
Timber Coulee Creek
Spring Coulee Creek
SPRING COULEE RD
Coon Valley
Coon Creek
Legend
Primary Highway
State/County Road
Major River
Fishing Access
City
N
Mississippi River
STODDARD
Flow
Westby
33
G
Y
H
X
P
14
61
35
162

Guide Bob Blumreich fishing a small brook trout stream near Timber Coulee.

Timber Coulee

If you find yourself dejected by the environmental degradation of our modern world, then give Dave Vetrano a call at 608-785-9009. Who is Dave Vetrano? He's the DNR fisheries biologist for Wisconsin's Coulee Counties—Crawford, Vernon, Monroe, and La Crosse. Why call him? Because he will tell you, with no self-aggrandizement, that streams in his region have, after years of being marginal fisheries, returned to a state more pristine than presettlement conditions. Colder water temperatures, more groundwater and springwater, and less erosion all account for this. He will get around to telling you that habitat work has been done on some of these streams—fish cribs, bank stabilization, reduction of grazing—but that a good part of it is luck and raised awareness regarding land-use.

The narrow valleys of this country are being farmed less intensively; in part because, sadly, small-scale farmers can't compete with mega-farms, but also because these valleys may have never been well suited to agriculture in the first place. Also, a good amount of this land is now recreational land, owned by both back-to-earth types and weekend hunters. This means less silt and less erosion—and, hence, more groundwater and colder, cleaner streams. Vetrano and his crew are also stocking wild-strain brookies and browns—brood fish taken from the area and stripped of milt and roe, their fingerlings reared in the Nevin Fish Hatchery and then released back into good habitat to be fruitful and multiply. So, in part by accident, in part by design, things are actually better now than they were 50 or even 100 years ago in these creek valleys.

Timber Coulee is perhaps the poster child for this trend. In the middle part of the century it was silty, shallow, and muddy; unfit to be a trout stream according to the DNR. Following a tradition begun in this valley in the 1930s by the Civilian Conservation Corps of encouraging contour farming and wooded hillsides to help conserve precious topsoil and maintain water quality, the Westby Rod and Gun Club undertook massive improvements on this stream. Local groups, the DNR, TU, and others worked hard in successive years to stabilize banks and add fish cribs.

No doubt the larger land-use trends of "greener farming" and the conversion of thousands of acres to recreational or set-aside land helped groundwater resources as well. Local-strain wild brown trout were also stocked, and by the mid-80s the stream had become a self-supporting wild trout fishery. Brown trout populations in some sections of the stream have quintupled in the last 30 years. What a difference a few decades can make!

Arising as a tiny spring creek just west of the village of Westby, Timber Coulee runs some miles to its confluence with Coon Creek. The banks of this stream are practically all under DNR lease, easement, or ownership. Fence stiles and gravel pullouts make for easy access and parking as the stream winds along County Highway P. Much of this stream runs through fairly open meadow country. An angler can indulge in actual fly casting and not just the tight roll casts and dapping so many of these streams demand. Below its confluence with Rullands Coulee, the stream widens. From County P upstream to Olstad Road, the stream is category 5—artificials only, catch-and-release. On all other parts of the stream, the daily bag limit runs from 3 to 5 with a maximum length of 12 inches. This rather liberal regulation is designed to thin out smaller trout, which are overabundant and perhaps taxing the stream's capacity to hold larger fish.

An interesting feature in this neck of the woods is the Rockin' K Farms Fly Shop just outside of Coon Valley, one of the few fly shops in this dairy country. (Check out local stream and hatch conditions on their website http://go.to/rocknk.) Owner Paul Kogut will be glad to trade information with you about coulee streams. He describes a regular progression of hatches on Timber Coulee; nearby Bohemian Valley and Rullands Creeks offer similar hatches. Kogut has observed Blue-Winged Olive hatches from February through December on Timber Coulee; he fishes a size 18 or 20 pattern early and late season and size 14 or 16 mid-season. Dark Hendricksons come off during April and May, and he fishes these larger mayflies with a size 12 or 14. Sulphur hatches are present from mid-May through mid-August, while Light Cahills occur between late May and late September.

Kogut describes June 5 or 6 as an etymological dividing line, with mainly mayfly action before that date and mainly caddis after. Kogut says you'll encounter just about every type of caddis here, and he recommends fishing subsurface patterns over dry flies for caddis. Carry an assortment of caddis imitations from size 12 to 16—Hare's

Ears, Pheasant Tails, and beadhead caddis all produce well. When the water's off, or toward dark, Kogut says anglers do well with large streamers, although he's no great fan of "hairy and scary" flies. Hopper fishing is good in August and September, especially in dry years, with cricket imitations producing well from July to season's end.

As to fish size, Dave Vetrano will tell you there's not a lot of variation here—most fish are in the 10- to 14-inch range. If you want big fish, he says, try the Kickapoo. If you want lots of fish, come to Timber Coulee. Since brown trout have done so well in the creek, Vetrano has slight regret that brookies weren't introduced here instead. He has no plans of tinkering with this great success. But watch out, Dave's busy trying to re-establish wild brook trout elsewhere in the area.

Stream Facts: Timber Coulee

Season

- The early season runs from the first Saturday in March to the last Sunday before the first Saturday in May; no-kill, single barbless hooks only. Regular season runs from the first Saturday in May at 5:00 am through September 30.

Regulations

- County P upstream to Olstad Road, category 5—no-kill, artificials only. The rest of the stream is also category 5 but under different regulations—5 trout may be kept with a maximum size of 12 inches.

Species

- Wild brown and brook trout

Miles of Trout Water

- 8 miles

Stream Characteristics

- Fast, cold stream running through woods and meadow; all wild trout; extensive stream improvements; fish densities of up to 5,000 per mile. Vast majority of fish are under 14 inches.

Access

- Numerous DNR holding on Highway P; most of the streambed is under DNR control.

Fly Shops

- Rockin' K Fly Shop, Gander Mountain (La Crosse), Cabela's, Driftless Angler

Maps

- *Wisconsin Atlas and Gazetteer*, page 40

This is a small tributary to Rullands Coulee Creek.

A bend on well-known Timber Coulee.

RULLANDS COULEE

Rullands Coulee Creek is an important feeder creek to the Timber Coulee/Coon Creek system. It has 4.5 miles of water supporting good populations of wild brown and brook trout. Rullands Coulee is category 5 (5-trout limit with 12-inch maximum size) for its entire length and boasts many of the same virtues held by its fellow coulees: abundant insect life, habitat improvements, generous public access, lush bluff scenery, and good doses of spring flow and groundwater. Hatches are similar to its bigger cousin, Timber Coulee, with Blue-Winged Olives (early spring and off and on throughout the season) followed by Hendricksons and Sulphurs. A beadhead caddis or small olive scud fishes well here. The stream begins near the small village of Cashton in southwest Monroe County and winds along Endicott Drive off County Highway P.

You can, in my experience, fish Rullands and other coulees during extended periods of rainy weather. With all the habitat work done on these streams, a minimum of topsoil washes into them, and they are pretty quick to return to a fishable level. For two seasons running my brother came from the East to fish Driftless streams, despite some wet weather. While we found those in Crawford and Grant Counties running like chocolate milk, we took trout on Spring Coulee, Bohemian Valley Creek, and Rullands Coulee. During good weather Rullands runs gin-clear to milky-limestone over sand, gravel, and watercress (home to scuds and cressbugs).

Is Rullands Coulee superior to other streams in the area? Well, it is sure highly regarded by Coon Valley flyfishers. Some of its trout—captured and stripped of milt and roe, their fingerlings reared in Nevin Fish Hatchery south of Madison—sired the strain of wild browns thriving in Timber Coulee and other local streams. This would suggest, correctly, that Rullands Coulee is a superior stream. Yet Dave Vetrano, area fisheries biologist, notes, "Get a motel in Viroqua, drive 50 miles in any direction. If it looks like a trout stream, it probably is." You may hit a few deadends. On the other hand, in a remote hollow reminiscent of the Ozarks, you may encounter the remnant strains of wild brook Vetrano hints at but refuses to give specific instructions to. There are thousands of miles of streams to explore in Driftless Country's hills and valleys and sloughs and swamps and little towns and forgotten farmsteads. Even if it were possible to catalog all of these—and it isn't because brook trout are expanding into waters no one ever thought possible—you would miss the point of exploring and fishing Coulee Country.

Stream Facts: Rullands Coulee

Season

- The early season runs from the first Saturday in March to the last Sunday before the first Saturday in May; no-kill, single barbless hooks only. Regular season runs from the first Saturday in May at 5:00 am through September 30.

Regulations

- Category 5—five trout limit with maximum size of 12 inches.

Species

- Wild browns and some brook trout, particularly near springs and tributaries.

Miles of Trout Water

- 4.5 miles

Stream Characteristics

- Fast, cold coulee running through woods and meadow; all wild trout; extensive stream improvements. Vast majority of fish are under 14 inches. Abundant insect life.

Access

- DNR holdings along Endicott Drive.

Fly Shops

- Rockin' K Fly Shop, Gander Mountain (La Crosse), Cabela's, Driftless Angler

Maps

- *Wisconsin Atlas and Gazetteer*, page 40

An angler fishing through the "mosquito hatch" on Bohemian Valley Creek.

Bohemian Valley Creek

This is a favorite creek of mine that contains good populations of wild brook and brown trout. Especially in its wooded upper reaches, with a Czech cemetery and church nearby, there is a sylvan enchantment here that I've known on no other stream. My wife and I once snuck up on our hands and knees to watch a pod of wild brook trout finning in a spring pond. I've also had tippet snapped more than a few times while trying to keep a bulldogging fish out of the timber. This is a special place, and I trust that other anglers will respect the delicate brook trout fishery here.

Beginning just to the west of Portland, Bohemian Valley Creek twists its way toward Timber Coulee for some 8 miles. This is category 5 water—5-trout limit with a maximum size of 12 inches. Where Bohemian Valley Creek, Timber Coulee, and Spring Coulee converge, the stream becomes known as Coon Creek, a siltier, slower, less scenic stream running through the town of Coon Valley and then on to the Mississippi.

In the 2 miles of Coon Creek after its juncture with Spring Coulee and downstream to the town of Coon Valley, there is plenty of good habitat and good trout numbers. However, downstream from Coon Valley, habitat and trout numbers fall off quickly. Access to this stretch is via Highway P.

You can fish the headwaters of Bohemian Valley Creek along Eldora-Muenzenberger Road, but this is so clear it's almost not worth your time. Follow

County G south toward Coon Valley. There are bridge crossings on Highway H and Highway G before it joins up with Timber Coulee. The Highway H bridge is a good place to begin; if memory serves there are remnants of an old mill dam here. An angler can fish up or down from here with good results or probe the underwater structure of the dam. Again, most of the usual aquatic invertebrates are here—scuds, caddis, and mayflies. It seems to me, though, that I've encountered fewer hatches on Bohemian Valley Creek than on other creeks in the system.

Private land is mixed with public land here so be sure to ask permission if you will be crossing someone's field. There's enough public access, especially in the lower reaches, that you'll never lack a public entry point to the stream. Look for fence stiles and/or gravel parking lots and yellow DNR stream-regulation signs. It's always a good idea to read these to make sure you are in compliance before entering a particular section of stream.

Stream Facts: Bohemian Valley Creek

Season

- The early season runs from the first Saturday in March to the last Sunday before the first Saturday in May; no-kill, single barbless hooks only. Regular season runs from the first Saturday in May at 5:00 am through September 30.

Regulations

- Category 5—five-trout limit with maximum size of 12 inches.

Species

- Wild browns and some brook trout, particularly near springs and tributaries.

Miles of Trout Water

- 8 miles

Stream Characteristics

- Begins as small, wooded headwater stream with deep pockets, broadens into meadow stream with riprapped banks. Of the three main coulee creeks—Timber, Rullands, and Bohemian Valley—this one perhaps holds the largest trout.

Access

- DNR holdings along Highway G.

Fly Shops

- Rockin' K Fly Shop, Gander Mountain (La Crosse), Cabela's, Driftless Angler

Maps

- *Wisconsin Atla s and Gazetteer*, page 40

The Upper Mississippi River near Ferryville.

The Mississippi River

La Crosse to Dubuque

A wide variety of warmwater species are present in this stretch of the Mississippi River, which is part of the Upper Mississippi River National Wildlife and Fish Refuge. Since this entire area is under federal ownership, access is extensive. Launch ramps can be found, north to south, in the following locations: La Crosse, Stoddard, Genoa, Ferryville, Lynxville, Prairie du Chien, Wyalusing, Bagley, Cassville, and McCartney. Species present are largemouth and smallmouth bass, northern pike, walleye and sauger, a variety of panfish, plus carp, catfish, and drum. A word to the wise: Stick to the backwaters if you don't have a truly seaworthy vessel. By this I mean a reliable outboard of 15-horsepower or more, a sound boat of no less than 14 feet, and a serviceable pair of oars. Strong currents and the locks and dams present on the river—together with frequent storms—can spell disaster for the ill-prepared or those in small crafts. You'll find walleye, smallmouths, and channel catfish in channels and near wing dams. Fish the extensive backwaters for panfish, northerns, and largemouths. While spin fishermen have the best chance at covering the main channel, flyfishers can work a streamer among lily pads for ornery northerns or fish poppers for bass and bluegill from a canoe or small boat.

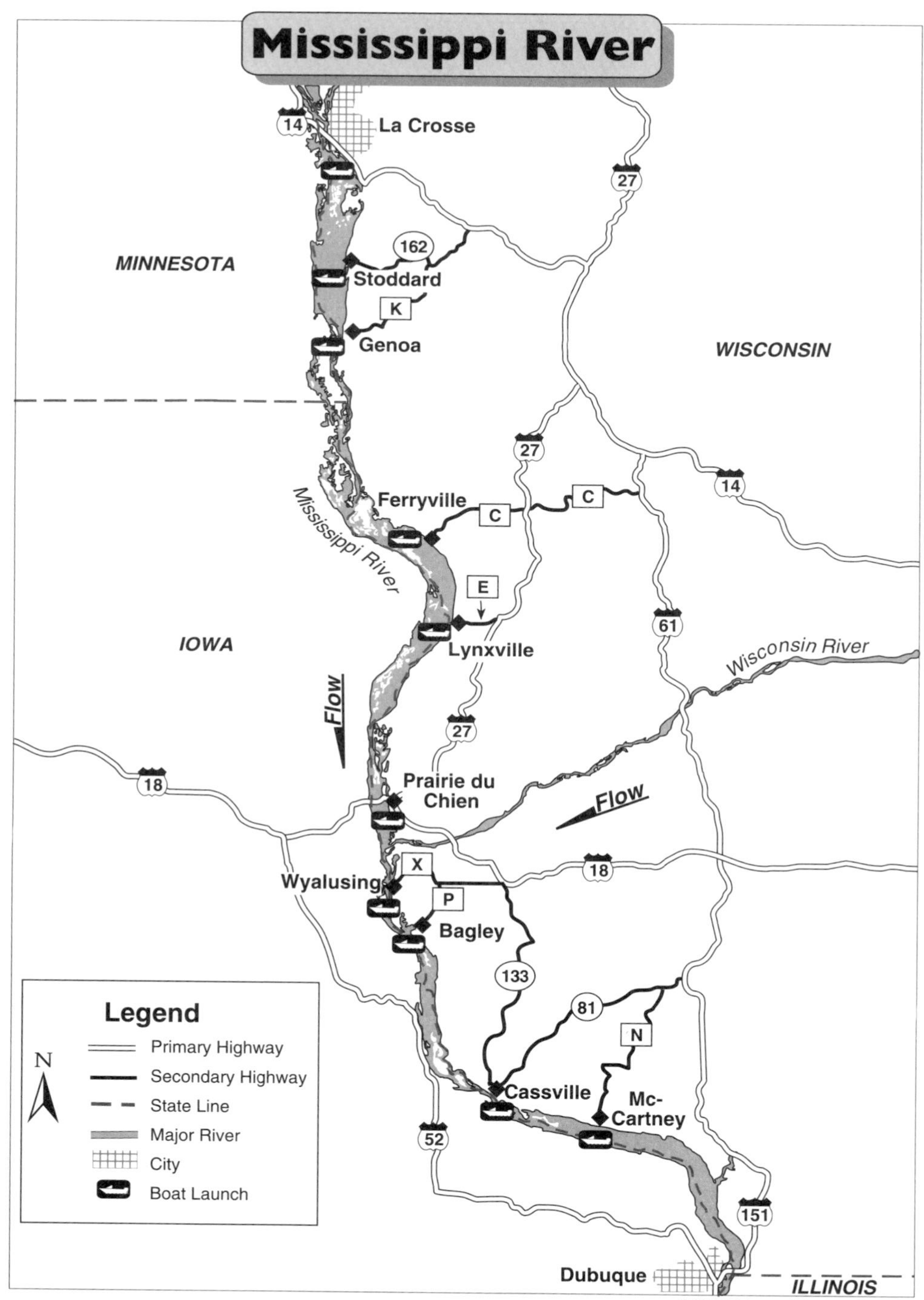

Mississippi River
La Crosse
14
27
162
MINNESOTA
Stoddard
K
Genoa
WISCONSIN
27
14
Ferryville
C
C
Mississippi River
E
Lynxville
61
IOWA
Wisconsin River
Flow
27
18
Prairie du Chien
Flow
X
18
Wyalusing
P
Bagley
133
81
N
Cassville
Mc-Cartney
52
151
Dubuque
ILLINOIS
Legend
N
Primary Highway
Secondary Highway
State Line
Major River
City
Boat Launch
© 2006 Wilderness Adventures Press, Inc.

Hub Cities: Westby and Coon Valley

Since the villages of Westby (pop. 1900) and Coon Valley (pop. 900) are so close together, I will treat them as one hub city. Good cafes, clean motels and bed and breakfasts, and a strong Norwegian heritage can be found in both towns. Each has a homey downtown section. They are very near the Coon Creek/Timber Coulee system. Don't miss "the Trout" in Dregne's Scandinavian Gifts and Hardware—a 10-pound brown taken from nearby Tainter Creek just after World War II. Norskedalen, a 400-acre nature and Norwegian heritage center, is located off County Highway PI outside of Coon Valley.

Accommodations

Di Sciacio's Cabins in downtown Coon Valley next to the award-winning restaurant; fireplace and Jacuzzi in more expensive cabin; 608-452-3182, $, $$

Old Towne Inn Supper Club, Highway 14, Westby; 800-605-0276; $$

Westby House Victorian Inn, 200 West State Street, Westby; 800-434-7439; $75-$150; $$$

Olstadalen, P.O. Box 142, Coon Valley; 608-452-3768; farmhouse located in scenic valley near coulee streams; $$

Stein Vatten Tourist Cottage, 30663 Oakland Road, Cashton; 608-452-3709; $$

Central Express Inn, Highway 14 & 27, Westby; 608-634-2950; $$

Campgrounds

Wildcat Mountains State Park, P.O. Box 98, Ontario; 608-337-4775; 20 miles east of

Westby Kickapoo Valley Reserve, 505 N. Mill St., La Farge; 608-625-2960; 15 miles east of Westby

Brush Creek Campground, S190 Opal Rd., Ontario; 608-337-4344; 20 miles east of Westby

West Fork Sports Club Campground, c/o Roger Widner, Avalanche; 608-634-2303; 10 miles east of Westby

Restaurants

Di Sciascio's Coon Creek Inn, 100 Central Ave, Coon Valley; 608-452-3182; critically acclaimed Italian food just a roll cast from Coon Creek; don't miss the eggplant caponata or chicken Marsala

Borgen's Cafe & Bakery, 109 S Main, Westby; 608-634-3516; good Norwegian-American cafe with Friday night smorgasbord

Central Express, Hwy 14 & 27, Westby; 608-634-2230

Nordic Lanes Inc., N Hwy 14, P.O. Box 36, Westby; 608-634-3985; tavern-style food in bowling alley

Old Towne Inn-Supper Club, S Hwy 14/61, Westby; 608-634-3991; good hearty supper club fare—steaks, fish, chicken

Westby House, 200 W State, Westby; 608-634-4112, 800-434-7439; hearty lunches,gourmet dinners by reservation

Westby Pharmacy, 104 W State, Westby; 608-634-3995; old-fashioned lunch counter in downtown Westby

Westby Rod & Gun Club, 215 S Main, Westby; 608-634-4314; burgers and bar food served up by conservation-minded folks

Back Door Cafe, 1223 Front St., Cashton; 608-654-5950; 10 miles east in Cashton, homestyle lunches, $5-$7; dinner by reservation only, entrees include roast duck, lamb, and beef medallions. good choice for fine dining in Coulee County; prices from $15.95 to $19.95

Outfitters/Sporting Goods

Jacquish Hollow Angler, 32491 Jaquish So. Rd., Richland Center; 608-585-2239

Rockin' K Fly Shop, 106 E. Roosevelt St, Coon Valley; 608 452 2142; rockinkflyshop.com; fly shop and guiding

Driftless Angler, 106 S. Main St., Viroqua; 608 637 8779; www.driftlessangler.com; fly shop and guiding

Streamside Outfitters, 2120 Main Street, Cross Plains; 608 295 6517; streamside-outfitters.com; fly shop and guide service on banks of Black Earth Creek

Bob's Silver Doctor Fly Fishing, P.O. Box 105, Viroqua; 608-637-3417

Cabela's, Highway 35, Prairie du Chien, 608 326 7163; full line of fly fishing gear and good source of information on Driftless streams

Madison Orvis, 1700 Deming Road, Greenway Station, Madison; 608-831-3181; full line of fly fishing gear on Madison's west side

Wal-Mart, Viroqua; 608-637-8514

Veterinarians

Veum Veterinary Clinic, 214 S Main St., Westby; 608-634-3993

Medical

Gunderson Lutheran Clinic, Viroqua; 608-637-3195

Bland Clinic, 100 Melby, Westby; 608-634-3126

Auto Rental

Enterprise Rent-a-Car, Viroqua; 608-637-3673

Automobile Repair

Car Care, 303 Bekkedal Ave., Westby; 608-634-3075

Eklov Mobil, 410 N Main St., Westby; 608-634-3958

Gratz Repair, S 2808 County Highway B, Westby; 608-634-2337

Heartland Country Coop, 405 S Main St., Westby; 608-634-3184

Air Service

Nearest airport Viroqua: RR 2, Viroqua; 608-637-2346

For More Information

Westby Chamber of Commerce
P.O. Box 94
Westby, WI 54667, 608-634-4011 www.westbywi.com

HUB CITIES: LA CROSSE AND ONALASKA

Anglers seeking to explore the coulee streams or explore warmwater opportunities on the Mississippi and nearby Black River from an urban setting may do so from the river towns of La Crosse (pop. 51,000) and Onalaska (pop. 11,000). Restaurants and motels abound. The Mississippi River here falls under the dominion of the U.S. Fish and Wildlife Service in the Upper Mississippi National Wildlife Refuge. While mainly managed as a refuge and breeding ground for migratory birds, refuge officials also manage the river for the good of fish, amphibians, furbearers, and a host of aquatic creatures. The locks and dams of the Mississippi offer excellent fishing for channel catfish and walleye. The lower reaches of the Black River offer some fine northern pike fishing.

Evidence of the French influence in the upper Midwest, the name "La Crosse" refers to the game French traders witnessed Indians in the area playing with ball and racquet. La Crosse is probably a corruption of the word for "crozier" or bishop's staff. The Great River Bike Trail and La Crosse River State Trail provide good opportunities for biking.

Accommodations

Days Inn Hotel and Conference Center, 101 Sky Harbour Drive, La Crosse; 608-783-1000; $$

Holiday Inn Express, 9409 Highway 16, Onalaska; 800-411-3712; $$

Midway Hotel/Best Western, 1835 Rose St., La Crosse; 800-528-1234; $$$

Econo Lodge, 1906 Rose St., La Crosse; 608-781-0200; $$

Hampton Inn, 308 Hampton court, Onalaska; 800-HAMPTON; $$

Microtel, I-90 & Hwy 16, Onalaska; 888-818-2359; $$

AmericInn Motel and Suites, 125 Buol Rd., West Salem; 800-634-3444; located 5 miles east of La Crosse off I-90; $$

Comfort Inn, 1223 Crossing Meadow Drive, Onalaska, 608-781-7500

Onalaska Inn, Highway 35, Onalaska; 888-359-2619; $$

Campgrounds

Perrot State Park, Route 1, P.O. Box 407, Trempealeau; 608-534-6409

Veterans Memorial Campground, Highway 16, La Crosse; 608-786-4011

Goose Island Campground, Highway 35, La Crosse; 608-788-7018

Pettibone Resort, 333 Park Plaza Drive, La Crosse; 608-782-5858

Neshonic Lakeside Campground, N5334 Neshonic Road Highway 16, West Salem; 608-786-1792

Restaurants

Lakeview Restaurant and Lounge, Highway 35 North, Onalaska; 608-781-0151; good food in panoramic setting overlooking Lake Onalaska; breakfast, lunch, and dinner

Piggy's, 328 South Front Street, La Crosse; 608-784-4877; world renown barbecue

Seven Bridges, 910 2nd Ave. North, Onalaska; 608-783-6103; "Dining with a view of the Mississippi Valley"

Old Country Buffet, 9417 Highway 16, Onalaska; 608-781-8478; Midwest chain serving garden-variety buffet for breakfast, lunch, and dinner
Buzzard Billy's Flying Carp Cafe, 222 Pearl St., La Crosse; 608-796-2277; New Orleans style food served in a 130-year-old hotel
Country Kitchen, 141 S. 7th St., La Crosse; 608-784-9660
Culver's Frozen Custard and Hamburgers, 4101 Mormon Coulee Rd., La Crosse; 608-787-5050; good burger and malt chain
Riverview Inn, N608 N. Bend Drive, Melrose; 608-488-5191; supper club located in rural setting on Black River, 10 miles from La Crosse

Fly Shops, Outfitters, Sporting Goods

Jacquish Hollow Angler, 32491 Jaquish So. Rd., Richland Center; 608-585-2239
Driftless Angler, 106 S. Main St., Viroqua; 608 637 8779; www.driftlessangler.com; fly shop and guiding
Rockin' K Fly Shop, 106 E. Roosevelt St, Coon Valley; 608 452 2142; rockinkflyshop.com; fly shop and guiding
Bob's Silver Doctor Fly Fishing, P.O. Box 105, Viroqua; 608-637-3417
Gander Mountain, 9519 Highway 16, La Crosse; 608-783-2820
R&L RiverSports, 111 Irvin St., Onalaska; 608-783-3349

Veterinarians

La Crosse Area Veterinary Clinic, 2128 Highway 16, La Crosse; 608-781-3466
Thomson Animal Medical Center, 4540 Mormon Coulee Road, La Crosse; 608-788-8820
Hillside Animal Hospital, W5706 Highway 33, La Crosse; 608-788-3425

Medical

Gunderson Lutheran Hospital, 1836 South Ave., La Crosse; 608-782-7300
Franciscan Skemp Health Care, 700 West Ave., La Crosse; 608-785-0940

Auto Rental

Avis Car Rental, La Crosse Municipal Airport; 608-781-7700
Enterprise Rent-a-Car, La Crosse; 608-781-7700
National Car Rental, La Crosse; 608-781-5678

Automobile Repair

Affordable Repair Service, 1303 8th. Street South, La Crosse; 608-785-0600
Brady's Auto Service, 2042 George St., La Crosse; 608-787-9241
Don's Towing and Repair, 816 Monitor Street, La Crosse; 608-784-5872

Air Service

La Crosse Municipal Airport, 2850 Airport Road, La Crosse; 608-789-7464

For More Information

La Crosse Visitors Bureau
410 Veterans Memorial Drive
La Crosse, WI 54601
877-568-3522 www.explorelacrosse.com

Hey, There's a Mouse in My Trout!

Last season I tussled with a fine heavy brown trout in the lower end of a favorite spring creek. I kept the fish and, upon cleaning him, found a crawfish in his stomach. This was no surprise. I've trapped crawfish in this stream and brought them home for midnight "crab" boils. What got my attention as I removed the gills was the mass of brown fur stopping up its mouth. "Hey, there's a mouse in my trout!" I said. (This helped dispel a little guilt for taking such a noble fish. Certainly Jonah the Mouse, in his last moments, did not think his predator very noble.)

There is a predilection for smallness among many flyfishers. There are special clubs for those who take fish over 20 inches on a size 20 or smaller fly. Moreover, if you asked these anglers what size trout they're after, they'd not likely say small trout. Yet, while trout below 12 inches subsist mainly on insects, those over 12 inches—browns in particular—want meat. According to Dave Vetrano, fisheries biologist for WDNR, forage fish, crawfish, other trout, amphibians, and, evidently, small rodents make up the bulk of a big trout's diet. While you may take a super-selective old brown on a small fly, it's like bagging a goose with a 20-gauge shotgun. Yes it can be done under certain conditions, but why not use what's more suited to the endeavor?

There's a related phenomenon that Vetrano points out—the predilection of big trout (20-inch-plus browns) to inhabit water that is marginal by classical trout standards, silty and scarce on riffles and gravel and insect life. But it's likely rich in other forms of aquatic life, such as the forage fish and crawfish these big carnivores favor. Perhaps big trout don't like to compete for their food. Perhaps they seek out solitude just like swamp bucks. And perhaps it's just cost-benefit analysis: It takes less energy to exist and eat the things they want to eat in these conditions. But Vetrano is unwavering in his recommendation. If you want big trout, fish the lower ends of trout streams with big flies.

What does this mean for the flyfisher prospecting Wisconsin's spring creeks for big browns? Don't slavishly adhere to the DNR trout map or exclusively fish the blue ribbon stretches of Castle Rock, the Blue River, and Timber Coulee. Talk to farmers. Talk to bait fishermen. Fish the lower ends of designated trout streams. Talk to the guy sitting next to you at the tavern. And for heaven's sake forget those size 20 dry flies! Give 'em a Muddler Minnow, or a crawfish or leech pattern. If all else fails, skitter a big hairy bass bug over a likely looking lair as night is falling. Who knows, maybe there'll be a mouse in your trout, too.

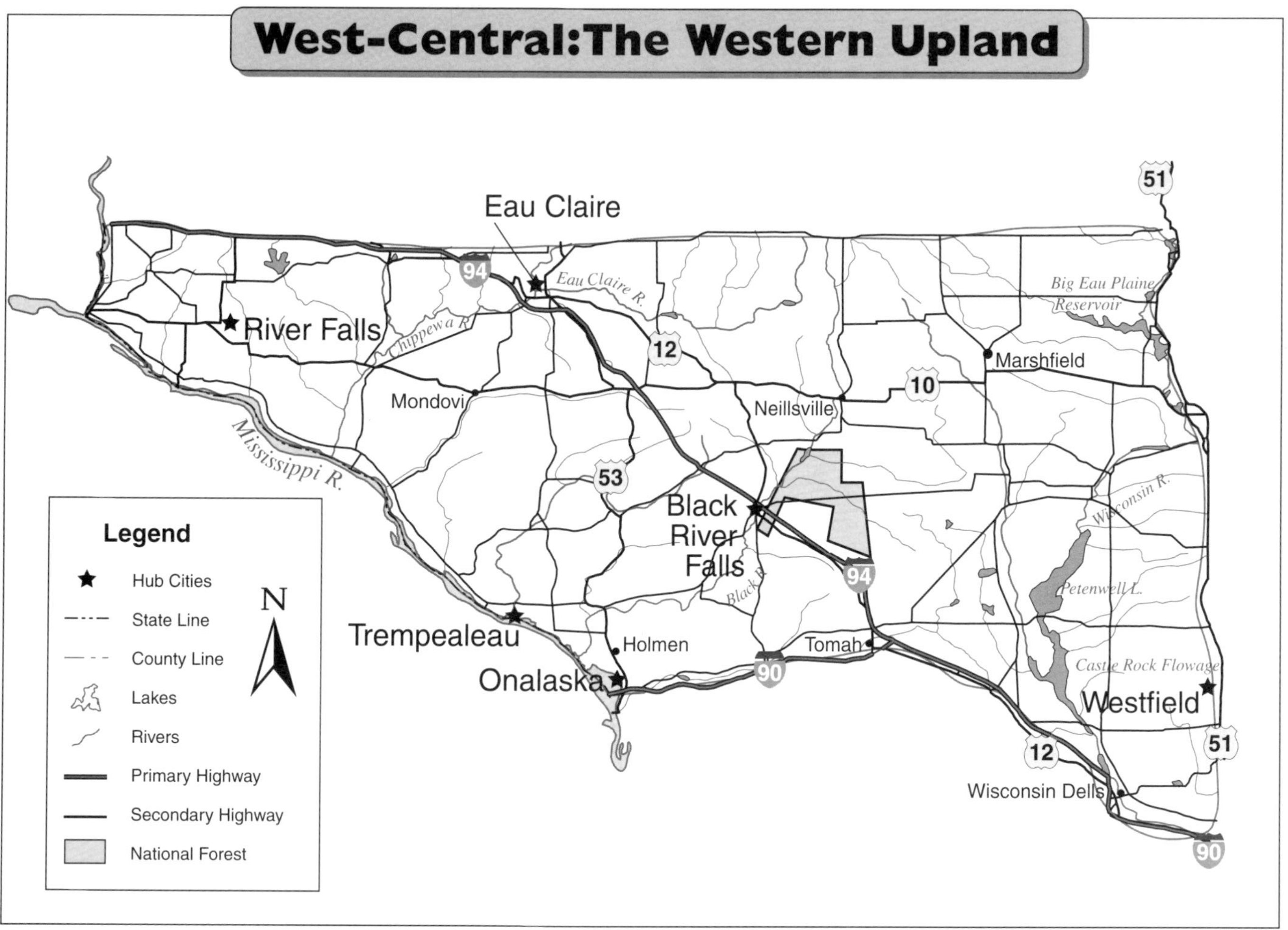
West-Central: The Western Upland
Eau Claire
Eau Claire R.
River Falls
Chippewa R.
Mondovi
Mississippi R.
Neillsville
Marshfield
Big Eau Plaine Reservoir
Black River Falls
Black R.
Trempealeau
Onalaska
Holmen
Tomah
Wisconsin R.
Petenwell L.
Castle Rock Flowage
Westfield
Wisconsin Dells
94
12
10
53
90
51
Legend
Hub Cities
State Line
County Line
Lakes
Rivers
Primary Highway
Secondary Highway
National Forest
N

West-Central Wisconsin: The Western Upland

The Western Upland is much like the Driftless region to the south. It is made up of ridges and valleys, has a long tradition of dairy farming, and—especially important for its trout streams—has a bedrock of limestone. Its springs and streams are thus infused, as are those of the Driftless area, with particulate limestone. Rich, fertile water supporting a host of plant life and aquatic invertebrates is the result. Scuds, stoneflies, caddisflies, mayflies, and crawfish are here in abundance. Hatches occur on a similar schedule to the Driftless region.

The main difference between the regions are that the Western Upland experienced some early glacial periods, which is noticeable in the slightly less craggy landscape. As a general rule, there are fewer upwellings of spring water and feeder creeks in the Western Upland, and its trout streams tend to be wider and longer. An

Tall grass and strong winds create ideal conditions for hopper fishing in late summer. (Tim Landwehr)

HATCH CHART—West-Central Wisconsin: The Western Upland

Insect/Food Source	J	F	M	A	M	J	J	A	S	O	N	D	Flies
Midges			■	■	■	■	■	■	■				Midge Pupa #16-22; Griffith's Gnat #16-22
Little Black Caddis			■	■	■								Micro Black Caddis #16-22; Caddis Larvae (dark) #16-22; Beadhead Caddis (dark) #16
Blue-Winged Olives (*Baetis*)				■	■	■	■	■	■				BWO Thorax, Sparkle Dun #16-22; Pheasant Tail #16-18
Hendricksons				■	■								Light Hendrickson, Spinners #12-14; Pheasant Tail #12-14
Sulphurs					■								Sulphur Dun, Pale Evening Dun, Spinner #16; Pheasant Tail Nymph #16
Caddis					■	■	■	■	■	■			Elk Hair Caddis #14-16; Sparkle Pupa, Beadhead Caddis, Caddis Larvae #16-20
March Brown					■								March Brown, Spinner, Hare's Ear Nymph #12-14
Hexagenia (Evening Hatch)						■	■						Hart Washer, Hex, Olive Drake #4-8; Hex Nymph, Strip Nymph #4-8/Late June #10
Red Quill				■	■								Red Quill, Rusty Spinner #14
Trico							■	■	■				Tiny White Wing Black, CDC Trico, Spent Wing Trico #24-28

HATCH CHART—West-Central Wisconsin: The Western Upland (cont.)

Insect/Food Source	J	F	M	A	M	J	J	A	S	O	N	D	Flies
White Mayfly (*Ephoron leukon*) (Evening Hatch)													White Wulff, White Miller #12-14
Other Stoneflies													Yellow Stimulator #10-12; Stonefly Nymphs #8-10
Scuds													Pink, Olive, Tan Scuds #14-18
Leeches													Marabou Leech, Strip Leech (Black, Olive, Brown) #4-10
Sculpin													Muddler Minnow, Olive or Brown Leech #8-10
Crawfish													Crayfish Patterns, Marabou Leech Olive/Brown #8-10
Ants, Beetles, Crickets													Standard Ant Patterns #14-20; Beetles #16-20; Crickets #8-10
Grasshoppers													Dave's Hopper, Parachute Hopper #6-10

average southwest coulee stream is about 5 miles long and 20 feet across, while the Rush River is some 30 miles long and the Willow is over 40 miles long.

These differences aren't very important, however, and what holds true for one region, from a fisherman's point of view, holds true for the other. The Rush, Kinnickinnic, and Trimbelle are excellent trout streams in the vicinity of River Falls. They have dependable hatches, good numbers of trout, and some large trout. The Kinnickinnic holds a whopping 5,000 trout per mile in some stretches.

The cluster of clear, sand-bottomed streams near Trempealeau are worth a look—the Trempealeau River, Beaver Creek, and the Buffalo River. You'll find lots of public land and little fishing pressure, even if they lack the fish densities of the more famous waters to the north and south.

For warmwater enthusiasts, there good opportunities in the Black River area. The Black River itself has good mixed-bag fishing. A number of cranberry flowages near Black River Falls offer first-rate bluegill and bass fishing, and you can check with the folks at Hardware Hank in Black River Falls for a list of which flowages allow anglers.

The Rush River

Seasoned angler Merlin Magnuson, who works at Bentley Outfitters in Eden Prairie, Minnesota, shared a plethora of information with me on the Rush. Perhaps it's strange to go to a Minnesota fly shop to get information on Wisconsin streams. Yet the thinly populated dairy country of western Wisconsin does not have its own fly shop, save the modest fly selection at Ace Hardware in River Falls.

The Rush holds big trout, especially browns. Magnuson said an 8- or 9-pounder usually wins the Rush River Sportsmen's Club contest for the largest trout. He routinely has 10- to 20-fish days on the Rush. What is his secret on a river that gets fished every weekend by Twin Cities anglers? Magnuson likes to fish weekdays, when pressure is less intense. He often fishes a mayfly imitation called the Merlin—named after its creator—heavily hackled, small (size 20), sometimes tied with mink underfur, often green or sulphur. If you can't get to Bentley Outfitters to buy a Merlin, use a size 18 Sulphur Dun with green tied into it.

Magnuson uses a variety of retrieves, including a dead drift, and also skitters and hops dries along the surface. This technique of imparting action to a fly, whether wet or dry, has roots in New York's Catskill fly fishing traditions. Watch an old-time fly fisherman sometime. Note that he will either let the fly hang at the end of its drift, skitter it along the surface, or do a painstakingly slow retrieve, gathering the line into figure-8s between his thumb and index finger as described in Ray Bergman's classic work, *Trout.* All of these retrieves impart subtle yet crucial action to the fly and are far superior to the nervous cast and retrieve one sees too often on streams today.

Andy Roth, manager of Bentley Outfitters, who studied entomology at nearby University of Wisconsin–River Falls, describes a regular hatch progression on the Rush. He says that hatches here are similar to those of coulee region streams near La Crosse, to the south. These streams have very high alkalinity, which makes them fertile and host to a good variety of aquatic life. Midges are present year-round. Blue-Winged Olives begin to hatch in April. Mother's Day marks the beginning of the Little

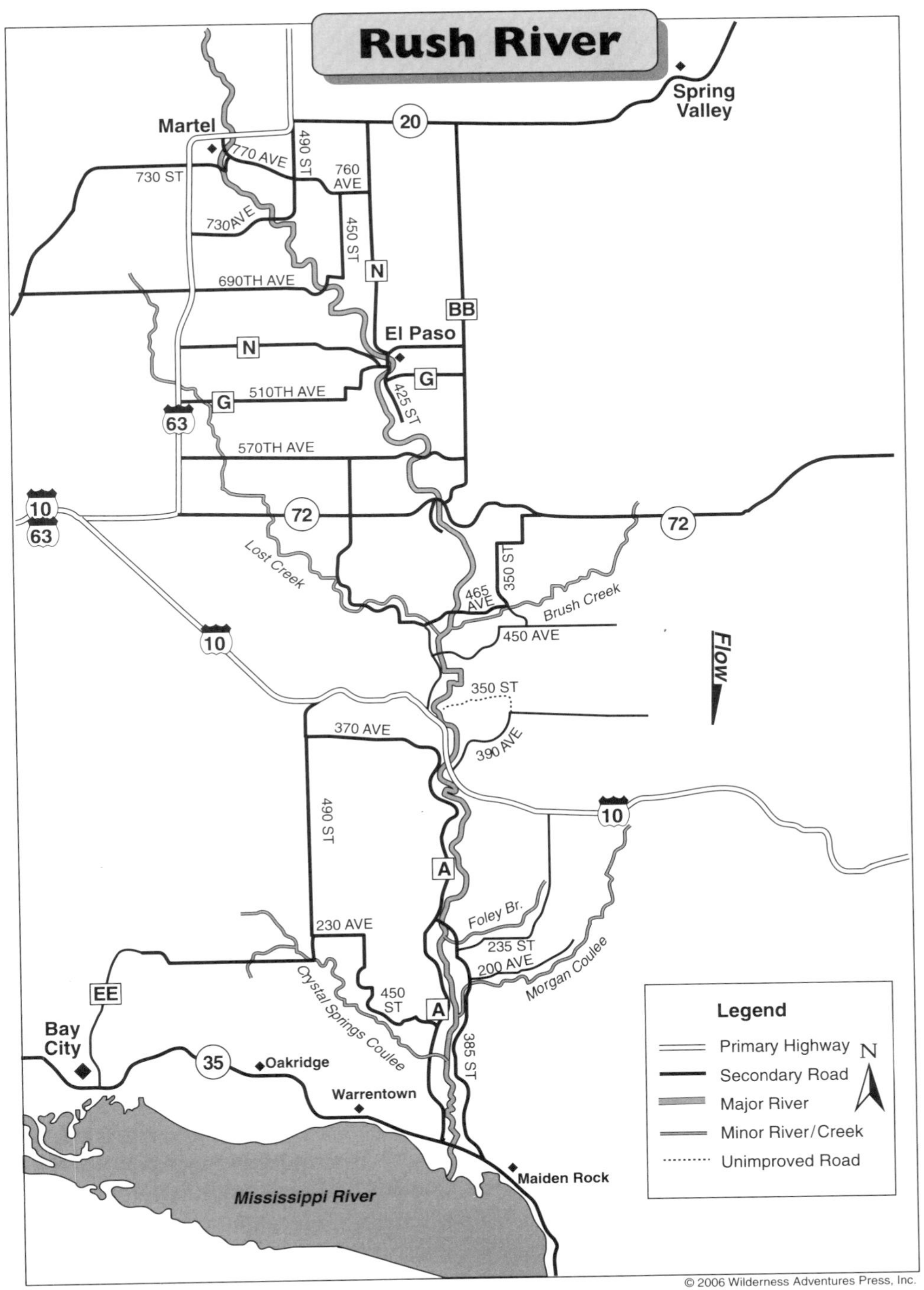
Rush River
Spring Valley
Martel
20
770 AVE
490 ST
760 AVE
730 ST
730AVE
450 ST
N
690TH AVE
BB
El Paso
N
G
510TH AVE
G
425 ST
63
570TH AVE
10
63
72
72
Lost Creek
350 ST
465 AVE
Brush Creek
450 AVE
10
Flow
350 ST
370 AVE
390 AVE
490 ST
10
A
Foley Br.
230 AVE
235 ST
200 AVE
Morgan Coulee
EE
450 ST
A
Crystal Springs Coulee
385 ST
Bay City
35
Oakridge
Warrentown
Maiden Rock
Mississippi River
Legend
Primary Highway
Secondary Road
Major River
Minor River/Creek
Unimproved Road
N
© 2006 Wilderness Adventures Press, Inc.

Black Caddis hatch, with various species hatching into September. Larval caddis are, of course, present year-round, making a caddis larvae (size 12 or 14) a good choice when no hatches are visible. May and June see Hendrickson and Sulphur activity, and you may find Trico hatches between July and September. Crawfish and sculpins thrive on the Rush's rocky bottom. Scuds are present in good numbers.

With all of this rich insect life and high alkalinity you'd expect terrific natural reproduction on the Rush. The jury is still out on this. The Rush receives plantings of all three trout species from the DNR and a local rod and gun club. And some say it doesn't produce trout. However, John Koch, a native of this area and operator of Western Wisconsin Fly Fishing Guide Service, says DNR shocking surveys have been turning up fish from a few inches to 25 inches, which he takes as a sign of natural reproduction. He's also been seeing Black Stoneflies, which are the bellwether of improving water quality.

Whatever their source, trout find plenty to eat in the Rush and grow to respectable, even prodigious, sizes. Fish density is good, with upwards of 2,000 trout per mile in some upper stretches. Browns predominate and fish in the 16-inch range are common. Roth likes to fish a two-fly rig with a bushy dry fly on top and caddis or midge larvae below. He also likes Prince Nymphs in size 16 to 22.

Beginning near the town of Martel east of River Falls and running to the Mississippi River at Maiden Rock, the Rush River covers some 25 miles from headwaters to mouth. The Rush's trout water begins near the St. Croix–Pierce County line above Highway 29 and extends below Highway 10 near the village of Salem.

Upstream from Highway 72, access can be had at 570th Avenue; at the village of El Paso along Highways G and N; and at 730th Avenue, Highway 63, and Highway 29 near Martel. Five-mile-long Lost Creek, joining the Rush below Highway 72, is planted with brook and brown trout; access it via 450th Street and Highway 10. Access the lower stretch of the Rush via Highway 10 and Highway A. While habitat falls off in these nether reaches, outsized browns can be found holding in the cover of fallen elms, growing fat on crawfish and chubs. Stalk them at dusk with a big streamer and heavy leader.

On a recent trip, I fished the middle section of the Rush above Highway 72 (upstream from that bridge), parking on a horseshoe road on the west side of the river that connects with Highway 72 in two places. (If you wish to access the north side of Highway 72, on Ellsworth Rod and Gun Club land, you will need to ask their permission. They are responsible for countless stream improvements and supplemental stocking.) There were a number of exceptional runs here, a number of them bordered by fallen trees. It was a September afternoon with aspen leaves turning golden, and I took a half-dozen browns to 14 inches on a beadhead caddis nymph. I broke the fly off on a larger fish and decided to call it quits for the day. There was so much habitat in this stretch that I covered just a hundred yards of water in two hours. The stream here was between 1 and 5 feet deep and very clear with a distinct hint of limestone.

The Rush is a fine western Wisconsin venue, especially if you are lucky enough to have an occasional weekday free to fish it.

Stream Facts: Rush River

Season

- The early season runs from the first Saturday in March to the last Sunday before the first Saturday in May; no-kill, single barbless hooks only. Regular season runs from the first Saturday in May at 5:00 am through September 30.

Regulations

- Category 4

Miles of Trout Water

- 25 miles

Stream Characteristics

- High-alkaline limestone stream that holds large browns; 50 feet wide in most places; scenic valleys and limestone outcrops.

Access

- Bridges on Highways 63, 72 and 10; bridges on county and secondary roads.

Fly Shops

- Gray Goat (Eden Prairie, MN); Bob Mitchell's Fly Shop (Lake Elmo, MN)

Maps

- *Wisconsin Atlas and Gazetteer*, page 58

The narrow Trimbelle River winds its way through pastureland.

A nice bend on the Trimbelle River.

TRIMBELLE RIVER

The Trimbelle River is one of a quartet of high-quality trout streams mentioned by Andy Roth of Bentley Outfitters in Eden Prairie, Minnesota. Bentley's is the largest fly shop in the Twin Cities metro area. If you need some last-minute gear while fly fishing western Wisconsin streams, going over the border in Minnesota is the quickest way to meet them. The Trimbelle is different from its better-know counterparts the Rush, Willow, and Kinnickinnic. It is smaller, more intimate water. It lacks the DNR easements and ownership that those other rivers enjoy. And it has less of a gradient. In setting, fertility, and gradient, it resembles some of the more isolated streams of Coulee Country a hundred miles south.

The Trimbelle's trout water begins along Highway 65, 7 miles southeast of River Falls. There are stream improvements downstream from the Highway 65 bridge—riprap, lunker-holding structures, and bank stabilization. Highways J and O and Avenues 650th, 640th, 870th, 570th, and 560th cross the river. Along O you will see the Trimbelle River Road and Gun Club. There's a wayside at Highway O and 560th Avenue that has some deep holes and bends—good fish-holding structure. From here Highway O follows the river as it flows toward the Mississippi. Deadfalls, sweepers, and bends afford cover in this stretch. However, below the bridge at 430th Avenue the water quality becomes marginal and trout few and far between.

A Prince Nymph is a good general fly choice here. A "Mother's Day" Little Black Caddis hatch is also fairly dependable, along with many of the typical hatches for this region. Natural reproduction of brook and brown trout does occur, but the river is also planted heavily with browns.

While there is limited public access, this beautiful stream offers some 15 miles of trout water and is not hit as hard as the nearby Rush and Kinni. Remember to ask permission if you plan on crossing private land.

The Willow River

When compared to the "big two" area streams—the Kinnickinnic and the Rush—the Willow River definitely brings up the rear. That's not to say that good trout fishing can't be had, but the Willow certainly lacks the trout density and water quality these other streams offer. Area guide John Koch sums it up well: "Its thermodynamics are not conducive to good trout habitat." Two dams in place on the Willow (one at Little Falls Lake in Willow River State Park and another at New Richmond) warm waters below them, and this is certainly bad for trout. That said, area DNR fisheries biologist Marty Engle caught a 13-pound brown on the Willow, which he describes as somewhere between a coldwater and warmwater fishery.

In past decades, the river used to be a first-tier trout stream. Koch speculates that heavy development in the area might be causing spring inflow to decline and stream temperatures to increase. Dams do not help. However, taken for what it is—a put-and-take fishery with some very large browns and smallmouth on its lower end—the

A fishy looking run on the Willow River.

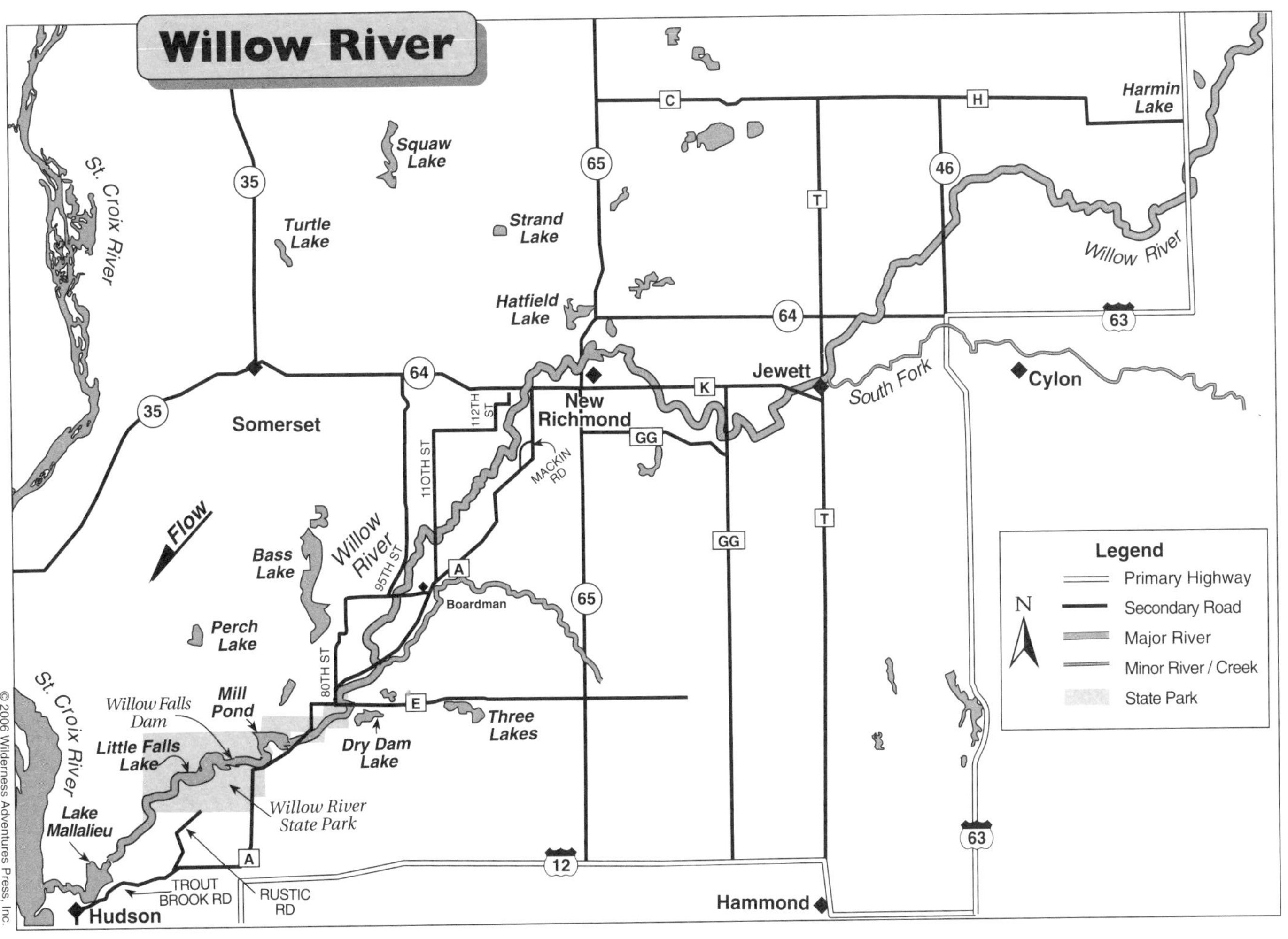
Willow River
St. Croix River
Squaw Lake
Turtle Lake
Strand Lake
Hatfield Lake
Harmin Lake
Willow River
Somerset
New Richmond
Jewett
South Fork
Cylon
112TH ST
110TH ST
95TH ST
80TH ST
MACKIN RD
Flow
Bass Lake
Willow River
Boardman
Perch Lake
Mill Pond
Willow Falls Dam
Little Falls Lake
Dry Dam Lake
Three Lakes
Willow River State Park
Lake Mallalieu
TROUT BROOK RD
RUSTIC RD
Hudson
Hammond
St. Croix River
Legend
Primary Highway
Secondary Road
Major River
Minor River / Creek
State Park
N
35
64
65
46
63
12
C
H
T
K
GG
A
E
© 2006 Wilderness Adventures Press, Inc.

Willow affords some fine fishing. The Willow is fished heavily by Twin Cities anglers during the first weeks of the regular trout season, and then pressure tapers off.

The Willow begins in earnest as a trout stream at the confluence of its north and south forks. The South Fork of the Willow is a trout stream in its own right. It has a population of native brook trout and rises near the town of Cylon, running for some 5 miles to its confluence with the North Branch near the town of Jewett. The South Fork is managed as a category 4 stream. I enjoyed good fishing for brook trout there on a late September afternoon using a Royal Coachman, picking up fish to 10 inches. Road crossings on the South Fork are at County O, Highway 63, and Highway 46. This small clear cold stream provides a contrast to fishing the larger, more fertile main branch of the Willow.

From the confluence of the forks at Jewett to the impoundment at New Richmond, a distance of some 6 miles, the Willow River flows through private land with bridge crossings at County T, County K, and County GG. Browns and rainbows are planted in this stretch. There is also a bit of natural reproduction among browns, and an occasional brookie slips down from the South Fork. The Willow is category 4 water for its entire length.

In the 10 miles of water between New Richmond and Willow River State Park, lots of forage fish and some big browns are present, according to Engle. It's stocked, with limited natural reproduction.

Willow River Falls.

A 5-mile stretch of the river runs through Willow River State Park. You need to buy a day pass or park sticker to fish here. This stretch begins with Highway A on the east side of the park and ends with Trout Brook Road on the park's west side. It is a pretty stretch of river, colored by limestone silt and flanked in places by steep-sided canyons.

Stream improvements and lunker structures have been made on the 2.5 miles of water between the Highway A bridge and Willow Falls. There's not much streamside cover in this stretch; save it for morning or evening hatch fishing. There's easy access here via trails and parking lots. Be aware that it sees a lot fishing pressure during the first few weeks of May.

Engle says the pocketwater immediately below Willow Falls, still in the park, offers some of the best habitat and fish densities on the river. Underground springs keep water temperatures low, and boulders provide good hiding places for trout. Access this stretch via the Willow Falls parking lot and trail.

A mile down from Willow Falls, the river widens into Little Falls Lake. Too warm to support trout, it does host northerns, bass, and panfish. There's a boat launch near the beach if you want to try your hand at a little warmwater flyrodding from a canoe.

Below the lake, trout habitat and densities pick up again (you can access this stretch via Trout Brook Trail) and the river splits into the Willow Branch and the Race Branch. The mile-long Race used to be one of the best trout streams in the state and is still a fair trout stream with some natural reproduction. A mixture of smallmouth and trout begin to show up in the warmer Willow Branch. The two branches join again at the western boundary of the park. The Willow shortly thereafter flows into Lake Mallilieu in Hudson, a fair smallmouth lake. Between the lake and the confluence of the two branches, a mixture of smallmouth and larger browns can be found. Access to Lake Mallilieu and the last part of the Willow is via Rustic Road along the river's south/east shore.

The progression of hatches on the Willow is like that of the nearby Kinni and Rush, with midges and *Baetis* present throughout the season, along with caddis. Forage fish play an important part in the Willow's food chain; keep some Muddlers and strip leeches in your fly box if you plan on fishing the Willow. Trout do not grow to be 13 pounds by sipping dainty mayflies. Streamers will do nicely for the smallmouth present in the river's lower reaches. Engle says smallmouths can run to 20 inches.

While the Willow may lack the numbers of its nearby counterparts, it has plenty of access within the state park, big browns in its middle reaches, a native brook trout fishery on its South Fork, and smallmouth in its lower reaches. Perhaps the twin to Engle's 13-pounder is still swimming in the Willow, growing fat on chubs.

Stream Facts: Willow River

Season

- The early season runs from the first Saturday in March to the last Sunday before the first Saturday in May; no-kill, single barbless hooks only. Regular season runs from the first Saturday in May at 5:00 am through September 30.

Regulations

- Category 2

Species

- Planted browns and rainbows in main branch; native brook trout in South Fork.

Miles of Trout Water

- 25 miles

Stream Characteristics

- Large browns present in middle reaches; river flows through scenic canyons in state park.

Access

- Willow River State Park; bridge crossings above state park.

Fly Shops

- Bob Mitchell's Fly Shop (Lake Elmo, MN); Gray Goat Fly Fishing (Eden Prairie, MN)

Maps

- *Wisconsin Atlas and Gazetteer,* pages 70, 71, 59

KINNICKINNIC RIVER

The storied Kinnickinnic is located in west-central Wisconsin, flowing through the town of River Falls. Some 25 miles from headwater to mouth and, in parts, supporting upwards as 6,000 fish per mile, the Kinni (as it's called locally) has a deserved reputation of one of the upper Midwest's (and perhaps the country's) finest trout streams. Add to this list of accolades a self-sustaining population of wild brown trout, extensive public access, hatches galore, and scenery ranging from northern lowland forests to steep-sided canyons. It's also within easy reach of any number of western Wisconsin cities (just off Highway 90/94) and a half-hour away from the Twin Cities. So, God is in his heaven and all's right with the Kinni. Right?

Religious questions aside, the answer is yes and no. While the Kinni is by anyone's estimation a great trout stream, such bliss was not always the case. Nor, with increased runoff from new construction and a burgeoning commuter population, is its future as a great trout stream 100 percent secure. Thick with native brook trout back in the early settlement days of the mid-1800s, the Kinni soon felt the effects of man. Logging meant tons of topsoil washing into the river. Farming meant riparian erosion and animal waste. Dams impeded the river's flow and robbed it of oxygen. Sewage and wastewater further polluted the river. A DNR survey in 1938 found the Kinni warm, sluggish, overgrazed, and oxygen-poor—literally and figuratively a dump.

But, as with Timber Coulee and Black Earth to the south, man can sometimes (with great effort and care) undo the damage he has done. This is no carte blanche to abuse resources and clean up later, but rather a reminder that conservation history is not always one-directional, that anglers, resource managers, and private groups can make a difference—a world of difference. In the mid-1900s, the River Falls Rod and Gun Club and the DNR began to clean up the Kinni: controlling grazing and erosion; improving in-stream habitat; leasing land from farmers; advocating for better wastewater disposal. By the late 1970s, water quality had improved, stream temperatures were some 10 degrees lower, a self-sustaining population of brown trout had established itself, and stocking was discontinued.

Today, the river has valuable allies in the local chapter of Trout Unlimited (KIAP-TU-WISH) and the Kinnickinnic River Land Trust (headquartered in a historic building in downtown River Falls and with radio personality Garrison Keillor among its members), which works with private landowners to ensure good conservation practices along the river. While the days of raw sewage and untold tons of manure and topsoil washing into the stream are gone, a more insidious if less direct opponent remains in the form of development and its accompanying runoff. If the amount of new paved surface can be limited and urban and farm runoff controlled (by retaining or directing it away from the river), then the future of the river may be as bright as the past. Let's hope the stream continues to bubble along at a cool 60 degrees year-round. Better yet, become a friend of the Kinnickinnic by joining the Kinnickinnic River Land Trust or by helping local TU chapters maintain this fine fishery.

The Kinnickinnic offers two distinct fisheries: from its headwaters to just above River Falls (some 15 miles) and from River Falls to its mouth at Prescott (some 10

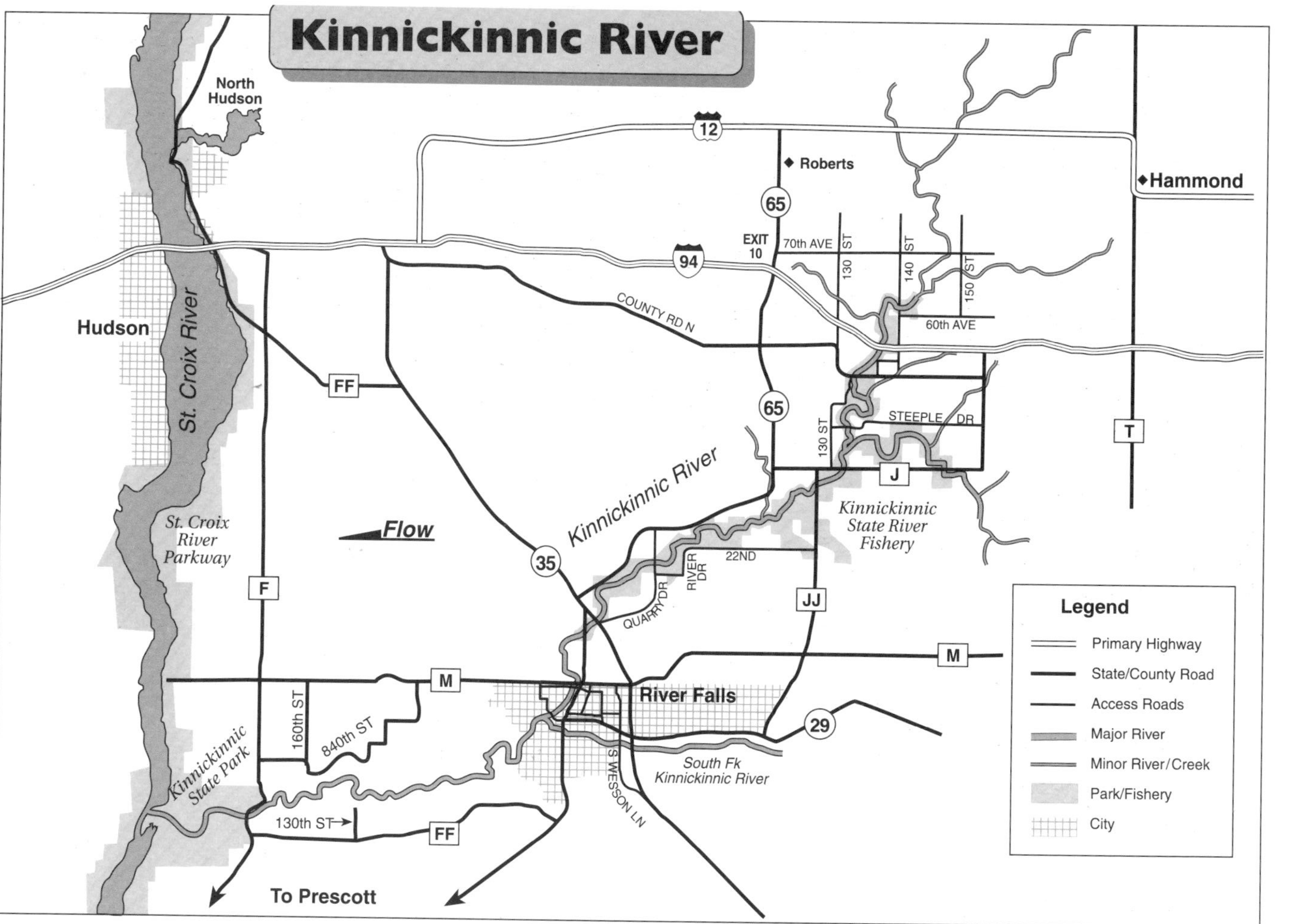
Kinnickinnic River
North Hudson
12
Roberts
Hammond
65
EXIT 10
70th AVE
130 ST
140 ST
150 ST
94
COUNTY RD N
60th AVE
Hudson
St. Croix River
FF
65
STEEPLE DR
130 ST
T
J
Kinnickinnic River
Kinnickinnic State River Fishery
Flow
St. Croix River Parkway
35
22ND
RIVER DR
QUARRY DR
F
JJ
M
M
River Falls
160th ST
840th ST
29
Kinnickinnic State Park
South Fk Kinnickinnic River
S WESSON LN
130th ST
FF
To Prescott
Legend
Primary Highway
State/County Road
Access Roads
Major River
Minor River/Creek
Park/Fishery
City

miles). According to Mike Alwin, proprietor of Bob Mitchell's Fly Shop across the St. Croix River in Lake Elmo, Minnesota, the upper Kinni is a classic sand-bottomed spring creek with a wide variety, if not huge numbers, of aquatic insects. It runs through thick lowland forest, and brook trout are occasionally caught near the confluence with Parker Creek.

The lower Kinni is a traditional spring creek with a rubble bottom and both variety and numbers of aquatic insects. The lower Kinni winds its way through wooded canyon bluffs. In addition, the lower river has populations of sculpin, forage fish, and stoneflies, which account for the larger trout in this stretch. Scuds are abundant in both stretches.

Not surprisingly, given its paucity of forage fish, the upper Kinni holds smaller fish. Expect *Baetis* hatches anywhere from the start of the early season in March to the end of the season in September. This can be fished with a Blue-Winged Olive pattern, size 16 or 18. Midges are abundant, according to Alwin, and May and June show a good evening Sulphur hatch. Caddis are relatively scarce in this stretch. If nothing is rising, a scud is a good choice in any of the standard colors—pink, olive, or tan. This stretch once hosted a good Hex hatch, according to Alwin, but no longer does.

While the lower Kinni holds browns in the 18-inch range, it's still not as much of a big-fish stream as, say, the nearby Rush. According to John Koch of Western Wisconsin Fly Fishing Guide Service, this is a function of a self-sustaining fishery. As with Timber Coulee to the south, good densities of wild fish mean fewer really large (20-inch-plus) fish.

As on the upper stretch, the lower Kinni has *Baetis* hatches throughout the season, with the heaviest activity in March/April and August/September. Stoneflies and caddis are abundant in this stretch, according to Alwin, and their imitations can be profitably fished in March and April. Caddis action continues into May and June, which is also the time for the Sulphur hatch. Two species of Sulphurs are present on the lower Kinni, according to Alwin: Evening Sulphurs and Pale Morning Duns. Look for good *Stenonema* spinner falls on June and early July evenings. Good terrestrial fishing can be had during late summer in sections of the river bordered by grass or meadow. The tiny *Plauditis* mayfly (size 26 or 28) hatches in August and September. Trico action can be good from July to September.

The upper Kinni starts just above Interstate 90/94. From the Highway 65 exit, take 70th Avenue to 140th Street to fish the small bit of water above the interstate. Below the interstate, the river can be reached by taking Highway 65 south. There is an access at County N, Steeple Drive, County J, Highway 65, River Drive, Quarry Road, Highway 35, and County MM. Parker Creek, bordered by Steeple Drive to the north and Highway J to the south, is a noted brook trout stream. Most of the land here is under DNR control; you will find parking at the above-mentioned access points.

There is no shortage of productive water in the town of River Falls, which is also home to the University of Wisconsin–River Falls. The river provides life-science students and faculty with endless research data; entomologist Dr. Clarke Garry is on the faculty and has an amazing command of insect life on the Kinni. In-town access is at the junction of Cedar and River Streets; in Glen Park; and at River Ridge Road. Below River Falls, access is at the Highway F bridge, which is part of Kinnickinnic State Park (a state park sticker is required to park here). The Kinni is category 5—5-trout limit; 5 trout under 10 inches or 4 trout under 10 inches and 1 trout over 14 inches.

Stream Facts: Kinnickinnic River

Season

- The early season runs from the first Saturday in March to the last Sunday before the first Saturday in May; no-kill, single barbless hooks only. Regular season runs from the first Saturday in May at 5:00 am through September 30.

Regulations

- Category 5—five-trout limit; five-trout limit; 5 trout under 10inches or 4 trout under 10 inches and 1 trout over 14 inches.

Species

- Native brown trout and occasionally brook trout.

Miles of Trout Water

- 20 miles

Stream Characteristics

- Upper, sand-bottom spring creek; lower, rock-bottom spring creek.

Access

- Upper, off Highway 65; in River Falls; lower, at Highway F or Kinnickinnic State Park.

Fly Shops

- Bob Mitchell's Fly Shop (Lake Elmo, MN); Gray Goat Fly Fishing (Eden Prairie, MN)

Maps

- *Wisconsin Atlas and Gazetteer*, page 58

The Red Cedar River

Starting below Chetek and flowing some 30 miles to Tainter Lake and Lake Menomin, the upper reach of the Red Cedar River is a top-quality smallmouth river—one of the best in the state, according to fisheries biologist Marty Engle. Throw in the possibility of a trophy northern, a decent population of walleye (more walleye further downstream below the impoundments), plus the chance to tangle with a log-sized brown trout at the mouth of Sand Creek, Hay Creek, or Eighteen Mile Creek, and the idea of a float trip on this west-central Wisconsin river looks even better.

In Barron County road crossings and access can be had along County Highway A and I. In Dunn County, Highway M follows the river down to Colfax along the east shore; Highway U and then Highway W follow the west shore. Below Colfax, Tainter Lake and Lake Menomin warm the river and lower its oxygen content, with walleye and catfish predominating.

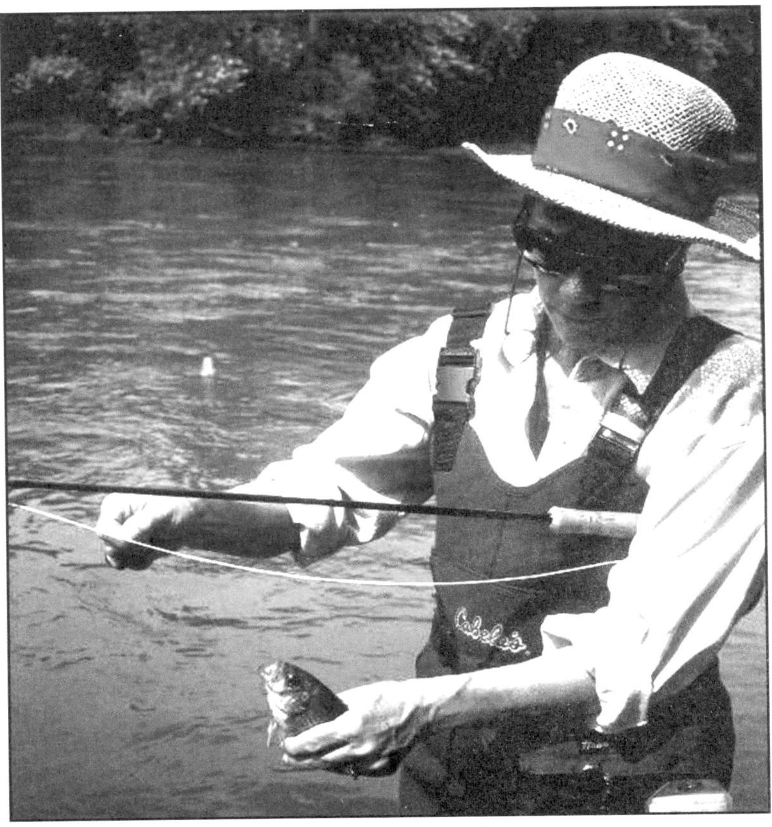

Warmwater species can be fun on a fly rod.

You're best served floating the upper river. Fish for smallmouth along log sweepers, at the mouths of creeks, and in its many gravel runs and oxbows. Use a streamer that imitates the forage fish and crawfish in the stream. Or if you are lucky enough to find smallmouth taking flies on top, match the hatch. The village of Sand Creek would be a good place to put in. Here an angler could try his hand at paddling up this category 4 trout stream of the same name or work the larger Red Cedar for a mixed bag of northerns, smallmouth, and walleye.

A bonus is the transitional western Wisconsin landscape, where bluffs and dairy farm mix with pine and aspen forests. Wisconsin is blessed with a plethora of rivers, many of which are simply not seen by the crowds following the beaten path to well-known lakes and trout streams. Those willing to do a bit of paddling can enjoy cooperative fish and an unspoiled setting on rivers like the Red Cedar. The minimum size for smallmouth is 14 inches with a daily bag limit of 5; they may be fished year-round.

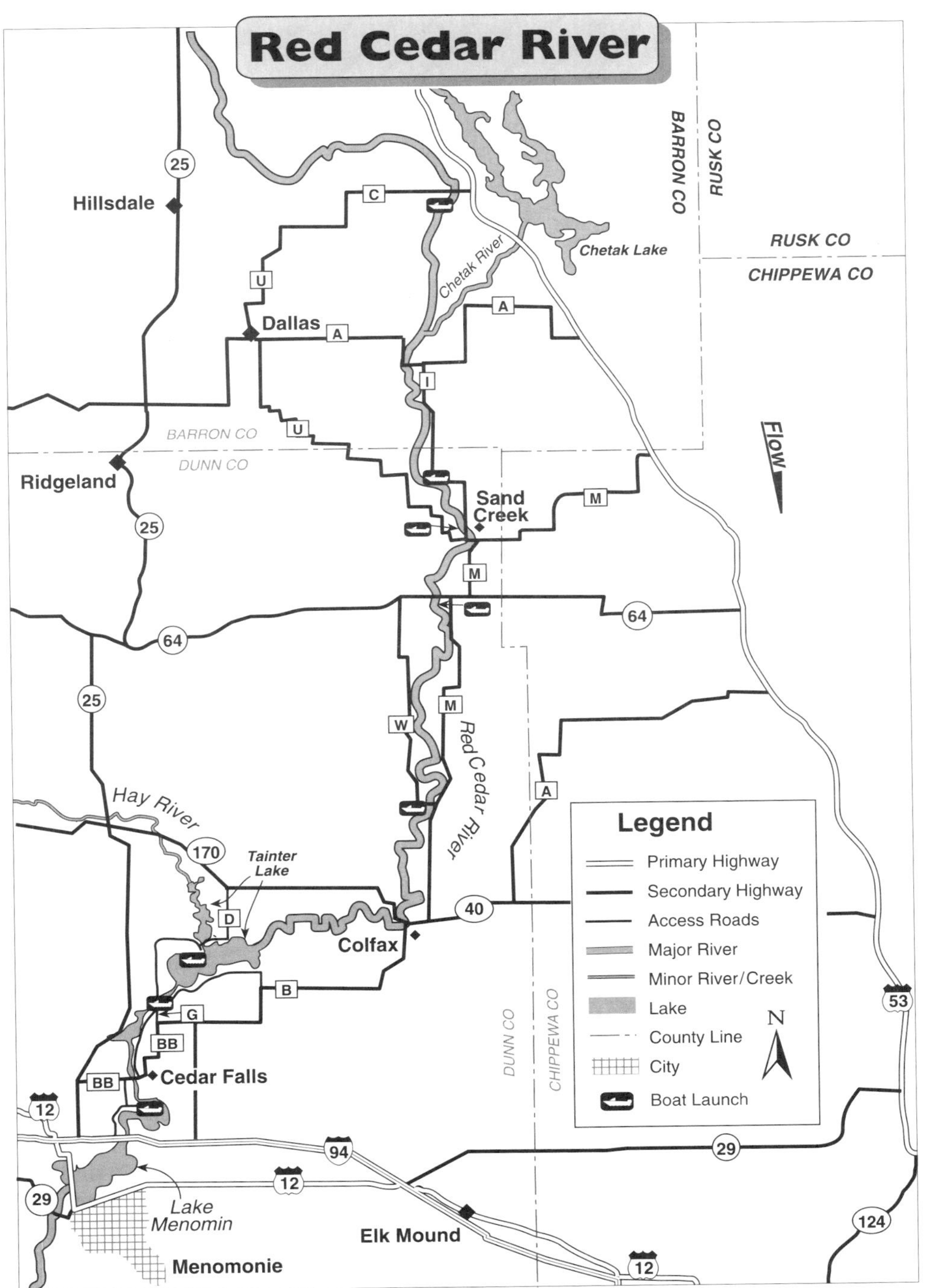
Red Cedar River
Hillsdale
Dallas
Ridgeland
Sand Creek
Colfax
Cedar Falls
Elk Mound
Menomonie
Chetak River
Chetak Lake
Hay River
Tainter Lake
Lake Menomin
Red Cedar River
BARRON CO
RUSK CO
CHIPPEWA CO
DUNN CO
Flow
Legend
Primary Highway
Secondary Highway
Access Roads
Major River
Minor River/Creek
Lake
County Line
City
Boat Launch
N
© 2006 Wilderness Adventures Press, Inc.

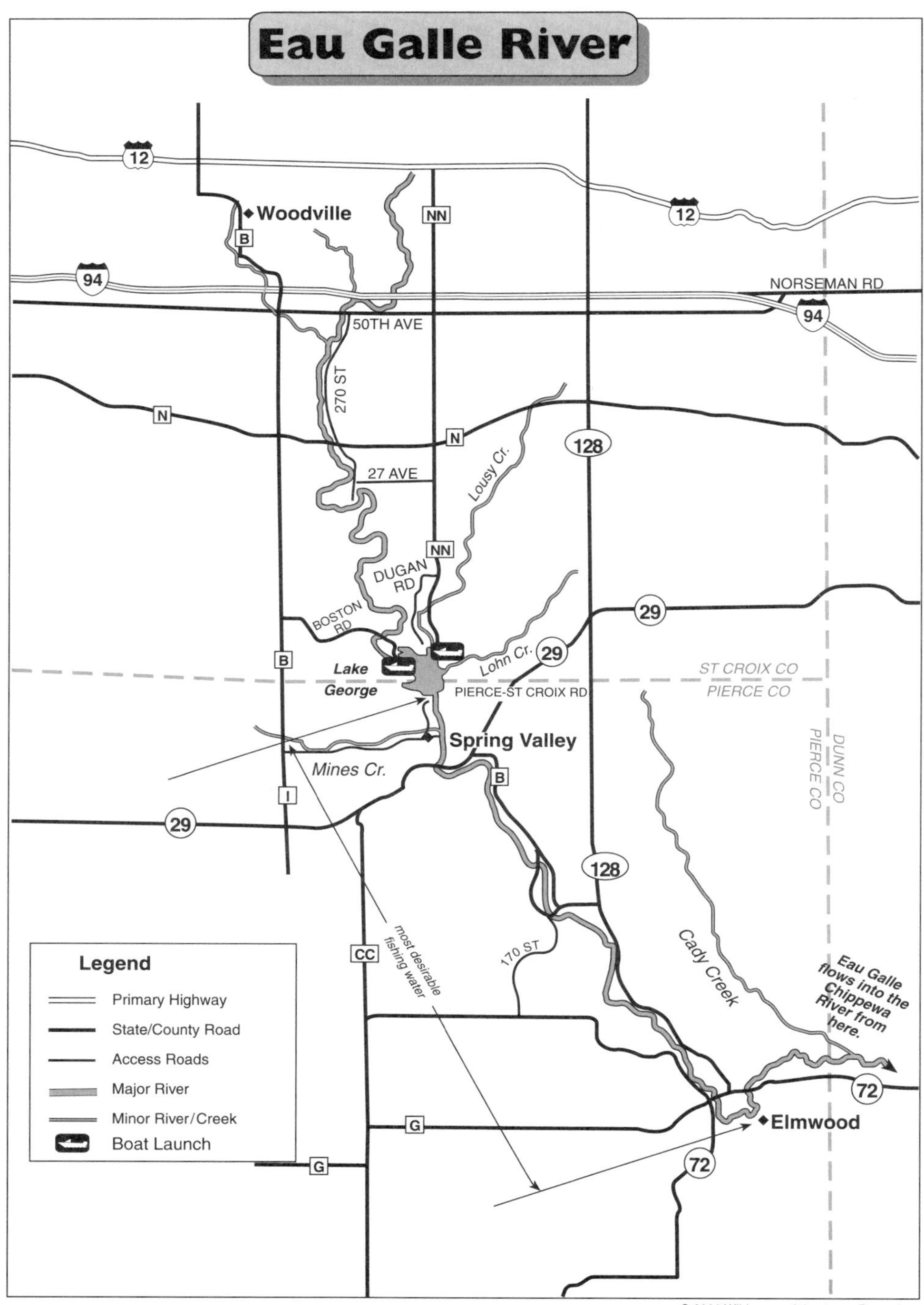

Eau Galle River
12
Woodville
B
NN
12
94
NORSEMAN RD
94
50TH AVE
270 ST
N
N
128
27 AVE
Lousy Cr.
NN
DUGAN RD
BOSTON RD
29
B
Lake George
Lohn Cr.
29
ST CROIX CO
PIERCE CO
PIERCE-ST CROIX RD
Spring Valley
DUNN CO
PIERCE CO
Mines Cr.
B
I
29
128
most desirable fishing water
170 ST
Cady Creek
CC
Eau Galle flows into the Chippewa River from here.
72
Elmwood
G
G
72
Legend
Primary Highway
State/County Road
Access Roads
Major River
Minor River/Creek
Boat Launch

Eau Galle River

John Koch, who formally ran Western Wisconsin Fly Fishing Guide Service, brought the Eau Galle River between Menomonie and River Falls to my attention—and provided a bit of fascinating conservation history.

The Eau Galle may well be the prodigal son of west-central Wisconsin trout streams. While the nearby Rush and Kinnickinnic have undergone impressive campaigns of self-improvement in the last few decades, the Eau Galle, until recently, has been in something of a slump. Water temperatures were up, trout numbers down. It was not the river old-timers remembered. In large part, this was due to U.S. Army Corps of Engineers flood control structures built in the late 1960s at Lake George in Spring Valley. In summer, warm surface waters from this impoundment were released into the Eau Galle, especially after rains. The results, until 2000, were summertime temperatures at or above lethal levels (79 degrees) and fish counts of just a few trout per mile.

In the late 1990s, groups such as the Eau Galle River Sportsman's Club voiced their opinion loud and clear: The Eau Galle is a trout stream in dire straits. The DNR and TU's KIAP-TU-WISH chapter undertook a study of the Eau Galle based on the premise that coldwater or subsurface draws from the reservoir might help river conditions. Sure enough, coldwater/subsurface releases into the Eau Galle lowered water temperatures by as much as 5 to 10 degrees and resulted in trout densities as much as 1,000 percent higher than levels before the subsurface draws. Water temperatures on the Eau Galle are now in the mid-60s year-round (perfect for brown trout, a bit high for brook trout) and trout densities now approach 500 per mile in some areas.

Of course, only time will tell if trout populations will continue to grow in response to lower temperatures on the Eau Galle. But the future looks bright. KIAP-TU-WISH has been improving stream habitat (29 lunker structures were installed in 2001) and the river has been brought into public scrutiny as an important coldwater resource. In addition, a $300,000 cost-sharing grant from the Corps of Engineers will provide funds for restoration of the Eau Galle between Lake George and Elmwood starting in 2002.

The best water on the Eau Galle is in the restoration area below Spring Valley (and Lake George). Access is available along Highway 128 between Spring Valley and Elmwood. It is a clear, sandy-bottomed stream that can be fished well with scuds or small nymphs. It is category 4 water for its entire length. If you are in the area and find the Rush too crowded, take Highway 29 or Highway 72 east and try the Eau Galle. The surrounding bluffs and small dairy farms, with their traditional red barns, have a quiet beauty, especially in fall when maples and aspens begin to show their colors.

Knapp Creek and Seven Pines Lodge

In addition to gourmet dining in a 1903 log cabin resort that is listed on the National Register of Historic Places, Seven Pines Lodge offers guests the chance to fish for rainbow, brook, or brown trout that reproduce naturally on the privately-managed mile of Knapp Creek that runs through the property. (This is unique in that Wisconsin streams and rivers are managed by the DNR and open to public use.) Call Andre Govrik at the lodge if you would like to come up for a fishing jaunt (715-653-2323). All fishing on the lodge property is catch-and-release; fishing is also restricted to lodge guests. Being spring-fed, the creek remains 48 degrees year-round.

Dependable caddis and Blue-Winged Olive hatches occur on the stream. Some 14 acres of virgin white pine remains on the property, with trees as old as 300 years. Outside the lodge property, Knapp Creek is not managed as a trout stream. However, as this stretch of stream has been stocked for a hundred years, trout probably do remain above and below the lodge.

A nice rainbow from the West-Central region.

Hub City: Hudson

Situated at the mouth of the St. Croix River, Hudson has been a strategic port for upper Midwestern trade and commerce for a century and a half. Early settlers and travelers noticed a resemblance between the Hudson River valley and the Saint Croix River valley, hence the name Hudson. Today, its main draws are an attractive main street and recreation opportunities on the St. Croix River. It's also a good base for exploring the nearby Rush, Willow, Kinnickinnic, and Trimbelle Rivers.

Just a half-hour from Minneapolis and St. Paul, Hudson has become a bedroom community for many who work in the Twin Cities. Motels are located right off the interstate, bed and breakfasts downtown. Hudson's downtown has a good variety of eateries; both your palate and your wallet will notice the proximity of the Twin Cities.

While Western Wisconsin Fly Fishing Guide Service and the Kinni Creek Lodge and Outfitters, both in Wisconsin, guide flyfishers, you'll need to go across the St. Croix to Minnesota to buy your flies. Bentley's and Bob Mitchell's are excellent fly shops with good information on Wisconsin streams. Wisconsin licenses are sold only in Wisconsin; try St. Croix Outpost, Lund's, or Consolidated Energy.

Accommodations

Super 8 Motel, 808 Dominion Drive, Hudson; 715-386-8800, 800-800-8000; $$

Best Western Hudson House, Highway 94, Hudson; 715-386-2394, 800-528-1234

Phipps Inn, 1005 Third Street, Hudson; 715-386-0800; another elegant and historic Hudson B&B; $$$

Kinni Creek Lodge and Outfitters, 545 N. Main Street, River Falls; 877-504-9705

Campgrounds

Kinnickinnic State Park, W11983 820th Avenue, River Falls; 715-425-1129

Willow River State Park, 1034 County A, Hudson; 715-386-5931

Apple River Camp Ground, 345 Church Hill Road, Somerset; 715-247-3378; private campground 20 miles north of Hudson

Restaurants

San Pedro Café, 426 Second Street, Hudson; 715-386-4003; Caribbean-style food, breakfast, specialty pizzas, fish and meat seared over wood fire in downtown Hudson

The Sub Club, 407 Second Street, Hudson; 715-381-9999; good fresh subs in downtown Hudson.

Barker's Bar and Grill, 413 Second Street, Hudson; 715-386-4123; friendly pub-style eatery next to Dragon Pearl Chinese Restaurant

Mama Maria's Italian Restaurant, 800 6th Street, Hudson; 715-386-7949; homestyle Italian restaurant located 2 miles north of downtown

Kentucky Fried Chicken, 1201 Coulee Road, Hudson; 715-386-9226; chain eateries located just off the interstate, as are following listings

Taco Johns, 710 11th Street, Hudson; 715-386-5522

Burger King, 2411 Center Drive, Hudson; 715-386-7155
Perkins Restaurant, 805 Crestview Drive, Hudson; 715-3869441

Fly Shops, Outfitters, Sporting Goods

Kinni Creek Lodge and Outfitters, 545 N. Main Street, River Falls; 877-504-9705; lodge and outfitter on the famed Kinnickinnic in River Falls; www.kinnicreeklodge.com
Gray Goat Fly Fishing/Andrew Roth; W10758 468th Ave, Prescott, Wisconsin; www.graygoatflyfishing.com; andy@graygoatflyfishing.com
Bob Mitchell's Fly Shop, 3394 Lake Elmo Avenue North, Lake Elmo, Minnesota;612-770-5854 ; www.bobmitchellsflyshop.com
Lund's Hardware, 201 S. Main, River Falls; 715-425-2415; fishing licenses
Consolidated Energy Coop, 10088 County A, Hudson; 715-386-8815; fishing licenses

Veterinarians

Hudson Pet Hospital, 751 Sommer, Hudson; 715-386-3511
Hillcrest Animal Hospital, 2215 Vine Street, Hudson; 715-386-1234

Medical

Hudson Medical Center, 400 Wisconsin, Hudson; 715-386-9321

Auto Rental

Enterprise Rent-a-Car, Stillwater, Minnesota; 651-351-0000, 800-736-8222
Ford Rent-a-Car, 2020 Crestview Drive, Hudson; 715-386-2334

Automobile Repair

Mike's Standard Service, 1313 Coulee Road, Hudson; 715-386-2494
Hilltop Service, 1000 O'Keefe Road, Hudson; 715-386-4000

Air Service

New Richmond Municipal Airport, Airport Road, New Richmond; 715-246-3201;15 miles north of Hudson
Minneapolis International Airport (half-hour west of Hudson)

For More Information

Hudson Area Chamber of Commerce
502 Second Street, Hudson, WI
800-657-6775 www.hudsonwi.org

HUB CITY: RIVER FALLS

In the last century and a half River Falls has undergone a number of economic changes: logging town, manufacturing center, and now a college town. Lately its identity has become closely linked to the Kinnickinnic River. The Kinnickinnic River Land Trust, which works with landowners to ensure good conservation practices and public access along the river, is also headquartered in downtown River Falls. Trout densities of up to 6,000 fish per mile make the Kinni a true destination stream.

The Rush, Trimbelle, and Willow Rivers are also nearby; and River Falls is a pleasant base from which to explore them. Again, Western Wisconsin Fly Fishing Guide Service and the Kinni Creek Lodge and Outfitters, both in Wisconsin, guide flyfishers on local waters, but you'll need to go across the St. Croix to Minnesota to buy your flies. Bentley's and Bob Mitchell's are excellent fly shops with good information on Wisconsin streams.

Accommodations

Super 8 Motel, 1207 St. Croix, River Falls; 715-425-8388, 800-800-8000; $$
River Falls Crossing Motel, 1525 Commerce Court, River Falls; 715-425-9500; $$
River Falls Motel, 1300 South Main, River Falls; 715-425-8181; $
Kinni Creek Lodge and Outfitters, 545 N. Main Street, River Falls; 877-504-9705; B&B with access to river and guide service; $$$

Campgrounds

Kinnickinnic State Park, W11983 820th Avenue, River Falls; 715-425-1129
Willow River State Park, 1034 County A, Hudson; 715-386-5931
Apple River Camp Ground, 345 Church Hill Road, Somerset; 715-247-3378; private campground 20 miles north of River Falls

Restaurants

Copper Kettle, 1005 South Main Street, river Falls; 715-425-2003; steaks, sandwiches, cocktails
South Fork Café, 116 South Main Street, River Falls; 715-425-2575; breakfast all day
West Wind Supper Club, 709 North Main, River Falls; 715-425-8100; Friday fish fry, prime rib, steak
Subway, 201 N. Main St., 715-425-7522
Hardees, 415 Oak, River Falls; 715-425-8783

Fly Shops, Outfitters, Sporting Goods

Kinni Creek Lodge and Outfitters, 545 N. Main Street, River Falls; 877-504-9705; lodge and outfitter located on the famed Kinnickinnic in River Falls; www.kinnicreeklodge.com
Bob Mitchell's Fly Shop, 3394 Lake Elmo Avenue North, Lake Elmo, MN; 612-770-5854; www.bobmitchellsflyshop.com

Gray Goat Fly Fishing/Andrew Roth; W10758 468th Ave, Prescott, Wisconsin; www.graygoatflyfishing.com; andy@graygoatflyfishing.com
Lund's Hardware, 201 S. Main, River Falls; 715-425-2415; fishing licenses
Consolidated Energy Coop, 10088 County A, Hudson; 715-386-8815; fishing licenses

Veterinarians
River Falls Veterinary Hospital, 1055 E. Cascade Avenue, River Falls; 715-425-2348

Medical
River Falls Area Hospital, 1629 E. Division, River Falls; 715-425-6155

Auto Rental
Enterprise Rent-a-Car, Stillwater, Minnesota; 651-351-0000, 800-736-8222
Ford Rent-a-Car, 2020 Crestview Drive, Hudson; 715-386-2334

Automobile Repair
Don's Auto, 235 Highway 35, River Falls; 715-426-0647
Swede's Union 76, 428 South Main, River Falls; 715-425-5377

Air Service
Minneapolis International Airport (half-hour west of River Falls)

For More Information
River Falls Chamber of Commerce
409 South Spruce
River Falls, WI 54022
715-425-2533

Eau Claire/Chippewa Falls Area Brook Trout Streams

Elk Creek

"Elk Creek is a fantastic brook trout stream," says Derrick Duchesneau, a former DNR fisheries biologist who grew up in Eau Claire. Elk Creek begins north of Chippewa Falls and flows beneath Interstate 94 before emptying into the Chippewa River west of Eau Claire. The upper half of the creek, above the interstate, is in Chippewa County. The lower half, below the interstate, runs along the Dunn–Eau Claire County border.

The upper reaches offer the best habitat on Elk Creek. The creek's headwaters are protected against development by the Elk Creek State Fishery Area. Access is via Highway N, Highway M, or Highway 29. Heading downstream, below Highway 29, you won't find another road crossing until 530th Avenue, a distance of 2.5 miles. This is a good stretch of the creek to wade. The next two crossings (Highway 12 and 490th Avenue) are within earshot of the interstate, which makes for noisy and unpleasant fishing. Pick Elk Creek up again, now in Dunn County, at Highway EE or 410th Avenue. The creek briefly crosses into Eau Claire County and then flows into Elk Creek Lake. Below the lake, water quality is poor.

Try fishing caddis and stonefly imitations over this sandy-bottomed stream. Look for shaded bends and woody debris. A minnow imitation fished in deep cuts might put some of the Elk's larger brook trout to the net. Elk Creek is category 5 (3 trout under 10 inches or 2 under 10 and 1 over 14 inches).

Wisconsin's dairyland heritage means you'll see a few cows when fishing in this region.

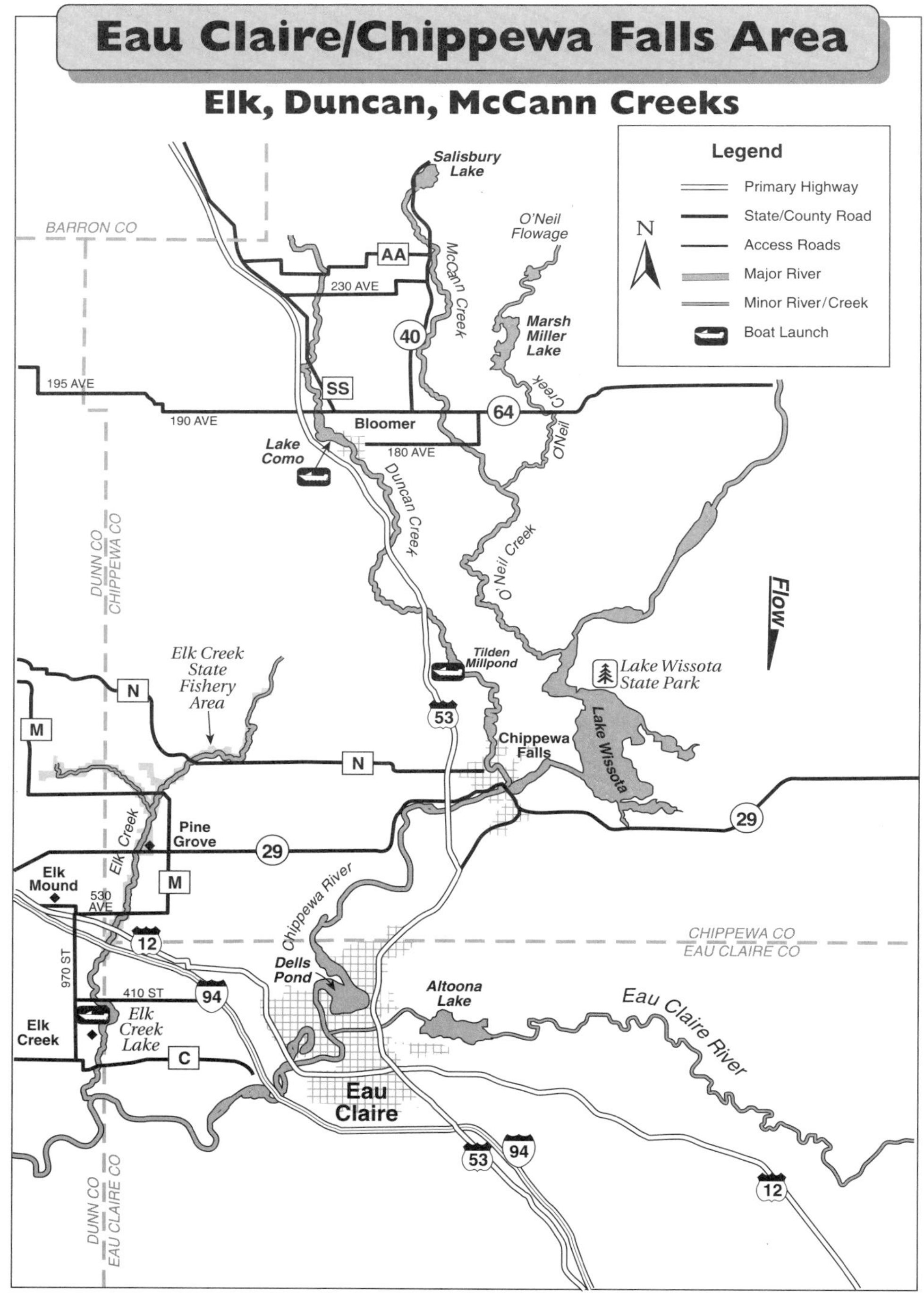

Eau Claire/Chippewa Falls Area
Elk, Duncan, McCann Creeks
Legend
Primary Highway
State/County Road
Access Roads
Major River
Minor River/Creek
Boat Launch
N
Salisbury Lake
O'Neil Flowage
BARRON CO
AA
230 AVE
McCann Creek
Marsh Miller Lake
40
195 AVE
SS
64
190 AVE
Bloomer
O'Neil Creek
Lake Como
180 AVE
Duncan Creek
O'Neil Creek
DUNN CO
CHIPPEWA CO
Flow
Elk Creek State Fishery Area
Tilden Millpond
Lake Wissota State Park
N
M
53
Lake Wissota
Chippewa Falls
N
29
Pine Grove
Elk Creek
29
Elk Mound
M
530 AVE
Chippewa River
12
CHIPPEWA CO
EAU CLAIRE CO
970 ST
Dells Pond
Altoona Lake
410 ST
94
Eau Claire River
Elk Creek
Elk Creek Lake
C
Eau Claire
53
94
12
DUNN CO
EAU CLAIRE CO

Outdoor writer Steve Miller on a Wisconsin stream.

Duncan Creek

Heading north from Chippewa Falls along Highway 53, you will encounter Duncan Creek. Its 8.5 miles above Lake Como/Bloomer sustain a naturally reproducing population of brook trout. From Lake Como, find bridge crossings at Highway 64, Highway SS, 230th Avenue, and Highway AA. If you continue north on 67th Street above the Highway AA crossing you'll be paralleling DNR land. Take a left turn to access it.

These upper reaches offer fishing in a marshy, secluded headwaters setting; farther downstream, the creek opens up. Caddis and stoneflies can be found along the sand and rock bottom; you'll find the usual *Baetis*, Hendrickson, Sulphur progression of mayfly hatches, plus terrestrials in summer. From its headwaters to the dam in Bloomer, Duncan Creek is category 5 (daily bag limit 3 trout; minimum length 8 inches). Below the dam in Bloomer, it is category 4.

McCann Creek

With 13 miles of wild brook trout water, McCann Creek, just east of Duncan Creek in western Chippewa County, shouldn't be ignored. McCann Creek is category 4 trout water for its entire length—from its inception below Salisbury Lake to its juncture with O'Neil Creek. Access DNR lands in the lower reaches of McCann via Highway SS or 180th Avenue. Highway 64 crosses it just south of Bloomer Municipal Airport. From here Highway 40 follows the creek to its headwaters; any number of right turns will take you to the creek. Fish caddis or stonefly nymphs, mayfly or terrestrial imitations as conditions dictate. If all else fails, try skittering a bushy dry over promising water to provoke a strike from an aggressive brookie.

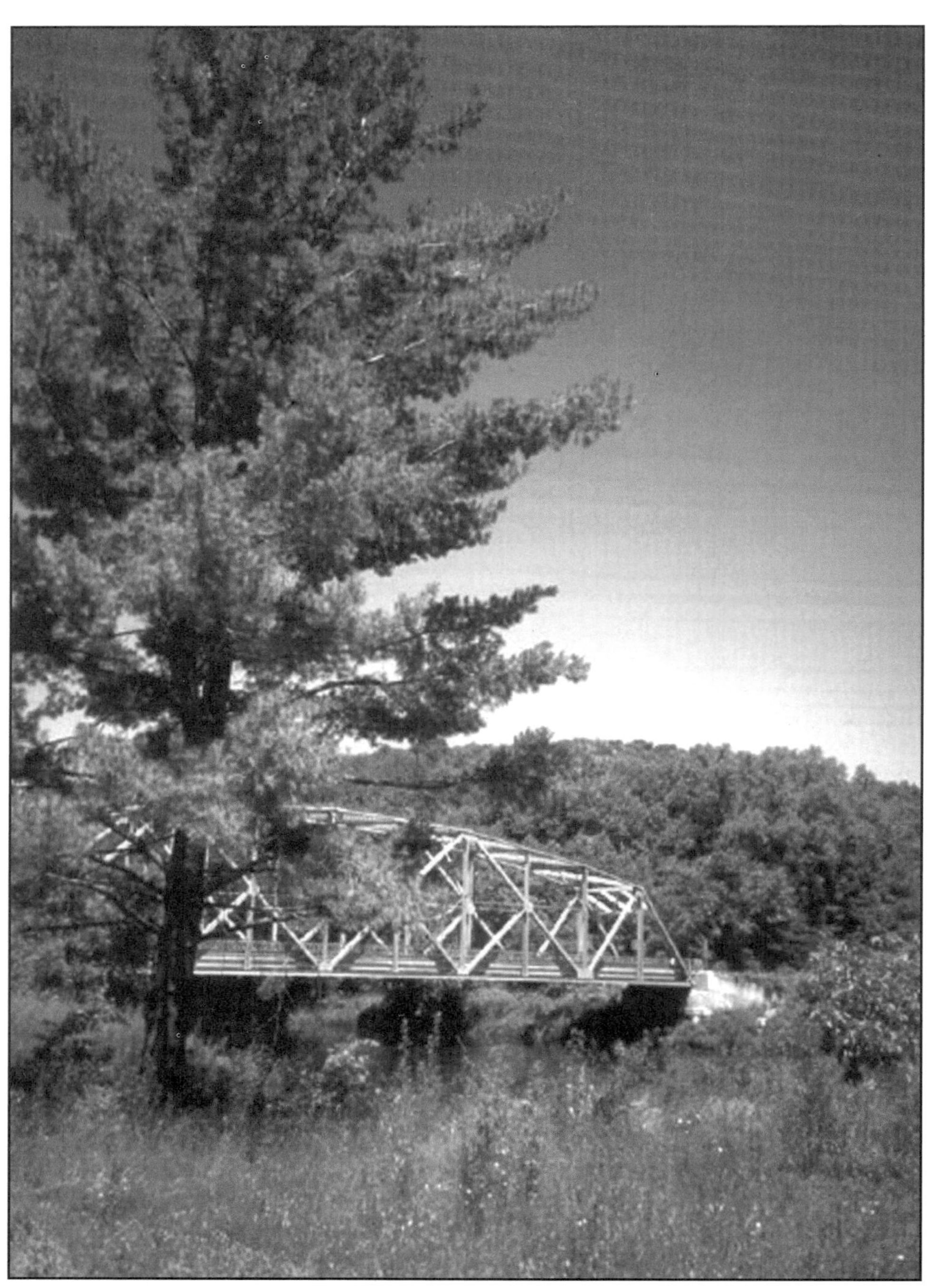

Red Cedar Trail on the Chippewa River.

CHIPPEWA RIVER

The Chippewa River runs for more than a hundred miles through west-central Wisconsin. In this stretch of river you will find the cities of Chippewa Falls and Eau Claire, two state parks (Brunet Island and Lake Wissota), and two extensive tracts of bottomland forest, (Dunnville Bottoms and Tiffany Bottoms). Smallmouth, thick throughout the Chippewa, are the main draw for flyfishers. Walleye, northerns, largemouth, muskie, panfish, and rough fish are also present.

This stretch of the Chippewa can be divided into two sections that offer two different experiences. The upper stretch (from the juncture with the Flambeau River to Eau Claire) is broken up by a series of dams and impoundments and has a rocky bottom. Flyfishers should cast their lines to likely looking cover, bring a tolerance for fishing in developed areas, and pretty much avoid (except as mentioned) the sprawling waters of the Holcombe Flowage and Lake Wissota.

From Eau Claire downstream to the Mississippi, the Chippewa is impoundment-free. Northerns, walleye, channel catfish, and rough fish are present in good numbers, and the bottom is a combination of rock and sand. As this is one of Wisconsin's larger river systems—with swift current and many holes over 20 feet deep—care should always be taken to have proper flotation aboard your boat. Also, give someone not in your party the estimated start and end times of your outings, as well as your launch site in case something should go wrong. If you fish with the proper respect, the Chippewa is a fine river offering some of the state's best smallmouth fishing.

Flambeau River to Chippewa Falls

As mentioned above, from the Flambeau River to Chippewa Falls the Chippewa River is basically a series of impoundments. Much of it is not small-boat or flyfisher friendly. However, flyfishers willing to work narrower areas between flowages will find lots of smallmouth. According to Terry Moulton at Mouldy's Archery and Tackle in Chippewa Falls, there is some great smallmouth fishing to be had. The stretch from the confluence of the Chippewa and Flambeau Rivers down to Highway D is excellent for smallmouth, according to Moulton. It is mainly rock bottom, and a streamer or large popper would work well. There is a launch just above the confluence on Highway D and another launch on Squaw Point Road. In the flowage itself, small-boat anglers should try the mouths of Birch Creek and Cranberry Creek and the accompanying islands off Highway CC on the west side of the flowage. Muskie, smallmouth, walleye, and crappy are present in this stretch.

Between the dam at Holcombe and the dam at Cornell (a stretch of about 6 miles known as Cornell Flowage) there is more good smallmouth fishing to be had, according to Moulton. And the water is small enough to be fished by the small-boat angler. You'll find lots of rocky riverbed and lots of smallmouth. Strip your streamer or leech and hold on. The area around Brunet Island State Park is a good area for muskie, Moulton notes. If you go after these big fellows, arm yourself with a 9-weight rod, a reel with plenty of backing, a heavy wire leader, and a Dahlberg Diver or very large streamer.

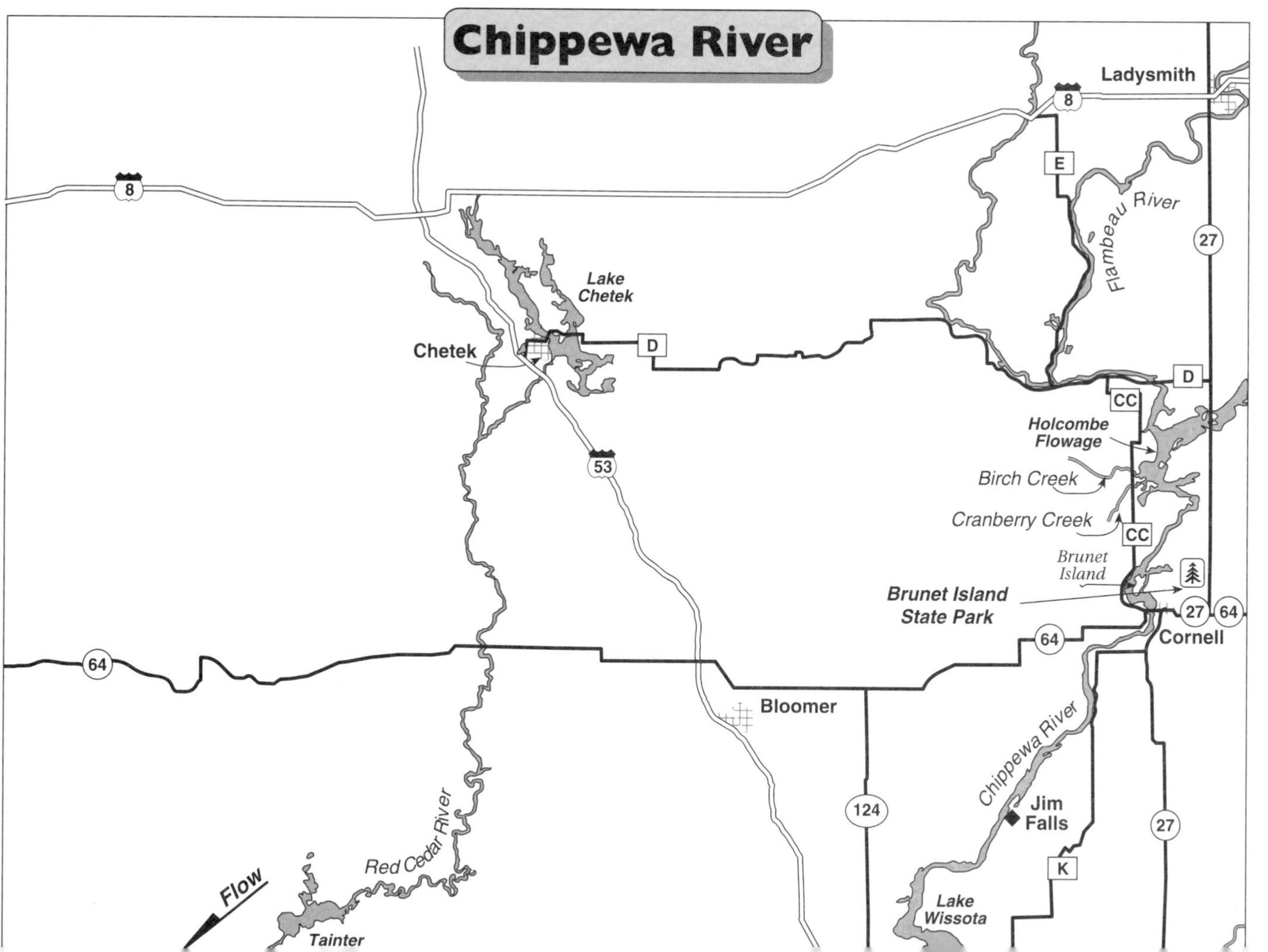
Chippewa River
8
Ladysmith
E
Flambeau River
27
Lake Chetek
Chetek
D
D
CC
Holcombe Flowage
Birch Creek
Cranberry Creek
CC
Brunet Island
Brunet Island State Park
27
64
Cornell
53
64
64
Bloomer
Chippewa River
124
Jim Falls
27
K
Lake Wissota
Red Cedar River
Flow
Tainter

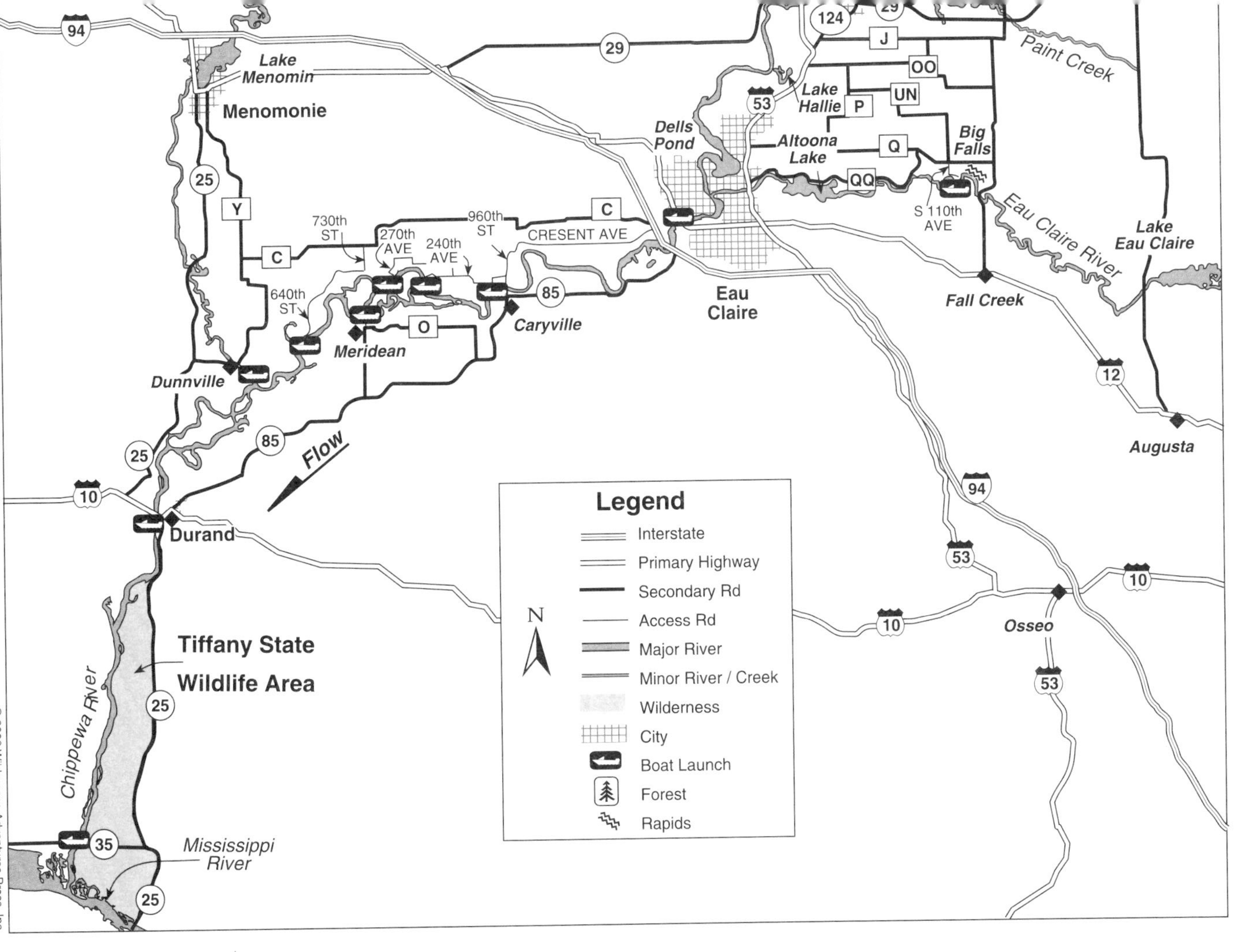
Lake Menomin
Menomonie
Dells Pond
Lake Hallie
Altoona Lake
Big Falls
Paint Creek
S 110th AVE
Eau Claire River
Lake Eau Claire
Fall Creek
Augusta
Eau Claire
730th ST
270th AVE
240th AVE
960th ST
CRESENT AVE
640th ST
Caryville
Meridean
Dunnville
Flow
Durand
Osseo
Tiffany State Wildlife Area
Chippewa River
Mississippi River
Legend
Interstate
Primary Highway
Secondary Rd
Access Rd
Major River
Minor River / Creek
Wilderness
City
Boat Launch
Forest
Rapids
N
94
29
124
J
OO
UN
P
Q
QQ
53
25
Y
C
O
85
12
10
35

Some good backwater opportunities exist on Lake Wissota. On the east side of the lake, the inlets of the Yellow River and Paint Creek, both shallow weedy habitats, provide good conditions for flyfishers seeking a mix of largemouth, panfish, and northerns. Access to these areas is via Highway K and Highway X. On the lake's west side, the area around O'Neil Creek, off Highway 178, provides similar habitat; this can also be fished from a small boat.

Those inclined to fish more in an urban setting can find some of the river's biggest smallmouth bass between the Chippewa Falls Dam and the Dells Pond in Eau Claire, according to Moulton. "Guys come up from Illinois to fish this section," he says. While most of the anglers you see in this area won't be flyfishers, smallmouth in the 3- to 5-pound range can be found here. Launches in this stretch are at Lake Hallie (on both sides of the river), and then at the widespread area known as Dells Pond (again, both sides of the river). Derrick Duchesneau, a friend and former DNR fisheries biologist, is a UW–Eau Claire graduate. He often did well catching walleye and smallmouth from the shoreline off Water Street near the university.

A sidelight worth mentioning, according to Duchesneau, is the Eau Claire River, a noted smallmouth fishery. A rocky and shallower stream than the Chippewa, the Eau Claire River joins the Chippewa below Altoona Lake in Eau Clair. The area between Big Falls and Altoona Lake (some 20 miles of river) is a popular float for smallmouth, according to Mike Buroker of Buroker Taxidermy in Eau Claire. Pick up bronzebacks by working the rocky shoreline trough with a Muddler Minnow, just as you would for trout. You can access the Big Falls area from Highway K via foot trails and dirt roads. There's a launch right below Big Falls off South 110th Avenue. Access to the Eau Clair downstream from Big Falls is via Highway QQ.

Eau Claire to the Juncture with the Mississippi River

Below the dam in downtown Eau Claire, the Chippewa River flows unimpeded to the Mississippi River some 50 miles to the southwest. Many of the same species are present as in the Flambeau-Eau Claire stretch, however, larger numbers of rough fish are present here as well. Between the Eau Claire Dam and Dunnville Bottoms, the river is rock and sand bottom; it is between 5 and 20 feet deep in the channels with some deeper holes at river bends. Look for gravel runs and riffles and you will find smallmouth. Fish them with weighted streamers.

Launches in this stretch are at Highway 12, Ferry Street just above Interstate 94 in Shawtown (southwest of Eau Claire), and at 960th Street in Caryville. Highway 85 loosely follows the south shore of the river. Moulton notes that 2001 was an exceptional year for channel catfish and flathead in this stretch of the river. While both species like to congregate below dams, channel catfish can be caught in many of the same places you catch smallmouths—in gravel runs, rock channels, or even right up against bridge embankments. Patient flyfishers willing to fish slow and deep can take their share of these fish.

The stretch known as Dunnville Bottoms is a rugged expanse of bottomland. Derrick Duchesneau, who turkey hunts this area, describes it as "underdeveloped with a few farms and limited access." Look for big northerns here, according to Terry

Moulton. Smallmouth, walleye, muskie, and catfish can also be found, along with good numbers of rough fish. You can gain access to this stretch (a small boat is your best bet) along the north side of the river via 240th Avenue, 270th Avenue, 640th Street, and County Y (Dunnville State Wildlife Area, where you launch near the mouth of the Red Cedar River). Access to the south side of the river is off Highway O just north of Meridean. Again, this is a remote area where help may be far away. As game wardens of an earlier age were wont to do, carry the means for making fire, extra food, and a space blanket.

Below Dunnville Bottoms, from Durand to the Mississippi River, there are only two bridge crossings: Highway 25 in Durand and Highway 35 at Tiffany Bottoms. There are two launches off Highway N on the west shore of the river, one at Dead Lake and one north of Ella; on the east side, the only launch is at Highway 35/Tiffany Bottoms. The fishery in this stretch of the Chippewa is similar to that of Dunnville Bottoms, with northerns, walleye, muskie, catfish, smallmouth, and rough fish present. The Tiffany Bottoms State Wildlife Area, 12,000 acres of public land, lies between the east shore of the Chippewa and Highway 25.

Consult the *Guide to Wisconsin Hook and Line Fishing Regulations* (available at license vendors) for a by-county listing of walleye and muskellunge bag and size limits. The Chippewa River is in the Northern Zone for pike and the Southern Zone for bass.

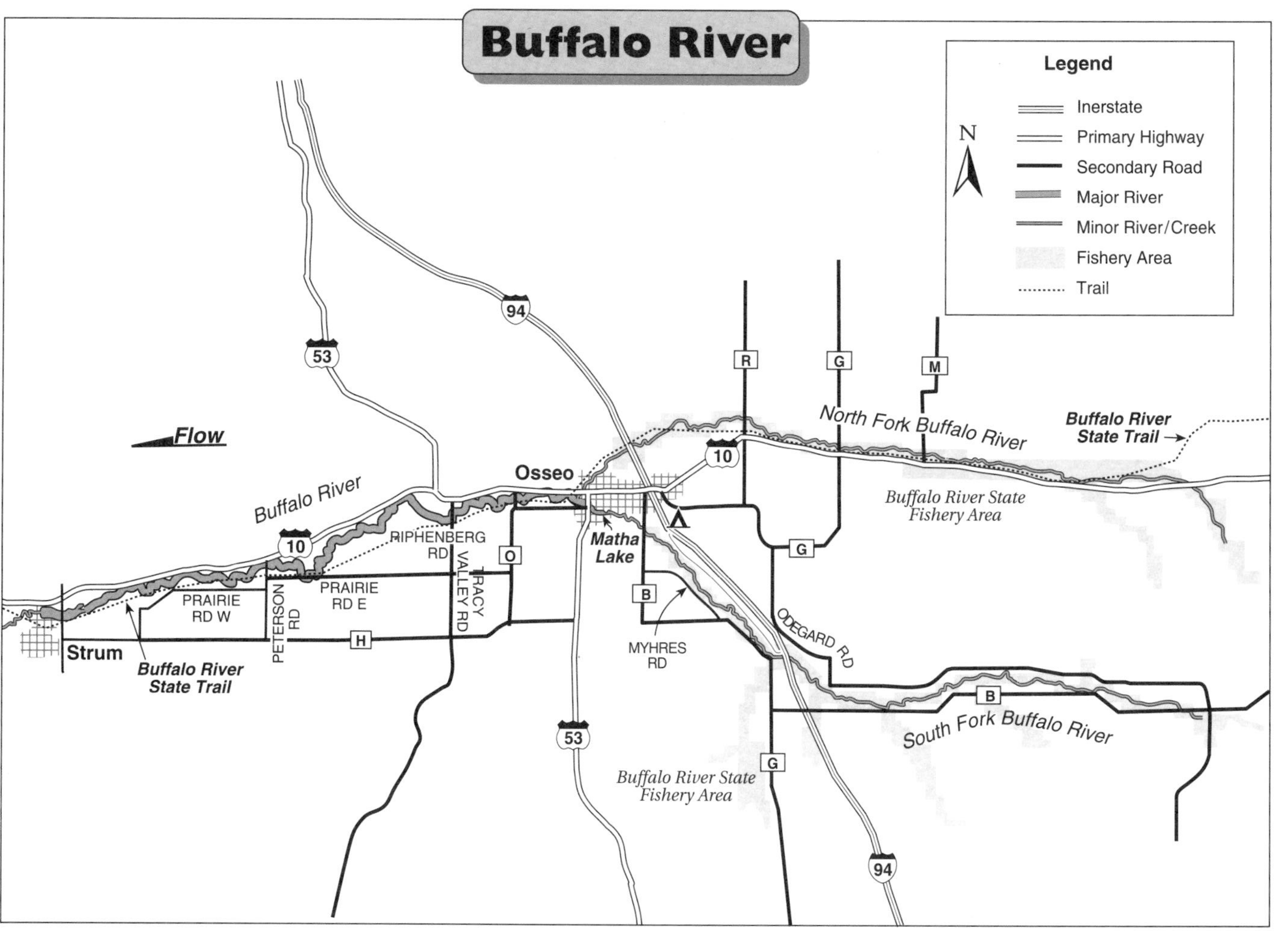
Buffalo River
Legend
Inerstate
Primary Highway
Secondary Road
Major River
Minor River/Creek
Fishery Area
Trail
N
Flow
Osseo
Buffalo River
North Fork Buffalo River
Buffalo River State Trail →
Buffalo River State Fishery Area
RIPHENBERG RD
TRACY VALLEY RD
PRAIRIE RD W
PRAIRIE RD E
PETERSON RD
Matha Lake
MYHRES RD
ODEGARD RD
South Fork Buffalo River
Strum
Buffalo River State Trail
Buffalo River State Fishery Area
94
53
10
R
G
M
O
B
H

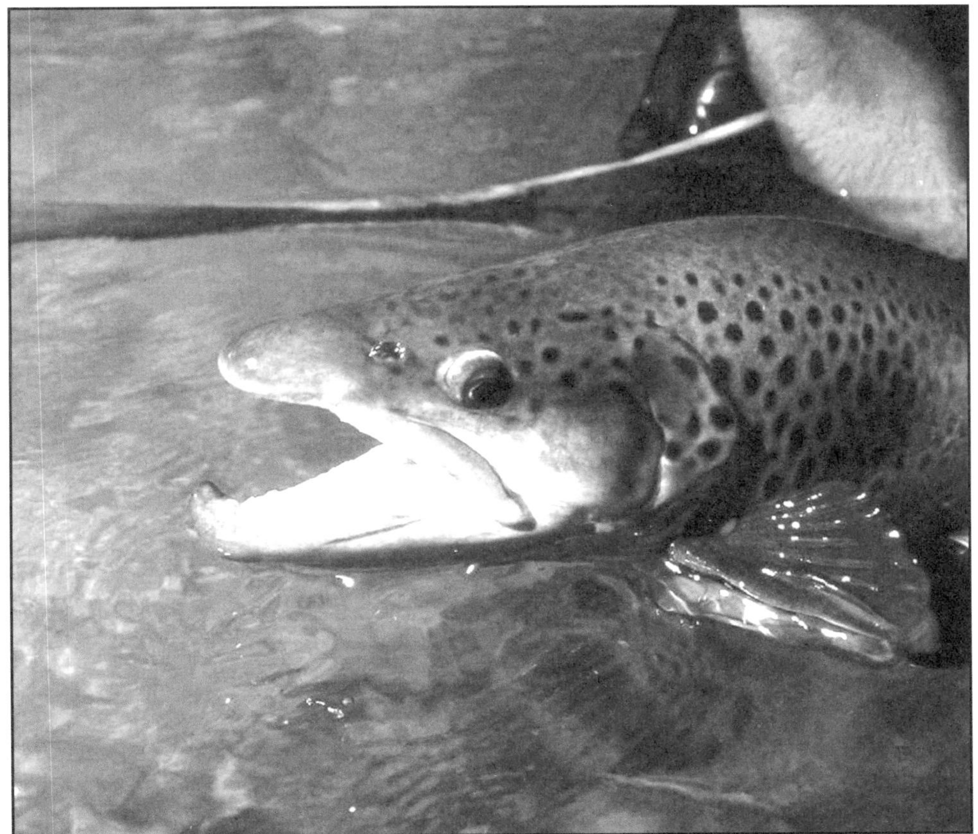

You can expect to catch some nice browns in the Buffalo River.

Buffalo River

The streams in the Black River basin may seem a bit lacking in comparison to the more fertile limestone-infused waters just to the north in the Rush/Kinnickinnic basin and just to the south in Coulee Country. The water, seeping up through sand instead of limestone, is not as fertile. There are fewer aquatic plants and insects, and, accordingly, lower trout densities and smaller trout on average. On the other hand, limestone streams set the bar pretty high. With a mix of natural reproduction and stocking, respectable angling for brook and brown trout can be had (with very little pressure) in this sand-pine-and-oak country. To boot, there's generous amounts of DNR land in these parts.

The North Fork and the South Fork of the Buffalo River both begin in eastern Jackson County and come together around the town of Osseo to form the main branch of the Buffalo. Between Osseo and Strum, the main fork is considered trout water. Below the impoundment in Strum, the Buffalo is no longer trout water; it runs some 40 miles to the Mississippi River at Alma with rough fish predominating. For warmwater opportunities in this area, best to try the Black River, Potters Flowage, the Mississippi, or the cranberry flowages covered later in this section.

The Buffalo River and both its forks are category 4 except for the stretch between County O and Town Road (between Osseo and Strum). This water is category 5 (artificials only; 2-trout limit; browns 18 inches; brook and rainbow 10 inches; only one brown may be kept).

To access the North Fork of the Buffalo River, use Highway 10 east of Osseo. A bonus here is the scenic Buffalo River Trail, which parallels the North Fork, allowing access to the river and a number of other recreation pursuits. Biking, hiking, cross-country skiing, hunting, and ATV and snowmobile use are all allowed in season on this rail-to-trail corridor.

Access to the South Fork is via Highway B out of Osseo. The Buffalo River State Fishery Area runs between the two forks. Between Osseo and Strum, access the river via Highway 10/53 and the Buffalo River Trail.

What can anglers expect from the Buffalo River? Decent trout and insect populations as well as very clear water (1 to 4 feet deep and 50 feet wide) flowing over a sandy bottom. There is natural reproduction among brook trout in the system and some among browns. The riffle-pool sequence one finds on high-gradient limestone streams to the south is replaced here by the bend-glide sequence. Look for fish at bends and corners and hanging around the abundant downed wood in the stream. During hatches fish may be found haunting the open glides as they boldly chase a meal. But during normal light conditions real caution and an eye toward stream cover is the way to go.

I fished the stretch right outside the town of Osseo and picked up browns and brookies (very brightly colored) in the 9- to 11-inch range. I fished during a late September evening, working slowly and methodically (avoiding wading when possible) and taking trout from dark pockets.

A mix of stoneflies, mayflies, caddisflies, and scuds inhabit the stream, according to Dan Hatleli, DNR fisheries biologist for the Buffalo, Trempealeau, and Black River basin. There are few forage fish and few crawfish, according to Hatleli, so trout may not attain the size or numbers like limestone streams to the north and south. Look for caddis and *Baetis* hatches in April, with *Baetis* picking up again in August and September; stoneflies, caddis, and scuds are present all year. Your best bet here, since mayfly hatches are not the mainstay, is a carefully fished scud or Prince Nymph.

While I found the stretch near Osseo productive, there is plenty of access on both forks and the main branch. When you've had your fill of the Buffalo, stop by Osseo's Norske Nook for a hot beef sandwich and a slice of its world-renowned pie.

Stream Facts: Buffalo River

Season
- The early season runs from the first Saturday in March to the last Sunday before the first Saturday in May; no-kill, single barbless hooks only. Regular season runs from the first Saturday in May at 5:00 am through September 30.

Regulations
- Main branch and both forks category 4, except for portion between County O and Town Road west of Osseo, which is category 5 (artificials only; 2-trout limit; browns 18 inches; brook and rainbow 10 inches; only 1 brown may be kept).

Species
- Planted and wild brook and brown trout.

Miles of Trout Water
- 10 miles main fork; 10 miles south fork; 10 miles north fork

Stream Characteristics
- Clear, sand-bottomed creek running through woods and meadow.

Access
- Off Highway 10/53; Buffalo River State Fishery Area, off County B.

Fly Shops
- Gander Mountain (Eau Claire); Bob Mitchell's Fly Shop (Lake Elmo, MN)

Maps
- *Wisconsin Atlas and Gazetteer*, page 60, 61

Hub City: Eau Claire

A 17th-century French translation of the Chippewa word for clear water, Eau Claire is now a medium-sized Wisconsin city at the juncture of the Chippewa and Eau Claire Rivers. The Eau Claire River has very clear water, hence the river (and city) name. In the 19th century, it was an important stop for loggers ferrying white pine along the Chippewa to the Mississippi, and also home to many of the lumber barons whose houses can still be seen in older parts of the city.

It is a good base city for exploring the Buffalo River to the south or the Chippewa River, which runs right through town. A notable area eatery is the Norske Nook in nearby Osseo, known the world over for its pies. The Joynt, 332 Water Street, is the standout tavern in a town known for its watering holes.

Accommodations

AmericInn, 6200 Texaco, Eau Claire; 715-874-4900; $
Days Inn, 2305 Craig Road, Eau Claire; 715-834-3193; $
Holiday Inn, 2703 Craig Road, Eau Claire; 715-835-2211; $$

Campgrounds

Brunet Island State Park, Route 2, Box 158, Cornell, 54732; 715-239-6888; located 15 miles west of Eau Claire on Cornell Flowage, an impoundment of the Chippewa River
Lake Wissota State Park, Route 8, Box 360, Chippewa Falls; 715-382-4574; located 10miles west of Eau Claire on the Lake Wissota, a flowage of the Chippewa River
Harstad Park, county park located east of Eau Claire and overlooking the Eau Claire River; from town of Augusta, take Highway 12 north to Highway HH; go north on Highway HH to Highway HHH and find park entrance off Highway HHH

Restaurants

Mike's Smoke House, 2235 Clairemont Street; 715-834-8153; generous portions of BBQ at good prices
Norske Nook, downtown Osseo 25 miles south of Eau Claire; 715-597-3069; world famous for pie, good hot beef sandwiches, Scandinavian specialties
Culvers, 4750 Golf Road, Eau Claire; 715 514 4655; quality Midwest burger chain
Heckel's Family Restaurant, 805 S. Hastings, Eau Claire; 715-834-2076; good basic food, good basic prices
Taco Johns, 242 Water Street, Eau Claire; 715-832-1149; good Mexican chain located in campus area

Fly Shops, Outfitters, Sporting Goods

Gander Mountain Sporting Goods, 6440 Sculy Drive, Eau Claire 715-834-4594; www.gandermountain.com

Scheel's All Sports, 4710 Golf Rd, Eau Claire; 715-833-1886; www.scheelssports.com

Mouldy's Archery and Tackle, 12127 Highway OO, Chippewa Falls; 715-723-3617

Veterinarians

Eau Claire County Animal Hospital, 2828 Mall Drive, Eau Claire; 715-835-5011

Medical

Luther Hospital-Mayo Health, 1221 Whipple Street, Eau Claire; 715-838-3242

Auto Rental

Avis Car Rental, 3800 Starr Avenue, Eau Claire; 715-835-7744

National Car Rental, 3000 Starr Avenue, Eau Claire; 715-835-2152

Automobile Repair

Affordable Auto Repair, 332 Truax Boulevard, Eau Claire; 715-832-8711

Don the Muffler Man, 1613 Harding Avenue, Eau Claire; 715-834-9302; dependable Wisconsin auto repair chain

Air Service

Eau Claire County Airport, 3800 Starr Avenue, Eau Claire; 715-839-4900

For More Information

Eau Claire Chamber of Commerce
3625 Gateway Drive, Suite B
Eau Claire, WI 54702
715-834-1204

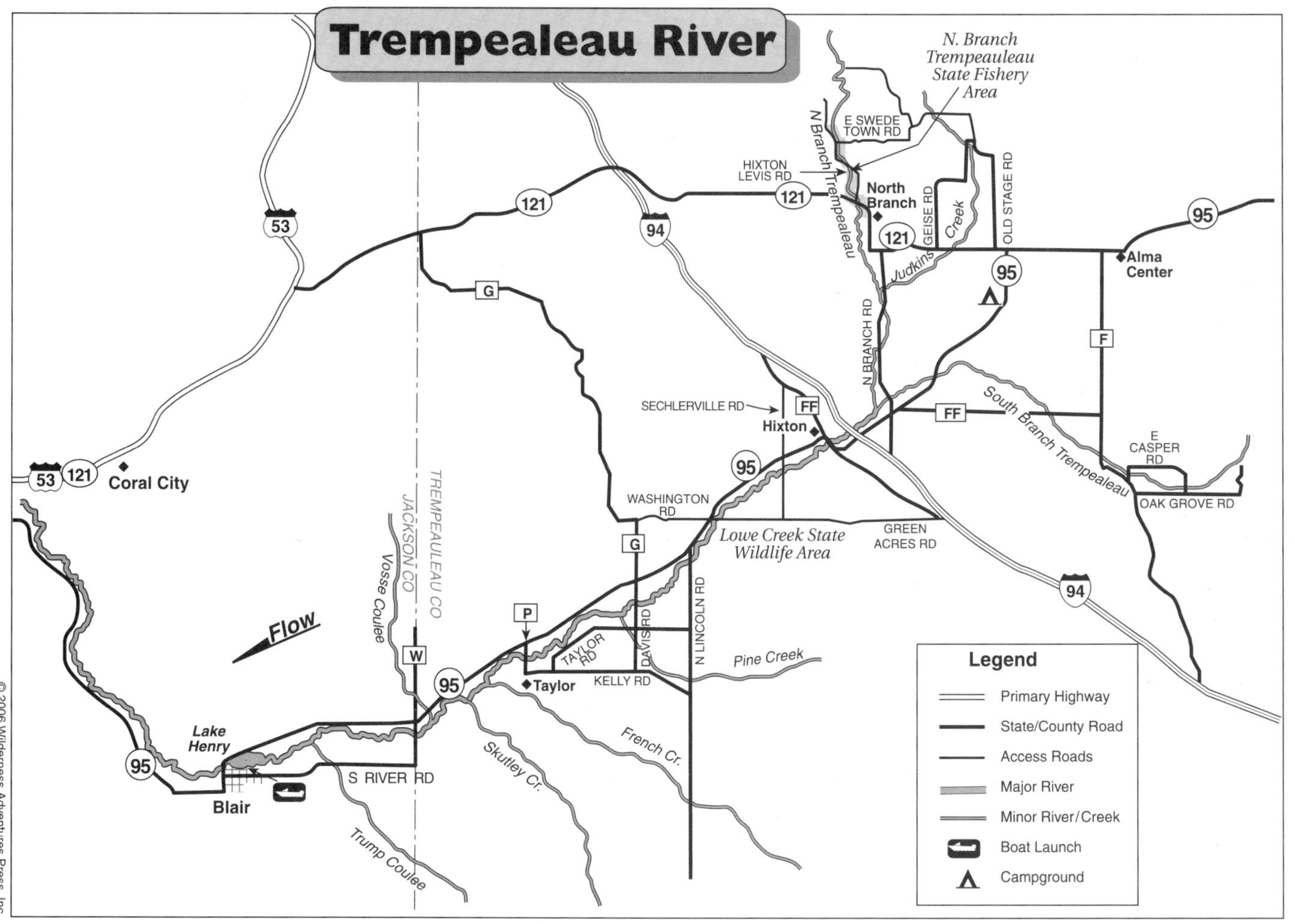
Trempealeau River
N. Branch Trempeauleau State Fishery Area
E SWEDE TOWN RD
HIXTON LEVIS RD
N Branch Trempealeau
North Branch
GEISE RD
Judkins Creek
OLD STAGE RD
Alma Center
N BRANCH RD
SECHLERVILLE RD
Hixton
South Branch Trempealeau
E CASPER RD
OAK GROVE RD
Coral City
WASHINGTON RD
Lowe Creek State Wildlife Area
GREEN ACRES RD
TREMPEAULEAU CO
JACKSON CO
Vosse Coulee
Flow
TAYLOR RD
DAVIS RD
N LINCOLN RD
Pine Creek
Taylor
KELLY RD
Lake Henry
Blair
S RIVER RD
Skutley Cr.
French Cr.
Trump Coulee
Legend
Primary Highway
State/County Road
Access Roads
Major River
Minor River/Creek
Boat Launch
Campground
95
121
94
53
F
FF
G
P
W
© 2006 Wilderness Adventures Press, Inc.

Stoneflies are prevalent on most gravel-bottomed streams. (Tim Landwehr)

TREMPEALEAU RIVER AND BRANCHES

Like Beaver Creek to the west and the Buffalo River to the north, the Trempealeau River is a clear, sand-bottomed stream with decent trout numbers (stocked and wild), healthy insect populations, and a fair amount of public access. The main branch of the Trempealeau begins at the confluence of its north and south branches in eastern Jackson County near the town of Hixton. The North Branch of the Trempealeau, some 7 miles in length, is a fine stream for wild browns and brookies. The South Branch, 5 miles in length, holds wild brook trout.

After the forks join, the river flows into Trempealeau County and empties into Lake Henry in the town of Blair, which marks the end of trout water—some 16 miles. Below Lake Henry, the Trempealeau River mainly supports catfish and rough fish, with a few northerns showing up near the river's mouth. The Black and Chippewa Rivers (described later in this section) are better warmwater fisheries by far. Below Lake Henry, the Trempealeau resembles a rough fish hook, as it rambles some 50 miles to the Mississippi River at the Trempealeau National Wildlife Refuge opposite Winona, Minnesota.

The main branch of the Trempealeau River is category 4 for the most part; the small section from Davis Road upstream to South Lincoln Road is category 5 artificials only, (2-trout limit, one of which may be a brown trout; minimum length for brown trout is 18 inches, brook and rainbow 10 inches). A small portion of the North Branch downstream from Cain Road is category 5 with the same regulations.

Access the North Branch via North Branch Road and Highway 121, the South Branch via Highway F, and the main branch via Highway 95. Public lands and access exist on the North Branch along Highway 121 at the North Branch Trempealeau River State Fishery Area, and on the main fork southeast of Hixton at Lowe Creek State Wildlife Area on Highway 95.

What are the highlights of this system? First, the creeks in this area are not heavily fished, so you will not find the crowds that you would on the Rush and Kinni farther north. The North Branch supports a good population of wild brook trout and browns. Combined with the extensive public lands on the North Branch, this allows the angler the intimacy of fishing small water in a natural setting. The rolling sandy ridges and copses of pine and oak provide a scenic backdrop while fishing for wary fish in clear water.

The lower reaches of the Trempealeau River, between the town of Taylor and Lake Henry, hold some brown trout in the 18-inch range. Highway P and Highway W provide road crossings in this stretch. As with many trout streams, the Trempealeau's lower trout reaches contain fewer (but larger) trout and higher numbers of forage fish.

According to Dan Hatleli, DNR fisheries biologist for the Black River Falls district, you will find lots of glides and corners and woody debris on this river. These cover pockets are where you will find fish. A mix of scuds, caddisflies, stoneflies, and mayflies make up the insect base. The Trempealeau's clear waters demand careful approach and a long fine leader.

Beaver Creek

If you find yourself bumming around the upper Mississippi River near Trempealeau, by all means give Beaver Creek a try. It's a sand-bottomed spring creek running through a pretty valley with both pasture and timber 10 miles west of Trempealeau.

Draining into Lake Marinuka in Galesville in Trempealeau County, Beaver Creek's main branch is 12 miles long and home to stocked and wild browns and brookies. Trout water ends at the lake, and there is little but rough fish below it. (Beaver's main branch begins at the juncture of the north and south forks at the town of Ettrick.) Because this creek lacks good cover, and thus hiding places for trout, concentrate your efforts in areas where cover is present, such as bridges, deadfalls, or undercut banks. Fish Beaver Creek early or late or during cloudy weather. Its clear water and open character make fishing during bright light very difficult.

You will find midge and Blue-Winged Olive hatches throughout the trout season, as well as some forage fish and scuds. Match the hatch if you see activity or try a scud or streamer if nothing is rising.

Steve Miller, a good friend and outdoor writer from Madison, fished the bridge at Crystal Valley Road some time ago. He reported strikes on 50 percent of his casts.

He was using a slow retrieve, mending the fly line end over end after it reached the end of the drift. The fish he caught were browns in the 9- to 12-inch range. Use this technique wherever you find cover on Beaver Creek and on other streams like it.

While lacking the trout densities of Timber Coulee to the south, Beaver Creek receives little pressure and is worth fishing if you're in the area. Access is at bridges heading north from Galesville: Highway 53, Crystal Valley Road, Highway 53, and at an unnamed road running between Highway 53 and Dopp Road outside the town of Ettrick. The main fork of Beaver is category 4.

The North and South Forks of Beaver Creek are small, brushy, and, at most, worth a glance in the early season when the cover's not so thick.

Lake Pepin

The Mississippi River Valley and Lake Pepin were formed when the large glacial Lake Agassiz began flowing southward, about 12,000 years ago. The massive flow of water decreased several thousand years later as the glacier receded and the waters began flowing in other directions. About 9,500 years ago, sand was deposited at the Chippewa River delta where it joined the Mississippi River and acted as a dam.

Lake Pepin straddles the Wisconsin-Minnesota border, running 30 miles from north to south. Its northern edge is roughly Pierce County Islands State Wildlife Area near Bay City, Wisconsin; the mouth of the Chippewa River is a rough southern boundary. Walleye, sauger, white bass, and panfish are the main draws of Lake Pepin. There are also largemouth and northerns "in the weeds," according to Gene Bokes of Gene's Tackle and Sporting Goods in Pepin. A 14-foot jonboat with a dependable outboard is a good minimum standard for fishing big water like Pepin. However, it's best to stay off the water if the wind is strong out of the north.

Right after ice-out, according to Bokes, walleye gather below dam #3. This is immediately upstream from Trenton on the Wisconsin side. You'll need a good anchor, warm clothes and good flotation devices to join in this sometimes-frigid fishery. Fish a fast-sinking line with a weighted streamer, or consider using a deep-diving plug. Spring-run walleye fishing is akin to opening day of trout season in New Jersey or salmon-run fishing in the Western states. It's often a shoulder-to-shoulder (or boat-to-boat) affair not for the agoraphobic. By the time May rolls around, walleye are dispersed throughout the lake. Channels and running sloughs are good places to look for them.

Bluegill and sunfish up to a half-pound are common on Lake Pepin, Bokes says. He recommends fishing anywhere off the dike road (Highway 26) between Nelson, Wisconsin and Wabasha, Minnesota. This is a popular year-round area for panfish, and you can fish right from shore with or without a boat. The sloughs in the Pierce County Islands State Wildlife Area are also a good bet for panfish, as are the backwaters just downstream from Pepin. Fish rubber spiders or poppers when the bluegills are on their beds; fish flashy nymphs near dropoffs after the spawn. You should be able to find crappies just about anywhere you find downed timber.

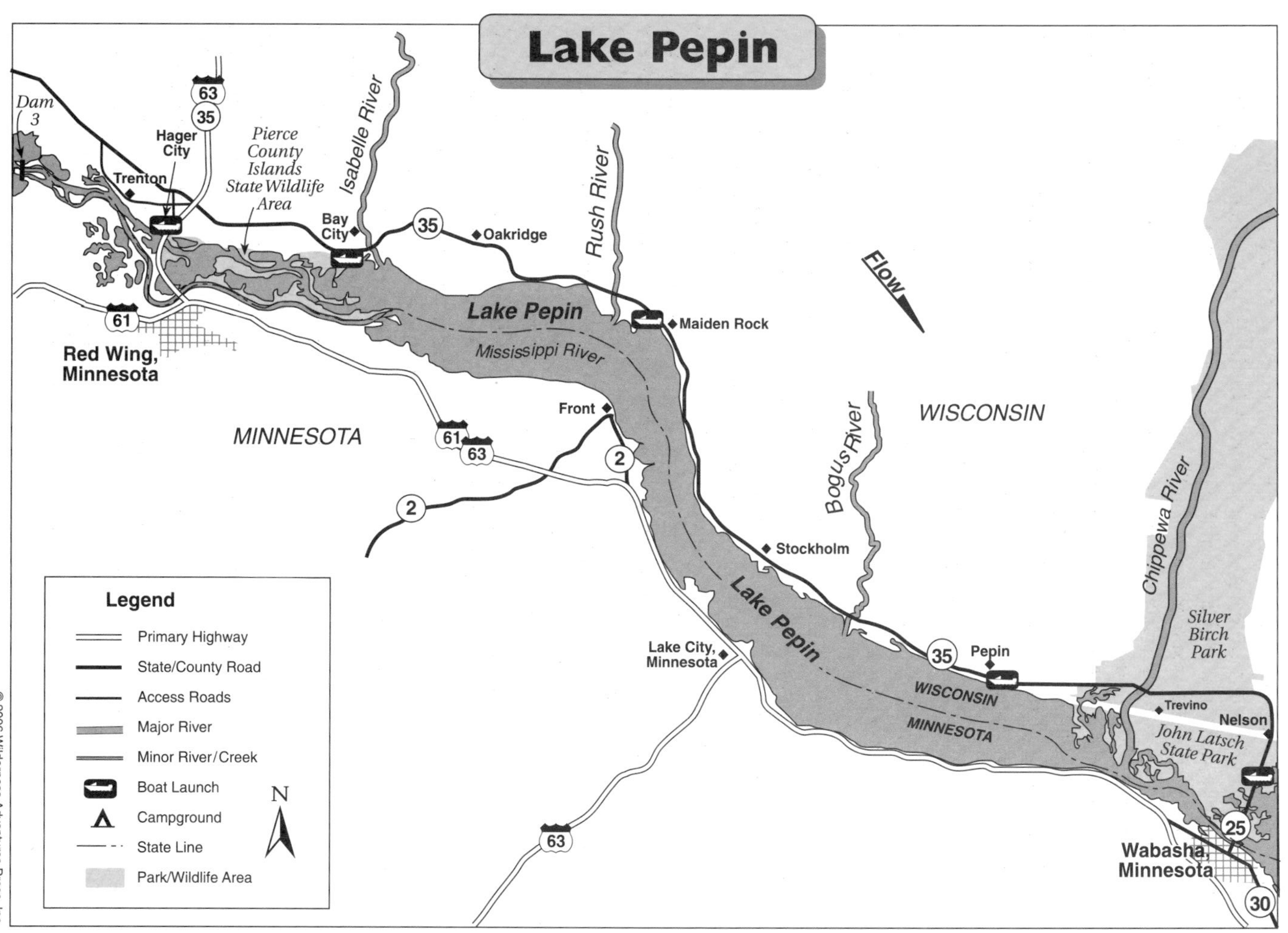
Lake Pepin
Dam 3
63
35
Hager City
Trenton
Pierce County Islands State Wildlife Area
Isabelle River
Bay City
35
Oakridge
Rush River
Flow
Lake Pepin
Mississippi River
Maiden Rock
61
Red Wing, Minnesota
Front
MINNESOTA
61
63
2
2
Bogus River
WISCONSIN
Stockholm
Lake Pepin
Lake City, Minnesota
35
Pepin
WISCONSIN
MINNESOTA
Chippewa River
Silver Birch Park
Trevino
Nelson
John Latsch State Park
25
Wabasha, Minnesota
30
63
Legend
Primary Highway
State/County Road
Access Roads
Major River
Minor River/Creek
Boat Launch
Campground
State Line
Park/Wildlife Area
N

White bass, or stripers, as they're called locally are feast-or-famine fish present in good numbers on Pepin. But when they are on, you can literally pick one up on every cast; use a minnow-imitation streamer or virtually anything with some silver tied into it. In my experience, white bass can be just about anywhere at any given time. I've caught them in fast rivers, weedy bays, and below dams during walleye runs. April/May and September/October are likely times to run into white bass schools. However, they will sometimes congregate and feed during the dog days of summer. Your best bet here is to check with locals on where the white bass have been recently.

For northerns, try creek mouths (Isabelle Creek, Rush River, Bogus Creek) during hot weather and weedy bays during the spring spawn. Northerns aren't numerous on Pepin, but they tend to run large. Pepin's northern and southern backwaters hold largemouths. Look for rubble bottom or sandbars to find smallmouths.

Boat launches, north to south, are at Hager City/Highway 63 (launch here to fish walleyes at dam #3), Bay City, Maiden Rock, Pepin, and along the dike road/Highway 25. Largemouth and smallmouth bass: minimum size 14 inches, daily limit 5; walleye and sauger: no minimum size sauger, 15-inch minimum walleye, daily limit 6; northern pike: no minimum size, daily limit 5; white bass: no minimum size, daily limit 25; panfish: no minimum size, daily limit 25. A Wisconsin fishing license (resident or nonresident) is valid for fishing Lake Pepin.

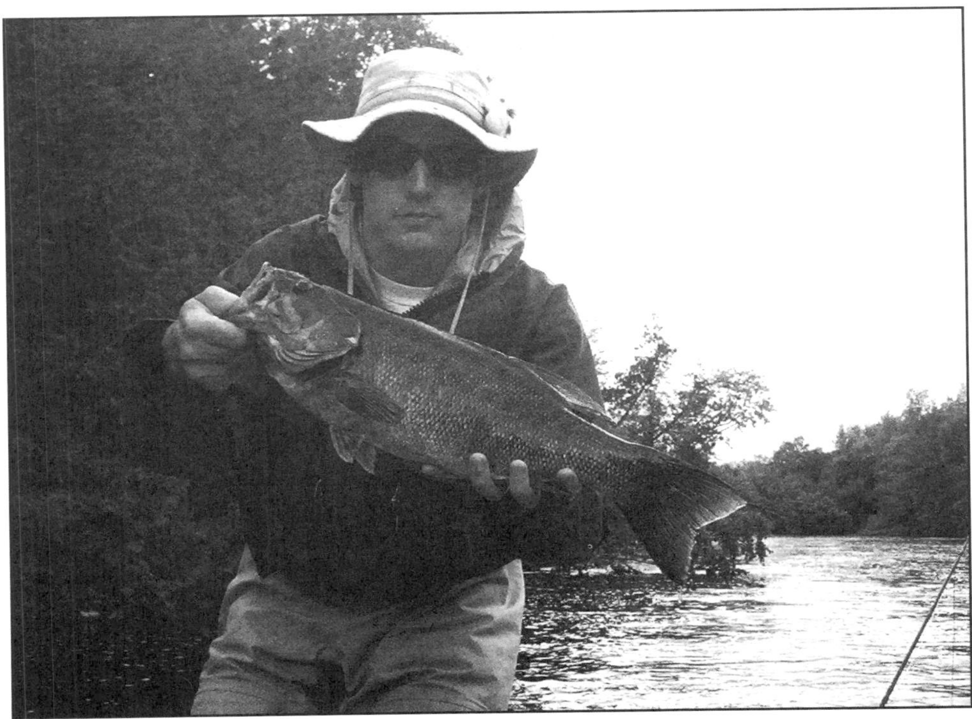

A huge fly-caught smallmouth bass. (Tim Landwehr)

PCBs have been a contaminant on the upper Mississippi River below the Twin Cities for many years, as they have been in many long-industrialized waterways. While water quality is improving somewhat on Lake Pepin, current DNR advisories for the lake recommend no more than one meal a week for walleye/sauger and northern pike over 30 inches; no more than one meal a month of white bass and northern pike over 30 inches; no limits are placed on the amount of panfish consumed. Consult the *Guide to Wisconsin Hook and Line Fishing Regulations* (available where you buy your license) for complete regulations.

Spring-run walleye fishing is very popular on Lake Pepin. (Mickey O. Johnson)

Mississippi River

Trempealeau to Lake Pepin

This 50-mile stretch of the Mississippi encompasses pools 5, 6, and 7—between Lake Pepin (near Red Wing, Minnesota) in the north to Lake Onalaska (near La Crosse) in the south. It's part of the 250-mile-long Upper Mississippi River Fish and Wildlife Refuge running between the Chippewa River mouth in Wisconsin to the Rock River mouth in Illinois. The lands within its boundaries are open to fishing, hunting, and camping, except as posted by the refuge. Primitive camping is allowed on sandbars and islands. While some shoreline and wade fishing is possible, a canoe or jonboat greatly expands the angler's options.

When I asked Brad Kaczorowski of West End Bait in Winona, Minnesota about backwater fishing on this stretch of the river, he said you could fish a whole summer and never leave the backwaters. Kaczorowski says this fishery is fairly diverse, with largemouth and smallmouth bass, northern pike, and panfish. There are also rough fish present such as freshwater drum, carp, sucker, and catfish. A variety of habitats can be found, including fallen timber, lotus beds, sloughs, and some wing dams. Kaczorowski says walleye congregate around dams in spring and fall, and smallmouth are just about everywhere. While flyfishers aren't common on these waters, more and more fly anglers are starting to realize the potential of areas like this.

Notable backwaters are the northern reaches of Lake Onalaska near Brice Prairie and the drainage of the Black River. Access this area via Highway Z, which heads northwest out of Onalaska, or via the Trempealeau Lake State Wildlife Area just south of the town of Trempealeau. May and June are the best times for panfish, as they strike aggressively while defending spawning beds. However, if the mosquitoes are tolerable, summer can also be a magical time to explore these fertile places. Launch at Perot State Park (you must pay a park admission fee).

Another notable backwater is the Whitman Dam State Wildlife Area between the towns of Fountain City and Cochrane. Launch at Merrick State Park (you must pay a park admission fee). A smaller complex of sloughs and backwaters can be found at the mouth of the Buffalo River near Alma. Largemouths and pike are also abundant throughout these backwaters.

Small poppers, rubber spiders, even flashy nymphs (weeds permitting) fished on a 4-weight rod will do nicely for panfish. Use a 6-weight rod with poppers and bass bugs if you want to pursue largemouth. For northerns, a 7-weight rod, heavy leader, and a collection of streamers (size 4 and up) will do the trick.

Fishing the main channel of the river is a different sort of experience—grand-scale to some, too big for others. As a rule, you'll be fishing from a boat, and you'll need a dependable outboard. Use a stout fly rod and a reel with a sinking line. Walleye gather below the dams during spring and fall. Dams at Whitman, Minnesota (Dam #5) and at Trempealeau, Wisconsin (Dam #6) are popular walleye spots. This is fast-water, cold-weather, and big-crowd fishing. Anchor among other boats and have at it.

In summer, look for walleye holding in channels, wing dams, and near rocky islands. Use a fast-sinking line and a weighted leech fly. You can find smallmouth in many of these habitats. You can also find smallmouth congregating near sandbars. Fish a minnow- or crawfish-imitation streamer. Pretend the Mississippi is a giant trout stream and work behind fallen trees, against old abutments, in eddies—anywhere that looks fishy. These habitats can sometimes be found near shore, sometimes right in town. For instance, Trempealeau has a good long stretch of riprapped water right at the end of Main Street.

Launches along the river (in addition to those specified in the discussion of backwater fishing) include one at Dam 5A north of Bluff Siding. There are a half-dozen launches between Cochrane and Alma, and a pair north of the Buffalo River in the section of the river known as Big Lake.

Bag limits are as follows for this stretch of the Mississippi. Largemouth and smallmouth bass: minimum size 14 inches, daily limit 5; walleye and sauger: no minimum size sauger, 15-inch minimum walleye, daily limit 6; northern pike: no minimum size, daily limit 5; white bass: no minimum size, daily limit 25; panfish: no minimum size, daily limit 25. A Wisconsin fishing license (resident or nonresident) is valid for fishing either the Wisconsin or Minnesota side of the river. Consult the *Guide to Wisconsin Hook and Line Fishing Regulations* (available where you buy your license) for complete regulations.

HUB CITY: TREMPEALEAU

A shortening of *La Montange qui trempe à l'eau,* the name given by French fur traders to the 425-foot-high bluff rising out of the Mississippi River, Trempealeau is now the name of both a county and a small Mississippi River town in west-central Wisconsin. The town has served variously as a stopping place for barges and the location of a noted house of ill-repute. It is now popular with recreation enthusiasts biking the Great River State Trail and canoeing the backwaters of the Mississippi.

For the angler, it affords good access to warmwater fisheries such as the Mississippi and Black Rivers, as well as a number of clear, sand-bottomed trout streams like Beaver Creek and the Trempealeau River. In spring and fall, the Trempealeau National Wildlife Refuge hosts thousands of migrating waterfowl; drive or bike over dirt roads to view these fertile backwaters.

With just over a thousand residents, Trempealeau lacks chain stores and some services (notably a hospital and veterinarian), but these can be found in nearby Winona, Minnesota or La Crosse, Wisconsin. The payoff is staying in a place where all the business is still done on Main Street.

Accommodations

Trempealeau Hotel, Main Street, Trempealeau; 608-534-6898; restored 1890s hotel with rooms upstairs from restaurant-bar, shared bathroom; live music on some summer weekends; $

Little Bluff Inn, 361 Main Street, Trempealeau, 608-534-6615; remodeled motel with whirlpool and indoor swimming pool; $$

Inn on the River, Main Street, Trempealeau; 608-534-7784; small clean motel with view of river; $

Campgrounds

Perrot State Park, Route #1 Box 407, Trempealeau; 608-534-6409; 97 campsites, scenic hiking, access to Great River State Trail (biking) and Mississippi River backwaters, boat launch

Merrick State Park, Box 182, Fountain City; 608-687-4936; 20 miles north of Trempealeau; located on Mississippi River; boat launch

Restaurants

Trempealeau Hotel, Main Street, Trempealeau; 608-534-6898; limited winter hours; full-service summer; vegetarian options, full menu

Eatery on Main, 220 Main Street, Trempealeau; 608-534-6886; basic down-home café, good food, good value

Ed Sullivan's, on road between Trempealeau Hotel and Perrot State Park; 608-534-7775; tavern-supper club menu with Irish theme and good prices

Hillside Fish House, Highway 35/54, Fountain City; 608-687-6141; great fish dinners in old Indian Agency Depot 10 miles north of Trempealeau

Fly Shops, Outfitters, Sporting Goods

Budget Mart, Highway 35, Trempealeau; 608-534-6554; sells fishing licenses and trout stamps

Gander Mountain, 9519 Highway 16, La Crosse; 608-783-2820

Veterinarians

Van Loon Animal Hospital, W7683 Highway 93, Holmen; 608-526-2210; located 10 miles south of Trempealeau

Medical

Community Memorial Hospital, 855 Mankato Avenue, Winona, MN; 507-454 3650; located 10 miles north of Trempealeau

Gundersen Lutheran, 811 Monitor Street, La Crosse; 608-791-8400; located 20 miles south of Trempealeau

Auto Rental

Enterprise Rent-a-Car, La Crosse; 608-781-7700, 800-736-8222

Automobile Repair

Magnussons, 24047 9th Street; 608-534-8320

Air Service

Municipal Airport, 2850 Airport Drive, La Crosse; 608-789-9385; closest airport of any size, 20 miles south of Trempealeau

For More Information

Trempealeau Chamber of Commerce
P.O. Box 212
Trempealeau, WI 54661
608-534-6780
www.trempealeau.net

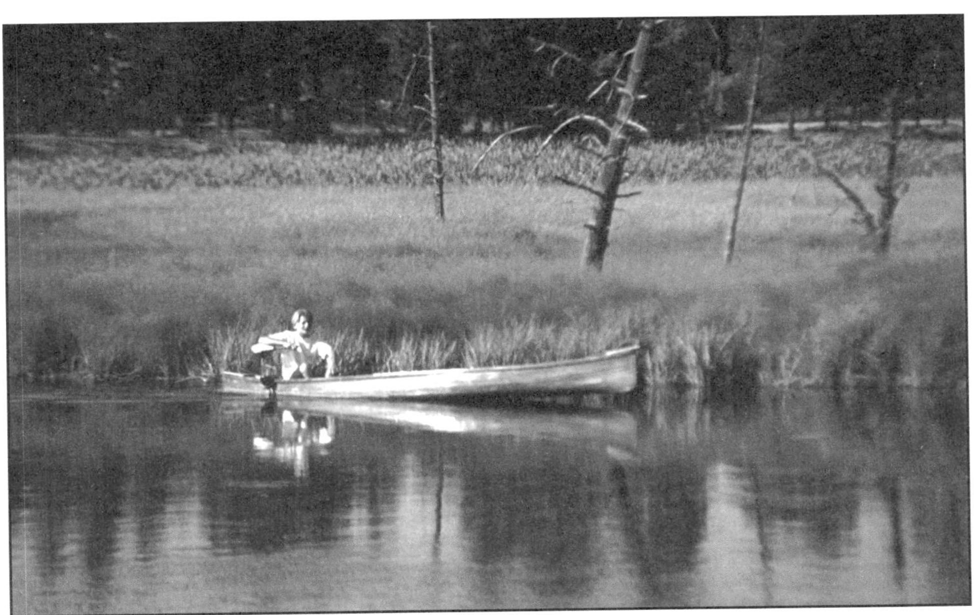

The Black River offers a number of float trips, with plenty of campsites available.

The Black River

Beginning above Neillsville north of Highway 10 and twisting, oxbowing, and meandering through a hundred miles of sand country to its delta at Van Loon State Wildlife Area north of La Crosse, the Black River offers a quintessential Wisconsin float trip ranging anywhere from a few hours to a week. You can camp on sandbars, fish channels for walleye and smallmouth, and ply backwaters for northern and panfish. Anywhere within the floodplain of the river is considered navigable water and is open to public use, including camping. And good chunks of its lower reaches flow through state-owned land, including Black River State Forest, with over a hundred developed campsites and motels just a short drive from the river.

From Black River Falls practically all the way to the river's confluence with the Mississippi, Highway 54 parallels the western shore of the river. You'll see a variety of different ecosystems, ranging from oak forests to pine belts, wooded swamps, and cattail marsh. Timber wolves, diminutive massasauga rattlesnakes, ruffed grouse, bald eagles and a variety of waterfowl call the river corridor home.

The Black River offers a wide variety of fish species and habitats. Fish the running channels for walleye and smallmouth; fish the mouths of creeks (Allen, Levis, Squaw) for the same, plus an occasional northern or brown trout. For larger quarry, a size #4 Muddler Minnow is a good bet. For panfish, try a flashy nymph, Glo-Bug, or fluorescent Woolly Bugger. While the creeks are classified by the DNR as trout streams, I would concentrate my efforts on the Black for warmwater species. Don't interrupt the flow of your float trip for marginal trout fishing.

Channel catfish are present in good numbers throughout the Black River. Right below the dam in Black River Falls is popular for walleye in spring and fall, though it is, to be sure, in-town fishing.

The river begins in earnest as a fishery below Lake Arbutus. The lake itself is a known walleye, northern, and panfish producer, but it is heavily traveled by motorboats so the flyfisher seeking solitude is best off sticking to the river. Below the lake, a popular float is to put in at Halls Creek canoe landing in the state forest, float 5 miles to the town of Black River, and take out before the dam; this would be a good day trip. A good overnight trip can be had by putting in below the dam (there are a number of canoe launches in town) and paddling some 5 miles to make camp for the night at Hawk Island (there are campsites there). Take out the next day at Irving, some 8 miles downriver.

Another float is between Irving and Melrose; this would take be a two-day affair, with Horseshoe Lake being a good stopover point. Horseshoe Lake north of Melrose has a large complex of sloughs associated with it—good panfish and northern fishing for those willing to explore some backwaters.

You can also float between Melrose and North Bend Bottoms; this is 5 miles or so, with good walleye and bass fishing available. Between North Bend Bottoms and Van Loon State Wildlife Area (mouth of the Black) is some 15 miles of less float-friendly water. Still, good numbers of bass, walleye, and, toward Van Loon, panfish and northerns are present.

A canoe or jonboat is the best way to fish the Black. Anything larger will be unwieldy in its numerous backwaters.

A word to the wise: Call Black River State Forest (715-284-5301) to ask about mosquitoes and black flies. They can ruin a trip in a hurry, especially during wet summers.

The La Crosse River

According to DNR fisheries biologist Dave Vetrano, the La Crosse River sits on a transition zone between sand-bottomed streams to the north (such as the Buffalo and Trempealeau Rivers) and the more fertile limestone, rubble-bottom coulees to the south (such as Timber Coulee). The La Crosse River begins above Fort McCoy near Tomah and flows southwest, more or less paralleling Interstate 90. It is category 2 for its entire 40-mile run. The La Crosse River empties into the Mississippi River at the city of La Crosse.

Impoundments along the river (Angelo Pond, Perch Lake, and Lake Neshonoc) adversely affect its ability to grow trout. However, a good trout fishery exists in the upper reaches, and some monster browns are found in tributaries of the La Crosse. For those interested in pursuing catfish, Vetrano says the La Crosse River has a dense population of flathead and channel cats (some to 40 pounds) between Lake Neshonoc and La Crosse.

On the La Crosse proper, trout fishermen should concentrate their efforts in the water above Angelo Pond. Access to this stretch is via the La Crosse River State Fishery Area off County I; look for the dirt track on your right hand side heading toward the river.

Farther upstream, you'll be in Fort McCoy. To fish this stretch you will need to obtain a permit from Fort McCoy's headquarters on Highway 21. There are brook and brown trout present in respectable numbers. Vetrano says that insect surveys in the stream have turned up very high populations of caddis, especially near woody debris. In fact, woody debris is the best (and sometimes the only) kind of cover to work in sand-bottomed streams like the La Crosse. Make careful approaches and fish a small Hare's Ear tight to cover. If you are after the La Crosse's larger brook trout or brown trout, tie on a Muddler Minnow or a leech and fish this clear stream during low-light conditions or after a rain. Scuds are present in modest numbers, as are forage fish and mayflies.

The stretch of the La Crosse between Rockland and Lake Neshonoc is noteworthy because of its big-fish-producing tributaries. Vetrano mentions the Little La Crosse River, which begins near Cashton and joins the La Crosse River downstream from Sparta, as a stream that's received recent habitat attention and holds some very large browns. Access to the Little La Crosse is via Highway 27; it is category 2.

Dutch Creek, another tributary of the La Crosse River, yielded a 11.25-pound, 28.5-inch brown trout recently, according to Vetrano. Dutch Creek runs between Middle Valley and Rockland along Highway 162; it is category 3. You can access the La Crosse River in this stretch at Highway J or Highway 162. Trout densities are not high here, but there is always the potential of nailing a real trophy on a minnow imitation.

Below Lake Neshonoc, you'll find mostly catfish and a few bass. Access is via Highway 16 and County M and County B. Vetrano said an electroshock survey turned up large numbers of catfish here, along with rough fish, and the cats were holding next to fallen trees. If you want to go after big cats on a fly rod (something you rarely hear discussed), this would be a good stream in which to do it, as it's fairly shallow and the fish can be reached by using a sinking line or by adding split shot above the fly. Try a leech pattern—the bigger, the better.

FISHING THE CRANBERRY FLOWAGES

Cranberries pay a number of dividends to central Wisconsin. They bring money to an area with few other sources of revenue. In fact, since the middle part of the 19th century, cranberries have been the backbone of the economy in this region—cranberry growers have been accorded special privileges dating back to the state constitution. The cranberry flowages, in addition to giving us something to eat with our turkey, can offer outstanding fishing. Big northerns and largemouths, as well as panfish the size of dinner plates, are typical flowage denizens. In addition, it's a peaceful (if somewhat unfamiliar) atmosphere, and you needn't worry about powerboats swamping your canoe.

What's the catch? They are private land and not covered under Wisconsin's navigable public water law. This doesn't necessarily mean they are inaccessible, but it does mean you need the owner's permission to fish them. There are a number of ways to go. Buy a plat map of the county you wish to fish for help in locating landowners. (Rockford Maps sells these for individual counties; call 815-399-4614 to order.) Or simply go farm to farm and ask permission (disadvantages: farmers are sometimes hard to find and you can't tell a barren flowage from a productive one just by looking). Better yet, ask for Bob (715-284-4621) at Moe Hardware on Main Street in Black River Falls. He's up to date on which growers allow fishermen, when bogs are being sprayed with pesticides, and when particular owners are harvesting.

There are dozens of flowages in Monroe and Jackson Counties alone, with more in Wood County toward Wisconsin Rapids. A canoe, jonboat, or belly boat will be a big help here, but you can still enjoy some fine fishing from shore or by wading. For panfish and bass in spring, fish the weedbeds with poppers. In summer, panfish tend to congregate around dikes and in deeper, cooler water; try for them with a flashy nymph or fluorescent Woolly Bugger. A good way to take bass and northerns is to fish toward shore from your boat. That means you will be working the cover and shade provided by the banks, but being in a boat will reduce the chance of spooking fish. Old stumpfields are another good area. For northerns, strip gaudy streamers through the shallows. For bass, try skittering a bass bug across the surface.

Enjoy this unique fishery, but make sure to respect the properties so other anglers can continue to enjoy it, too.

Potters Flowage

A fairly isolated flowage on the outskirts of Black River State Forest, 350-acre Potters Flowage offers a lively mixed bag of fishing. Dave Hatleli, area DNR fisheries biologist, says it is predominantly a panfish fishery, holding good numbers of black crappie and bluegill. Black crappie are ubiquitous in central Wisconsin flowages, according to Hatleli, and can tolerate the relatively infertile water and dearth of cover better than many other panfish species.

Hatleli says Potters is also planted with muskies, which are sometimes gulped down by the flowage's eat-anything northerns. Largemouth bass are present in good numbers, as well. Efforts at tracking growth rate and reproduction among muskies are in the beginning stages, according to Hatleli. Periodic winterkills and lack of forage fish do not help the fledgling population of muskies here, but panfish, northerns, and bass don't seem to be bothered much.

To reach Potters Flowage, take Interstate 94 to Millston, find North Settlement Road, and follow it approximately 20 miles to Potters Road. There is a launch on Jensen Road on the north end of the flowage and one on Potters Road on the south. A small boat will open up your fishing possibilities here.

Flowages have their detractors and advocates. Those who dislike them say they are manmade, lack cover, and are infertile. Perhaps, but the other side of the coin is that they are, when small like Potters, easy to read: concentrate your efforts in the stumpfields and weeds along the shorelines; ignore the deeper middle sections, which lack cover and food.

The nice thing about the fish being relatively concentrated is the chance to pick up a variety of species. The angler would be best to divide his targets, however, into panfish-bass and muskie-northern. The former can be taken on a 5-weight rod, fishing a light leader and small spiders, poppers, or bass bugs. Poppers are the way to go when Potters weeds up in summer. The east and west ends of Potter have good weeds and good bass and panfish populations.

As for big game, use an 8-weight rod with plenty of backing and heavy leaders. Gaudy streamers will get their attention. Inflows and outflows, along with deeper holes at the edge of cover, are good spots to work for pike and muskie.

Muskie must be a minimum of 40 inches and only one may be kept. Otherwise, Potters Flowage follows the bag and size limits for Wisconsin's Southern Zone. So, while some write off central Wisconsin flowages as infertile and artificial, I like to fish them for a variety of species. Don't let your fly rod gather dust after trout season is over or if the finicky salmonoids aren't cooperating. And as you may find yourself at Potters Flowage in autumn, bring your duck or grouse gun. You can wander among the aspen stands or gun the various flowages within Black River Falls State Forest for mallard, wood duck, teal, and an occasional black duck.

A canoe, jonboat, or belly boat will be a big help flyfishing the weedbeds in Wisconsin's flowages.

Hub City: Black River Falls

The first white settlers came to the area in 1819, establishing a camp at the prominent falls on the Black River. In the mid-19th century, Black River Falls was a lumbering and sawmilling center with high populations of Scandinavian, German, and Eastern European immigrants. Cranberries are a major cash crop and have been for 150 years. Modest farming operations have tried to make a go of it in the sandy soil, with potatoes and corn being major products.

Now, Black River Falls is an ideal base for recreation on the 50,000-acre Black River Falls State Forest. For the flyfisher, the Buffalo and Trempealeau Rivers are good nearby trout streams with plenty of public access. The Black River hosts a good mix of warmwater species and is an ideal water to fish on a float trip. The cranberry flowages can be terrific for panfish and northerns. If you plan to camp at Black River Falls State Forest, check with the ranger station about bugs. I've had to check into a motel on a few occasions while visiting the area because of mosquitoes and black flies, which can be brutal in June and July.

A cluster of hotels and chain restaurants are located off the interstate at Exit 116. Older businesses are located on Main Street near the falls.

Accommodations

Best Western Arrowhead Lodge, 600 Oasis Road, Black River Falls; 715 284 9471; comfortable lodging with adjoining restaurant, right off interstate

Super 8 Motel, W10090 Highway 54, Black River Falls; 715-284-3320, 800-800-8000; located right off interstate; $$

Falls Economy Motel, 512 E. Second Street, Black River Falls; 715-284-9919; located in quiet area just outside of town, convenient to public lands; $

Trails End Cabins and Resort, County J, Hatfield/contact Donna Austin; 888-269-6118; modern cabin north of Black River Falls; $$

Campgrounds

Black River Falls State Forest, Route 4, Box 18, Black River Falls; 715-284-5301

Merlin Lambert County Park and Campground, 20 campsites, take Highway 54 east to McKenna Road, south on McKenna Road 4 miles

Spaulding Pond, located on Highway 54 east, 22 miles from interstate

Restaurants

Perkins, Highway 54 and Interstate 94 (Exit 116), Black River Falls; 715-284-2223

Orange Moose Inn, 600 Oasis Road; 715 284 9471; restaurant connected to Best Western Arrowhead Lodge

Country Café, 18 Main Street, Black River Falls; 715-284-1636; good breakfast, in downtown

Castle Hill Supper Club, Highway 12, Black River Falls; 715-333-5901; steaks, seafood, drinks located north of Black River Falls

Fly Shops, Outfitters, Sporting Goods

Moe Hardware, Main Street, Black River Falls; 715-284-4621; talk to Bob to inquire about fishing local cranberry flowages

Dugan's How-to and Rent-it Center, 306 E. Main Street, Black River Falls; 715-284-4815

Gander Mountain, 9519 Highway 16, La Crosse; 608-783-2820

Veterinarians

Hart Veterinary Service, 310 County A, Black River Falls; 715-284-4424

Medical

Black River Falls Memorial Hospital, 711 W. Adams Street, Black River Falls; 715-284-5361

Auto Rental

Riverside Auto Rentals, N5856 Highway 54, Black River Falls; 715-284-4525

Enterprise Rent-a-Car, La Crosse; 608-781-7700, 800-736-8222

Automobile Repair

Black River Falls Auto Sales, 303 County A, Black River Falls; 715-284-2918

Air Service

Municipal Airport, 2850 Airport Drive, La Crosse; 608-789-9385; closest airport of any size is 30 miles west of Black River Falls

For More Information

Chamber of Commerce
120 N. Water Street
Black River Falls, WI 54615
715-284-4658
www.blackrivercountry.net

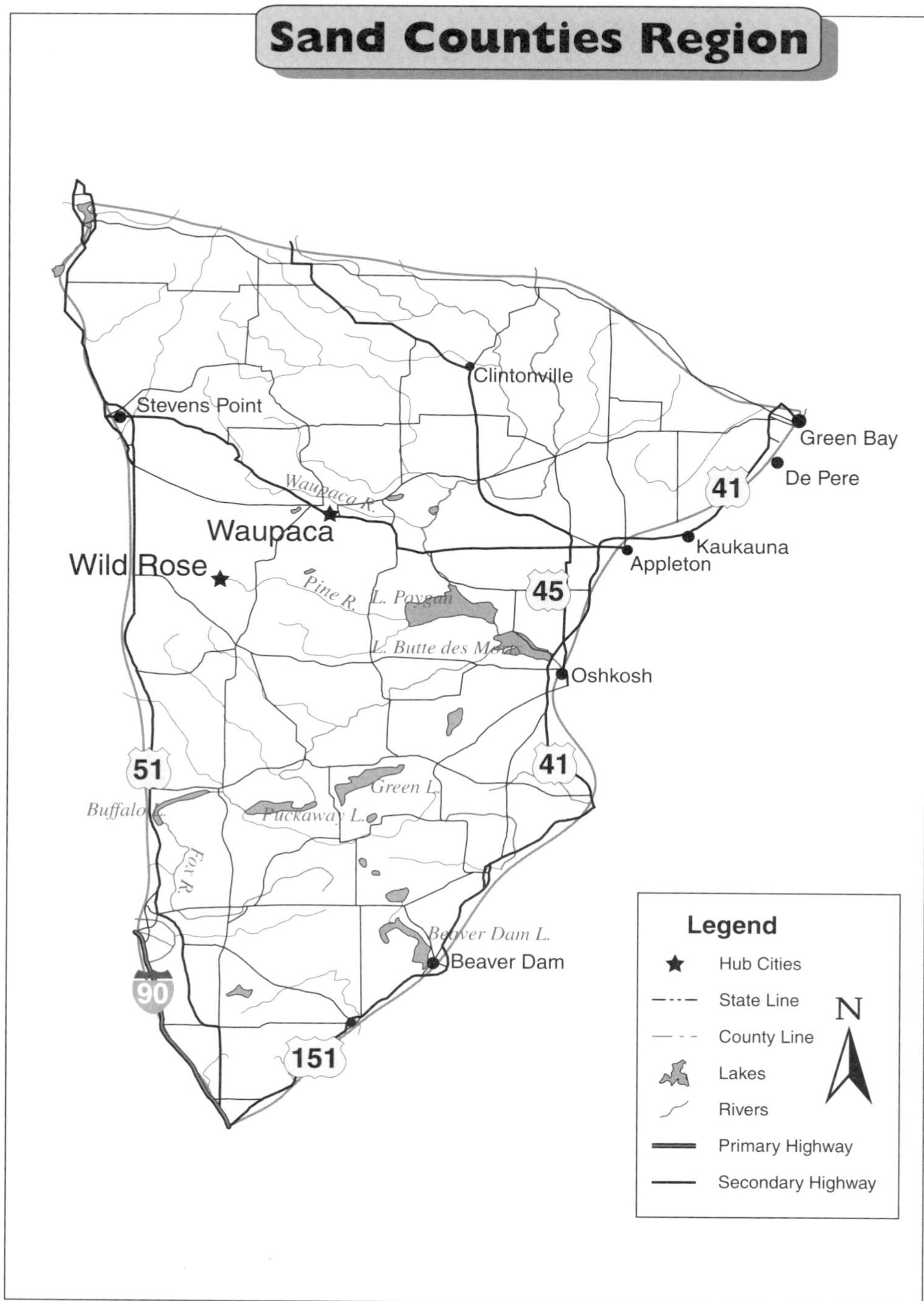
Sand Counties Region
Clintonville
Stevens Point
Green Bay
De Pere
41
Waupaca R.
Waupaca
Wild Rose
Kaukauna
Appleton
Pine R.
L. Poygan
45
L. Butte des Morts
Oshkosh
51
41
Green L.
Buffalo L.
Puckaway L.
Fox R.
Beaver Dam L.
Beaver Dam
90
151
Legend
Hub Cities
State Line
County Line
Lakes
Rivers
Primary Highway
Secondary Highway
N

Central Wisconsin: The Sand Counties

Beginning an hour north of Madison and stretching northward to the southern fringes of pine country near Wausau, Wisconsin's Sand Counties were immortalized in Aldo Leopold's nature classic *Sand County Almanac.* Columbia, Adams, Marquette, Waushara, and Waupaca Counties all evince the gently rolling sandy terrain, once part of vast glacial Lake Wisconsin. Many fine Sand County streams rise from the glacial moraine running northeast of Westfield and visible from Highway 51—all fed by the vast Central Sands Aquifer. The same water that feeds these trout streams is of interest to the global spring water bottling giant, Perrier. "No Way, Perrier!" is a bumper sticker that reflects local sentiment, and so far no well has been tapped. But this is an ongoing concern, and appeals for such things can drag on for decades. We can only hope that no well is sunk here, and we can support organizations aligned with preserving the aquifer.

The Mecan River with its slow glides and clear sandy water is a classic Sand County stream, as are its feeders, such as Chaffee and Caves Creek. The silt-loving *Hexagenia* mayfly makes its home along the banks of the Mecan and then erupts into an explosive evening hatch, typically during the last week of June. This is traditionally fished at night with large bushy dry flies like the White Wulff, although big nymphs

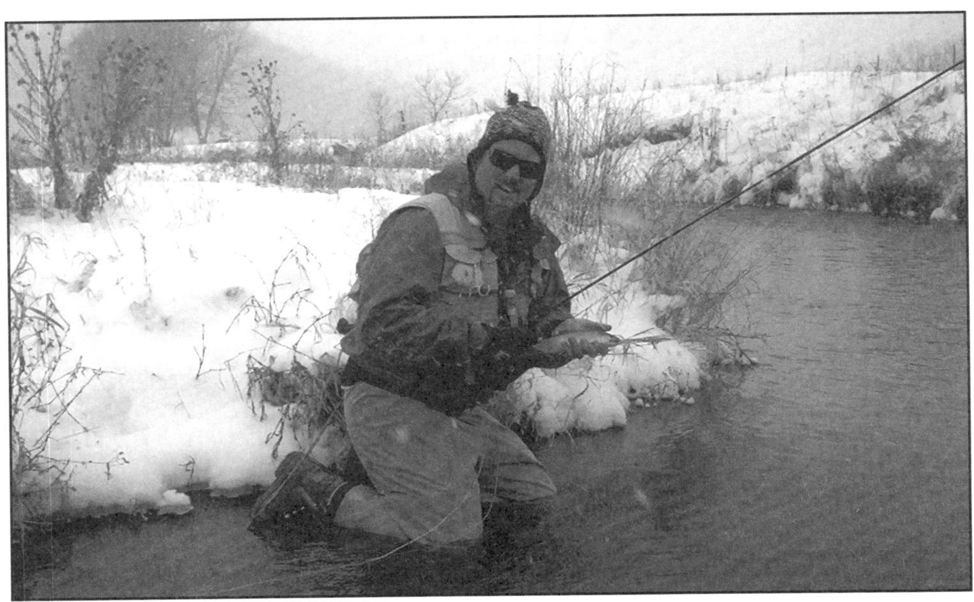

Bart Landwehr fishing during the early season. (Tim Landwehr)

HATCH CHART—Central Wisconsin: The Sand Counties

Insect/Food Source	J	F	M	A	M	J	J	A	S	O	N	D	Flies
Midges			■	■	■	■	■	■	■				Midge Pupa #16-22; Griffith's Gnat #16-22
Little Black Caddis			■	■	■								Micro Black Caddis #16-22; Caddis Larvae (dark) #16-22; Beadhead Caddis (dark) #16
Willow Stonefly (*Leuctra*)			■	■	■	■							Tiny Black Stone #14-18; Prince Nymph #14-16
Blue-Winged Olives (*Baetis*)				■	■	■	■	■	■				BWO Thorax, Sparkle Dun #16-22; Pheasant Tail #16-18
Hendricksons				■	■								Light Hendrickson, Spinners #12-14; Pheasant Tail #12-14
Sulphurs					■								Sulphur Dun, Pale Evening Dun, Spinner #16; Pheasant Tail Nymph #16
Caddis					■	■	■	■	■				Elk Hair Caddis #14-16; Sparkle Pupa, Beadhead Caddis, Caddis Larvae #16-20
March Brown					■								March Brown, Spinner, Hare's Ear Nymph #12-14
Hexagenia (Evening Hatch)						■	■						Hart Washer, Hex, Olive Drake #4-8; Hex Nymph, Strip Nymph #4-8/Late June #10

HATCH CHART—Central Wisconsin: The Sand Counties (cont.)

Insect/Food Source	J	F	M	A	M	J	J	A	S	O	N	D	Flies
Red Quill				■	■								Red Quill, Rusty Spinner #14
Trico							■	■	■				Tiny White Wing Black, CDC Trico, Spent Wing Trico #24-28
White Mayfly (*Ephoron leukon*) (Evening Hatch)							■	■	■				White Wulff, White Miller #12-14
Other Stoneflies					■	■	■	■	■				Yellow Stimulator #10-12; Stonefly Nymphs #8-10
Scuds			■	■	■	■	■	■	■				Pink, Olive, Tan Scuds #14-18
Leeches			■	■	■	■	■	■	■				Marabou Leech, Strip Leech (Black, Olive, Brown) #4-10
Sculpin			■	■	■	■	■	■	■				Muddler Minnow, Olive or Brown Leech #8-10
Crawfish			■	■	■	■	■	■	■				Crayfish Patterns, Marabou Leech Olive/Brown #8-10
Ants, Beetles, Crickets					■	■	■	■	■				Standard Ant Patterns #14-20; Beetles #16-20; Crickets #8-10
Grasshoppers							■	■	■				Dave's Hopper, Parachute Hopper #6-10

and emergers can be fished during the day with some success. Other Sand County Hex favorites are the White and the Tomorrow. Tiny Lawrence Creek outside of Westfield is a gem of a brook trout stream that has improved greatly over the years through DNR efforts and careful study.

Good early stonefly and caddis hatches can be found on many of these streams during the March and April season. But be sure to consult page 1 of the *Wisconsin Trout Fishing Regulations and Guide* to make sure the water you plan to fish is open to fishing during this early season, as certain portions of streams are closed during this season. A complex of glacial kettle lakes just to the east of Oxford provides good two-tier fishing, with trout taken in the early season and bass and bluegill biting later on. These are Wolf, Deep, Parker, and Jordan Lakes.

There is a quiet poetry to the strawberry and potato farms, clear streams, and sand swales of this region. I hope you will get out to see just how special they are. One point that can't be stressed enough is that these streams are gin-clear. Light leaders, careful wading, and low-light conditions will all increase your chances for taking Sand County brookies and browns.

Lawrence Creek

A fine central Wisconsin brook trout stream that has received much habitat work and study under former DNR fisheries biologist Robert Hunt, Lawrence Creek straddles the Adams-Marquette County line. Lawrence Creek drains toward Lake Michigan along the Lake Michigan–Mississippi River drainage line marked by the glacial moraine snaking through central Wisconsin.

From its headwaters to Lawrence Lake—some 3 miles—Lawrence Creek is category 2. From Lawrence Lake downstream for 6 more miles to where the creek is known as Westfield Creek, it is category 3. The upper part of Lawrence Creek runs through the 961-acre Lawrence Creek Wildlife Area, accessible via Eagle Avenue. You'll be fishing among the classic central Wisconsin scenery of bogs, spring ponds, marsh, and oak forest. Clear water and limited cover mean you will need to present your fly with care. The brook trout of Lawrence Creek are colorful little jewels. Savor them and the scenery, and think of Aldo Leopold, father of wildlife ecology, whose legacy lives on in restoration work on Lawrence Creek.

A rich mix of insect life makes itself at home in the sand and marl bottom of Lawrence Creek. Stoneflies and caddis are present in good numbers, and they begin to emerge in March and April. A small Prince Nymph or dark beadhead caddis fished tight to cover will do well during these early months. Caddis larvae imitations are another logical choice. Carry midges and Blue-Winged Olives in your fly box as they are present all season on Lawrence Creek. Sulphurs and Hendricksons show up, respectively, in May and June.

Terrestrial fishing is good on Lawrence Creek, too. While July and August are good times to float a Dave's Hopper up against the bank, beetle and ant flies can be fished anytime and crickets are effective as early as June. Depending on the year, you may find the *Ephoron leukon*, or White Mayfly, hatch during August, which can be fished effectively with a size 14 White Wulff.

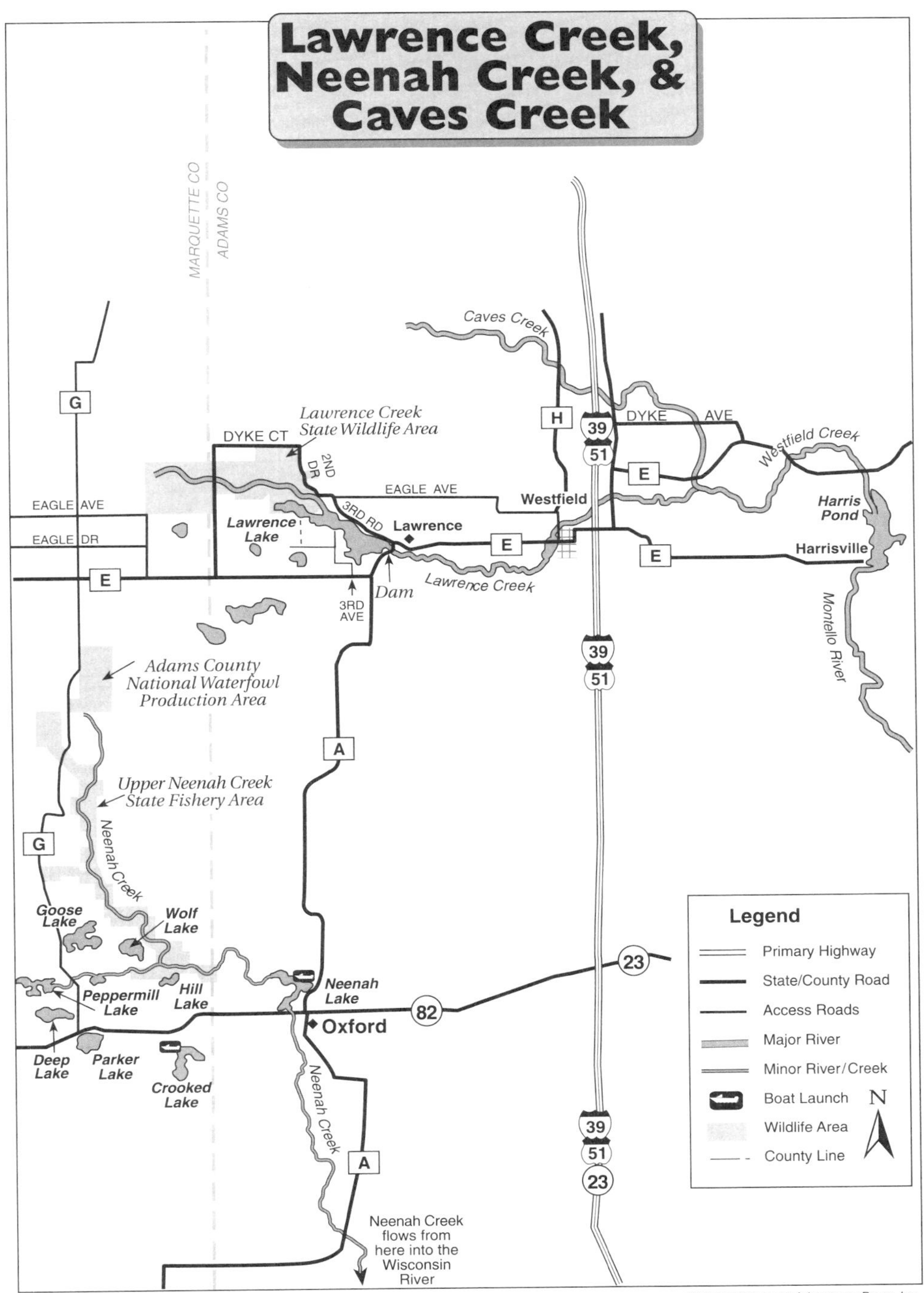

Lawrence Creek, Neenah Creek, & Caves Creek
MARQUETTE CO
ADAMS CO
Caves Creek
Lawrence Creek State Wildlife Area
DYKE CT
2ND DR
DYKE AVE
Westfield Creek
EAGLE AVE
3RD RD
Westfield
Lawrence Lake
Lawrence
Harris Pond
EAGLE AVE
EAGLE DR
Harrisville
Dam
Lawrence Creek
3RD AVE
Montello River
Adams County National Waterfowl Production Area
Upper Neenah Creek State Fishery Area
Neenah Creek
Goose Lake
Wolf Lake
Peppermill Lake
Hill Lake
Neenah Lake
Oxford
Deep Lake
Parker Lake
Crooked Lake
Neenah Creek
Neenah Creek flows from here into the Wisconsin River
Legend
Primary Highway
State/County Road
Access Roads
Major River
Minor River/Creek
Boat Launch
Wildlife Area
County Line
N

A bonus fishery here is Lawrence Lake, an impoundment of Lawrence Creek. You'll want to fish this weedy pond from a canoe or belly boat. There are boat launches off Eagle Avenue on the eastern shore of the lake and off the road running along the west shore. Anglers can try for the usual warmwater species such as northern pike, largemouth bass, and panfish among shoreline weedbeds and stumps. Try a small popper or any flashy nymph for bluegills; go with a deer-hair streamer for bass and pike. There's also the chance of tying into a brook trout grown fat on forage fish.

If you're after brook trout, fish with big streamers just above the dam or in the lake channel right after ice-out. After Lawrence Lake's waters warm in June, brookies move back upstream to the colder waters of Lawrence Creek.

Below the dam, Lawrence Creek becomes Westfield Creek, a category 3 trout stream. The stream flows through Westfield, beneath Highway 51, and ultimately into Harris Pond. Access Westfield Creek via Highway E.

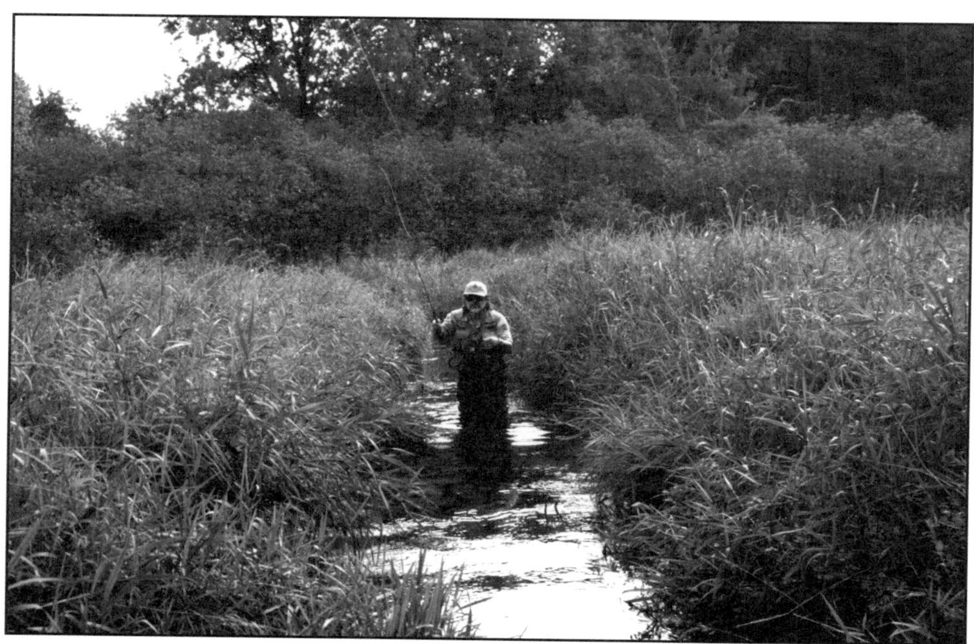

Lawrence Creek. (Chris Halla)

Stream Facts: Lawrence Creek

Season

- The early season runs from the first Saturday in March to the last Sunday before the first Saturday in May; no-kill, single barbless hooks only. Regular season runs from the first Saturday in May at 5:00 am through September 30.

Regulations

- Above Lawrence Lake, category 2; below Lawrence Lake, category 3.

Species

- Wild brook trout

Miles of Trout Water

- 9 miles

Stream Characteristics

- Clear sand-bottom creek, much studied and worked on by Wisconsin DNR; impoundment at Lawrence Lake with chance for larger brook trout and warmwater species.

Access

- Lawrence Creek State Wildlife Area off of Eagle Avenue west of Westfield; boat launches on Lawrence Lake.

Fly Shops

- Tight Lines Fly Fishing Company

Maps

- *Wisconsin Atlas and Gazetteer*, page 43, 44

Neenah Creek

Another fine Sand County trout stream is Neenah Creek. You will find it near Oxford straddling the Marquette-Adams County border. Highway 82 and Neenah Lake Dam separate category 5 (artificials only 2-trout limit with minimum size of 14 inches) from the category 3 water. Concentrate your efforts in the category 5 area, as water quality below Neenah Lake is much poorer due to the impoundment. You'll still have 6 miles of stream to fish, much of it running through public land. Take Highway E north out of Oxford to Highway A and follow A into the Upper Neenah Creek Fishery Area.

Like Rocky Run and Rowan Creek to the south and Lawrence Creek to the north, Neenah Creek is a cold, spring-fed stream running over a combination of sand and gravel bottom with muck in some areas. And like its Sand County counterparts it needs to be fished with much care, in low light, and/or during cloudy weather. A tiny nymph on a long leader is the name of the game here. A minnow imitation fished around logjam might coax out one of Neenah Creek's larger browns.

Neenah Creek is open to fishing during the March and April catch-and-release season.

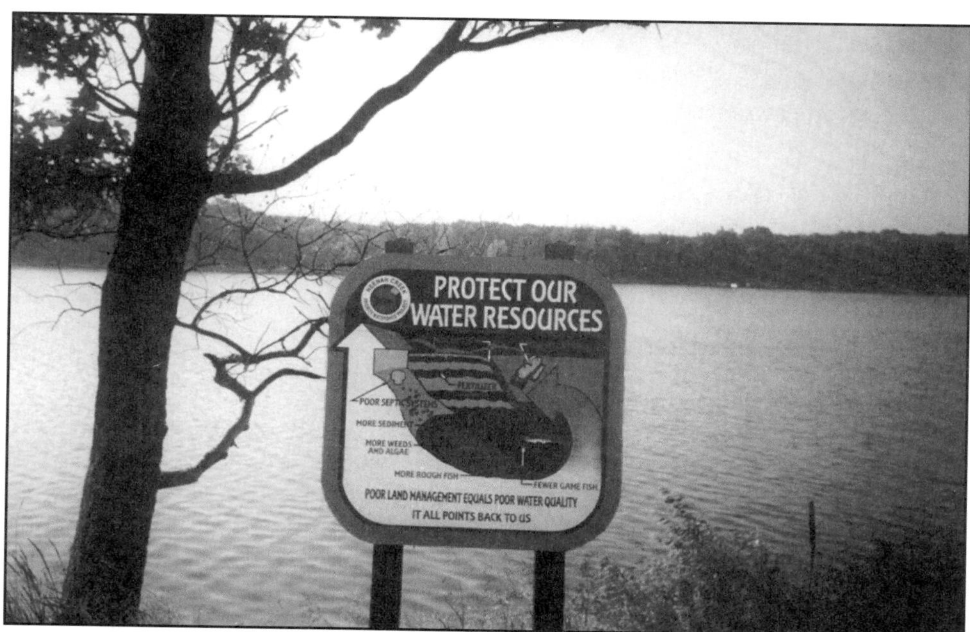

Good land use is no accident.

Caves Creek

This 6-mile brook trout stream flowing just to the east of Westfield is worth the angler's time. It can be reached by taking Highway J to Highway JJ and turning onto the dirt track that leads to DNR land. Some of my best fishing has been in this immediate stretch. A Prince Nymph is a good fly here on brookies that run between 8 and 11 inches. Fish Caves during the early season and into May; consider it again after September's cool has diminished the mosquito and deer fly swarms. Caves Creek is category 2. You can also access Caves on Dyke Avenue, which comes of Highway JJ to the east.

Mecan River

Beginning in the headwater spring pond known as Mecan Springs and emptying into Germania Marsh, a broad central Wisconsin wetland flecked by islands of wild rice, the storied Mecan River provides the flyfisher with 17 miles of trout water in which to ply his trade. All three species of trout are present and reproduce naturally in these 17 miles. Warmwater anglers can work the 20 miles between the marsh and the Mecan's confluence with the Fox River.

Glacial ridges and scrubby pine and oak woods characterize the surrounding area known as the Central Sands region. In fact, according to retired DNR land purchasing agent Elward Engle, you can see a ridge of glacial moraine running between Coloma and Plainfield; it marks the Lake Michigan–Mississippi River drainage. Streams to the east of this line (like the Mecan) drain toward Lake Michigan, those to the west (like Roche a Cri) drain toward the Mississippi River. Both partake of the pure waters of the vast Central Sands Aquifer.

This quality water source, bubbling up through sandy moraine, is one reason for the pure water of streams like the Mecan. The DNR owns 6,000 acres bordering the Mecan and its key tributaries, helping to secure this fishery for generations to come. However, even the most rudimentary grasp of water ecology tells you that depletion of the Central Sands Aquifer could potentially have devastating impacts upon area streams. Local citizens of broad stripe argue that despite what scientists say and despite promises from Perrier, who wants to tap into the aquifer, one mistake is all it takes to ruin what Sand County farmers, citizens, and sportsmen depend on: clear water. And that's hard to argue against.

The Mecan begins below Mecan Springs as a wide river, between 50 and 75 feet across, and is best known for explosive nighttime Hex fishing in mid-June. Here, of a mid-June evening, reserved German brown trout, which normally spook at the slightest mis-step in these gin-clear waters, feed with abandon on the big Midwestern mayfly. How do you know when the Hex hatch is in full swing? According to Elward Engle, it usually peaks between June 10 and June 15. The exact date depends on the number of warm days around this time. A warm (but not hot) evening helps, he says. Action really gets going about 9:30 and can last until midnight. If an angler can maintain equilibrium amid the bats, darkness, and brick-size trout smacking the

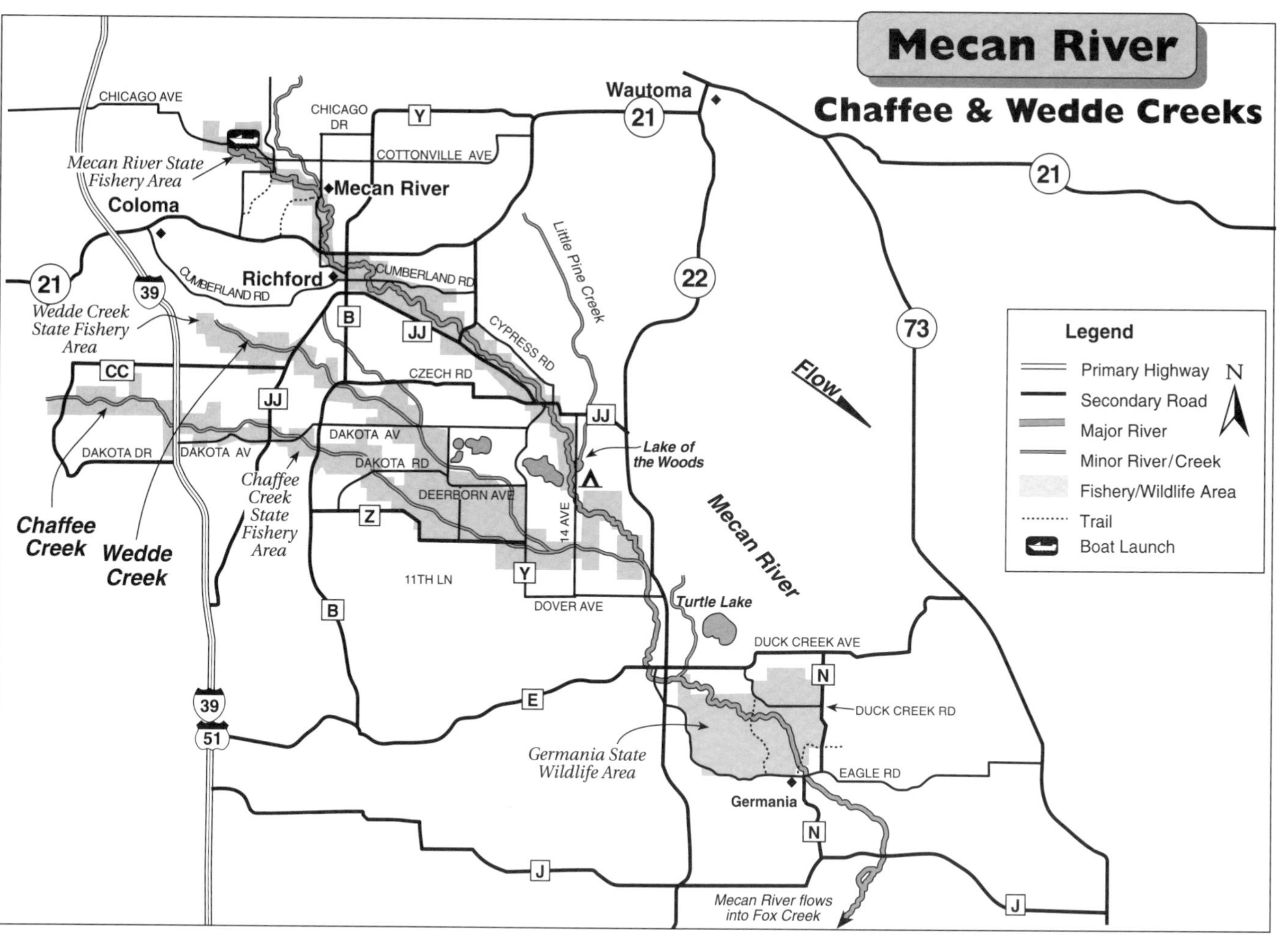
Mecan River
Chaffee & Wedde Creeks
Legend
Primary Highway
Secondary Road
Major River
Minor River/Creek
Fishery/Wildlife Area
Trail
Boat Launch
N
Flow
Wautoma
CHICAGO AVE
CHICAGO DR
COTTONVILLE AVE
Mecan River State Fishery Area
Mecan River
Coloma
Richford
CUMBERLAND RD
Little Pine Creek
CYPRESS RD
Wedde Creek State Fishery Area
CZECH RD
DAKOTA AV
DAKOTA RD
DAKOTA DR
Lake of the Woods
DEERBORN AVE
14 AVE
Chaffee Creek State Fishery Area
Chaffee Creek
Wedde Creek
11TH LN
DOVER AVE
Mecan River
Turtle Lake
DUCK CREEK AVE
DUCK CREEK RD
EAGLE RD
Germania State Wildlife Area
Germania
Mecan River flows into Fox Creek
21
22
73
39
51
Y
B
JJ
CC
Z
E
N
J

Checking out the water from the launch ramp at Mecan Springs.

water, he or she might take one of the 5-pound trophies the Mecan coughs up each year at Hex time.

Tim Landwehr, owner of Tight Lines Fly Fishing Company in De Pere, adds that you can pick up trout during the day during Hex time by fishing Hex nymphs or emergers. He notes that Hex nymphs (present year-round) are going to be active a few weeks before and after the peak of the hatch. A fly called the Gray Leech, tied by Wisconsin angler Ross Mueller, does a good job of imitating a Hex nymph.

A "little sister" to *Hexagenia limbata* is *Hexagenia atrocaudata*; this mayfly hatches well into July and can be imitated with a size 10 version of any Hex pattern. This hatch can also be nymphed in the manner described above. With a willingness to fish nymphs and smaller flies, an angler can turn what's normally viewed as a one-night-stand into a fishing courtship that lasts a month or more.

While the Mecan's not necessarily known as a big-trout stream, it does yield sizable browns each year during the Hex hatch. Fishing the Hex must be done with care, not so much for the sake of the fish (who are feeding ravenously and not overly selective), but for the sake of keeping your limbs intact. Scout the area you plan to fish while there is still daylight and mark obvious deadfalls and holes. Carry a small flashlight and consider going out with a fishing chum.

The Mecan is no one-hatch wonder, though. Stonefly and caddis hatches occur as early as March and April. The first hatches of the year offer the angler a chance to pursue fish that are a bit rusty. Landwehr says you can use halfbacks, beadhead caddis, generic stonefly imitations, as well as the tried and true Prince Nymph. Caddis larvae patterns in size 12 or 14 are also productive. Blue-Winged Olives and midges are present all season. The peak emergence for Hendricksons is mid-May to mid-June, with Sulphurs about a month later.

You can fish beetles and ants as early as May, according to Landwehr. He fishes parachute-style imitations close to the bank. Landwehr also fishes a Dave's Hopper or Parachute Hopper during July and August. As dace and sculpins are present in good numbers, you'll want to have some Marabou Muddlers (yellow, white, and black) and a variety of leech imitations in your box. When all else fails, according to Landwehr, skitter an Elk Hair Caddis over promising water and you're likely to provoke a strike. The White Mayfly hatch in August can be very lively, but Landwehr cautions against overstressing trout in water temperatures that might rise into the dangerous mid-70s. Fish this hatch on top with a White Wulff in size 12.

Access the upper Mecan and Mecan Springs via Highway GG from the dirt track just east of GG off Highway 21 (east of Coloma) or from the Highway 21 bridge. This upper section of the stream has numerous gravel-bottom runs, fast riffles, and small pools—perfect spawning habitat. Highway JJ also follows the stream southeast. As it widens, gravel gives way to sand as the dominant bottom structure. Seek out undercut banks, fallen trees, or canopies created by tag alders flecking the stream. Caddis and stonefly nymphs do well if fished close to fallen trees.

Fourteenth Avenue is the next bridge crossing, which also crosses Wedde/Chaffee Creek. This marks the dividing line on the Mecan between category 3 water upstream, and category 5 water downstream. (The category 5 stretch is artificials only; 3 trout may be kept with a 12-inch minimum size. Only 1 trout over 15 inches may be kept.)

Wedde and Chaffee Creeks are excellent streams in their own right and important trout-rearing tributaries; careful nymphing (try a Prince Nymph) is a good way to explore these clear feeder streams. Wedde Creek is category 2. Road crossing are County B, Dakota Avenue, 11th Drive, County Z, County Y, and 14th Avenue. It's a small creek with a sandy bottom fringed with tag alders.

Chaffee Creek is crossed by Highway B, then paralleled by Highway Z. Upstream from County B, Chaffee Creek is category 2; from B to the Mecan River it is category 3. Both Chaffee and Wedde Creek have good public access via public lands along Highway B. Wedde Creek is open during the early March and April season, as is the portion of Chaffee downstream from Highway B.

The Mecan River State Wildlife Area is located below 14th Avenue. Highway 22 follows the river in this stretch. Dixie Road, Dover Road, Highway E, and finally Highway 22 cross the river before it enters the Germania Marsh Wildlife Area, a stopover point for migrant ducks and geese. A dirt track running between Eagle Road to the south and Duck Creek Road to the north provides access and a launch.

This lower portion of the Mecan is a lovely float. It's at the lower end of trout water, but trout are still present, especially early in the year. You're also likely to tie into a northern pike or smallmouth bass. The dam at the outlet of Germania Marsh marks the end of trout water. The Mecan River below Germania Marsh is mainly known as a duck hunter's float. Eagle Road, Highway J, Highway N, Highway 23, and Highway

C cross it before it joins the north of Lake Puckaway. Adventurous anglers will find northern pike and smallmouth bass in its reedy bends and oxbows.

Curiously, Mecan Springs in the Mecan's headwaters is also a known producer of bass, big northern pike, and panfish; trout are present when water temperatures cool, and it is managed as category 3. You can put in a canoe or belly boat from the boat launch on the north end of the springs. Follow Highway GG north from Highway 21, crossing the Mecan just below the springs, and take your first left. This is Chicago Road; the launch will be on your left, most of the way up the pond.

The Mecan is also a popular canoe route, especially during summer. And justifiably so, as it's a beautiful river. As frustrating as this may be for anglers, these folks have a right to use the river, too. If they are canoeing in the proper spirit, quietly slipping along among the tag alders, trout should not be much disturbed. One way around this is to fish early or late in the day, during the week, or in September. Midday can be a tough time to fish bright, clear water.

Also, only the portion of the Mecan upstream from Highway 22 is open to trout fishing during the March and April season; below Highway 22 it is open to trout fishing from the first Saturday in May.

Stream Facts: Mecan River

Season
- The early season runs from the first Saturday in March to the last Sunday before the first Saturday in May; no-kill, single barbless hooks only. Regular season runs first Saturday in May at 5:00 am through September 30.

Regulations
- Above 14th Avenue, category 3; below, category 5 (artificials only; 3 trout limit with a 12-inch minimum; 1 trout over 15 inches). The only portion open to fishing in the early season is between 11th Road and Highway 22.

Species
- Wild brook, brown, and rainbow trout above Germania Marsh; warmwater species below Germania Marsh.

Miles of Trout Water
- 17 miles

Stream Characteristics
- Sand-bottom creek, especially clear; known for Hex hatch

Access
- Mecan River State Wildlife Area off of Highway 21 and Highway 22.

Fly Shops
- Tight Lines Fly Fishing Company

Maps
- *Wisconsin Atlas and Gazetteer*, page 44, 53

Tagatz Creek

For its 16 miles of trout water, Tagatz Creek offers anglers a crack at wild browns and brook trout in a classic Sand County setting—a clear creek running over a sand bottom against a backdrop of birch, aspen, scrub oaks, and jackpine. Like nearby Caves, Chaffee, and Wedde Creeks, Tagatz does not boast large trout. However, what these trout lack in size they make up for in color—red-spotted, olive-backed browns and purple-black brookies. Fish for them with small dark nymphs, or on the surface with a midge or Cahill pattern. Try hopper flies during August and September.

Tagatz is a brushy creek, so a short rod is the way to go. The creek's mirror-like clarity demands a careful approach and presentation. It begins east of Highway 51 and north of Westfield, where you can access it via Dakota Drive, 4th Road, or Highway H. After crossing Highway 51, you can pick it up again on County Z, JJ, and finally County B. It flows into Harris Pond in Harrisville. It is category 2. There is DNR access at the juncture of JJ and Z, and then again just before the creek crosses B north of Harrisville. Tagatz Creek is open to fishing during the March and April season.

Chaffee Creek

Beginning south of the town of Coloma and ultimately feeding into the Mecan River, Chaffee Creek supports some 12 miles of trout water and has received extensive habitat work from the DNR and local conservation groups. Bank stabilizing, fish-holding structures and current deflectors all help make Chaffee a first-class fishery. To access the Chaffee Creek Fishery Area west of Highway 51 (category 2 water), take County CC to 4th Avenue. East of Highway 51 (category 3 water), there is DNR access along Dakota Avenue, County B, and County Z. Only the portion of Chaffee Creek downstream from Highway B is open to fishing during the March and April season.

Don't expect the riffle-run configuration found on southwest Wisconsin limestone creeks. Instead, you'll find long glides, deep slower sections, and lots of streamside brush and trees. Nor does Chaffee (or other Sand County creeks for that matter) seep up through limestone, so the water is gin-clear and not forgiving of careless angling.

Chaffee is small-water fishing and one of the finest area creeks, its banks almost entirely under public ownership. Above Highway B, I've enjoyed good early season midge and Blue-Winged Olive hatches. (For the Hex hatch, you are better off on the Mecan, the White or Tomorrow Rivers.) I fish caddis nymphs and wet flies all season, with Pheasant Tail Nymphs and dark Hare's Ears being good choices. Meadow sections of Chaffee play host to good numbers of crickets and hoppers, which show up on the stream in July and August, and hopper fishing for wild brookies on Chaffee is terrific fun. Small beetles and ant imitations can be fished anytime. On such small water, I don't bother with bigger meat patterns.

Chaffee Creek offers extensive public access, fine quality trout habitat, and good populations of modest-sized native brook and brown trout. There is a certain poetry to these Sand County streams. Savor the clear water and sandy bottom, and thank the DNR for preserving and improving them.

Big Roche a Cri Creek

Big Roche a Cri might be called a two-tier fishery. From its Waushara County headwater at Highway 39/51 near Plainfield to its widening at Roche a Cri Lake just east of Castle Rock Flowage in Adams County, Big Roche a Cri Creek contains 20 miles of trout water. From the lake down to Castle Rock Flowage (a distance of 15 miles) warmwater fishing opportunities exist.

This low-gradient stream has an interesting trout fishery, according to retired DNR land purchasing agent Elward Engle of Wautoma, Wisconsin, in that wild brown trout and brook trout coexist. Engle says this is unusual since browns tend to outcompete brook trout. But here, like distinct ethnic groups in a big city, Roche a Cri browns and brookies have their own separate neighborhoods. Above County W, the fishery is predominantly brook trout; from County W downstream to Big Roche a Cri Lake, it's mostly browns. Most of the water above County W is public. Concentrate your efforts in the brook trout water. It's the prettiest stretch of stream, holds a stable wild brook trout population (something of a rarity this far south in Wisconsin), and features stream improvement courtesy of the DNR. Access to this stretch is via 4th Avenue, Highway KK, 2nd Avenue, 1st Avenue, County G, and County W.

If you want to explore the lower trout reaches of Big Roche a Cri, you can take one of the many eastbound roads from Highway 13. On a recent trip to Castle Rock Flowage, I took a side jaunt to explore lower Big Roche a Cri. I found many bridge crossings blocked off by strands of barbed wire and posted signs (according to Wisconsin law, bridges are public right-of-ways for accessing streams and rivers). I saw nothing particular to recommend about this lower trout stretch.

Big Roche a Cri's hatch pattern follows that of other Sand County streams. Midges and Blue-Winged Olives are active all season. Roche a Cri's sandy bottom is rife with caddis and stonefly nymphs, imitations of which can be fished all season. Sculpins and dace are present and can be mimicked effectively with a Muddler Minnow. The creek holds scuds, too, though not in the numbers of limestone creeks to the south. All portions of Roche a Cri are open during the March and April season.

If Roche a Cri's trout are not cooperating, try Big Roche a Cri Lake. This widening of Big Roche a Cri Creek begins just east of Highway 13. There's a boat launch off the northern shore of the Highway 13 bridge. You'll find the typical southern Wisconsin mix of largemouth bass, northern pike, and panfish. Fish the creek mouth for northerns in spring, the stumps for crappie, and the weeds for bass. There's a dam at the outlet of the lake. From there, Big Roche a Cri Creek flows another 15 miles (impounded again midway at Arkdale Lake) to Castle Rock Flowage. It's an important nursery for walleye and northern pike, which can be found, respectively, in deeper bends and weedy margins. Access to this stretch is at Highway 21, Highway Z, and a number of crossings on smaller roads. Roche a Cri State Park is just a stone's throw away, offering 45 wooded campsites, hiking trails and a chance to see Native American petroglyphs.

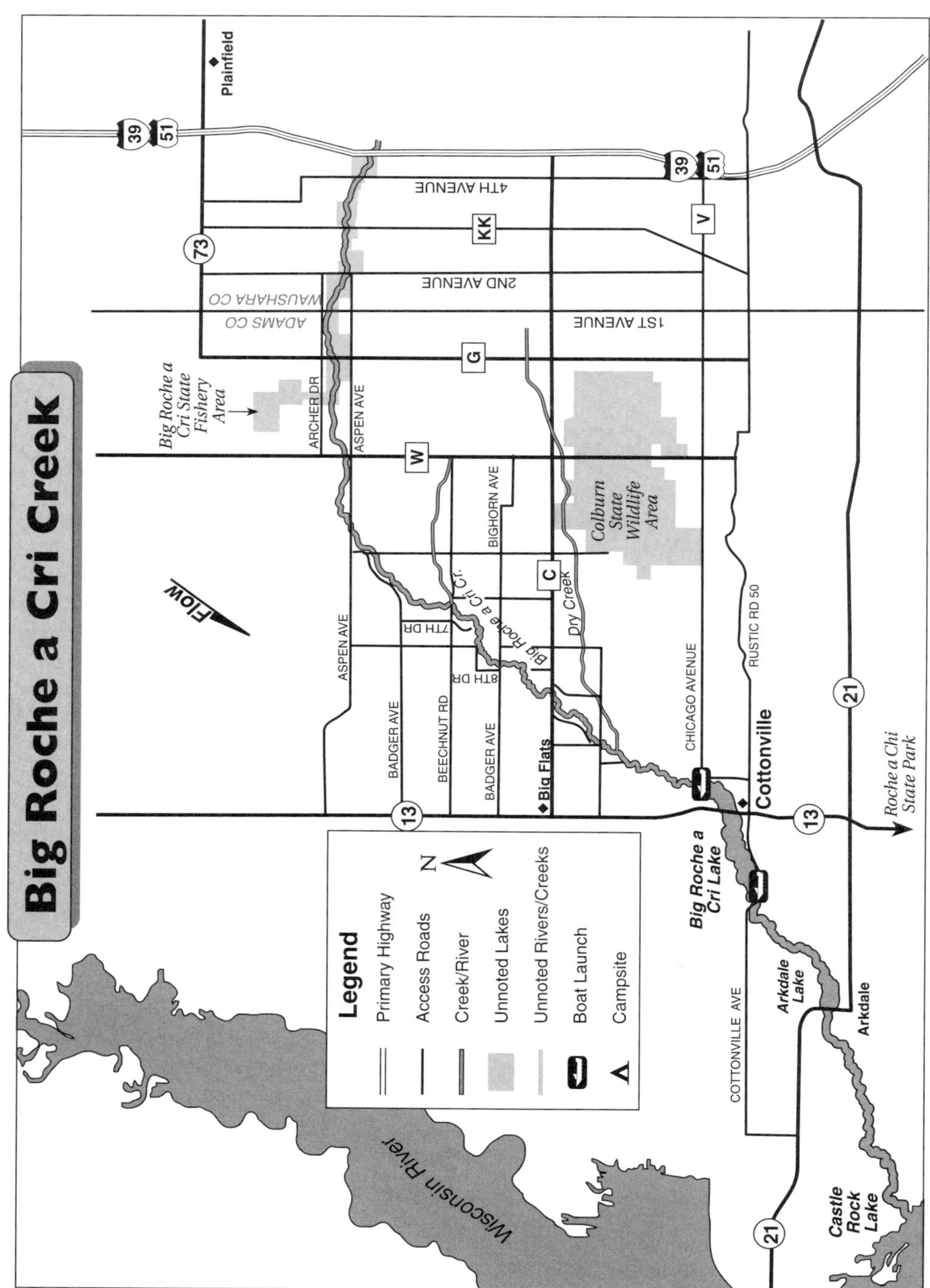
Big Roche a Cri Creek
Legend
Primary Highway
Access Roads
Creek/River
Unnoted Lakes
Unnoted Rivers/Creeks
Boat Launch
Campsite
N
Flow
Plainfield
39
51
73
KK
V
G
W
C
13
21
4TH AVENUE
2ND AVENUE
1ST AVENUE
WAUSHARA CO
ADAMS CO
Big Roche a Cri State Fishery Area
ARCHER DR
ASPEN AVE
BIGHORN AVE
Colburn State Wildlife Area
Big Roche a Cri Cr.
Dry Creek
7TH DR
8TH DR
BADGER AVE
BEECHNUT RD
Big Flats
CHICAGO AVENUE
RUSTIC RD 50
Cottonville
Roche a Chi State Park
Big Roche a Cri Lake
COTTONVILLE AVE
Arkdale Lake
Arkdale
Castle Rock Lake
Wisconsin River

Stream Facts: Big Roche a Cri Creek

Season

- The early season runs from the first Saturday in March to the last Sunday before the first Saturday in May; no-kill, single barbless hooks only. Regular season runs from the first Saturday in May at 5:00 am through September 30.

Regulation

- Above Highway W, category 2; Highway W downstream to Big Roche a Cri Lake, category 3. All of Big Roche a Cri is open during the March and April season.

Miles of Trout Water

- 20 miles; 15 miles containing warmwater species below Big Roche a Cri Lake.

Species

- Wild brook and brown trout above lake; panfish and warmwater gamefish below lake.

Stream Characteristics

- Sand-bottomed creek with native brook trout in headwaters, browns in lower reaches; warmwater opportunities in Big Roche a Cri Lake and downstream to Castle Rock Flowage.

Access

- Big Roche a Cri State Fishery Area above County W.

Fly Shops

- Tight Lines Fly Fishing Company (De Pere)

Maps

- *Wisconsin Atlas and Gazetteer*, page 52

A typical Sand County brook trout stream.

Dell Creek

If you find yourself in the Dells with a fly rod and a few hours to kill, try Dell Creek. Located just west of Wisconsin's tourist capital, Wisconsin Dells, Dell Creek offers scenic solitude and some 10 miles of trout water surrounded by the 2,125-acre Dell Creek Wildlife Area. Brown and brook trout are present through a combination of stocking and natural reproduction.

Dell Creek is a tannin-stained stream twisting its way through a variety of cover; wade carefully or, if possible, make your approach from the bank. For the most part the streambed is sand bottomed with a few riffles running over gravel here and there. Nymphing with a caddis imitation is a good way to start fishing. In the lower reaches, where forage fish are present, you might go with a streamer. You will be doing a good amount of stream crossing and bog trotting so use waders instead of hip boots here.

The upper part of Dell Creek can be accessed via County HH, H, and P; the lower part via Coon Bluff Road and Highway 23. Dell Creek resembles Rocky Run near Poynette, another stream in the Wisconsin River drainage. Other than a few grouse and woodcock hunters in September, you will pretty much have the creek to yourself. Dell Creek is category 3, except for the portion between Coon Bluff Road and South Avenue, which is catch-and-release and artificials only.

Devil's Lake

This Devil's Lake is not the waterfowl mecca sprawling across north-central North Dakota, but it is an interesting glacial phenomenon in its own right. Located just a stone's throw from Wisconsin's tourist capital of Baraboo and the Wisconsin Dells, 9,000-acre Devil's Lake State Park is one of the most-visited parks in the state system. It's easy to see why. The ancient Baraboo Range (1.5 billion years old) towers 500 feet above the lake; backfilled by the retreating Wisconsin Glacier 10,000 years ago, this basin pocket filled with water. It's now 357-acre Devil's Lake. Yes, there are sunbathers and a crowded swimming beach, and, yes, reservations for campsites fill up a year in advance, but it is also one of the few lakes in southern Wisconsin where gas and diesel motors are prohibited (electric motors only). Anglers willing to launch and paddle away from the crowds can still enjoy solitude in a pretty setting. It is also a deep, spring-fed lake with a good mixed fishery. Walleye, smallmouth, northern pike, bluegills, and perch (few in number, jumbo in size), as well as trout (browns and rainbows), inhabit this 50-foot-deep basin.

So what is the best way for a fly angler to approach this lake? First, a small boat is a big help. Bring your own or rent one at the concessions near the two launches. Launch at the south shore off South Lake Road or the north shore from the park road running south from Highway DL. (You will need to purchase a park permit in either case.) A boat will get you away from the shoreline commotion and give you access to the crucial dropoffs where fish congregate in Devil's Lake. Fishing a mix of weeds and dropoffs (giving wide berth to the swimming beaches) is a good strategy.

Use a sinking line because Devil's Lake is deep. Leeches, minnows, and night crawlers are sold in spades at local bait shops. Choose a streamer that imitates one of these—a strip leech is usually a good bet. Finally, consider fishing Devil's Lake during the week, off-season, or at night. Up and down the lakeshore on summer nights, lanterns can be seen like scattered fireflies. Night fishing at Devil's Lake is a time-honored tradition, and a good many walleye, northern, and trout are taken by anglers when the fish move into the shallows to feed.

Devil's Lake is no secret, but those willing to fish during off times (nights, weekdays, autumn) can enjoy some fine fishing with impressive natural history for a backdrop. Trout may be taken between the first Saturday in May and March 1 with a minimum size of 9 inches and a daily bag of 3 fish. Northerns must be 32 inches, and only one may be kept. Otherwise, regulations follow the general guidelines for Wisconsin's Southern Zone.

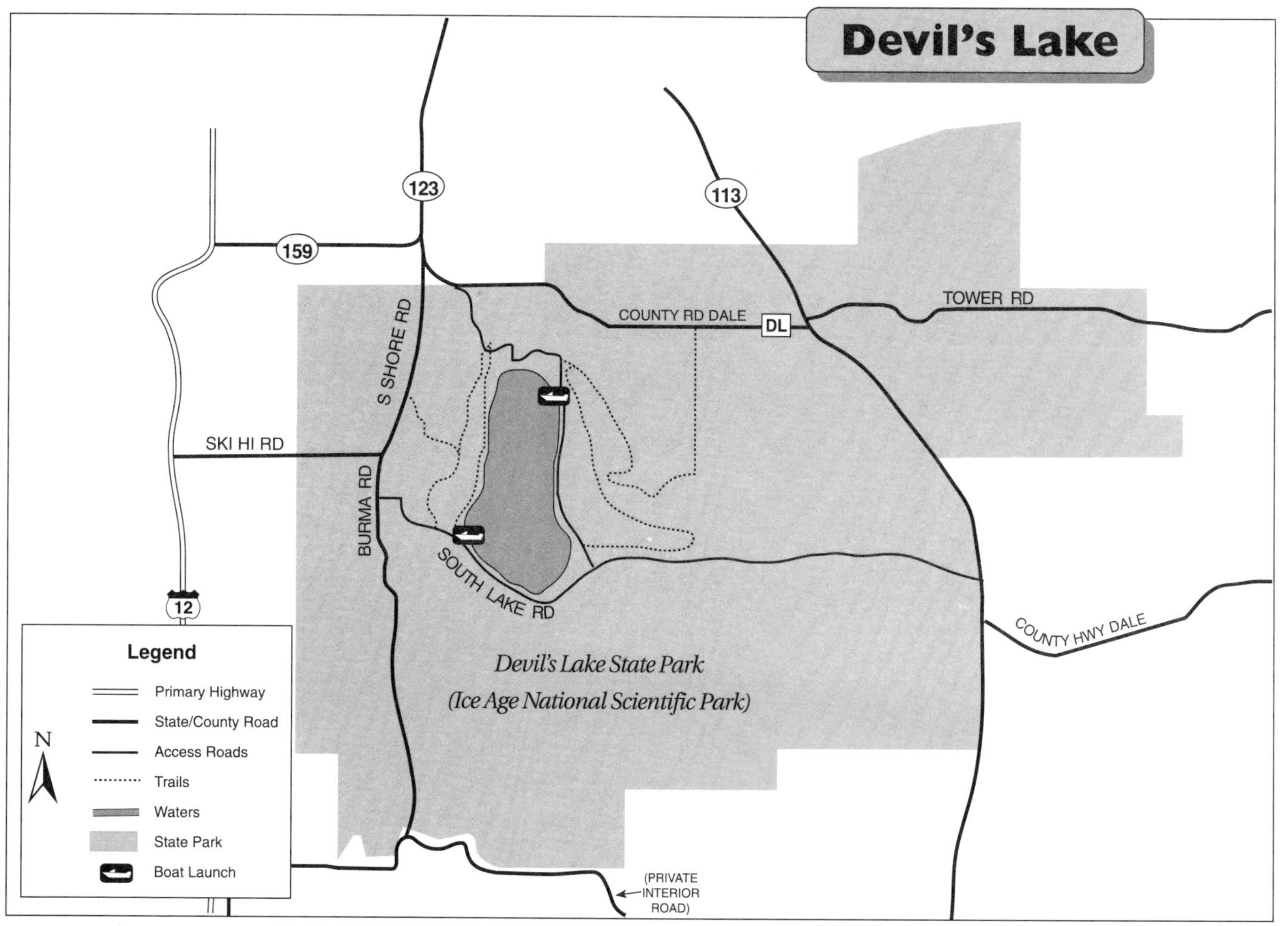
Devil's Lake
123
113
159
TOWER RD
COUNTY RD DALE
DL
S SHORE RD
SKI HI RD
BURMA RD
SOUTH LAKE RD
12
COUNTY HWY DALE
Devil's Lake State Park
(Ice Age National Scientific Park)
(PRIVATE INTERIOR ROAD)
Legend
Primary Highway
State/County Road
Access Roads
Trails
Waters
State Park
Boat Launch
N

A pair of fat Mason Lake bluegills.

Mason Lake

Located on the Marquette-Adams County line just east of Wisconsin Dells, Mason Lake is a good fly-rod bluegill lake, according to Chuck Wenzel of Wisconsin Rapids. Wenzel is an avid outdoorsman who's lived in central Wisconsin for the last 50 years. Wenzel said that Mason Lake's bluegills were running a bit smaller last year than in previous years, but they were still prolific and big enough to fish for. If the fish are on their spawning beds (as they are likely to be from mid-May to early June), he fishes rubber spiders and poppers. Another favorite bluegill fly of Wenzel's is the White Miller.

There are also crappie and perch off the main point on Mason's northeast side; fish them with minnow-style streamers. There are plenty of weeds—perhaps too many—on shallow Mason Lake. They all pretty much contain bluegills. Mason is also a good northern pike producer. Wenzel advises fly anglers to fish Mason Lake early in the season before it weeds up. Launch ramps can be found on the north, south, and east sides of the lake. You might try it again in the fall for northerns if you're experiencing the "can't fish for trout blues."

Sunset on a Central Wisconsin Lake.

Wolf Lake

You will not be bothered by water skiers or motorboats on 47-acre Wolf Lake, located east of Oxford off Highway A. No gas motors, no electric motors, no motors period are permitted here. Largemouth bass are present in very good numbers and some reach considerable size, according to Terry Berndt of Coddington Hardware in nearby Oxford. Berndt, who lives in the area, has talked to property owners who catch bass at will right off their docks.

Wolf Lake is also managed as a trout lake (season runs from the first Saturday in May to first Saturday in March; category 3). Black crappie and bluegill are present as well. There is a public boat launch on the west side of the lake off Highway A. Wolf Lake is best fished from a canoe or belly boat as much of the shoreline is private. Work the weeds along the south and east shore for bass and panfish in spring when the fish are on their beds. Fish a nymph or streamer in the deep water (which tops out at 58 feet) east of the launch for trout.

Parker Lake

I found out a number of interesting things about Parker Lake (west of Oxford and just south of Highway 82) after talking to Terry Berndt at Coddington Hardware in Oxford. First among them is the bass fishery. Berndt has talked to a number of divers

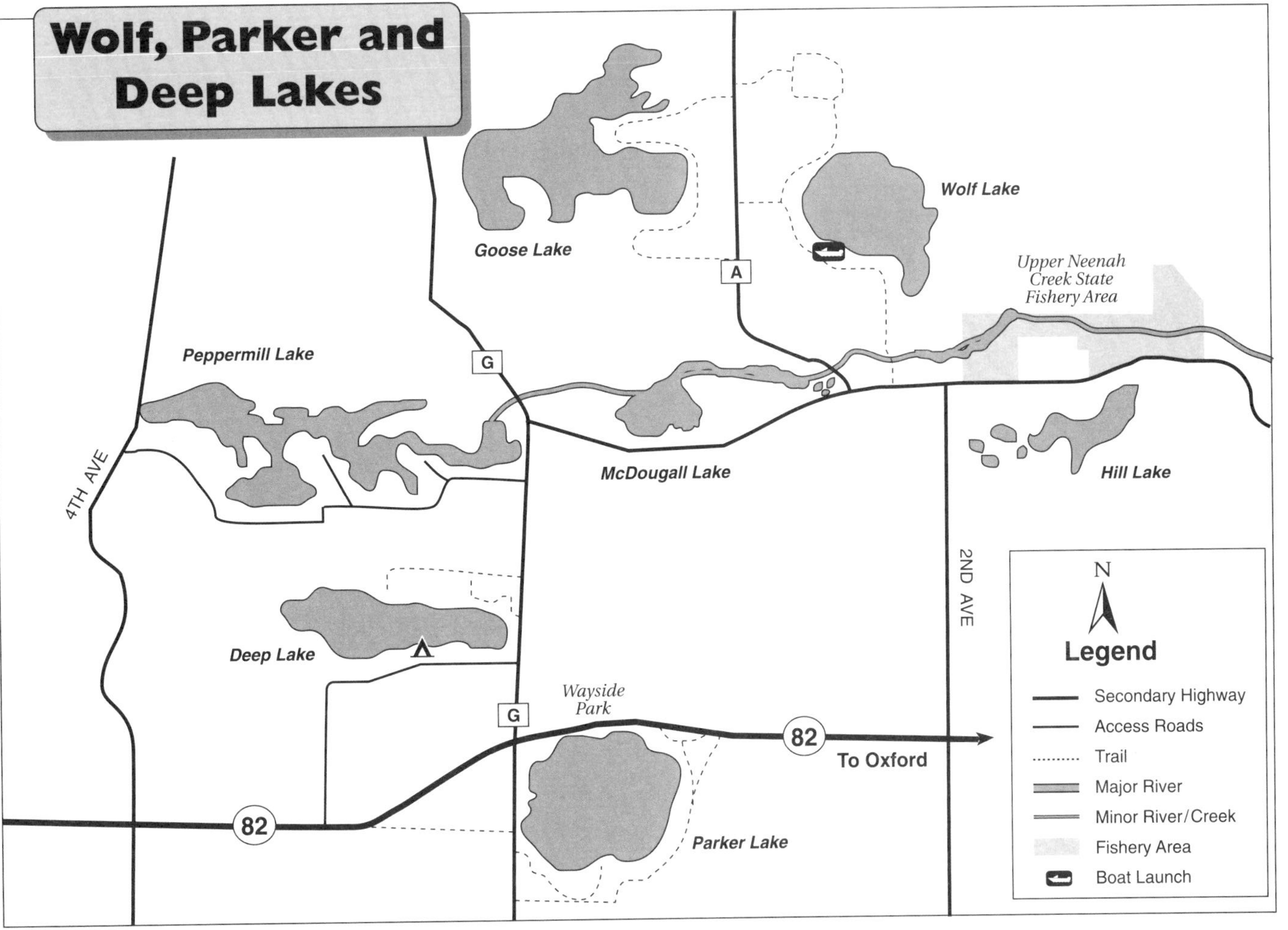
Wolf, Parker and Deep Lakes
Goose Lake
Wolf Lake
A
Upper Neenah Creek State Fishery Area
Peppermill Lake
G
McDougall Lake
Hill Lake
4TH AVE
2ND AVE
Deep Lake
Wayside Park
G
82
To Oxford
82
Parker Lake
N
Legend
Secondary Highway
Access Roads
Trail
Major River
Minor River/Creek
Fishery Area
Boat Launch

who use Parker Lake because of its sandy bottom and deep, clear water. One reported seeing a largemouth bass in the 8- to 10-pound range. In case you're wondering, the state record largemouth is just over 11 pounds. Berndt says he's sure the fish will be caught someday and it will be all over the papers. But that won't be the first big bucketmouth taken from Parker's 63 acres.

Parker is locally known as a terrific largemouth bass lake, and there are even a number of bass tournaments held there now. It also has northern pike (which tend to run small, according to Berndt) and panfish. The DNR also manages Parker Lake for trout (season runs from the first Saturday in May to first Saturday in March; category 3).

The other interesting thing is that Parker is now a no-wake lake by local ordinance; property owners seem to be enjoying the quiet. Berndt said he's curious (and hopeful) about the results of this, as motors had been tearing up the lake weeds that are important cover and spawning habitat. The no-wake rule also makes the lake more attractive to small boaters.

Launch at Parker Lake Resort on the lake's north shore, just off Highway 82. Fish the downed trees and vegetation early on for Parker's big bass, then move out deeper as the shallows warm. The folks at the resort may also have some helpful hints.

Deep Lake

True to its name, Deep Lake is another clear, sandy-bottom lake near Oxford with depths up to 50 feet. Both trout and warmwater species are found in Deep Lake, which is also home to Deep Lake Resort, where you can rent a cabin for a few days or a week. (See the description in the hub city of Westfield.)

Deep Lake is located just north of Highway 82 off Highway G. Trout are one fishery (season: first Saturday in May to first Saturday in March; category 3) on this 35-acre, oblong lake. Bass, bluegill, and northerns round out the fishery. Access is at the campground off Highway G, where you can also launch for a small fee. There's also a public launch on the north side of the lake.

Despite its depth, Deep Lake isn't very big. "You can practically throw a rock across it," says Terry Berndt. A cartop boat is handy on small water like this. In a morning or evening, you'll be able to cover most of the promising water. Fish a sinking line with a weighted nymph if you're after trout. Otherwise, try the shoreline weeds.

Crooked Lake

Crooked Lake is shallower than Wolf, Deep, and Parker and lacks the trout population present in these lakes. It's a great bass and bluegill lake, however, with northern pike also present. Wade along the weedy south shoreline casting bass bugs or poppers, or fish the patterns from the small boat (launch at the north side of the lake). This shallow weedy lake is not often frequented by the powerboat crowd. You'll find Crooked Lake south of Highway 82 and just west of Oxford.

Buffalo Lake

Narrow, weed-choked, and brown are three words that come to mind for 2,200-acre Buffalo Lake, an impoundment of the Fox River near the town of Montello in central Wisconsin. A harvester runs all summer long to keep the weeds down. "It's great for northerns, bass, and panfish," according to Jerry Ross of Holliday True Value in Montello. You have three options for fishing this weedy lake, all of which are best done from a skiff or canoe powered by a small outboard.

Fish in spring when it's just weeding up, and enjoy some fantastic panfish and bass action on poppers in the shallows. In summer, fish what Ross calls pockets—bits of open water amid the weeds. This can be productive, especially if you can place your popper accurately. Finally, in October and November, the weeds die down and fishing for bass and northerns picks up. And while there's always a carp-removal program underway at Buffalo Lake, there are also always carp. You can have some exciting sight-fishing for Buffalo's carp in the shallows with medium to small nymphs.

In springtime, fish Buffalo's northerns in weedy shallows where they spawn. Fish the creek mouths and the springs on the north shore off Highway C as things warm up in summer. Northerns seek out the cool, oxygen-rich water in these holes.

Panfish are ubiquitous on Buffalo Lake. "Cruise the lake until you run into good-sized fish," Ross suggests. Since Buffalo Lake is a long narrow body of water, a small boat equipped with an outboard is very helpful. Work right in the weeds in springtime and hit the channels just outside the weeds come summer. Crappie like the structure provided by bridge or railroad pilings.

You can find Buffalo's largemouths scattered among pockets of open water. Don't neglect water near boat launches. A 5-pounder isn't uncommon on Buffalo.

There are two launches off County C west of Montello; a launch off County D south of Packwaukee; and one off Highway T near Endeavor. While this weedy gumbo of a lake isn't pretty to look at, it's amazingly fertile, has good numbers of trophy northerns and largemouths, and a solid base of panfish.

Buffalo Lake is open to fishing year-round for all species except muskellunge.

Lake Puckaway

Like Buffalo Lake to the west, Lake Puckaway is a shallow, weedy impoundment of the Fox River. Also like Buffalo Lake, it's full of northerns, bass, and panfish. In fact, the state-record northern was caught here in 1952, weighing in at a whopping 38 pounds. At just over 5,000 acres, Puckaway is definitely big water; it looks like (and is, come fall) a giant duck marsh. A small boat equipped with an outboard is obviously going to be helpful for fishing here.

Cathy Vales, of Mike and Cathy's Good Old Days Resort, recommends the west end of Puckaway for northerns. "Fish the mouth of the Fox River for bass and northerns in springtime," says Jerry Ross of Holliday True Value in Montello. (This is the area off Puckaway Road, the very southwest corner of the lake.) Vales says you will find panfish off the sandbars, and Ross advises anglers to fish the reed beds. Bass are spread throughout Puckaway's shallow waters (maximum depth of 5 feet). Fish pockets of open water for bucketmouths.

Launches can be found at the town of Marquette and off Lake View Drive on the south shore; on the north shore, there is a launch off Highway C. Lake Puckaway is managed as a trophy northern lake (32-inch minimum, bag limit of 1). Otherwise, it is governed by the standard regulations for Wisconsin's Southern Zone.

Columbia Lake

Where do you go when you are itching to throw a fly in the dead of Wisconsin winter, with trout season months off and warmwater venues frozen solid? Columbia Lake, of course, which is formed by warmwater discharge from the Columbia Lake Power Plant just south of Portage. It stays free of ice—in the mid-70s—all year. Launch a cartop boat via the access road off County Highway VJ (just west of Highway 51); shoreline anglers can access Columbia Lake here, too. The lake is popular with float-tube fishermen. One angler described winter float tubing Columbia Lake—with its ambient steam from temperature contrast—as akin to being in a giant hot tub with fish. What kind of fish? Striped bass are present, and largemouth and smallmouth bass are abundant, as are panfish, carp, and catfish. As for flies, bring the garden-variety streamer assortment: Mickey Finns, Muddler Minnows, Clouser Minnows, and Marabou Leeches. The power plant and surrounding 3,000 acres are currently managed by Alliant Energy and are open to fishing. Columbia Lake is open to fishing all year; the size limit on largemouth and smallmouth bass is 18 and the daily bag limit is 1; for striped bass and white bass the daily bag limit is 3.

Rocky Run Creek

Rocky Run Creek begins in Columbia County just west of Mud Lake Public Hunting Ground south of Rio as a narrow, marshy rivulet; this part of the stream is not trout habitat and is not worth your time. The DNR classifies Rocky Run as trout water between Highway 22 and Highway 51, and these 7 miles (all category 3) are where you should fish. I've caught small browns at the pool below the Highway 22 culvert.)

Next, the creek flows beneath Cuff Road a half-mile downstream from Highway 22, and this stretch is heavily posted. You can legally fish here if you keep your feet wet, or you can access the creek via Rocky Run Public Hunting Ground just to the north on Highway 22. Once you're in the parking area of the hunting ground, follow the main trail for about a half-mile until you get to the creek (pleasant in cool weather, laborious with waders on during the dog days). This stretch is lightly fished but thick and difficult to get through.

To explore Rocky Run downstream, follow Highway 22 just north of the public hunting ground and turn left on Phillips Road. Go 3 miles on Phillips Road and then turn left onto Dunning Road, where you will find another bridge. The next bridge crossing is at Highway 51, which marks the end of trout water. The public hunting ground runs south of Phillips Road and ends before Highway 51. You can access the

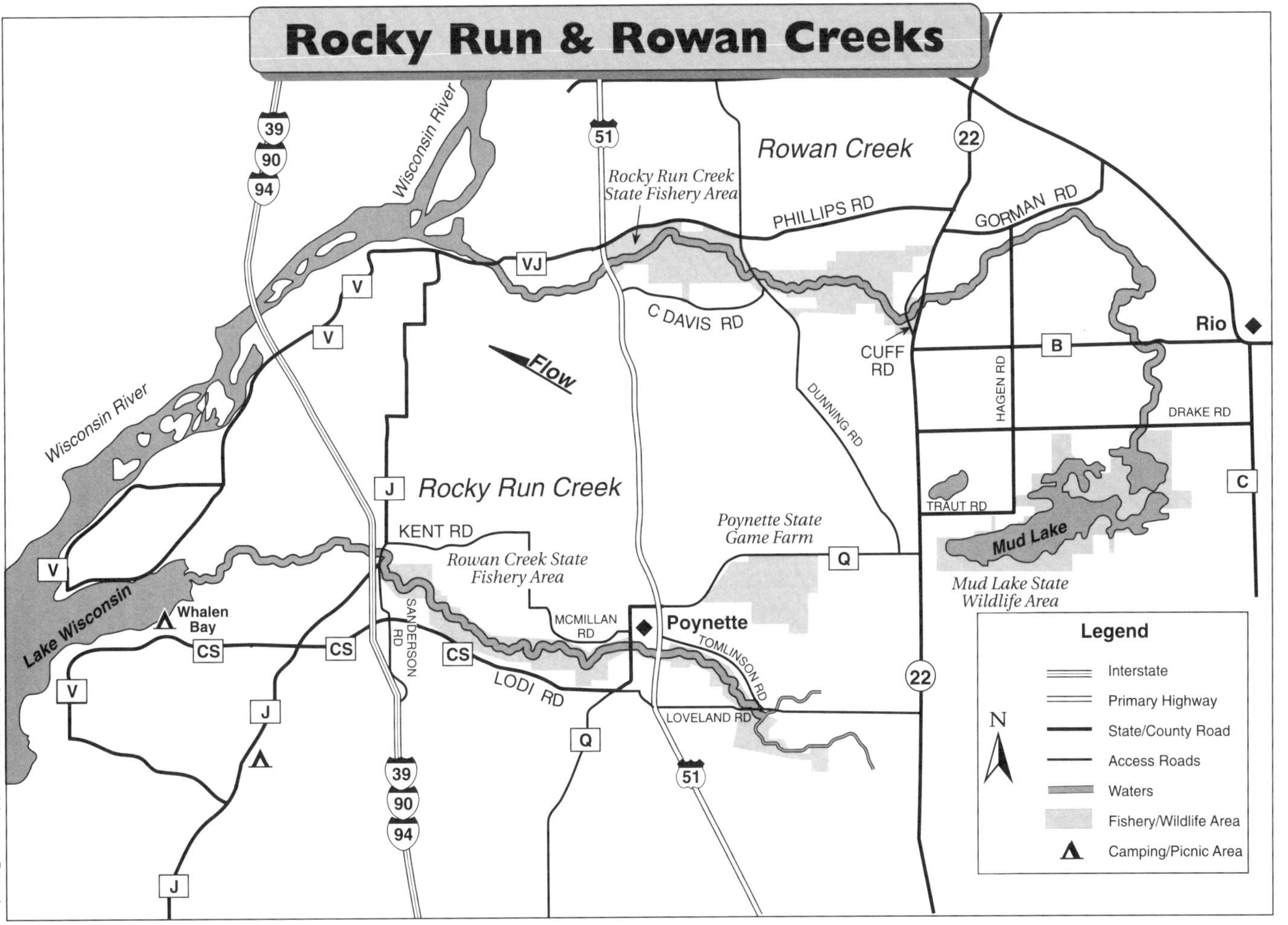
Rocky Run & Rowan Creeks
Rowan Creek
Rocky Run Creek State Fishery Area
PHILLIPS RD
GORMAN RD
Wisconsin River
Wisconsin River
VJ
C DAVIS RD
CUFF RD
Rio
B
HAGEN RD
DRAKE RD
DUNNING RD
Flow
Rocky Run Creek
TRAUT RD
C
Mud Lake
Mud Lake State Wildlife Area
KENT RD
Rowan Creek State Fishery Area
Poynette State Game Farm
Q
Lake Wisconsin
Whalen Bay
SANDERSON RD
MCMILLAN RD
Poynette
TOMLINSON RD
LODI RD
LOVELAND RD
CS
V
J
22
51
39
90
94
Legend
Interstate
Primary Highway
State/County Road
Access Roads
Waters
Fishery/Wildlife Area
Camping/Picnic Area
N

creek by heading south through the public lands, but be warned, it can be a killer on hot days.

Is all the trouble worth it? Yes. The restrictive access keeps casual anglers out and makes for some unspoiled fishing for pretty wild browns. According to a local taxidermist, Rocky Run was one hell of a brook trout stream before browns were introduced and out-competed the natives. The trout I've caught here have been browns under 10 inches, all brightly colored. I like to fish here in fall when the mosquitoes are gone. Mostly, I nymph my way along very slowly, often letting the fly hang at the end of a drift. Birch and aspen leaves rustle in the breeze, and a grouse might flush from the pin oaks as you pass.

Rocky Run is a good stream to explore if you are fishing nearby Rowan Creek, which is more heavily fished. I've seen lots of caddis and stoneflies in the stream, and hoppers are abundant in meadow sections off Phillips Road. My recommendation is to fish early or late in the season, keep your expectations modest, and enjoy the Sand County scenery. As with anything in its natural state, Rocky Run is not fish-by-the-numbers.

Rowan Creek

Rowan Creek is a central Wisconsin trout stream bordering Driftless streams to the west and Sand County streams to the north. Characteristics typical of both areas can be seen along its 12 miles of trout water, which begin above Highway 51 just east of the town of Poynette and end at the confluence with the Wisconsin River at Whalen's Grade. Good public access exists along the upper half of the creek, and this is where anglers should concentrate their efforts.

Rowan is a small meadow stream above Highway 51 and can be reached along Loveland and Tomlinson Roads at DNR easements. Here you will find populations of small brown and brook trout, largely wild and quite skittish due to the water's relatively open nature. A parking lot on Highway 51 is a good location from which to explore the water up and downstream. Here the stream takes on a rocky cast, and tumbling a scud or wet caddis in likely pocketwater will take fish. You will see Poynette High School on your right, and then a bit of town land and a picnic area at the road crossing near downtown Poynette.

The stream next winds its way into a marsh under first town and then DNR ownership. This is the meat of the stream for my money. Angling pressure falls off here because access is walk-in only from various points along Highway CS, which parallels the stream's west bank. The cross-country skiing and hiking trail just after the intersection of County Q is a good way to access water. Various DNR pull-offs can also be seen along the highway and trails lead to the stream (sometimes circuitously).

This stretch of water is not an easy stretch to fish. It is clear and you are often betrayed in advance by your footsteps along the stream's marshy edge. Try fishing it during a cloudy day after a rain; that is when I've had the best luck. A pink or olive scud seems to be the fly to use here. You might also try flipping a streamer through some of the deeper holes. Browns in the 12-inch range are common, although one rainy afternoon I slid the net under a 20-inch hook-jawed beauty.

A DNR parking area on Highway J marks the end of DNR land. I have taken fish here by running streamers and nymphs tight to the banks where the trout like to hide.

While the lower 5 miles are classified as trout water, you will have to access them via private land—securing permission first—along Kent Road (which joins up with Highway J). I tried to float this stretch in a canoe but turned around because of the abundance of barbed wire and fallen trees blocking passage downstream.

Rowan Creek is best fished subsurface—with nymphs, scuds, caddis wets, and streamers. Its woody debris and rocks hold lots of aquatic insects. After fishing here for over 10 years, I have yet to observe a hatch that drew much attention from Rowan's trout.

Crooked Lake offers good crappie fishing.

A spring day on Rowan Creek.

Stream Facts: Rowan Creek

Season

- The early season runs from the first Saturday in March to the last Sunday before the first Saturday in May; no-kill, single barbless hooks only. Regular season runs from the first Saturday in May at 5:00 am through September 30.

Regulations

- Category 3

Species

- Wild brook and brown trout

Stream Characteristics

- Sand-bottomed creek flowing through meadow, over rocks, then through marsh.

Access

- DNR parking areas on Highway CS and 51.

Fly Shops

- Fontana Sports

Maps

- *Wisconsin Atlas and Gazetteer*, page 36, 37

HUB CITY: WESTFIELD

Westfield is a good base from which to explore the cluster of lakes around Oxford to the south, Neenah Creek, Caves Creek, and the Mecan River and its tributaries.

Accommodations

Halls Wood Lake Resort, W7115 Dakota Avenue, Westfield; 608-296-3200; on spring-fed lake just outside Westfield with chance to do some warmwater fishing, near Mecan River; bar and restaurant on premises; $$

Deep Lake Resort, 3261 County G, Oxford; 608-586-5835; cabins on productive panfish lake described in this section; $$

Nature Glen Motel, 227 Park Street, Westfield; 608-296-3022; $

Pioneer Motor Inn, 242 N. Pioneer Park, Westfield; 608-296-2135; $$

Campgrounds

Roche a Cri State Park, 1767 Highway 13, Adams-Friendship; 608-339-6881; state park on trout stream 20 miles northwest of Westfield

Castle Rock Park, on Castle Rock Flowage; take Highway 13 to County F; take County F west to County Z; sprawling Castle Rock Lake, impoundment of the Wisconsin River, offers flyfishers shoreline smallmouths and stream-inlet panfish and northern pike

Hartman Creek State Park, N2480 Hartman Creek Road, Waupaca; 715-258-2372; located 25 miles north of Westfield

Camp Shin Go Beek, N7015 24th Lane, Waupaca; 715-258-2271; Boy Scout camp on Twin Lake, described in this section

Restaurants

Haystack Supper Club, W7457 County E, Westfield; 608-296-3200; good fish and steaks and Sunday brunch

Pioneer Family Restaurant, 244 N. Pioneer Park, Westfield; 608-296-3121; longtime family restaurant

Subway, 219 W Pioneer Park, Westfield; 608-296-2067

Halls Wood Lake Resort, W7115 Dakota Avenue, Westfield; 608-296-3200; good resort with restaurant bar just north of town, great fish fry and steaks

Fly Shops, Outfitters, Sporting Goods

Coddington's True Value, Highway 82, Oxford; 608-586-4361; fishing licenses, talk to Terry Berndt for warmwater fishing information

True Value Hardware, Main Street, Westfield; 608-296-2444; fishing licenses

Tight Lines Fly Fishing Company, 1534 Mid Valley, De Pere; 920 336 4106; located one hour east of Sand Couties; excellent source of information and gear for Sand County, Driftless, tributary, and smallmouth; 5 fulltime guides on staff

Veterinarians

Sand County Vet Clinic, W6597 County M, Westfield; 608-296-2333

Medical

Wild Rose Community Memorial, 601 Grand Avenue, Wild Rose

Auto Rental

Enterprise Rent-a-Car, Waupaca; 715-256 2668, 800-736-8222; auto rental at Madison, Appleton, and Oshkosh airports

Automobile Repair

Lucky's Auto Repair, 526 S. Main, Westfield; 608-296-3040
Precision Collision, 433 Industrial Drive, Westfield; 608-296-3600

Air Service

Wautoma Municipal Airport, W8471 Cottonville Avenue, Wautoma; 920-787-3030
Airports also at Madison, Appleton, and Oshkosh.

For More Information

Westfield Chamber of Commerce
317 S. Main Street
Westfield, WI 53964
608-745-1555

Pine River

From its brook-trout-rearing headwaters above Wild Rose Millpond to its nether reaches in the pike-and-duck marsh country of Lake Poygan, the Pine River offers some 30 miles of water (the upper 20 miles of which hold trout) running west to east across Waushara County. An outdoor companion of mine from Oshkosh has been fishing the Pine for 15 years and has taken brook trout to 16 inches and browns better than 20 inches. DNR shocking surveys confirm the presence of big browns and brook trout. While hardly a secret, the Pine, with its robust population of forage fish, may be the big-trout stream among Sand County waters. Wild browns and brookies comprise the bulk of the upper Pine's fishery; the lower reaches see a mix of wild and planted fish.

Trout are regularly taken from Wild Rose Millpond, which the fly shop overlooks. Fish it from a belly boat or canoe (launch at County AA) and look for dimplings in the water toward evening. The pond is category 2 water with an open season from the first Saturday in May to the first Saturday in March. Above the pond are the nip-and-tuck headwaters of the Pine. Headwater access is via the bridge crossing on 17th Drive and the old railroad grade running toward Stevens Point.

Above Wild Rose Millpond, the Pine is category 2; below the millpond it's category 3. Only the portion of the Pine River from County K (above Saxeville) to Poysippi Millpond is open to fishing during the March and April trout season.

For my money, the best part of the Pine is the stretch between Wild Rose Millpond and the impoundment at Saxeville—10 miles of stream. And within this stretch the DNR lands off Aniwa Road and Apache Avenue are good access points. Look for water that's siltier than other Sand County streams. Also, as there is not an overabundance of structure on the Pine, don't overlook deep holes near bridges. These can serve as concentration points for trout. Apache Road, County K, Aniwa Road, Apache Avenue, County A, and 24th Lane (west to east) offer bridges in this stretch. Try swinging a leech pattern tight to the abutments in the morning or evening. Otherwise, look for fish wherever there's woody debris, bank cuts, or deep-shaded holes.

Between Saxeville and the village of Pine River, a distance of 5 miles, is the place to look for large browns. Follow County EE south of Saxeville and take your first left, which follows the river and affords access to another DNR parcel. Below the village of Pine River there aren't enough trout to warrant your attention, as impoundments degrade water quality beyond what trout can tolerate. Northern pike, however, are present in fair numbers in the river from the village of Pine River downstream 10 miles to Poygan Marsh. Access this stretch via Highway H.

Caddis and stonefly hatches are the early highlights on the Pine, followed by the Hex hatch in mid-June. Any dark caddis or stonefly nymph in size 10 or 12 will do the trick. If you don't feel like night-fishing during the Hex hatch, try a size 6 Hex nymph pattern (fished as you would a leech pattern) during the day. Browns will be keyed in on the Hex and all its phases for the entire month of June.

The Pine is a fine hopper stream in July and August, and you can fish beetle, ant, and cricket imitations as early as May. Streamers are an excellent choice on the Pine, as both big trout and forage fish are abundant. You may notice, of an August evening, what looks like a snowfall of white mayflies. Don't worry. Wisconsin winter is at least a month off. You're probably seeing a hatch of *Ephoron leukon*, or White Mayfly. Fish this hatch with a size 12 White Wulff.

Be mindful of trout and water temperatures on the Pine. If stream and air temperatures are particularly high and fish seem sluggish, consider quitting for the day. Trout are extremely fragile during these times.

Stream Facts: Pine River

Season

- The early season runs from the first Saturday in March to the last Sunday before the first Saturday in May; no-kill, single barbless hooks only. Regular season runs from the first Saturday in May at 5:00 am through September 30.

Regulations

- Pine River upstream from Wild Rose Millpond, category 2; Wild Rose Millpond (open first Saturday in May to first Saturday in March); Pine River downstream from millpond, category 3. Only portion open during early season: Highway K downstream to Poysippi Millpond.

Species

- Brook and brown trout, wild and stocked.

Miles of Trout Water

- 20 miles

Stream Characteristics

- Sand-bottomed creek, somewhat silty; producer of large trout.

Access

- Pine River State Fishery Area off Apache Road, DNR lands, and bridge crossings.

Fly Shops

- Tight Lines Fly Fishing Company

Maps

- *Wisconsin Atlas and Gazetteer*, pages 53, 54

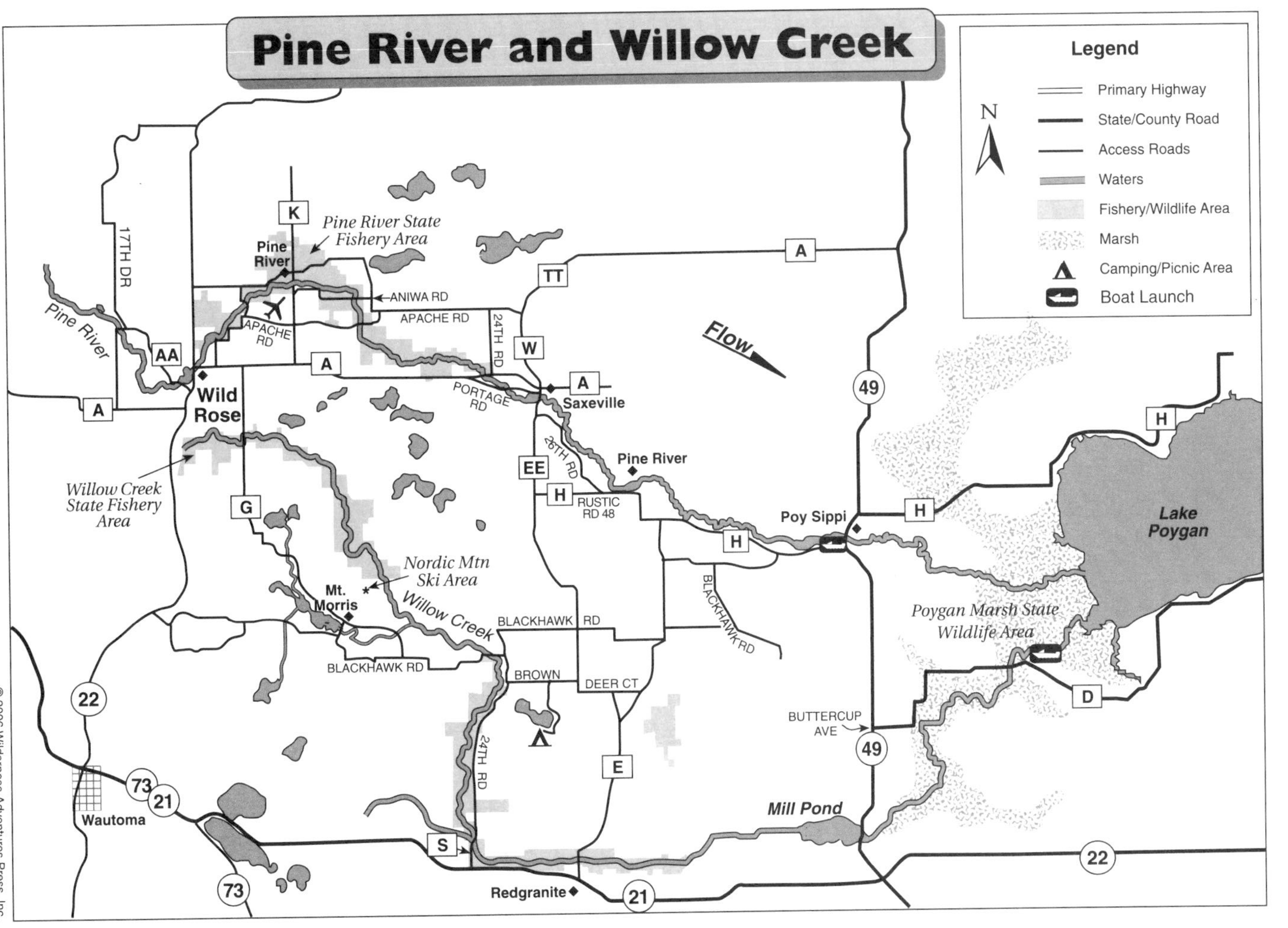
Pine River and Willow Creek
Legend
Primary Highway
State/County Road
Access Roads
Waters
Fishery/Wildlife Area
Marsh
Camping/Picnic Area
Boat Launch
N
Flow
Pine River State Fishery Area
Pine River
ANIWA RD
APACHE RD
APACHE RD
24TH RD
17TH DR
Pine River
Wild Rose
Saxeville
PORTAGE RD
26TH RD
Pine River
RUSTIC RD 48
Poy Sippi
Lake Poygan
Willow Creek State Fishery Area
Nordic Mtn Ski Area
Mt. Morris
Willow Creek
BLACKHAWK RD
BLACKHAWK RD
BLACKHAWK RD
BROWN
DEER CT
Poygan Marsh State Wildlife Area
BUTTERCUP AVE
24TH RD
Mill Pond
Wautoma
Redgranite
K
A
TT
AA
W
A
A
A
EE
H
H
H
H
G
D
E
S
49
49
22
22
73
21
73
21

Hexagenia mayflies provide one of the most exciting hatches of the year in Wisconsin. (Tim Landwehr)

Willow Creek (Waushara)

Willow Creek is a Waushara County stream similar to the Pine. It's highly regarded and heavily fished by sportsmen from the Fox River Valley. However, many of these folks quit fishing by early June, leaving the Willow wide-open for the Hex hatch and the remainder of the summer.

Willow Creek begins near Wild Rose and offers some 20 miles of trout water. Like the Pine, it has siltier waters and offers larger brook and brown trout than other Sand County streams. Upstream from Blackhawk Road east of Morrisville, category 2 regulations govern; downstream from Blackhawk Road, it's category 3. Blackhawk Road also marks the rough dividing line between the all-wild upstream fishery and a wild-plus-stocked fishery downstream. Access DNR lands on the upper Willow via Highway G; the middle reaches via Highway W and 24th Road; and the lower stretch via Highway S.

Early season caddis and stonefly hatches are good on the Willow. A Prince Nymph or caddis larvae pattern is a good bet, even if bugs aren't visibly hatching. The Willow's also known for its Hex hatch. If fishing bushy dries at night doesn't catch your fancy, try stripping a Hex nymph or leech pattern through one of the Willow's deep lies. I once kept a nice brown from the Willow during Hex time and found its stomach full of Hex nymphs.

Fish streamer patterns in low-light conditions for the Willow's big browns and brookies. Try hopper patterns in hot weather anywhere the Willow winds through a meadow. Ant or beetle imitations can be fished throughout the season.

Stream Facts: Willow Creek (Waushara)

Season

- The early season runs from the first Saturday in March to the last Sunday before the first Saturday in May; no-kill, single barbless hooks only. Regular season runs from the first Saturday in May at 5:00 am through September 30.

Regulations

- Above Blackhawk Road, category 2; below, category 3. Only portion between Blackhawk Road and 29th Lane open during early March and April season.

Species

- Wild and planted brook and brown trout.

Miles of Trout Water

- 20 miles

Stream Characteristics

- Sand-bottomed creek, siltier than most Sand County streams.

Access

- Upper Willow via Highway G; middle reaches via Highway W and 24th Road; lower stretch via Highway S.

Fly Shops

- Tight Lines Fly Fishing Company

Maps

- *Wisconsin Atlas and Gazetteer*, page 53

West Branch of the White River

A number of fishing opportunities exist in the vicinity of the West Branch of the White River: fishing the West Branch itself for small wild trout; fishing the West Branch Millpond for trout; fishing the upper main branch of the White for large trout and the White's lower reaches for warmwater species.

The West Branch of the White River near Wautoma is a noted Sand County trout stream. It's only 5 miles long, but it contains a naturally reproducing population of all three species of trout (a rarity in these parts since each species has its own distinct habitat requirements). West Branch rainbows are particularly handsome fish with an abundance of black spots, elongated bodies, gently forked tails, and blood-red stripes.

Gin-clear water is a hallmark of the West Branch. Fish near woody debris, around mats of floating vegetation, or along its shaded banks. The West Branch is not big-trout water but a place to hone your skills on wary native fish; it is category 2 for its entire length. Access and DNR lands can be found at County T, County C, County Y, and Highway 22. The West Branch is mainly a caddis, stonefly, and terrestrial stream with sporadic mayfly activity. You'll find a Hex hatch here but not the large browns offered on the Tomorrow, Mecan, Willow, Pine, or mainstem White. The West Branch of the White River is closed to fishing during the March and April season.

The West Branch Millpond, while not prime trout water, does hold trout. It is open to trout fishing from the first Saturday in May to March 1, giving fall and winter anglers a shot at trout. You can try fishing to rises and matching the hatch or dragging a Prince Nymph, slowly, over its sand bottom. There's a launch off 13th Avenue on the pond's eastern shore.

Gin-clear water is a hallmark of the West Branch.

Stream Facts: West Branch White River

Season
- The early season runs from the first Saturday in March to the last Sunday before the first Saturday in May; no-kill, single barbless hooks only. The regular season runs from the first Saturday in May at 5:00 am through September 30.

Regulations
- West Branch, category 2; West Branch Millpond, category 2 (open first Saturday in May to first Saturday in March).

Species
- Wild brook, brown, and rainbow trout

Miles of Trout Water
- 20 miles

Stream Characteristics
- Clear, sand-bottomed creek.

Access
- Upper Willow via Highway G; middle reaches via Highway W and 24th Road; lower stretch via Highway S.

Fly Shops
- Tight Lines Fly Fishing Company

Maps
- *Wisconsin Atlas and Gazetteer*, page 53

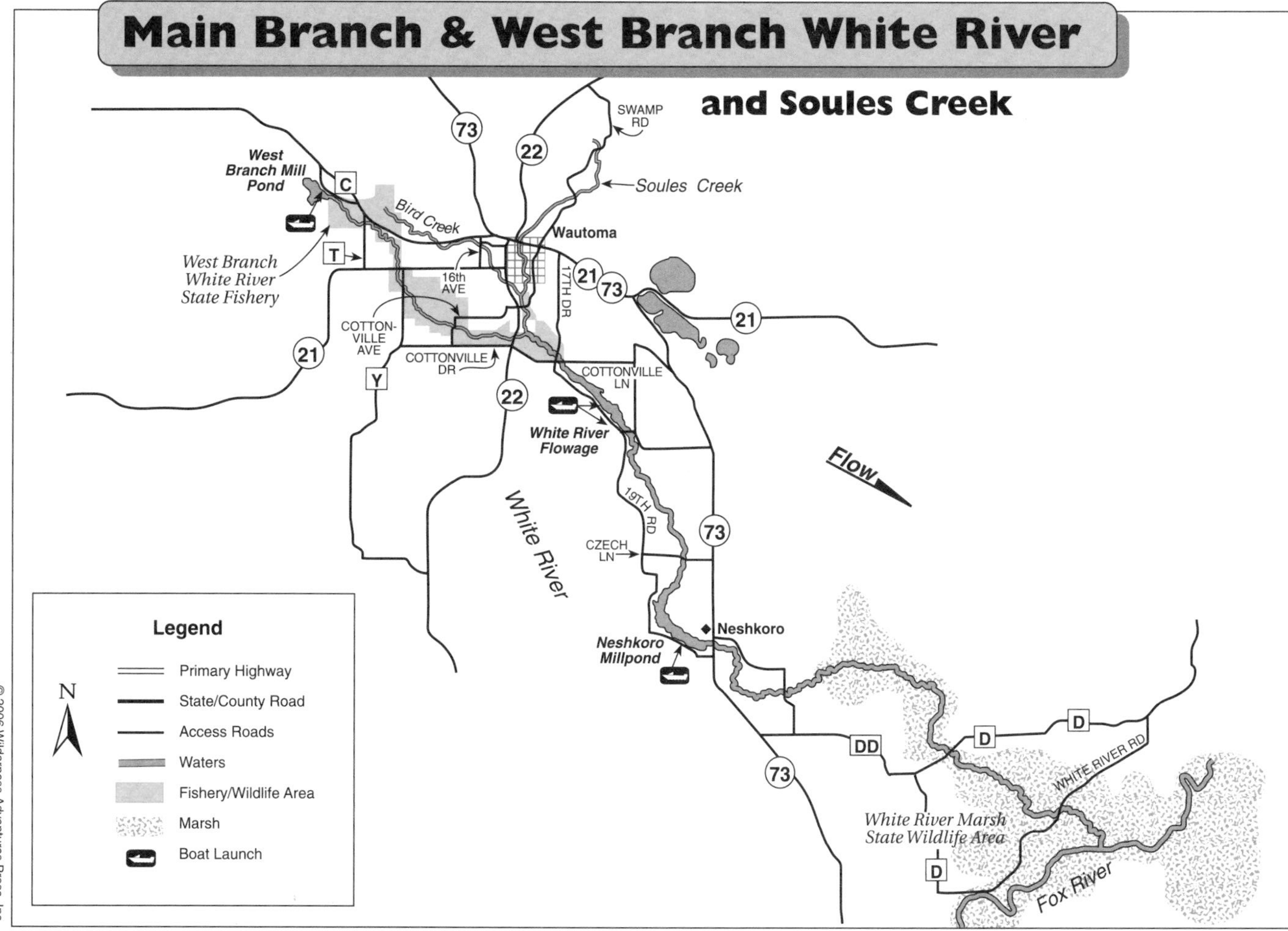

Main Branch & West Branch White River
and Soules Creek
SWAMP RD
Soules Creek
West Branch Mill Pond
Bird Creek
Wautoma
West Branch White River State Fishery
16th AVE
17TH DR
COTTON-VILLE AVE
COTTONVILLE DR
COTTONVILLE LN
White River Flowage
White River
19TH RD
CZECH LN
Neshkoro
Neshkoro Millpond
Flow
WHITE RIVER RD
White River Marsh State Wildlife Area
Fox River
73
22
21
C
T
Y
D
DD
Legend
Primary Highway
State/County Road
Access Roads
Waters
Fishery/Wildlife Area
Marsh
Boat Launch
N

Main Branch of the White River

The main branch of the White is known in DNR circles as a producer of large browns and rainbows and a good place to try your hand during the Hex hatch. Its trout water is between the town of Wautoma (where it begins, fed by Soules and Bird Creeks) to the White River Flowage, a distance of about 5 miles. The main branch of the White River is category 5 (artificials only, 3-trout limit with only 1 fish over 15 inches, minimum size 12 inches). Only the portion of the White River between Highway 21 and the White River Flowage is open to trout fishing during the March and April season.

There are DNR lands on the main branch of the White at Cottonville Lane/17th Drive, just above the White River Flowage, which marks the end of the White's trout water. Below the flowage, the White River winds into Neshkoro Millpond (off Highway 73) and then into the White River State Wildlife Area (accessible via County D). While the lower White is mainly known as a duck float, you'll find northerns, largemouth, and rough fish in the river and its two impoundments.

Soules Creek

Soules Creek drains a large swamp northeast of Wautoma before joining the West Branch of the White River. It comes highly recommended from retired DNR land agent Elward Engle as a place to catch native brook and brown trout in a wild setting. The stream in found within lowland cover types (tamarack, ash, basswood, and tag alder). It has a low gradient and a bottom of sand and marl, and it is fed by a number of tributaries in its upper reaches.

Soules Creek is located along Swamp Road, with good DNR access for most of its 5 miles. The creek is category 2, no longer catch-and-release, artificials only. If you've ever fished trout in a swamp in the upper Midwest you know that exquisite care is a prerequisite for success. One careless footstep along these marshy margins sends trout scurrying. The typical Sand County mix of caddis, stoneflies, scuds, and mayflies thrive in the mud-sand bottom. Try a Prince Nymph on a long leader. If all else fails, Tim Landwehr of Tight Lines Fly Fishing Company says you can usually provoke a strike by skittering an Elk Hair Caddis over promising water.

Soules Creek is open to fishing during the March and April season.

Wisconsin Rapids Area Ditches

If you drive to northern Wisconsin in the dead of winter, you'll notice tiny ribbons of open water, ditches really, crossing Highway 51/39 between Plainfield and Stevens Point. Open water in winter? These must be spring-fed—and if they're spring-fed they must be trout streams. If your mind works like mine, this is probably what you thought upon seeing them. However, with the exception of Ten Mile Creek, these haven't been first-rate trout fisheries since the FDR administration.

To understand these ditches, one has to look back in time, according to retired DNR land purchasing agent Elward Engle. Free-flowing streams 70 years ago, these ditches were straightened (and the accompanying wetlands drained) in the name of productive farming. Before this, they provided outstanding recreational opportunities. Engle spoke of a retired railroad man who, in pre-Depression days, took his fill of mallard ducks, prairie chickens, and brook trout along these ditches. Now, however, the ditches suffer from siltation, farm runoff, and the effects of periodic drainage. While brook trout do reproduce in some of them, these are not of the caliber of streams like the nearby Roche a Cri, Mecan River, Chaffee Creek, or Lawrence Creek.

In Engle's tenure at DNR he supervised extensive improvements along Ten Mile Creek. Engle says the South Branch of Ten Mile Creek has not been ditched and has a very nice brook trout population. It crosses Highway 51/39 just south of Bancroft. Access it east of the highway on County D or Harding Avenue and west of the highway on Central Sands Road or Taft Road. The DNR holds perpetual easement rights on the upper South Branch of Ten Mile Creek.

The DNR has also been improving the lower portion of Ten Mile, according to Engle. The main branch flows west from the Wood-Portage County line toward the Wisconsin River. Access Ten Mile Creek at the following road crossings: Highway U, Highway 73, Bell Avenue, Highway 13, Range Line Road, and County Z.

To sum up, Ten Mile Creek is the creek to fish among the Wisconsin Rapids area ditches, especially its upper reaches. As it has clear water without much cover, fish it in low light with a scud or wet caddis on a long leader. While an angler with lots of time on his hand could find brook trout in other ditches, he's better served fishing streams in the Mecan area. These ditches are category 2, with the exception of Ten Mile Creek downstream from Rangeline Road, which is category 5 (artificials only; 1 trout 16 inches or longer).

A Profile of Wisconsin Rod Maker Don Schroeder

Wisconsin rodmaker Donald Schroeder splitting bamboo.

When I phoned Don Schroeder to arrange a meeting, we had to plan around a shipment of bamboo he was expecting. I pictured a few neat sticks—you know, what your grandparents used to stake tomato plants, or perhaps something a little longer. But when Don opened his garage door, I did a double take. On the cement floor were a hundred poles as wide as a man's arm and as long as an aspen tree—and these were the rejects! The prime specimens, five score of them, rested in a neat cradle of 2x4s attached to the ceiling. Now, I'm no stranger to raw material. I've selected Portuguese cork, smelling sharp and minty, for decoys from a dim warehouse; I've seen my brother's tying bench flush with gadwall feathers, vices, silken threads, and lacquers. Each craft has its tack. But the sheer physicality of the bamboo canes, all hand-split by Schroeder, drove home that making bamboo rods is real work. Lots of it. Clearly, I had much to learn.

Schroeder, a former auto mechanic and factory worker, is no stranger to work. He stands six feet tall, round at the shoulders, with woodworker's hands and forearms. His basement shop is a testament to work in the old-time craftsman sense. You won't see bulging Home Depot bags, dirty caulk guns, or haphazard stacks of drywall. You walk down the steps leading to the basement and enter another world. The room is long and narrow, like a ship's galley. On the right, running the length of the workbench, is a milling machine that fashions strips of bamboo into the requisite triangle shape needed for rod construction. On the left is a wood-topped workbench with a red vice. Gouges, files, rasps, pliers, awls, and picks rest on hooks in pegboard. What looks like a card catalog from an old library contains rod ferrules. A small cubby at the far end of the room holds paints and stains. And in a shelf along the left wall are a variety of stocks bought from gunsmiths or knifemakers—some tiger maple, other's Schroeder's Claro walnut trademark—that will become reel seats.

How do you make a bamboo rod? Where does bamboo come from? I only have room here for a thumbnail sketch, but there are several excellent books available that delve into this complex craft. The type of bamboo used in rod making comes from the hilly Tonkin cane growing area, which covers some 42,000 acres northwest of Canton, China. The cane is harvested and floated down the Yangtze River in large rafts—in the manner that white pine was floated down the Wisconsin River in logging days—and shipped out of Shanghai. It is then purchased by a wholesaler, such as Demerest Industries in New York, from whom Schroeder gets his bamboo. Rod makers like Schroeder pay roughly $20 a culm, a swath of bamboo 2.5 inches in diameter and 12 feet long. How does a $20 culm turn into a $1500 fly rod? Perhaps 50 percent of the cane meets Schroeder's standards, and a Schroeder rod takes roughly a month to complete.

The typical bamboo fly rod is a three-piece affair. (By tradition, an extra end-segment, called a mirror-image tip, is included with the rod.) Each segment is in turn composed of six triangular filaments fitted and glued together. Schroeder sands all nodes and imperfections from these filaments before they are glued into segments. I held a magnifying glass to a segment of the rod blank Schroeder was working on. Only after a great deal of convincing from him was I able to say for sure that this segment was not a solid piece—this is how good the craftsmanship was! Each segment must adhere to certain graded measurements (down to the thousandth of an inch) to ensure proper taper and balance. Once the rod blank is complete, Schroeder installs ferrules, eyelets, and cork. He then places the rod on an automated pulley system that he designed. At a painstaking rate of 4.5 inches per second, the pulley lowers the rods into and out of a varnish tank. After the varnish dries, Schroeder puts on the reel seat and sews the rod bag, and then the package is complete.

I recall something Don said earlier about the artistry of rod making. "After a point, you're not making things, you're making art." It takes no New York art critic to discern fine aesthetics in his work. And anyone with half a whit of taste will agree that every Schroeder rod definitively crosses over into the art side of the dichotomy. But while Don has been making fine rods for a quarter of a century, and as a full-time business for a third of that time, I sense that he is on a larger journey, one that reaches back to boyhood and at the same time finds its articulation in the last third of his life. As we sit in his den surrounded by mounts, trout and salmon prints, and fish carvings, he describes catching his first brook trout. He was fishing a red and white streamer (one that he tied himself) on a blue Garcia fiberglass rod. He fished the spring ditches near Necedah. "The fish was so bright," he says wistfully. "I was addicted." Despite a shock of gray hair, he begins to look like a boy. Every journey to something new is a return to something old.

If you are interested in owning a fine bamboo rod, contact Schroeder at: D. G. Schroeder Rod Co., 3822 Brunswick Lane, Janesville, Wisconsin 53546; 608-752-1520; dgschroederrod.com

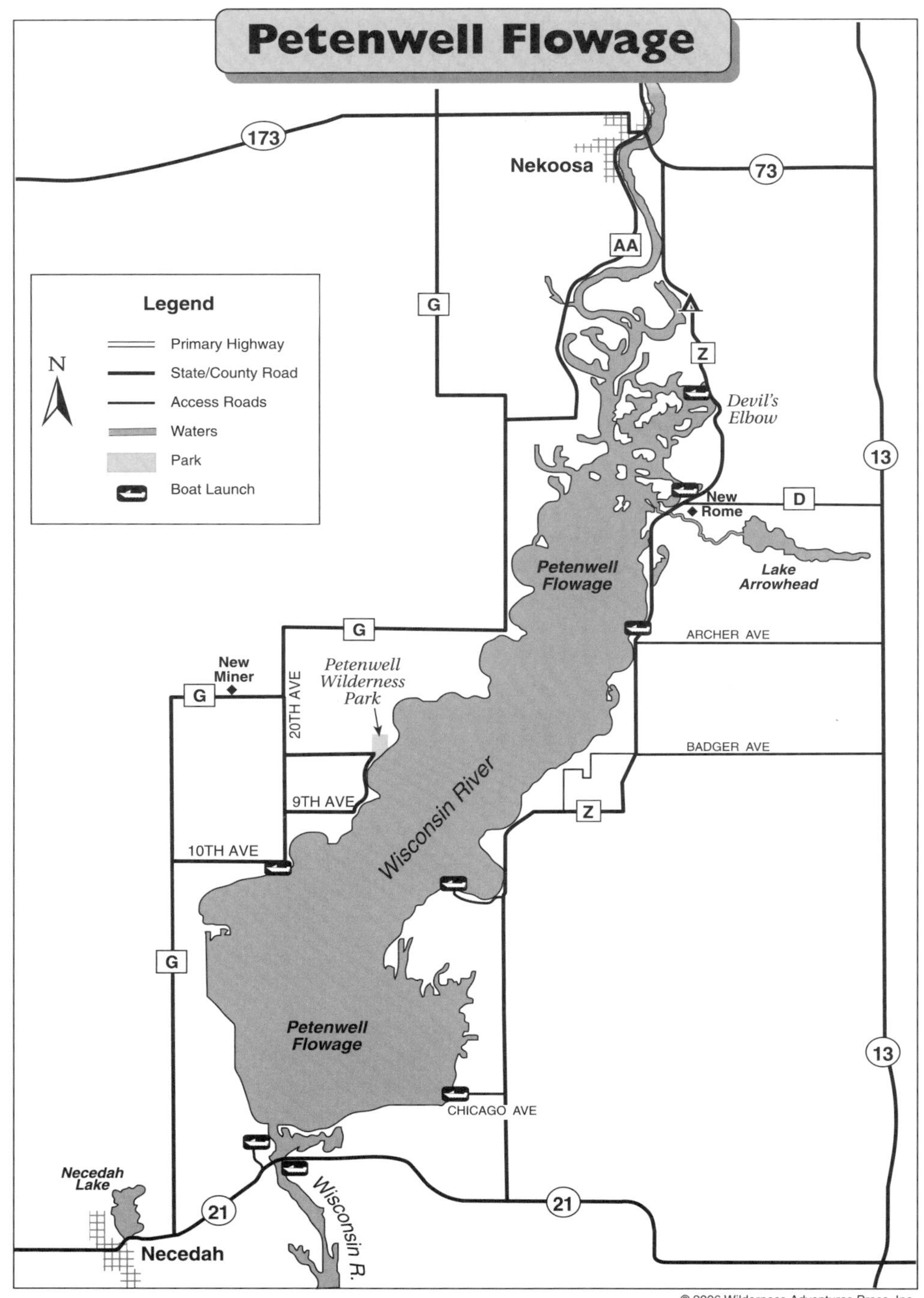

Petenwell Flowage
Legend
Primary Highway
State/County Road
Access Roads
Waters
Park
Boat Launch
N
173
Nekoosa
73
AA
G
Z
Devil's Elbow
13
New Rome
D
Petenwell Flowage
Lake Arrowhead
G
ARCHER AVE
New Miner
G
20TH AVE
Petenwell Wilderness Park
BADGER AVE
Wisconsin River
9TH AVE
Z
10TH AVE
G
Petenwell Flowage
13
CHICAGO AVE
Necedah Lake
21
21
Wisconsin R.
Necedah

PETENWELL FLOWAGE

At first glance Petenwell Flowage, a huge impoundment dating back to the 1940s when the Wisconsin River Power Company dammed up this stretch of the Wisconsin River for hydroelectric power, appears to have a number of strikes against it for the fly angler. At 23,000 acres (Wisconsin's second largest inland lake), it's a massive body of water without much obvious structure and with a dearth of aquatic vegetation. PCBs and mercury are present in walleye, carp, white bass, and smallmouth from years of industrial and papermill pollution. (Children and women of child-bearing age should avoid eating gamefish from Petenwell, and others should limit their intake according to DNR guidelines. For a complete rundown, consult the DNR publication *Important Health Information for People Eating Fish from Wisconsin Waters* or visit http://www.dnr.state.wi.us/org/water/fhp/fish/advisories.) In addition, much of this water is just too big to fish from a small boat.

At this point the reader may be wondering why I included Petenwell Flowage in this book. Well, there are two interesting niche fisheries for the long-rod angler to explore on this lake. Petenwell has an excellent smallmouth fishery along its rocky shorelines, according to DNR fisheries biologist Scott Ironside. There's also good bluegill and crappie fishing around the islands and backwaters on the northeast side of the flowage (locally known as Devil's Elbow) according to Chuck Wenzel, a Wisconsin Rapids angler.

To help prevent erosion, the power company has undertaken a massive riprap campaign at Petenwell and nearby Castle Rock Flowage over the years. And since the power company is using a public resource (water) it must, by law, give something back to the public. Thus, the 100-foot buffer, which is largely boulder for the southern half of Petenwell, is public access for recreational use, including fishing. The unintended byproduct of this, according to Scott Ironside, is a tremendous smallmouth fishery. Ironside often takes his kids to "fish the rocks" for smallmouths, and they usually run into fish. This is like a dentist endorsing a brand of chewing gum—a reliable expert's vote of confidence. While Ironside says that most anglers use diving plugs or live bait here, flyfishers can do well here, too.

Leave the boat at home, and concentrate your fly-fishing efforts on the rocky shore of Petenwell, which is basically the southern half of the lake. A sinking line with a weighted streamer or leech pattern will do the trick. Walleye also congregate in this rocky habitat; these would be a bonus fish to tie into.

When I spoke to Ironside about fly fishing here, he had two more suggestions: target white bass and carp. White bass are a school fish and can be seen just about any time of the year chasing baitfish toward the surface in the manner of their saltwater cousin, the striped bass. Look for effervescent clouds of minnows bubbling toward the surface and you've probably found a white bass school. Any flashy minnow-style streamer will do the trick. White bass give a good tussle and can reach 2 pounds or more; their bulldogging fight is not unlike that of striped bass. While white bass are not a species you would set out to fly fish for specifically, they are another nice bonus fish.

Trash or treasure depending on your point of view, carp are almost ubiquitous here. Look for them in the sun-warmed shallows in spring. Sight-cast to them with a nymph. Throughout the remainder of the year carp can be just about anywhere. Look for the telltale splash.

The rock buffer is basically along the southern half of Petenwell. Just look for rock and you've found access and smallmouth bass. Ironside says you can catch smallmouth just about anywhere there are rocks. This fishing is akin to angling from jetties or breakwater on the East Coast, so wear non-slip footwear and consider bringing a long-handled net. The eastern and western shores both have rock. To fish the eastern shore, take Highway G north out of Necedah and take any of the east-west roads west toward the lake. On the western shore, work the area around Strong Prairie. The minimum size for northern pike is 32 inches, with a daily bag limit of one; otherwise regulations for General Inland Waters (Southern Zone) apply.

To fish bluegills, launch at the area known as Devil's Elbow off County Z. There are lots of islands here and some weeds and stumps. Look for bluegills in weeds and crappie among the stumps. Petenwell crappies can attain impressive proportions. I learned this one day while ice fishing with Chuck Wenzel in early 2002, long after I was forced to hang up my fly rod for the winter. Wenzel took a crappie that was close to a pound and tossed it on the ice with mild disappointment. His buddy Wayne pulled up a slabside that must have gone a pound and a half. Again not much of a fish, they agreed. It was only after a shot-and-beer warm-up at the nearby Lure Inn that I beheld what a Petenwell crappie should look like. Stringers of mounted crappies—each fish easily 2 pounds—adorned the walls of the tavern. So twitch a small streamer among the stumps in Devil's Elbow. You might just catch yourself a 2-pounder.

Castle Rock Flowage

Much of what holds true for larger Petenwell Flowage just to the north can be said about Castle Rock Flowage, also a massive impoundment of the Wisconsin River. As with Petenwell, PCB and mercury counts are high on certain species. If you want to eat fish from Castle Rock, consult the DNR publication *Important Health Information for People Eating Fish from Wisconsin Waters* or visit http://www.dnr.state.wi.us/org/water/fhp/fish/advisories. Also like Petenwell, Castle Rock's sheer size can intimidate anglers.

Fortunately there are ways for shoreline and small-boat anglers to succeed on Castle Rock: fishing the shoreline rocks for smallmouth and fishing river inlets for a variety of species. Fish smallmouth from the rocks with a sinking line and a weighted leech pattern or streamer; you might also pick up a walleye or run into a white bass school. The riprap on Castle Rock Flowage can be accessed from County Z between the lower dam and Dyke Road.

A bonus on this flowage is the large number of stream and river inlets. Big Roche a Cri, Little Roche a Cri, and Klein Creek feed into Castle Rock's east shore, with the Yellow River on the northwest shore. These are northern pike nurseries and also good areas to try for walleye, crappie, and white bass. You'll find launches convenient

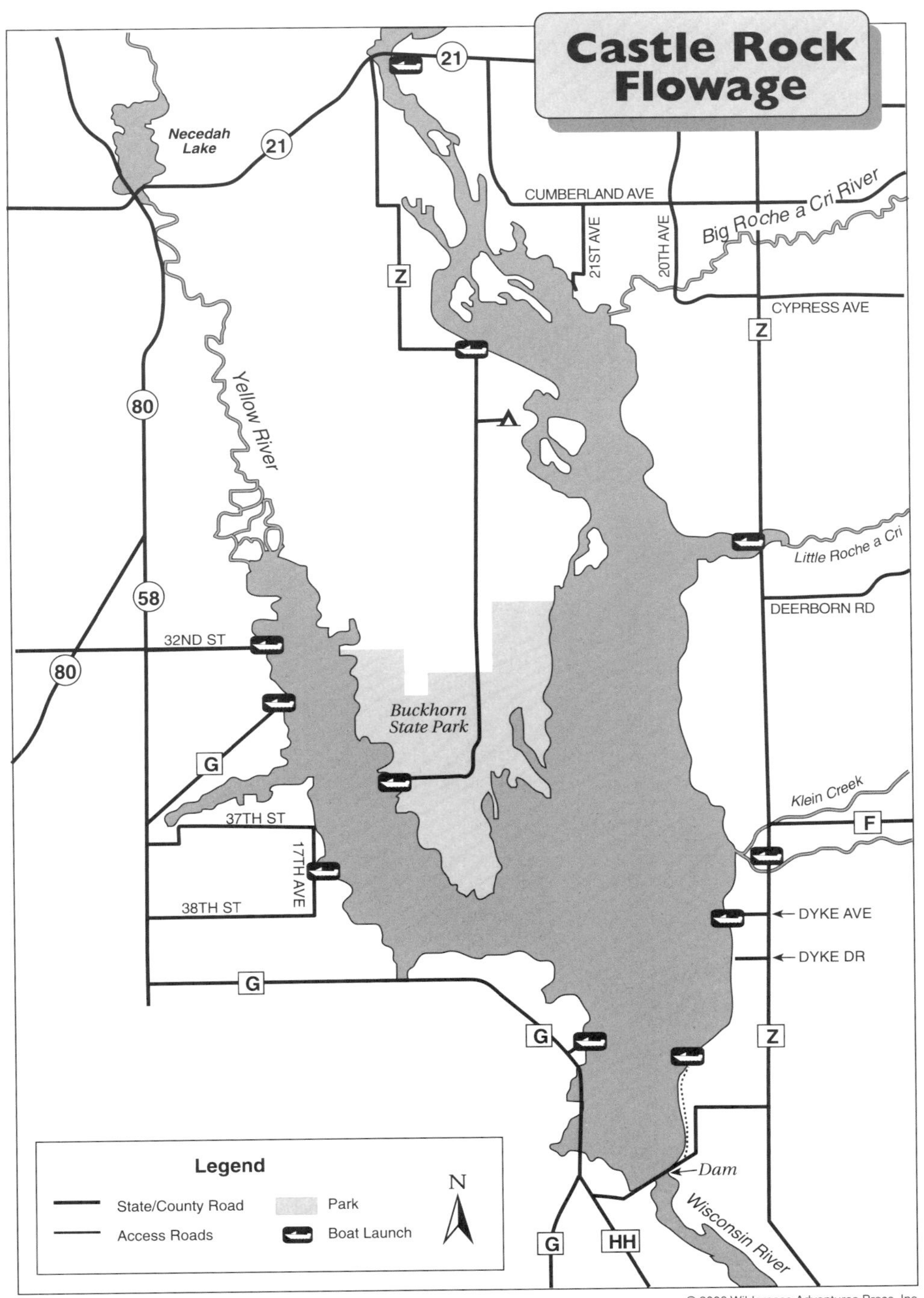
Castle Rock Flowage
Necedah Lake
21
CUMBERLAND AVE
21ST AVE
20TH AVE
Big Roche a Cri River
CYPRESS AVE
Z
80
Yellow River
58
80
32ND ST
Little Roche a Cri
DEERBORN RD
Buckhorn State Park
G
37TH ST
17TH AVE
38TH ST
Klein Creek
F
DYKE AVE
DYKE DR
G
HH
Dam
Wisconsin River
Legend
State/County Road
Access Roads
Park
Boat Launch
N

to each area. Launch at 32nd Street (off Highway 80) to fish the Yellow River mouth; launch from County F to fish the Klein Creek mouth; off Deerborn Road for Little Roche a Cri; or 21st Avenue to fish Big Roche a Cri. To venture forth on the larger waters of Castle Rock, you'll want a stable boat and dependable outboard; things can whip up pretty quick. To fish the inlets, a jonboat or canoe will suffice.

Chuck Wenzel, an avid outdoorsman from Wisconsin Rapids, has floated the Yellow River both for ducks and fish. He has encountered walleye, northern pike, and crappie in the stretch between Castle Rock Flowage and the Necedah Dam. The river is quite serpentine in character and often requires the angler to portage his boat around fallen timber. Launch either below Necedah Lake in the town of Necedah or near the Yellow River mouth from 32nd Street.

On Castle Rock, there's a 32-inch minimum size for northern pike with a bag limit of one; otherwise follow regulations for General Inland Waters, Southern Zone.

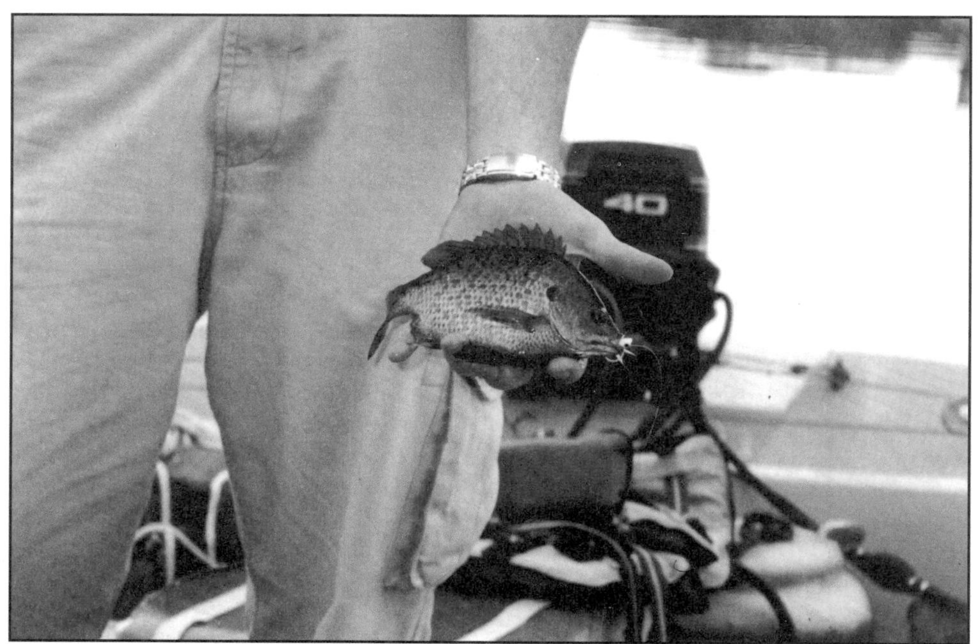

A nice Central Wisconsin bluegill. (Craig Amacker)

WISCONSIN RIVER

Castle Rock Lake Dam to Prairie du Sac Dam

This stretch of water on the Wisconsin River is nearly 60 miles long, starting at the outlet of Castle Rock Dam and ending at Prairie du Sac Dam. While it's not universally friendly for fly fishing, some good backwater and rockpile opportunities do exist between the Columbia Lake power plant and the dam at Prairie du Sac. The rocky river channel through Wisconsin Dells holds smallmouth and walleye, but I would not recommend fishing for them in anything less than a 14-foot V-hulled boat. The pleasure and tour boat traffic don't mix well with anglers trying to get some quiet fishing in from canoes.

Downstream from the Dells is the productive area around Dekorra and the Columbia Lake power plant. (See the description of Columbia Lake on page 226.) Follow the Interstate to Highway V and take V east (you'll be following the southern shore of the Wisconsin River). Launch at one of the ramps on County V. A wide variety of fish habitats can be found here, including rocky dropoffs, sand bars, backwaters, and islands. Walleye and smallmouth are thick in rock and sand cover; crappie, bluegills, and northerns are equally abundant in the backwaters.

The bays on Lake Wisconsin are another area of interest to the flyfisher in a small boat. The majority of backwater habitat on Lake Wisconsin is on the southeast shore. Continue along Highway V (this time west of the Interstate) to Whalen's Grade, which will be on your right. You can easily launch a cartop boat here. Just follow parking regulations, as you will receive a hefty ticket if you don't. Whalen's Grade is classic panfish and bass water. I've also taken lots of small northerns here and seen good catches of crappie, white bass, and walleye taken by bridge fishermen.

The backwaters around Okee and Harmony Grove, also off Highway V, provide a similar fishery. On the northwest shore of Lake Wisconsin is the area known as Wiegans Bay/Moon Valley. Reach this area from Highway 78 north of Sauk City or cross from the east side of the lake on the Merrimac Ferry and pick up Highway 78 south. Try the rockpiles here for smallmouth, walleye, and crappie.

TWIN LAKE

Brad Skupe, of Skupe's Corner in Wautoma, says that summer lake fishing in central Wisconsin can be tough. Skupe's Corner is a good place to stop for gas, a snack, fishing licenses, or warmwater fishing information. Brad is a very knowledgeable angler. Don't miss the collection of old Fox River gunning decoys and mounted fish and game adorning the store. There are literally hundreds of lakes within an hour's drive of Wautoma, but most are overrun by water skiers and speedboats. Skupe's answer to this quandary is to find and fish lakes with restrictive access, where the chore of hauling in a canoe or skiff will keep you among like-minded anglers (those who put a premium on fishing in a natural setting and are willing to work for it.) Twin Lake in northern Waushara County, some 10 miles northwest of Wild Rose, is such a lake. It is

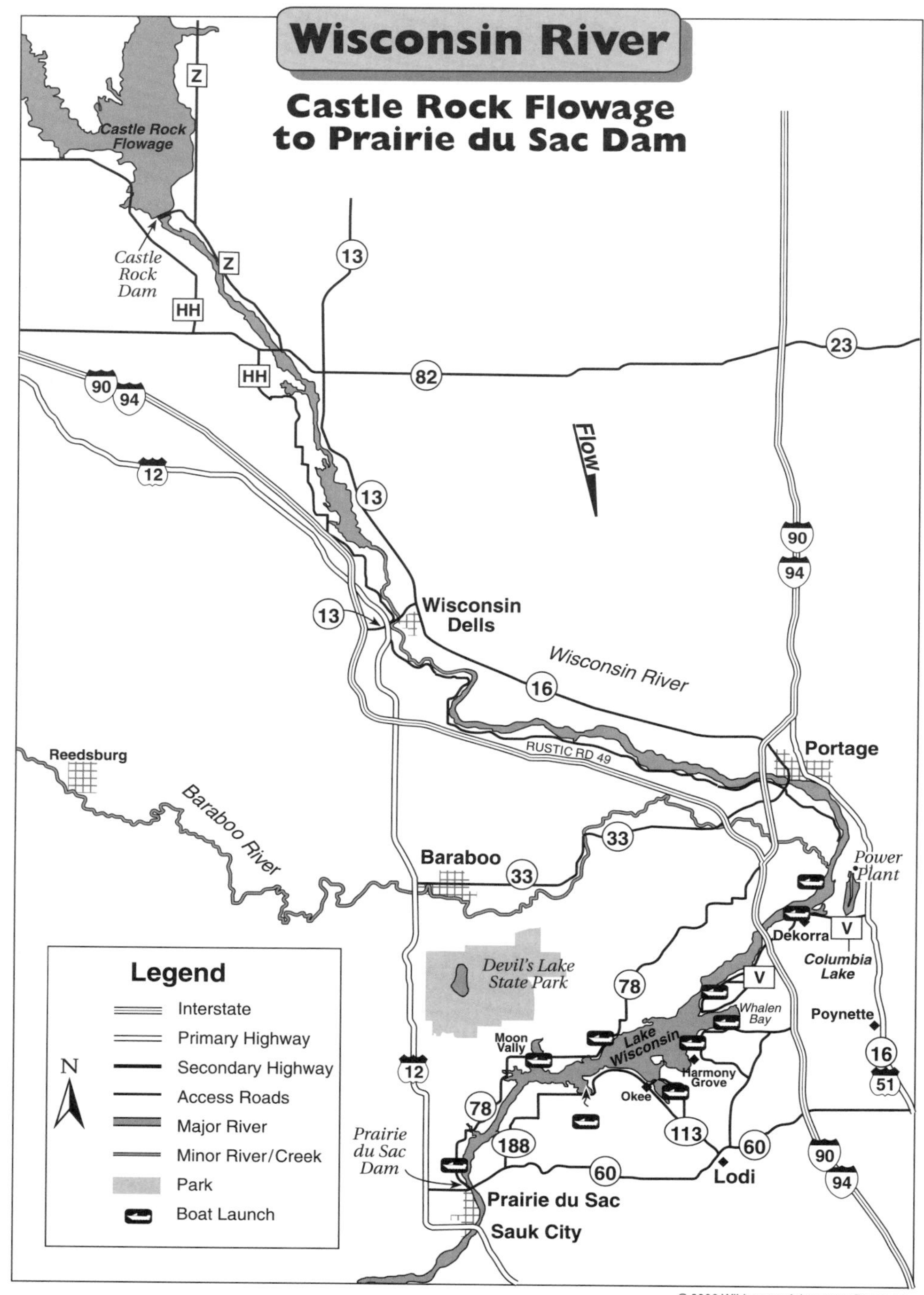
Wisconsin River
Castle Rock Flowage to Prairie du Sac Dam
Castle Rock Flowage
Castle Rock Dam
Z
HH
13
82
23
90
94
12
Flow
Wisconsin Dells
Wisconsin River
16
RUSTIC RD 49
Portage
Reedsburg
Baraboo River
Baraboo
33
Power Plant
Dekorra
V
Columbia Lake
Devil's Lake State Park
78
Whalen Bay
Poynette
Moon Vally
Lake Wisconsin
Harmony Grove
Okee
51
113
60
188
Prairie du Sac Dam
Lodi
Prairie du Sac
Sauk City
Legend
Interstate
Primary Highway
Secondary Highway
Access Roads
Major River
Minor River/Creek
Park
Boat Launch
N
© 2006 Wilderness Adventures Press, Inc.

surrounded by a scout camp, a Sand County mix of pine and oak, and not much else.

Follow County K north from Wild Rose to Akron Avenue and take your next right, which leads to the only public launch on the lake. The launch is suitable for a cartop boat. May to early June and autumn are good times to fish this shallow, weedy lake. While the weeds can make for tough fishing in summer, they also make for phenomenal northern pike and largemouth bass habitat. Expect lots of northerns here; however, many will be below the general Wisconsin 26-inch size limit for pike.

At just 93 acres, Twin Lake isn't big, but it has quality northern pike and bass water in a pretty and secluded setting. You should have plenty of elbowroom to throw a streamer or bass bug into its weedy shallows; work the deep water (up to 12 feet) south of the launch ramp as the lake weeds up. Falling just south of Highway 10, Twin Lake is located within the DNR's Southern Zone. Largemouth bass must be a minimum of 14 inches and a total of 5 may be kept; northerns must be a minimum of 26 inches and 2 may be kept. The season for both species runs from the first Saturday in May to the first Saturday in March.

The author shows off a nice northern pike.

HUB CITY: WILD ROSE

Wild Rose is a good base for exploring such noted waters as the Pine, Willow, and Mecan. In fact, you might even see trout dimpling the surface of the millpond right in town. Skupe's Corner is a good place to buy a license and get information on warmwater fisheries. Don't expect chain establishments in this small, homey community.

Accommodations

Krahl Inn, 415 Main Street, Wild Rose; 920-622-5900; $

Lickman's Landing Cottages, W6456 Highway H, Wild Rose; 920-622-3062; $

Wild Rose Hotel and Bar, 350 N. Main St., Wild Rose; 920-622-3479; historic hotel with shared-bath rooms; $

Koch's Cottages, W5607 Aspen Road, Wild Rose; 920-622-3716; $$

Silver Lake Resort, Route 2, Wild Rose; 920-622 3596; $$

Halls Wood Lake Resort, W7115 Dakota Avenue, Westfield; 608-296-3200; on spring-fed lake just outside Westfield with a chance to do some warmwater fishing right on premises, near Mecan River; bar and restaurant on premises; $$

Campgrounds

Roche a Cri State Park, 1767 Highway 13, Adams-Friendship; 608-339-6881; state park on trout stream 20 miles northwest of Westfield

Castle Rock Park, on Castle Rock Flowage; take Highway 13 to County F; take County F west to County Z; sprawling Castle Rock Lake, impoundment of the Wisconsin River, offers flyfishers shoreline smallmouths and stream-inlet panfish and northern pike

Hartman Creek State Park, N2480 Hartman Creek Road, Waupaca; 715-258-2372

Camp Shin Go Beek, N7015 24th Lane, Waupaca; 715-258-2271; Boy Scout camp on Twin Lake

Restaurants

Chatter Box, 457 Main St., Wild Rose; 920-622-3189; down-home café in downtown Wild Rose

Red Fox Food and Spirits, N5285 E. Little Silver Lake Rd., Wild Rose; 920-622-5300; supper club–style food located on Little Silver Lake

Wild Rose Hotel and Bar, 350 N. Main Street, Wild Rose; 920-622-3479; historic hotel with good home cooking

Springwater Resort, W5565 Springwater Drive, Wild Rose; located 5 miles east of Wild Rose on Kussel Lake; pizza, chicken, steak

Halls Wood Lake Resort, W7115 Dakota Avenue, Westfield; 608-296-3200; good resort with restaurant bar just north of town, great fish fry and steaks

Fly Shops, Outfitters, Sporting Goods

Tight Lines Fly Fishing Company, 1534 Bid Valley Rd., De Pere; 920-336-4106; www.tightlineflyshop.com; good source of information on area streams and hatches located about 1 hour east of most streams in this region

Pamida Discount Store, N2585 Plaza Road; Wautoma; 715 787 7709; fishing licenses

Skupe's Corner, 605 S. Cambridge Avenue; 920-787-3816; licenses sold, good source of warmwater fishing information, ask for Brad

Mr. Ed's, W6964 County GH, Wild Rose; 920-622-4939

True Value Hardware, Main Street, Westfield; 608-296-2444; fishing licenses

Veterinarians

Town and County Veterinarian, N1883 Highway 22, Wautoma; 920-787-3991; located 10 miles from Wild Rose

Sand County Vet Clinic, W6597 County M, Westfield; 608-296-2333

Medical

Wild Rose Community Memorial, 601 Grand Avenue, Wild Rose; 920-622-3257

Auto Rental

Enterprise Rent-a-Car, Waupaca; 715-256-2668, 800-736-8222

Automobile Repair

L&L Automobile Repair, W4645 County A, Wild Rose; 920-622-4173

Air Service

Wautoma Municipal Airport, W8471 Cottonville Avenue, Wautoma; 920-787-3030

Airports also at Appleton and Oshkosh.

For More Information

Wautoma Chamber of Commerce
Box 65
Wautoma, WI 54982
920-787-3488

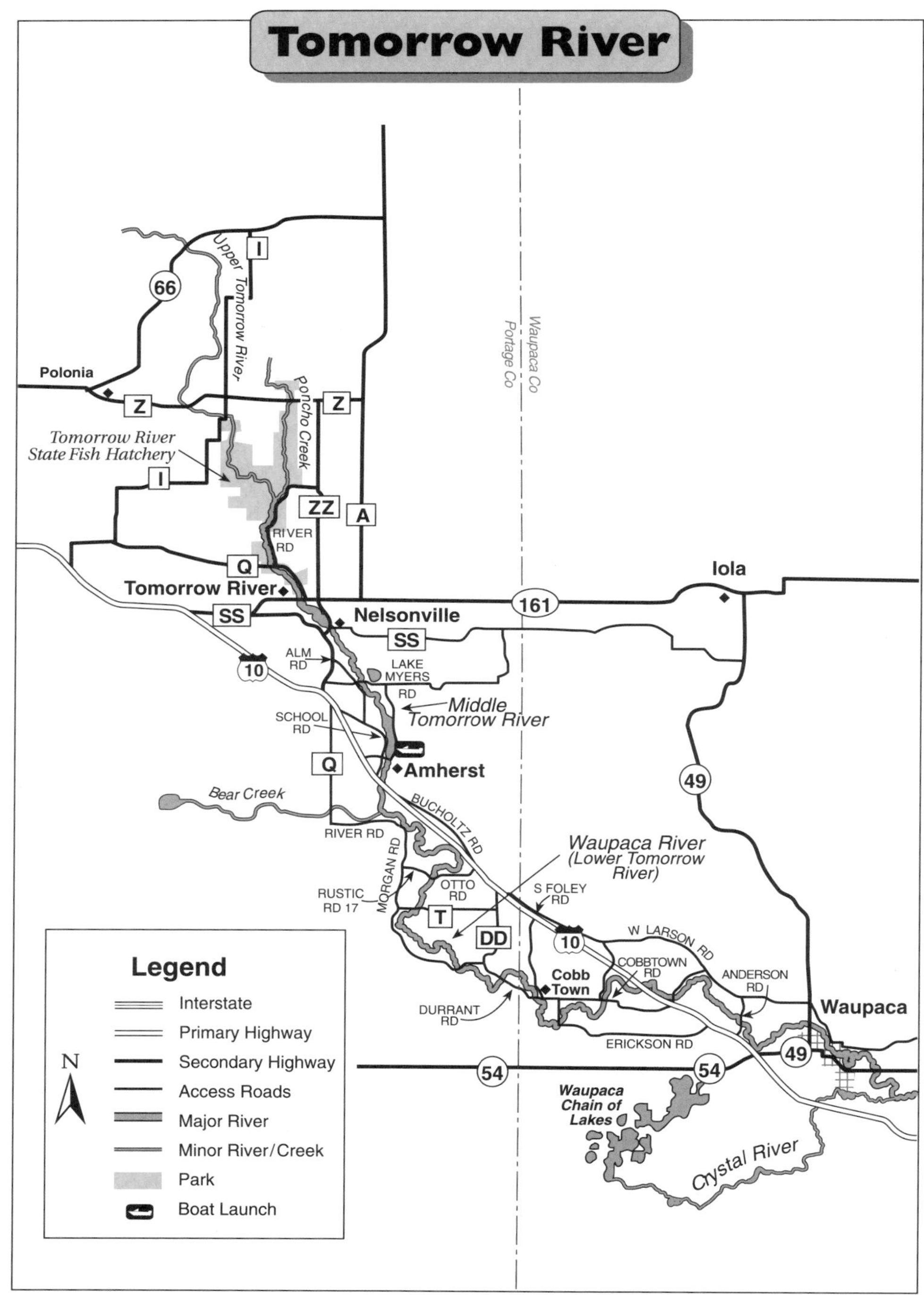

Tomorrow River
Upper Tomorrow River
Poncho Creek
Waupaca Co
Portage Co
Polonia
Tomorrow River State Fish Hatchery
RIVER RD
Tomorrow River
Nelsonville
Iola
ALM RD
LAKE MYERS RD
Middle Tomorrow River
SCHOOL RD
Amherst
Bear Creek
BUCHOLTZ RD
RIVER RD
MORGAN RD
RUSTIC RD 17
OTTO RD
Waupaca River (Lower Tomorrow River)
S FOLEY RD
W LARSON RD
COBBTOWN RD
ANDERSON RD
Cobb Town
DURRANT RD
ERICKSON RD
Waupaca
Waupaca Chain of Lakes
Crystal River
Legend
Interstate
Primary Highway
Secondary Highway
Access Roads
Major River
Minor River/Creek
Park
Boat Launch
N

The brushy banks of the upper Tomorrow River.

The Tomorrow River

Offering some 35 miles of trout water, a variety of scenery and stream conditions, and noteworthy hatches of *Hexagenia* and other insects, the Tomorrow River is one of the centerpieces of Sand County trout fishing. "It's really three different rivers in one," according to Tim Landwehr, owner of Tight Lines Fly Fishing Company in De Pere. I will describe the river separately for its three sections—upper, middle, and lower.

The Upper Tomorrow River

Rising in swampland near Polonia (named for the area's Polish population), the upper Tomorrow offers what Landwehr calls "U.P.-style brook trout fishing." For those unfamiliar with trouting in Michigan's Upper Peninsula, this means fishing in dense cover, possibly approaching on your hands and knees and trying to drop a fly through the net of tag alders. Much of these headwaters run through the 1,200-acre Richard J. Hemp Fishery Area and contain a mix of wild brook and brown trout. Access is at DNR lands along County I, River Road, and along County Q.

The confluence with Poncho Creek, off River Road, is a good place to begin your efforts as the Tomorrow increases in flow and size after this point. You can also try prospecting up Poncho Creek, a good brook trout stream in its own right, from DNR access along Highway Z. For this nip-and-tuck fishing, try something buoyant and visible like an Elk Hair Caddis or Parachute Hopper. This kind of fishing is the rule

Matt Rogge fishing on the Tomorrow River.

downstream to Nelsonville and Highway 161, the site of a former dam. The water is exquisitely clear in this stretch and runs at a low gradient over sand bottom.

Don't be put off by the reference to U.P.-style brook trout fishing unless you feel graceful casts are *de rigueur* for fly fishing. There's a certain grace and skill to fishing small, tight waters and a satisfaction in taking the brightly colored wild fish that live there. Not only are you fishing for wild fish, you're fishing in a wild setting. Much northern swampland has been left alone because it's too damn difficult to do anything with, a blessing for the hunter or angler who wants to pursue native quarry in its proper surroundings.

I think it's fair to say that headwater fishing is to grouse hunting as open-water fishing is to pheasant hunting. The former depends on economy of motion and often split-second timing. The latter take place on a wider playing field that permits more errors.

The Middle Tomorrow River

The section of the Tomorrow River between Nelsonville and the dam in Amherst might be described as the middle portion of the river. Here, streamside cover is less thick, the bottom is silt and sand, and the population balance shifts from brook to brown trout. However, both species do naturally reproduce in this stretch. Removal of the longstanding dam in Nelsonville (and stream improvements by the DNR in the stretch immediately below it) has helped this stretch of the Tomorrow.

Why are millponds bad for trout streams? It's not merely the presence of the dam that's harmful, but the way most small dams work. They release sun-warmed, oxygen-poor surface water into the stream—increasing temperatures and reducing water quality below them. However, if water is drawn from colder, oxygen-rich water below (say from a depth of 25 feet), as on Lake George on the Eau Galle River in western Wisconsin, the effect on the stream is actually positive. Think of tailwater fisheries like the White River in Arkansas: they're not natural trout streams but the byproduct of cold-water releases into the river, which make for constant water temperature and flow below—perfect growing conditions for trout. Unfortunately, I'm not aware of plans to remove the dam at Amherst.

Access to this stretch of the Tomorrow is via DNR lands along Highway SS and at Lake Meyers Road.

The Lower Tomorrow (Waupaca) River

As in many watersheds, downstream reaches of the Tomorrow (called the Waupaca River on most maps) have lower trout densities, little natural reproduction, and the river's biggest trout. This area is stocked with brown, brook, and rainbow trout. Tim Landwehr says it yields browns in the 20-inch-plus range every year.

The lower Tomorrow takes on some freestone characteristics, with boulders and pocketwater and a higher gradient than upstream. Forage fish densities also increase here, so make sure you have a good selection of streamers in your fly box. This stretch runs some 15 miles from the dam in Amherst to the confluence with the Crystal River in Waupaca, and for the most part, it's followed by Highway 10. Downstream from the Waupaca County line the Tomorrow becomes marginal for trout (stream temperatures reach the mid-70s by summer). Concentrate your efforts in the 10 miles of water between Amherst and the Waupaca-Portage County line. Access here is at waysides and bridge crossings on County A, Buckholz Road, Otto Road, Morgan Road, and Durant Road.

The Tomorrow has a wide variety of insect life and hatches. Often overlooked is the early season stonefly hatch in March and April. Most people think of the Tomorrow as a Hex stream, according to Landwehr, and they miss the smorgasbord of hatches it offers. Landwehr recommends a generic stonefly pattern in size 10 to 14. Halfbacks, Prince Nymphs (black or natural), and Little Black Caddis will all do the job.

Landwehr also notes that the fish in the early season are not keyed on specific imitations, so something close will do. Caddis action is good in May, June, and off and on throughout the season. Landwehr likes to fish caddis larvae imitations, size 12 or 14. Hendricksons (mid-April to mid-May) and Sulphurs (end of May to mid-June) are minor hatches on the Tomorrow. Blue-Winged Olive hatches can happen any time during the season, with spikes in April/May and August/September.

The Tomorrow is probably best known for its *Hexagenia* hatch. Most people think of it as strictly a nighttime, mid-June activity—and they are missing some fine fishing, according to Landwehr. The hatch usually straddles a few weeks on either side of the magic mid-June date. Fish can be taken on Hex spinner or emerger imitations on evenings when the hatch is not on full-bore. Landwehr also fishes Hex nymphs during the day. Trout are not going to ignore those big meaty nymphs, even if the sun is shining. There's also a sister fly to the larger *Hexagenia limbata* (*Hexagenia atrocaudata*), which hatches well into July. For the main Hex hatch, you'll want to fish big, size 4 or 6; for the smaller version, size 8 or 10 is about right. Landwehr ties a pattern called Tim's Hex, which is well known locally and made of foam and deer hair.

Terrestrial fishing is traditionally done in the heat of summer. While there is certainly good hopper and cricket fishing during these times on the Tomorrow, you can fish an ant or beetle imitation with good results as early as May. Landwehr likes parachute-style terrestrials fished tight to the bank.

The *Ephoron leukon* is a sleeper hatch on the Tomorrow. This is a White Mayfly hatch (a White Wulff size 14 mimics it well) and a real hot-weather event, occurring in the doldrums of August. Trout need to be played quickly and released with special care during this time. Landwehr even encourages anglers to quit fishing if the fish seem especially sluggish and stream temperatures are in the mid-70s. Any stress in these conditions can be fatal for trout, which are especially vulnerable during times of extreme heat and cold or low or high water. Streamers are a good year-round bet on the Tomorrow, with Marabou Muddlers and leech patterns being good imitations of the stream's prolific dace and sculpins.

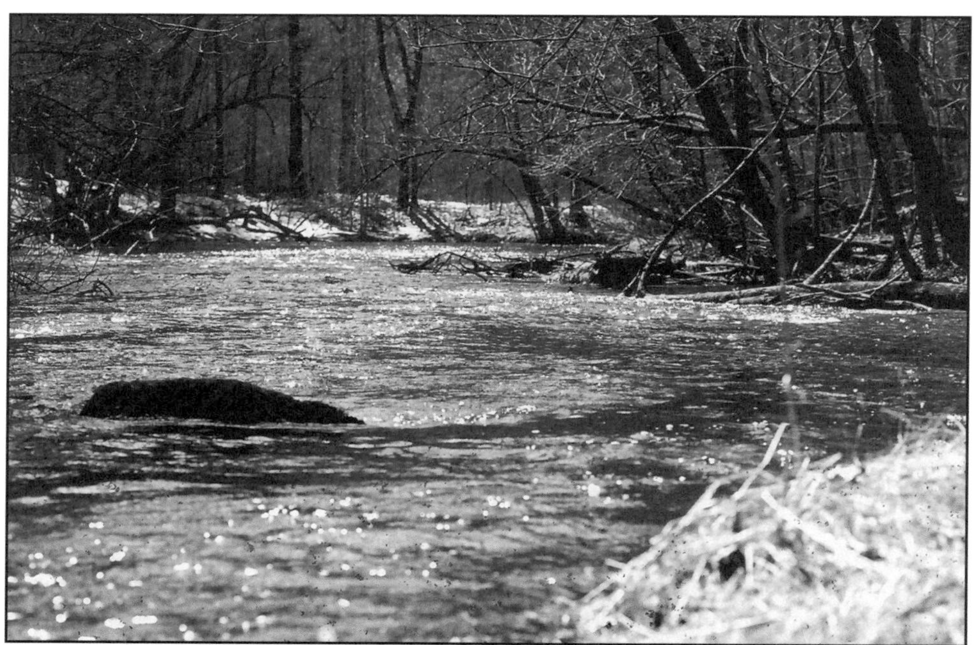

Pretty water on the Tomorrow River. (Tim Landwehr)

Stream Facts: Tomorrow River

Season

- The early season runs from the first Saturday in March to the last Sunday before the first Saturday in May; no-kill, single barbless hooks only. Regular season runs from the first Saturday in May at 5:00 am through September 30.

Regulations

- Primarily category 4. Category 5 at Old Railroad Bridge north of Amherst (artificials only; 3 trout limit; 3 trout between 10 inches and 13 inches or 2 trout between 10 inches and 13 inches and 1 trout over 20 inches). Category 5 between Durant Road and River Road (artificials only, 1 trout limit, brook trout minimum 12 inches, brown trout minimum 18 inches).
- Early season Tomorrow River: open only from Amherst to Durant Road in Portage County; open only from Frost Valley Road to Highway 54 in Waupaca County.

Species

- Wild and planted brook and brown trout.

Miles of Trout Water

- 35 miles

Stream Characteristics

- Sand-bottomed creek, especially clear; known for Hex hatch.

Access

- Tomorrow River State Fishery Area upstream and downstream from Nelsonville; road access downstream from Amherst.

Fly Shops

- Tight Lines Fly Fishing Company

Maps

- *Wisconsin Atlas and Gazetteer*, pages 65, 53

Whitcomb Creek

Rising just to the east of Big Falls and joining the Little Wolf near Union, Whitcomb Creek offers 14 miles of self-sustaining brook trout water in north-central Waupaca County. While it resembles nearby Flume Creek, it has not, for some reason, made it into the cannon of central Wisconsin trout streams.

Whitcomb offers tight tag-alder fishing, sometimes in swamps, sometimes in upland, and receives little pressure. Try a Pass Lake or other bushy dry fly fished close to the bank; or skitter your dry along likely looking cover to provoke a strike from *Salvelinus fontinalis*. Caddis or stonefly nymphs fished on a long, fine leader are also effective. Fish ants and beetles anytime; try hopper and cricket patterns during the doldrums. Access to Whitcomb Creek is at the following road crossings: Highway G, Highway E, Campbell Lake Road, Swamp Road, and Jossie Road. Whitcomb Creek is open to trout fishing during the early March and April season.

Flume Creek

Flume Creek is similar to the better-known Tomorrow River to the west, according to Tim Landwehr of Tight Lines Fly Fishing Company. Its upper half offers U.P.-style brook trout fishing: swampy margins, sand bottom, bright fish, tight quarters. Its lower reaches, flecked by boulders and whitewater, begin to look like a freestone stream, with the population balance giving way to brown trout. The former sort of fishing can be found in Portage County, the latter in Waupaca County.

I first noticed Flume Creek while driving through central Wisconsin's scrub pine and potato farms on the way to an outdoor writer's conference. On that cool June morning, I picked up several brilliant-colored brook trout on a Royal Coachman skittered along the tag alders below the village of Rosholt. (To reach that spot, take Highway A south out of Rosholt, turn right onto Mill Road and look for an access road on your right; there's public access here through a DNR holding.) However, once the light of day exposed my operation, the fish quit biting.

Heading east on Flume Creek between Linden Road and Highway 49 one notices that the stream takes on a swampy cast. This section can be productive for larger brook trout—and the pressure is almost non-existent—but it's tough going in summer when mosquitoes and horse flies are present. Try it during the early season or on a cool September day. There's more DNR land east of Highway 49 and the village of Northland. Take Highway C east and cross the river at Lund or Drake Road—bigger and deeper water here with brown trout displacing brook trout and plenty of whitewater pockets to fish. A few miles east of Northland, Flume empties into the Little Wolf River, a fine trout stream in its own right.

Fish wet stonefly or caddis imitations in the lower reaches; try bushy dries like a Parachute Adams in the tight upper reaches. The swampy middle parts of the Flume, west of Highway 49, are a good place to fish the mid-June Hex hatch. As on many Sand County streams, a tiny black ant or beetle imitation can be just the ticket when nothing else seems to work. There's also good hopper and cricket fishing on Flume

Creek from July to September. The creek offers 18 miles of category 3 trout water and supports native brook trout and brown trout.

HUB CITY: WAUPACA

Waupaca is a larger central Wisconsin community with more services than Westfield and Wild Rose. It is convenient to many of the trout streams described in this region, particularly the Tomorrow River, Flume Creek, the Willow, and the Pine.

Accommodations

Baymont Inn and Suites, 110 Grand Seasons Drive, Waupaca; 715-258-9212; $$
Village Inn Motel, 1060 W. Fulton Street, Waupaca; 715-258-8526; $$

Campgrounds

Hartman Creek State Park, N2480 Hartman Creek Road, Waupaca; 715-258-2372; located on Chain o Lakes
Roche a Cri State Park, 1767 Highway 13, Adams-Friendship; 608-339-6881; state park on trout stream 40 miles southwest of Waupaca
Castle Rock Park, on Castle Rock Flowage; take Highway 13 to County F; take County F west to County Z; sprawling Castle Rock Lake, impoundment of the Wisconsin River, offers flyfishers shoreline smallmouths and stream-inlet panfish and northern pike
Camp Shin Go Beek, N7015 24th Lane, Waupaca; 715-258-2271; rural Boy Scout camp on Twin Lake

Restaurants

Country Inn Bar and Restaurant, N 4004 Highway 49, Waupaca; 715-258-2901; country tavern and grill with chicken, steak, and fish
Simpson's Indian Room Restaurant, 222 S. Main Street, Waupaca; 715-258-2330; good supper club food
Wheel House, E1209 County Q, Waupaca; 715-258-8289; friendly restaurant with pasta, pizza, and sandwiches
Culvers, 1045 W. Fulton St., Waupaca; 715-256-0066; quality Midwest hamburger and frozen custard chain
Pizza Hut, 1080 W. Fulton St., Waupaca

Fly Shops, Outfitters, Sporting Goods

River Bend Sport Shop, 230 Grand Seasons Drive; Waupaca, 715-258-2514; fishing licenses
Tight Lines Fly Fishing Company, De Pere; 920-336-4106; www.tightlineflyshop.com; good source of information on area streams and hatches located about 1 hour east of most streams in this region

Veterinarians

Waupaca Veterinary Service, 780 Bowling Lane, Waupaca; 715-258-3343

Medical

Riverside Medical Center, 800 Riverside Drive, Waupaca; 715-258-1119

Auto Rental

Enterprise Rent-a-Car, Waupaca; 715-256-2668, 800-736-8222
Auto rental at Madison, Appleton, and Oshkosh airports.

Automobile Repair

Bill's Auto Repair, 303 W. Fulton, Waupaca; 715-256-0601

Air Service

Waupaca Municipal Airport, Highway 10 and 49; 920-987-3201
Airports at Madison, Appleton, and Oshkosh.

For More Information

Waupaca Chamber of Commerce
221 S. Main Street
Waupaca, WI 54981
715-258-7343

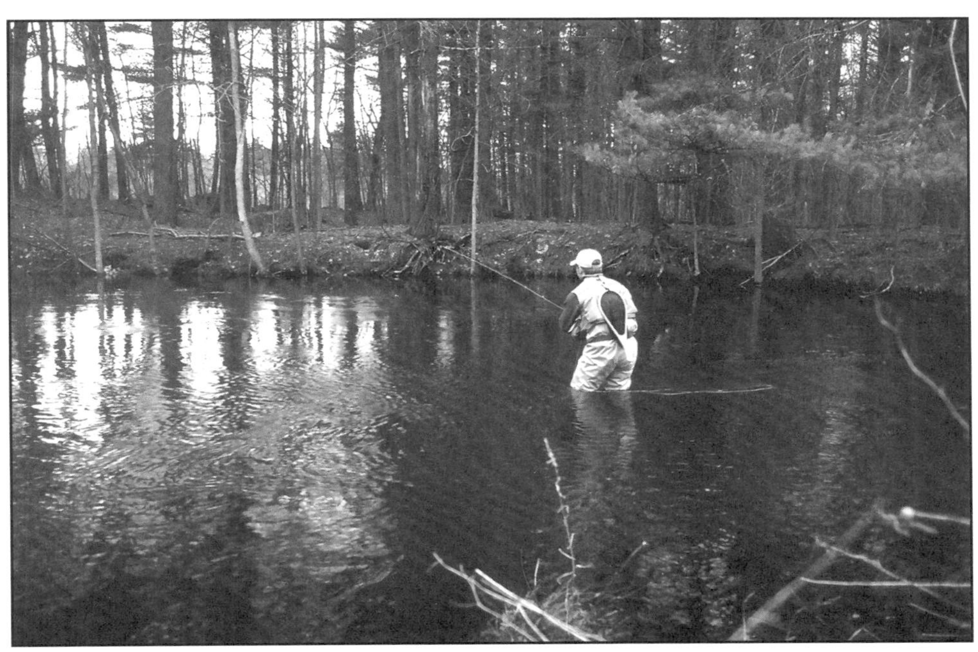

Bart Landwehr fishing a deep pool on the Waupaca. (Sarah Landwehr)

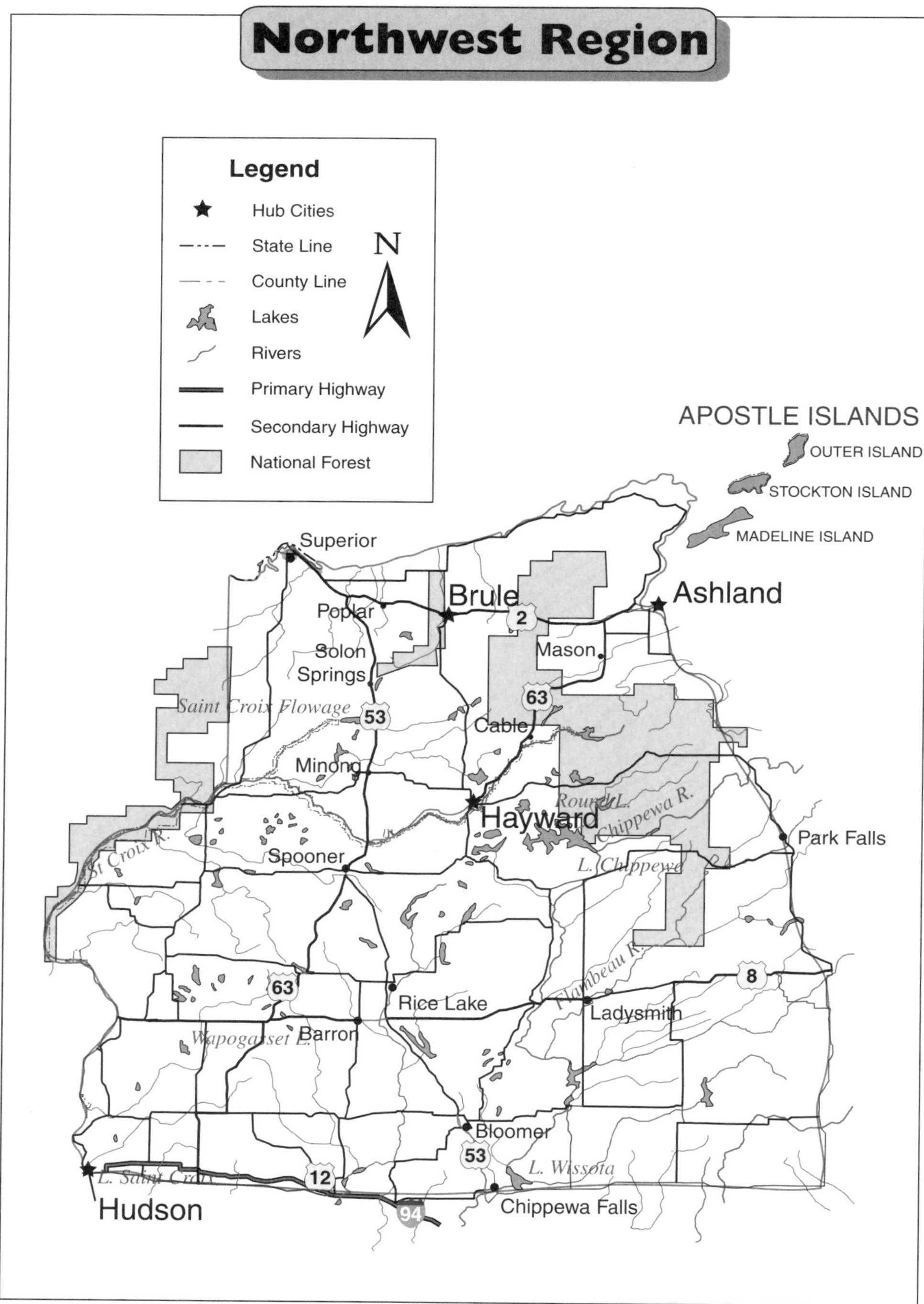
Northwest Region
Legend
Hub Cities
State Line
County Line
Lakes
Rivers
Primary Highway
Secondary Highway
National Forest
N
APOSTLE ISLANDS
OUTER ISLAND
STOCKTON ISLAND
MADELINE ISLAND
Superior
Brule
Ashland
Poplar
2
Mason
Solon
Springs
63
Saint Croix Flowage
53
Cable
Minong
Round L.
Chippewa R.
Hayward
Park Falls
St Croix R.
Spooner
L. Chippewa
Flambeau R.
8
63
Rice Lake
Ladysmith
Wapogasset L.
Barron
Bloomer
53
L. Wissota
L. Saint Croix
12
Hudson
94
Chippewa Falls

Northwest Wisconsin: Indianhead Country

A friend of mine religiously hits the Brule River for the trout opener. In most of the state, the first Saturday in May can be anything from cool and rainy to hot and sunny. Only in Brule County are snow and ice real possibilities. Be prepared if traveling to Wisconsin's far northwest. Pack a down vest and long underwear for May, a wool sweater even in summer, and heavy outerwear if you're brave enough to fish fall steelhead. Gore-Tex is a must year-round to protect against wind-driven rain and snow.

Northern latitude and proximity to Lake Superior make for short growing seasons and colder weather than elsewhere in the state. Another result of this northerly climate is later hatches—early Blue-Winged Olive and midge hatches so common in central and southern streams are almost absent here. Hendricksons don't really get underway here until early May. The Hex hatch, for which the White River is known, peaks a week to two weeks later than it does in central parts of the state—early July rather than late June.

A beautiful steelhead ready for release. (Craig Amacker)

HATCH CHART—Northwest Wisconsin: Indianhead Country

Insect/Food Source	J	F	M	A	M	J	J	A	S	O	N	D	Flies
Stoneflies (Peak in April/May)				X	X	X	X	X	X				Yellow Stimulator #10-12; Black Stonefly #10-14; Stonefly Nymphs #8-10
Caddis				X	X	X	X	X	X				Elk Hair Caddis #14-16; Sparkle Pupa, Beadhead Caddis, Caddis Larvae #16-20
Blue-Winged Olives (*Baetis*) (Peaks May 1-15)					X	X	X	X	X				BWO Thorax, Sparkle Dun #16-22; Pheasant Tail #16-18
Hendricksons (Peaks May 1-15)					X								Light Hendrickson, Spinners #12-14; Pheasant Tail #12-14
Brown Drake (Peaks June 14-21/Evening Hatch)						X							Brown Drake, Spinner, Emerger, Nymph #10-12
Sulphurs					X	X							Sulphur Dun, Pale Evening Dun, Spinner #16; Pheasant Tail Nymph #16
Hexagenia (Evening Hatch)						X	X						Hart Washer, Hex, Olive Drake #4-8; Hex Nymph, Strip Nymph #4-8/Late June #10
Trico (Peaks July 15-Aug 7/Morning Hatch)							X	X	X				Tiny White Wing Black, CDC Trico, Spent Wing Trico #24-28

HATCH CHART—Northwest Wisconsin: Indianhead Country (cont.)													
Insect/Food Source	**J**	**F**	**M**	**A**	**M**	**J**	**J**	**A**	**S**	**O**	**N**	**D**	**Flies**
Terrestrials (Ants, Beetles, Crickets, Grasshoppers)							■	■	■				Green Hoppers #6-10; Letort Cricket #10; Ants #14-20; Beetles #18-20
Crawfish			■	■	■	■	■	■	■				Crayfish Patterns, Marabou Leech Olive/Brown #8-10
Leeches			■	■	■	■	■	■	■				Marabou Leech, Strip Leech (Black, Olive, Brown) #4-10
Sculpin			■	■	■	■	■	■	■				Muddler Minnow, Olive or Brown Leech, Black-Nosed Dace #8-10
White Mayfly (*Ephoron leukon*) (Evening Hatch/Peaks early August)								■	■				White Wulff, White Miller #12-14

The Bayfield Peninsula is known for clear, sand-bottomed streams.

While there are fewer trout streams in this part of the state, these streams—notably the Brule, Namekagon, and White—harbor some of the densest populations of big trout (over 15 inches) east of the Mississippi. Namekagon browns are legendary for their size. The Brule holds large resident fish. And Bibon Marsh, in the middle reaches of the White, is a destination for fishing the Hex hatch.

Wild lake-run trout and salmon run up the Brule, lower White, and some of the smaller Lake Superior tributaries on the Bayfield Peninsula in spring and fall. Many are open between the last Saturday in March and November 15 to allow anglers to try for lake-run trout and salmon. Check the *Wisconsin Trout Fishing Regulations and Guide* to be sure the county in which you are fishing is open.

If you're from Wisconsin, or have spent time here, you know the world-record muskellunge (69 pounds, 11 ounces) was taken from the Chippewa Flowage in 1949. And while the Chippewa Flowage is fished intensively for muskellunge by anglers using conventional tackle, a growing number of anglers have come to pursue muskellunge using fly rods. Hayward guide Drake Williams (715-462-9650) specializes in guiding fly-rod anglers for muskies. He feels it may even be easier to "get right into the slop" with fly tackle.

If you don't find the solitude you want on the flowage, try Teal, Ghost, and Lost Land Lakes, which are managed with no-wake, minimal shoreline development, and a low-fly zone to protect nesting eagles. The Flambeau and Chippewa River systems provide good muskellunge and smallmouth fishing, especially for the angler who doesn't mind paddling for his fish. The St. Croix, which forms the Wisconsin-

Minnesota border for 55 miles, is a popular float for smallmouth and wild scenery. Polk, Burnett, and Washburn Counties abound with glacial lakes. And Lake Superior's Chequamegon Bay offers some of the finest smallmouth fishing anywhere. Fly shops can be found in Ashland, Brule, and Hayward.

Streams of the Bayfield Peninsula

The streams north of Highway 2 on the Bayfield Peninsula can be treated as a group because they are similar in many respects. They drain into Lake Superior or Chequamegon Bay and support runs of anadromous trout and salmon. They all rise in the peninsula's clay soils and thus have problems with erosion and sediment, especially during floods. While they do support modest populations of wild brown and brook trout, they are not first-tier trout fisheries like the nearby Brule or Namekagon.

As venues for wild lake-run browns and rainbows, they offer good fall and spring fishing on a beautiful and wild peninsula. In addition, chinook, coho, and pink salmon (in even years) visit these streams in fall. Egg patterns are a good bet for steelhead and browns. Bright Woolly Buggers work on salmon, as well as trout. A tandem rig with an egg pattern trailing behind a Woolly Bugger is an effective way to prospect high and low in the water column. But keep in mind that tandem rigs foul-hook more fish, and the second hook can catch on snags.

The following size and bag limits apply to these streams. Daily bag limit is 5 trout and salmon; only 2 may be brown trout over 15 inches, and only 1 may be a rainbow trout. Size limits are 8 inches for brook trout, 10 inches for brown trout, 12 inches for salmon, and 26 inches for rainbow trout.

Salmon and steelhead runs in Lake Superior tributaries follow a calendar not unlike that of Lake Michigan. Coho and king salmon, as well as brown and brook trout, make their way up Superior's tributaries from the middle part of September to ice-up in November. Steelhead runs are a springtime affair in Superior country, with the vanguard of fish coming up rivers in early April and continuing until the middle part of May. Just after a good October rain and after a modest snowmelt in spring are good times to strike out on a salmon or steelhead outing. However, muddy water may keep the fish dormant and your flies hard to see.

Use an 8- or 9-weight rod and sturdy leaders. Egg patterns, big nymphs, and Woolly Buggers in a variety of colors are good salmon and steelhead patterns. Steelhead average about 5 pounds while salmon, especially kings, usually weigh in at better than 10.

The main difference between Lake Michigan and Lake Superior fishing is that natural reproduction occurs among Superior steelhead and, to a lesser extent, among its salmon, while population levels in the Lake Michigan system are maintained by a steady stocking of fingerlings.

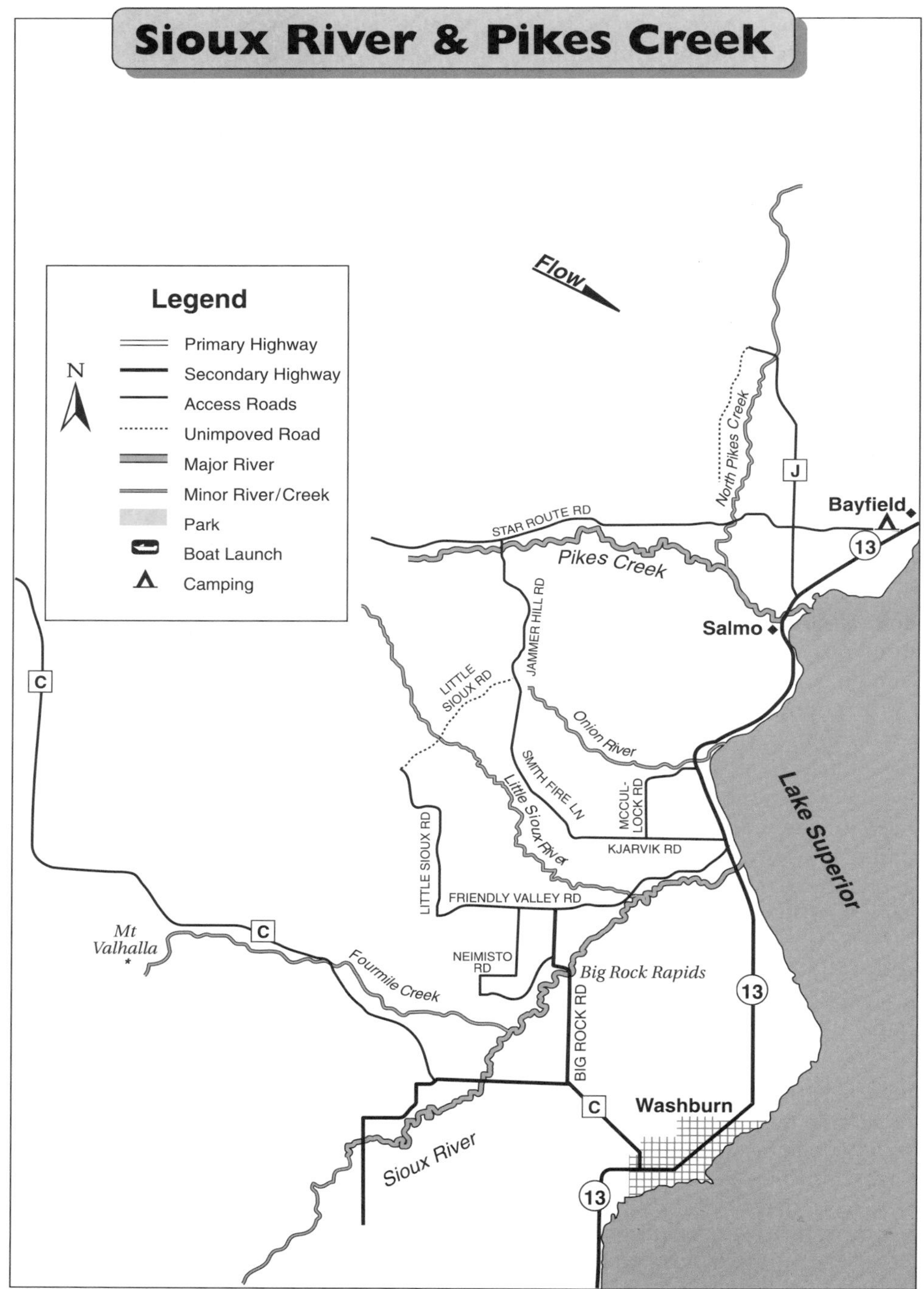
Sioux River & Pikes Creek
Legend
Primary Highway
Secondary Highway
Access Roads
Unimpoved Road
Major River
Minor River/Creek
Park
Boat Launch
Camping
N
Flow
North Pikes Creek
J
Bayfield
13
STAR ROUTE RD
Pikes Creek
Salmo
JAMMER HILL RD
LITTLE SIOUX RD
Onion River
SMITH FIRE LN
MCCUL-LOCK RD
Little Sioux River
KJARVIK RD
Lake Superior
LITTLE SIOUX RD
FRIENDLY VALLEY RD
C
Mt Valhalla
C
Fourmile Creek
NEIMISTO RD
Big Rock Rapids
BIG ROCK RD
13
C
Washburn
Sioux River
13

Sioux River

Located just outside the town of Washburn halfway between Ashland and Bayfield is the Sioux River. Upstream to Big Rock Falls, it is open from the last Saturday in March to November 15. It is a basically a spring steelhead stream. Access it at Highway 13 and Big Rock Road. The smaller Onion River just to the north is also worth a look for spring steelhead.

Pikes Creek

Just west of the town of Bayfield, Pike's Creek can be reached by taking Highway J west to Star Route Road. Below the Red Dam, the season runs from the first Saturday in May to November 15; above the dam, the season runs from the first Saturday in May to September 30. Pikes Creek has a good fall fishery for king and coho salmon, as well as lake-run browns.

Cranberry River

The Cranberry River runs through the Cranberry State Wildlife Area south of Herbster off Lenawee Road. Downstream from the Lenawee Road bridge, the Cranberry River is open to fishing from the last Saturday in March to November 15. Above the bridge, the season runs from the first Saturday in May to September 30. The Cranberry is probably the best of the lot as far as holding decent numbers of resident brook trout. It's also a very pretty stream with good in-stream cover and lots of hiding places for resident and lake-run fish. The Cranberry sees good fall runs of king and coho salmon.

Flag River

The Flag River flows through the town of Port Wing into Lake Superior. The Flag River Fishery Area is east of Port Wing. To reach the fishery area, take Flag Road east from Highway 13. From the confluence with East Fork of the Flag River downstream to the mouth at Lake Superior, the river is open from the last Saturday in March to November 15. Above the East Fork, the river is open to fishing from the first Saturday in May to September 30. The Flag is a good-sized river system that sees fall salmon runs and spring steelhead runs.

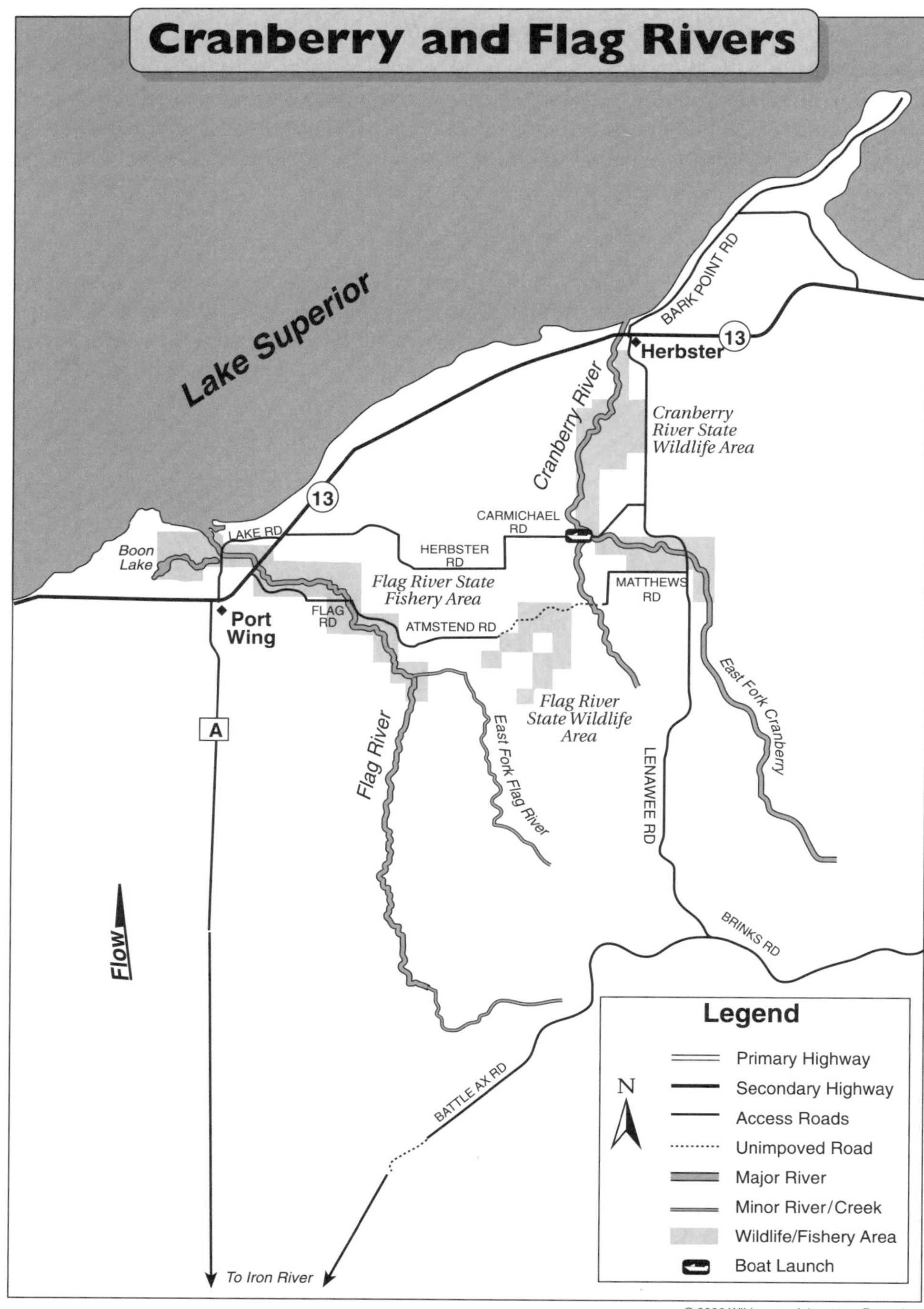
Cranberry and Flag Rivers
Lake Superior
BARK POINT RD
13
Herbster
Cranberry River
Cranberry River State Wildlife Area
13
CARMICHAEL RD
LAKE RD
Boon Lake
HERBSTER RD
Flag River State Fishery Area
MATTHEWS RD
Port Wing
FLAG RD
ATMSTEND RD
East Fork Cranberry
Flag River State Wildlife Area
A
Flag River
East Fork Flag River
LENAWEE RD
Flow
BRINKS RD
Legend
Primary Highway
Secondary Highway
Access Roads
Unimpoved Road
Major River
Minor River/Creek
Wildlife/Fishery Area
Boat Launch
N
BATTLE AX RD
To Iron River

Chequamegon Bay

It's hard to know where to begin when describing the fishery in an 84,000-acre bay on the world's largest body of fresh water. Fortunately, there's an easy answer. Ask any upper Midwest angler worth his or her salt, and you'll get the same response. Smallmouth bass—big, chunky bronzebacks averaging 2 to 3 pounds.

Thanks to intelligent management from the DNR and the bay's fertile water, Chequamegon Bay is home to some of the world's finest smallmouth bass fishing. As good as it is, it's probably not what you're expecting. Whereas smallmouth are usually found around rocks, Chequamegon Bay is mostly sand and weeds. Smallmouth hold here in the wild rice, cabbage, celery, and bulrush beds throughout the bay. Guide Roger La Penter, owner of Anglers All in Ashland, says the downed timber in the east end of the bay is also an excellent area for smallmouths. You're also likely to catch walleye and northern pike while chasing smallies. And early on, just after ice-out, you'll find trout and salmon on a post-winter feed, pursuing smelt and shiners.

A nice smallmouth from Northwest Wisconsin waters.

The right gear is crucial for any safe and successful fishing outing, particularly on big water like Chequamegon Bay. A minimum standard for Lake Superior is a deep V-hull of 16 feet with a strong outboard. On calm days, you might get by with a small craft like a canoe. The only problem with this is that you don't know when the weather will change. Winds and seches (the equivalent of tides on the Great Lakes) can change from placid to whitecapped in a matter of minutes, leaving the small boater in big trouble. It is therefore crucial to have a marine radio and to keep an eye on the weather.

Hiring a guide is not a bad idea for your first time on Chequamegon. Another point to bear in mind is that the wild rice beds in the vicinity of Kakagon Slough are a no-motor zone. These rice beds, occurring on the land of the Bad River band, have

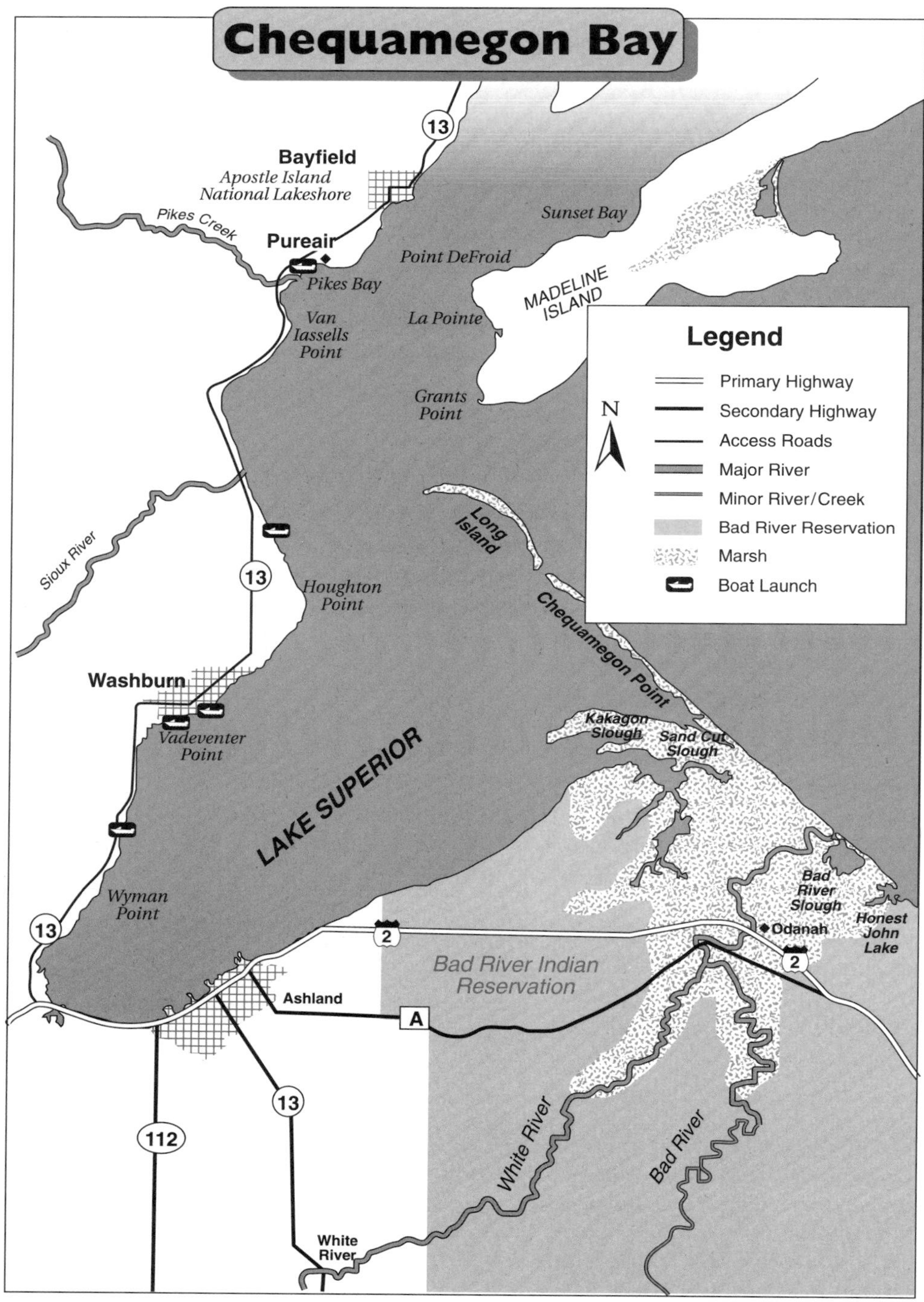
Chequamegon Bay
Bayfield
Apostle Island National Lakeshore
Pikes Creek
Pureair
Pikes Bay
Van Iassells Point
Point DeFroid
Sunset Bay
La Pointe
MADELINE ISLAND
Grants Point
Sioux River
Long Island
Houghton Point
Chequamegon Point
Washburn
Vadeventer Point
Kakagon Slough
Sand Cut Slough
LAKE SUPERIOR
Wyman Point
Bad River Slough
Odanah
Honest John Lake
Ashland
Bad River Indian Reservation
White River
Bad River
White River
13
2
A
112
Legend
Primary Highway
Secondary Highway
Access Roads
Major River
Minor River/Creek
Bad River Reservation
Marsh
Boat Launch
N
© 2006 Wilderness Adventures Press, Inc.

been a source of nourishment to the Bad River people for hundreds of years. They are also host to a variety of migrant and nesting waterfowl and shorebirds. You will need to pushpole your boat through the rice beds, as propellers wreck havoc on them. This is per town and tribal ordinance, and the boundary of the rice beds should be marked with buoys. If you are in doubt as to the tribal boundary in this area, pushpole your boat. Kakagon Slough, at 16,000 acres, is one of the largest intact natural wetland systems in the upper Midwest—and we should all work to keep it that way.

An 8- or 9-weight rod will allow you to throw big flies into the wind. For the topwater bite in midsummer, fish a floating line. Otherwise, you're better off with a sinking line, as smallmouth usually feed in the lower part of the water column. Leech, minnow, and crawfish imitations (size 2 to 6) are the flies to use. In summer, watch for rises and fish them with a good-sized dry like a White Wulff or Hex.

Since the bay is clear and relatively shallow, sight-fishing with the aid of polarized glasses is a good way to take fish. La Penter compares fishing on Chequamegon's sand flats to sight-fishing bonefish in the Caribbean. If you want to fish structure, look for downed timber, dropoffs, sand flats, and weedbeds. Find cover and you'll find fish. For the angler without a boat, shoreline fishing can be good around the cities of Ashland and Washburn. Trout can be taken just after ice-out, and smallmouths will hang around until the middle of July in a typical summer, later in a cool one. Look for them around piers, rocks, and breakwater.

There are numerous boat launches along the bayshore, off Highway 2/13 in the vicinity of Ashland and off Highway 13 near Washburn. Season dates vary by species in the bay. Smallmouth and largemouth bass fishing is catch and release between the first Saturday in May and the middle Saturday in June; a 1-fish, 22-inch limit is in effect from the following Sunday to the first Saturday in March. Walleye may be fished year-round in the bay itself; daily bag is 5 with a minimum length of 15 inches and only 1 fish over 20 inches. In tributaries and connected sloughs the season runs from the first Saturday in May to March 1. Northern pike may be fished year-round in the bay itself with a daily bag of 2 and a minimum length of 26 inches; in tributaries and connected sloughs up to the first dam the season runs from the first Saturday in May to March 1.

Trout may be fished year-round, except lake trout, which may be fished from December 1 to September 30 only. Daily bag is 5 for trout of which 3 may be lake trout and 1 rainbow trout. Rainbow trout must be a minimum of 26 inches. Other trout must be 15 inches. Only 1 lake trout larger than 25 inches may be kept. Salmon may be fished year-round, with a daily bag of 5 and a minimum length of 15 inches.

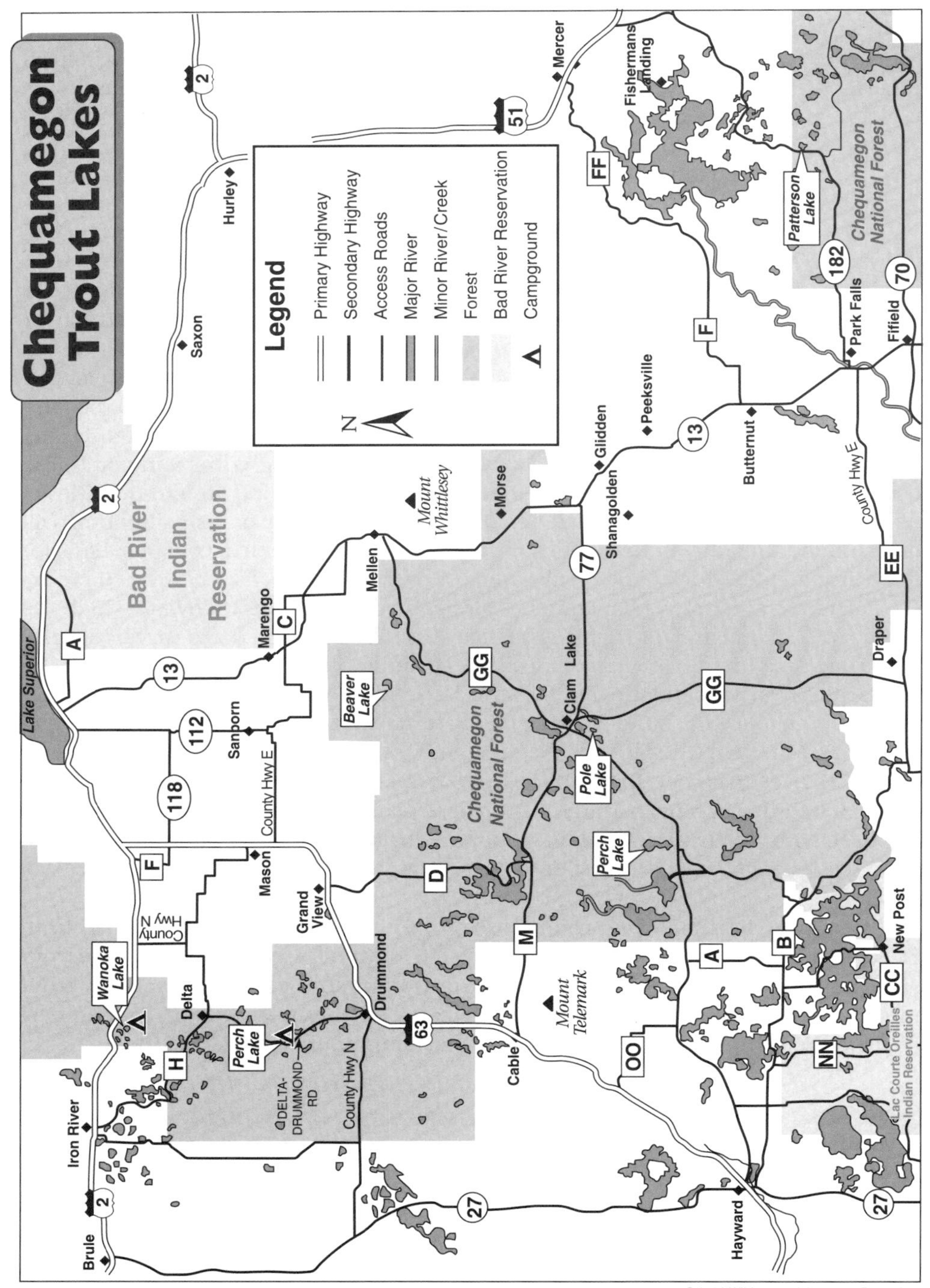

Chequamegon Trout Lakes
Legend
Primary Highway
Secondary Highway
Access Roads
Major River
Minor River/Creek
Forest
Bad River Reservation
Campground
N
Lake Superior
Bad River Indian Reservation
Chequamegon National Forest
Lac Courte Oreilles Indian Reservation
Mount Whittlesey
Mount Telemark
Brule
Iron River
Delta
Drummond
Grand View
Mason
Sanborn
Marengo
Saxon
Hurley
Mercer
Fishermans Landing
Mellen
Morse
Glidden
Shanagolden
Peeksville
Butternut
Park Falls
Fifield
Clam Lake
Draper
Cable
Hayward
New Post
Wanoka Lake
Perch Lake
Beaver Lake
Pole Lake
Patterson Lake
DELTA-DRUMMOND RD
County Hwy N
County Hwy E

Wanoka Lake

TROUT LAKES OF THE CHEQUAMEGON NATIONAL FOREST

Chequamegon National Forest is the equivalent of Nicolet National Forest in northeast Wisconsin—big, wild, and dotted with lakes. Unfortunately, many of these lakes are sterile seepages that never contained fish. Other cold, deep lakes are planted with trout, though natural reproduction is generally poor or nonexistent. Many of these lakes offer a two-tier fishery, with bass, northern, and panfish present. The following is a sampling of Chequamegon's best trout lakes (presented from north to south).

Wanoka Lake

Just east of Iron River on Highway 2 is tiny 15-acre Wanoka Lake. Take Fire Road 234 to the lake, where access is via trail. Wanoka Lake is stocked with brook and rainbow trout, some of which attain considerable size. It is a category 2 trout lake with an open season running from the first Saturday in May to first Saturday in March. A belly boat or canoe will help you make careful approaches to Wanoka's wary trout.

Perch Lake

Perch Lake offers a two-tier fishery with planted rainbow and brook trout, as well as resident walleye, bass, and panfish. It covers 70 acres, with a maximum depth of

77 feet. From the village of Drummond, take Delta-Drummond Road to reach the boat launch and USFS campground. It is a category 2 trout lake with an open season running from the first Saturday in May to first Saturday in March. The boat launch will accommodate larger boats.

Beaver Lake

Thirty-five-acre Beaver Lake in western Ashland County north of Clam Lake offers fishing for both planted brook trout and panfish. With a maximum depth of just 10 feet, it does suffer from winterkill in years of extreme cold. From Clam Lake, take Highway GG north to the intersection with Clam Lake Road. Follow this to the juncture with Mineral Lake Road. Go left at the fork and follow what will now be Coffee Lake Road to Beaver Lake. There is also a USFS campground and a boat launch. Beaver Lake is a category 2 trout water open from the first Saturday in May to first Saturday in March.

Perch Lake

Located east of Lost Land Lake and Teal Lake in Sawyer Lake, this Perch Lake is tiny and offers a fishery for stocked brook trout. It lies north of Highway 77 off Fire Road 203. Perch Lake is a category 3 trout lake open from the first Saturday in May to first Saturday in March.

Pole Lake

Just south of Clam Lake, you'll find tiny Pole Lake, which covers just 13 acres. It's walk-in access only and holds trout and panfish. Take Highway GG south from Clam Lake to Fire Road 1275. Stay right (north) at the fork. Pole Lake will be on your left after about a half-mile walk. Bring the belly boat to this one, since carrying a canoe for a half-mile is no fun. Pole Lake is category 2 trout water open from the first Saturday in May to First Saturday in March.

Patterson Lake

Located in northern Price County just south of the Ashland County line off Highway 182, Patterson Lake is a trout lake that sees good growth in its holdover fish. Brook trout to 14 inches are taken most years, as are rainbows and browns to 20 inches. It's a category 2 trout water open from the first Saturday in May to first Saturday in March.

Twin Lake

Just east of Patterson Lake in eastern Price County is Twin Lake, at just 20 acres. It holds panfish and trout. From Highway 70, take Shady Knoll Road (also marked as Fire Road 144) north to the juncture with Twin Lakes Road and continue east on Twin Lakes Road to Twin Lake, where you'll find a boat launch and USFS campground. It's a category 2 trout water open from the first Saturday in May to first Saturday in March.

THE WHITE RIVER

The White River is a premier North Country trout stream that rises as a small brook trout stream near the community of Delta in Bayfield County and flows 30 miles to join Lake Superior near Odanah in Ashland County. Like the Namekagon, it offers anglers the chance to tangle with large resident brown trout. Like the Brule just to the west, the White offers a spring and fall fishery for lake-run trout and salmon, which make it as far upstream as the White River Flowage on the Bayfield-Ashland County line.

The White is also rich in coldwater tributaries that keep its water temperatures down and serve as nurseries for wild brook and brown trout. Fish it during the Hex hatch, haunt its cold upper reaches for dark-backed brook trout, or throw big nymphs and streamers in rugged weather for sleek steelhead.

Some very large northern pike prowl the White. Delta and Basswood Lakes near the White's headwater, White River Flowage, and Chequamegon Bay all have good northern populations so it's little surprise they show up in the White. When your streamer gets ravaged and your fly rod bends double, it may be an outsized brown or *Essox lucius* on the end of your line. From the point of view of trout density, you're doing the White a favor by keeping northerns. And a northern pike taken from cold clean water makes fine eating. If you're worried about bones, steak the fish or pickle it in brine.

Just east of the community of Delta, the south, west, and east forks of the White River join to form the main branch. While none of these branches are over 2 miles long, they are all good, cold brook trout streams. They lie just west of Delta-Drummond Road. The South Fork is off an unmarked dirt track, the West Fork off Cutoff Road, and the East Fork off West Delta Road.

Kern and Bolen Creeks, 2 miles downstream from Delta and south of Highway H, are also worth a look. They both cross White River Road before joining the White. These streams offer the kind of close-in brook trout fishing you either love or hate. Whatever your feelings about this kind of fishing, these feeders infuse the White River with cold oxygenated water that sustains its fishery for brook and brown trout.

The Bayfield County portion of the White River has three distinct faces. The 6-mile stretch from the headwaters to Bibon Marsh is classic brook trout water. The 8-mile stretch called Bibon Marsh is known for big brown trout and limited access. From Bibon Marsh downstream to White River Flowage, some 8 miles, is fast, freestone water.

The limited access in the upper portion of the White River makes floating it in a canoe a good option. Put in at Pike River Road and take out 4 miles downstream at Townline Road in Sutherland at the start of Bibon Marsh. Banks will be brushy here so consider using a short rod. This section fishes well all season. Wet or dry caddis patterns will take fish, as will terrestrials during the summer heat.

Johnson and Hanson Creeks feed into the south bank of the White from the west. They are accessible via the dirt road heading south of Sutherland Road and are worth a look if you like small-water brook trout fishing. Hanson joins the White ¾ mile

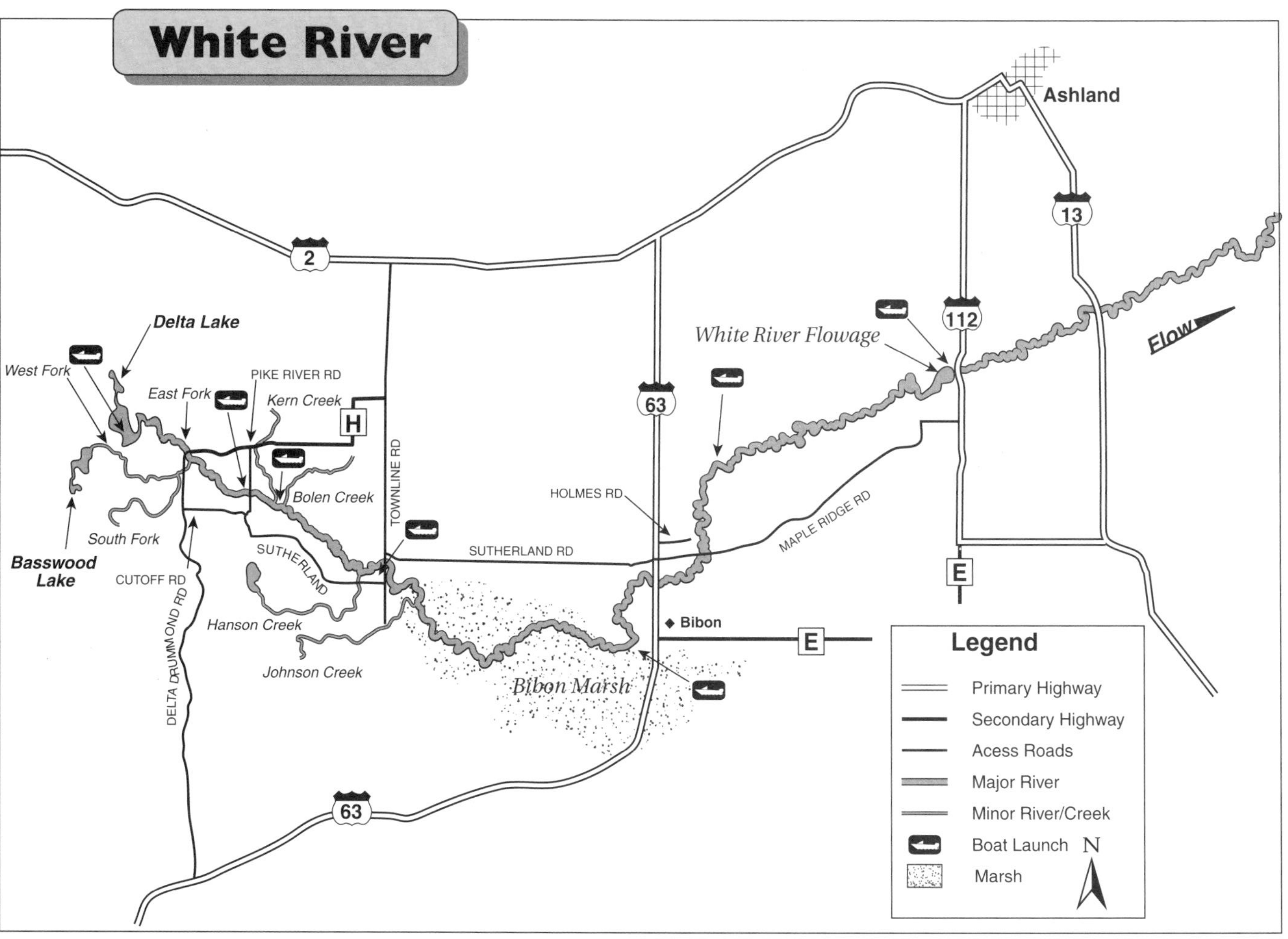
White River
Ashland
13
2
112
White River Flowage
Flow
Delta Lake
West Fork
East Fork
PIKE RIVER RD
Kern Creek
H
63
TOWNLINE RD
Bolen Creek
HOLMES RD
MAPLE RIDGE RD
South Fork
Basswood Lake
SUTHERLAND RD
CUTOFF RD
SUTHERLAND
E
Hanson Creek
Bibon
E
DELTA DRUMMOND RD
Johnson Creek
Bibon Marsh
Legend
Primary Highway
Secondary Highway
Acess Roads
Major River
Minor River/Creek
Boat Launch
Marsh
N
63

upstream from Townline Road. Johnson joins 1½ miles downstream from Townline Road in Bibon Marsh.

Fishing Bibon Marsh is a different proposition. It's a 9-mile float from the bridge at Townline Road to the Bibon Road, the two access points for this stretch of river. You can work this two ways. Go halfway into the marsh and paddle back against the current to your vehicle. (If you do this, mark all forks in the river with a piece ribbon, so you know which way to return. Yes, all marshes do look the same after a long day of paddling.) Or arrange to have your vehicle shuttled to the other bridge. Given the vast nature of Bibon Marsh, float it first during the day, and then consider going back to fish it at night after you are more familiar with it.

The White is known for big browns, and there are plenty in Bibon Marsh. There are also plenty of mosquitoes in every marsh and swamp in Wisconsin from May to September so bring repellent and a head net. There's nothing worse than getting halfway into a paddle or hike and realizing, after being beset by bugs, that things are going to get worse before they get better. Allow a good half-day to float Bibon Marsh. This stretch of river is recommended by DNR fisheries technician Cordell Manz, son of trout fishing guide Ron Manz.

From the end of Bibon Swamp to White River Flowage, the river changes character again. This time, it begins to look like the lower portions of the Brule, fast and rocky. Road crossings in this stretch are at the village of Mason, just downstream from here at Highway 63, and then 2 miles farther downstream at Maple Ridge Road. The next road crossing is at the White River Flowage on Highway 112. Below, Highway 112, road crossings are at Highway 13 and 10 miles downstream at Highway 2.

Below White River Flowage, the river is open to fishing from the last Saturday in March to November 15. The closure during winter allows fish to spawn. Egg patterns, streamers, and big nymphs will all take fish. Check with a local fly shop, such as Anglers All or Brule River Classics, to see how the run is doing before you come up. Look for steelhead runs from early April to mid-May and for salmon runs from mid-September to mid-November.

If you're willing to brave the cold Aprils in this part of the state, you will find good stonefly hatches on the White, in addition to good caddis activity. (The portion of river upstream from Pike River Road is closed during the early season.) Chances are good that Hendricksons will be active around opening day. Oddly enough, cold weather doesn't seem to bother them. Look for a Brown Drake hatch in early June.

The much-awaited Hex hatch can occur anytime from the third week in June to early July. As on so many northern and central Wisconsin rivers known for their Hex hatch, you can catch fish during the day on Hex nymphs. Prior to emerging, these mayflies are present in their nymphal stage for several weeks. Naturally, big browns are not going to pass up a meal of this size just because it's offered during lunchtime instead of dinnertime. Bibon Marsh is known for it Hex hatch.

Caddis imitations—whether dry or wet or pupael—will take fish all summer if fished in the surface film. Terrestrials are productive starting in July. And don't neglect minnow and crawfish patterns, especially in September when fish are bulking up for winter.

Stream Facts: White River

Season
- Bayfield County portion (except above Pike River Road) open to fishing during catch-and-release March-April season; Ashland County portion open Last Saturday in March to November 15.

Regulations
- Upstream from Pike Road, category 2; from Pike Road to White River Dam, 3 trout over 9 inches with only 1 brown trout over 15 inches. Below White River Dam, 5 trout and salmon. Brook trout must be over 8 inches, brown trout over 10 inches, salmon over 12 inches, and rainbow trout over 26 inches; only 1 rainbow trout and 1 brown trout over 15 inches.

Miles of Trout Water
- 22 miles

River miles
- To Sutherland, east end Bibon Marsh, 6 miles; to Mason, west end of Bibon Marsh, 14 miles; to White River Flowage, 22 miles.

Stream Characteristics
- Upper reaches, clear brook trout water; middle reaches, Bibon Marsh known for big brown trout; fast pocketwater from swamp to flowage; lake-run trout and salmon below flowage.

Access
- Pike River Road, Townline Road, Highway 63, Highway 112, Highway 13, Highway 2.

Fly Shops
- Boulder Lodge (Hayward); Anglers All (Ashland); Brule River Classics (Brule)

Maps
- *Wisconsin Atlas and Gazetteer*, pages 94, 95, 103

Hub City: Bayfield

Known as La Pointe when settled by the French in the 17th century, Bayfield was renamed after a British admiral in the mid-19th century. It has since been a fishing port and vacationing spot. Local orchards, favored by cool Lake Superior breezes, produce an array of fruits in summer. Bayfield makes a good base for exploring the peninsula's steelhead streams (the Brule, Pikes Creek, the Sioux River, the Cranberry River, and Flag River) in fall and spring and is just 20 miles north of the famed smallmouth flats in Chequamegon Bay. For those who prefer a village with a touch of artistic flavor, Bayfield is the place.

Accommodations

Greunke's First Street Inn, 17 Rittenhouse Avenue; 800-245-3072; historic inn in downtown Bayfield; $$

Winfield Inn and Suites, 100 Lynde Avenue; 715-779-3252; motel and cabins just north of town; $$

Woodfield Cottages, P.O. 494; 715-779-5600; just south of Bayfield; $$

Campgrounds

Chequamegon National Forest—nearest campsites Birch Grove west of Washburn and Wanoka Lake, known for its brook trout, west of Ashland off Highway 2

Apostle Islands View Campground, 715-779-5524

Buffalo Bay Campground, 715-779-3743

Dalrymple Campground, c/o Bayfield City Hall; 715-779-3743

Restaurants

Hurricane Hut, 222 Rittenhouse Street; 715-779-5522; beer, pizza, sandwiches, breakfast; open early and late

Wild Rice Restaurant, 84860 Old San Road, Bayfield; 715 779 9881; gourmet restaurant with emphasis on local ingredients; www.wildricerestaurant.com

Greunke's First Street Inn, 17 Rittenhouse Avenue; 800-245-3072; good food in historic hotel

Fly Shops, Outfitters, Sporting Goods

Angler's All, 2803 Lake Shore Drive, Ashland; 715-682-5754; guides for smallmouth on Chequamegon Bay

Outdoor Allure, Route 2, Washburn; 715-373-0551

Apostle Islands Outfitters, 10 S. Broad Street, Bayfield; 715-779-3411; licenses

The Superior Fly Anglers, 310 Belknap Street, Superior; 715-395-9520

Veterinarians

Countrycare Vet Hospital, Range Road, Ashland, 800-408-7387; 20 miles south of Bayfield

Medical

Memorial Medical Center, 1615 Maple Lane, Ashland; 715-682-4563; 20 miles south of Bayfield; ambulance service, 715-373-6120

Auto Rental

Enterprise Superior, 3215 Tower Avenue #107, Superior; 715-395-9900

Automobile Repair

Superior Petrol, 407 Rittenhouse Avenue; 715-779-5412
Ron's Welding and Auto, County J, Bayfield; 715-779-5260

Air Service

Duluth International Airport, 4701 Grinden Drive, Duluth MN; 218-753-2968; 30 miles northwest of Brule

For More Information

Bayfield Chamber of Commerce
P.O. Box 138
Bayfield, WI 54814
800-447-4094
www.bayfield.org

HUB CITY: ASHLAND

Originally named Whittlesey after its first postmaster and impresario, Ashland is now a major shipping port, commercial fishing center, and base for outfitters who explore Chequamegon Bay and the outlying Apostle Islands. Where Bayfield is quaint, Ashland is down-to-earth, with coal stacks and shipping concerns dominating the lakefront. It's the most convenient port to Chequamegon Bay's smallmouth bass fishing (Anglers All guides for bronzebacks on the bay) and is also convenient to the White River, which is known for its Hex hatch and big browns. It's also just a half-hour east of the Bois Brule.

Accommodations

Hotel Chequamegon, US Highway 2; 800-727-2776; luxury hotel located on Lake Superior; $$$
Super 8 Motel, 1610 Lake Shore Drive; 715-682-9377
AmericInn, 3009 Lakeshore Drive; 715-682-9950; $$
Crest Motel, US Highway 2 and Sandborne Avenue; 715-682-6603; Mom and Pop, cheap and clean; $

Campgrounds

Chequamegon National Forest—nearest campsites on Namekagon Lake, Lake Owen
Moose Lake, Day Lake; all roughly 20 miles from Hayward

Kreher Park, 36 RV sites, on the lakeshore in Ashland
Prentice Park, 19 sites on the lakeshore in Ashland
Copper Falls State Park, P.O. Box 438, Mellen; 715-274-5123; located 20 miles south of Ashland

Restaurants

Deepwater Grill, 800 West Main Street; 715-682-4200; new brewpub with full menu
Hotel Chequamegon, US Highway 2; 800-727-2776; fine restaurant inside elegant hotel
County Kitchen, 400 Lake Shore Drive; 715-682-4543; dependable chain

Fly Shops, Outfitters, Sporting Goods

Angler's All, 2803 Lake Shore Drive, Ashland; 715-682-5754; guides on Chequamegon Bay for smallmouth and on inland waters, full-service fly shop
Outdoor Allure, Route 2, Washburn; 715-373-0551
Apostle Islands Outfitters, 10 S. Broad Street, Bayfield; 715-779-3411; licenses
The Superior Fly Anglers, 310 Belknap Street, Superior; 715-395-9520

Veterinarians

Countrycare Vet Hospital, Range Road, Ashland; 800-408-7387; 20 miles south of Bayfield

Medical

Memorial Medical Center, 1615 Maple Lane, Ashland; 715-682-4563; ambulance service, 715-373-6120

Auto Rental

Enterprise Superior, 3215 Tower Avenue #107, Superior; 715-395-9900

Automobile Repair

Eder Brothers, 1301 Lake Shore Drive; 715-682-3066

Air Service

Duluth International Airport, 4701 Grinden Drive, Duluth MN; 218-753-2968; 30 miles northwest of Brule

For More Information

Ashland Chamber of Commerce
805 Lake Shore Drive
Ashland, WI
715-682-2500

A pretty marsh near Lake Superior.

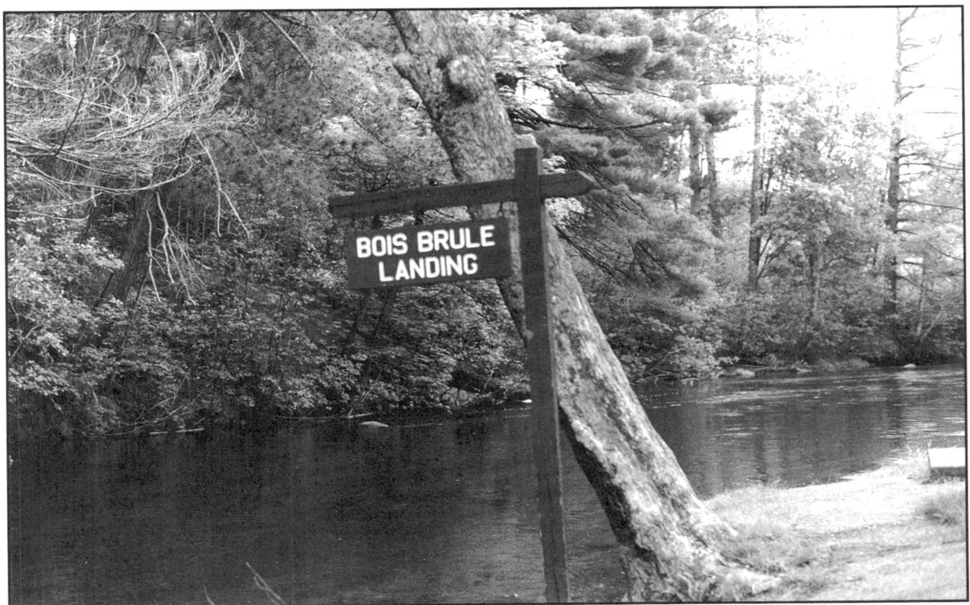

The Brule River offers some fantastic fishing.

The Bois Brule River

If you can't be happy trout fishing on the 44 miles of Wisconsin's Bois Brule River, you might as well give up the sport of fly fishing, because this river offers just about every kind of trout fishing experience an angler could ask for. Do you like tangling with big, wild Lake Superior steelhead and salmon? The lower sections of the Bois Brule offers some of the finest fishing for anadromous trout and salmon in the state. If you like pursuing wild brook trout in a remote setting, fishing small flies in clear water over a sandy bottom, you'll find that on the upper Brule. And if hatches are your thing, the Brule boasts everything from tiny Blue-Winged Olives to Giant Michigan Mayflies. And the Brule has tackle-busting browns, too, in the widening of the river known as Lucius Lake.

History buffs will delight in knowing that it has been an Ojibway, voyageur, and logger route between Lake Superior and the Mississippi River via the St. Croix River. Ulysses S. Grant, Grover Cleveland, Herbert Hoover, Calvin Coolidge, and Dwight Eisenhower have all wet lines here.

In a far-sighted act of conservation, the state acquired some 50,000 acres of land along the river to form Brule River State Forest. Thus, anglers, paddlers, hunters, and wildlife enthusiasts will be able to enjoy the river's beauty and bounty for generations to come. Continuing the legacy of conservation, the DNR and Brule River Sportsman's Club continues to improve spawning redds by removing silt and adding gravel. Gravel in the upper portions of the Brule, where smaller resident trout spawn, is pea-sized.

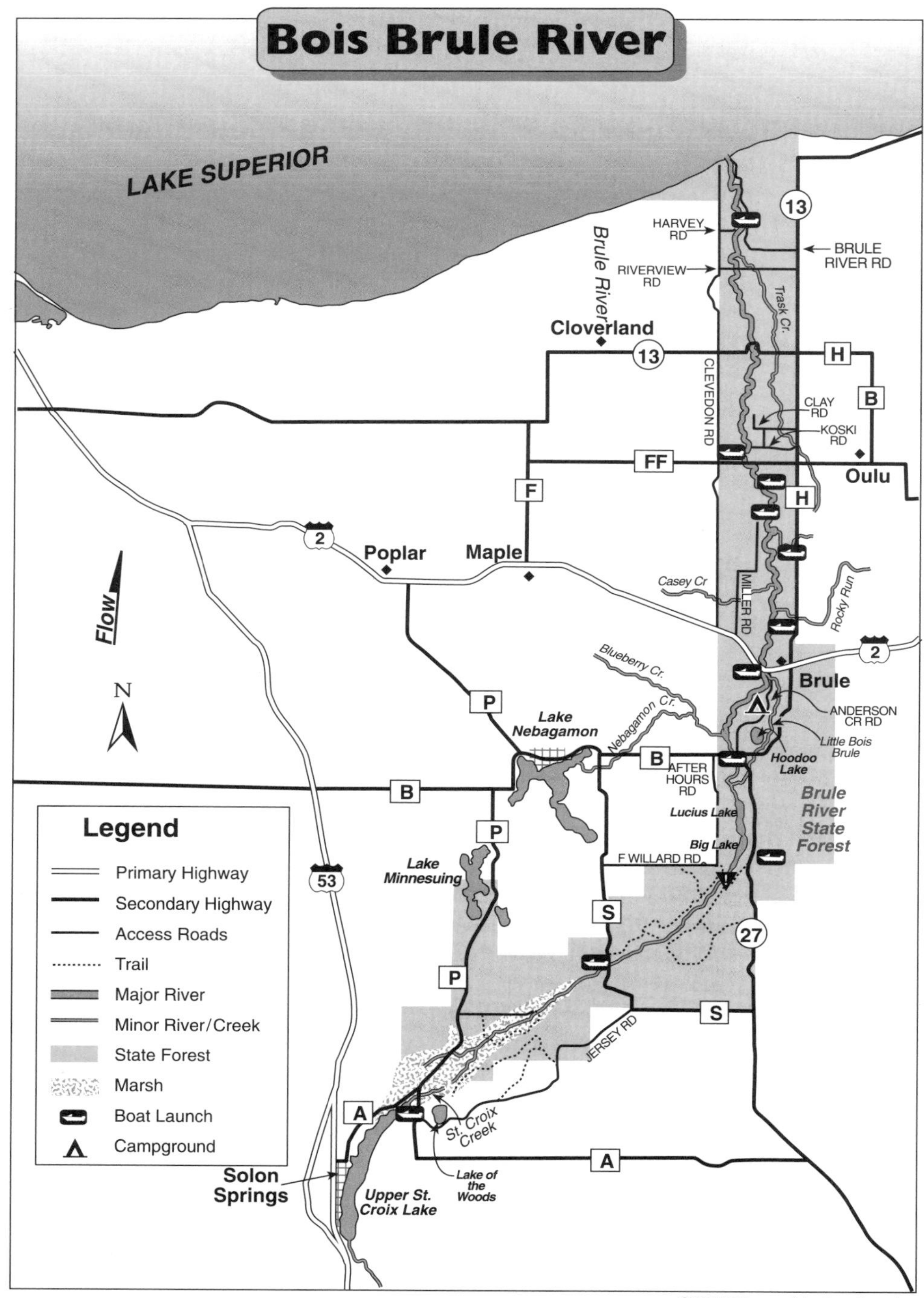
Bois Brule River
LAKE SUPERIOR
Brule River
Cloverland
HARVEY RD
RIVERVIEW RD
BRULE RIVER RD
Trask Cr.
CLEVEDON RD
CLAY RD
KOSKI RD
Oulu
Poplar
Maple
Flow
Casey Cr
MILLER RD
Rocky Run
Blueberry Cr.
Nebagamon Cr.
Brule
ANDERSON CR RD
Little Bois Brule
Hoodoo Lake
Lake Nebagamon
AFTER HOURS RD
Lucius Lake
Big Lake
Brule River State Forest
F WILLARD RD
Lake Minnesuing
JERSEY RD
St. Croix Creek
Lake of the Woods
Solon Springs
Upper St. Croix Lake
N
Legend
Primary Highway
Secondary Highway
Access Roads
Trail
Major River
Minor River/Creek
State Forest
Marsh
Boat Launch
Campground
© 2006 Wilderness Adventures Press, Inc.

Gravel in the lower portion of the Brule, where larger lake-run trout and salmon spawn, is golf ball–sized.

From an angling perspective, the Brule might be described as a two-tier fishery. Below Highway 2 the fishery is mainly for lake-run trout and salmon. Above Highway 2 the river holds wild resident brook, brown, and rainbow trout. Highway 2 also serves as a rough line of geographic demarcation, according to Ron Johnson who owns and operates nearby Iron River Trout Haus. North of Highway 2, which basically encompasses the Bayfield Peninsula, soils are heavy red clay. South of Highway 2, the sandy loam of northern Wisconsin predominates.

It is not a coincidence that resident trout thrive above Highway 2, and this is only enhanced by the cold tributaries above the highway. But equally important is the fact that clay soil has bad effects on trout water. Especially during periods of heavy rain, it washes into the river and causes siltation, lowering the oxygen content and causing the water to warm. As can be seen in streams fed by the Central Sands Aquifer (like the Mecan), water seepage through sand is usually clear and cold.

Not only are the upper reaches of the Brule fed by cold tributaries, they are home to a wide variety of aquatic foods. Hatches here in the far northwest corner of the state occur about two weeks later than they do farther south. In fact, anglers sometimes find the mouth of the Brule River ice-choked on opening day and spend the day picking ice from the guides on their fly rods. In other years they shed mackinaws and down vests and strip down to T-shirts in 80-degree heat.

Stoneflies and caddis start hatching in April. While the river is technically open during the early March and April season, few anglers venture forth. March 21 may mark spring on the calendar, but it's likely to see 2 feet of snow and sub-freezing temperatures in Brule River country. Still, by the time the regular trout season opens on the first Saturday in May, caddis will still be active and there's a fair chance you'll see a stonefly or two. If there are no visible stonefly hatches don't rule out stonefly nymphs, as they are common, particularly in rocky sections of the middle and lower Brule.

Brule mayfly hatches, according to area fly tier Dick Berge, begin with Blue-Winged Olives and Hendricksons, which continue roughly into mid-May. Berge was careful to talk about all these hatches with the caveat "if the weather is right," meaning highs in 50s around opening day. Spring cold snaps can set hatches back, and heat spells can accelerate them. Toward the middle and latter part of May, Hendricksons begin to hatch. Typically, they will be active until early June. While matching the hatch is great when there is a visible hatch, spinner, emergers, and nymphs should not be neglected at other times.

Brown Drakes typically come off around the second or third week in June and stick around until early July. This is Hex time on the Brule, and browns cast off their selective trout PhD's for a week of wanton carnage. If you find yourself in Brule Country during Hex time but can only fish during the day, by all means tie on a Hex nymph or emerger—even a strip leech. The flies that hatch at night have to come from somewhere, right? This is a neglected opportunity during the Hex and other hatches.

If you had to pick a date by the calendar to fish the Hex hatch on the Brule you wouldn't go too far wrong with the Fourth of July. You may be left wondering, Was that a firework from the town of Brule or a 5-pound brown slapping down in the water? Don't look for the Hex on the lower Brule, where red clay soils are not attractive to the nymphal stage of this mayfly. Instead, fish above Highway 2 over rock or sand bottom. Highway S is a good place to try nighttime Hex fishing, provided you've scouted out the area you plan to fish while there's still daylight.

During mid and late July, look for tan caddis and the smaller Blue-Winged Olives. You'll find Tricos hatching on the Brule throughout August and September. Terrestrial fishing on the Brule can be terrific. Crickets, green hoppers, ants falling from riverside tree limbs, Asian beetles, even moths make up this rich mix. There is nothing like a big, twitching hopper imitation to rouse an indolent brown from the doldrums.

Late summer and early fall are pleasant times for floating rivers like the Brule. Look for long glides or water surrounded by meadow cover and float a Parachute Hopper tight to the bank. Big trout are taken every year on minnow and crawfish imitations. These are good flies to drift around obstructions like rocks and deadfalls, where larger trout are wont to hide.

Tactics for taking Brule steelhead, browns, and salmon differ little from fishing other Great Lakes tributaries. However, anglers should not hesitate to throw a nymph or minnow imitation at these fish. Spawning and over-wintering habitat—not to mention food supplies—on the Brule are among the best on the Great Lakes. Fish tend to enter the river a bit earlier and stay a bit later because the digs are so good. Skamania-strain steelhead and lake-run browns begin to enter to the river in early fall. (Again, as water temperatures are suitable for trout reproduction, they may be in the river earlier than they would be farther south.) Coho and chinook salmon are also fall spawners, entering the river in September and October. Of an October afternoon, an angler might do battle with any or all of these species and still have time to hunt grouse in the aspens of Brule River State Forest.

Spring runs of steelhead begin as early as there is passage up the river mouth from the lake. The season framework is meant to allow angler the opportunity to take advantage of these runs without endangering spawning fish. Thus the season is open from March 30 through the first Saturday in May and then again from October 1 to November 15. Egg flies are always good choices for Great Lakes salmon and steelhead. Big nymphs or strip leeches are also a safe bet. Leave the 5-weight trout stream rod back in the motel and fish an 8-weight equipped with sinking line and a good amount of backing.

The Brule begins below the outlet of Upper St. Croix near the town of Solon Springs as a boggy brook trout stream. From the headwaters to the Highway S bridge, a distance of roughly 6 miles, the river is swampy and fed by numerous springs. This is a good area to fish for wild brook trout, and occasionally larger browns seeking cooler water later in the season. Highway S is the first access point to the river. Given its swampy margins, you'll probably want to float this stretch by putting in at S.

Five miles below S, you will encounter a series of natural lakes (Big Lake and then Lucius Lake) preceded by rapids. Resident browns and rainbows displace brook trout in this stretch. The next road crossing is Highway B at Winneboujou, 6 miles downstream from Big Lake. Look for fast pocketwater from Highway B to Highway 2 at Brule, a distance of 4 miles. This stretch is more conducive to wading.

Downstream from Highway 2, you will encounter a slower, grassy section known as The Meadows, a good area to fish during terrestrial time. Fast freestone water resumes after the Copper Range campground off Highway H and continues for the next 10 miles to the river mouth. Red clay soil is another notable characteristic of this stretch of the Brule.

While the last 10 miles support good runs of anadromous trout and salmon, there's too much silt and too little oxygen for resident fish to reproduce here in any numbers. Below Highway 2, access to the river is at Copper Range Campground, the Highway FF bridge, the Highway 13 bridge, and along Brule River Road. Highway H and Highway 13 parallel the east shore of the river. Clevedon Road parallels the west shore.

An angler working a run on the Brule.

Stream Facts: Bois Brule River

Season

- Below Highway 2, Last Saturday in March to November 15. Above Highway 2, first Saturday in March to last Sunday before the first Saturday in May is catch-and-release, artificials only with barbless hooks; regulations stated below apply from first Saturday in May to September 30.

Regulations

- Between Highway B and Highway S, category 5 (artificials only; 3 trout and salmon, only 2 of which may be brown trout and only 1 of which may be a rainbow trout; brook trout 10 inches and longer, brown trout 15 inches and longer; salmon 12 inches and longer; rainbow trout 26 inches and longer); all other portions, category 5 with no gear restrictions (5 trout and salmon may be kept, only 2 of which may be brown trout larger than 15 inches and only 1 of which may be a rainbow trout; brook trout 8 inches or longer, brown trout 10 inches or longer, salmon 12 inches and longer, rainbow trout 26 inches and longer).

Miles of Trout Water

- 30 miles

River miles

- Headwaters to Lucius Lake, 6 miles; to County B/Winneboujou, 9 miles; Highway 2, 12.5 miles; mouth of Brule/Lake Superior, 30 miles.

Stream Characteristics

- Sand-bottomed and spring-fed in upper third (brook trout the main species); natural lakes and freestone water in middle third (resident browns and rainbows); mainly fast freestone water below Highway 2 (good steelhead, lake-run brown and salmon fishery).

Fly Shops

- Anglers All (Ashland)

Maps

- *Wisconsin Atlas and Gazetteer*, pages 93, 101

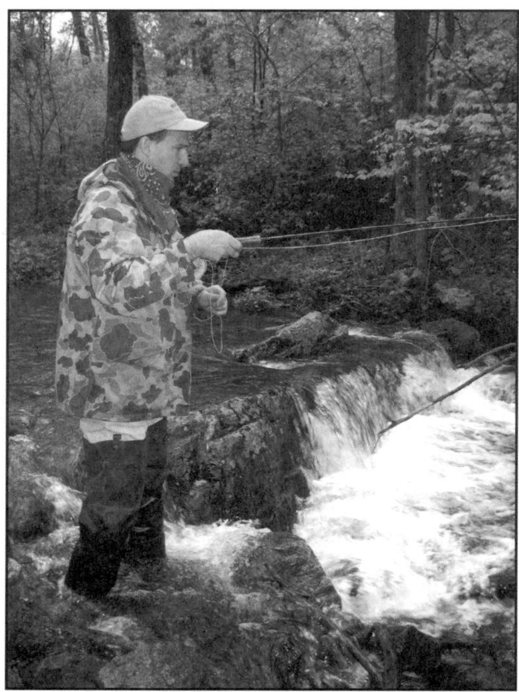

The author on a favorite brook trout stream.

Blueberry Creek

Blueberry Creek is a tributary of Nebagamon Creek, which joins the Brule River just northwest of Winneboujou and the Highway B bridge. It contains naturally reproducing populations of all three species of trout, so it is not stocked. To fish for these wild trout, access the creek at After Hours Road or farther upstream at Bellwood Pit Road. Blueberry Creek is 5 miles long, all of it category 2 trout water. As with many tributary streams, the brush gets thick in summer, so fish with a short rod and a lot of patience.

Nebagamon Creek

Nebagamon Creek also has 5 miles of trout water. It supports populations of all three trout species, augmented by some stocking. Its source is Nebagamon Lake, a warmwater fishery containing good populations of northern pike, largemouth bass, and panfish. At almost a thousand acres—the largest inland body of water for some distance—it draws heavy boat traffic. Flyfishers might find solitude here off-season or on a rainy weekday, otherwise its best left to the boaters. Nebagamon Creek can be accessed at Highway B and via the old railroad grade north of County B. It is a category 2 trout stream.

A nice brook trout taken in the Northwest region.

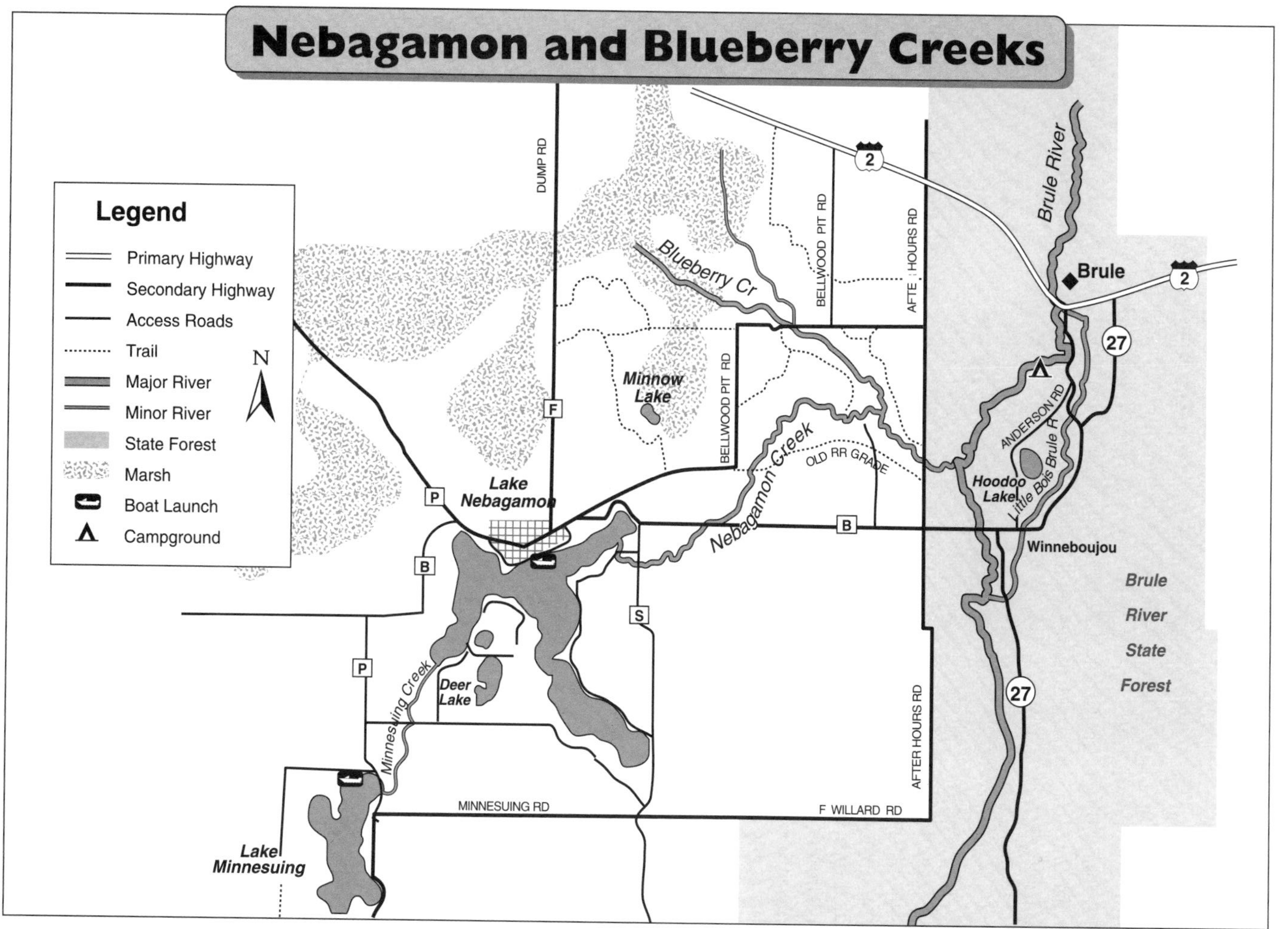
Nebagamon and Blueberry Creeks
Legend
Primary Highway
Secondary Highway
Access Roads
Trail
Major River
Minor River
State Forest
Marsh
Boat Launch
Campground
N
DUMP RD
Blueberry Cr
BELLWOOD PIT RD
AFTE HOURS RD
2
Brule River
Brule
27
Minnow Lake
ANDERSON RD
Little Bois Brule R
Hoodoo Lake
Nebagamon Creek
OLD RR GRADE
F
P
Lake Nebagamon
B
Winneboujou
Brule River State Forest
S
Minnesuing Creek
Deer Lake
AFTER HOURS RD
MINNESUING RD
F WILLARD RD
Lake Minnesuing

Iron River

The Iron River offers a diverse fishery. Flowages on the system—Iron and Moon Lakes near its headwaters south of Highway 2 and Orienta Flowage just upstream from Lake Superior—offer warmwater fishing for bass, pike, and panfish. The Iron River between the sea lamprey barrier at the former site of the Orienta dam and Lake Superior sees runs of trout and salmon. It's a larger stream, and is dependable even in low-water years. This 4-mile stretch of the Iron River is open to trout and salmon fishing from March 30 to November 15; 5 trout and salmon may be kept in total. Size limits are 8 inches for brook trout, 10 inches for brown trout, 12 inches for salmon, and 26 inches for rainbow trout; only 1 rainbow trout may be kept and only 2 brown trout over 15 inches may be kept. The lower Iron also sees June and October runs of walleye, and northern pike hang around its bulrush beds all year. The run from Highway 2 downstream to Orienta Flowage holds resident trout.

Of particular interest on the trout portion of the Iron is the property owned by Ron and Cindy Johnson, who operate the Iron River Trout Haus. (The Johnsons run fly casting clinics for beginners. Guests staying at the Trout Haus for two nights get to catch trout from their trout pond for breakfast.) The Johnsons, along with the Brule River Sportsman's Club, have worked with the DNR on improving the Iron River on their 40 acres. Wing dams, log structures, and bank covers have been installed, making for fine habitat. In exchange for the habitat improvement, the Johnson's granted a DNR fishing easement on the property. The easement (and Johnson property) begins just north of the old railroad grade at Highway 2. Give it a try. To fish downstream, follow Fairground Road north to Town Line Road and cross the river at Cheese Factory Road or Highway B. Continue west on Highway B from the bridge to Airport Road if you want to explore the lower reaches of Iron River. You'll find wild brookies and browns along with planted rainbows.

The Iron sees a late June/early July Hex hatch and a July and August Trico hatch and has good populations of stoneflies and forage fish. The East Fork of the Iron, beginning near Iron River National Fish Hatchery, holds wild brook, brown, and rainbow trout over its 12 miles. The Iron River between Moon Lake and Orienta Flowage and the East Fork of the Iron River are category 3 trout streams.

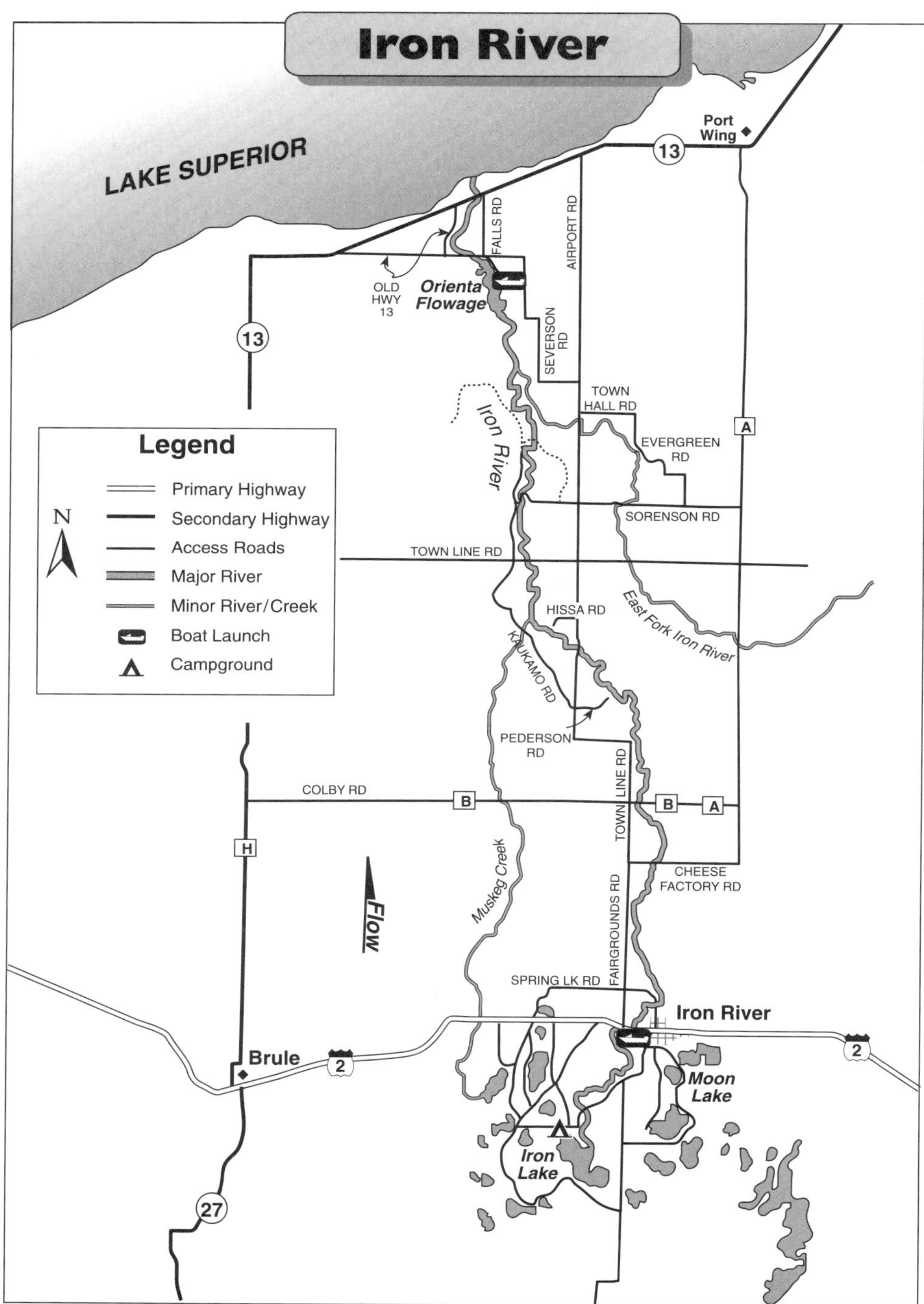
Iron River
LAKE SUPERIOR
Port Wing
13
FALLS RD
AIRPORT RD
OLD HWY 13
Orienta Flowage
SEVERSON RD
TOWN HALL RD
Iron River
EVERGREEN RD
A
SORENSON RD
TOWN LINE RD
HISSA RD
East Fork Iron River
KAUKAMO RD
PEDERSON RD
COLBY RD
B
TOWN LINE RD
H
Muskeg Creek
Flow
CHEESE FACTORY RD
FAIRGROUNDS RD
SPRING LK RD
Iron River
2
Brule
Moon Lake
Iron Lake
27
Legend
Primary Highway
Secondary Highway
Access Roads
Major River
Minor River/Creek
Boat Launch
Campground
N

THE NAMEKAGON RIVER

I will drive past McKinney's drug store there in Cable and over to the river, and just as I'm arriving at Squaw Bend four cars with Illinois license plates will be pulling out. These will be city fishermen who don't know any better than to fish for Namekagon browns in broad daylight. They will be sore at the river. They will tell me there ain't a brown in the river—never was. They will go away from there, leaving it just when I want it, as the fishing gets good.

Gordon MacQuarrie, "Now, in June"

Beginning at the outlet of Lake Namekagon (a 3,200-acre warmwater fishery) and continuing as a first-rate trout stream for some 18 miles to Hayward Lake, the upper Namekagon River is just one level of a multi-layered fishery. Lake Hayward, while somewhat developed, also offers good warmwater fishing, and the tailwaters below it offer a seasonal tailwater fishery for big browns. And from Trego Flowage to the Namekagon's confluence with the St. Croix River at the town of Danbury, the river offers a fine fishery for smallmouth bass.

The Namekagon, being an important tributary of the St. Croix, falls within the St. Croix National Scenic Riverway, safeguarding it against future development and ensuring quality recreation to those who fish, hunt, paddle, and camp along its banks. In addition, Senior DNR fisheries biologist Frank Pratt says its fishery for trophy brown trout (30 fish over 15 inches per mile in some stretches) is unrivaled east of the Mississippi. It also has something of a literary heritage—having been written about by now-deceased *Milwaukee Journal* outdoors columnist Gordon MacQuarrie in his short story "Now, in June" and by Ernest Schwiebert in "Night Comes to the Namekagon."

Lake Namekagon

Were it not the headwaters of the famed Namekagon River, Lake Namekagon would be just another good warmwater fishery in northwest Wisconsin. Fish it for crappie and bluegill in May and early June. Or try your luck for northern and muskie in summer, when the upper Namekagon warms into the 70s. Much of the shoreline of Lake Namekagon is dominated by weeds. Fish these for northerns, which are small but numerous, and bluegills, which are average-sized. Work deeper water for Namekagon's walleyes.

Being one of the larger bodies of water in this corner of the state, Lake Namekagon sees heavy boating and water skiing pressure during summer weekends; fish it early in the morning or during the week. Highway D and Garden Road follow the east shore of the lake, and boat launches can be found off each road. There is no minimum length on walleye, but only one fish over 14 inches may be kept. Minimum length on muskellunge is 50 inches.

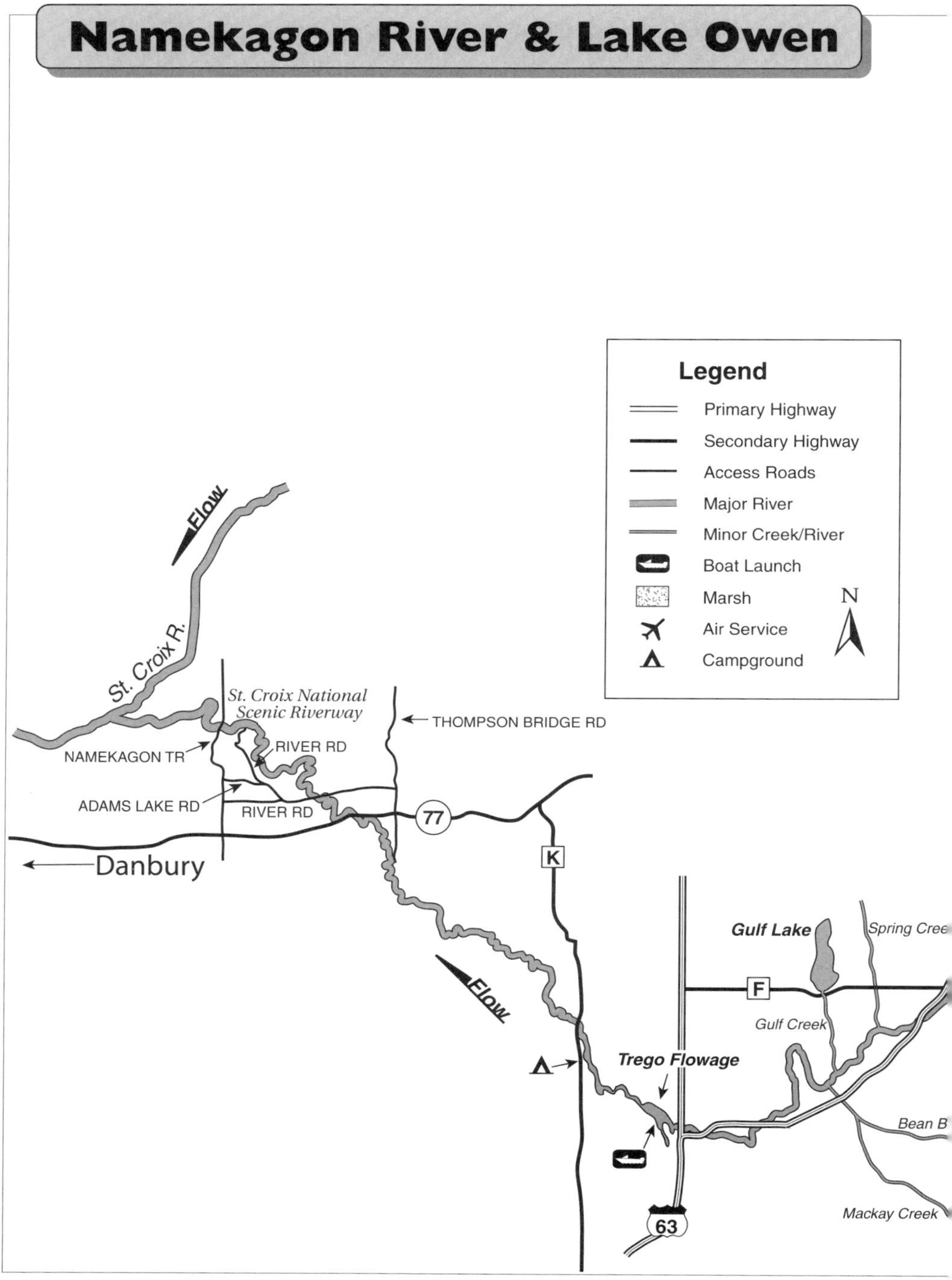

Namekagon River & Lake Owen

Legend
Primary Highway
Secondary Highway
Access Roads
Major River
Minor Creek/River
Boat Launch
Marsh
Air Service
Campground
N

Flow
St. Croix R.
St. Croix National Scenic Riverway
THOMPSON BRIDGE RD
RIVER RD
NAMEKAGON TR
ADAMS LAKE RD
RIVER RD
77
Danbury
K
Flow
Gulf Lake
Spring Cree
F
Gulf Creek
Trego Flowage
Bean B
Mackay Creek
63

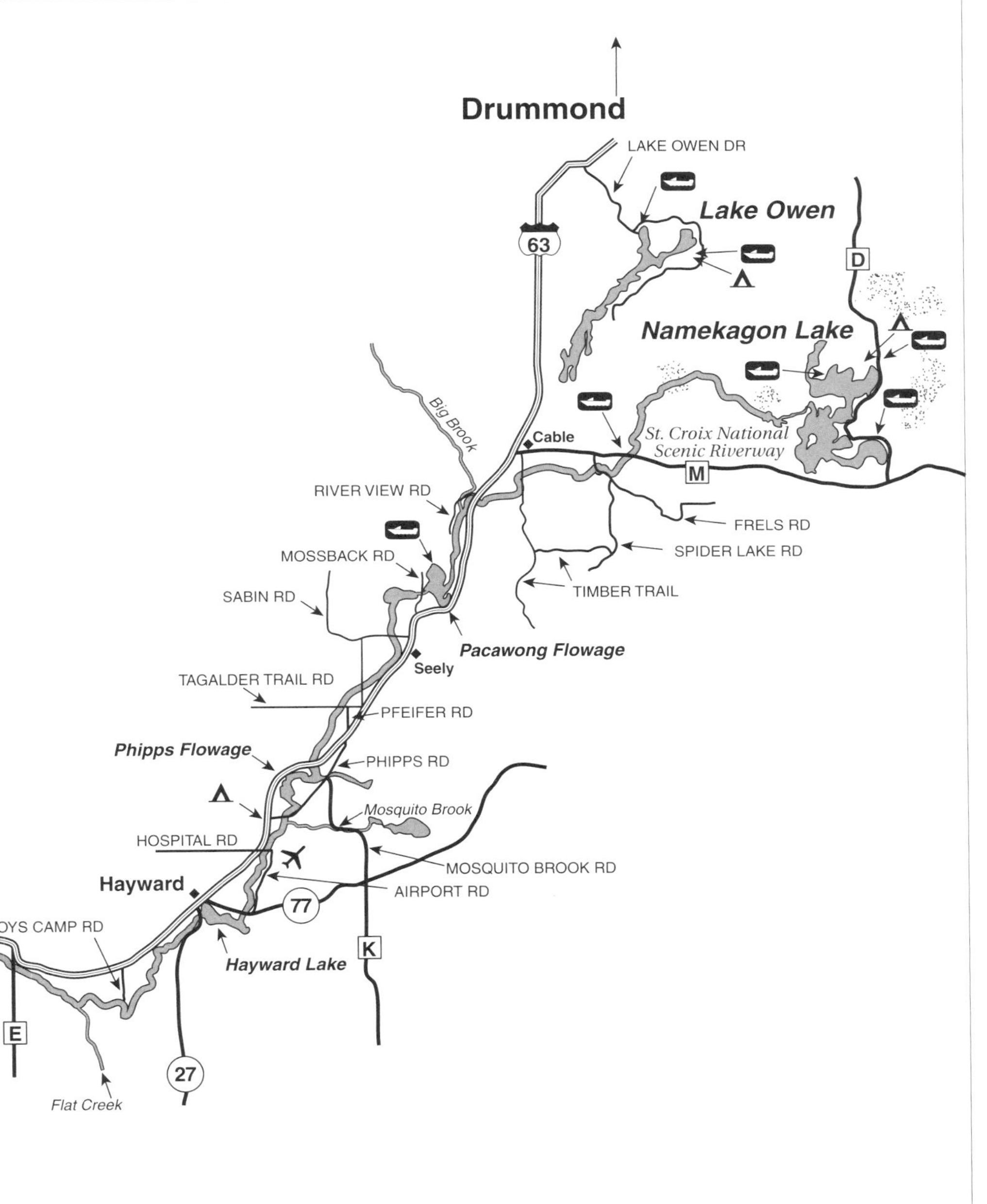
Drummond
LAKE OWEN DR
Lake Owen
63
D
Namekagon Lake
Big Brook
Cable
St. Croix National
Scenic Riverway
M
RIVER VIEW RD
FRELS RD
SPIDER LAKE RD
MOSSBACK RD
TIMBER TRAIL
SABIN RD
Pacawong Flowage
Seely
TAGALDER TRAIL RD
PFEIFER RD
Phipps Flowage
PHIPPS RD
Mosquito Brook
HOSPITAL RD
MOSQUITO BROOK RD
AIRPORT RD
Hayward
77
BOYS CAMP RD
K
Hayward Lake
E
27
Flat Creek

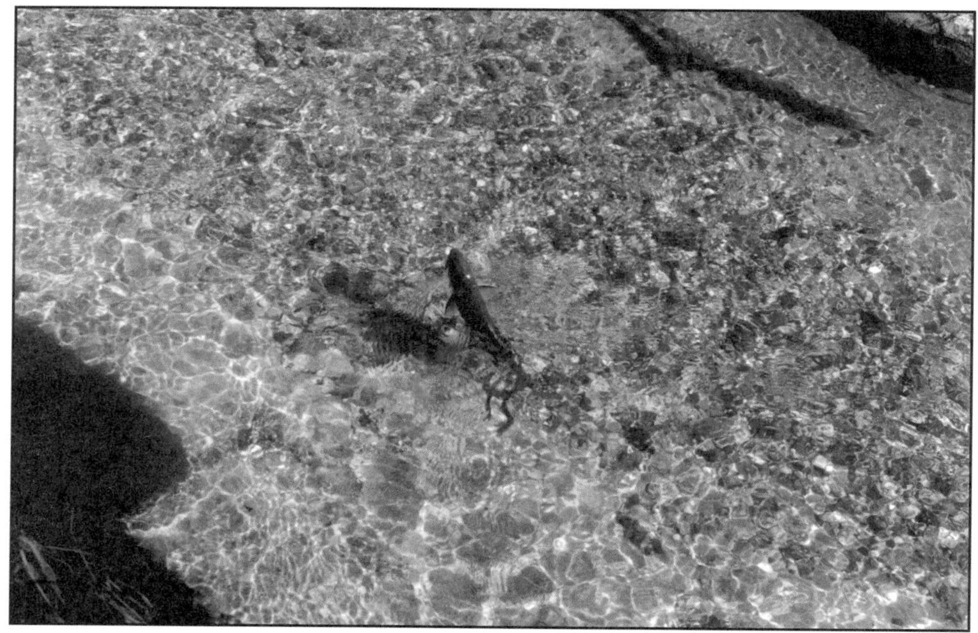

A nice brookie comes to net on the Namekagon River.

The Namekagon River—Cable to Hayward

According to Frank Pratt, the 18 miles of the Namekagon between Cable and Hayward can be looked at as three fisheries: The upper part of the river in Bayfield County has good populations of small wild brook and brown trout. The middle section of the river near the town of Seely is known for trophy browns, and the section downstream from Phipps Flowage, which has been recovering from overharvesting, has plantings of hatchery-reared, Namekagon-strain brown trout.

Bring a stream thermometer with you when fishing the Namekagon. If you find daytime water temperatures above 70 degrees, you are better off trying the area's numerous warmwater options or finding a cold brook trout stream like Big Brook near Cable. During the dog days of summer (July and early August), the Namekagon's trout go into a shutdown mode, feeding selectively on the morning Trico hatch. Where do they go? They're probably sulking in one of the river's feeders or with their bellies low against cool sand in a deep hole. Just go elsewhere to find productive fishing when the Namekagon warms up.

Between the outlet of Lake Namekagon and Highway M there are 6 miles of unproductive water—too warm for trout and not populated by much beyond rough fish and stunted northern pike. However, below Highway M an infusion of spring water doubles the river's volume and drops its temperature by 10 degrees. Big Brook and Schultz Springs are the main spring tributaries. This stretch is near the town of

Cable, and road crossings are at Highway M, Frels/Spider Lake Road, and Timber Trail just outside of Cable. According to Pratt, this is a good section to fish for numbers of fish, especially brook trout. Trout numbers remain relatively stable because of spring flow.

From Highway M downstream 9 miles to the Sawyer County below Cable, the Namekagon is under category 3 regulations. Below Cable, access is along Highway 63 and Riverview Road. Arising to the northwest of Cable, Big Brook is a category 2 stream that holds good populations of wild brook trout.

If you want trophy browns, fish the Namekagon near Seeley. Pratt notes that every 3 or 4 years during the early March and April season there is a phenomenal stonefly hatch. Apparently, these big, twitching and emerging bugs drive browns wild, and every time the hatch is on fish of 25 inches are taken. Your best bet on this one is to check with a local outfitter (like Boulder Lodge in Hayward) in mid-March to see if the stoneflies are out.

Electroshocking surveys in this part of the stream have turned up 30 browns per mile over 15 inches. While this may not raise eyebrows out West, east of the Mississippi it's really something. The White River tailwater fishery in Arkansas and the Upper Delaware River in New York State are the only other fisheries in the East that might make that claim. This stretch is governed by special regulations to preserve large browns. From Highway 63 above Phipps Flowage to Pacawong Dam, one trout may be kept with a minimum size of 15 inches.

Next is the 7-mile catch-and-release section. Highway 63 follows the east bank of the river here, and road crossings are at Mossback Road, Sabin Road, River Road, and Tag Alder Tail Road. Pacawong Flowage on the upper end of this area holds a few pike and panfish. According to Pratt, the dam is not being managed and at some point—through attrition or removal—this stretch of the Namekagon will be free-flowing.

The section between Hayward Lake and Phipps Flowage had been suffering from low trout numbers, but Pratt says catch-and-release regulations and the reintroduction of wild-strain Namekagon browns have helped the fishery recover in this stretch. A good place to begin fishing here is near the confluence with Mosquito Brook off Phipps Road below the flowage. If you find the Namekagon too warm, you can always prospect up category 2 Mosquito Brook (off Mosquito Brook Road) in search of brook trout. There's also a campground off Phipps Road, which is part of the St. Croix National Scenic Riverway. Highway 63 follows the west side of the river and road crossings are at Airport Road and Phipps Road.

While fishing Hayward Lake is not exactly wilderness fishing, you will find good numbers of northern pike, smallmouth, and panfish here. If the trout aren't rising on the Namekagon, throw your canoe or float tube into 257-acre Hayward. Below the lake there is a seasonal fishery for big brown trout. From Hayward Lake downstream to the Washburn County line, this fishery is category 3 during the regular trout season and catch-and-release from October 1 to the start of the regular trout season the next year. Access to this stretch of the river can be had at Highway 27 and Boys Camp Road.

The Namekagon plays host to a rich gumbo of aquatic foods. As described above, stoneflies can be a very important hatch to fish in the early season, although there is only a "superhatch" every few years. Caddis are active throughout the season. In fact, Pratt's failsafe fly on the Namekagon is a size 10 soft-hackled caddis fished in the surface film. Hendricksons can be a terrific hatch on the Namekagon, roughly corresponding to the opening of the regular trout season in May. Don't hesitate to nymph this hatch during the day with a Hare's Ear, Pratt says, as trout may be stuffed from feeding subsurface by the time the evening hatch occurs. There's also a Sulphur hatch in mid to late May.

Pratt calls the June Brown Drake hatch unimpressive. You're just as well served fishing nymphs or emergers during this one. The Hex hatch is not a hatch of great importance on the Namekagon, as the silt they thrive in is almost absent on this river. Try the White River or Brule for a better Hex hatch.

As water temperatures warm during July and early August, the river shuts down a bit. You may take an occasional fish on a Trico early in the day or on a terrestrial, but you are better off fishing a cold tributary (like Mosquito Creek or Big Brook) or fishing the lower river for smallmouth. When autumn begins to cool water temperatures by the middle of August, it's time to pull out the big guns—Muddlers, Matukas, leech or crawfish patterns—as fish are bulking up for winter. The Seeley section fishes well this time of year. As the tailwaters below Hayward Dam are open to trout fishing in fall, you might try them with large streamers, as well.

The Namekagon River—Hayward to St. Croix River

The 20 miles of river from the Washburn County line downstream to Trego have a "little bit of everything and a lot of nothing," according to Pratt. Your efforts are better served floating the 30 miles below the impoundment at Trego, where there's prime smallmouth fishing all the way downstream to the confluence with the St. Croix. Muskellunge and walleye are also present, with northern pike showing up in some of the marshy stretches.

Look for smallmouths in the typical hiding places—in riffles, against boulders and logs, and near rocky areas of streambed. Fish them with leech, crawfish, or minnow patterns. Rugged bluff and woods scenery is another reward. Below Trego, there is a put-in at Highway K, at Thompson Bridge Road 10 miles downstream, and at Highway 77 near the Washburn-Burnett County line 3 miles farther down. Below the county line, there's access at River Road and Namekagon Trail. Namekagon Trail is the last take-out before the confluence with the St. Croix.

Stream Facts: Namekagon River

Season

- From Highway M in Bayfield County to Lake Hayward in Sawyer County, open to catch-and-release, artificials-only fishing with barbless hooks first Saturday in March to last Sunday before the first Saturday in May. From Lake Hayward to Washburn County line, catch-and-release, artificials-only season from October 1 to first Saturday in May. Regular season is from the first Saturday in May to September 30.

Regulations

- Highway M in Bayfield County to Sawyer County line, category 3. Highway 63 upstream to Pacawong Dam, 1 trout over 15 inches, artificials only. Airport Road to Phipps Dam, artificials only, catch-and-release. From Lake Hayward to Washburn County line, category 3.

Miles of Trout Water

- 22 miles

River miles

- Cable to Lake Pacawong, 6 miles; to Seeley, 10 miles; to Phipps Flowage, 16 miles; Phipps Flowage to Hayward Lake, 22 miles; to Trego Flowage, 50 miles, Highway 77, 70 miles; to confluence with St. Croix River, 85 miles.

Stream Characteristics

- Trout stream with reputation for producing large browns; brook trout in upper reaches; warms in dog days of summer but returns to fishable temperatures by mid-August; good smallmouth fishing in lower reaches.

Access

- Highway M, Highway 63; part of St. Croix National Scenic Riverway.

Fly Shops

- Boulder Lodge (Hayward); Anglers All (Ashland)

Maps

- *Wisconsin Atlas and Gazetteer*, pages 94, 84, 93

Diana Rudolph with a nice Chequamegon Bay smallmouth. (Tom Andersen)

Lake Owen

Lake Owen in southern Bayfield County is recommended by Craig Amacker of Planet Trout Guide Service as an excellent smallmouth lake, especially when bad weather makes Chequamegon Bay to the north unfishable. Fish the rock bars on the east and west ends of the lake for smallmouth using a sink-tip line and leech, crawfish, or minnow flies in size 4 or 6. The smallies may not run as big as those in Chequamegon Bay, but Amacker says he's had a ball catching and releasing 17-inchers. And if you want to safeguard Owen's smallmouths for future generations, practice catch-and-release here. They grow slowly, taking four years to mature, and as a fishery that's recently come into fashion in the Badger State, they are vulnerable to overharvest. Walleye are often found in these rocky habitats, too, so they are a bonus for fly-rod anglers. If you want fish for the pan, keep some of the lake's abundant panfish or northern pike. And keeping a walleye or two won't hurt the population.

Smallmouths find relief from the summer heat in Lake Owen's depths, which top out at almost a hundred feet. And while the lake does see boat and recreational traffic in summer, finding a quiet cover shouldn't be too much of a problem early and late in the day on the lake's 1,300 acres. The fall smallmouth bite on Lake Owen is good, too.

From Highway 63 in Drummond, take Lake Owen Drive east to the boat ramp on the west side of the lake or continue along Lake Owen Drive to the Two Lakes campground, where you'll find another launch.

HUB CITY: BRULE

Located on the Brule River, which has been luring trout fishermen for over a hundred years, the village of Brule has basic goods and services, motels, and eateries. You'll need to go to Superior, Wisconsin about 30 miles to the west for car repair or hospital visits. Iron River a few miles to the east has a wider choice of restaurants.

Brule River Classics fly shop has everything a flyfisher needs.

Accommodations

Brule River Motel and Campground, 13844 Highway 2; 715-372-4815; $$

Brule River Classics, 6008 Highway 27; 715-372-8153; cabins for rent, guiding available; $$

Iron River Trout Haus, 205 W. Drummond Road, Iron River; 888-262-1453; bed and breakfast and cabins 10 miles east of Brule; $$

Campgrounds

Brule River State Forest, Ranger Station; 715-372-4866

Big Bay State Park, P.O. Box 589, Bayfield; 715-747-6425; located 10 miles north on Chequamegon Bay

Pattison and Amnicon Falls State Parks, Route 2 Box 435, Superior; 715-399-8073; located 20 miles northwest of Brule

Copper Falls State Park, P.O. Box 438, Mellen; 715-274-5123; located 30 miles east of Brule

Chequamegon National Forest—nearest campsites on Wanoka Lake Namekagon Lake, Lake Owen

Campsites also available along the Namekagon River, part of the St. Croix NationalScenic Riverway

Restaurants

River House Restaurant, P.O. Box 126; 715-372-5696; fish and Cajun specialties, open daily 6:30 am to 9 p.m.

Twin Gables Motel and Restaurant, Highway 2 and Highway 27; 715-372-5000; Open 7 days a week with dinner on weekends

Round Up North, Maple Street; 715-372-4875; Italian specialties, Friday fish

Fly Shops, Outfitters, Sporting Goods

Anglers All, 2803 E. Lakeshore Drive, Ashland; 715-682-5754; great fly selection, specializing in both smallmouth and trout; guide service available

Boulder Lodge, Highway 77, Hayward; 888-462-3002; Orvis and Scott dealer fly shop 40 miles west of Boulder Junction

The Superior Fly Anglers, 310 Belknap Street, Superior; 715-395-9520

Veterinarians

Northland Veterinary Service, 8560 Topper Road, Iron River; 715-372-5590; 9 miles east of Brule

Medical

St. Mary's-Superior, 3500 Tower Avenue; 715-395-5400; 27 miles northwest in Superior

Auto Rental

Enterprise Superior, 3215 Tower Avenue #107, Superior; 715-395-9900

Automobile Repair

Baillie Oil Company, First Avenue; 715-372-4800; automobile repair located in Brule

Air Service

Duluth International Airport, 4701 Grinden Drive, Duluth MN; 218-753-2968; 30 miles northwest of Brule

For More Information

Iron River Area Chamber of Commerce
Highway and 100 Mill Street
715-372-8558

CHIPPEWA FLOWAGE AND UPPER CHIPPEWA RIVER SYSTEM

At 17,000 acres, the Chippewa Flowage, also called Lake Chippewa, is Wisconsin's third largest lake behind Lake Winnebago and Petenwell Flowage. Big Chip, as it's known locally, is also vast in the sense that anglers can get lost, big-time, in its channels, meanders, and stumpfields. That's not hard to do, so stay close to shore at first and don't venture out without reliable topographical maps or a GPS system, available at outfitters in Hayward. Hiring a guide for your first trip here is not a bad idea. It will increase your chances for fishing success and eliminate the worry of getting lost.

That said, the Big Chip is Wisconsin's premier muskie lake, with good populations of panfish, walleye, and northern pike, all of which relate to the lake's ubiquitous structure. The world-record muskellunge, caught here in 1949, weighed in at just under 70 pounds.

We'll take a closer look at the main tributaries to the flowage, the east and west forks of the Chippewa River, and the main branch of the river between the flowage dam in Winter and the confluence with the Flambeau River. However, a brief history of the making of the flowage, and some devastating consequences that followed in its wake, are in order.

The Making of the Flowage

The Chippewa Flowage came into existence when the Wisconsin-Minnesota Power and Light Company (now Northern States Power) dammed the East Fork of the Chippewa River in 1923. If this sounds simple, its history and consequences are anything but that. In 1916, W-MPL was granted flowage rights by the U.S. Government for 6,000 acres in an area traditionally known as "Valley of the Chiefs" to the Lac Courte Oreilles tribe. This acquisition was subject to LCO approval. W-MPL approached the LCO community in 1919 with two offers to buy this land. The LCO rejected both offers.

Chief among the many reasons for this rejection was concern for the vast wild rice beds in the area. The largest wild rice beds in North America, these had been a source of physical and spiritual sustenance for the LCO band for centuries. Not coincidentally, the Federal Power Act was passed by Congress in 1920. This gave the Federal Power Commission (now the Federal Regulatory Commission) jurisdiction over waterways (including those on tribal land) for purposes of energy regulation for up to 50 years. This freed W-MPL from having to obtain LCO approval. W-MPL agreed to re-establish damaged wild rice beds and move graves that were in danger of being flooded.

Fluctuating water levels dealt irrevocable harm to the rice beds, and a majority of graves were not removed. It's not hard to understand why the LCO community has a very different take on the construction of the flowage than do many anglers and resort owners. However, there's a postscript to this story. After years of contesting the

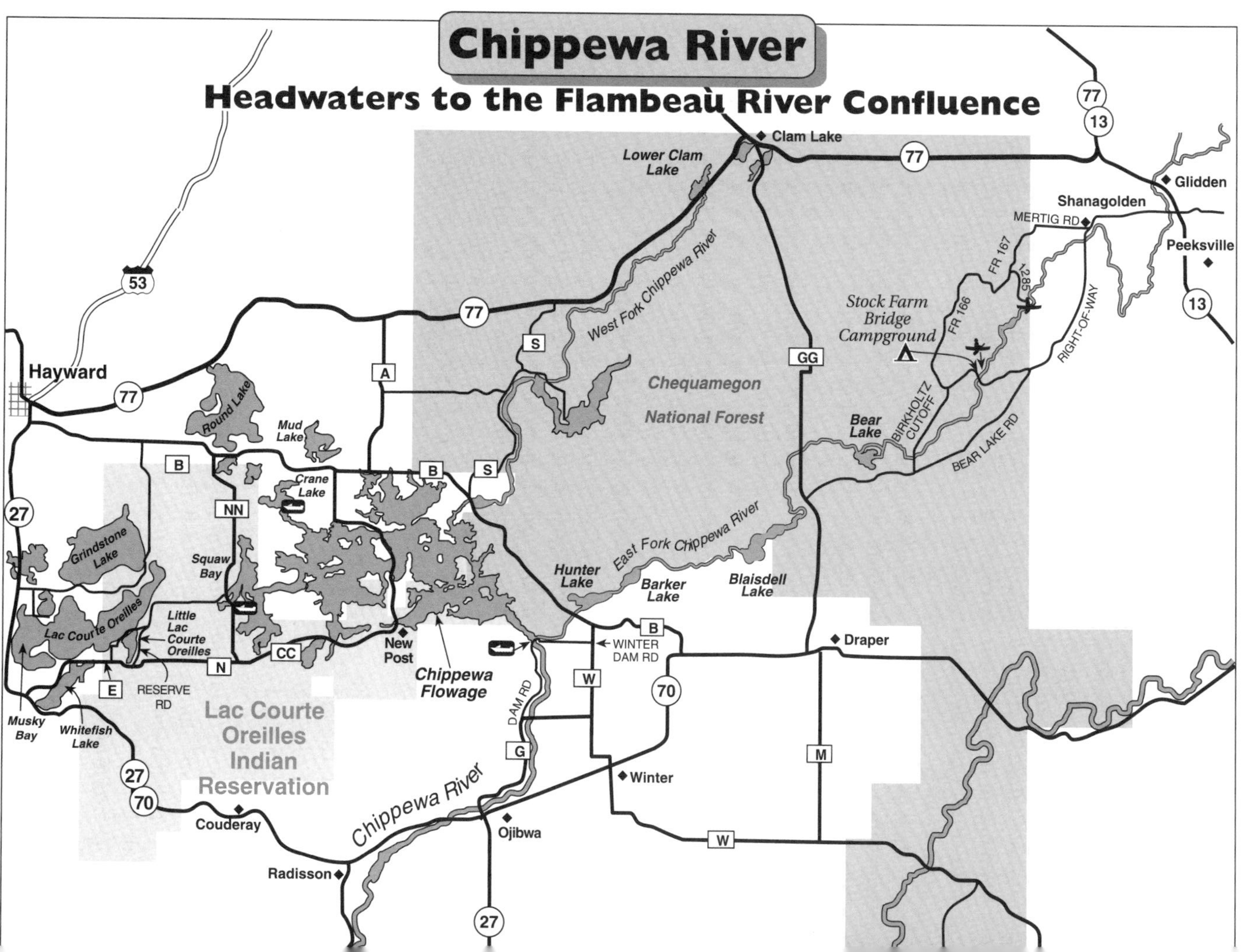
Chippewa River
Headwaters to the Flambeau River Confluence
Clam Lake
Lower Clam Lake
Glidden
Shanagolden
MERTIG RD
Peeksville
FR 167
1285
FR 166
Stock Farm Bridge Campground
RIGHT-OF-WAY
West Fork Chippewa River
Chequamegon
National Forest
Bear Lake
BIRKHOLTZ CUTOFF
BEAR LAKE RD
Hayward
Round Lake
Mud Lake
Crane Lake
East Fork Chippewa River
Hunter Lake
Barker Lake
Blaisdell Lake
Grindstone Lake
Squaw Bay
Lac Courte Oreilles
Little Lac Courte Oreilles
New Post
Chippewa Flowage
WINTER DAM RD
Draper
RESERVE RD
Musky Bay
Whitefish Lake
Lac Courte Oreilles Indian Reservation
DAM RD
Winter
Couderay
Chippewa River
Ojibwa
Radisson
77
13
53
27
70
S
A
GG
B
NN
CC
N
E
W
G
M

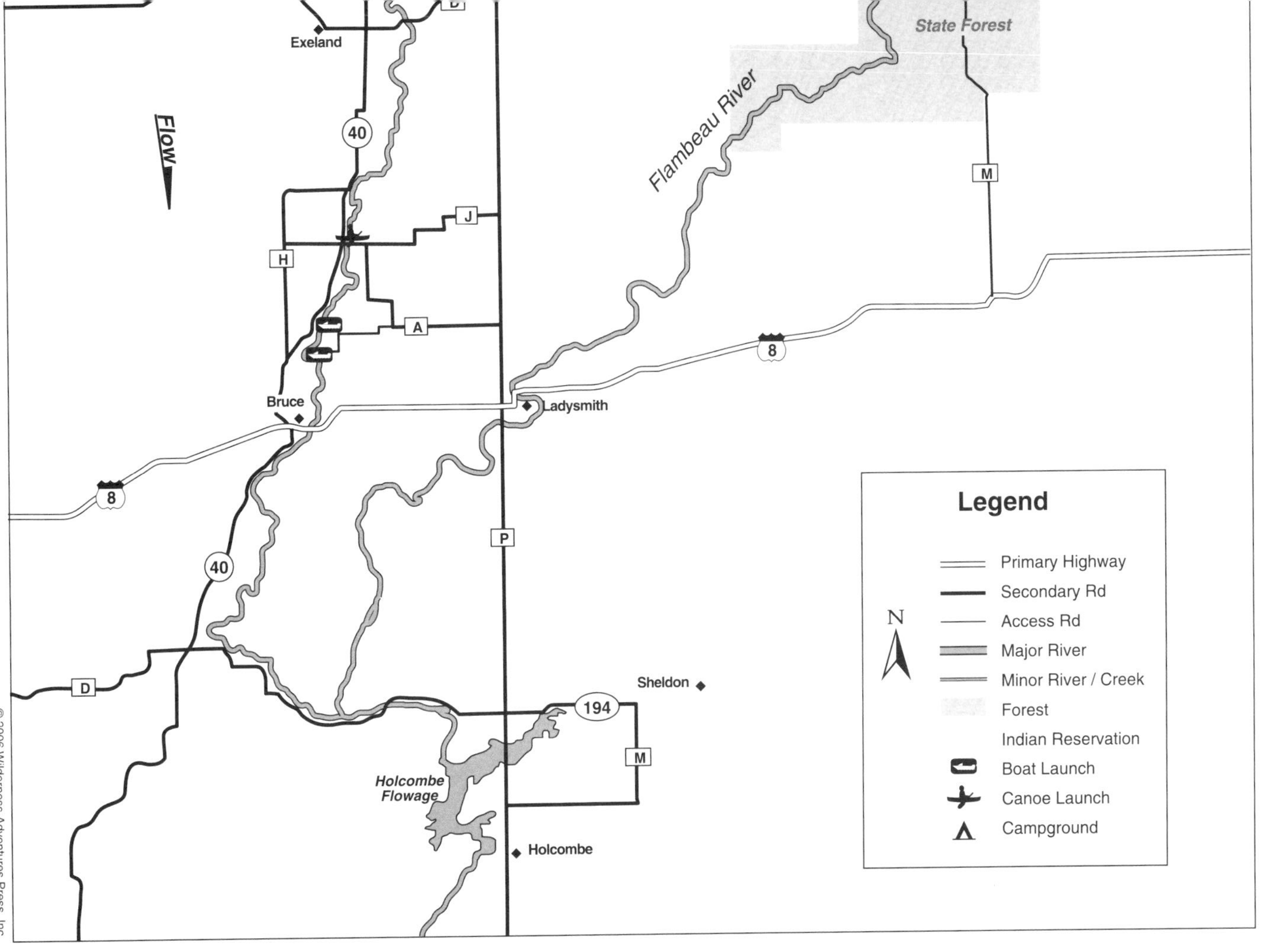
Exeland
Flow
40
J
H
A
Bruce
Ladysmith
8
8
P
40
D
Holcombe Flowage
194
M
Sheldon
Holcombe
State Forest
Flambeau River
M
Legend
Primary Highway
Secondary Rd
Access Rd
Major River
Minor River / Creek
Forest
Indian Reservation
Boat Launch
Canoe Launch
Campground
N

re-licensing of NSP's flowage rights, the LCO community was awarded the right to construct, maintain, and sell electricity from its own dam. LCO Hydro now stands next to the Winter Dam—a bit of closure on what has been a very painful event for some of Wisconsin's original people.

The Chippewa Flowage

Drake Williams, who guides fly-rod anglers on the flowage, has thought quite a bit about his craft and the gear necessary for it. As trout fishermen match the insect hatch at hand, fly-rod muskie anglers do well to adapt their offerings to what Mother Nature has in season. Williams sees fly fishing for muskie as similar to fly fishing for trout, except for the larger offerings and wire leaders, of course. Smaller, more subtle flies (tadpoles and small panfish imitations) are best during post-spawn in late May and early June. Topwater offerings will razz muskies in the doldrums, with frogs and mice being good patterns. Fall anglers should graduate to big flies, sucker imitations in the 6- to 8-inch range.

As for gear, Williams recommends a 9/10-weight rod and a reel loaded with floating line (switch to sinking or sink-tip if fish are deep). A weed guard on hooks is a must, allowing you to "get right into the slop." This is an advantage fly anglers have over plug-slingers: treble hooks bog down in weeds, which is where muskies are found a good portion of the time, while a fly with a weed guard can be thrown just about anywhere.

Finally, you'll want a 6-foot length of heavy monofilament (20- or 30-pound line) with a foot and a half of heavy-duty leader attached. Williams sells Tiger Leaders, which he says can handle anything. A standard wire leader will work, but casting and turnover are awkward. Don't try a vertical hook set as you would naturally do on trout. Muskies have mouths full of teeth and you're not likely to hit cartilage. Instead, set the rod into your chest—and hard. This will put the hook into the more vulnerable (and less toothy) corner of the mouth.

Williams likes shallow bays and river channels ("fish highways," in his parlance) for muskies. So when in doubt, try these areas. Productive sections of the flowage are Crane Lake on the northwest side and Squaw Bay on the southwest. Crane Lake also has a good largemouth and northern fishery. Cranberry, Wagon Wheel, and Church Islands and their accompanying bars are standbys on the southeast corner of the flowage.

Crappie can be found just about anywhere there is downed wood. Look for smallmouth and walleye off rocky points and shorelines. Do release muskies and smallmouths, both of which grow slowly. If you want fish for the pan, try walleye (no minimum length), northern pike, and panfish (limit 25 a day with a maximum of 15 crappies from opening day to November 30). The minimum length for muskellunge is 34 inches with a daily bag of one. If you really want a memory of your muskie, snap a photo and have a carving done.

The Big Chip lies 15 miles southeast of Hayward. Highway CC cuts through the center of the flowage and provides access to numerous launches. Crane Lake's launch is off Kelsey Road (from Highway CC). The launch for Squaw Bay is off Highway NN.

East and West Forks of the Chippewa River

The two main tributaries, which were originally flooded by Northern States Power to create the flowage, are the East Fork and the West Fork of the Chippewa River in eastern Sawyer County. Smallmouth and muskie guide Steve Cervenka sees them as first-rate fisheries in their own right. The faster and cooler East Fork is excellent smallmouth water, while the wide, lake-like West Fork is prime muskie water.

The West Fork begins at the dam on Lower Clam Lake below Highway 77; access is along Highway 77 and Highway S. The East Fork, which begins near Glidden and Shannagolden below Highway 13, runs through a wilderness setting in the Chequamegon National Forest for some 40 miles. There are a number of put-in opportunities in the Glidden/Shannagolden area where the river takes on a marshy cast. Below Shannagolden there are put-ins at Fire Road 1265 (off Mertig Road, which turns into Fire Road 167) and at Stock Farm Bridge Campground on Stock Farm Road. Below Highway GG, the river passes through a series of lakes—Blaisdale, Hunter, and Barker—and into the flowage at the Winter Dam. You'll find mostly muskie and northern in these lakes and a mix of smallmouth and muskie above them.

Main Branch of the Chippewa River

Below the Chippewa Flowage, the river hosts a similar fishery. Smallmouth are common, and muskellunge are present in good numbers. While river muskies are smaller than lake and flowage muskies as a rule, they are good game, especially on a fly rod. Smallmouths in the 5-pound range are taken every year from this stretch of the Chippewa, with fish in the 1- to 2-pound range common. You'll also find walleye and sauger in the river channel. The Chippewa is known for a good channel catfish population, and panfish are found in Radisson Flowage.

Between the Winter Dam and the confluence with the Flambeau River south of Highway 8, there are 60 miles of river. From the flowage to the town of Ojibwa, access to the river is via Dam Road and then County G. From Radisson to Bruce, Highway 40 follows the west shore of the river. Ten miles south of Bruce, Highway D intersects Highway 40. Highway D then follows the west shore of the river. Popular put-in/take-outs are below the Winter Dam, at the village of Ojibwa, at the town of Bruce, and along Highway D. Ojibwa State Park has 6 self-register campsites and is located 1 mile east of the village of Ojibwa on Highway 70.

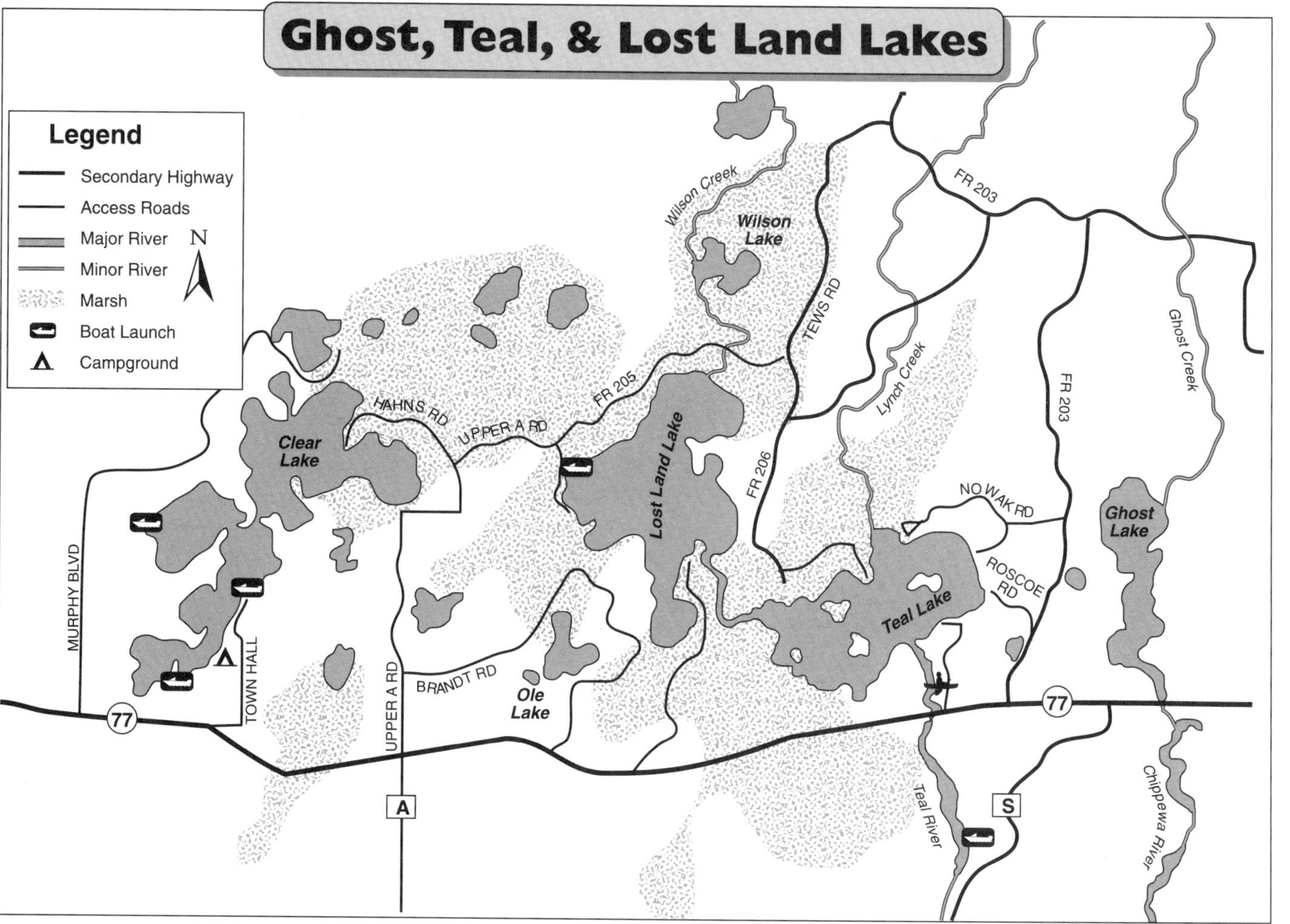
Ghost, Teal, & Lost Land Lakes
Legend
Secondary Highway
Access Roads
Major River
Minor River
Marsh
Boat Launch
Campground
N
Wilson Creek
Wilson Lake
TEWS RD
FR 203
FR 203
Ghost Creek
Lynch Creek
HAHNS RD
UPPER A RD
FR 205
Clear Lake
Lost Land Lake
FR 206
NOWAK RD
Ghost Lake
ROSCOE RD
Teal Lake
MURPHY BLVD
TOWN HALL
UPPER A RD
BRANDT RD
Ole Lake
77
77
A
S
Teal River
Chippewa River

GHOST, TEAL, AND LOST LAND LAKES

These three Sawyer County waters have been designated as "quiet lakes" by the Quiet Lakes Resort Association, a group of area business people committed to quality fishing and nature experiences. Rules governing these Quiet Lakes are a 10 mph speed limit for all boats and no water skiing; a buffer strip of 200 feet between dwellings and lakeshore; and a 500-foot no-fly zone to protect nesting eagles.

Besides cutting down on noise pollution and crowding, this has paid big dividends for anglers. Gamefish and panfish populations are up compared to pre-regulation levels. The reason for this is simple. Less boat traffic means more weeds and more weeds mean more fish. By contrast, northern Wisconsin lakes with heavy shoreline development and liberal boating laws have seen major declines in gamefish (not to mention waterfowl and amphibian) populations.

The Quiet Lakes Resort Association strongly advocates catch-and-release for muskellunge. On the Teal River from its confluence with the Chippewa River upstream and including Teal Lake and Lost Land Lake, there is no minimum length on walleye. (As the DNR regulations imply, Lost Land and Teal Lake are connected by the Teal River.) Ghost Lake is a separate body of water that feeds the West Fork of the Chippewa River. These are definitely boat lakes. If you haven't brought your own, many resorts offer boats—free to their guests or with a fee to day-users.

Take Highway 77 east from Hayward to Upper A Road to Lost Land Lake. The boat launch is just beyond the gravel pit on your right. Look for muskies in shallow bays early in the season in 1,300-acre Lost Land Lake, the biggest of these three bodies of water. "Fish right in the slop," says area guide Drake Williams. Start with smallish tadpole or panfish patterns (3 or 4 inches) and graduate to frogs and mice (patterns, that is) and deeper water as summer progresses. Fish deep troughs with big minnow patterns in fall as the lakes turn over and muskies bulk up for fall. In addition to muskies, you'll find a variety of panfish and a good population of largemouth bass. Look for them in the shallow weedy areas along the southern half of the lake.

To fish Teal Lake you can either motor over from Lost Land Lake or launch at the ramp on Larson Road on the east shore of the Teal River. Teal Lake is fairly big water, with just over 1,000 acres. The river channels—between Lost Land and Teal Lakes and between Teal Lake and the Teal River—are fish highways for all species from muskies to panfish. Don't neglect the weedbeds or islands.

The Teal River itself contains muskies, panfish, bass, and northerns. Its weeds are actually a bonus for small boaters in that bigger boats with large propellers can't navigate it. Fish wherever you find open water.

Ghost Lake is not part of the Teal–Lost Lake chain. In fact, it was named by a logger who saw it for the first time in an early morning mist. It contains muskellunge, bass, and panfish. The structure of this narrow, 370-acre lake is essentially a weedy shoreline, so boat along the outside edge of the weedline and cast toward shore. The launch on Ghost Lake can be found just upshore from the dam on the east side of the lake. As you pass the dam on Highway 77 at the outlet of Ghost Lake, look for your next left turn, which follows the east shore of the lake and will take you to the boat launch.

Lac Courte Oreilles and Little Lac Courte Oreilles

At 5,000 acres and with fairly heavy recreational traffic, Lac Courte Oreilles, located south of Hayward, is not what you'd call a flyfisher's paradise. Still, you can fish its shallow bays (such as Musky Bay) with good success for a mix of warmwater species in May and June. Minimum length here on muskellunge is 50 inches. For some solitude, you're better served launching a cartop boat off Highway E and fishing Little Lac Courte Oreilles for a mix of northern pike and panfish.

Grindstone Lake

At 3,200 acres, Grindstone Lake is also big water. It's located just north of Lac Courte Oreilles but somehow doesn't see as much fishing pressure. Focus your efforts on the weedy area near the launch ramp off Highway K for northern pike, largemouth bass, and panfish. If you venture into the lake's deeper water, fish a leech or crawfish pattern off the rock shelves on a sinking line. This will put you in the midst of Grindstone's smallmouth and walleye.

Windigo Lake

Located just to the west of Grindstone Lake, Windigo Lake offers a good fishery for northern pike, panfish, and smallmouth bass. Larger gamefish taken from Windigo should not be eaten because of high mercury content; consult DNR advisories for details. Its smaller size and limited access translate to less pressure than the two big lakes just to the east. You can launch off Highline Road (take County K east from Highway 27) on the lake's southwest side.

Sand Lake

Located at the juncture of Highway 70 and Highway 27 just south of Lac Courte Oreilles, Sand Lake offers a fishery for muskellunge and panfish along its weedy southern shoreline. The launch ramp is located off Highway E just south of Highway 70. Minimum length on walleye is 28 inches with a bag limit of 1.

The Flambeau River

Beginning at the outlet of Turtle-Flambeau Flowage and meandering to join the Chippewa River below Ladysmith 120 miles downstream, the Flambeau River is known as a good producer of smallmouth bass and muskellunge, with occasional walleye, northern pike, and panfish showing up in its impoundments. A good portion of the river system runs through Flambeau River State Forest, which offers numerous campsites. Expect to see groups of paddlers on the river during summer, but with all the elbowroom everyone can find space to do his or her thing.

For angling purposes, the river has three segments: from Turtle-Flambeau Flowage to the confluence with the South Fork of the Flambeau (a stretch sometimes called the North Fork), roughly 70 miles; the South Fork of the Flambeau, roughly 80 miles; and the main branch of the Flambeau from the confluence with the South Branch through Dairyland Reservoir and downstream to the confluence with the Chippewa River, roughly 40 miles. Steve Cervenka, who guides on the Flambeau River, favors the first segment, which he says holds the biggest smallmouths and some good muskies. The South Fork, an enjoyable float, has much smaller bass and fewer muskies. The lower segment of the river holds fish, but it's less wild than the upper two.

Turtle-Flambeau Flowage and the North Fork

To start at the beginning of things, Turtle-Flambeau Flowage covers over 14,000 acres of water in western Iron County. The standard cautions for boating on big water apply here, so keep your eye on the weather and the shoreline if your craft is on the small side (14 feet or under). Small northerns are dispersed throughout the flowage's many weedbeds, making them a good fly-rod target. Smallmouth and largemouth bass are present, too, and don't be surprised if you take an occasional walleye as you fish deep for smallmouths. You'll also find muskellunge and panfish.

The following regulations are in place in the flowage. There is no minimum length for walleye. Minimum length on muskellunge is 40 inches. After June 14, the minimum length for largemouth and smallmouth bass is 15 inches, with a daily bag limit of 2. There is a total combined limit of 10 for bluegill, crappie, pumpkinseed, and yellow perch. The minimum length of crappie is 10 inches. On all forks and impoundments of the Flambeau River downstream from Turtle-Flambeau Flowage, follow general DNR seasons, sizes, and bag limits for the Northern Zone, except that there is no minimum size on walleye and only 1 fish over 14 inches may be kept.

Between the Turtle-Flambeau Flowage Dam and the town of Park Falls is 18 miles of prime smallmouth water. You'll also find Class 2 rapids, which should only be attempted by experienced canoers. You'll want to fish smallmouth in this stretch as if you were fishing for big brown trout. Cast around fallen timber, in eddies, and along rocky shelves. Woolly Buggers, Strip Leeches, and big stonefly nymphs are all good fly choices. Steve Cervenka ties a brown Woolly Bugger with yellow legs, similar to the Western pattern known as the J.J. Special. Cervenka says 2-pound smallmouth are common on this stretch, and that on most trips he runs into a 4-pounder. Deerhair or hard-body poppers are also productive on Flambeau smallmouths.

The slower water on this stretch holds muskies; the 5 miles above Park Falls are good, slow muskie water. A Lefty's Deceiver fished on a wire leader is Cervenka's favorite fly-rod muskie offering. There's river access for a cartop boat at County FF below the flowage dam. Ten miles downstream there's a launch/take-out at Holt's Landing off Creamery Road on the west side of the river. As you approach Park Falls, River Road offers several put-ins or take-outs on the west side of the river.

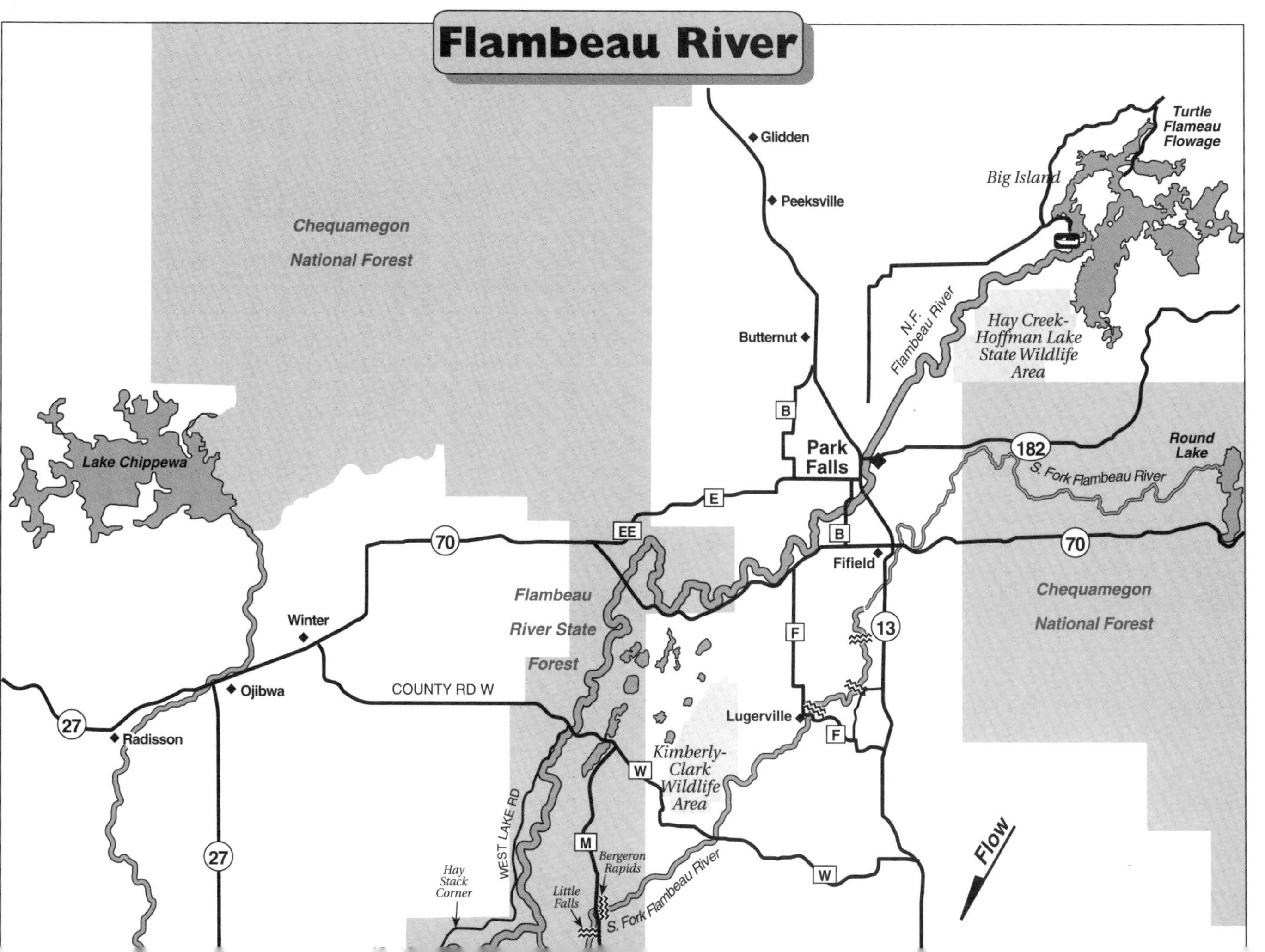
Flambeau River
Chequamegon National Forest
Glidden
Peeksville
Butternut
Turtle Flameau Flowage
Big Island
N.F. Flambeau River
Hay Creek-Hoffman Lake State Wildlife Area
Park Falls
182
Round Lake
S. Fork Flambeau River
Lake Chippewa
E
EE
B
70
Fifield
Chequamegon National Forest
Flambeau River State Forest
F
13
Winter
Ojibwa
COUNTY RD W
27
Radisson
Lugerville
Kimberly-Clark Wildlife Area
W
WEST LAKE RD
M
Bergeron Rapids
Hay Stack Corner
Little Falls
S. Fork Flambeau River
Flow

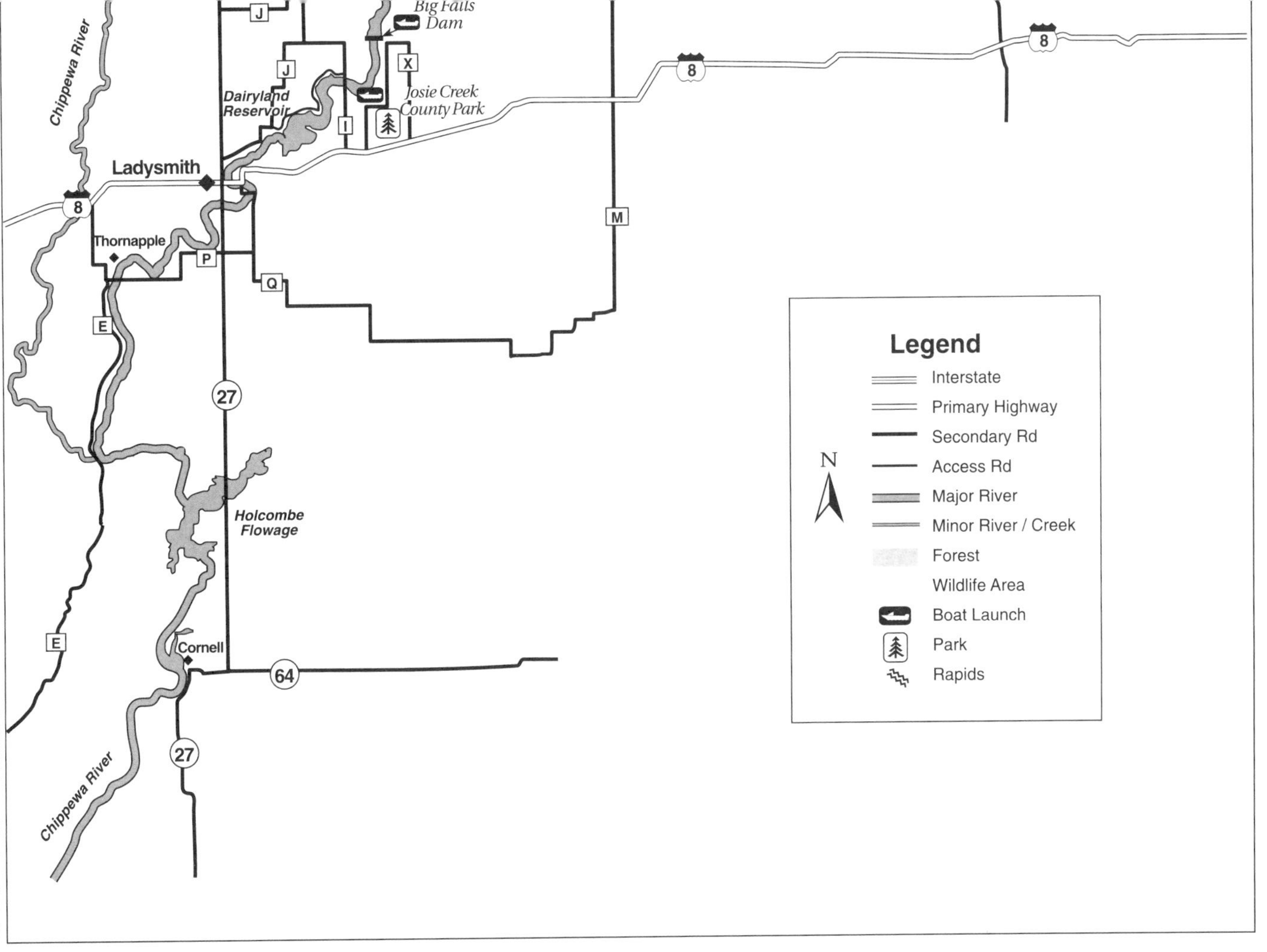
Legend
Interstate
Primary Highway
Secondary Rd
Access Rd
Major River
Minor River / Creek
Forest
Wildlife Area
Boat Launch
Park
Rapids
N
Big Falls Dam
Josie Creek County Park
Dairyland Reservoir
Ladysmith
Thornapple
Holcombe Flowage
Cornell
Chippewa River
Chippewa River
8
8
8
M
X
I
J
J
Q
P
E
E
27
27
64

The 60-odd miles of the North Fork between Park Falls and the confluence with the South Fork offer a mix of flowages and rapids. Fish smallmouths in the fast water, muskies, walleye, and panfish in the pool-like stretches. Much of this falls within the Flambeau River State Forest. Group campsites requiring reservations (715-332-5271) can be found within the forest at Connor Lake and Lake of the Pines. Fourteen primitive canoe campsites can be found along the North Fork in the forest.

Above the forest, access to the river—and landings for small boats—can be found at Highway 13 south of Park Falls and along Highway 70. Within the forest, Highway W and West Lane Road give access to the river.

South Fork of the Flambeau River

Beginning as a small stream at the outlet of Round Lake in eastern Price County, the South Fork gradually gains size and flow as it approaches the confluence with the North Fork. It is 60 miles in length. The 30 miles above Fifield is comprised of small water, often too low for floating in summer. Between Fifield and the confluence with the North Fork, the river is larger and has more dependable flows. Bergeron and Little Falls Rapids in the vicinity of Highway M are dangerous; best to portage around them. Scenery is excellent, with mixed pine and hardwoods and very little development. However, the average size of smallmouths and muskies in this stretch is much smaller than those on the North Fork, according to Steve Cervenka.

Flambeau River to Confluence with Chippewa River

The 15 miles of the Flambeau from the confluence of forks to Big Falls Flowage offer a fishery and scenery similar to that of the North Fork—smallmouth in the fast water, muskellunge in the slower water. Put-in/take-outs for this stretch are Cedar Rapids, east of Haystack Corners on Flambeau Road; at Flambeau River Lodge; and just above Big Falls Dam. There is a fee for parking at the Flambeau Lodge take-out off Flambeau Road at the head of Big Falls Flowage. You can also arrange for boat and/or car shuttle service through the lodge (715-532-5392).

Below Big Falls Dam is the impoundment known as Dairyland Reservoir. A good muskie and smallmouth fishery exists here, with fair numbers of walleye. Josie Creek County Park off County X offers a boat landing at the head of the reservoir, and there are several other landings along Dairyland's east shore.

From Ladysmith to the confluence with the Chippewa River is a distance of roughly 15 river miles. You can put in at Highway 27 and take out at the confluence on County E. The fishery remains similar here, with walleye becoming more numerous. There is more development here than on upper stretches of the river. Access can be had along Highway E.

St. Croix River

The St. Croix Flowage, which gives birth to the river of the same name, receives heavy fishing pressure. However, the St. Croix River affords anglers plenty of solitude. The upper portion of the river falls within the St. Croix National Scenic Riverway, ensuring protection against development along its banks. According to DNR fisheries biologist Rick Cornelius, the river above St. Croix Falls is traditional smallmouth water. Below St. Croix Falls, it is larger and wider and, in species and habitat, essentially like the Mississippi River. Scenery and fly fishing are superior on the upper stretch of the river, which runs roughly 85 river miles.

Popular put-ins are: Gordon Dam below the St. Croix Flowage; Highway T just above Beaver Creek (10 miles); St. Croix Trail (16 miles); Highway 35 (23 miles); the town of Danbury (30 miles); Highway 77/48 (35 miles); the former gaging station off Highway F (50 miles); Highway 70 (63 miles); Highway O (70 miles); and St. Croix Falls (85 miles). The most significant rapids are on the first 15 miles of water (above the confluence with the Namekagon), occurring just below Highway T and just above St. Croix Trail. Portage your canoe if this looks like more than you can handle. Primitive campsites are available at the site of the old Coppermine Dam above Highway T in Douglas County, just above Highway 35 at Hay Creek on the Minnesota side, at Norway Point, and at Interstate Park off Highway 70 on the Minnesota side of the river.

Smallmouth fishing is good throughout this stretch. You'll find an occasional walleye in deep holes, along with northern pike in marshy areas and river deltas like the Clam and the Yellow. The St. Croix forms the border between Wisconsin and Minnesota and is subject to Wisconsin-Minnesota Boundary Water Regulations in *Guide to Wisconsin Hook and Line Fishing Regulations.*

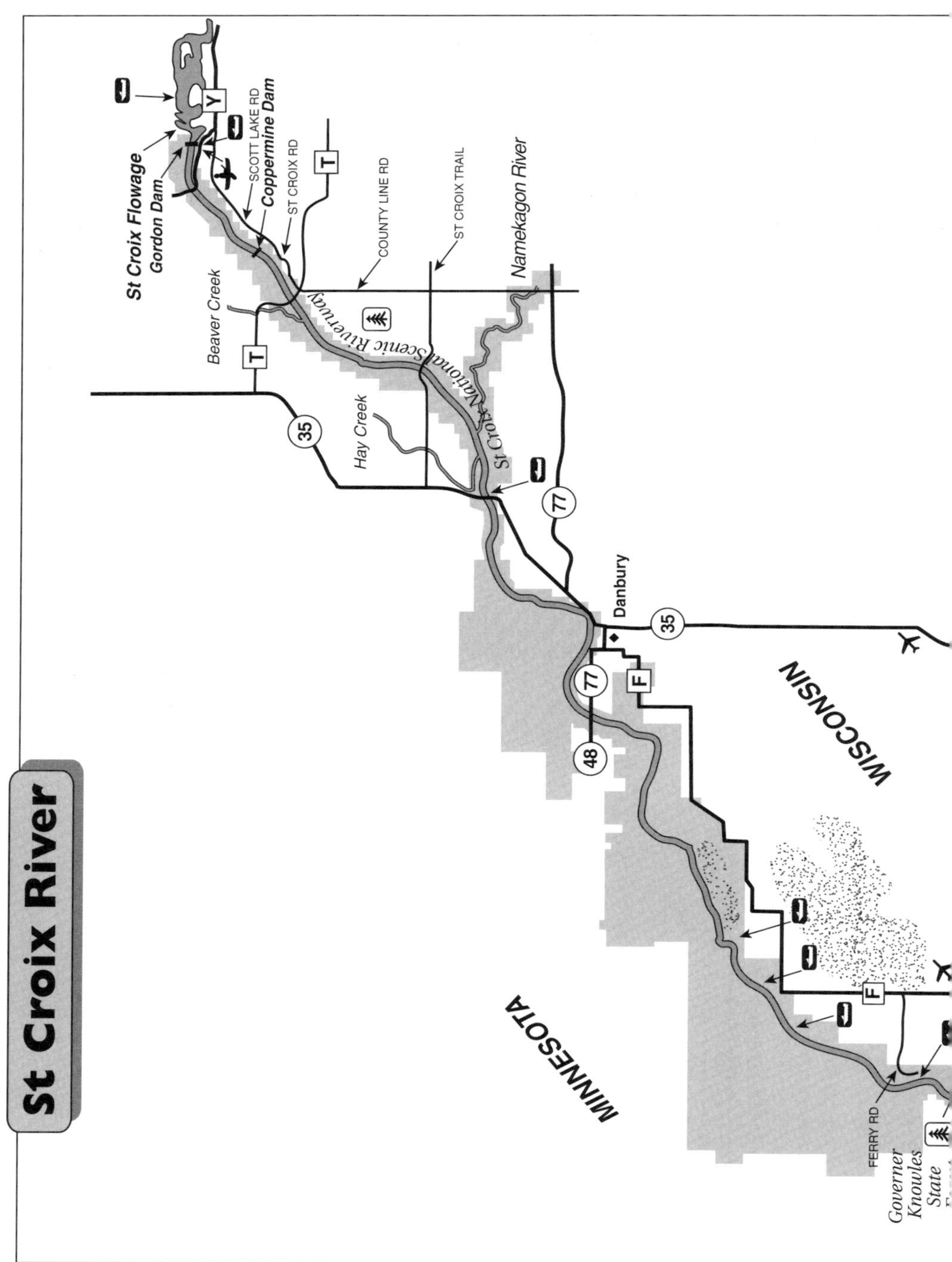
St Croix River
St Croix Flowage
Gordon Dam
Y
SCOTT LAKE RD
Coppermine Dam
ST CROIX RD
T
COUNTY LINE RD
ST CROIX TRAIL
Namekagon River
Beaver Creek
St Croix National Scenic Riverway
T
35
Hay Creek
77
Danbury
35
77
F
48
WISCONSIN
MINNESOTA
F
FERRY RD
Governer
Knowles
State

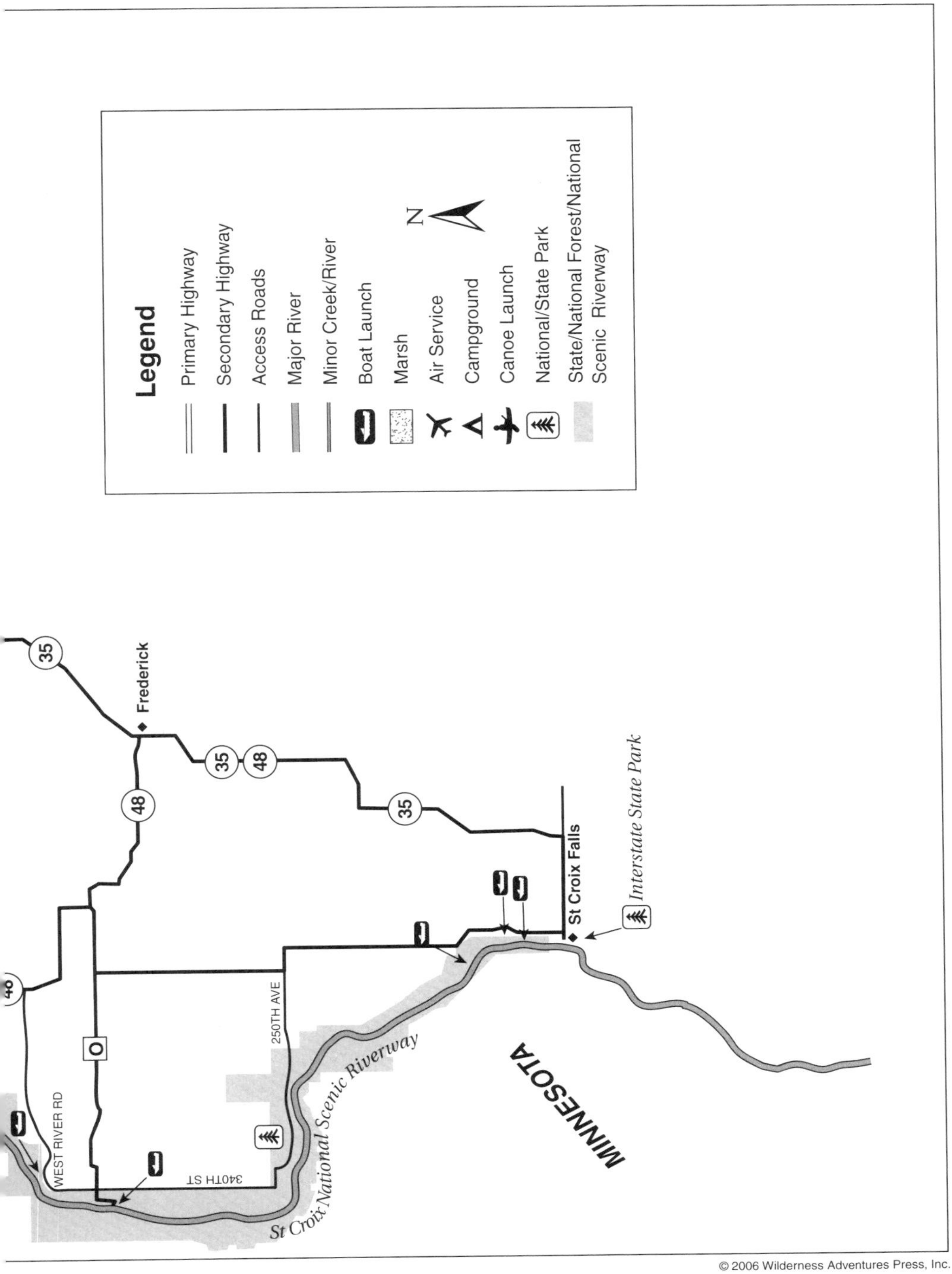

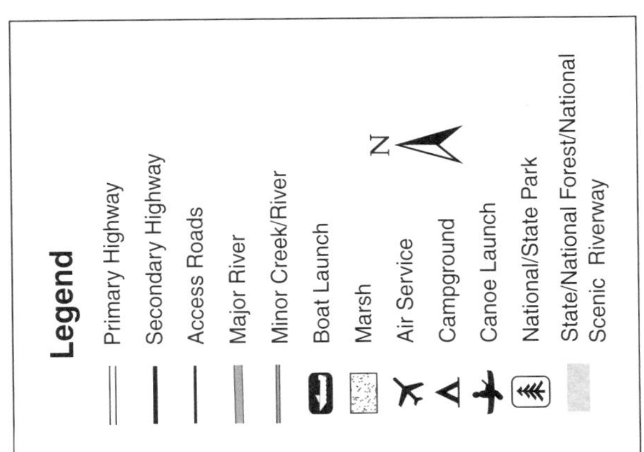
Legend
Primary Highway
Secondary Highway
Access Roads
Major River
Minor Creek/River
Boat Launch
Marsh
Air Service
Campground
Canoe Launch
National/State Park
State/National Forest/National Scenic Riverway
N
Frederick
St Croix Falls
Interstate State Park
250TH AVE
340TH ST
WEST RIVER RD
St Croix National Scenic Riverway
MINNESOTA
35
48
O

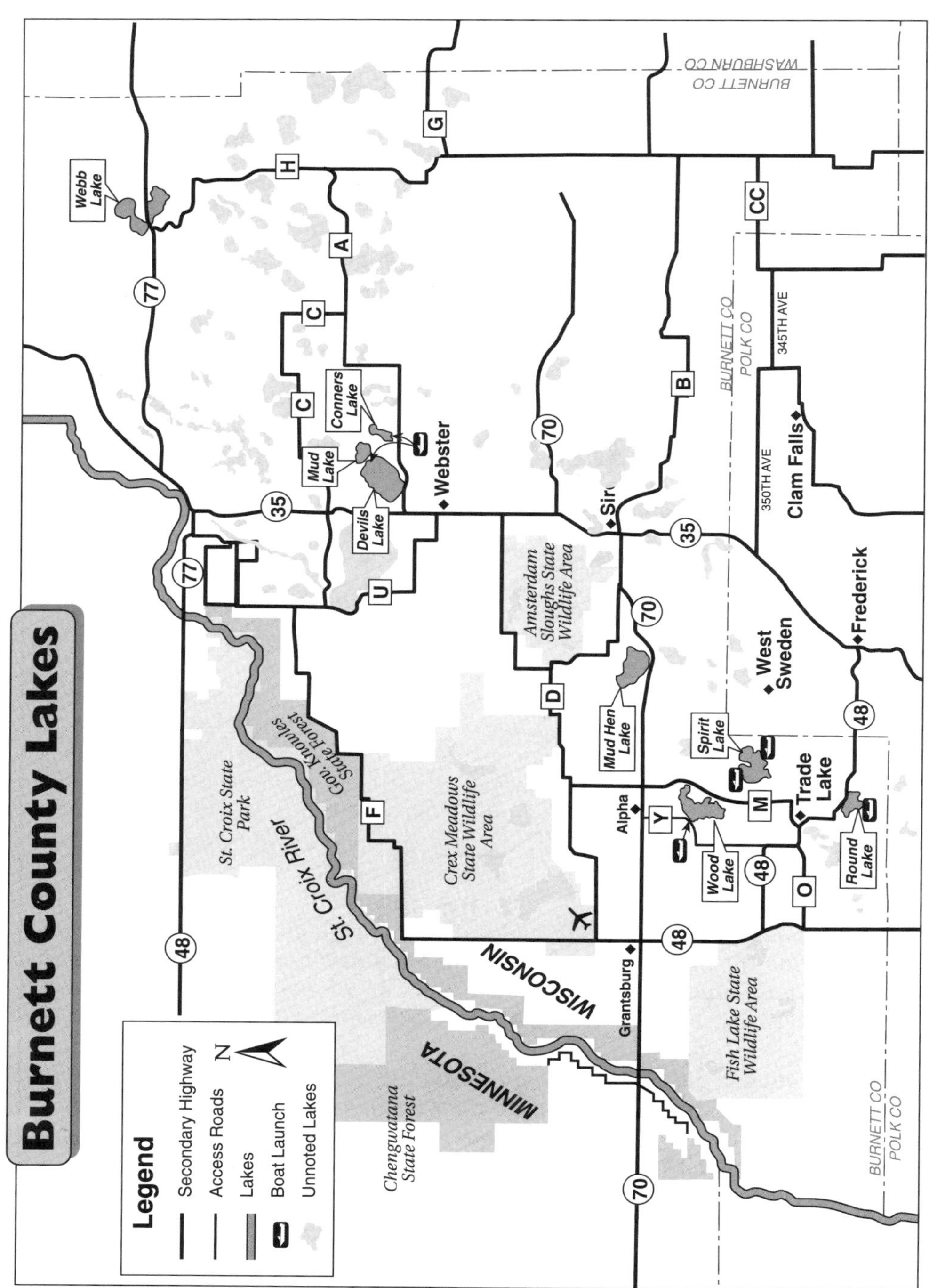

Burnett County Lakes
Legend
Secondary Highway
Access Roads
Lakes
Boat Launch
Unnoted Lakes
N
Webb Lake
Conners Lake
Mud Lake
Devils Lake
Webster
Sir
Clam Falls
350TH AVE
345TH AVE
BURNETT CO
POLK CO
WASHBURN CO
Amsterdam Sloughs State Wildlife Area
Mud Hen Lake
West Sweden
Frederick
Spirit Lake
Trade Lake
Round Lake
Wood Lake
Alpha
Grantsburg
Crex Meadows State Wildlife Area
St. Croix State Park
Gov. Knowles State Forest
St. Croix River
WISCONSIN
MINNESOTA
Chengwatana State Forest
Fish Lake State Wildlife Area
77
35
70
48
G
H
A
C
U
D
F
B
CC
Y
M
O

Lakes of Burnett County

Burnett County is blessed with many small, out of-the-way lakes that provide excellent fishing for the belly-boat or canoe angler seeking warmwater species. A bonus here is the abundance of wild rice and marsh, which play host to a variety of waterfowl, shorebirds, and mammals.

Heavy recreational pressure is the rule during summer on larger waters like Clam Lake, Yellow Lake, and Sand Lake. However, there are many small, often weedy, bodies of water that offer the fly-rod angler a bit of solitude and good populations of warmwater gamefish.

The best bets for fishing the smaller lakes in the county are described below.

Round Lake

Located west of Frederic and just south of Highway 48, 204-acre Round Lake offers a good fishery for largemouth bass and panfish. There is a launch off Round Lake Road. Fish the weeds on the western side of the lake.

Spirit Lake

Just to the north of Round Lake, Spirit Lake, at 593 acres, offers good bass and bluegill fishing, too. From Highway 48 in Frederic, take a right turn on County Line Road and follow it for 3 miles to Whispering Pines Road. Take your first right, which will lead you to the launch ramp.

Mud Hen Lake

Named after the freshwater coot that migrate through the Mississippi–St. Croix Flyway, 563-acre Mud Hen Lake holds good numbers of largemouth bass and panfish along its weedy shores. There's a launch off Highway 70 on the southeast corner of the lake.

Wood Lake

To reach 520-acre Wood Lake, take Highway 70 west from Siren to the town of Alpha. Take Highway Y south from Alpha and look for signs to the launch. You'll find largemouth bass, bluegills, and some northern pike in Wood Lake. Little Wood Lake, just to the south, offers a similar fishery.

Devils Lake

Located north of Webster off Highway 35, 1,000-acre Devils Lake is a larger body of water that is often overlooked by anglers who fish better-known Yellow Lake and Sand Lake. Fish the weed edges for bass, walleye, and panfish. From Highway 35 in Webster, continue north to Devils Lake Road (which may be marked as Highway C on some maps). Turn right on Devils Lake Road, and continue to the launch ramp.

Conners Lake

To reach Conners Lake, continue on Devils Lake Road along the north shore of Devils Lake. Follow the access road to the boat launch on Conners. You'll find plenty of bluegill, northern pike, and largemouth bass. At only 100 acres, you could easily cover the weeds of Conners Lake in a float tube.

Webb Lake

Located off Highway 77 in northern Burnett County, Webb Lake slips under the radar screen of guidebooks and fishermen, despite its size of almost 800 acres. One reason may be lack of developed launch facilities. Your best bet is to cartop a boat or put-in with a belly boat from Highway 77. Good bass, panfish, and northern pike fishing can be had here.

Small Lakes of Washburn County

While Washburn County's big water (notably Long Lake, Shell Lake, and Spooner Lake) sees lots of fishing pressure, there are a number of small weedy lakes, some with rough access, waiting for the canoe or belly-boat angler. Here are eight good bets. Try them if things are slow on the Namekagon or if you find the bigger waters near Hayward off-putting.

Little Devil Lake and Big Devil Lake

These two weedy lakes are accessible via only one launch ramp—at 56-acre Little Devils Lake off Highway P southeast of Spooner. You'll find plenty of largemouth bass, northern pike, and panfish in both lakes. Little Devils Lake is almost entirely surrounded by wetlands, and the shoreline on 162-acre Big Devil Lake is also rimmed by weeds. Nice to see in this age of shoreline development!

Pavlas Lake

A bass lake just east of Sarona on Highway D, little 44-acre Pavlas Lake packs some good-sized bucketmouths as well as northern pike and panfish. Launch at the juncture of Highway P and Highway D on the west shore of the lake. You can pick up Highway D headed east in Shell Lake.

Ripley Lake

Largemouth bass are abundant in this 190-acre lake. It's just east of Sarona off County D, with a launch suitable for a cartop boat on the southern end of the lake and a better launch on the north side off the road that heads due west out of Sarona.

Potato Lake

Located just north of Highway 70 and east of Spooner, 222-acre Potato Lake hosts a good population of northern pike, panfish, and largemouth bass. There's an access road and launch on the east side of the lake.

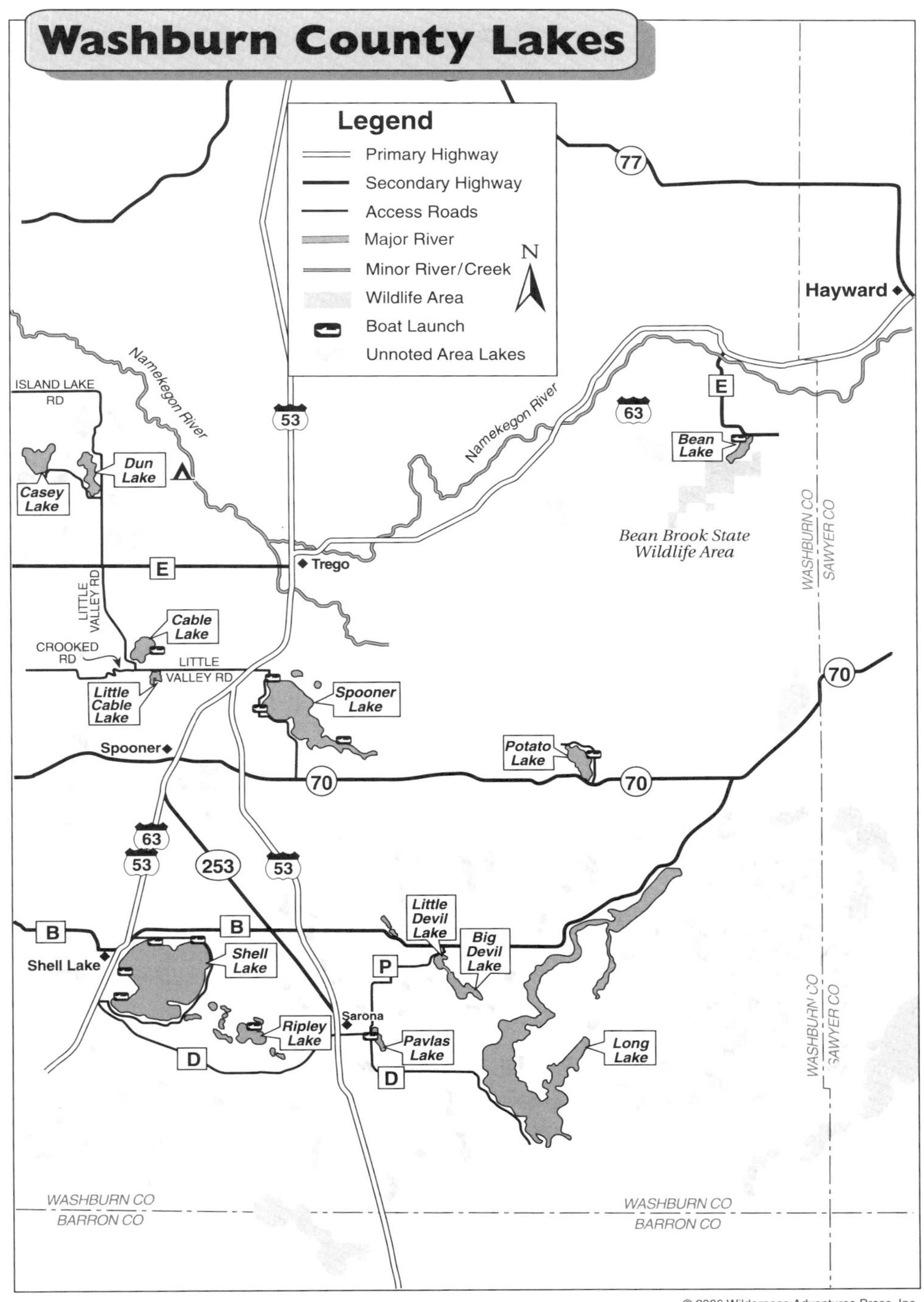
Washburn County Lakes
Legend
Primary Highway
Secondary Highway
Access Roads
Major River
Minor River/Creek
Wildlife Area
Boat Launch
Unnoted Area Lakes
N
77
Hayward
E
63
Namekegon River
Bean Lake
53
ISLAND LAKE RD
Dun Lake
Casey Lake
Bean Brook State Wildlife Area
WASHBURN CO
SAWYER CO
Trego
LITTLE VALLEY RD
Cable Lake
CROOKED RD
LITTLE VALLEY RD
Little Cable Lake
Spooner Lake
70
Spooner
Potato Lake
253
B
Little Devil Lake
Big Devil Lake
Shell Lake
P
Sarona
Ripley Lake
Pavlas Lake
D
Long Lake
BARRON CO

Bean Lake

Bean Lake, in the Bean Brook State Wildlife Area, offers a similar fishery to Potato Lake. Take Highway 63 southwest from Hayward and turn left (south) on Highway E. The lake and launch are off Bean Brook Road. Bean Lake covers 100 acres.

Cable Lake

Located northeast of Spooner, 185-acre Cable Lake is surrounded by marsh and offers a good fishery for largemouth bass and panfish. Take Highway 63 north from Spooner, turn left on Little Valley Road (which turns into Crooked Road), and look for the access road and launch on the right.

Dunn Lake

Located north of Cable Lake off Highway K, 193-acre Dunn Lake is another weedy bass, northern pike, and panfish lake that also holds walleye. Take Highway K north out of Spooner. At the juncture with Highway E, turn left and continue to Island Lake Road. Follow this to the south shore of Dunn Lake and turn left along the south shore to the get to the launch.

Casey Lake

To reach 100-acre Casey Lake, continue on Highway E to Lower MacKenzie Lake Road and follow this to North Casey Lake Road. There's an access road leading to the launch ramp from this road. Casey Lake has a fishery similar to other small Washburn County lakes, with bass, northern pike, and panfish all present.

Balsam Lake

Recommended by DNR fisheries biologist Rick Cornelius, 300-acre Balsam Lake in southwestern Washburn County near Birchwood is a good lake to fish for largemouth bass and bluegill. While it does see its share of boat traffic, you can find enough nooks and crannies to cast a line. Try the marshy east arm of the lake. Both largemouth bass and panfish should be on their spawning beds in late May and early June in Balsam Lake. Look for northern pike in this marshy area, as well as near the inlet of Birch Creek. There are boat launches on the southwest and northeast ends of Balsam Lake, which is located 15 miles northeast of the community of Rice Lake.

Red Cedar Lake

Larger Red Cedar Lake, connected to Balsam Lake by a small channel, is a fine smallmouth bass lake. On this 1,800-acre body of water, you'll want to look for shoreline dropoffs. Chances are good you'll also run into an occasional walleye. Work leech and crawfish patterns along these dropoff areas and you should do well. Most of Red Cedar Lake is over 20 feet deep, so you'll need to fish a sinking line.

There are two boat launches off Highway 48 on the west side of the lake. If you're looking to fish smallmouth bass in a bit more solitude, float the Red Cedar

River between Red Cedar Lake and Rice Lake. Road crossings are at 25th Avenue, 24th Avenue, 23rd Street, and Highway 48.

Bear Lake

Bear Lake is located on the Washburn-Polk County border just to the northwest of Haugen off Highway 53. The best bet for flyfishers on this 1,350-acre body of water is to fish along the weedy west shore of the lake. You'll find a mix of northern pike, largemouth bass, and panfish. From the town of Haugen, take 26th Avenue headed west. A mile from town, take a right turn on the lake access road and take the jug handle that will put you on the southwest shore of the lake. From here, simply motor or paddle the shoreline and cast until you find fish.

Chetek Chain of Lakes

Located south of the community of Rice Lake and just east of Highway 53 in northwest Wisconsin, the Chetek Chain of Lakes is as dense with bluegills as southwestern Wisconsin streams are with brown trout. This five-lake chain totaling just under 4,000 acres teems with bluegill and its close relative, pumpkinseed sunfish. The shallow, tinted water warms early and its weeds attract large quantities of zooplankton, a favorite food of sunfish. Fish in the 8- to 10-inch range are common, and you'll probably nail a few bigger ones.

Prairie Lake, at 1,500 acres, makes up the western boundary of the chain. Mud and Pokegama Lakes, covering 1,100 acres, lie just to the east of Prairie Lake. The southern end of the Chetek Chain, covering some 1,200 acres, is comprised of Lake Chetek and Ten Mile Lake. Lake Chetek is the best-known of the chain for panfish, but all the lakes are good producers.

In a typical year, Memorial Day weekend marks the start of the panfish bite, with fish moving onto their spawning beds. However, depending on weather, the bite can begin as early as mid-May or as late as mid-June. Warm fronts often signal good fishing, while cold fronts give panfish a case of lockjaw. You should be able to find fish on weedbeds most of the summer.

There is shoreline access in the town of Chetek and at boat ramps, but the best fishing is from a small boat or a float tube. Launches are numerous up and down the chain.

The Chetek Chain would be a super place to introduce a youngster to fly fishing. Bring them to a weedbed where you've had luck the day before. Fast action and the willingness of a bluegill to take a fly will get things off to a good start. A White Wulff or small popper will take them on top; a Prince Nymph will take them below.

You'll also find bass and northern pike in the chain's weedy shallows. The minimum length on northern pike is 26 inches, with a daily bag of 2 fish; the minimum length on muskellunge is 40 inches, with a daily bag of 1 fish.

You'll enjoy fine panfish fishing on this chain, but do expect company. If you find yourself on the way to the Kinnickinnic or to Bayfield with a canoe on the car, stop by the Chetek Chain for a day or two of panfishing.

Hub City: Hayward

In addition to being the self-proclaimed Musky Capital of the World, Hayward has much to recommend to anglers. A location on the banks of the Namekagon, known for coughing up spaniel-sized brown trout, doesn't hurt. Nor does the town's proximity to the Flambeau and Chippewa Rivers and Lake Superior's Chequamegon Bay—top-notch smallmouth fisheries all.

Hayward's Boulder Lodge is a certified Orvis dealer and a well-stocked fly shop. Drake Williams guides flyfishers on the Chippewa Flowage, which yielded the state record muskellunge in 1949, weighing 69 pounds, 11 ounces. All in all, a fisherman's paradise.

Accommodations

AmericInn of Hayward, 15601 Highway 63, Hayward; 715-634-2700; $$
Best Western Northern Pine Inn, 9966 West Highway 27 South, Hayward; 800-777-7996; $$
Chip-wa Motel, 9651 N. County CC, Hayward; 715-462-3859; $
Chippewa Pines Resort, 7230 N. Sandy Pines Road, Couderay; 715-945-2776; located on Chippewa Flowage; $$
Comfort Suites, 15586 County B, Hayward; 715-634-0700
Boulder Lodge, Highway 77, Hayward; 715-462-3002; $$

Campgrounds

Lake Chippewa Campground, 8380N County CC, Hayward; 715-462-3672; located on the Chippewa Flowage
Ojibwa State Park, P.O. Box 187, Winter; 715-266-3511; located 35 miles southeast of Hayward
Chequamegon National Forest—nearest campsites on Namekagon Lake, Lake Owen,
Moose Lake, Day Lake; all roughly 20 miles from Hayward
Campsites also available along the Namekagon River, part of the St. Croix National Scenic Riverway

Restaurants

Famous Dave's BBQ Shack, Highway B, Hayward; 715-462-3352; excellent Midwest BBQ chain, try the Buffalo chicken wings
Norske Nook, Highway 27, Hayward; 715-634-4928; Wisconsin franchise famous for its pies and from-scratch cooking
The Cook Shanty, 15546 W. County B, Hayward; 715-934-2345; another Wisconsin franchise with family menu
Chippewa Inn, 9702 County B, Hayward; 715-462-3648; supper club menu with German flare
Angler's Bar and Grill, Main Street, Hayward; 715-634-4700; burgers, pizza, Mexican, and beer

Fly Shops, Outfitters, Sporting Goods

Boulder Lodge, Highway 77, Hayward; 715-462-3002; Orvis and Scott dealer, fly shop 40 miles west of Boulder Junction

Happy Hooker, 12272 N. Upper A Road, Hayward; 715-462-3984; sells licenses

Hayward Fly Fishing Company, 15849 Second St., Hayward; 715 634 8149; also provides guiding

We Tie It Fly Shop & Northern Adventure Guide Service, Boulder Junction; 715-385-0171; the Northwoods fly shop, plus guiding for trout and warmwater species

Veterinarians

Hayward Animal Hospital, 15226 W. County B, Hayward; 715-634-8971

Medical

Hayward Area Memorial Hospital, 11040N Highway 77, Hayward; 715-634-1115

Auto Rental

Gillis Motors, Highway 63, Hayward; 715-634-2651

Automobile Repair

Fischer Automobile Repair, 10518 Lakewood Drive, Hayward; 715-634-0188

Air Service

Hayward Airport, 10930 N. Airport Rd., Hayward; 715-634-4624; facilities also at Minneapolis, MN and Duluth-Superior

For More Information

Hayward Area Chamber of Commerce
P.O. Box 726
Hayward, WI 54843
715-634-8662
www.haywardlakes.com

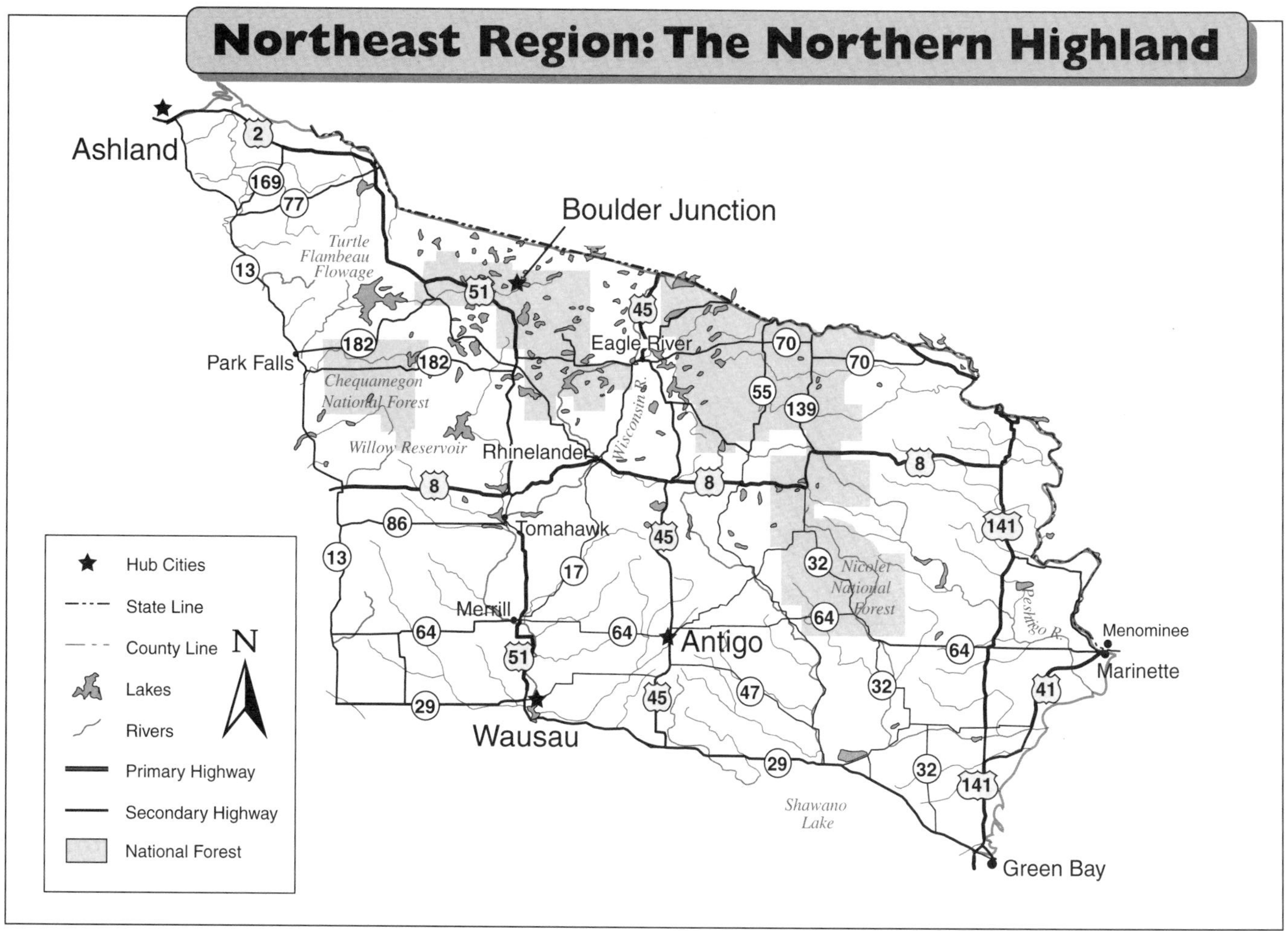
Northeast Region: The Northern Highland
Ashland
Boulder Junction
Turtle Flambeau Flowage
Park Falls
Chequamegon National Forest
Willow Reservoir
Rhinelander
Eagle River
Wisconsin R.
Tomahawk
Merrill
Wausau
Antigo
Nicolet National Forest
Peshtigo R.
Menominee
Marinette
Shawano Lake
Green Bay
2
169
77
13
51
45
182
70
55
139
8
141
86
17
64
32
47
29
41
Hub Cities
State Line
County Line
Lakes
Rivers
Primary Highway
Secondary Highway
National Forest
N

Northeast Wisconsin: The Northern Highland

Look at the Wolf, Pine, Popple, or Peshtigo Rivers in May and you'll think you have entered a smaller version of Colorado—big brawling freestone water with precipitous drops. In May, you will find good numbers of trout in these big rivers. But visit the same rivers in the doldrums of summer and you will wonder where the trout have gone. This is the mystery of fishing this dark wooded country. Come hot weather, the trout seem to disappear.

Plunging a stream thermometer into the water can dispel a lot of that mystery. These streams warm into the 70s and sometimes hit the 80-degree mark in summer. DNR surveys have recorded fish traveling as much as 40 miles on northern Wisconsin river systems. These rivers are shallow and lack deep holes that provide relief in the heat. Fish them early in the season and then again in September.

The Pike is probably the best of these rivers. The Wolf can have some very fine hatches, particularly March Browns, before it warms. A number of smaller river systems in Marinette County offer good brook trout fishing, including the Pemebonwon and the Wasaukee. In the Antigo area the East Branch of the Eau Claire River is a good bet. The Prairie River near Wausau is now dam-free for its entire length and holds a mix of wild brook and brown trout.

The region is also rich in wilderness lakes, with hundreds in the Northern American Highlands State Forest and Nicolet National Forest—some of which hold trout, others a mix of trout and warmwater species, still others hold only warmwater species, and some are just plain barren of fish. I've included a sampling of some of the most productive waters in the Nicolet and Northern Highland.

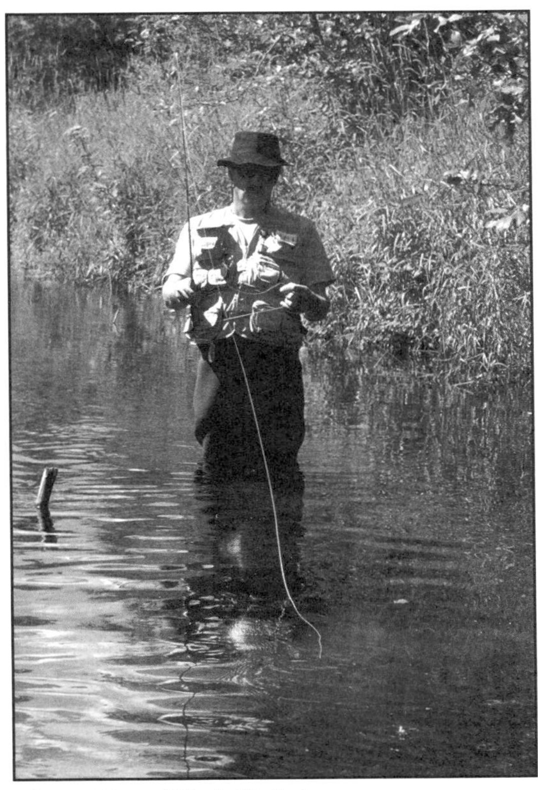

Plover River. (Chris Halla)

HATCH CHART—Northeast Wisconsin: The Northern Highlands

Insect/Food Source	J	F	M	A	M	J	J	A	S	O	N	D	Flies
Blue-Winged Olives (*Baetis*)				■	■	■	■	■	■				BWO Thorax, Sparkle Dun #16-22; Pheasant Tail #16-18
Hendricksons				■	■	■							Light Hendrickson, Spinners #12-14; Pheasant Tail #12-14
Mahogany Dun					■								Blue Quill #16-18; Leadwing Coachman #14-16
Leadwing Coachman (*Isonychia bicolor*)					■	■							Gray Drake, Leadwing Coachman #14-16
Sulphurs					■	■							Sulphur Dun, Pale Evening Dun, Spinner #16; Pheasant Tail Nymph #16
Black Quill					■	■							Black Quill #14
Red Quill					■	■							Red Quill, Rusty Spinner #14
Brown Drake						■							Brown Drake, Spinners, Emergers #10-12
March Brown & Gray Fox					■	■	■						March Brown, Spinner, Hare's Ear Nymph #12-14; Gray Fox #12

HATCH CHART—Northeast Wisconsin: The Northern Highlands (cont.)													
Insect/Food Source	**J**	**F**	**M**	**A**	**M**	**J**	**J**	**A**	**S**	**O**	**N**	**D**	**Flies**
Hexagenia (Evening Hatch)						■	■						Hart Washer, Hex, Olive Drake #4-8; Hex Nymph, Strip Nymph #4-8/Late June #10
Light Cahill					■	■	■						Light Cahill #12; Hare's Ear Nymph #12
Little Golden Drake						■	■						Cream-Colored Mayfly #14-20; Hare's Ear Nymph #16
Trico(Peaks mid-June to mid-July)						■	■	■					Tiny White Wing Black, CDC Trico, Spent Wing Trico #24-28
White Mayfly (*Ephoron leukon*) (Evening Hatch/Peaks early August)								■	■				White Wulff, White Miller #12-14
Little Black Caddis			■	■	■								Micro Black Caddis #16-22; Caddis Larvae (dark) #16-22; Beadhead Caddis (dark) #16
American Grannom					■	■							Elk Hair Caddis, Sparkle Pupa #12-14; Caddis Larvae #18-20

HATCH CHART—Northeast Wisconsin: The Northern Highlands (cont.)													
Insect/Food Source	J	F	M	A	M	J	J	A	S	O	N	D	Flies
Green Caddis (*H. Slossonae*)				■	■								Green Caddis #12-14; Green Sparkle Pupa, Green Caddis Larvae #16-20
Caddis (*H. borealis*)						■	■						Elk Hair Caddis, Spent Partridge Caddis #16; Tan Sparkle Pupa #18-20
Stoneflies				■	■	■	■	■					Brown, Yellow, Olive Stimulators #8-12; Stonefly Nymphs #6-8
Terrestrials (Ants, Beetles, Crickets, Grasshoppers)							■	■	■				Hoppers #6-10; Crickets #8-10; Ants #14-20; Beetles #18-20
Sculpin			■	■	■	■	■	■	■				Muddler Minnow, Olive or Brown Leech #8-10
Crawfish			■	■	■	■	■	■	■				Crayfish Patterns, Marabou Leech Olive/Brown #8-10
Leeches			■	■	■	■	■	■	■				Marabou Leech, Strip Leech (Black, Olive, Brown) #4-10

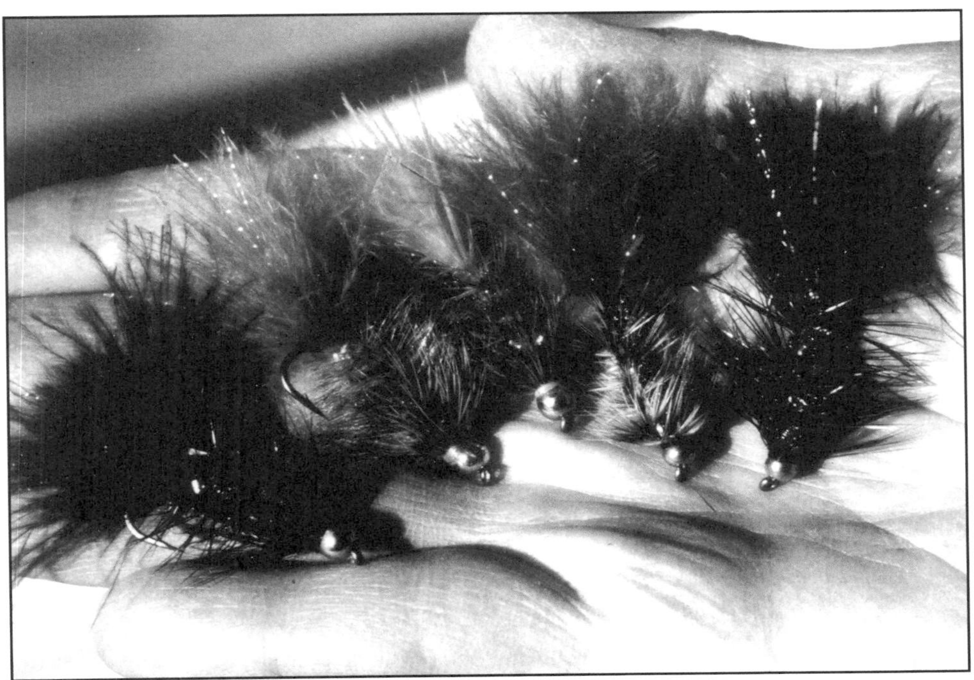

Beadhead Woolly Buggers will take virtually all of Wisconsin's major gamefish.

Plover River

Like the Little Wolf and Comet Creek to the south, the Plover River is a brook trout stream of the first order. It contains 25 miles of trout water, and wild brook and brown trout can be found throughout. It is also stocked with rainbow trout. The Plover River is located in Marathon County, and given its proximity to the East Branch of the Eau Claire River, an angler looking to a pass a weekend in the Antigo or Wausau area would need to look no further than this trio of sleeper streams to stay busy.

There's something special about waters with a long history in fishing literature (like the Wolf and the Prairie). On the other hand, trying one's hand on lesser-known waters provides the angler with that intangible sense of discovery. You might scare up a pair of wood ducks from a bankside eddy or catch a beaver lazing in a slow pool. Also, your chance of running into scores of anglers is diminished. That's the nice thing about fishing in a state with 10,000 miles of trout water and 15,000 lakes. You can always find solitude if that's what you prefer. Having grown up in New Jersey, where trout streams are scarce and anglers abundant, I have a special appreciation for all of Wisconsin's elbowroom. There's always another stream, another bend to explore.

Trout water on the Plover begins just above Highway 52 east of the town of Hogarty. This is small, tight, brook trout water with a fairly dense canopy. Most of the

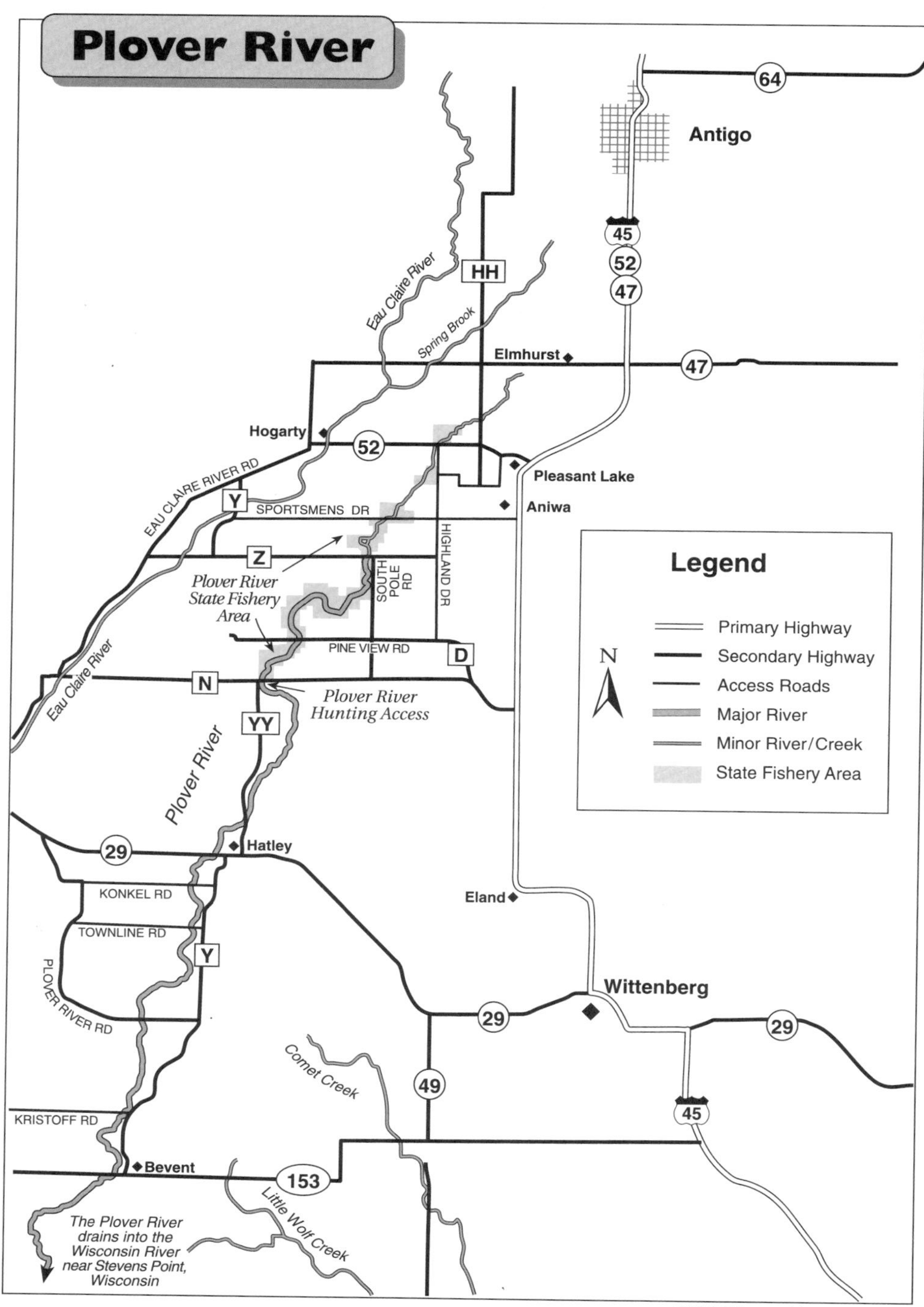
Plover River
64
Antigo
45
52
47
HH
Eau Claire River
Spring Brook
Elmhurst
47
Hogarty
52
EAU CLAIRE RIVER RD
Pleasant Lake
Aniwa
Y
SPORTSMENS DR
HIGHLAND DR
Z
SOUTH POLE RD
Plover River State Fishery Area
PINE VIEW RD
D
Eau Claire River
N
Plover River Hunting Access
YY
Plover River
Legend
Primary Highway
Secondary Highway
Access Roads
Major River
Minor River/Creek
State Fishery Area
N
29
Hatley
KONKEL RD
TOWNLINE RD
Eland
Y
PLOVER RIVER RD
Wittenberg
29
29
Comet Creek
49
45
KRISTOFF RD
Bevent
153
Little Wolf Creek
The Plover River drains into the Wisconsin River near Stevens Point, Wisconsin

land on the upper Plover is contained within the Plover River State Fishery Area, so you'll be on public ground if you decide to step outside the stream. You can also access this stretch on Highway HH just upstream from Highway 52 and on Sportsman's Drive just downstream from Highway 52.

On streams such as the upper Plover, I wade very slowly, being careful not to stir up silt, and drift a streamer downstream against bankside cover. It's a technique I developed in my worming days, and it seems to apply quite well to fly fishing. Even fish that are not actively feeding will zap an undulating streamer out of curiosity or aggression.

There's also access on County Z, South Pole Road, Pine View Road, and County N. The Plover widens below Highway N, with rocky pocketwater becoming more common. Trout water continues below Highway N for another 15 miles to the village of Bevent and Highway 153. Follow Highway Y, south from Highway N, if you're looking to explore the lower reaches of the Plover. You'll hit the village of Hatley and Highway 29. Highway Y continues to Bevent, with road crossings at Konkel, Townline, Plover River, and Kristoff Road. The streambed becomes wider as you move downstream on the Plover. The river warms, and brown trout begin to displace brook trout as the dominant species.

Hatches on the Plover are similar to other Sand County and northeast Wisconsin streams. Early season caddis, stonefly, and Blue-Winged Olive hatches can be had in March and April. The water between Highway 29 and Highway 153 is open during

A beautiful brook trout. (Chris Halla)

the early season; otherwise, the Plover opens to trout fishing the first Saturday in May. Toward the latter part of April and into May you will encounter Hendricksons. Sulphurs appear from the middle part of May through June.

The lower reaches of the Plover see a Hex hatch anywhere between mid and late June. If you are fishing the Plover during the day in June, try a big Hex nymph. The Plover's larger browns will be eating Hex nymphs before and after the hatch. Look for a White Mayfly hatch in July and August. Don't neglect caddis imitations on the Plover, either; green, black, and tan are good color choices. Brown and yellow stonefly nymphs are also a good bet on the lower Plover. As always, keep a few crawfish patterns and streamers in your fly box.

Stream Facts: Plover River

Season

- The early season runs from the first Saturday in March to the last Sunday before the first Saturday in May; no-kill, single barbless hooks only. Regular season runs from the first Saturday in May at 5:00 am through September 30. The Plover River is open during the early trout season only between Highway 29 and Highway 153.

Regulations

- Upstream from Totten Springs outlet is category 2; between Totten Springs and County Z is category 5 (artificials only, 3-trout limit, all trout kept must be between 10 and 13 inches); between Highway Z and Highway 153, category 4.

Species

- Wild brook and brown trout

Miles of Trout Water

- 25 miles

Stream Characteristics

- Narrow headwater fishing above Highway N; wider and rockier below.

Fly Shops

- We Tie It Fly Shop (Boulder Junction)

Access

- Plover River State Fishery Area along Highway Y.

Maps

- *Wisconsin Atlas and Gazetteer*, pages 77, 65

The upper reaches of the Prairie River.

Prairie River

In addition to yielding a state-record brook trout just under 10 pounds (9 pounds, 15 ounces, to be exact) in 1944, the Prairie River continues to provide excellent fishing for wild brook and brown trout. What's more, with the Prairie Dells Dam removed in the early 1990s and Ward Papermill Dam now removed, the Prairie is dam-free for the first time in a hundred years.

"The Prairie is on the rebound," says area DNR fisheries biologist Dave Seibel. Trout can now move about the river freely. Come winter, they can fatten up on forage fish in the Prairie's lower reaches and in the Wisconsin River, in summer they can move back upstream to the Prairie. Dam removal also means colder water, more oxygen, and better trout habitat. The entire river now sees some degree of natural reproduction, from its headwaters in northwestern Langlade County to its juncture with the Wisconsin River near Merrill.

Wild brook trout predominate in the upper stretches, with browns showing up as you move downstream. The lower reaches of the Prairie also receive plantings of brook and brown trout. While elder anglers may wax rhapsodic about the good old days of trout fishing—certainly there were fewer anglers (and people) 75 years ago—the best days of the Prairie appear to be in the future, not the past. So much so that Seibel has plans to discontinue stocking trout in the Prairie. And if you tire of the 30.9 miles of trout water, you can always try the North Branch of the Prairie, a fine brook trout stream in its own right.

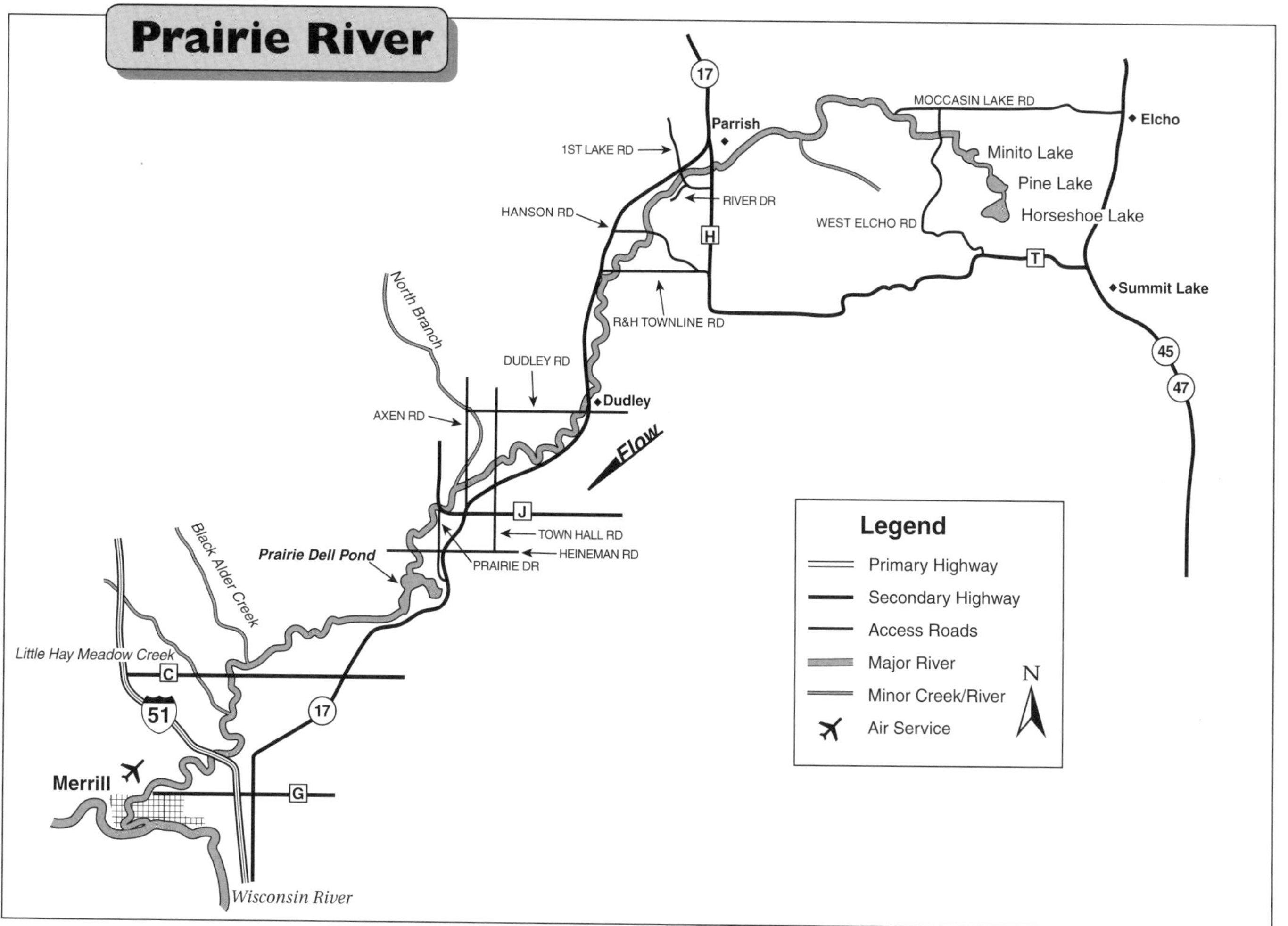
Prairie River
17
Parrish
MOCCASIN LAKE RD
Elcho
1ST LAKE RD
Minito Lake
Pine Lake
RIVER DR
HANSON RD
Horseshoe Lake
WEST ELCHO RD
H
T
Summit Lake
R&H TOWNLINE RD
North Branch
DUDLEY RD
45
47
Dudley
AXEN RD
Flow
J
TOWN HALL RD
Prairie Dell Pond
HEINEMAN RD
PRAIRIE DR
Black Alder Creek
Legend
Primary Highway
Secondary Highway
Access Roads
Major River
Minor Creek/River
Air Service
N
Little Hay Meadow Creek
C
51
17
Merrill
G
Wisconsin River

Access to the Prairie is generally good, but it's limited in the upper reaches. Here, the river rises from boggy Horseshoe, Pine, and Minito Lakes west of Highway 45/47 and the community of Summit Lake. There are two principal road crossings in the headwater section. From Summit Lake, take Highway T to West Elcho Road and take West Elcho Road 5 miles to cross the river. From the community of Elcho on Highway 45/47, Moccasin Lake Road ends at the river after continuing west for about 6 miles. Access improves as you head downstream on the river. Beginning in the village of Parrish, DNR lands and Highway 17 provide good access to the river down to Dudley. Highway 17 follows the Prairie down to Merrill and most any right turn will take you over the river. There are numerous parking lots and good access is available at bridges.

The Prairie is good wading water, with boulders, riffles, side channels, and fallen trees. It has a gentler character and lower gradient than the Wolf to the east, which roars with whitewater in spring but warms dangerously in summer. The Prairie's trout certainly benefit from these stable conditions.

Tim Landwehr of Tight Lines Fly Fishing in De Pere has fished the Prairie quite a bit. The Prairie serves up a full range of insects and forage fish from the early season in March and April through the dog days of summer and into the cool of September. Landwehr says hatches on the Prairie are similar to those on the Tomorrow/Waupaca River to the south. You should see some midge activity as early as March, and midges continue pretty much throughout the season. Little Black Stoneflies begin to emerge in March and continue into April; a black Elk Hair Caddis in size #14 is a dependable imitation for this hatch, especially early on when fish haven't gotten educated.

After the first warm spell in March, you're likely to start seeing Blue-Winged Olives. Hendricksons tend to emerge between mid-April and mid-May, with Sulphurs following in June. A good black caddis hatch comes off in May, which you can fish with a caddis pupae or any generic black caddis dry in size 18. The Prairie is not known for its Hex hatch, as are some central Wisconsin streams like the Tomorrow and Mecan. However, there is a strong White Mayfly hatch between mid-July and early August.

Terrestrials fish well on the Prairie; hopper patterns are good in meadow stretches in July and August, but beetles, spiders, ants, and crickets can be fished tight to bankside cover just about all season. Landwehr also fishes streamer patterns (small Muddlers or Black-Nosed Dace) down and across current. These can be fished just about anytime, provoking aggressive strikes from the Prairie's numerous brook trout.

Seibel has noted trout densities in the Prairie between 2,000 and 6,000 fish per mile, depending on the year. (Warm summers and cold winters are hard on trout populations.) That compares favorably with other noted trout streams like Black Earth, Timber Coulee, and the Kinnickinnic. Lots of cold groundwater feeds the Prairie, keeping its upper reaches in the low 60s and its lower reaches below the 70-degree mark in summer.

An interesting dynamic occurs here between brook and brown trout. The Prairie has received much habitat attention, such as overhead bank cover, from the local chapter of TU and from the DNR. Browns, being more aggressive, tend to occupy prime habitats. This drives brook trout into less than ideal habitat, leaving them more vulnerable to predation and anglers. Thus, while the river has the potential to grow very large brook trout, many are caught before they reach maximum size. If browns weren't present, who knows, maybe the Prairie would produce another 10-pounder.

Stream Facts: Prairie River

Season

- The early season runs from the first Saturday in March to the last Sunday before the first Saturday in May; no-kill, single barbless hooks only. Regular season runs from the first Saturday in May at 5:00 am through September 30. The Prairie River is open during the early trout season from Highway J downstream only.

Regulations

- Category 4

Species

- Wild brook and brown trout

Miles of Trout Water

- 30.9 miles

Stream Characteristics

- Freestone river with coldwater seepage and tributaries; all dams removed; very rich in insect life with good and reliable hatches.

Fly Shops

- We Tie It Fly Shop (Boulder Junction)

Access

- Prairie River State Hunting and Fishing Grounds, Highway 17.

Maps

- *Wisconsin Atlas and Gazetteer*, page 76

THE LITTLE WOLF RIVER

Beginning near the town of Galloway and joining the Wolf River at Big Falls, the Little Wolf is a sleeper brook trout stream, according to Bill Sherer of We Tie It Fly Shop and Northern Adventure Guide Service of Boulder Junction. Fed by groundwater seeping up through a sand bottom, it resembles nearby Flume Creek and Comet Creek more than its namesake the Wolf River, a large freestone stream that warms beyond comfortable trout temperatures in July and August. From its beginnings in Marathon County, the Little Wolf flows briefly through Portage County.

A good stretch to fish is the Little Wolf River State Wildlife Area off Highway 49 and Wigwam Road in Portage County. Swing streamer patterns along the densely wooded banks. Over the Waupaca County line, road crossings are at Highway P, Little Wolf Road, Ness Road, Highway C, and Highway J before the town of Big Falls. Below the impoundment in Big Falls, it is too warm for trout but supports smallmouth and northern pike down to its confluence with the Wolf River downstream from New London, some 50 miles south. Highway 110 parallels the lower Little Wolf.

Early on, caddis and stonefly imitations are good bets. Hendrickson hatches take place in late April and early May, with Sulphurs coming about a month later. Fish the mid-June Hex hatch by day with Hex nymphs and by night with bushy dries like a White Wulff. Terrestrial fishing is also good on the Little Wolf. Crickets and beetles will take fish from June on. July, August, and September are prime hopper time.

During the March and April season, only the portion of the Little Wolf between County P and County J (in Waupaca County) is open to trout fishing; the rest of the river is closed to trout fishing during this early season. Category 4 regulations are in place for the majority of the stream during the regular trout season. However, the water from Ness Road downstream to County J (in Waupaca County) is category 5; only artificial lures may be used and 1 trout with a minimum length of 14 inches may be taken per day.

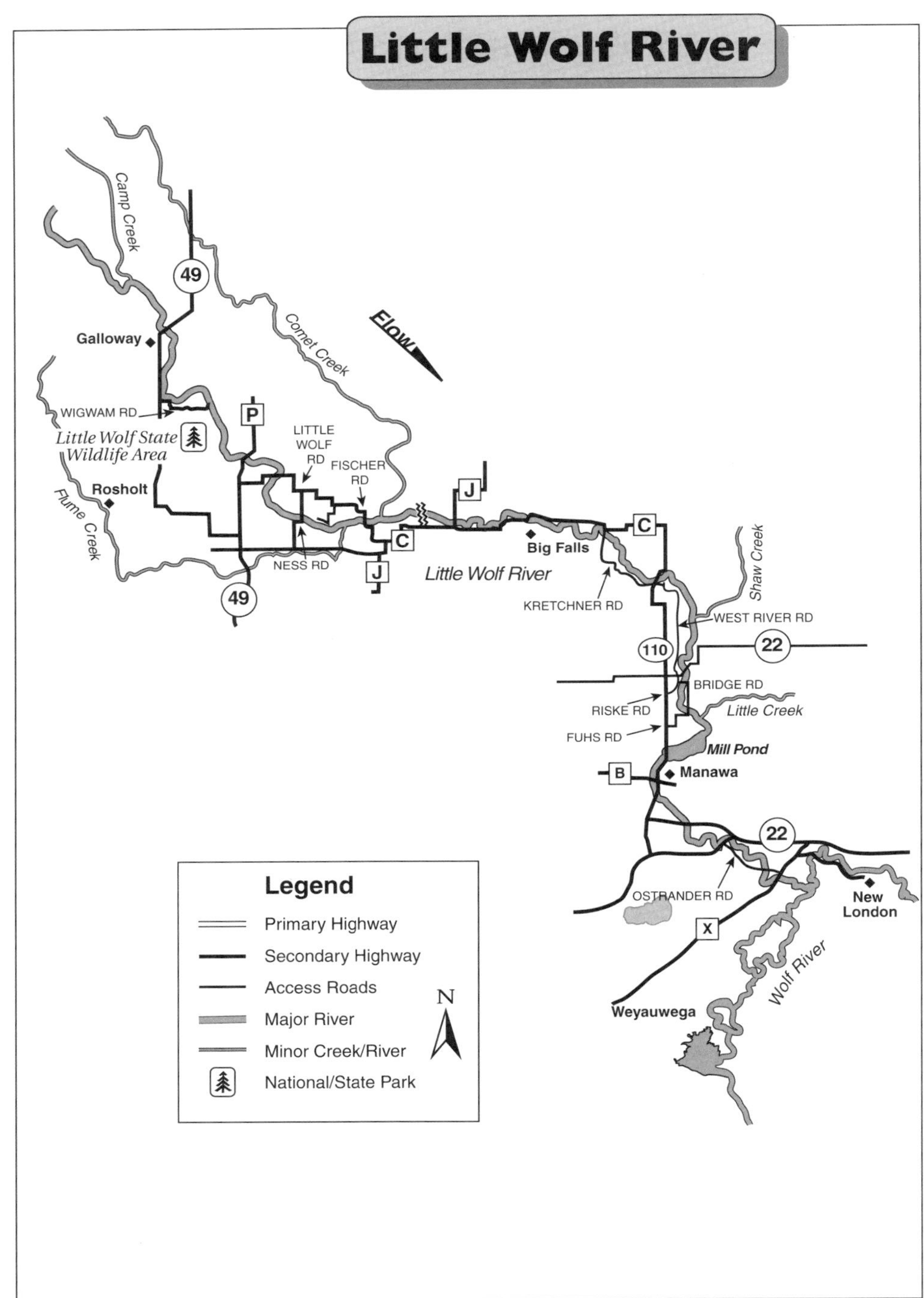
Little Wolf River
Camp Creek
49
Comet Creek
Flow
Galloway
WIGWAM RD
P
Little Wolf State Wildlife Area
LITTLE WOLF RD
FISCHER RD
Rosholt
Flume Creek
J
C
NESS RD
J
49
Big Falls
C
Little Wolf River
KRETCHNER RD
Shaw Creek
WEST RIVER RD
22
110
BRIDGE RD
RISKE RD
Little Creek
FUHS RD
Mill Pond
B
Manawa
22
OSTRANDER RD
New London
X
Wolf River
Weyauwega
Legend
Primary Highway
Secondary Highway
Access Roads
Major River
Minor Creek/River
National/State Park
N

Stream Facts: Little Wolf River

Season

- Regular season runs from the first Saturday in May at 5:00 am through September 30. Closed during March-April season.

Regulations

- Category 4 except between County J and Ness Road, where it is category 5 (1-trout limit, minimum size 14 inches, artificials only).

Species

- Brook trout, with smallmouth and northern pike in the lower reaches.

Miles of Trout Water

- 20 miles

Stream Characteristics

- Sand-bottomed brook trout stream; very clear.

Fly Shops

- We Tie It Fly Shop (Boulder Junction)

Maps

- *Wisconsin Atlas and Gazetteer*, page 76, 77

Hub City: Wausau

Wausau was founded by George Stevens in the late 1830s as a sawmilling center for northern Wisconsin timber. German and Polish immigrants settled Wausau and worked its mills in the late 19th century; in the last 20 years, immigrants from southeast Asia are the area's newest group. Agriculture and forestry in surrounding Marathon County are the principal land uses. The Wausau metropolitan area, with a population of 70,000, makes a good base city for exploring the nearby Prairie River, Plover River, the East Branch of the Eau Claire River, and spring ponds in Marathon, Lincoln, and Langlade Counties. The Wisconsin River offers the boat angler excellent fishing for smallmouth bass.

Accommodations

Super 8 Motel, 2006 Stewart Avenue, Wausau; 715-848-2888, 800-800-8000; $

Days Inn, 116 S. 17th Avenue, Wausau; 715-842-0641; $

Best Western Midway, 2901 Martin Avenue, Wausau; 715-842-1616, 800-528-1234; $$

Campgrounds

Marathon Park, juncture of Stewart Avenue/Highway 52 and 17th Street

Dells of the Eau Claire County Park, Highway Z, 14 miles east to Highway Y north

Nicolet National Forest, campgrounds at Boulder Lake, Boot Lake, Ada Lake, and Fanny Lake; forest headquarters, 68 South Stevens Street, Rhinelander; 715-362-1300 or 877-444-6677 to make a reservation; campgrounds throughout forest

Veteran's Memorial Park, take Highway 45/47 12 miles north of Antigo and follow Highway J east to campground on Jack's Lake

Council Grounds State Park, 1110 E. 10th Street, Merrill; 715-536-8773; located 10 miles north of Wausau on Wisconsin River

Rib Mountain State Park, 5301 Rib Mountain Road, Wausau; 715-359-4522

Restaurants

Great Dane Brewpub, 2305 Sherman Street, Wausau 715 845 3000; brew pub offering full menu

Annie's American Café, 305 S. 18th Avenue, Wausau; 715-842-0846; chain restaurant serving full menu

2510 Restaurant, 2510 Stewart Avenue, Wausau; 715-845-2510; breakfast, sandwiches, dinner

Kobe Restaurant, 1127 E. Grand Avenue, Rothschild; 715-355-4232; fine Asian cuisine and sushi

Fly Shops, Outfitters, Sporting Goods

We Tie It Fly Shop & Northern Adventure Guide Service, Boulder Junction; 715-385-0171; the Northwoods fly shop, plus guiding for trout and warmwater species, located 1.5 hours north of Wausau

Gander Mountain, 1560 County Road XX, Rothschild; 715-355-5500

Veterinarians

Wausau Animal Hospital, 1006 Townline Road, Wausau; 715-845-9637

Medical

Wausau Hospital Center, 333 Pine Ridge Boulevard, Wausau; 715-847-2121

Auto Rental

Avis (715-693-3025) and **National** (715-693-3430) located at Wausau Airport

Automobile Repair

Rosemurgy Repair, 1700 Business Highway 51, Wausau; 715-675-7775; works on foreign cars

Air Service

Wausau Airport (715-693-2147) located 8 miles south of Wausau in Mosinee

For More Information

Wausau-Central Wisconsin Convention and Visitor's Bureau
10204 Park Place
Suite 8
Mosinee, WI 54455

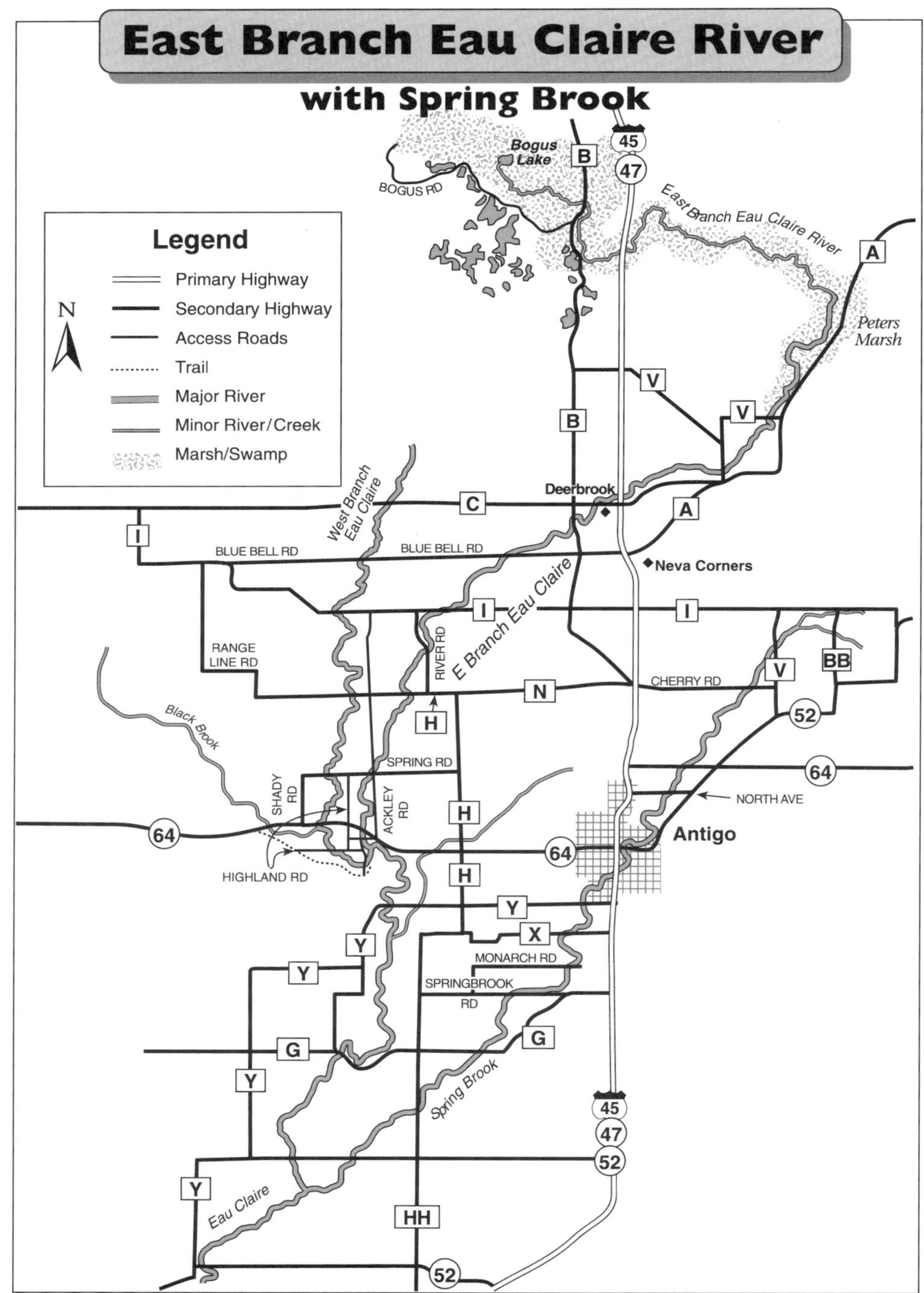
East Branch Eau Claire River
with Spring Brook
Legend
Primary Highway
Secondary Highway
Access Roads
Trail
Major River
Minor River/Creek
Marsh/Swamp
N
Bogus Lake
BOGUS RD
East Branch Eau Claire River
Peters Marsh
Deerbrook
Neva Corners
West Branch Eau Claire
BLUE BELL RD
BLUE BELL RD
E Branch Eau Claire
RANGE LINE RD
RIVER RD
CHERRY RD
Black Brook
SPRING RD
SHADY RD
ACKLEY RD
NORTH AVE
Antigo
HIGHLAND RD
MONARCH RD
SPRINGBROOK RD
Spring Brook
Eau Claire
© 2006 Wilderness Adventures Press, Inc.

East Branch of the Eau Claire River

While no longer a secret, the East Branch of the Eau Claire River, with 15 miles of wild brook trout water, is still a consistent producer. Bill Sherer of Northern Adventure Guide Service goes so far as to say that the East Branch of the Eau Claire may be the best-managed brook trout stream in the state. It's not as cold as some brook trout streams, but it's got plenty of cover and shade.

This stream was a favorite of fly-fishing employees at the now defunct Steve Gerhardt's Sporting Goods of Madison. Its swampy headwaters rise north of the town of Neva in Langlade County and angle southwest, joining the Eau Claire River west of Antigo. There is DNR land in the upper reaches (north of Neva) along Highway A; otherwise, access is at road crossings. Highway V crosses the stream in Neva, Highway C and Highway B just below Neva. The last road crossings are Highway I, Highway H, Spring Road, and Highway 64.

Despite intensive agriculture in the surrounding area, the East Branch's banks are stabilized with riprap and trees, and there is good in-stream cover. A small Prince Nymph bounced through the stream's dark pockets is a good way to prospect for fish; a bushy attractor dry (such as a White Wulff) floated along riprapped banks will also take fish. Beetles, crickets, and grasshopper patterns are good late-summer flies. You'll find Sulphur and Hendrickson hatches in May on the East Branch. You can also take East Branch brook trout by fishing streamers tight to likely looking cover. Forage fish abound on the East Branch.

From Bluebell Road downstream to River Road is category 3; otherwise the East Branch is category 5 (2-trout limit, artificials only, minimum size 12 inches). The river is closed to fishing during the early March and April season.

The East Branch of the Eau Clair is full of little brook trout.

Spring Ponds of Langlade County

Langlade County has over 200 spring ponds. These are upwellings of cold, high-quality groundwater through the local sandy soil known as Antigo Loam. They can range in size from a quarter of an acre to 20 acres. The county's larger spring ponds are listed in *Wisconsin Trout Fishing Regulations and Guide,* available at sporting goods stores and DNR offices. These vary in quality, according to DNR fisheries biologist Dave Seibel. Some contain few if any trout. Most contain at least some naturally reproducing brook trout; a few contain brown trout. "They're harder to fly fish than streams," says Seibel, "because they're so clear."

The best fishing can be had from a lightweight portable canoe or belly boat in low-light conditions—early or late in the day or during rainy or drizzly weather. Fish a small nymph or larvae imitation on a long leader. Work structure such as shoreline slopes, fallen trees, or brush overhangs.

Six of the county's best spring ponds can be found in the Woods Flowage State Fishery Area, according to Seibel. These are: Woods Flowage, Hoglee Springs #1, Hoglee Springs #2, Stark's Springs, Nixon Springs, and Hoglot Springs. They are all walk-in only. All are category 3.

Take Highway 64 east out of Antigo through the town of Polar. Woods Flowage is located off Polar-Evergreen Road south of Highway 64 and is accessible via a walking trail. The other spring ponds are located off Blackhawk Road (take Muraski Road, the next right turn after Polar-Evergreen Road, to Blackhawk Road) and are also accessible via a walking trail leading from the south end of the wildlife area.

Lakes of Langlade County

McGee Lake

This is a larger spring pond (22 acres) popular with locals early in the season because of its easy access. It contains wild brook trout and stocked rainbow trout. After the first few weeks of the season things quiet down and McGee offers the fly caster in a belly boat or canoe larger water to work.

From the town of Elton west of Polar on Highway 64, take Elton South Road. You will see McGee Lake on your left at 2.5 miles. There is a jug-handle access road on the north side of the lake off Elton South Road; there is also access on the southeast side of the lake off Harmon Road. McGee Lake is category 5, artificials only. You may keep 2 trout with a minimum size of 12 inches.

Rollingstone Lake

Shallow Rollingstone Lake offers a good fishery for northern pike, panfish, walleye, and some largemouth bass. It covers almost 700 acres and is located east of the Mole Lake Indian Reservation and Highway 55 in northern Langlade County. Minimum length on walleye is 18 inches with a daily bag limit of 3 fish.

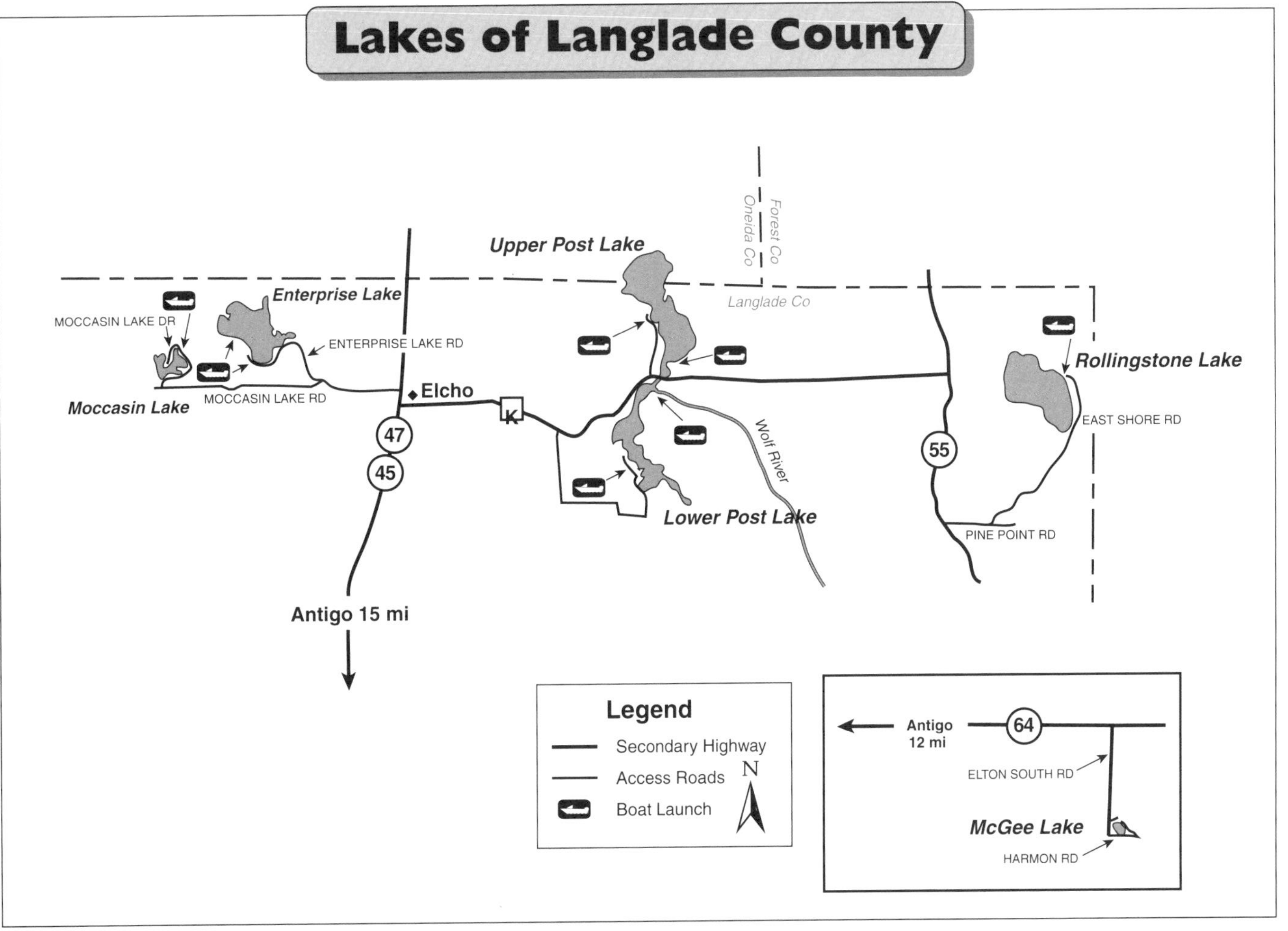

Lakes of Langlade County
Upper Post Lake
Forest Co
Oneida Co
Langlade Co
Enterprise Lake
MOCCASIN LAKE DR
ENTERPRISE LAKE RD
Rollingstone Lake
Elcho
Moccasin Lake
MOCCASIN LAKE RD
K
47
45
55
EAST SHORE RD
Wolf River
Lower Post Lake
PINE POINT RD
Antigo 15 mi
Legend
Secondary Highway
Access Roads
Boat Launch
N
Antigo
12 mi
64
ELTON SOUTH RD
McGee Lake
HARMON RD

Given its shallow marshy nature, you will be limited to fishing patches of open water in summer, which is fine as this is where the fish should be. From Highway 55, take Pine Point Road to East Shore Road to the boat launch. And you'll want a boat here, as the lakebed is too soft to wade.

Enterprise Lake

Dark, murky Enterprise Lake holds good populations of smallmouth bass, muskellunge, and walleye. It can be found west of Elcho and Highway 45/47. Find ramps on the south shore of the lake on Enterprise Lake Road. It is 550 acres with a maximum depth of 27 feet.

Moccasin Lake

Just to the west of Enterprise Lake is 111-acre Moccasin Lake. This is essentially full of weeds in summer, so fish it in spring and fall or consider flies with a weedless hook guard. You'll find walleye, panfish, bass, and muskellunge here. Fish the weed edges with bass bugs and you never know what will swirl at your fly. The boat launch is on the north side of the lake, off Moccasin Lake Drive.

Upper Post Lake and Lower Post Lake

These narrow, shallow lakes cover 1,100 acres on the border of Oneida and Langlade Counties. If you like to fish weeds, try Lower Post. If you prefer more open water, try Upper Post. I've never minded casting rubber spiders and bass bugs right in the slop. I love to see the swirl as something comes up to grab the fly. You'll find pike, muskies, panfish, and largemouth bass in this chain.

A fly plate for the Wolf River tied by the late Ed Haaga. (Tim Landwehr)

Wolf River

There were a variety of reasons for including individual waters in this guidebook. Some merited inclusion simply on the basis of fish populations, some because of striking scenery, some because they exemplified certain environmental issues. While the Wolf does suffer from persistent habitat problems—it lacks deep holes to provide relief from summer heat and winter ice—it could be included here on any of the above criteria. What's more it has a mythological, larger-than-life quality. The banks of this 200-mile-long waterway have played host to every activity crucial to the state identity: fishing, hunting, logging, rafting, mining, cheesemaking, even the development of Wisconsin's state dog, the American water spaniel, bred by market hunters along the lower Wolf in the mid-1800s.

Like the animal after which it is named, the Wolf is a big, elusive, many-mooded creature, now fast and savage, now indolent and slow. And like *Canis lupus,* it has suffered as the state was transformed from wilderness to settled ground. While both the river and the animal enjoy certain protections (the timber wolf is classified as a threatened species and the banks of the upper Wolf are under DNR and Menominee Nation control), their status continues to hang in the balance. Heat waves, winter ice flows, and the threat of sulfide discharges from a proposed Exxon mine at the village of Crandon loom in the background as dangers to the river's trout. Wisconsin's timber wolf population remains vulnerable to poaching, and there's talk of a proposed

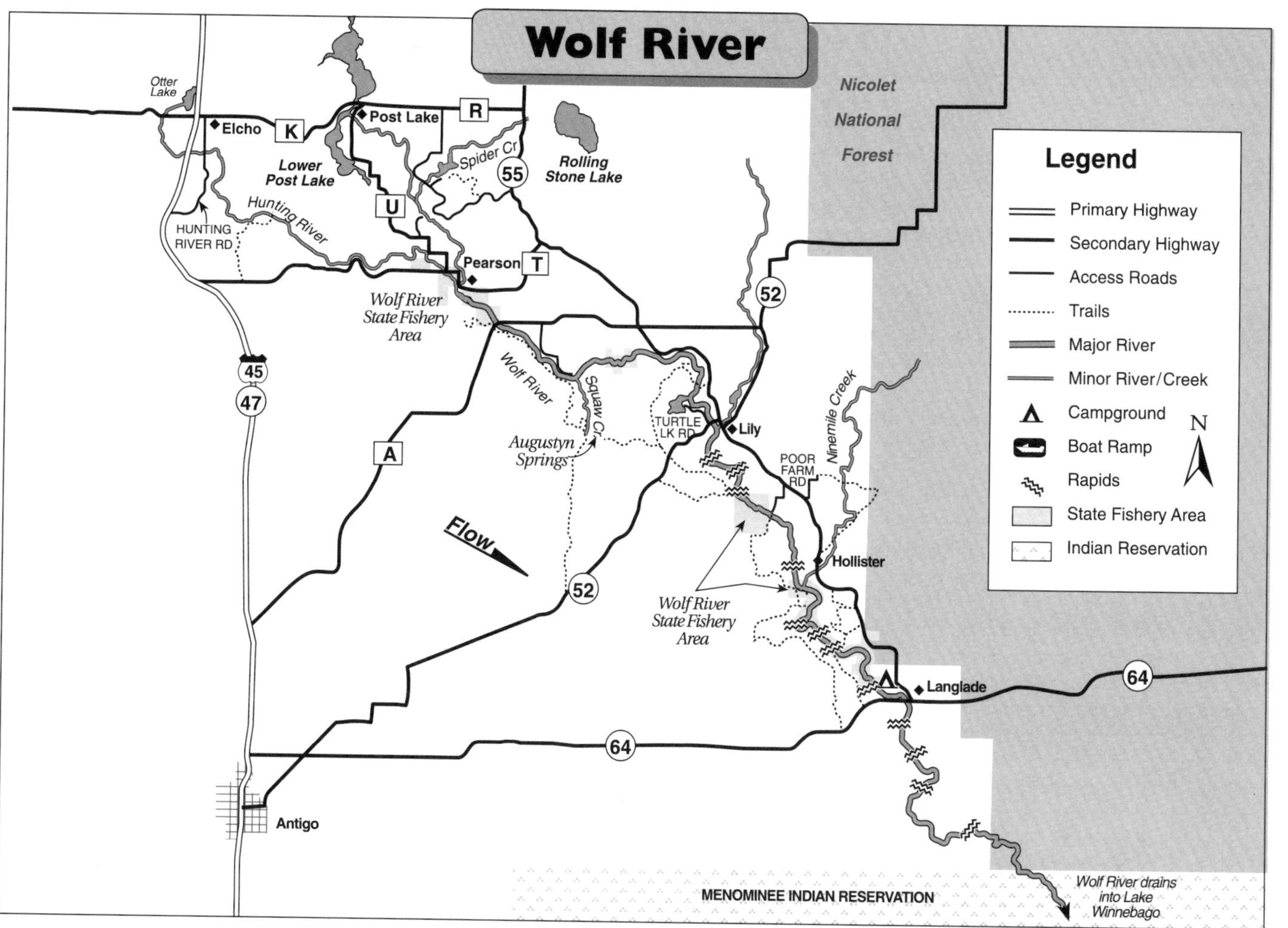
Wolf River
Otter Lake
Elcho
K
Post Lake
R
Lower Post Lake
U
Spider Cr
55
Rolling Stone Lake
Nicolet National Forest
Legend
Primary Highway
Secondary Highway
Access Roads
Trails
Major River
Minor River/Creek
Campground
Boat Ramp
Rapids
State Fishery Area
Indian Reservation
N
Hunting River
HUNTING RIVER RD
Pearson
T
52
Wolf River State Fishery Area
45
47
Wolf River
Squaw Cr.
TURTLE LK RD
Lily
Ninemile Creek
POOR FARM RD
Augustyn Springs
A
Flow
Hollister
52
Wolf River State Fishery Area
Langlade
64
64
Antigo
MENOMINEE INDIAN RESERVATION
Wolf River drains into Lake Winnebago

hunting season following complaints of wolf predation on livestock, deer, and hunting dogs. Still, even at the advent of the 21st century, wild rivers and predators somehow manage to survive in the pine and popple darkness of northeast Wisconsin.

From its headwaters near the village of Pearson in northern Langlade County to its mouth at Lake Poygan in the Fox River Basin, the Wolf River meanders some 200 miles through coniferous forests and tribal lands and then dairy farms and duck marshes. An angler may swing a Muddler Minnow through fast pocketwater near Lily or fish white bass at night from a lit houseboat near Fremont, the "white bass capital of the world."

I will concentrate on the 34 miles of trout water in Langlade County. Just to the south of Langlade County, the Wolf enters the Menominee Reservation. The 27 miles that run through this reservation are under the jurisdiction of the Menominee Nation. Angling by nontribal members is not permitted. However, this section of the Wolf has been designated by Congress and the state of Wisconsin as a National Wild and Scenic River, a designation due in part to the world-renowned conservation and timber-harvesting practices of the Menominees. The lower reaches of the Wolf, particularly in the vicinity of Fremont, provide a diverse warmwater fishery.

The thermodynamics of the Wolf River have been hurt by its use as a log highway. The river is twice as wide as it was a hundred years ago, according to DNR fisheries biologist Dave Seibel. Logs were floated from the upper Wolf down to Appleton at Lake Winnebago. Obstructions were blasted out, and with them, much of the riparian cover. This resulted in a wider, shallower river prone to warming in summer and with few deep holes in which trout might over-winter.

The scoured streambed is only one problem. The climate of the Northern Highlands (the northeast corner of the state) is harsh and landlocked. The region is blanketed under heavy snows and ice in winter and fairly swelters, with the moderating effect of Lakes Superior and Michigan almost a hundred miles away, in summer. The effect of heat is obvious on a shallow river with a rock basin. The surrounding granite heats up, and since the water is rarely over 4 feet deep, so does the river. Stream temperatures upwards of 80 degrees aren't uncommon, and this sends trout scurrying toward tributaries and groundwater seepages. What few deep holes do exist in the river often freeze solid; trout are thus forced into whitewater pockets and tributaries.

Dislodged ice sheets further scour the streambed, uprooting trees and habitat projects as they travel downstream, and push trout downstream into marginal water. Seibel says the DNR is trying to combat these conditions with the construction of bankside covers and by stocking wild-strain brown and brook trout. However, the Northern Highland climate and shallow river channel are persistent problems that will likely hamper the Wolf in decades to come. Thus, the river is mainly a put-and-grow fishery, with natural reproduction occurring principally in its small cold tributaries.

Despite the above limitations, trout do survive and attain considerable size here, providing good sport in May, June, and September, as well as during an extended catch-and-release season from October 1 to November 15. Insect life on rivers of the

Northern Highlands is amazingly diverse, with 17 species of mayflies, 14 species of caddis, and 12 species of stoneflies, according to Bill Sherer of Northern Adventure Guide Service.

There is also a strong population of crawfish and forage fish on the Wolf, and terrestrial fishing can be very productive both in late summer and early fall with hopper patterns and just about anytime with beetle, ant, and cricket imitations. This smorgasbord of food options, according to Sherer, results in fish that are generally less keyed-in on a particular kind of food and more receptive to a wide variety of offerings. Herb Buettner, owner of the renowned Wild Wolf Inn, TU chapter president, and a 60-year veteran of the Wolf, gives a similar view of fishing the river.

It offers the typical hatches, like a May Hendrickson hatch and June Sulphur hatch, but it follows its own schedule, too. Buettner noted a mid-June evening fishing the Brown Drake hatch with Wisconsin outdoor personality Dan Small. In less than an hour Small caught and released 20 fish over 15 inches on a spinner pattern. Buettner also described an August evening fishing a Dave's Hopper pattern during which "every damned trout in the river wanted to kill that thing." However, he also described trips where all the conditions were right—hatching bugs and low light—and nary a fish could be raised.

The Wolf is known for toying with the fragile psyches of anglers. What does this mean for the flyfisher? Carry the standard imitations but don't be afraid to try something creative like a nymph fished below a big dry fly. Streamers and attractor patterns work well in the fast, dark waters. And the Wolf tends to fish best early, late, and during cloudy or drizzly weather. Fish a wilderness lake in the nearby Nicolet or try a cold brook trout tributary by day, and fish the Wolf mornings and evenings. This is also important because rafting trips, for which the river is also known, start after 8 am and must finish by 7 pm by local ordinance. This is to minimize conflict between these two groups of river users.

A stream thermometer comes in handy on the Wolf, especially in summer; it will help find cool stretches of the river that are fed by hidden spring seeps. Find cool water and you'll find fish.

The Wolf River offers 34.5 miles of trout water in Langlade County and some 9,200 acres along the Wolf make up the Wolf River Fishery Area. The river begins in earnest as a trout stream below the juncture with the Hunting River at Pearson.

The Hunting River is a first-class tributary offering miles of stream improvements and wild brook trout. It begins west of Highway 45/47 near the community of Elcho and flows 16 miles to its confluence with the Wolf River at Pearson. Upstream from Fitzgerald Dam Road, the Hunting River is category 2; below this it is category 5, catch-and-release and artificials only. Only 1 trout of each species may be kept; minimum length for brook and rainbow trout is 12 inches, and minimum length for brown trout is 18 inches.

Access is at Highway T, Fitzgerald Dam Road, Hunting River Road, and Highway 45. Fisheries manager Dave Seibel recommends it as a fine wild brook trout stream, superior in water quality and trout numbers to the Wolf. Other upper Wolf tributaries recommended by Seibel are Squaw Creek, the Lily River, and Ninemile Creek. These are coldwater brook trout streams. Squaw Creek is just upstream from the town of Lily and is category 4, the Lily River, joining the Wolf at the town of Lily, is category 4 in Langlade County and category 1 in Florence County. Ninemile Creek, just downstream from Lily, is category 2.

Returning to the Wolf River, access can be found at the small towns of Pearson, Lily, Hollister, and Langlade. Follow Highway 55 along the east side of the river to reach these towns. Along the west side, there is a good trail from Pearson to Langlade; anyone willing to do a bit of walking can find solitude on the river, especially early and late in the day when the rafters are gone.

This is all big freestone water. It should be waded carefully. The upper third of the river from Pearson to Lily is considerably slower, with only a handful of rapids; from Lily to the Menominee Reservation, there are 20 rapids on the river and an elevation loss of over 400 feet, making for abundant pocketwater, boulders, islands, and oxbows. Devotees of Western freestone rivers will feel at home on the Wolf and other northeast Wisconsin rivers like the Pike, Popple, and Brule.

The river is planted with some 30,000 brown and brook trout yearly from DNR and conservation club stocking. Herb Buettner has been encouraging the DNR to consider planting more rainbow trout, which spawn in winter and spring and have a better chance of survival in the Wolf. Eggs of fall-spawning brook and brown trout freeze for several months and only produce a very limited hatch.

Fish the Wolf early and late in the season or in overcast weather. Avoid it during hot summer days when rafters will be more common than trout. Try the Hunting, Lily, Ninemile, or Squaw instead; these coldwater tributaries should hold fish even during the doldrums.

Stream Facts: Wolf River

Season

- The early season runs from the first Saturday in March to the last Sunday before the first Saturday in May; no-kill, single barbless hooks only; applies to entire Wolf River in Langlade County. Regular season runs from the first Saturday in May at 5:00 am through September 30. The extended season runs from October 1 through November 15; catch-and-release, artificials only.

Regulations

- All portions of the Wolf River in Langlade County are category 4, except for Soo Line Railroad Bridge downstream to Dierk's Irrigation Hole, which is category 5, catch-and-release, artificials only.

Miles of Trout Water

- 34 miles

Stream Characteristics

- Large Western-style freestone river, typically 50 yards wide.

Access

- Wolf River State Fishery Area, access at Pearson, Lily, Hollister, and Langlade.

Fly Shops

- Sherer's We Tie It Fly Shop (Boulder Junction); Boulder Lodge (Hayward)

Map

- *Wisconsin Atlas and Gazetteer*, pages 77, 78

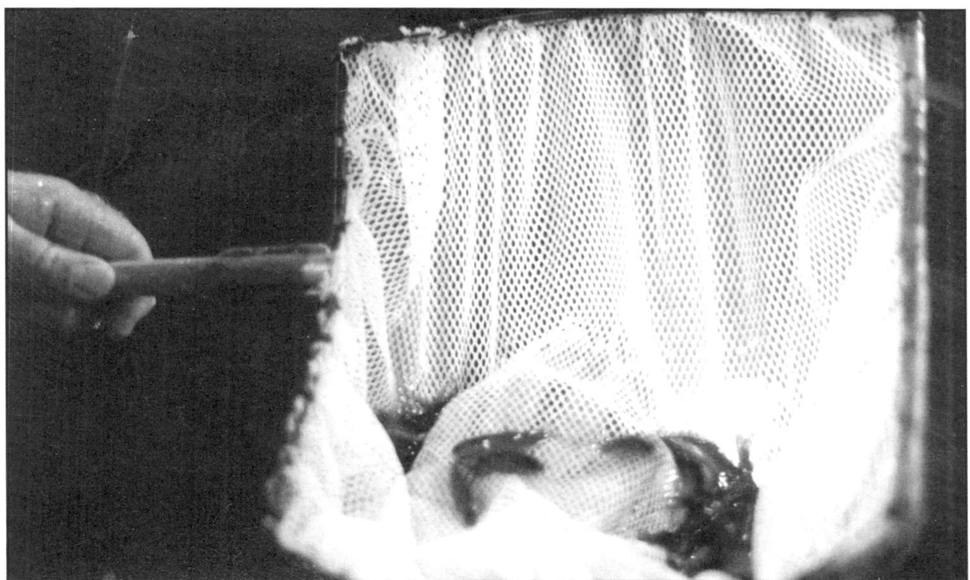

Trout frye destined for the Oconto River.

Oconto River

The Oconto River system can be described as a three-story fishery. Its north and south branches are good trout streams. Its main branch is a mixed fishery, with marginal trout populations below the confluence of the north and south branches and warmwater species between the town of Pulcifer and the dam in the town of Stiles. From Stiles to its mouth at Green Bay, the Oconto is a lake-run trout and salmon stream.

North and South Branches of the Oconto River

Running along the Langlade-Forest County line east of the Wolf River, through the Menominee Reservation, and joining the Oconto at the town of Suring in Oconto County, the South Branch of the Oconto is by far a better trout stream than the larger main stem. The DNR has tracked trout migrating 40 miles from spring to summer in search of cool water on the Oconto. The Oconto, like the nearby Wolf and Peshtigo Rivers, is a relatively shallow river that suffers from warming in summer. Fish it anytime after the first few weeks in May and you're likely to catch suckers and a handful of smallmouth bass.

Water quality is much better on the South Branch. Beginning near the Fanny Lake Campground in Nicolet National Forest, the South Branch flows to the west of Highway T. It crosses Highway 64 west of Mountain and continues along Highway T before entering Menominee lands, where fishing by nontribal members is prohibited.

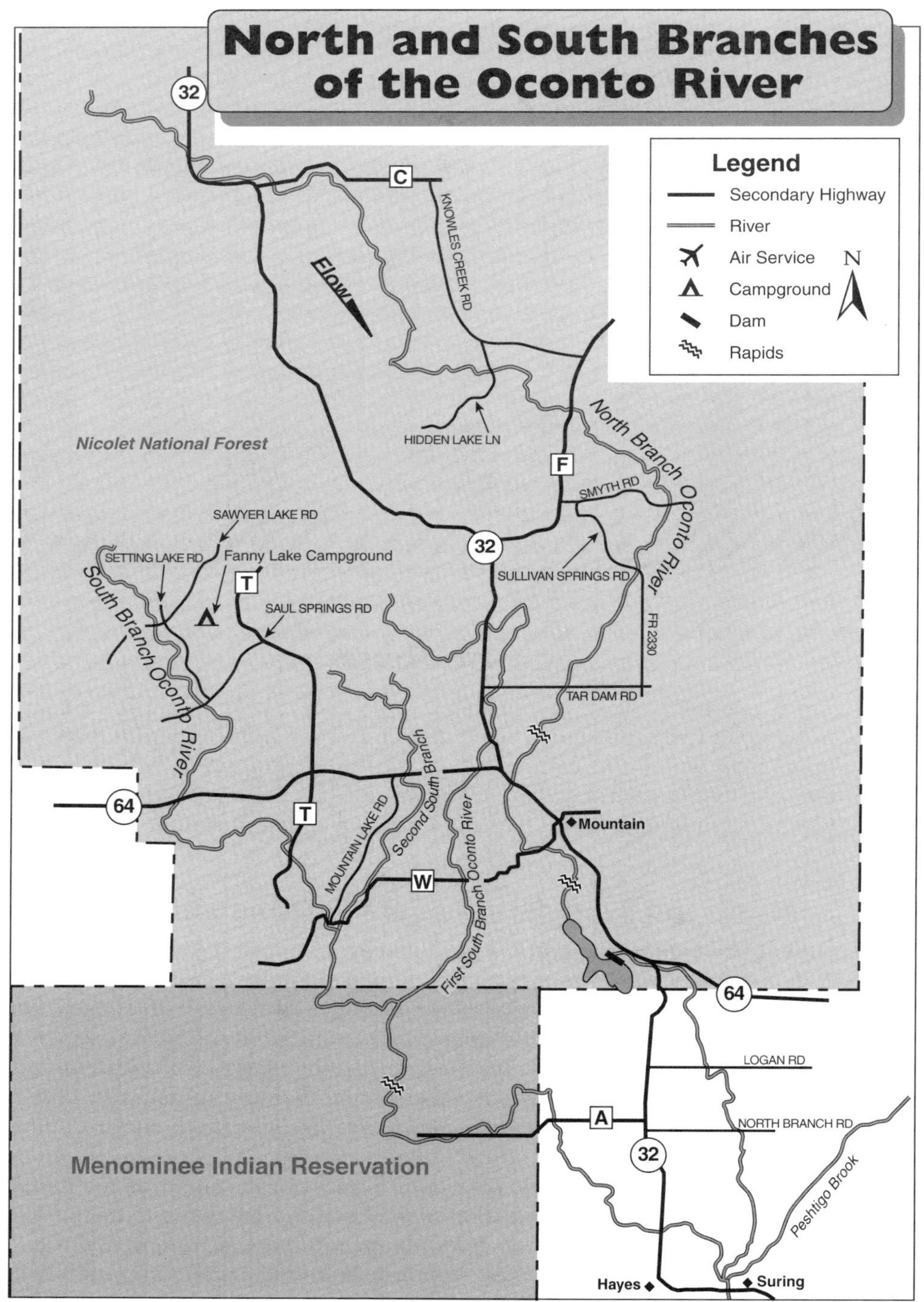

North and South Branches of the Oconto River
Legend
Secondary Highway
River
Air Service
Campground
Dam
Rapids
N
32
C
KNOWLES CREEK RD
Elow
HIDDEN LAKE LN
Nicolet National Forest
North Branch Oconto River
F
SMYTH RD
SAWYER LAKE RD
32
SETTING LAKE RD
Fanny Lake Campground
SULLIVAN SPRINGS RD
T
SAUL SPRINGS RD
South Branch Oconto River
FR 2330
TAR DAM RD
Second South Branch
64
T
MOUNTAIN LAKE RD
First South Branch Oconto River
Mountain
W
64
LOGAN RD
A
NORTH BRANCH RD
32
Menominee Indian Reservation
Peshtigo Brook
Hayes
Suring

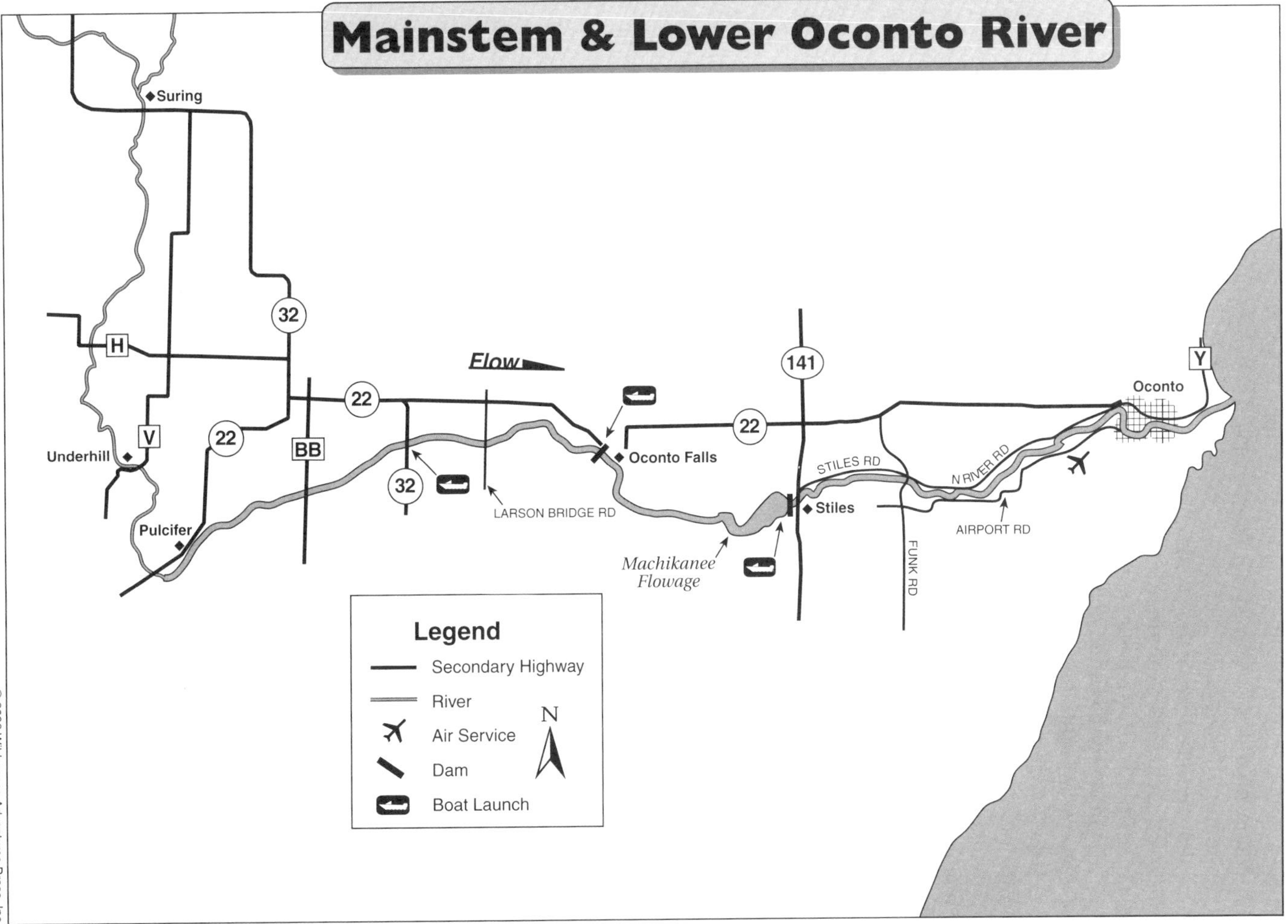
Mainstem & Lower Oconto River
Suring
32
H
Flow
141
Y
Oconto
22
22
V
Underhill
22
BB
Oconto Falls
STILES RD
N RIVER RD
32
Stiles
LARSON BRIDGE RD
AIRPORT RD
Pulcifer
Machikanee Flowage
FUNK RD
Legend
Secondary Highway
River
Air Service
Dam
Boat Launch
N

It then enters Oconto County and flows through the South Branch of the Oconto State Wildlife Area west of Highway 32. You can reach it by any number of east-west roads intersecting Highway 32.

The South Branch of the Oconto is managed as category 4 above the Menominee Reservation; below the reservation it is category 5 (artificials only, brook and rainbow trout 12 inches, brown trout 18 inches, and rainbow trout 6 inches; limit 1 trout).

The First South Branch of the Oconto and the Second South Branch of the Oconto, off Highway W and south of Highway 64, are good brook trout producers.

The North Branch of the Oconto River begins in the Potawatomi Reservation north of Wabeno, where fishing by nontribal members is prohibited, and flows 60 miles south to the juncture with the South Branch at the town of Suring. As a trout stream, it's worth fishing in May and again in mid-September, as it warms into the 70s during June, July, and August. What trout the North Branch does have can be found in summer at the mouths of cold feeder creeks and spring seeps. Test for temperature with your stream thermometer. Smallmouth are also present in the North Branch of the Oconto.

It can be accessed from east-west roads off Highway 32, which parallels the river from Wabeno to Suring. The North Branch is a category 2 stream.

Small wild brook trout are the main fishery in the South Branch and its tributaries, while stocked trout of all three species are present in the North Branch and mainstem; a handful of holdover browns on the North Branch attain considerable size (2 pounds or more) by feeding on the river's crawfish and forage fish. The branches of the Oconto are similar in size to the East Branch of the Eau Claire or the Little Wolf; both branches are 40-50 feet across, sand-bottomed, and moderately clear to tannin-stained.

Mainstem Oconto River

The Oconto River begins at the juncture of its north and south branches at Suring. It is not a prime trout stream, and the best water can be found immediately below the confluence of its two branches where the cooling effects of the south branch hold sway for a few miles. Highway V runs from Suring to just west of Pulcifer, crossing the Oconto at the town of Underhill. The other road crossing is on County H. This stretch of the Oconto is a category 2 trout stream. Smallmouth are a better bet than trout on the Oconto between Suring and Pulcifer.

From Pulcifer to Stiles, the river changes in character to a wider, slower stream. There is a dam at the Scott Paper Company at Oconto Falls and one in Stiles at the outlet of the Machikanee Flowage. Highway 22 runs between Pulcifer and Stiles. Road crossings are at Highway BB, Highway 32, Larson Bridge Road in the town of Oconto Falls, and Highway 141.

Mixed-bag fishing, typical of warmwater rivers, exists on this stretch of the Oconto: northern pike, walleye, bass, and panfish are all present here. Launch possibilities for a small boat exist at the Highway 32 bridge, Oconto Falls, and just above the dam in Stiles. Check DNR advisories for PCBs and mercury before keeping fish in this stretch. While cleanup efforts are underway, toxins released from papermill pollution are slow to exit the food chain.

The Lower Oconto River

The stretch from Stiles to the river's mouth at Green Bay is best known as a highway for migrating trout and salmon in fall, winter, and spring. The dam in Stiles is a popular spot for anglers trying for these lake-run fish. Between Stiles and Oconto, Stiles Road/Funk Road/N. River Road follows the north bank of the river; Airport Road runs along the south bank. Main Street/Highway Y follows the north bank of the river to near its terminus. There is a road crossing at Highway S and a small road (unmarked in the Wisconsin Atlas & Gazetteer) leading to the river mouth. As well as trout and salmon, pike, walleye, and smallmouth also make their way into the Oconto, providing a year-round fishery.

Skamania-strain steelhead push their way up the lower Oconto after the first cold snap in September. October and November runs of Chambers Creek–strain steelhead, coho and king salmon, and brook and brown trout follow. Things are pretty quiet on the Oconto in the dead of winter, but it picks up again with Ganaraska-strain steelhead entering the river in March. Fish these lake-run brawlers with a 9-weight rod, stout leaders, and a sink-tip line. (Poly leaders on a floating line will also work.) Egg patterns and Woolly Buggers in a variety of colors are your best bets on the Oconto. Purple and black are standard colors, but it's a good idea to experiment with other colors, too. Steelhead average about 5 pounds and the average salmon weighs in at about twice that.

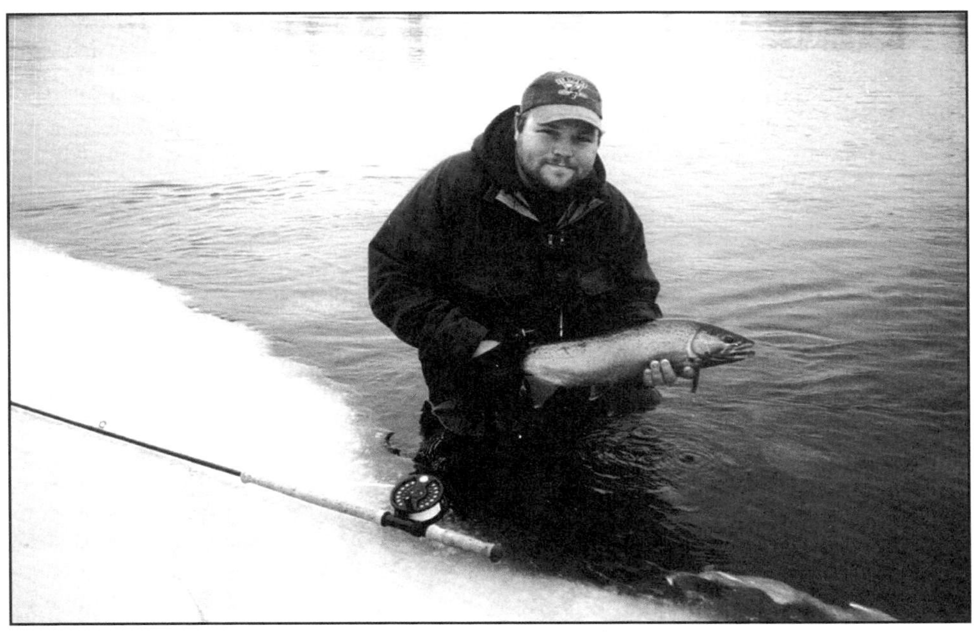

A nice steelhead ready for release. (Stephen R. Nelson)

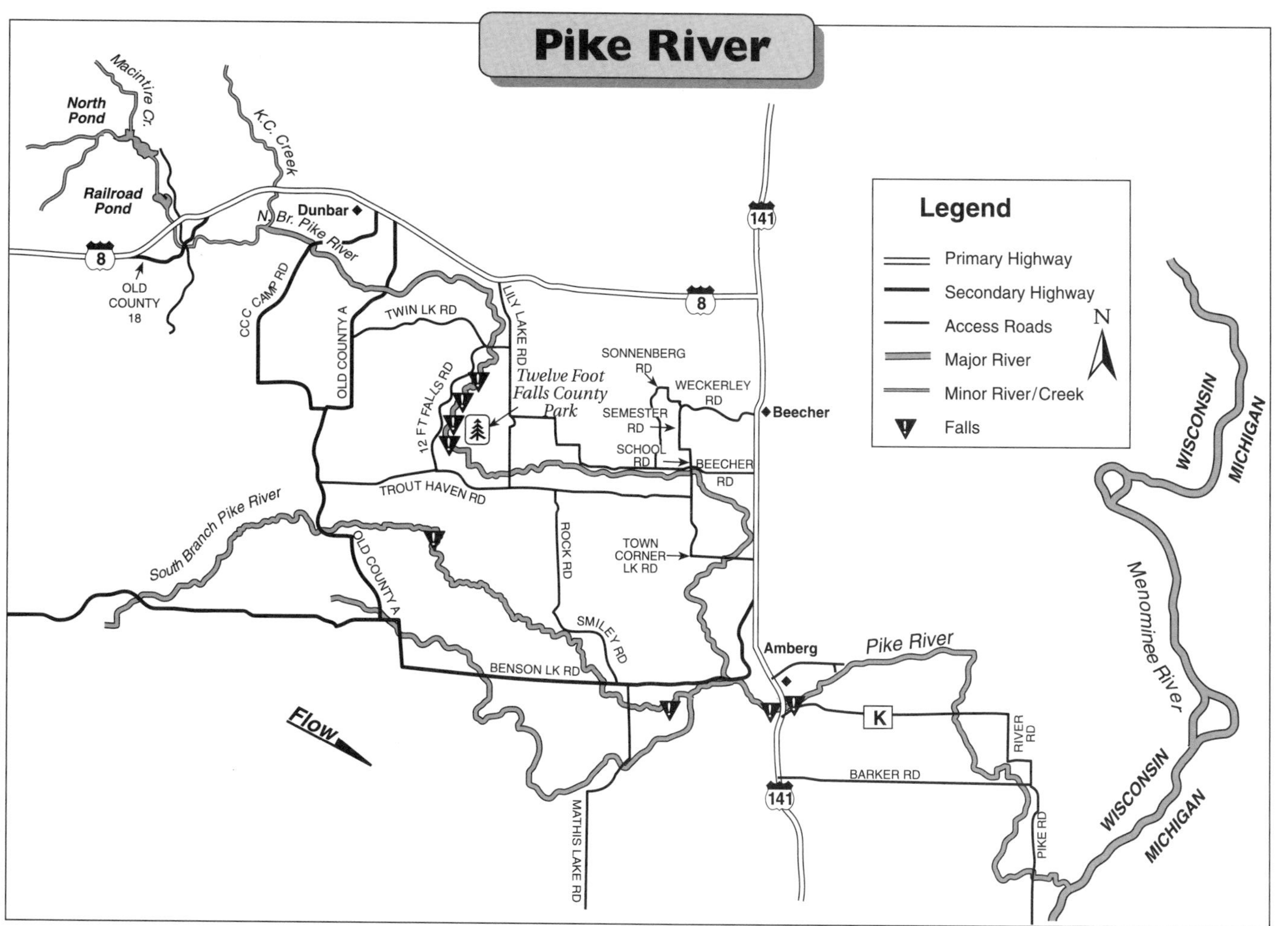
Pike River
Macintire Cr.
North Pond
K.C. Creek
Railroad Pond
Dunbar
N. Br. Pike River
8
OLD COUNTY 18
CCC CAMP RD
OLD COUNTY A
TWIN LK RD
LILY LAKE RD
8
141
12 FT FALLS RD
Twelve Foot Falls County Park
SONNENBERG RD
WECKERLEY RD
Beecher
SEMESTER RD
SCHOOL RD
BEECHER RD
TROUT HAVEN RD
South Branch Pike River
OLD COUNTY A
ROCK RD
TOWN CORNER LK RD
SMILEY RD
BENSON LK RD
Amberg
Pike River
K
RIVER RD
BARKER RD
141
MATHIS LAKE RD
PIKE RD
Flow
Legend
Primary Highway
Secondary Highway
Access Roads
Major River
Minor River/Creek
Falls
N
WISCONSIN
MICHIGAN
Menominee River
WISCONSIN
MICHIGAN

Pike River

Among the long, northeastern Wisconsin watersheds included in this book—such as the Wolf, Pine, Popple, Peshtigo, and Oconto Rivers—the Pike is the standout for trout fishing. According to DNR fisheries technician Greg Kornely, trout in the Pike are more likely to stay put than those in other rivers in the region. The reason for this is habitat. The Pike has a deeper, narrower streambed and is less prone to warming than other rivers. It is also fed by numerous high-quality tributaries, including the north and south branches of the Pike River.

The scenery on this river is unrivaled. Designated a Wild and Scenic River by the Wisconsin Legislature, the Pike is protected from shoreline development and flows through a mix of northern hardwoods and conifer forests. From the confluence of the North Branch and South Branch west of Amberg to the bridge at Highway K (7 miles) is managed as category 4 trout water. The branches of the Pike hold good populations of wild brook trout, while the Pike proper hosts a mix of stocked and wild fish of all three species.

If you are floating the Pike, you should be aware of some of its more formidable rapids. There are two sets of rapids that should be portaged around—Dave Falls at Dave Falls County Park just west of Highway 141 and Powerline Rapids a mile east of Highway 141.

From Highway K to the mouth of the Pike at the Menominee River, northern pike and smallmouth are the dominant species along with rough fish and the occasional stray brown trout. Between Highway K and Barker Road to the south, there are a half-dozen rapids; be on the look out. Road crossings in this stretch are at Highway 141, Highway K, Barker Road, and Pike River Road. With all of this whitewater, the angler must be ready to share the Pike with paddlers and kayakers, most of whom are also good stewards of this river.

The Pike has a rich mix of insect life and forage fish. Stoneflies and caddisflies cleave to its rocky bottom. You will some good hatches in April and then off and on throughout the season. Sulphurs and Brown Drakes come off, respectively, in June and July. However, in big fast water like the Pike it's more important to give fish something visible and attractive than to match a hatch exactly. A White Wulff works well at evening. A well-presented leech or large nymph will draw strikes as well. Sculpins and minnows are common, making Muddler Minnows a good choice.

The lower Pike holds a good population of smallmouth bass, which trade back and forth between the Menominee River and the Pike. Large leech, minnow, and crawfish patterns will work on them.

The North Branch and the South Branch of the Pike are also fine wild brook trout streams, as good or better than the main river, but smaller and tighter. The South Branch can be found along Old County A Road and Benson Lake Road west of Amberg. It begins as a small, low-gradient stream, draining from swampland upstream from Old County A Road and gradually shifts over to a freestone stream with moderate gradient as it joins the North Branch near Amberg. The South Branch is a category 2 trout stream.

The North Branch, with 30 miles of prime brook trout water, begins at the juncture of K.C. Creek and McIntyre Creek west of Dunbar and just south of Highway 8. It crosses Old County A Road shortly after it starts and then flows into a series of waterfalls (Bulls Falls, Eighteen Foot Falls, Twelve Foot Falls, Eight Foot Falls) along Twelve Foot Falls Road. There is good access to the river via walking trails. Fish the pocketwater beneath the falls with a Prince Nymph and a little split shot.

To reach more water, take Trout Haven Road to the east along the river and follow Semester School Road south to Town Corner Lake Road, which is the last road crossing before the two branches join. The North Branch of the Pike River is category 4.

Stream Facts: Pike River

Season

- The early season runs from the first Saturday in March to the last Sunday before the first Saturday in May; no-kill, single barbless hooks only. Regular season runs from the first Saturday in May at 5:00 am through September 30. Pike River between County V and County K only is open to trout fishing during early season.

Regulations

- Main stem, category 4; South Branch, category 2; North Branch, category 4.

Species

- Wild brook trout in North and South Branches; brook, brown, rainbow (stocked and wild) in main branch; smallmouth and northern pike in lower reaches of main branch.

Miles of Trout Water

- 7 miles on main branch; 40 miles (combined) on north and south branches.

Stream Characteristic

- Fast freestone river with deep stream channel, good habitat, and numerous cold-water tributaries.

Fly Shops

- We Tie It Fly Shop (Boulder Junction)

Maps

- *Wisconsin Atlas and Gazetteer*, pages 91, 99

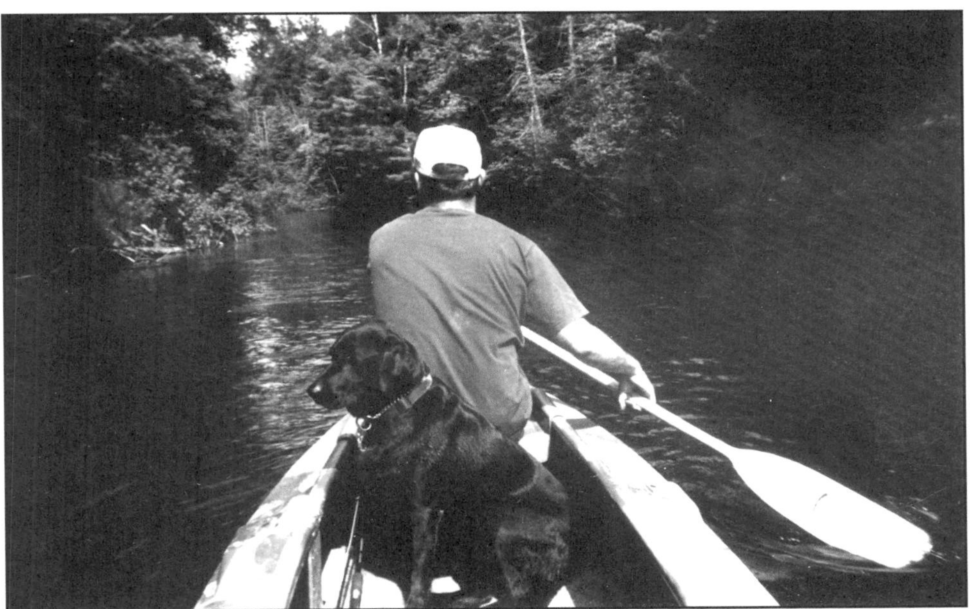

The best companions on float trips never make fun of your casting.

Lakes and Streams of the Nicolet National Forest Area

The fisheries present in the Nicolet National Forest lakes have much in common with those of the Northern Highlands American Legion State Forest to the north. There are over a thousand lakes across Forest, Florence, Oneida, Langlade and Oconto Counties, some with only walk-in access. Some are first-rate small remote seepage lakes rich with bass, panfish, and northerns. Others are large, developed lakes that happen to fall within the boundary of the national forest. Still others are stocked trout lakes, and a good many are simply barren of fish because of winterkill or sterile water. No list could ever be truly complete and up-to-date because the fisheries in these lakes are always changing—fishing pressure, year classes of fish, and severity of winters all affect what a lake holds in a given year.

The more popular lakes are covered here, roughly north to south. The adventuresome angler, armed with a belly boat and topographical map, might want to explore the Nicolet further.

Spectacle Lake

Stocked trout and naturally reproducing bass and panfish round out the fishery here. Find the lake south of Phelps in the northern Nicolet. From Highway 17 south of Phelps, take Highway A east to Fire Road 2196 headed south. Follow Fire Road 2572 to the campground and boat launch. You may keep 5 trout with a minimum size of 12 inches; trout may be fished on 171-acre Spectacle Lake between the first Saturday in May to March 1.

Stevens Lake

West of Tipler off Highway 70, 297-acre Stevens Lake holds northern pike, bass, and panfish. There is a boat launch and a USFS campground on the west side of the lake off Stevens Lake Road.

Lost Lake

Lost Lake is an undeveloped lake located in the Nicolet National Forest near the town of Tipler off Halsey Lake Road. With a maximum depth of 45 feet and covering 92 acres, Lost Lake is stocked with trout and also contains warmwater species, predominantly panfish. A boat launch can be found on the west shore of the lake, and only electric motors are permitted on Lost Lake. It is category 3 trout water with an open season from the first Saturday in May through March 1. A USFS campground is located on the northern end of the lake.

Keyes Lake

Keyes Lake (202 acres) is located just up Highway 101 northeast of Patten Lake and is a good bass and panfish lake. There is a boat launch on the east side of the lake off Highway 101. The water is very clear and demands careful canoe or belly boat approaches. Find the launch ramp off Highway 101.

Sea Lion Lake

Sea Lion Lake is shallow for most of its 122 acres and has good populations of bass, northerns, and panfish in its abundant weedbeds. It's located off Highway 101, south of Keyes Lake. There's a boat launch off Sea Lion Park Road.

Sand Lake

Located south of Commonwealth in Florence County, Sand Lake is a category 2 trout lake. Open season for trout is from the first Saturday in May to March 1. The lake also contains largemouth bass and is 25 acres with a maximum depth of 28 feet. Access is via a walking trail from Sand Lake Road. A belly boat is your best bet for fishing Sand Lake.

Anvil Lake

At just under 400 acres, Anvil Lake is a large Nicolet National Forest lake. It's located off Highway 70 east of Eagle River, with a developed boat ramp on the south side of the lake. Walleye, bass, northerns, and panfish are present. There is no minimum length on walleye, but none between 14 and 18 inches may be kept. Only one walleye over 18 inches may be kept. A USFS campground is located on the southern end of the lake.

Julia Lake

Located primarily within the Nicolet, narrow 300-acre Julia Lake is just east of Three Lakes. The boat ramp is located on Lake Julia Road off Highway 32 in eastern Oneida County. As to species present, you name it, Julia Lake has it—muskie, northerns, trout, walleye, panfish, and bass. There is no minimum length of walleye and a 40-inch minimum on muskellunge.

Pine Lake

Located in western Forest County, Pine Lake holds a mixed bag of panfish, bass, and northern pike. The western and northern shorelines are essentially undeveloped marsh. You can pick up all three species by working the weeds. Pine Lake is one of the larger Nicolet lakes, covering just under 1,700 acres with a maximum depth of just 14 feet. You can find Pine Lake west of Argonne, off Highway 32. There is a boat launch and a USFS campground on the west side of the lake.

Little Rice Lake

A similar fishery to Pine Lake just to the north, Little Rice Lake spreads over 1,300 acres with a maximum depth of 10 feet. It is surrounded by the Little Rice Lake State Wildlife Area. Expect company from duck hunters if you plan on fishing Little Rice in fall. The same aquatic vegetation that provides food for ducks gives spawning habitat to the lake's northerns, largemouths, and panfish. Find it west of Crandon and north of Highway 8.

Lake Lucerne

Lake Lucerne, east of Crandon and south of Highway 8/32, is a 1,000-acre lake with a maximum depth of 73 feet, which provides cold water for its trout during the heat of summer. You'll also find bass, walleye, northern pike, and panfish here. Minimum length on walleye is 18 inches with a daily bag limit of 3. By fishing the shallows early, you might tie into some of Lucerne's big browns and lakers. Lake trout must be a minimum of 26 inches, brown trout a minimum of 16 inches. Lake trout season runs from the first Saturday in May through September 30. The season for other trout runs from the first Saturday in May through March 1. The daily bag is 1 for lake trout and 3 for brown trout.

Richardson Lake

Located on Highway W west of Wabeno, Richardson Lake is a small drainage lake covering just over 50 acres. You'll find northern pike, largemouth bass, and panfish in this shallow lake. You'll find pike at the inlet and outlet of the lake, which connects to Richardson Creek. There is a boat launch and a USFS campground off Richardson Lake Road.

Lakes of Nicolet National Forest
Phelps
A
FR 2196
FR 2572
Spectacle Lake
17
70
Anvil Lake
Eagle River
70
H
Sand Lake
32
45
Julia Lake
JULIA LAKE RD
Pine Lake
Nicolet
National
Forest
Stevens Lake
STEVENS LAKE RD
Tipler
70
Lost Lake
HALSEY LAKE RD
Commonwealth
Keyes Lake
Sea Lion Lake

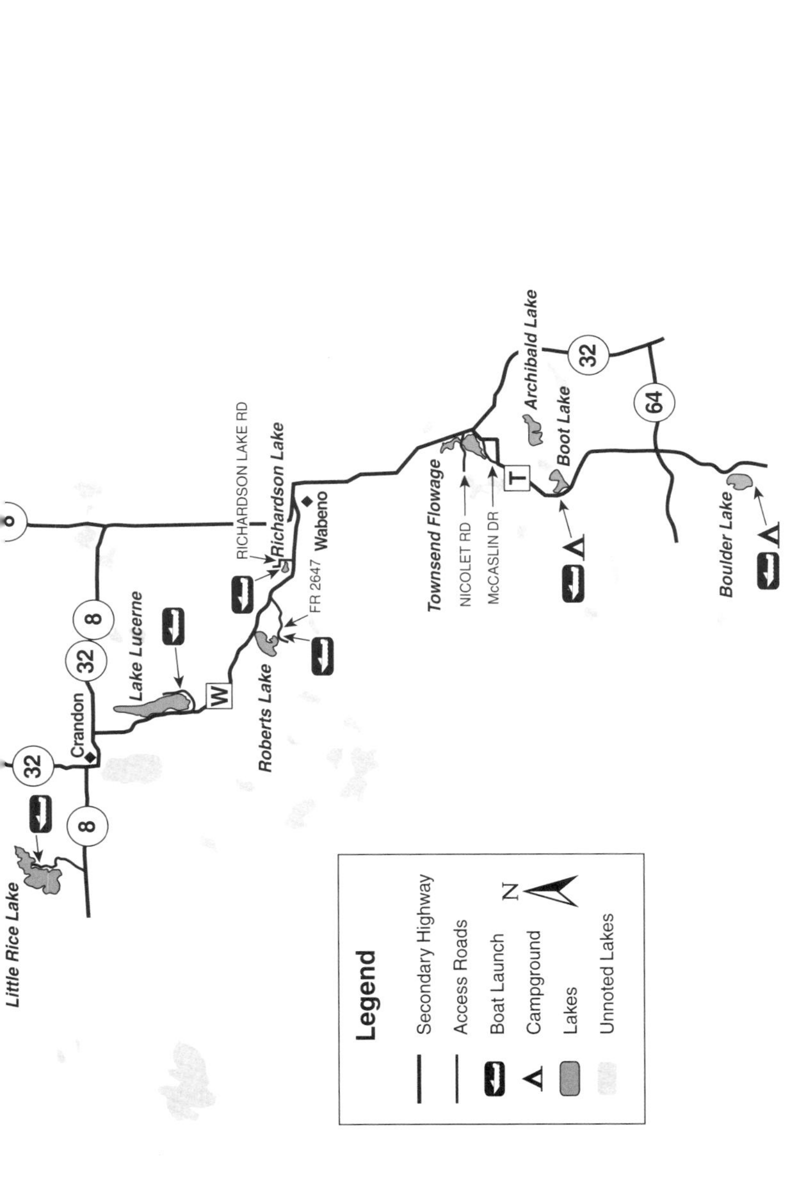
Little Rice Lake
8
32
Crandon
32
8
Lake Lucerne
W
Roberts Lake
FR 2647
RICHARDSON LAKE RD
Richardson Lake
Wabeno
Townsend Flowage
NICOLET RD
McCASLIN DR
T
Boot Lake
Archibald Lake
32
64
Boulder Lake
Legend
Secondary Highway
Access Roads
Boat Launch
Campground
Lakes
Unnoted Lakes
N

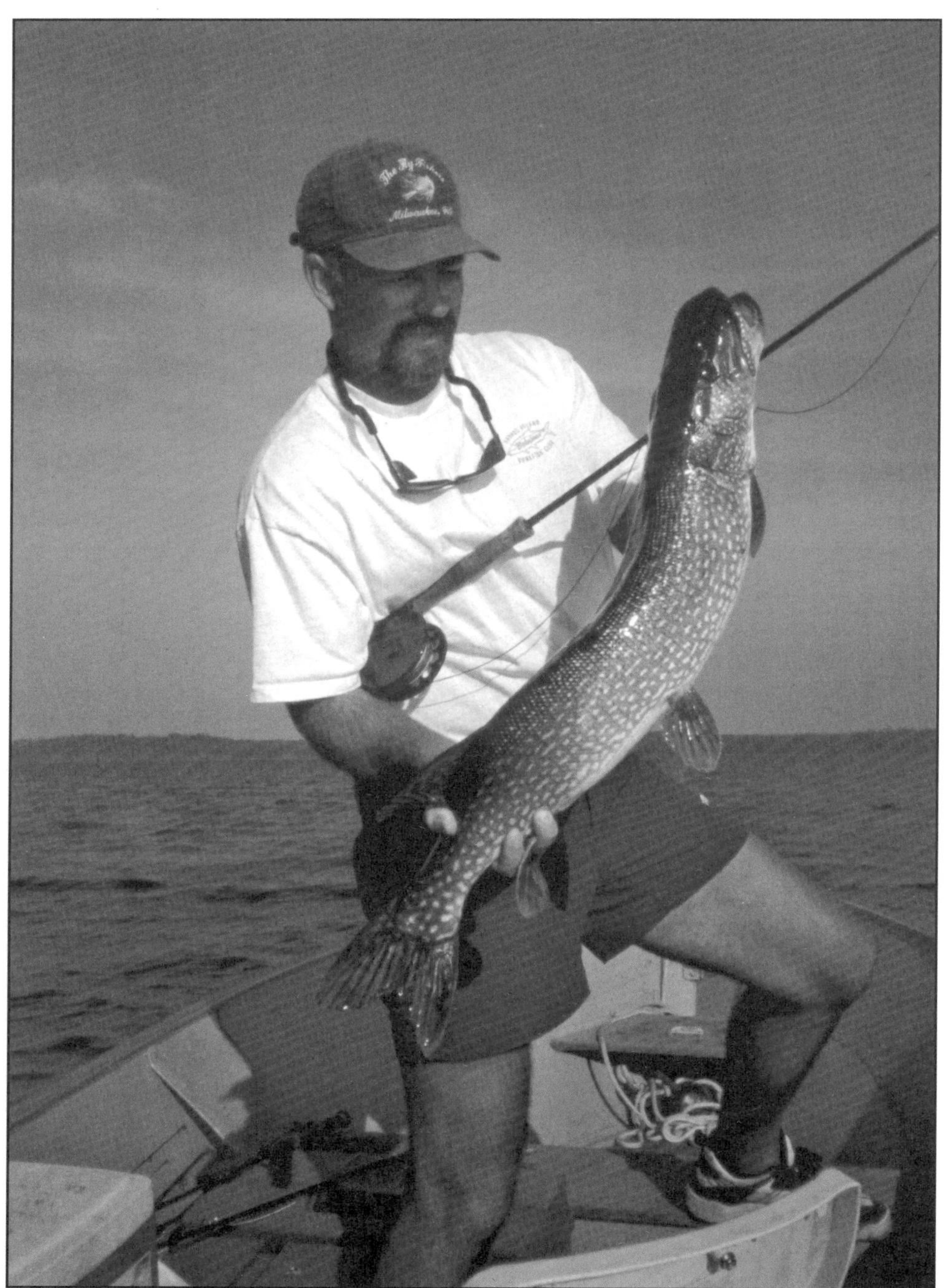

Pat Ehlers, guide and owner of the Fly Fishers, with a hefty northern.

Roberts Lake

Six miles west of Richardson Lake off Highway W is larger Roberts Lake—a spring-fed lake of 415 acres with a maximum depth of 32 feet. It holds northern pike, muskellunge, walleye, bass, and panfish. There's a launch ramp off Fire Road 2647.

Townsend Flowage

This shallow impoundment of McCaslin Brook offers a good fishery for northern pike, largemouth bass, and panfish. It's located just west of Townsend. Rough launches can be found off McCaslin Drive (off County T) on the south end of the flowage and off Valley View Road (off Nicolet Road) on the north end of the flowage.

Archibald Lake

Muskie, largemouth, and panfish can be found on 393-acre Archibald Lake south of Townsend Flowage located off County T. The minimum length on muskie is 40 inches. Maiden Lake to the southwest holds bass and panfish.

Boot Lake

You'll find muskellunge, walleye, panfish, and largemouth bass at 235-acre Boot Lake off Highway T. There is a USFS campground and a boat launch off Highway T on the west side of the lake. Maximum depth here is 38 feet.

Boulder Lake

Ten miles south of Boot Lake off Highway T is 362-acre Boulder Lake. With a median depth of 7 feet, it's a much shallower lake than Boot. It supports a wide variety of warmwater species, including muskellunge. Located in the extreme southern Nicolet, it gets a bit more pressure in summer than lakes farther north within the Nicolet. There is a USFS campground on the lake.

Middle Inlet Creek

Middle Inlet Creek is a productive brook trout stream in this region, according to Bill Sherer of Northern Adventure Guide Service. It's located just north of Crivitz and crosses Highway 141 on a northwest-southeast diagonal. It is 15 miles long from its headwaters to its mouth at Lake Noquebay. Like many Marinette County brook trout streams, it is full of dark pocketwater and drains from the area's numerous cedar swamps. Access is at Highway A, Moonshine Hill Road, Highway X, and Highway 141. It is category 4.

Beaver Creek

Beaver Creek, just north of Coleman in southern Marinette County, is a small, productive creek with wild brook and brown trout. It is formed by the juncture of the north and south branches of Beaver Creek. Dense stream canopy can make Beaver

Creek tough to fish in summer, so fish it early in the season or use a short rod.

The North Branch of Beaver Creek can be found north of Highway P. The banks of the North Branch are, for the most part, under DNR ownership as part of the Beaver Creek Public Hunting Ground. Access is at Highway P, Highway 141, 25th Road, and a dirt road running between 37th Road (west side of the creek) and 27th Road (east side of the creek). The North Branch is 10 miles long, ending at the juncture with the South Branch. Above 25th Road, the North Branch is category 2; below 25th Road it is category 4.

The South Branch of Beaver Creek is a category 2 trout stream. It runs roughly parallel to, and then crosses, Highway 64 near the village of Pound. Other road crossings, downstream to upstream, include Highway P, Highway 141, 25th Road, 24th Road, Highway Q, and Highway Z. The South Branch is 9 miles long, all of it trout water.

Beaver Creek, below the confluence of its two branches, is 4 miles long and is category 4. It runs between Highway 64 (south bank) and Highway P (north bank). Road crossings are at 15th Road, 11th Road, and Highway P.

The Wausaukee River

Running through the town that shares its name, the Wausaukee River is a 25-mile-long trout stream that contains wild brook and brown trout. While it is relatively small compared to the nearby Pike, it's known to produce larger trout than you'd expect.

Follow Highway C northeast out of Wausaukee toward the village of Athelstane to fish the Wausaukee upstream from the town of Wausaukee. Follow Jamros Road out of Wausaukee to fish the river downstream, with a road crossing at Freele Road providing access.

The Wausaukee is a category 4 trout stream. Since it's a narrow, brushy stream, you might want to spend some time driving to find a stretch of the stream with sufficient casting room. The Wausaukee comes recommended as a quality trout stream from DNR fisheries technician Greg Kornely.

Shawano Lake

Covering over 6,000 acres, Shawano Lake is one of northeast Wisconsin's larger bodies of water. The lake has lots of weeds and, accordingly, good panfish and largemouth bass populations. However, it's proximity to Green Bay and the Fox River valley make it a destination lake in an area where fishing ranks a close second behind the Green Bay Packers. It sees less pressure in fall than during the summer, and fishing on weekdays is a good option for avoiding the crowds. You'll find launch ramps off Highway H and Highway 22.

Lake Noquebay

Marinette County's largest lake, at 2,500 acres, Lake Noquebay holds muskellunge, largemouth bass, northern pike, and panfish. Fish beadhead nymphs for bluegills, Muddler Minnows for crappie, and Dahlberg Divers for pike and largemouths. Working the weeds on the lake's southern edge will produce all species but muskellunge, which cleave to Noquebay's deeper holes. The lake is located off Highway GG east of Crivitz. The boat landing can be reached from Boat Landing Lane.

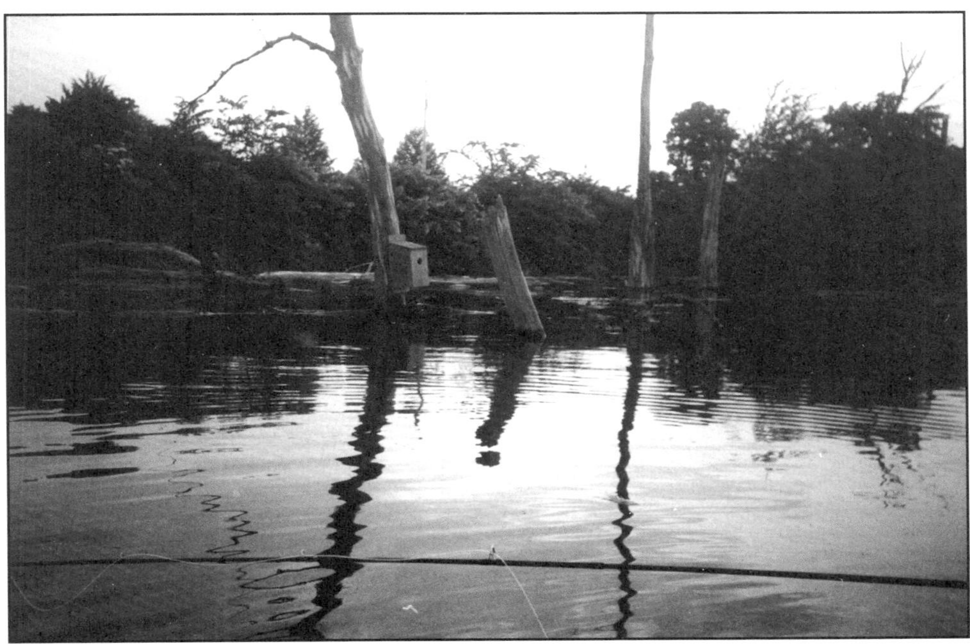

Good shoreline habitat on Lake Noquebay.

Hub City: Antigo

The county seat of Langlade County, Antigo is a city of 8,500 catering to hunters in fall, snowmobilers and cross-country skiers in winter, and fishermen in spring and summer. The name Antigo is a corruption of the Chippewa word for evergreen. Besides being home to the Mepps Corporation (known for its line of spinners), the town is conveniently located to good fishing. The Wolf River, local spring ponds, and a number of smaller and/or tributary streams hold small brook trout and larger browns. Spring Brook, which runs through the center of Antigo, is an excellent brook trout stream, as are the Little Wolf and East Branch of the Eau Claire Rivers. Jesse's Wolf River Inn is a storied Northwoods resort on the shores of that river.

Accommodations

Super 8 Motel, 535 Century Avenue, Antigo; 715-623-4188, 800-800-8000; $

Sleep Inn, 525 Memory Lane, Antigo; 715-623-0506; $$

Bear Paw Inn, N3494 Highway 55, White Lake; 715-882-3502; rustic cabins and rooms 15 miles east of Antigo on Wolf River; $$

Jesse's Wolf River Inn, N2119 Taylor Road, White Lake; 715-882-2182; turn-of-the-century lodge adorned with sporting art, 15 miles east of Antigo; $$$

Buettner's Wild Wolf Inn, Highway 55, White Lake; 715-882-8611; $$

Campgrounds

Nicolet National Forest, campgrounds at Ada Lake, Boot Lake, Fanny Lake and Boulder Lake; Forest Headquarters, 68 South Stevens Street, Rhinelander; 715-362-1300, 877-444-6677 to reserve; campgrounds throughout forest

Veteran's Memorial Park, take Highway 45/47 12 miles north of Antigo and follow Highway J east to campground on Jack's Lake

Restaurants

Dixie Lunch, 716 5th Avenue. Antigo; 715-623-4634; open early and late, good down-home café in downtown Antigo

The Refuge, Highway 64 and 45, Antigo; 715-623-2249; feast your eyes on the 300-gallon aquarium with local species plus replicas of state-record fish on walls in this homey tavern-restaurant

Country Kitchen, Highway 45, Antigo; 715-617-4394; dependable chain serving meals all day

Taco Johns, 2405 Highway 45; 715-627-0500; Midwest Mexican food chain

Jesse's Wolf River Inn, N2119 Taylor Road, White Lake; 715-882-2182; reservations-only, fixed-price gourmet dinners

Bear Paw Inn, N3494 Highway 55, White Lake; 715-882-3502; open for breakfast and lunch, on the Wolf River

Buettner's Wild Wolf Inn, Highway 55, White Lake; 715-882-8611

FLY SHOPS, OUTFITTERS, SPORTING GOODS

We Tie It Fly Shop & Northern Adventure Guide Service, Boulder Junction; 715-385- 0171; the Northwoods fly shop, plus guiding for trout and warmwater species, located 1 hour north of Antigo

Fleet Farm, Highway 45, Antigo; 715-623-2063; fishing licenses

Bob's Amoco Standard, 335 Superior Street, Antigo; 715-623-2709; fishing licenses

Veterinarians

Antigo Vet Clinic, 610 Amron Avenue, Antigo; 715-623-4116

Medical

Langlade Memorial Hospital, 112 E. 5th Street; 715-623-2311

Auto Rental

Parson's of Antigo, Amron Avenue; 715-627-4888Auto rentals are also available in Wausau at airport.

Automobile Repair

Bob's Standard Amoco, 335 Superior Street; 715-623-2709

Air Service

Langlade County Airport, Highway 52 and Highway 64, Antigo; 715-623-5901

For More Information

Antigo Chamber of Commerce
P.O. Box 339
Antigo, WI 54409
888-526-4523

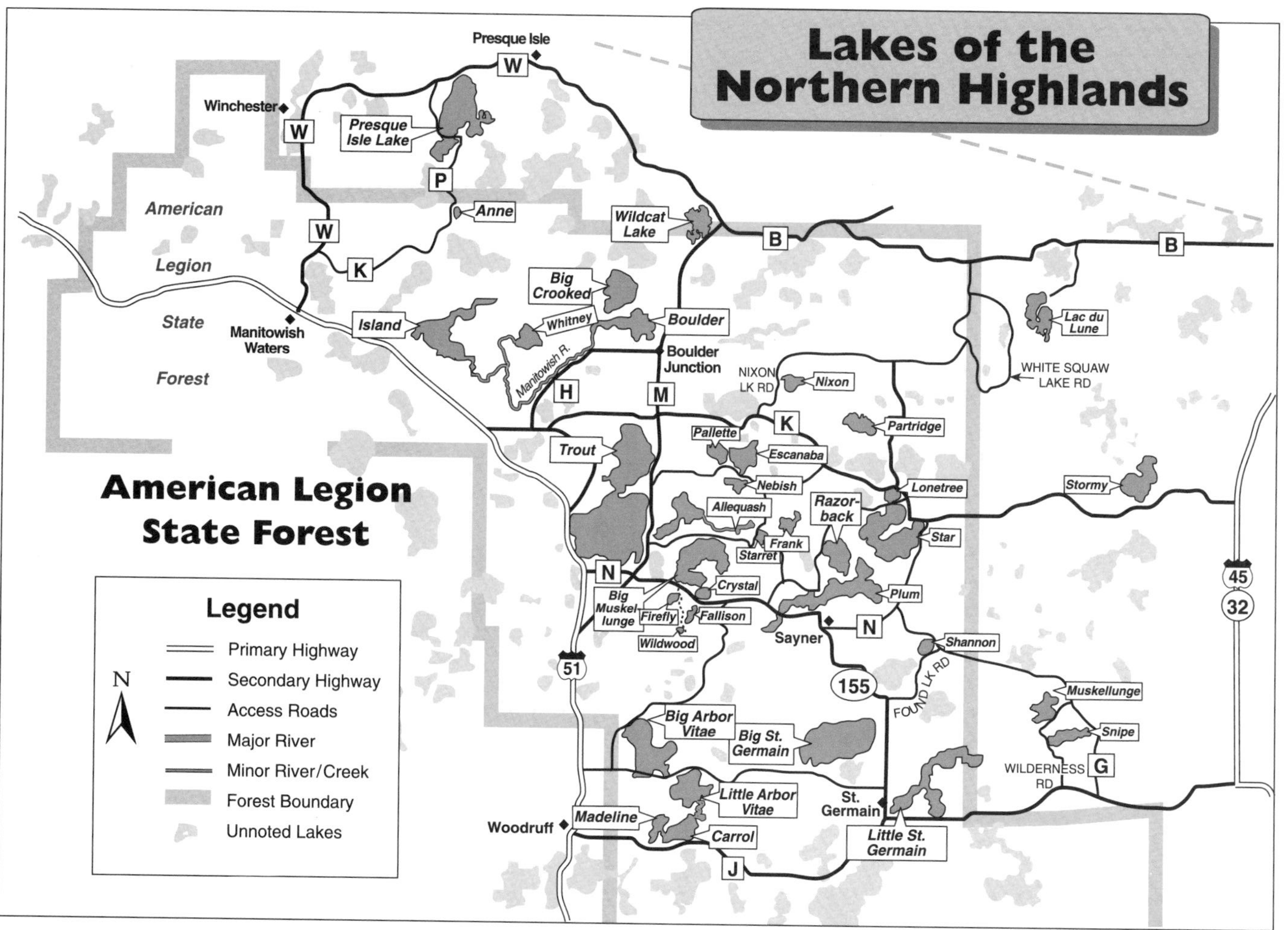
Lakes of the Northern Highlands
American Legion State Forest
Legend
Primary Highway
Secondary Highway
Access Roads
Major River
Minor River/Creek
Forest Boundary
Unnoted Lakes
N
Presque Isle
Winchester
Manitowish Waters
Boulder Junction
Sayner
St. Germain
Woodruff
American
Legion
State
Forest
Presque Isle Lake
Anne
Wildcat Lake
Big Crooked
Whitney
Island
Boulder
Manitowish R.
Lac du Lune
WHITE SQUAW LAKE RD
NIXON LK RD
Nixon
Partridge
Pallette
Escanaba
Trout
Nebish
Lonetree
Stormy
Allequash
Razor-back
Frank
Starret
Star
Crystal
Plum
Big Muskel-lunge
Firefly
Fallison
Wildwood
Shannon
FOUND LK RD
Muskellunge
Snipe
WILDERNESS RD
Big Arbor Vitae
Big St. Germain
Little Arbor Vitae
Madeline
Carrol
Little St. Germain
W
P
K
B
H
M
N
G
J
45
32
51
155

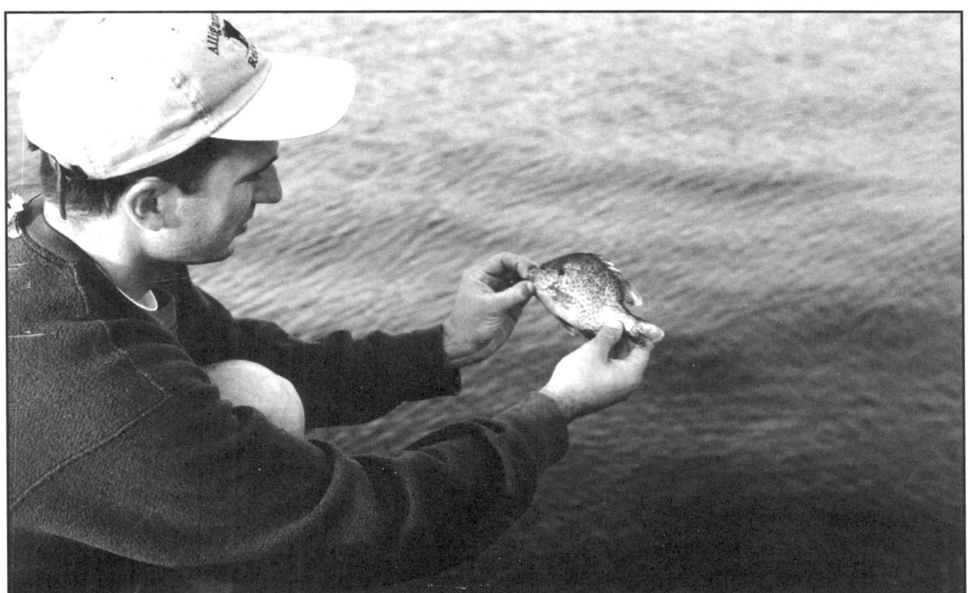

The author releases a little bluegill from a Northern Highlands Lake.

LAKES OF THE NORTHERN HIGHLANDS AMERICAN LEGION STATE FOREST

Hosting over a thousand lakes and 200,000 acres of wilderness, this forest was created in 1925 to protect the headwaters of the Flambeau and Wisconsin Rivers. If this area sounds like an outdoorsman's dream—well, it is. Bear, moose, grouse, deer, and eagles thrive in its spruce swamps and aspen ridges. All manner of gamefish swim in its waters. Miles of wilderness trails beckon to backpackers.

As with any vast holding, there is a certain *terra incognita* quality here. An angler's hike in, or bushwhack, is sometimes rewarded with memorable fishing. Other times, he ends up bug-stung and fishless. This is the agony and ecstasy of wilderness fishing. To further complicate things, most lakes in this region are remote and difficult to survey. Even information that's a year old can be out of date. A hard winter might freeze shallow lakes and result in a fish kill or fishermen may over-harvest a lake, decimating its breeding fish.

However, there are ways to tap the potential of wilderness lakes. Anglers interested in fishing the lakes of the Northern Highlands can try three approaches. They can fish the lakes described below. These lakes are managed by the DNR for trout and/or warmwater species. While these lakes are not secrets, they should all contain fish. And given that many of them require at least some effort to reach—and the fact that wilderness anglers tend to be good about catch-and-release—you should do well on them.

Another option is to hire a guide. Bill Sherer of Northern Adventure Guide Service in Boulder Junction (715-385-0171) has been fishing and guiding these waters most of his life. For a few hundred dollars, you're likely to be rewarded with a day of spectacular scenery and fishing as good as a remote Canadian wilderness.

For the stout of heart and limb, there's the do-it-yourself approach. This requires a topographical map, compass, and emergency provisions. Locate the lake you want to fish, consult the *Wisconsin Lakes* booklet published by the DNR to make sure it has fish in it, and have at it. Start with short hikes and work up to longer ones if you are an inexperienced hiker.

What follows is a sampling of the lakes in the forest, with an emphasis on motor-restricted waters. I have included special regulations for each lake. Except as noted, size and bag limits on these waters are the same as those for inland waters in the Northern Zone. Exhaustive coverage of every Northern Highlands lake would require its own book and might well take the fun out of exploring some of the more remote wilderness waters.

Anne Lake

Besides bearing the same name as my daughter, this remote 37-acre lake just south of the Michigan border offers a good mixed fishery for trout and the usual warmwater suspects. Anne Lake is category 2 trout water. Take Highway W out of Manitowish Waters to Highway K, and follow K to Highway P and turn onto Big Lake Road. You'll need to carry your float tube or canoe into Anne Lake, as it has no developed facilities. This little bit of work will put you far from the madding crowd and in the midst of good fishing.

Crystal Lake

Crystal Lake is one of a number of no-motor lakes along Highway N east of Highway 51 and north of Arbor Vitae within the Northern Highlands American Legion State Forest. It is stocked with lake trout and has self-sustaining population of bass and panfish. The lake is 88 acres with a maximum depth of 67 feet. Lake trout must be 26 inches long and there is a daily bag limit of 1; they may be fished from the first Saturday in May to September 30. There is a USFS campground on the lake.

Firefly Lake

Just to the west of Crystal Lake off Highway N is Firefly Lake; it is 27 acres with a maximum depth of 46 feet and holds both stocked trout and assorted warmwater species. It is managed as a category 2 trout lake. There's a USFS campground on the lake and motors are not permitted.

Wildwood Lake

It is a half-mile walk or portage into 16-acre Wildwood Lake, which contains stocked brown trout and naturally reproducing largemouth bass. Artificials only are permitted here; 5 trout may be taken, with a minimum size of 12 inches. It's open to fishing from the first Saturday in May to November 15. Continue down the road from Firefly Lake to reach Wildwood Lake.

Fallison Lake

Also off County N near Crystal Lake is 53-acre, 43-foot-deep Fallison Lake. It is a walk-in brook trout lake, a quarter-mile from County N. Only battery-powered motors are allowed on the lake. It's open to fishing from the first Saturday in May to November 15; 5 trout may be kept with a minimum size of 8 inches. As it's been chemically treated prior to stocking, trout are the only fish found here.

Plum and West Plum Lakes

Off Highway N just west of Sayner, West Plum Lake, essentially a small bay of 1,000-acre Plum Lake, is planted with trout and allows only battery-operated motors. West Plum Lake is managed as a category 2 trout lake.

Larger Plum Lake offers standard boat accommodations and wide variety of warmwater gamefish and panfish. There is no minimum length on walleye, but walleye from 14 to 18 inches may not be kept, and only 1 fish over 18 inches is allowed. After June 14, the minimum length on largemouth and smallmouth bass is 18 inches with a daily bag limit of 1.

Shannon Lake

Northeast of St. Germain (take Highway 155 to Found Lake Road), Shannon Lake offers a mixed fishery for bass, bluegill, and brown trout. It is 36 acres with a maximum depth of 30 feet. Trout fishing is open from the first Saturday in May to March 1; 5 trout may be kept with a minimum size of 12 inches.

Muskellunge and Snipe Lakes

Located southwest of Shannon Lake off County G, these two lakes offer a good fishery for muskellunge, panfish, and northern pike. Muskellunge Lake is 272 acres, and Snipe Lake is 239 acres.

Allequash Springs

A category 4 spring pond with brook and brown trout, 10-acre Allequash Springs can be reached via a quarter-mile hike from Big Muskellunge Lake Road, which is just north of Firefly and Crystal Lakes. Take Highway N to Highway M to Big Muskellunge Lake Road. Allequash Lake has abundant panfish.

Escanaba and Nebish Lakes

Located off Nebish Lake Road, these two lakes are managed by the DNR as experimental fisheries and you will need to obtain a permit from the ranger station at Escanaba Lake before fishing them. On 293-acre Escanaba Lake, fishing is open year-round with no daily bag limit or minimum size.

Nebish Lake, at 98 acres, is open year-round for its best-known species, smallmouth bass. There is no minimum length on smallmouth, but fish between 9 and 12 inches must be released.

Pallette Lake

An excellent smallmouth bass fishery, 173-acre Pallette Lake is accessible via the Escanaba Trail off Nebish Lake Road east of Trout Lake. It is a walk-in-access-only lake, so using a belly boat is a good way to fish here. Lake trout season is currently closed on Pallette Lake. Smallmouth bass fishing is permitted year-round; 2 fish may be kept with a minimum size of 16 inches. (For other species, size and bag limits are the same as those for other inland waters in Wisconsin's Northern Zone.) Catch-and-release is highly recommended here, as smallmouth bass are slow-growing fish, especially in cold northern waters. Snap a photo if you want a memory of your fish.

Starrett Lake

This lake, located on Big Muskellunge Lake Road, has a USFS campground. It is 66 acres, with a maximum depth of 19 feet, and has good populations of bass and panfish.

Frank Lake

A half-mile down the road from Starrett Lake is 141-acre Frank Lake. It is accessible via a hiking trail and contains a variety of warmwater gamefish and panfish. Only battery-powered motors are allowed. Given the mile hike to reach the lake, you're probably best served fishing from a belly boat.

Nixon Lake

Nixon Lake is 110 acres but shallow, with a maximum depth of 5 feet—perfect habitat for the bass and panfish here. You'll have to bushwhack to it from Nixon Road off County K. In a cold winter, shallow Nixon Lake sometimes suffers from winterkill.

Razorback Lake

Located just east of Frank and Nixon Lakes on Razorback Road is Razorback Lake. At 362 acres, it is one of the larger lakes in the forest and offers a good mix of muskie, pike, bass, walleye, and panfish. The launch ramp is located on the northwest side of the lake. Gas motors are permitted.

Lonetree Lake

Located off Highway K north of Star Lake, 121-acre Lone Tree Lake is a good bass lake that allows electric motors only. Panfish are also present.

Partridge Lake

This lake hosts a variety of gamefish and panfish and has good weed cover; it is 220 acres with a maximum depth of 14 feet. The lake can be worked from a belly boat or canoe and has a developed launch ramp. It's located between Nixon Lake and Lonetree Lake. From County K, take Camp Road 2 to Wechler Road and follow signs for the boat launch.

Stormy Lake

Farther east on County K, Stormy Lake is planted with brown trout and has a good smallmouth bass population. It's larger than many forest lakes at 522 acres, with a maximum depth of 60 feet. Trout may be fished for from the first Saturday in May to March 1; 5 trout may be kept with a minimum size of 12 inches.

Lac du Lune

Located off Highway B just south of the Michigan border, Lac du Lune is another larger forest lake with a standard boat ramp. It is 426 acres with a maximum depth of 65 feet. You'll find stocked brown trout, abundant panfish, and a few bass here. Trout may be fished for from the first Saturday in May to March 1; 5 trout may be kept with a minimum size of 12 inches.

Carol and Madeleine Lakes

This pair of lakes is located in the southern part of the Highlands Forest just west of Woodruff and north of County J. Panfish are abundant in both lakes, as are northern pike and largemouth bass. Carol Lake, at 352 acres, has a campground on its southern shore just off County J. Madeleine Lake is 159 acres.

Wildcat Lake

Located off Highway M northeast of Boulder Junction is 300-acre Wildcat Lake. It is an excellent lake in which to fly fish for muskies, according to Joe Sherer who guides in the area. Most fish are in the 25- to 30-inch range, but each year Wildcat coughs up a few legal (34-inch-plus) muskies. Use wire leaders and big streamers like Dahlberg Divers. Open season for muskellunge in Wisconsin's Northern Zone runs from May 25 to November 30. The launch ramp is located on the eastern side of the lake off Highway M.

Manitowish River

An opportunity that shouldn't be overlooked is the mixed muskellunge, northern pike, and bass fishery in the Manitowish River, which runs between Fishtrap Lake, Boulder Lake, and Whitney Lake. Launches on the river can be found off Dam Road east of Boulder Junction and on Wool Lake Lane (off of County K) west of Boulder Junction. A canoe or skiff will work well for floating the Manitowish. On Fishtrap and Boulder Lakes, there is no minimum size on walleye, but only 1 fish over 14 inches may be kept. On Whitney Lake, after the middle Saturday in June, the minimum length limit on smallmouth and largemouth bass is 18 inches and the daily bag limit is 1; minimum length on northern pike is 26 inches with a daily bag limit of 2.

Presque Isle Lake

Located a few miles south of the Michigan border in far northeast Wisconsin, Presque Isle Lake is a large body of water (just shy of 1,300 acres) full of smallmouth bass. Joe Sherer, who grew up here and has guided in these parts, says it's one of the finest smallmouth lakes around. Most of the east shore is shallow, making it a good place to fish for early smallmouths. As the weather warms, fish for them near dropoffs with a sink-tip line and a weighted leech pattern. Boat ramps are located on the east side of the lake, off Bayview Road, and on the southwest corner of the lake on Highway P.

Walleye on Presque Isle Lake have no minimum size, but you may keep only one over 14 inches. While Presque Isle is clear, it is also rocky. For your safety and your boat's sake, pick up a lake map at Sherer's Northern Adventure Guide Service in Boulder Junction. There are lots of boulders out there waiting to do violence to your boat's propeller.

Smallmouth bass season is catch-and-release in the Northern Zone of Wisconsin between the first Saturday in May and June 14. Between June 15 and March 1, 5 bass in aggregate may be kept with a minimum length of 14 inches. Do consider releasing your smallmouths. They're slow-growing, especially in these northern waters, taking up to 5 years to reach maturity. Keep a walleye or some panfish if you want a fish dinner.

Larger Area Lakes

In the northern part of the forest, Trout Lake, Star Lake, Big Muskellunge Lake, and Upper and Lower Buckabutton Lakes are some of the larger bodies of water. Big St. Germain Lake and Big Arbor Vitae Lake are large lakes in the southern part of the forest. Having well-developed facilities, they tend to be heavily used, especially on summer weekends. Summer weekdays and fall are better times to fish these lakes, since fly fishing from a small boat or float tube requires a certain amount of quiet.

Lower Buckabutton Lake is shallow and weedy and good for northern pike; Upper Buckabutton is deeper and holds bass, walleye, muskie, and panfish. Buckabutton Creek is an excellent producer of smallmouth and largemouth bass.

True to its name, Big Muskellunge Lake contains muskie as well as bass and panfish; it covers 920 acres.

Trout Lake, at 3,800 acres, holds lake trout, panfish, and all warmwater gamefish.

Big Arbor Vitae Lake, adjacent to the community of the same name, weighs in at just under 1,100 acres; its fertile waters host lots of good-sized panfish and a host of gamefish.

Big St. Germain Lake, at 1,600 acres, is known as a consistent walleye producer with good populations of muskie and panfish.

Having coughed the state-record tiger muskellunge at 51 pounds, 3 ounces, Lac Vieux Desert on the Wisconsin-Michigan border also holds big panfish and a decent population of smallmouth bass.

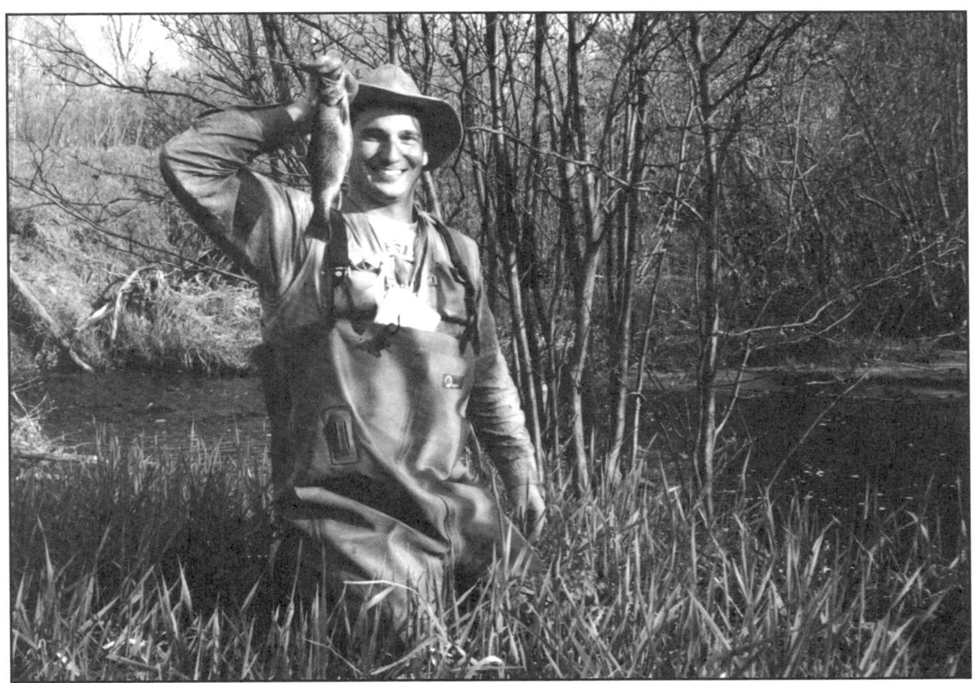

The streams of Marinette County are full of brook trout.

A canoe will help you reach prime water on the Wisconsin River. (Craig Amacker)

Wisconsin River

Beginning near Land O' Lakes in extreme northeast Wisconsin, the Wisconsin River travels 400 miles southwest to its juncture with the Mississippi at Prairie du Chien. Little wonder it served as a trade-goods highway for Indians and the French during the 17th and 18th centuries and as a route for pine logs from the Northwoods in the 19th century.

The river has changed in many ways during the last three hundred years, mostly for the worse. Sawmills in the Wausau/Stevens Point area created small impoundments and log rafts widened the streambed, creating a wider, shallower river. But the paper companies that came in the early 20th century, whose byproducts were released untreated into the air and water, had a far more profound effect. The quest for hydroelectric power in the 1940s and 1950s prompted the creation of dams and impoundments along the river (notably Rainbow, Rhinelander, Spirit River, Lake Dubay Flowages).

Slow to void from a large river system, PCBs and mercury lodged in these slow-moving waterways and their fish. The DNR and EPA have since enforced stricter emission and effluent standards, and gradually things have begun to improve. Still, be sure to check DNR fish advisories when eating fish (especially walleye, smallmouth, and white bass) from the Wisconsin.

This gloomy history does not strike a death knell for fly fishing on the river, though. While anglers can no longer float down a pristine undammed Wisconsin, they can still find good fishing for smallmouth and walleye in the stretches between dams, particularly the scenic headwaters area north of Eagle River. Those with a 14-foot or larger boat equipped with a reliable outboard motor might give the bigger river flowages a try. Concentrate your efforts around structure in these large bodies of water—weeds, rocks, islands, fallen shoreline timber, stumpfields, or lily pads. You'll find a good mix of smallmouth bass, northern pike, muskellunge, and panfish. Fishfinders or advice from a local tackle shop will help you avoid fishing unproductive water on these flowages.

The Wisconsin River begins at the Michigan border below Birch Lake, Crystal Lake, and Lac Vieux Desert. The first road crossing and launch opportunity is Highway 45/32. A good long day float would be from this bridge 9 miles downstream to Highway K outside Conover. An outboard will help you get to productive water, although a canoe was the traditional Chippewa and voyageur mode of transport and is still a viable option. Modern or traditional, you will enjoy one of the wildest sections of this river while fishing for good populations of smallmouth, walleye, and the occasional northern pike. Muddler Minnows, streamers, leech patterns, or poppers will all take fish.

Below Conover there are 12 miles of undammed river with no road crossings until Highway G outside Eagle River. Terrain and species are similar to the first stretch of river described. Below G, the river widens into Watersmeet Lake, which sees lots of boat traffic given its proximity to Eagle River. Skip Watersmeet and float the water between the outlet of the lake and the upper part of Rainbow Flowage along Highway

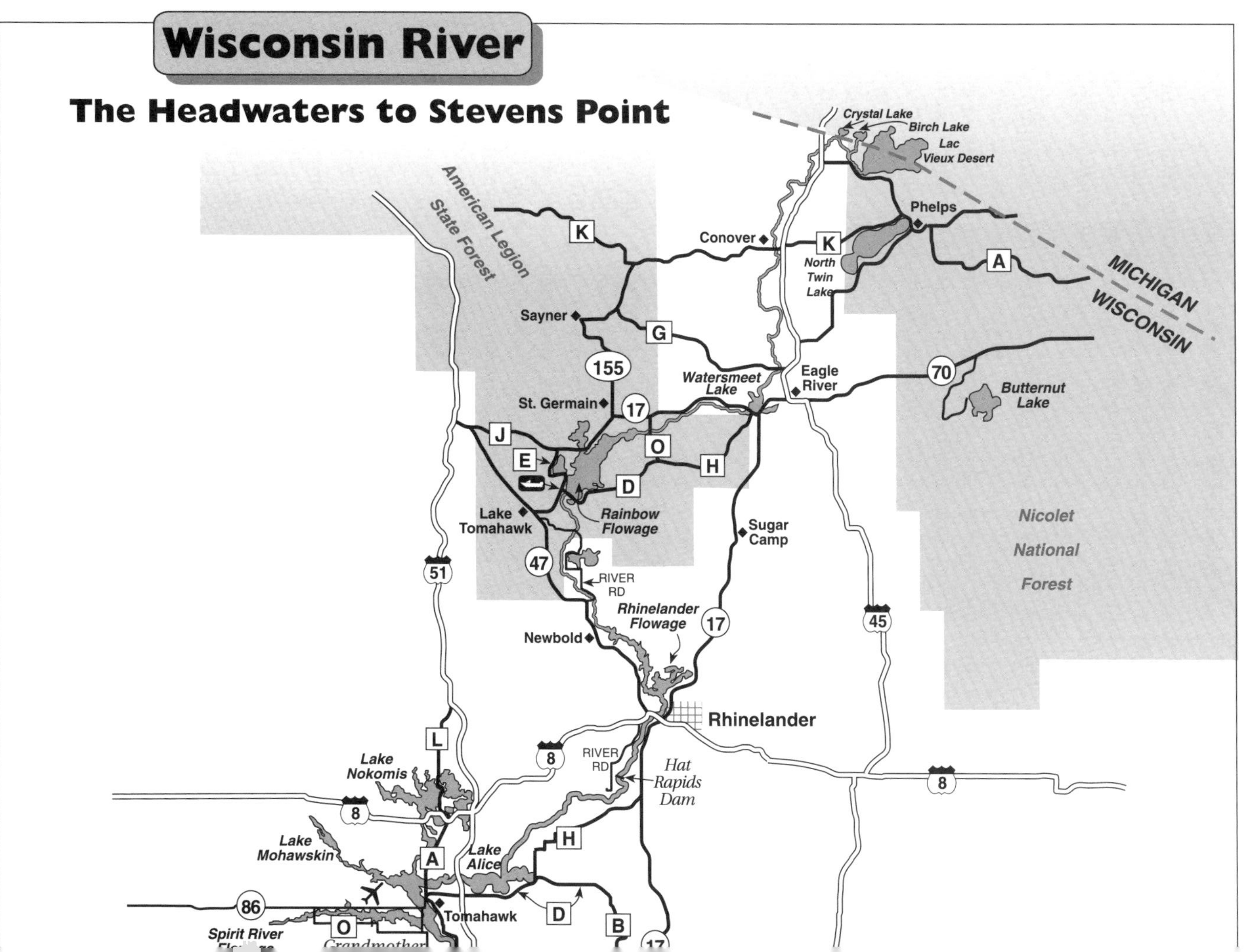

Wisconsin River
The Headwaters to Stevens Point
Crystal Lake
Birch Lake
Lac Vieux Desert
Phelps
MICHIGAN
WISCONSIN
American Legion State Forest
K
Conover
K
North Twin Lake
A
Sayner
G
155
Watersmeet Lake
Eagle River
70
Butternut Lake
St. Germain
17
J
O
E
H
D
Lake Tomahawk
Rainbow Flowage
Sugar Camp
Nicolet National Forest
51
47
RIVER RD
Rhinelander Flowage
17
45
Newbold
Rhinelander
L
8
RIVER RD
Hat Rapids Dam
8
Lake Nokomis
8
H
Lake Mohawskin
A
Lake Alice
86
Tomahawk
D
B
O
Spirit River

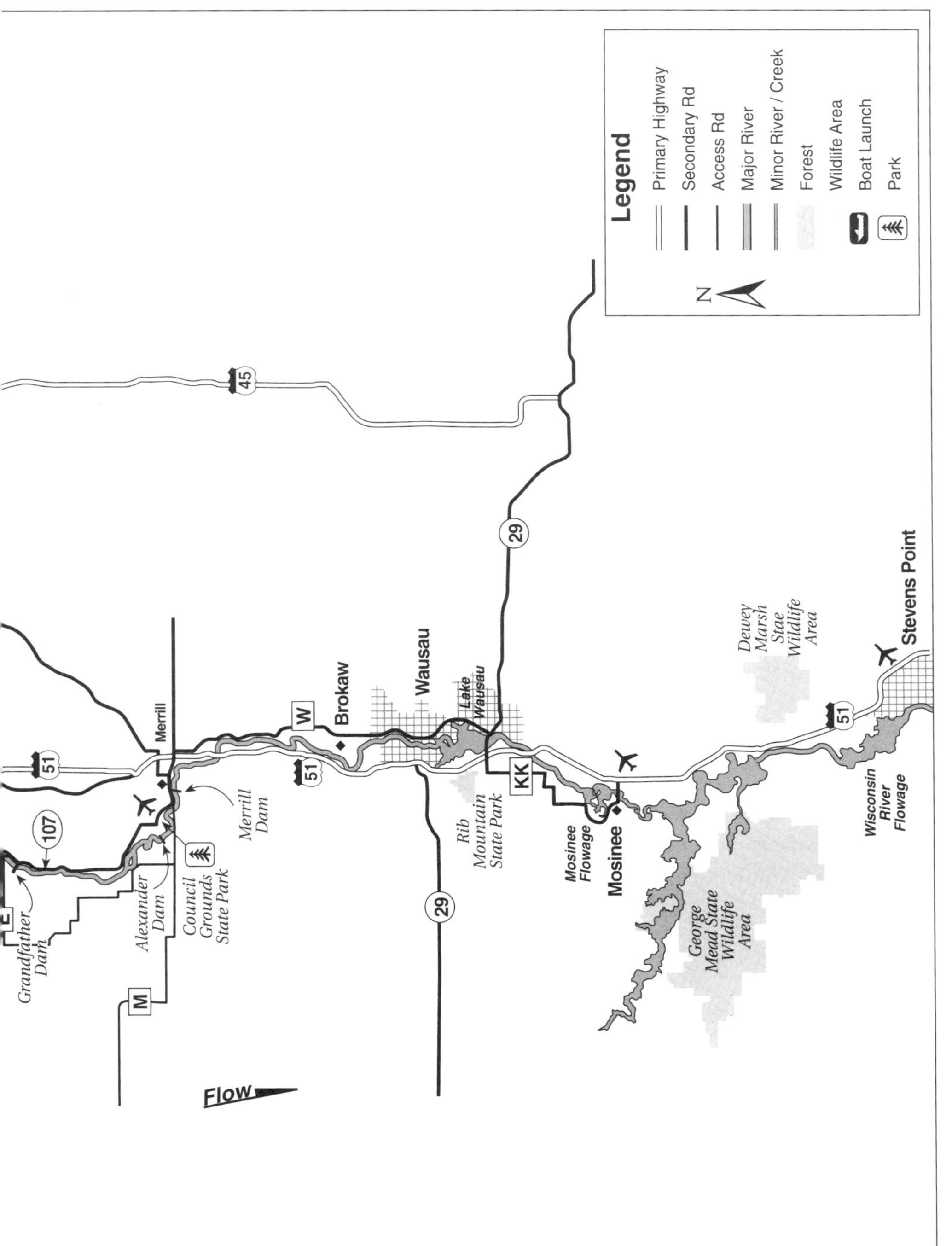
Legend
Primary Highway
Secondary Rd
Access Rd
Major River
Minor River / Creek
Forest
Wildlife Area
Boat Launch
Park
N
Flow
Grandfather Dam
Alexander Dam
Council Grounds State Park
Merrill Dam
Merrill
Brokaw
Wausau
Lake Wausau
Rib Mountain State Park
Mosinee Flowage
Mosinee
George Mead State Wildlife Area
Dewey Marsh Stae Wildlife Area
Wisconsin River Flowage
Stevens Point
107
51
45
29
W
KK
M
E

70. Highway O is a good takeout point. You'll find more pike and muskie in this stretch. Rainbow Flowage (2,000 acres) can be accessed from Highway J or Highway E with a launch on J. Fish Rainbow's shoreline rocks for smallmouth, its weeds for pike and panfish. Rainbow's islands and channels are noted magnets for its robust population of walleye.

Another 15 miles of river fishing is available between the outlet of Rainbow Flowage and the head of Rhinelander Flowage. There's a launch at Highway D, just below Rainbow, and access to the river along River Road, which continues along Rhinelander Flowage with a number of launch ramps. Rhinelander Flowage is about half the size of Rainbow with a similar mix of species and habitat.

Below Rhinelander, there's 30 miles of good river fishing to Tomahawk. Road crossings are at Highway 47 and Highway 8 just south of Rhinelander; Rapids Road off Highway 17 crosses the river below Hat Rapids Dam. At Tomahawk the Wisconsin River widens into the Lake Alice-Lake Mohawskin-Spirit River Flowage complex. From the town of Tomahawk, you can reach Lake Alice on Highway D, Lake Mohawskin off Highway 86, and Spirit River Flowage off Highway O. These flowages offer the typical warmwater Wisconsin mix of smallmouth bass, northern pike, and panfish. Highway 107 follows the east shore of the Wisconsin from Tomahawk to Merrill, some 40 miles. This is a favorite stretch of Pat Ehlers of the Milwaukee Area Fly Fishers. He floats it in a jonboat and fishes for smallmouth and muskie. Smallmouths can be taken on leech and minnow patterns, muskies require a 9-weight rod and steel leader with heavy-duty streamers. As this is a series of four flowages, look for smallmouth in the upper riverine sections of each. Those floating the river should be on the lookout for four dams in this stretch: Grandmother Dam, Grandfather Dam, Alexander Dam (just upstream from Council Grounds State Park) and Merrill Dam. Council Grounds State Park is popular with camping fishermen. Its campsites fill up early on summer weekends so book early or stay during the week or off-season.

The stretch between Merrill and Wausau is another good float-trip stretch. Highway W follows the east shore of the river; Highway 51 runs along the west shore. Between Wausau and Stevens Point the river is impounded into Lake Wausau, Mosinee Flowage, Big Eau Plaine Reservoir, Lake Dubay, and Wisconsin River Flowage, all of which can be reached via Highway 51/39. These are big-water fisheries like the others along the Wisconsin River, with walleye congregating in deep channels, smallmouths frequenting rocky dropoffs, and northerns and panfish in the weedy shallows.

Butternut Lake

DNR fisheries biologist Bob Young recommends 1,300-acre Butternut Lake as one of the finest smallmouth fisheries in northern Wisconsin—and in a land known for great smallmouth fishing that's saying something. Young recommends fishing Butternut during the catch-and-release bass season from the first Saturday in May to middle Saturday in June when bass are on and around their spawning beds. (From the middle Saturday in June to the first Saturday in March in the Northern Zone, 5 smallmouths with a minimum size of 14 inches may be kept.)

Young has seen bass up to 6 pounds during shocking surveys, and he says 20-inch smallies aren't uncommon. You'll find fish off rocky dropoffs and points. A streamer fished on a sink-tip line or poly leader will take fish. Find Butternut Lake northeast of Eagle River, south of Highway 70, and east of the Vilas-Florence County line. Boat landings are on the east side of the lake off Divide Road.

Spread Eagle Chain of Lakes

Located just north of the town of Spread Eagle on Highway 2/141, the Spread Eagle Chain is comprised of eight lakes and covers 550 acres. It offers a diverse fishery of smallmouth, walleye, northern pike, and panfish. The only catch is that this lake is heavily used during summer and has only one public boat ramp. Fish it during May or in the fall. The launch ramp can be found on North Lake off North Lake Road. The weeds on North and West Lakes hold pike and panfish. Find walleye and smallmouth around rocky dropoffs.

Deerskin River

The Deerskin River, a fine brook trout stream made even better by the removal of the McDermott Dam in its middle reaches in 2001, runs between Long Lake and Deerskin Flowage (just northeast of Eagle River). A sediment trap is in place and stream improvements are planned once water levels stabilize. The Deerskin now flows unimpeded between these two lakes for some 12 miles. According to Bill Sherer, owner of We Tie It Fly Shop and Northern Adventure Guide Service in Boulder Junction, this dam removal boosts the number of miles of trout water in Vilas County by one-third.

The Deerskin is a pretty tannin-dark Northwoods brook trout stream with lots of cover and a good population of 6- to 10-inch brook trout. The stream also holds some big browns, according to Sherer. I've taken brookies on the Deerskin by snaking streamer flies beneath grassy banks and logjams. While I've never taken any fish over 10 inches here, I enjoy catching and releasing these small wild fish. The river's upper reaches are in the scenic Nicolet National Forest, not far from the Michigan border.

Starting upstream, access can be found at County A, Fire Roads 2538, 2178, 2199, Rangeline Road, and North Carpenter Road. A number of hiking trails in the vicinity of Blackjack Creek and Springs provide access to the Deerskin for anglers willing to walk. These trails will also take you along lightly fished stretches of the creek. From the juncture with Blackjack Creek downstream to Rangeline Road is category 5 (3-trout limit, artificials only, a maximum of 2 brook trout larger than 12 inches and 1 brown trout larger than 18 inches may be kept). Otherwise, the Deerskin River is a category 2 stream.

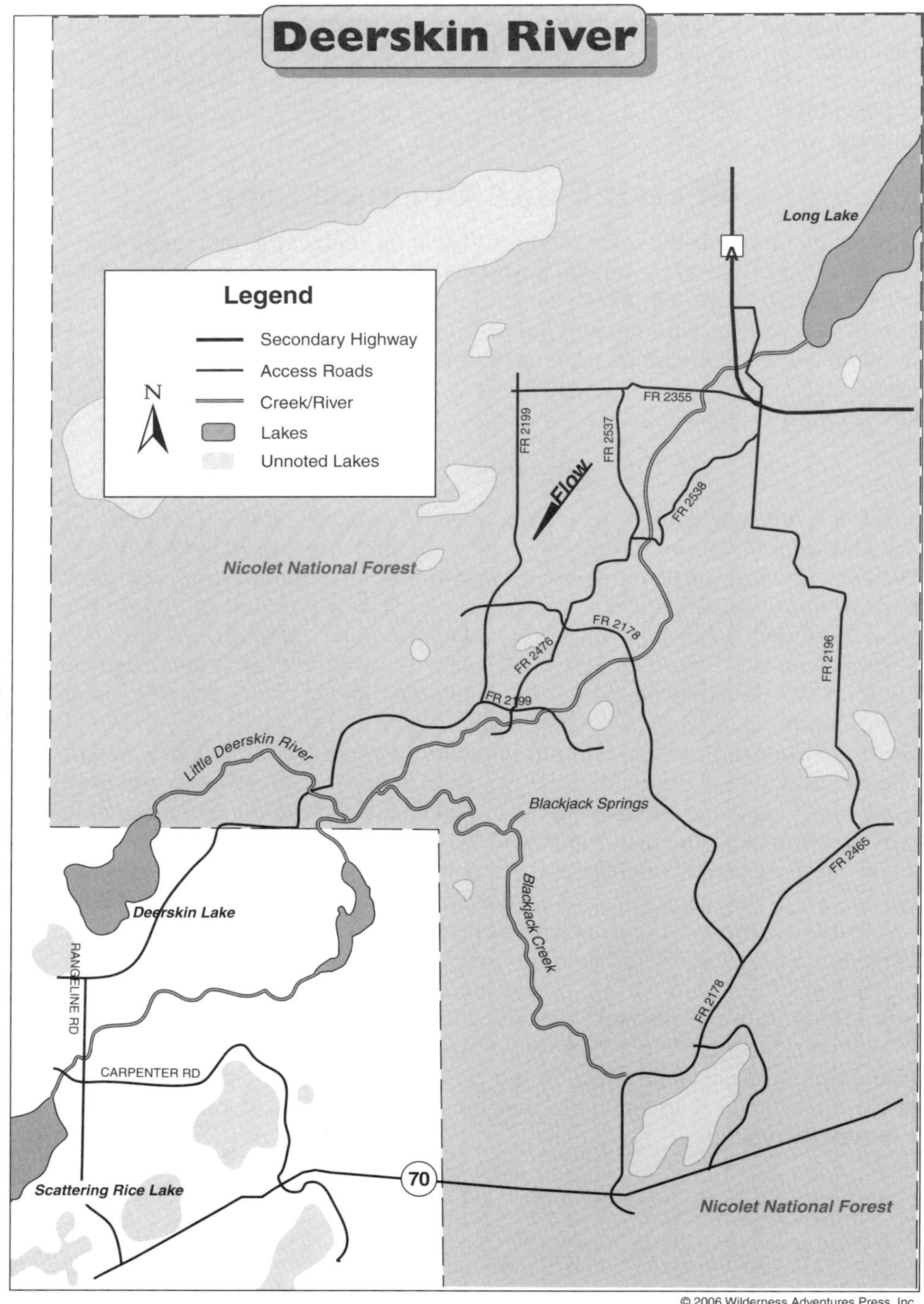

Deerskin River
Legend
Secondary Highway
Access Roads
Creek/River
Lakes
Unnoted Lakes
N
Long Lake
Flow
FR 2355
FR 2199
FR 2537
FR 2538
Nicolet National Forest
FR 2178
FR 2476
FR 2199
FR 2196
Little Deerskin River
Blackjack Springs
FR 2465
Deerskin Lake
Blackjack Creek
RANGELINE RD
FR 2178
CARPENTER RD
70
Scattering Rice Lake
Nicolet National Forest

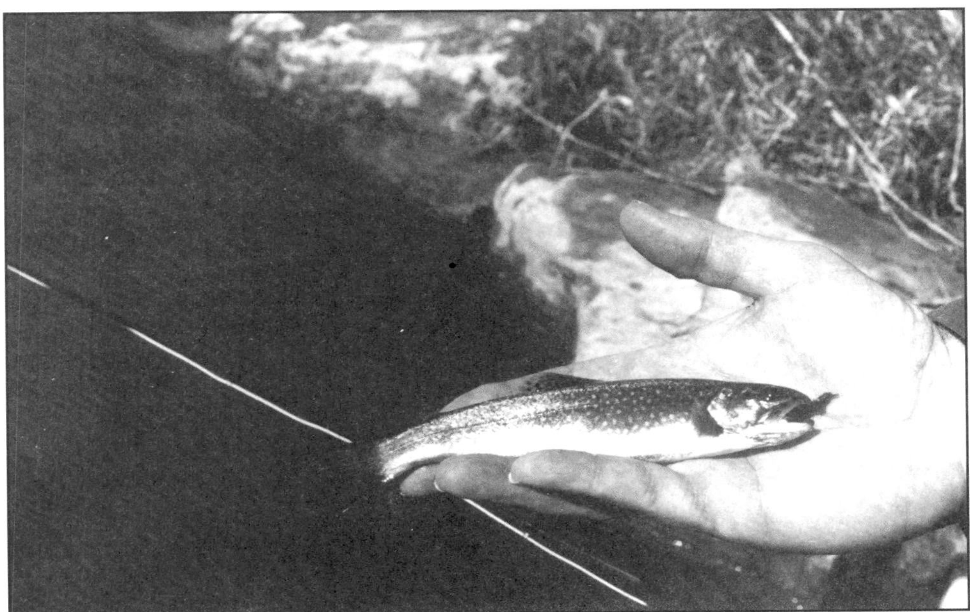

A tiny but beautiful brook trout from the Deerskin River.

Stream Facts: Deerskin River

Season

- Regular season runs from the first Saturday in May at 5:00 am through September 30. Closed to fishing during March-April season.

Regulations

- From the juncture with Blackjack Creek downstream to Rangeline Road is category 5 (3-trout limit, artificials only, a maximum of 2 brook trout larger than 12 inches and 1 brown trout larger than 18 inches may be kept). Otherwise, the Deerskin River is a category 2 stream.

Miles of Trout Water

- 12 miles

Stream Characteristics

- Small, tea-colored river with good population of native brook trout.

Fly Shops

- We Tie It Fly Shop (Boulder Junction)

Maps

- *Wisconsin Atlas and Gazetteer*, pages 91, 99

Boundary Brule River

The Brule River in Forest and Florence Counties in northeastern Wisconsin shares a boundary with Michigan for 40 miles. It's sometimes known as the Boundary Brule, not to be confused with the famous Bois Brule in northwest Wisconsin.

The Brule is a scenic freestone river located in the Nicolet National Forest, with small brook trout and some large brown trout. The Brule's popularity with canoers, however, has hurt its capacity to produce and hold trout, according to Bill Sherer, of We Tie It Fly Shop. Paddlers and paddling clubs have removed fallen trees from the river over the years, increasing erosion and siltation and reducing crucial fish (as well as bird and amphibian) habitat. Coupled with the tendency of area freestone streams, which often lack cold groundwater seepage, to warm over the summer, this has resulted in a deteriorating trout population over the years.

On the bright side, the Wisconsin DNR and Michigan DNR are working together to install boom covers and lunker structures along the river to provide cover for trout. Sherer says the Brule has seen more stream improvement over the last two years than in the past decade.

It's best to fish the Brule in May and early June, before water temperatures warm and fish are disturbed by canoe traffic. Floating is a good way to cover lots of water, find pods of fish, and fish high-quality tributaries. Sherer recommends Elvoy Creek, accessible via Highway A near the Brule's headwaters, and Allen Creek, just north of Highway 70 near the village of Alvin.

Access to the Brule in Forest County can be had at Highway 73 near the village of Nelma, and on Fire Roads 2172, 2454, and 2594. Highway 189 north of Tipler, Daumitz Road, and Fire Road 2150 cross the Brule in Florence County. Highway 2/141 (north of Florence) crosses the river just north of the town of Florence. The river ends a few miles from here at its confluence with the Paint River Pond where fishing is for warmwater species.

Both residents and nonresidents must posses a valid fishing license for the state in which they are fishing. The Brule is open to trout fishing from the last Saturday in April until September 30. Above Highway 2/141, you may keep 5 trout (brook trout, 8-inch minimum; brown trout 12-inch minimum). Below Highway 2/141, 7 trout may be kept with a minimum size of 7 inches.

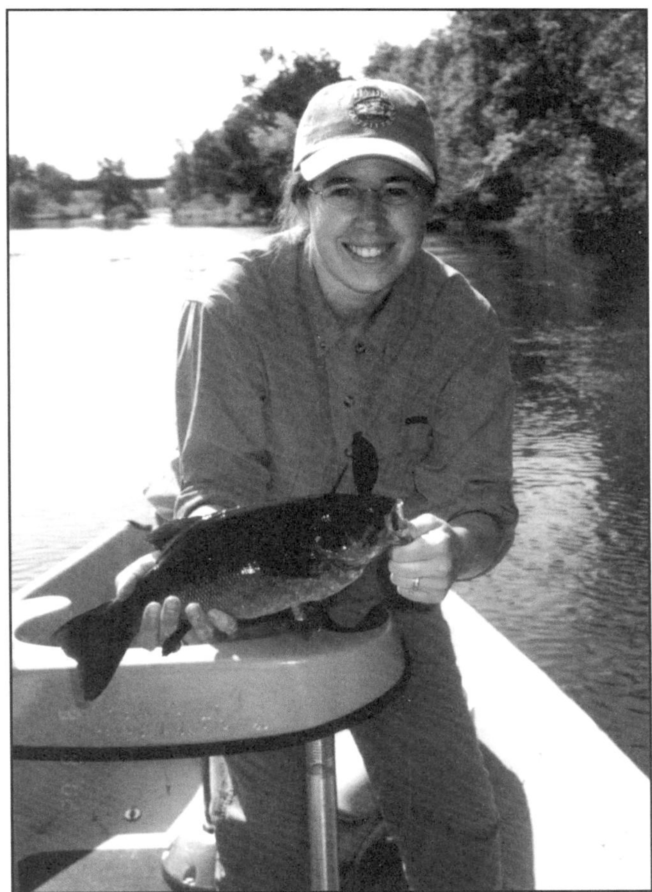

Sarah Landwehr shows off a nice smallmouth. (Tim Landwehr)

MENOMINEE RIVER

The Menominee River may be described as a two-story fishery: its upper 100 miles are a series of flowages hosting warmwater gamefish; its lower reaches see Lake Michigan trout and salmon runs in spring and fall.

Beginning at the confluence of the Brule River and the outlet of Michigamme Lake in Michigan's Upper Peninsula northeast of Iron Mountain, the Menominee River forms the Michigan-Wisconsin border for over a hundred miles and empties into Green Bay at the cities of Marinette/Menominee. A river in name, the Menominee is actually a series of flowages, narrow and riverine in their upper reaches, broad and lake-like in their lower reaches. Smallmouth bass are the main draw for flyfishers

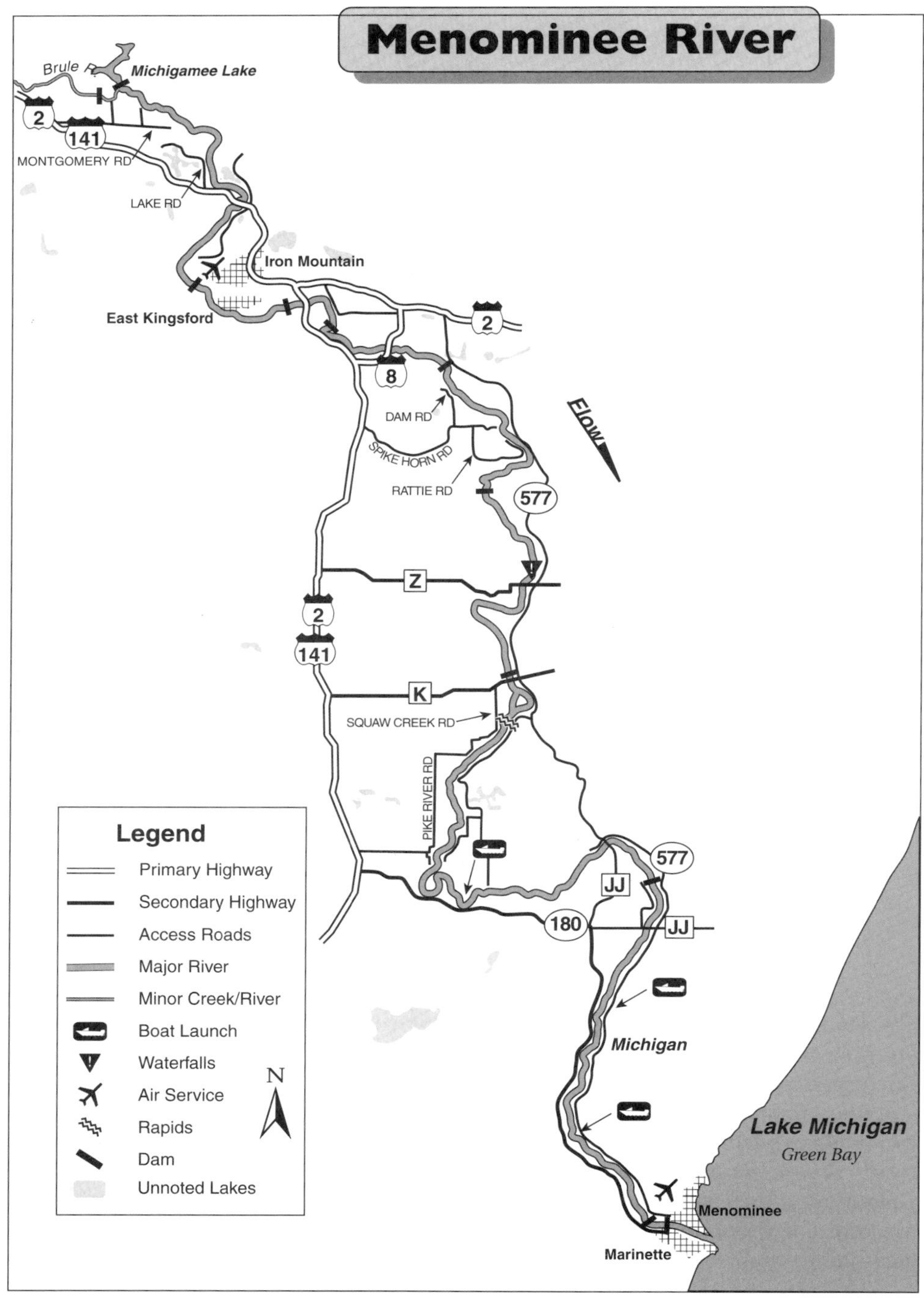
Menominee River
Brule R.
Michigamee Lake
2
141
MONTGOMERY RD
LAKE RD
Iron Mountain
East Kingsford
2
8
DAM RD
SPIKE HORN RD
RATTIE RD
577
Flow
Z
2
141
K
SQUAW CREEK RD
PIKE RIVER RD
577
JJ
180
JJ
Michigan
Lake Michigan
Green Bay
Menominee
Marinette
Legend
Primary Highway
Secondary Highway
Access Roads
Major River
Minor Creek/River
Boat Launch
Waterfalls
Air Service
Rapids
Dam
Unnoted Lakes
N

here. DNR fisheries technician Greg Kornely says there is tremendous smallmouth fishing just about anywhere on the Menominee.

Fish Menominee bronzebacks near rocky dropoffs and fast riffles using a sink-tip line and a #4 leech pattern. Hammerhandle pike will be hanging around stumpfields, lily pads, and creek mouths. Walleye can be found in many of the same rocky haunts as smallmouth.

The extreme lower reaches of the Menominee River—from its mouth in Green Bay to the Haitie Street Dam in Marinette—see fall and spring runs of steelhead and salmon. Staging trout and salmon can also be picked up by working streamer patterns in and around Marinette/Menominee Harbor. Brown trout, steelhead, and splake frye are all planted in the lower part of the river, to return after maturing in the lake.

Highway 2/141 gives access to the upper part of the Menominee, and Highway 180 access to the lower part. Camping is available for a nominal fee on power company land along the river. Under Wisconsin law, utility companies must provide public benefit in exchange for harnessing hydroelectric power from dammed rivers. Thus, the launch ramps and campgrounds along the upper Menominee.

Flowages on the Menominee are best fished from a small boat—jonboat, V-hull, or canoe. An outboard helps anglers move around to find fish, but those willing to paddle or row aren't at much of a disadvantage. In fact, oars or paddles make for a quiet, subtle approach and spook fewer fish.

Another fact about the Menominee: it's full of crawfish. I've found the stomachs of walleye packed with them, and sitting by the water at night by lantern light, you can see crawfish cruising the shallows in search of food. Be sure to carry a few crawfish imitations in your fly box.

Largemouth and smallmouth bass are open to catch-and-release fishing only from the first Saturday in May to the middle Saturday in June; from the middle Saturday in June to November 30, the combined daily bag limit for largemouth and smallmouth bass is 5. There is no minimum size limit for northern pike; the daily bag is 5, and open season is the first Saturday in May to March 1. Walleye must be 15 inches to keep, with a daily bag of 5 and an open season from the first Saturday in May to March 1.

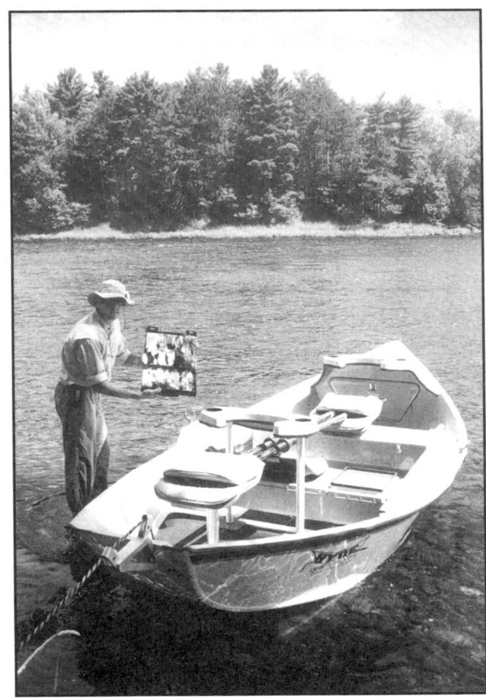

Tight Lines Guide Service offers float trip smallmouth fishing on the beautiful Menominee River. (Kay Adams)

Wisconsin residents need a Wisconsin license to fish the Menominee; Michigan residents need a Michigan license; nonresidents may purchase either a Wisconsin or Michigan license. To fish below Haitie Street Dam in Marinette, you'll need to have a Wisconsin Great Lakes Trout and Salmon Stamp.

South Branch of the Pemebonwon River

This tributary of the Menominee River begins north of Dunbar in northern Marinette County. It flows some 25 miles before joining the North Branch of the Pemebonwon near Kremlin just east of the Menominee River. The South Branch runs parallel to Highway O north of Dunbar and crosses Highway 8 at Pembine. East of Highway 8, you can cross the river on Smith Lake Road before it joins the North Branch.

The South Branch is a category 2 stream with a strong population of wild brook trout. It can get pretty brushy in summer so fish with a short rod if you have one. Since the banks are so thick, you'll have to wade in the stream. Fishing a Royal Coachman or hopper pattern tight to bankside cover can be deadly on Pemebonwon brook trout.

Once, while enjoying a June afternoon on the Pemebonwon catching small brook trout, I watched a large old Buick pull up. An old woman greeted me in a thick East European accent. In one hand she held a red coffee can, in the other a stout spinning rod. When I turned my head, she had disappeared into the thick underbrush. I continued to work my fly along the bankside cover picking up small fish here and there. Half an hour later I saw the old woman emerge from the brush. She now held both the coffee can and spinning rod in her right hand. In her left hand she carried a switch of willow sagging beneath the weight of three hook-jawed brook trout. "Da big ones," she said, "they like the worms." I nodded. It was hard to argue. She opened the trunk and put the three big slabs into a Coleman cooler.

North Branch of the Pemebonwon

Another fine brook trout stream, according to DNR fisheries technician Greg Kornely, is the North Branch of the Pemebonwon. You can find it above the South Branch off County O (road crossings at Camp 12 Road, Walton Road, and County O). It then crosses Highway 8 north of Pembine and tumbles down a series of waterfalls—Smalley Falls and Long Slide Falls.

There is good access to the west bank of the river at Long Slide Falls County Park (take Highway 141 to Morgan Park Road). Spikehorn Road and Pemene River Road follow the east side of the river before it joins the South Branch south of Kremlin. The North Branch is category 2 water, with wild brook trout present in good numbers. Look for nice pocketwater in the vicinity of Smalley Falls and Long Slide Falls.

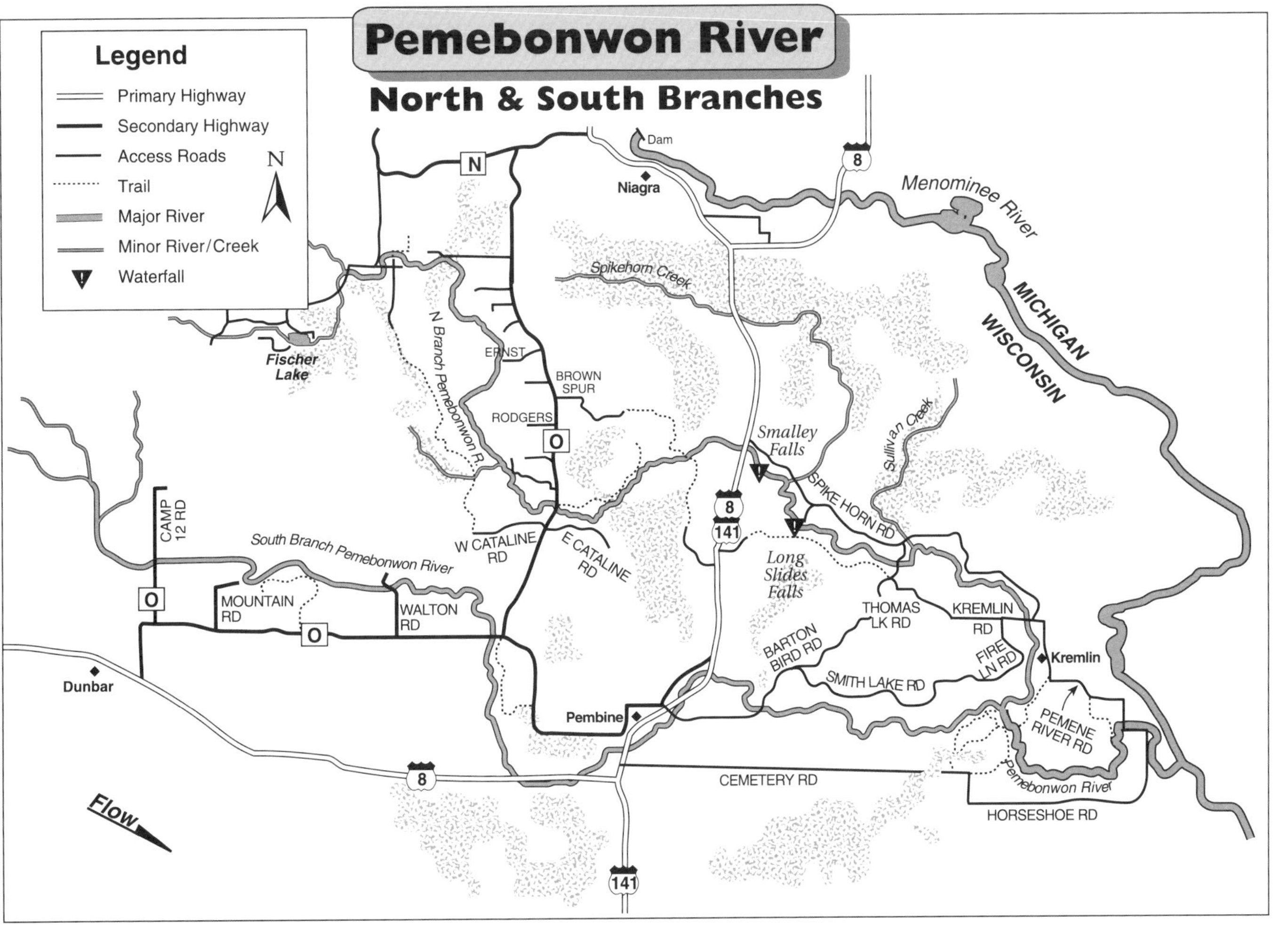
Pemebonwon River
North & South Branches
Legend
Primary Highway
Secondary Highway
Access Roads
Trail
Major River
Minor River/Creek
Waterfall
N
Dam
Niagra
8
Menominee River
MICHIGAN
WISCONSIN
Spikehorn Creek
Fischer Lake
N Branch Pemebonwon R.
ERNST
BROWN SPUR
RODGERS
O
Smalley Falls
Sullivan Creek
SPIKE HORN RD
141
Long Slides Falls
CAMP 12 RD
South Branch Pemebonwon River
W CATALINE RD
E CATALINE RD
MOUNTAIN RD
WALTON RD
THOMAS LK RD
KREMLIN RD
BARTON BIRD RD
FIRE LN RD
Kremlin
SMITH LAKE RD
Dunbar
Pembine
PEMENE RIVER RD
CEMETERY RD
Pemebonwon River
HORSESHOE RD
Flow

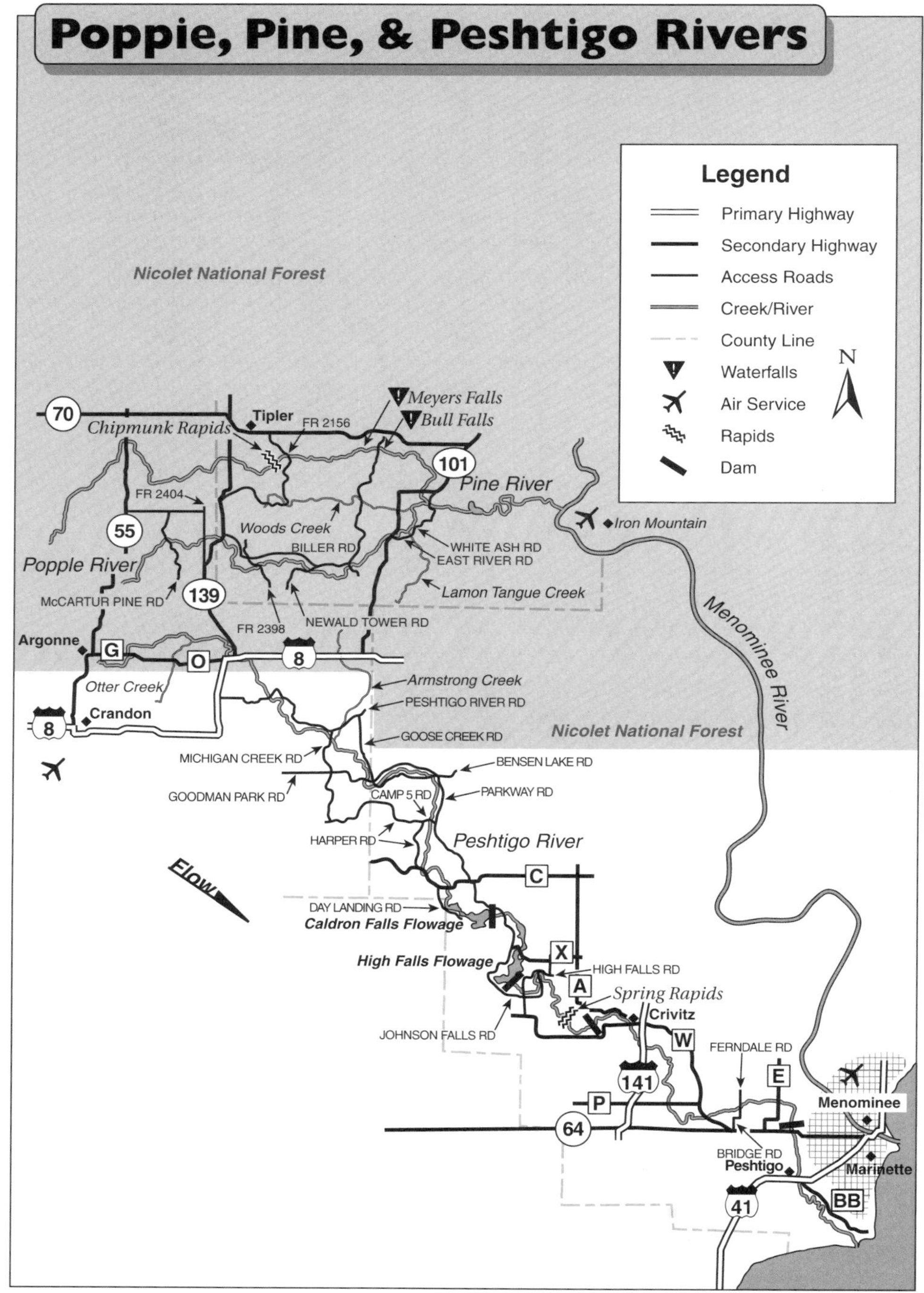
Poppie, Pine, & Peshtigo Rivers
Legend
Primary Highway
Secondary Highway
Access Roads
Creek/River
County Line
Waterfalls
Air Service
Rapids
Dam
N
Nicolet National Forest
70
Tipler
FR 2156
Meyers Falls
Bull Falls
Chipmunk Rapids
101
Pine River
FR 2404
55
Woods Creek
BILLER RD
WHITE ASH RD
EAST RIVER RD
Iron Mountain
Popple River
McCARTUR PINE RD
139
Lamon Tangue Creek
FR 2398
NEWALD TOWER RD
Argonne
G
O
8
Menominee River
Armstrong Creek
Otter Creek
PESHTIGO RIVER RD
Crandon
GOOSE CREEK RD
Nicolet National Forest
MICHIGAN CREEK RD
BENSEN LAKE RD
GOODMAN PARK RD
CAMP 5 RD
PARKWAY RD
HARPER RD
Peshtigo River
Flow
C
DAY LANDING RD
Caldron Falls Flowage
High Falls Flowage
X
HIGH FALLS RD
A
Spring Rapids
Crivitz
JOHNSON FALLS RD
W
FERNDALE RD
141
E
Menominee
P
64
BRIDGE RD
Peshtigo
Marinette
41
BB
© 2006 Wilderness Adventures Press, Inc.

Popple, Pine, and Peshtigo Rivers

These three rivers are treated as a group because they are very similar. Large, long freestone rivers, they all provide suitable habitat for trout for the first and last months of the season. But they warm precipitously during July and August, sending trout looking for relief in cooler groundwater swells and feeder creeks.

From a fishing standpoint, these rivers can be looked at more as part of a habitat network than as self-sustaining ecosystems in themselves. Thus, the flyfisher frequenting these rivers for trout in summer should carry a stream thermometer to check for suitable trout water. He might also try tributary streams. This trio of rivers might not bear mentioning as serious trout water if they didn't yield big trout and have such a rich base of caddis, mayflies, stoneflies, crawfish, and forage fish. Aesthetically, they are also lovely rivers, tumbling through northern forests of birch, hemlock, pine, and aspen, with lots of waterfalls and whitewater. The lower portions of the Pine and Popple are designated Wild Rivers by the state of Wisconsin. This means there is minimal shoreline development.

Popple River

The Popple River, named for the aspen that are so common in the Northwoods, begins in Forest County and joins the Pine River some 30 miles later in Florence County. The Popple looks like prime trout water, especially when its waterfalls are running full-bore in spring. It does support trout, especially in its tributaries and upper reaches; however, fish its middle reaches in summer and you'll be unhooking chubs, not trout. Put your stream thermometer in and you're likely to get readings in the mid to upper 70s.

Where do the trout go? According to Bill Sherer of We Tie It Fly Shop in Boulder Junction, DNR telemetry studies show that trout travel as much as 40 miles in summer in search of cool water. In September they do the reverse—working back to the deeper water downstream in search of food. Freestone streams like the Popple are fed by snow and rain and thus reflect northeast Wisconsin's ambient temperature—warm in summer and cold in winter.

Unlike Driftless and Sand County streams to the south and west, groundwater and spring flow contribute relatively little to northeast Wisconsin watersheds. Concentrate your efforts in tributaries and headwaters during warmer months and fish the main branch only during cooler weather.

Road crossings in Florence County are McCarthur Pine Road, Fire Road 2404, and Highway 139. In Florence County, Fire Road 2398, Newald Tower Road, and Highway 101 cross the river. The Popple River is category 2 for its entire length.

La Montagne Creek, arising near the town of Fence, and Woods Creek (called Halsey Lake Woods Creek on the DNR map) join the Popple just upstream from the Popple's confluence with the Pine. Both of these creeks come highly recommended by Bill Sherer as good wild brook trout streams. Outside of Fence in southern Florence County, Highway C parallels and then crosses the upper reaches of La Montagne

Creek. Take Highway 101 to East River Road to White Ash Road to cross the lower reaches of La Montagne. Halsey Lake Road, Biller Road, and Highway 101 cross Woods Creek.

Pine River

The Pine River begins as a swampy, low-gradient stream in Forest County. It then flows faster and rockier on its westward journey below Highway 55 and the Florence County line. It joins the Menominee River near Iron Mountain, Michigan. The main branch of the Pine River extends some 40 miles. Like the Popple and Wolf, it is a long watershed that suffers from warming in summer and lack of over-winter habitat in cold weather. Still, it contains some big holdover trout, and native brook and brown trout frequent its many tributaries.

The key to fishing the Pine in summer is finding cool water in the form of spring seeps and tributaries. A stream thermometer is also helpful in finding upwellings of cold groundwater that may be invisible to the eye. Summer temperatures of 70 or below are comfortable for brown trout; mid-60s and below are right for brook trout.

Access to the Pine is from road crossings and fire lanes. Since the upper Pine falls within the Nicolet National Forest, you are also free to bushwhack cross-country to the river from roads or trails. Take a compass if you plan to do this.

To reach the Pine River from the south, take Highway 55 north from Crandon through the crossroads town of Argonne and continue 15 miles north, crossing

An angler works the riffles and runs of the Pine River. (Chris Halla)

the Pine. You can reach middle and downstream portions of the Pine by following Highway 8/32 east from Crandon and either taking Highway 139 north or Highway 101 north to river crossings. If you want to backtrack from Highway 101, take Highway 70 east (which follows the north bank of the Pine) toward Tipler, where you can rejoin Highway 139. A series of Forest Service roads (locally called fire lines) give access to the south shore of the river. You will find a Forest Service campground on the Pine River at Chipmunk Rapids off FR 2156.

In Forest County, the Pine River is category 2; in Florence County, down to the Pine River Flowage, it is category 4. Large nymphs, strip leeches, and Muddler Minnows are all good bets on the Pine. The North Branch of the Pine, west of Highway 55, contains native brook trout and planted browns and might be worth a try if water temperatures on the main branch are high. You also might consider floating the Pine. You'll be able to cover more water and investigate promising tributaries.

A good 9-mile float is the stretch between Chipmunk Rapids and Goodman Grade. Take Highway 70 heading east from Tipler to Fire Road 2450 south. Take this to Fire Road 2156 south (Chipmunk Rapids Road) and cross the Pine at Chipmunk Rapids. A Forest Service campground will be on the south bank of the river. Meyers Falls, a half-mile from the take-out at Goodman Grade, will require a portage. Fish both the feeder creeks on the north side of the river and the river itself. A Muddler Minnow with a bit of tinsel tied in is deadly on North Country brook trout. The Goodman Grade take-out is reached by following the road to Bull Falls south from Highway 70; continue on this road (skipping the fork to Bull Falls) and cross the Pine.

Peshtigo River

The Peshtigo River is the longest of this troika of northeast Wisconsin rivers, with some 60 miles of trout water in Forest and Marinette Counties; it is then dammed into a series of flowages, mainly providing a warmwater fishery below this point. Otter Creek and Armstrong Creek, both coldwater tributaries of the Peshtigo in Forest County, hold wild brook trout.

The upper Peshtigo is much like the Pine and Popple in that it's a boulder-strewn whitewater river popular with paddlers and suffers from high temperatures during the summer months. It begins near the village of Argonne and Highway 55; Highway G and Highway O follow this upper stretch of the river. South of the village of Cavour on Highway 8, follow Peshtigo River Road east along the river. From Peshtigo River Road, take Michigan Creek Road south to Goodman Park Road. Goodman Park Road, after Goodman County Park, becomes Parkway Road and follows the river.

From Highway 8 in Forest County to Highway C in Marinette County, the Peshtigo River is category 3. This section is open between October 1 and November 15 to artificials-only, catch-and-release fishing.

Parkway Road continues along Caldron Falls and High Falls Flowages (impoundments) on the river. Both flowages offer good fishing for bass along their extensive shorelines, which can be fished from a small boat. Boat landings can be

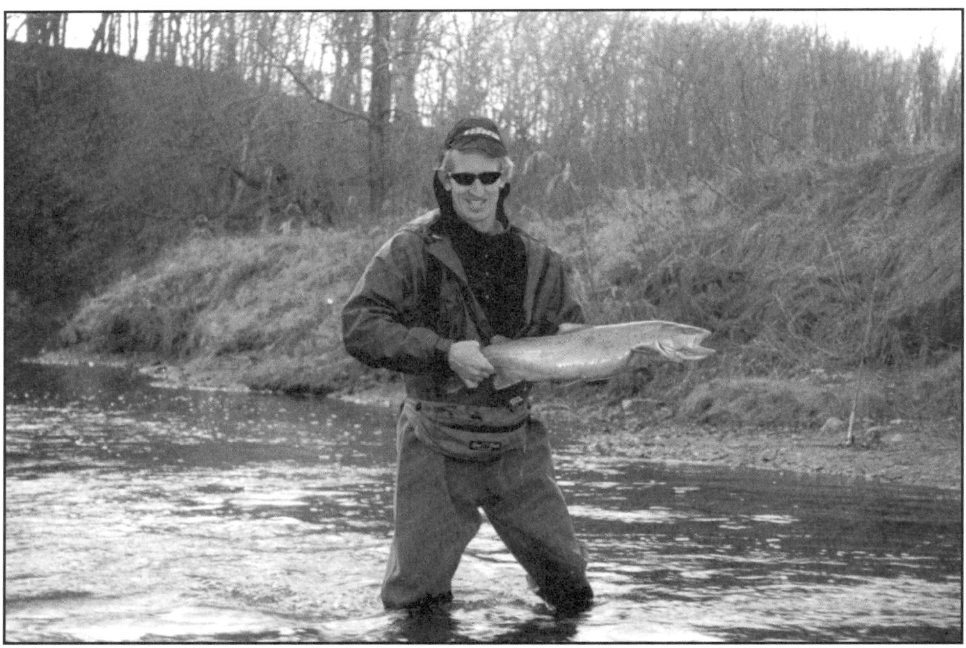

A nice fish from one of Lake Michigan's tributary streams. (Craig Amacker)

found off Parkway Road. Of the two flowages, Caldron Falls, at 1,200 acres, sees less boat traffic. Its shoreline is mostly wild and undeveloped. It also offers a fishery for muskie, northern pike, and panfish. High Falls Flowage, to the north and twice the size of Caldron, sees considerable recreational boat traffic during summer weekends. Fish it early in the season, on weekdays, or during the fall.

Below the flowages there is a brief section of trout water between Johnson Falls and Spring Rapids. All three species of trout are planted, and browns often attain considerable size. It is artificials only with a daily bag of 2 trout; brown trout must be 18 inches or longer; rainbow and brook trout 12 inches or longer. This is big, fast water—a good place for streamers, leeches, or attractor patterns. From Parkway Road, access this stretch via High Falls Road and Johnson Falls Road. There are a number of walking trails that lead into the river, offering anglers a chance at fishing solitude.

Warmwater gamefish are present in the river between Crivitz and Peshtigo (site of the infamous Peshtigo fire in 1871), but this stretch is lightly fished. Road crossings include Highway 141, Highway W, Highway E, and Highway 64.

Gamefish from Green Bay make it up the Peshtigo River as far as the Peshtigo Dam at Highway 41. There's a fall run of trout and salmon and a spring steelhead run. Smallmouth bass and pike grown fat on Green Bay smelt can also be caught in the lower reaches of the Peshtigo. The last few miles of the river is part of the Green Bay Shores State Wildlife Area and can be accessed from Harbor Road and Highways B and BB out of Peshtigo.

ONEIDA COUNTY LAKES

Perch, Squash, Crescent, and Emma Lakes

On Perch and Squash Lakes, anglers may fish for trout from the first Saturday in May to March 1; you can keep 5 with a minimum length of 12 inches. Perch and Squash are planted with trout, and while these trout do not reproduce, they do attain considerable size. Bass and panfish are bonus fisheries, with northerns present at Squash Lake.

The lakes are located off Highway 8 near Woodboro. Take Washburn Lake Road to Trout Creek Road to get to the launch on Perch Lake. Squash Lake, just east of Highway 8, can be reached by taking Crescent Lake Road to Long Lake Road to the launch ramp. On Squash Lake there is no minimum length on walleye, but only 1 fish over 14 inches may be kept.

Crescent Lake, northeast of Squash Lake and east of Highway 8, is a good muskie, walleye, and panfish lake. Tiny Emma Lake, between the Wisconsin River and Crescent Lake, offers bass and panfish. On Crescent Lake, there is no minimum size on walleye, but only 1 over 14 inches may be kept. After June 14, the minimum length for largemouth bass caught on Crescent Lake is 18 inches with a daily bag of 1.

Indian and Jennie Weber Lakes

Just outside the town of Sugar Camp in Oneida County you'll find Indian Lake and Jennie Weber Lake. The former sits just to the north of town, the latter just to the south. Both lie just to the east of Highway 17. You'll find pike and panfish in the lakes, plus smallmouth in Indian Lake.

Indian Lake has vegetation and rocks, while Jennie Weber is mostly weeds. Launch right off Highway 17 to fish Jennie Weber and off Indian Lake Road (turn right from Highway 17) to fish Indian. Given that Jennie Weber is a mere 7 feet deep, a low-draft boat or float tube is the way to go. Indian Lake is bigger and deeper, allowing for larger craft.

Birch, Bearskin, and Little Bearskin Lakes

Located between the village of Goodnow and Highway 51 south of Woodruff, these three lakes offer different fisheries. Rocky Bearskin Lake is rife with smallmouth bass, while weedy Little Bearskin holds largemouth, panfish, and northern pike. Birch is a wilderness lake with no developed facilities, which cuts down fishing pressure; it holds mainly panfish, largemouths, and northern pike. Launch a canoe or belly boat off Lakewood Road to fish Birch. Continue on Lakewood Road to Bearskin Lake's launch ramp. The access road for Little Bearskin Lake is off Highway 51.

Hub City: Boulder Junction

A small Northwoods crossroads town of 950 for nine months of the year, Vilas County's Boulder Junction (Musky Capital of the World) swells to 8,000 residents in summer. Vilas County alone has over 1,300 lakes, and this is the main draw. The large lakes see heavy boat traffic, but the Northern Highland American Legion State Forest offers a wealth of small quiet lakes. Do-it-yourselfers can fish dozens of remote lakes in the state forest and Nicolet National Forest.

Bill Sherer of Northern Adventure Guide Services describes the Northern Highland Plateau as one of the most diverse freshwater fisheries in the world. Plenty of resorts and Northwoods eateries make Boulder Junction a fine base camp for flyfishers.

Accommodations

Zastrow's Linx Lodge, P.O. Box 2777L, Boulder Junction; 800-882-5969; quality, established Northwoods resort; $$

Sunrise Resort, HC1 Box 463, Presque Isle; 715-686-2414; scenic resort located on Michigan-Wisconsin border; $$

Volinek's Upper Gresham Resort, 4880 Highway 51, Boulder Junction; 715-385-2578;another fine, established Northwoods resort; $$

Boulder Junction Motor Lodge, 10432 Main Street, Boulder Junction; 715-385-2825; comfortable woodsy motel with hot tub, fire place, continental breakfast; $$

Campgrounds

Nicolet National Forest Headquarters, 68 South Stevens Street, Rhinelander; 715-362-1300, to make reservations 877-444-6677; campgrounds throughout forest

Northern Highlands American Legion State Forest, P.O. Box 440, Woodruff; 715-356-5211; camping throughout forest

Camp Holiday, Inc., P.O. Box 57, Boulder Junction; 715-385-2264; commercial campground with RV and electrical hook-ups

Restaurants

Little Bohemia Restaurant, Highway 51 southbound, Manitowish Waters; 715-543-8800; excellent food with strong Eastern European emphasis; 10 miles southwest of Boulder Junction

The Granary, 5367 Park Street, Boulder Junction; 715-385-3736; good breakfast and lunch in downtown Boulder Junction

Guide's Inn, Highway M southside of Boulder Junction; 715-385-2233; good supper club fare: steaks, fish, cocktails

JJ's Pub and Grub, downtown Boulder Junction; 715-385-0166; burgers, sandwiches, beer

Fly Shops, Outfitters, Sporting Goods

We Tie It Fly Shop & Northern Adventure Guide Service, Boulder Junction; 715-385-0171; the Northwoods fly shop, plus guiding for trout and warmwater species

Boulder Lodge, Highway 77, Hayward; 715-462-3002; Orvis and Scott dealer, fly shop 40 miles west of Boulder Junction

Coontail Corner, downtown Boulder Junction; 715-385-2582; fishing licenses

Wal-Mart, Highway 70 West, Minocqua; 715-356-1609; fishing licenses, 20 miles west of Boulder Junction

Veterinarians

Northwoods Animal Hospital, 223 Highway 51, Manitowish Waters; 715-543-2860

Medical

Howard Young Medical Center, Maple Street, Woodruff; 715-356-8000

Auto Rental

Enterprise, 3620 Highway 47, Rhinelander; 715-369-8880

Automobile Repair

Long's Boulder Service, Boulder Junction; 715-385-2127

Air Service

Lakeland Airport, North Farming Road, Woodruff; 715-356-3891; paved runway, 20 miles west of Boulder Junction

For More Information

Boulder Junction Chamber of Commerce
Highway M
800-GO-MUSKY;
www.boulderjunction.org

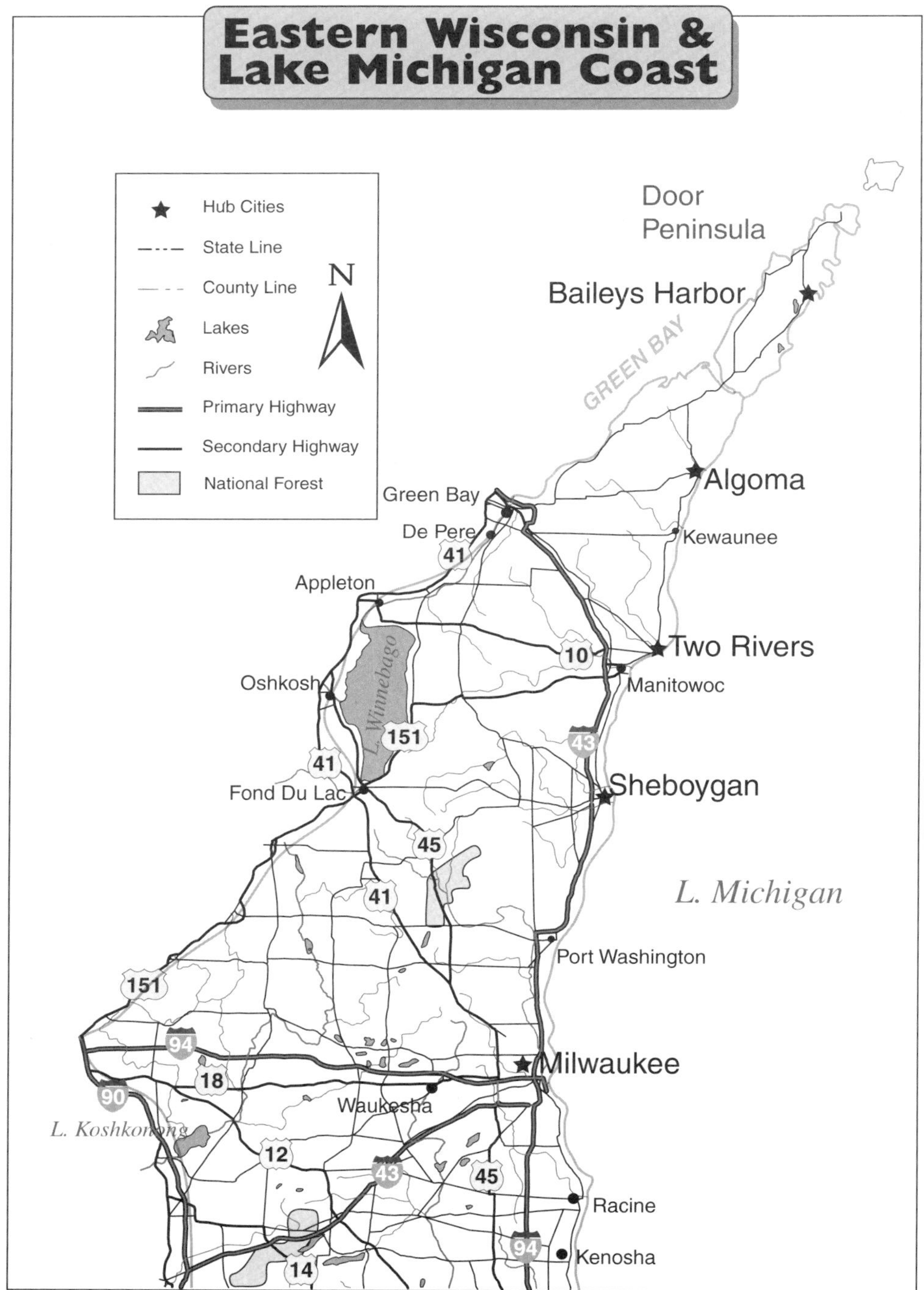
Eastern Wisconsin & Lake Michigan Coast
Hub Cities
State Line
County Line
Lakes
Rivers
Primary Highway
Secondary Highway
National Forest
N
Door Peninsula
Baileys Harbor
GREEN BAY
Algoma
Green Bay
De Pere
Kewaunee
41
Appleton
Two Rivers
10
Manitowoc
Oshkosh
L. Winnebago
151
43
41
Sheboygan
Fond Du Lac
45
L. Michigan
41
Port Washington
151
94
Milwaukee
18
90
Waukesha
L. Koshkonong
12
43
45
Racine
94
Kenosha
14
© 2006 Wilderness Adventures Press, Inc.

Eastern Wisconsin and Lake Michigan Coast

While most of this book focuses on inland trout and warmwater opportunities, eastern Wisconsin and the Lake Michigan shoreline provide a different landscape and a different set of challenges. First, this is the most industrialized part of Wisconsin, with over a million people in the Milwaukee area and hundreds of thousands more in the suburbs and cities adjacent to the lake. Green Bay, Appleton, and Oshkosh in the Fox River valley form their own urban belt, whose economy revolves around papermills and, of course, the Green Bay Packers.

Don't be put off by appearances; or, rather, don't think industrialized landscapes mean barren waters. If you're willing to fish in urban surroundings, you can enjoy some of the state's finest fishing. Kleftzsch Park on the Milwaukee River is a favorite with salmon and steelhead fishermen and is just a long cast away from some of Milwaukee's amenities. Racine's Root River, Kenosha's Pike River, and the Sheboygan River all offer high-quality salmon and steelhead fishing in urban settings. The

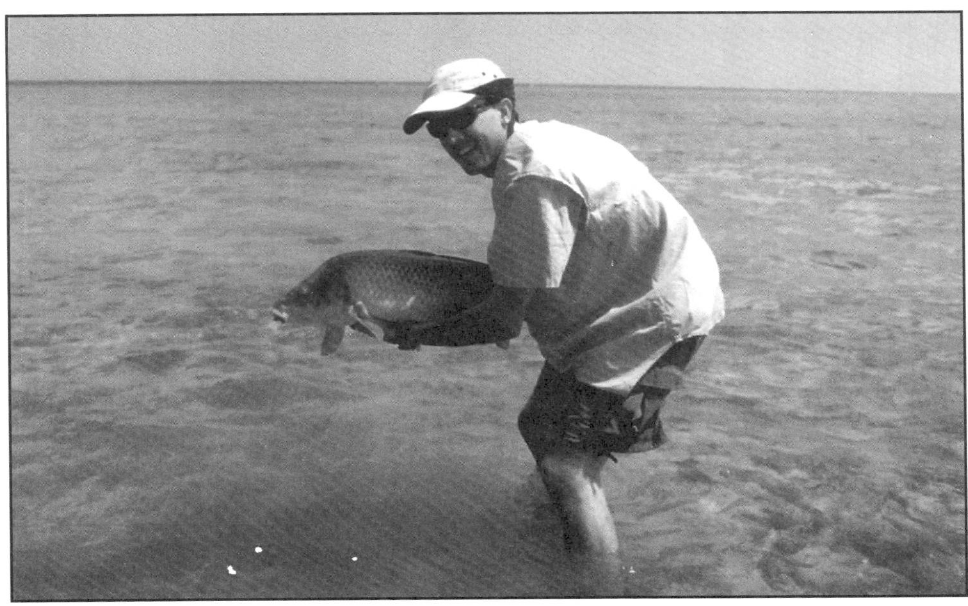

In addition to offering excellent steelhead and salmon fishing in its tributaries, Lake Michigan can yield huge carp to patient flyfishers who work the flats. (Sarah Landwehr)

HATCH CHART—Eastern Wisconsin and Lake Michigan Coast

Insect/Food Source	J	F	M	A	M	J	J	A	S	O	N	D	Flies
Midges	■	■	■	■	■	■	■	■	■	■	■	■	Midge Pupa #16-22; Griffith's Gnat #16-22
Blue-Winged Olives (*Baetis*)			■	■	■	■	■	■	■	■	■		BWO Thorax, Sparkle Dun #16-22; Pheasant Tail #16-18
Hendricksons				■	■								Light Hendrickson, Spinners #12-14; Pheasant Tail #12-14
Sulphurs					■								Sulphur Dun, Pale Evening Dun, Spinner #16; Pheasant Tail Nymph #16
Hexagenia (Evening Hatch)						■	■						Hart Washer, Hex, Olive Drake #4-8; Hex Nymph, Strip Nymph #4-8/Late June #10
Caddis			■	■	■	■	■	■	■				Elk Hair Caddis #14-16; Sparkle Pupa, Beadhead Caddis, Caddis Larvae #16-20
Stoneflies			■	■	■	■	■	■	■				Stimulators #10-12; Black Stonefly, Stonefly Nymphs #8-10
White Mayfly (*Ephoron leukon*) (Evening Hatch)						■	■	■					White Wulff, White Miller #12-14
Scuds	■	■	■	■	■	■	■	■	■	■	■	■	Pink, Olive, Tan Scuds #14-18

HATCH CHART—Eastern Wisconsin and Lake Michigan Coast (cont.)													
Insect/Food Source	**J**	**F**	**M**	**A**	**M**	**J**	**J**	**A**	**S**	**O**	**N**	**D**	**Flies**
Terrestrials							■	■	■				Hoppers #6-10; Crickets #10; Ants #14-20; Beetles #18-20
Crawfish	■	■	■	■	■	■	■	■	■	■	■	■	Crawfish Imitations #6-10; Brown/Olive Marabou Leech #4-8
Sculpin	■	■	■	■	■	■	■	■	■	■	■	■	Muddler Minnow, Woolly Bugger #4-10
Leeches	■	■	■	■	■	■	■	■	■	■	■	■	Marabou Leech, Strip Leech (Black, Olive, Brown) #4-10

entire lower Fox River from Appleton to its mouth at Green Bay, smokestacks notwithstanding, is rife with smallmouth and walleye, some attaining trophy size. If you like to pursue lake-run trout and salmon in prettier surroundings, drive a few hours north to fish the Kewaunee, Ahnapee, or the spring-run streams of Door County.

You should keep a few things in mind when fishing for Lake Michigan trout and salmon. These fish are not really eating, so the notion of matching the hatch can be discarded. They are here in an attempt to spawn—these streams are too warm to rear wild salmon and steelhead, so populations are maintained by stripping milt and roe and raising fingerlings in hatcheries—and basically have breeding on the mind. One biologist compared them to college students on spring break. Therefore, you have to entice, some would say harass, them into striking by floating bright streamers and egg patterns over them. Steelhead may feed a bit on eggs present in the streams, but annoyance and defending territory are their primary motives for striking. Purple Woolly Buggers, Egg Sucking Leeches, and egg patterns (all in sizes 4 through 10) are good bets for lake-run trout and salmon.

Leave the 5-weight at home and graduate to an 8- or 9-weight equipped with a reel that has lots of backing; you'll be fishing for salmonoids anywhere between 4 and 20 pounds. Another difference is the time of year you'll be fishing. Fall-run fish (Skamania and Chambers Creek steelhead as well as coho and chinook salmon and brown trout) start moving into Lake Michigan tributaries once the cold fronts of fall begin to sweep across Wisconsin. Spring-run steelhead (Ganaraska-strain) move into rivers as ice begins to go out in late winter. This means water temperatures from the 50s right on down to the mid-30s. Warm waders and insulated underwear are a must.

You will also need to purchase a Great Lakes Trout and Salmon stamp. Since these fish don't reproduce naturally, you will not affect populations by keeping an occasional fish for the grill. However, consult the DNR pamphlet *Choose Wisely: A Health Guide for Eating Fish in Wisconsin* before deciding to keep anything for the table. Because of PCBs found in Lake Michigan predator fish, women of child-bearing age and children need to be particularly mindful of these guidelines. In any case, trim away all fat and skin and use high-heat methods like grilling or broiling, as PCBs lodge in the fat of fish. None of this should interfere with the thrill of doing battle with a sleek silvery steelhead on a cold autumn day.

The Northern and Southern Units of Kettle Moraine State Forest also offer quality fishing opportunities in this region. Paradise Springs in the Southern Unit, just half an hour west of Milwaukee, is open from the first Saturday in January to September 30, giving trout fishermen somewhere to go in the dead of winter. The Northern Unit of Kettle Moraine State Forest has a number of no-motor lakes—good quiet venues for casting a fly to bluegills and bass. The shoreline of Door County, both the Green Bay and Lake Michigan sides, are smallmouth magnets. Look for rocks and you'll find smallmouth.

This steelhead is headed for the dinner table.

Root River

Fishing Racine's Root River is not for everyone. You may find yourself elbow-to-elbow during fall and spring steelhead runs. And the river's scenery, running through a city with 100,000 inhabitants, ranges from hardcore urban to suburban parks and golf courses. That said, however, it is planted with thousands of steelhead and salmon yearlings each year (making it one of the most-planted Lake Michigan tributaries) which grow big in Lake Michigan and return in an attempt to spawn several years later.

Anglers willing to tolerate crowds and less-than-pristine scenery might tussle with steelhead that routinely top 10 pounds and chinook salmon pushing 20 pounds. If fishing for you is primarily about solitude it might be best to sit this one out. I'd encourage anglers sitting on the fence to give this a try. Hooking a 10-pound steelhead gets the pulse pounding. If you don't like it, salve the sting at one of Milwaukee fine ethnic restaurants.

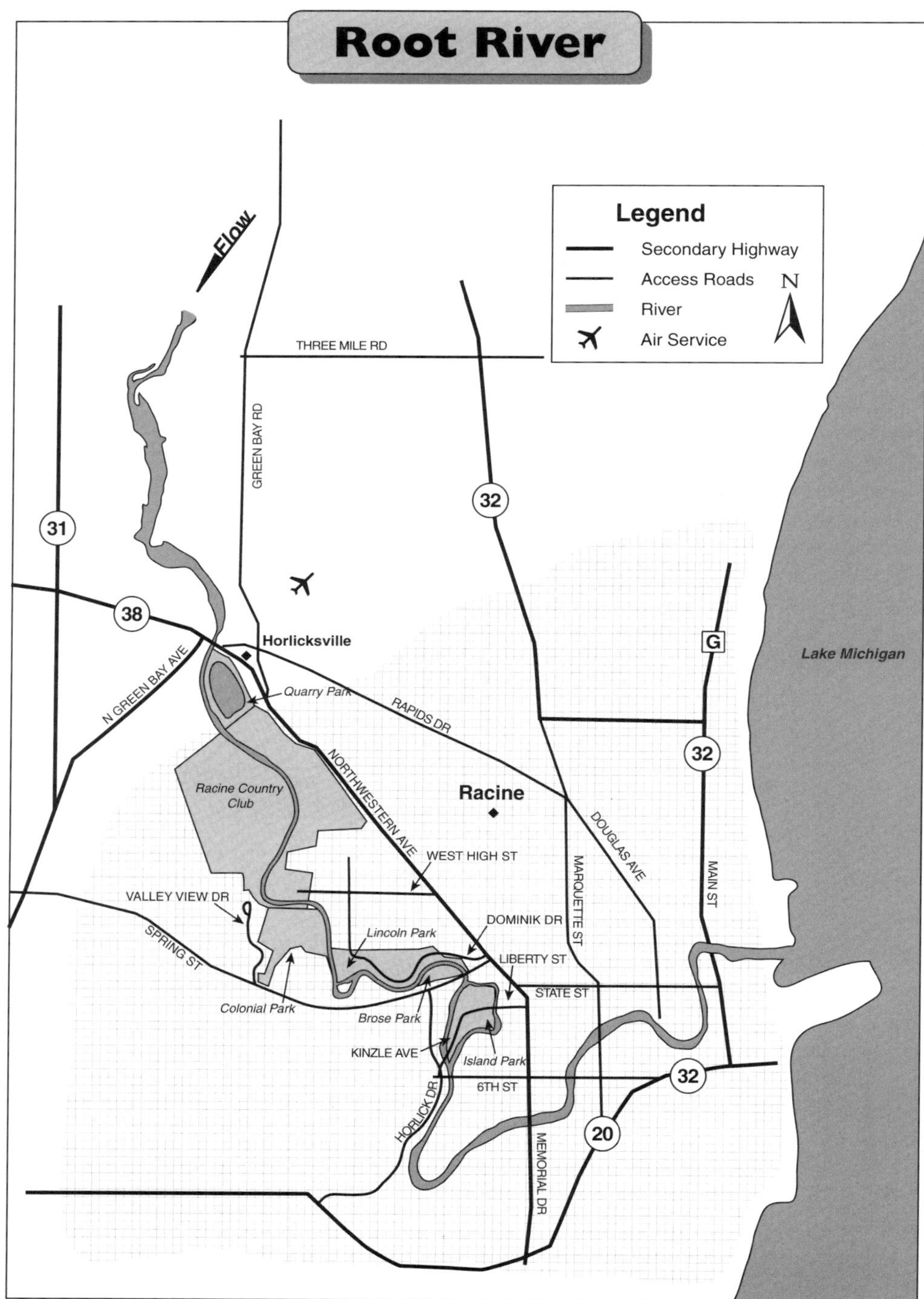
Root River
Legend
Secondary Highway
Access Roads
River
Air Service
N
Flow
THREE MILE RD
GREEN BAY RD
32
31
38
Horlicksville
G
Lake Michigan
N GREEN BAY AVE
Quarry Park
RAPIDS DR
32
NORTHWESTERN AVE
Racine Country Club
Racine
DOUGLAS AVE
WEST HIGH ST
MARQUETTE ST
MAIN ST
VALLEY VIEW DR
DOMINIK DR
SPRING ST
Lincoln Park
LIBERTY ST
STATE ST
Colonial Park
Brose Park
KINZLE AVE
Island Park
32
6TH ST
HORLICK DR
20
MEMORIAL DR

The Root River begins in Waukesha County near the suburb of New Berlin. It then runs some 40 miles southeast through Milwaukee and Racine Counties and empties into Lake Michigan at Racine Harbor. The majority of the Root River is not worth your time; it contains a few carp and suckers and not much else. The 8 miles (from the dam at Horlicksville to the mouth in Racine Harbor) are a temporary home to thousands of steelhead and salmon. Skip the upper reaches and concentrate your efforts here.

Pacific-strain salmon and steelhead were introduced to Lake Michigan in the 1960s and 1970s to boost a sagging lake trout fishery and to help control the alewife population. The DNR soon learned that these salmonoids grew to hefty proportions on alewife, and the resurgence of Lake Michigan's fishery began. However, Lake Michigan tributaries in Wisconsin lack the oxygen, cold water, and gravel beds for spawning. Thus, the DNR collects milt and roe from returning fish and raises fingerlings in hatcheries, which are eventually stocked back into Lake Michigan tributaries. Fish are detained at the weir in Lincoln Park on the Root River for this purpose. It's quite a thrill to see one of these big fish, let alone catch one.

The best fishing on the Root River—which does have its share of gravel runs, deep holes and fallen timber—occurs in a series of parks upstream from downtown Racine: Island Park, Brose Park, and up to the weir in Lincoln Park; above the weir in Colonial Park, the Racine Country Club, and Quarry Park. There are fewer fish above the weir—subject to what the DNR allows to pass upstream—and also fewer anglers.

The stretch of the Root River that runs through the Racine County Country Club is private; ask the country club for permission or keep your feet wet. The Horlicksville Dam, just above the country club, marks the end of salmon and steelhead water on the Root.

Access to Island Park can be had via Kinzie Avenue. Access to Brose and Lincoln Park is via Spring Street on the river's south side and Domanik Drive on the north side. To fish Colonial Park, use Valley View Drive (off Spring Street) on the south bank and West High Street (off Domanik Drive) on the north side. Access to the country club stretch is via the water in Colonial Park. Access to Quarry Park and the Horlicksville Dam is via Highway 38 and Highway MM.

Polarized sunglasses are helpful, as they allow the angler to spot finning fish and target them specifically. You can either sight-fish to those you see or fish structure. Deep holes, gravel runs, fallen trees, and overhanging banks provide good holding spots for fish. Think of places where a fish would rest undisturbed to store up energy for its fight against the current. Or look for would-be redds. The Root is a fairly small stream, usually 40 feet across or less, so wading works well. Consider piling on wool trousers or an extra pair of long underwear, as you'll be fishing in spring and fall water that is between 35 and 50 degrees.

Fishing for these large salmonoids presents a peculiar challenge. To begin with, these fish are not actively feeding, which makes attractor patterns an obvious choice. Woolly Buggers, Polar Shrimp, and Zonkers (size 4 to 10) are good choices. Even if these fish want to eat—a source of debate among anglers and biologists—these tributary streams generally lack the aquatic invertebrates that trout like. What they do have, in spades, is roe—eggs from salmon, eggs from steelhead, eggs from brown and brook trout, as well as eggs from suckers. Any pattern that imitates an egg or a clump of eggs will take fish. A Glo-Bug is a great fly.

Craig Amacker of Planet Trout Guide Service, and also the fishing manager of Fontana Sports in Madison, swears by a fly called Schmid's Egg Sucking Leech with a medium Marabou tail, a light hackle of peacock hurl, and a strand of two of chenille tied into the body. He also likes flies in the color purple because of their visibility. Black, red, orange, and white also fish well.

Amacker recommends a sinking line and a weighted leader called a poly leader (available for about $8 per leader at most fly shops) or a quad-tip ($120). Quad-tips are tie-on leader heads, carried in a wallet, that allow anglers to change the depth at which they fish by changing leader heads instead of entire lines. Split shot and a floating line will get you by in a pinch. Fish an 8- or 9-weight rod and a reel with plenty of backing. Steelhead tend to be more line-shy than salmon. You'll need to go down to a tippet of about 10-pound test.

The DNR stocks different strains of trout and salmon with the goal of providing a year-round fishery. Spring and fall are best, especially after heavy fall rain or spring snowmelt when home-scented water runs into Racine Harbor and activates the spawning instinct of these fish. Skamania-strain steelhead are summer spawners, which means they may be in the river as early as July or August.

Skamania runs peak when water temperatures begin to drop with the first cold front in September. Chambers Creek steelhead come into the Root in fall and winter. Ganaraska-strain steelhead typically spawn in April and May.

Steelhead will attempt to spawn from maturity until death. Coho and chinook salmon, fall spawners, have a fixed lifecycle of three and four years, respectively. They die after their attempt to spawn. Some large brown trout also make their way up the Root in an attempt to spawn in fall.

Stream Facts: Root River

Season
- All year

Regulations
- Daily bag limit 5 trout and salmon in total, only 2 may be lake trout; size limit 10 inches; from September 15 to May 1, fishing is prohibited a half-hour after sunset to a half-hour before sunrise

Miles of Trout Water
- 8 miles

Stream Characteristics
- Flows through urban setting with some park land; good pools and riffles and holding cover for salmon and steelhead; fish go as far as dam at Horlicksville.

Access
- Island Park, Lincoln Park, Colonial Park

Fly Shops
- The Fly Fishers, Laacke & Joy

Maps
- *Wisconsin Atlas and Gazetteer*, page 39

Pike River & Oak Creek

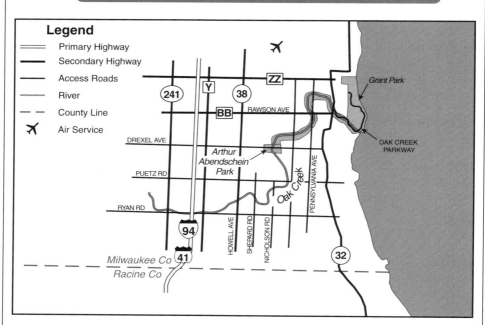

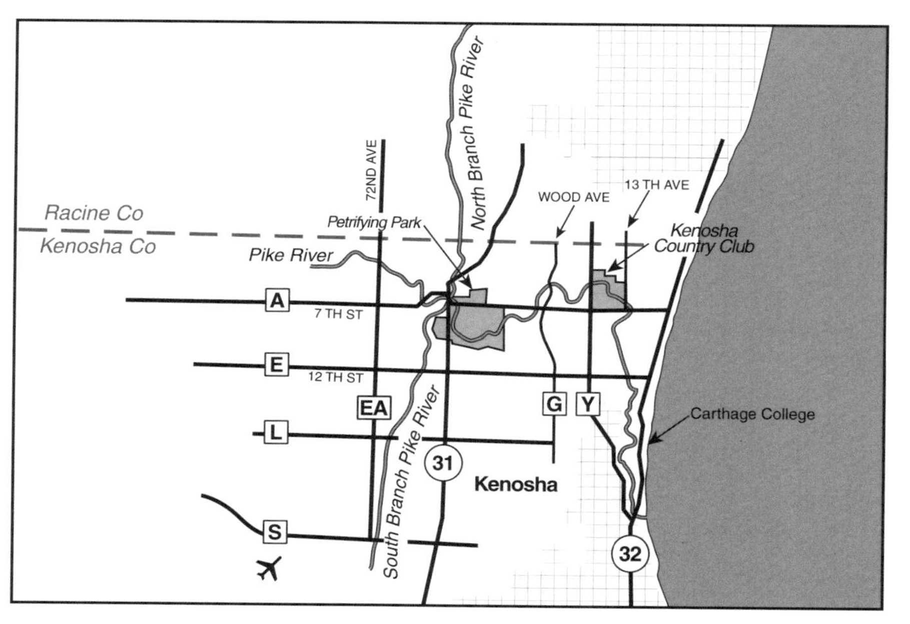

A happy angler releases a steelhead on the Pike River. (Craig Amacker)

Pike River

The Pike River in Kenosha and Racine Counties is another Lake Michigan tributary in an urban setting. You might call it a second-tier stream, as it is a smaller tributary that sometimes suffers from low flows and becomes blocked at the mouth by a sandbar.

The best fishing on the Pike is from Kenosha Harbor upstream to Petrifying Springs County Park. A few steelhead and salmon make it into the north and south branches of the Pike above Petrifying Springs County Park but not in sufficient numbers to warrant much attention.

Angler access is good at Kenosha Harbor and at the Pike River mouth, both on city land off Sheridan Road. Just upstream from here is Carthage College, along Highway 32 (Sheridan Road), and they are gracious about letting anglers fish on campus land along the river.

On what might be called the middle stretch of the Pike, between County E (12th Street) and Wood Avenue, land is private—owned by farmers, a golf course, and the Kenosha County Country Club. You will either need to gain permission or keep your feet wet here. A city bike path cuts through this stretch (between 13th Avenue and 7th Street) and provides a narrow ribbon of public access near the country club and dam.

Farther upstream is Petrifying Springs County Park, between Wood Avenue and Highway 31. There are several miles of access within the park and lots of good runs and holding water for steelhead and salmon; the surroundings are also pleasant and tree-lined.

Fewer fish are present on the north and south branches of the river. East-west roads bisecting Highway 31 provide access to these branches.

A word to the wise: landowner and angler relations (especially in tight urban quarters) only remain cordial when both parties respect each other. Do your part by avoiding trespassing and leaving the riverbank cleaner than you found it. And whatever you do, don't leave rough fish on the bank!

The Pike is planted generously with coho and chinook salmon, as well as three strains of steelhead. Brook and brown trout also find their way here in fall. While rain and snowmelt give the river enough flow to draw in fish from the harbor in most springs, the Pike often suffers from low water in fall. Call a Lake Michigan fly shop (The Fly Fishers in Milwaukee is a good bet at 414-259-8100) or visit the Internet to check the gaging station (www.crh.noaa.gov) on local rivers.

The usual assortment of egg patterns and leeches in sizes 6 to 10 will work well on the Pike. Given its small size, you'll need a finer leader (2X or 3X, 8-pound tippet). A sink-tip line is the best choice, but a floating line with a few split shot clipped to the leader will do in a small stream like the Pike. To fish the river mouth or harbor, you'll want to stick to a sinking or sink-tip line and an assortment of streamers. Racine and Kenosha Harbors are known for their coho populations.

Salmon, steelhead, brook, and brown trout are also present, as is the occasional smallmouth bass.

Oak Creek

Oak Creek is a small tributary that empties into Lake Michigan at South Milwaukee Harbor. It is some 15 miles in length, but only the lower 3 miles offer steelhead and salmon fishing; the other 12 miles comprise an urban river of little interest to the angler. The dam just above Mill Road prevents fish from going upstream, where carp and suckers are the predominant species. Since only a small portion of the creek sees steelhead and salmon runs, these fish are more concentrated than on the Milwaukee River to the north and the Root River to the south.

Access to this portion of Oak Creek is good since it flows mainly through Grant Park. And this makes for pleasant enough surroundings in which to fish. From north-south Highway 32, take Oak Creek Parkway to the east and you'll cross Oak Creek twice. Mill Road is the last road crossing before the dam.

Fish the usual assortment of egg patterns (orange or pink) and flashy (pink, black, or purple) Marabou Leeches. The 26 lunker structures and streambank stabilization completed by the DNR in 1990 help Oak Creek hold more fish.

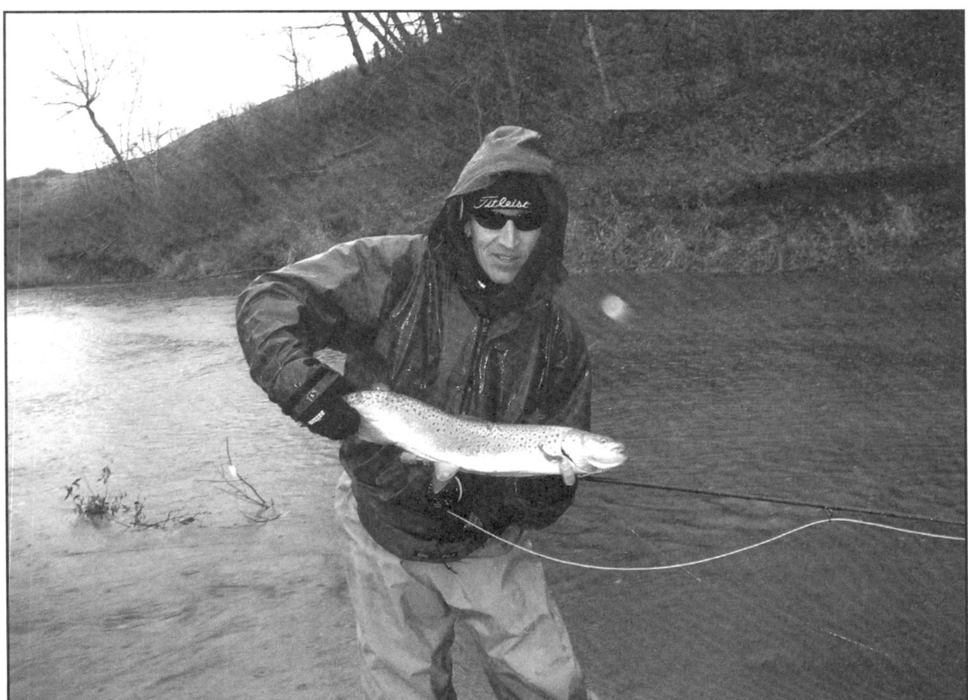

A nice lake-run brown. (Craig Amacker)

Pat Ehlers of The Fly Fishers, a Milwaukee fly shop, finds rainbow and brook trout congregating near the mouth of Oak Creek in spring and fall. He fishes from shore with a 5-weight with a sink-tip line. A Mickey Finn is his fly of choice for picking up fish in the 12- to 15-inch range. Oak Creek is a small stream that is good to fish when larger tributaries are too high. It also warms faster than the larger tributaries and, hence, sees runs of fish as early as late February or early March.

Milwaukee River

If you don't mind fishing smack dab in the middle of Wisconsin's largest city you can enjoy some fine steelhead and salmon fishing on the Milwaukee River. With the breaching of Milwaukee's North Avenue Dam in 1997, salmon and steelhead go as far upstream as Grafton, adding 20 miles of river to the fishery. County parks in North Milwaukee afford good access to the river. Both Craig Amacker of Planet Trout and Pat Ehlers of The Fly Fishers comment on the surprising aesthetics of fishing the Milwaukee River. Fishing in these tree-lined parks, they say, the angler might forget he's in a metropolitan area home to over a million people.

I'll describe the Milwaukee County parks from south to north. Hubbard Park is located just south of East Capitol Drive (called Highway 190 on some maps). Follow

North Humboldt Avenue to fish the west side of the river; follow North Oakland Avenue for the east side. The next park north is Estabrook Park, located between East Capitol Drive and East Hampton Road (Highway EE on some maps). Craig Amacker likes this stretch, which contains lots of riffles and spawning gravel and (if one stretches the imagination a bit) could be taken for a Western freestone river.

There is plenty of room to throw a cast in most of the county parks, and crowding, ironically enough, is not much of an issue. The next county park to the north is Kleftzsch Park in Glendale. This park contains a small waterfall, which can be a fish barrier in low-water years. Find Kleftzsch Park between West Bender Road and Green Tree Road. This is another pretty park with good riffles and gravel and holding places for fish.

Depending on water levels, fish may or may not make it above the waterfall in Kleftzsch Park. Even in a wet year fish populations are denser below the waterfall. Another obstacle for the angler is the dearth of public land above Kleftzsch. Above Brown Deer Road and in the village of Mequon, the Milwaukee River runs through some pretty exclusive real estate. Public access from here north is limited to road crossings: County Line Road, Mequon Road, Highland Road, Pioneer Road/County C, and Lakefield Road/County T.

The rocky Milwaukee River is also home to smallmouth bass, even above Grafton, where access is easier. Highway 57 and then Highway H follow this upper stretch of the Milwaukee.

Pat Ehlers of The Fly Fishers notes that purple has been a good fly color for Lake Michigan salmon and steelhead in recent years. He believes, however, that presentation is more important than color. Gracefully drop a fly in front of a steelhead's nose, and there is a good chance he'll strike, even if it's unfamiliar. Make a sloppy cast with the right fly and you're not likely to hook-up. Pat likes to fish a size 8 or 10 caddis larvae on a dropper, 12 to 18 inches off a larger attractor pattern such as a Woolly Bugger.

Plantings of three strains of steelhead in the Milwaukee River help to provide fall, over-winter, and spring fishing. Browns, brook trout, and salmon are also present. Stream improvements made in 1997 (bank stabilization, planting of trees, placing boulders in the stream) help to provide resting places and cover for trout and salmon.

Stream Facts: Milwaukee River

Season
- All year

Regulations
- Daily bag limit 5 trout and salmon in total, only 2 may be lake trout; size limit 10 inches; from September 15 to May 1, fishing is prohibited a half-hour after sunset to a half-hour before sunrise.

Miles of Trout Water
- 25 miles

Stream Characteristics
- Flows through urban setting with some park land; good pools and riffles and holding cover for salmon and steelhead; fish go as far as dam at Grafton.

Access
- Hubbard, Estabrook, and Kleftzsch Parks

Fly Shops
- The Fly Fishers, Laacke & Joy

Maps
- *Wisconsin Atlas and Gazetteer*, page 39

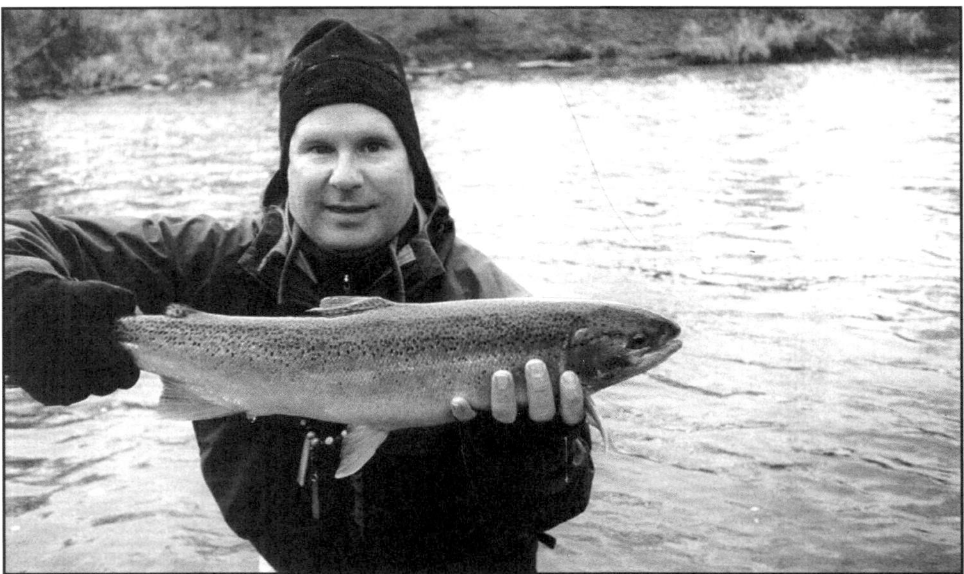

Steelhead are a blast on a fly rod. (Craig Amacker)

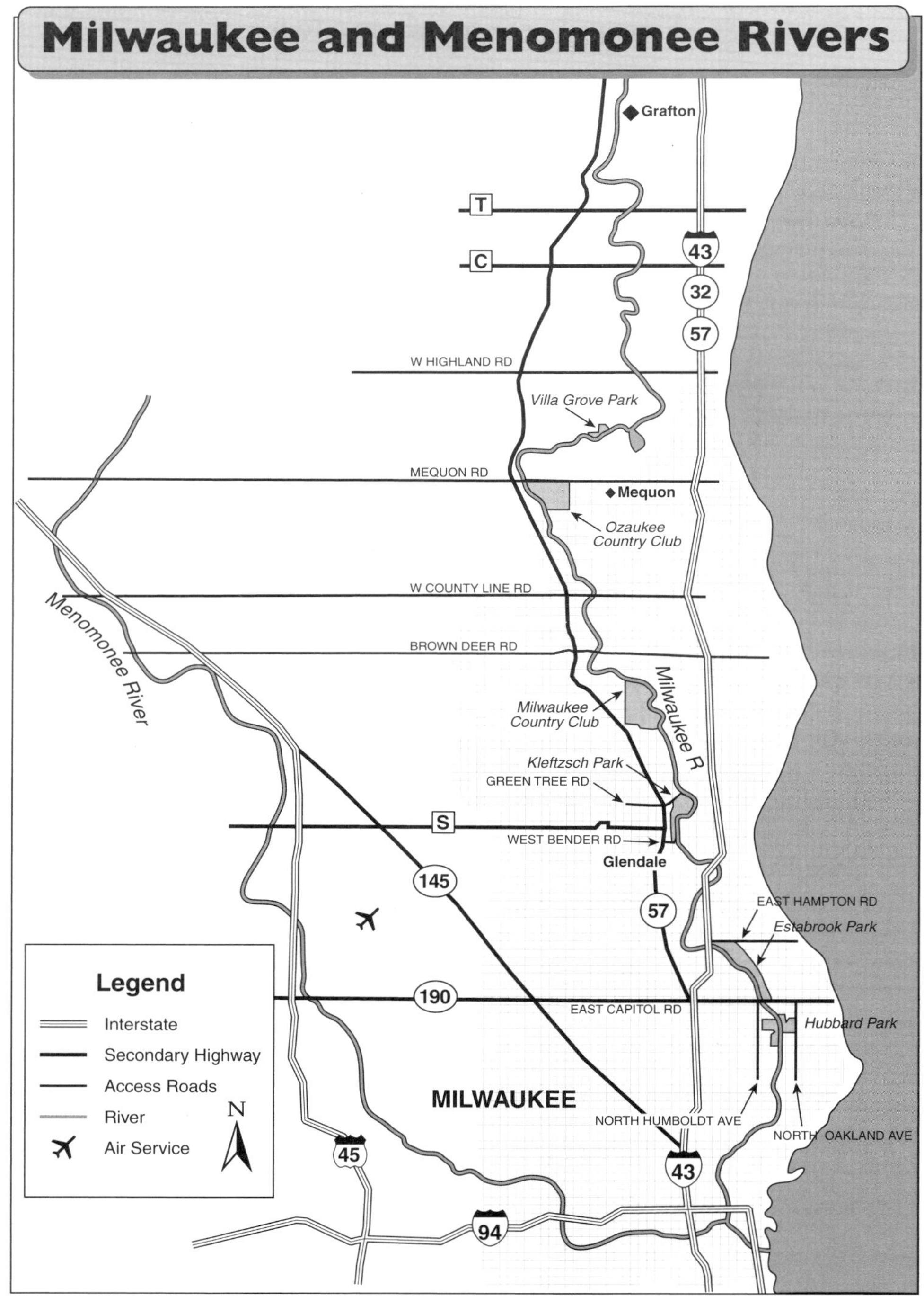
Milwaukee and Menomonee Rivers
Grafton
T
43
C
32
57
W HIGHLAND RD
Villa Grove Park
MEQUON RD
Mequon
Ozaukee Country Club
W COUNTY LINE RD
Menomonee River
BROWN DEER RD
Milwaukee R
Milwaukee Country Club
Kleftzsch Park
GREEN TREE RD
S
WEST BENDER RD
Glendale
145
57
EAST HAMPTON RD
Estabrook Park
Legend
Interstate
Secondary Highway
Access Roads
River
Air Service
190
EAST CAPITOL RD
Hubbard Park
MILWAUKEE
N
NORTH HUMBOLDT AVE
NORTH OAKLAND AVE
45
43
94

The Menomonee River

The Menomonee River is another urban fishery located on the western edge of Milwaukee and flowing into the Milwaukee River from the northwest. The best stretch of the Menomonee is near Miller Park Stadium (once known as County Stadium) off Interstate 94. This stretch has seen recent clean-up and habitat work. Take the Miller Park Way exit from Interstate 94 toward the river where you will find plenty of parking on county ground.

According to Pat of The Fly Fishers, water levels on the Menomonee rise and fall quickly. Fish it during a rain, as water levels are coming up, and you should find fresh-run fish. It's also a good stream to hit once it falls if the larger Milwaukee and Root are too high. The Menomonee sees both spring and fall runs of steelhead and salmon.

Fox River

Pat Ehlers of The Fly Fishers in Milwaukee recommends the Fox River in western Racine County as a good stream to wade for smallmouth. Pat is a guru of Wisconsin warmwater fly fishing, so his recommendations should be well-heeded. A good smallmouth rod for medium-sized rivers like the Fox is an 8-foot, 6-weight. Fish leech or minnow patterns with a bit of split shot on a floating line. Pat often fishes a dropper rig for smallmouth, a size 8 nymph 18 inches below a popper; the popper acts as both a strike indicator and a potential meal. Sweep this rig past rocky ledges or deadfalls and keep your eye on the popper!

The Fox River exits Tichigan Lake in Waterford and flows south some 30 miles before crossing the Illinois border. Pat fishes the stretch between Waterford and Burlington, about 10 miles of water. Smallmouth are also present in smaller numbers in the 20 miles between Burlington and the Illinois line. This lower stretch flows through the scenic Karcher Marsh State Wildlife Area near New Munster. White bass, northern pike, and rough fish are also present in the Fox River.

Access to the Waterford-Burlington stretch is via Highway 36; below Burlington, Highway 83 (then Highway B) runs along the river. The Fox is just a short drive from Milwaukee on Highway 36. From Beloit/Janesville, take Highway 43 north to Highway 11 west, which joins Highway 36 in Burlington. From Madison, take Interstate 90 east to Waukesha and take Highway 164 south to Waterford.

Kettle Moraine State Forest–Southern Unit

Kettle Moraine State Forest's southern unit features 18,000 acres of wooded land with long glacial ridges known as moraines and bowl-shaped depressions known as kettles. The landscape is the result of retreating glaciers ten thousand years ago. Hiking, mountain biking, and cross-country skiing opportunities abound. A number of good fly fishing opportunities exist here as well, which seems almost amazing given its proximity to Milwaukee.

Paradise Springs offers winter trout fishing for wild and planted fish. The South Branch of the Scuppernong River, just west of Paradise Springs, is a respectable little trout stream. Ottawa Lake is a no-motor lake stocked with trout and with a self-sustaining population of bass and panfish. Rice Lake, located near the town of Whitewater, offers a quiet fishery for bass and panfish in its weedbeds. Bluff Creek just to the north of Rice Lake holds trout.

Paradise Springs

Paradise Springs makes good on its name in at least one respect: it offers anglers a place to try for trout while Wisconsin's inland streams are closed to trout fishing. Located in the Southern Unit of Kettle Moraine State Forest just 30 miles west of Milwaukee, it is a small spring pond open to trout fishing from January 1 to the end of the regular trout season on September 30. Fishing here is catch-and-release and artificials only.

Water conditions are ideal for trout—47 degrees year-round with a spring that pumps out 5,000 gallons a minute of cold water; snails, sowbugs, and caddis abound in its weeds and sandy bottom. Wild brown and brook trout, bolstered by stocking, are also present. You can reach it from the town of Eagle in southwestern Waukesha County by taking Highway N north from Highway 59. You will need a park day pass or sticker to fish Paradise Springs, which you can buy at park headquarters in Eagle.

The outflow of Paradise Springs, from County N to its juncture with the Scuppernong River, is a category 3 trout stream. It's open to catch-and-release, artificial-only trout fishing with barbless hooks from the first Saturday in March to the last Sunday before the start of May gamefish season.

Paradise Springs trout are not naïve Northwoods brookies. They live within a half-hour of the state's largest city and have the sophistication to show for it. Most have been caught by anglers; all have seen a variety of flies and spinners tossed at them. Use fine tippet, make careful casts, and keep your profile down. You might try presenting an unorthodox attractor pattern new to these discriminating fish. At the very least you'll be able to wallow in the novelty of winter trout fishing in Wisconsin. The remains of an old hotel and springhouse hint at its past status as a fishing preserve for the well-heeled. Access to the pond is good from a paved trail. There's also a handicapped casting platform on the pond.

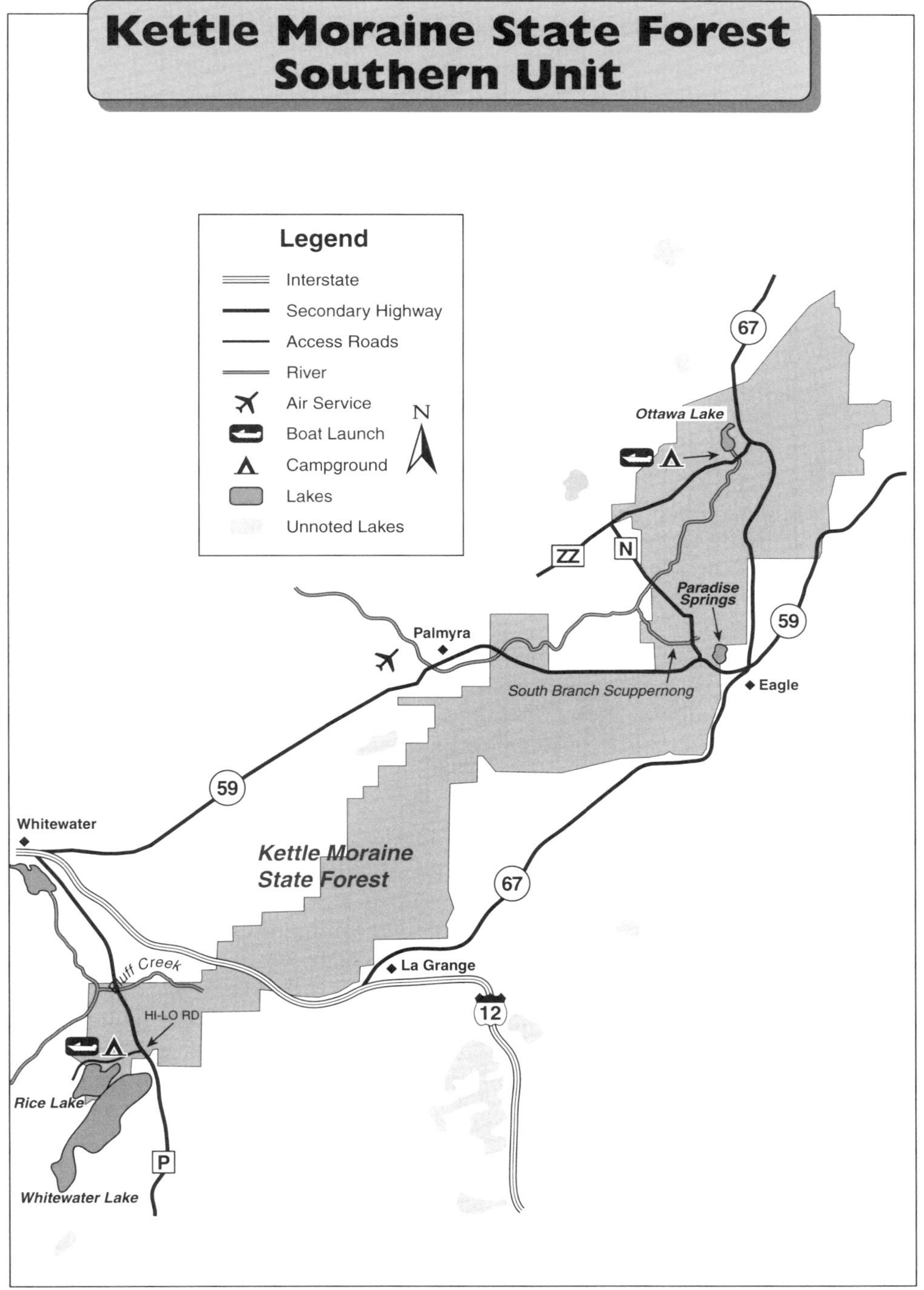
Kettle Moraine State Forest
Southern Unit
Legend
Interstate
Secondary Highway
Access Roads
River
Air Service
Boat Launch
Campground
Lakes
Unnoted Lakes
N
67
Ottawa Lake
ZZ
N
Paradise Springs
59
Palmyra
South Branch Scuppernong
Eagle
59
Whitewater
Kettle Moraine State Forest
67
uff Creek
La Grange
12
HI-LO RD
Rice Lake
P
Whitewater Lake

South Branch of the Scuppernong River

This 1.5-mile tributary of the Scuppernong River crosses Highway 59 in Waukesha County just east of the Jefferson County line and joins the Scuppernong River about a mile north of the road crossing. It's a narrow stream containing wild and planted brown trout, and it runs through the Scuppernong Wildlife Area within the Kettle Moraine State Forest.

Given its clarity and small size, anglers will need to approach it with care in order to take fish. It is a category 3 trout stream—open to catch-and-release, artificials-only trout fishing with barbless hooks from the first Saturday in March to the last Sunday before May gamefish season; from the first Saturday in May to September 30, 3 trout may be kept with a minimum size of 9 inches. This stream is noteworthy because southeast Wisconsin has few trout streams; if it occurred in trout-rich western or central Wisconsin, it probably wouldn't bear mentioning.

Ottawa Lake

Tiny Ottawa Lake, at just under 40 acres, packs a good wallop as far as fly-fishing opportunities are concerned. First, only electric motors are allowed, making for a quiet atmosphere conducive to fly fishing. Trout are planted in this spring-fed lake and can be taken on egg, nymph, or streamer patterns. Trout season runs from the first Saturday in May to September 30; 3 trout may be kept with a minimum size of 9 inches.

Bass and panfish frequent the weeds around the lake, as do a few northern pike. There is a launch on the southwest side off County ZZ, and Ottawa Lake's small size means a canoe or belly-boat can cover its water in a morning or afternoon. Ottawa Lake campground (showers, flush toilets, and some sites with electricity) and a swimming beach are also located on the lake.

Rice Lake

Located on the western edge of the Kettle Moraine State Forest in Walworth County, Rice Lake is a shallow lake with moderate boat traffic. Paul Sandgren, the superintendent for the Southern Kettle Moraine, recommends it as a lake with good panfish and bass populations in its numerous shoreline weeds. Sandgren says that even though it is used by motorboats the lake's shallow nature keeps boat traffic down. Find it off Highway P south of the town of Whitewater; a launch can be found on the northern edge of the lake off Hi-Lo Road as well as at the state forest campground.

Larger Whitewater Lake, connected by a small channel, is another good bass, panfish, and pike lake. However, it sees heavy boat traffic and is best fished very early in the morning.

Bluff Creek

Located just south of the town of Whitewater, Bluff Creek is a small stream with a population of stocked and wild brown trout. Paul Sandgren, superintendent for the

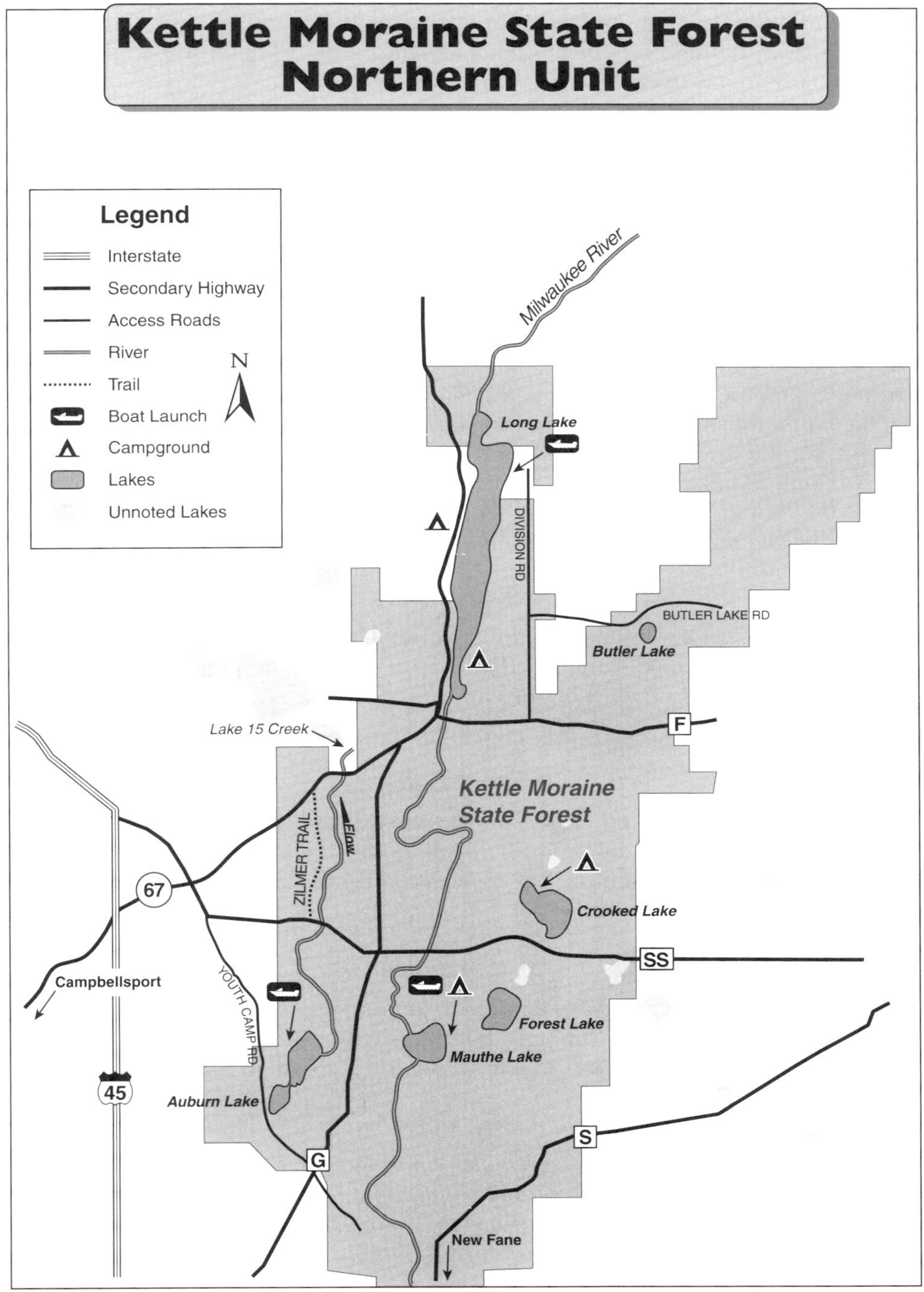
Kettle Moraine State Forest
Northern Unit
Legend
Interstate
Secondary Highway
Access Roads
River
Trail
Boat Launch
Campground
Lakes
Unnoted Lakes
N
Milwaukee River
Long Lake
DIVISION RD
BUTLER LAKE RD
Butler Lake
Lake 15 Creek
F
Kettle Moraine
State Forest
ZILMER TRAIL
Flow
67
Crooked Lake
SS
Campbellsport
YOUTH CAMP RD
Forest Lake
Mauthe Lake
45
Auburn Lake
S
G
New Fane

Southern Kettle Moraine, recommends it as a good trout stream. Trout are found above Highway P. Bluff Creek is category 4. During the early March and April season it is open to catch-and-release fishing with barbless flies.

Kettle Moraine State Forest—Northern Unit

A number of the lakes within the Northern Unit of the Kettle Moraine State Forest offer something special to the angler who likes quiet canoe fishing: no motors and restricted-wake lakes in a beautiful glaciated setting. There's also a brook trout stream here, Lake 15 Creek, with planted and wild fish.

Mauthe Lake

Located off Highway S just north of the town of New Fane in Fond du Lac County, no-motor Mauthe Lake offers 78 acres of unspoiled fishing for anglers willing to paddle for their fish. There are northern pike, largemouth bass, walleye, and panfish present. It's a kettle lake without a lot of obvious structure. Fish the shoreline weeds and dropoffs. Mauthe Lake is popular with flyfishers who wade along the shoreline, says Deb Coblantz, chief law enforcement ranger for the Northern Kettle Moraine. A canoe or belly boat would also work well.

Auburn Lake

Auburn Lake is just a stone's throw off Highway G. The lake covers 107 acres with a maximum depth of 29 feet. You'll find northern pike, walleye, largemouth, and panfish. Access is off County G on the east side of the lake and off Scout Camp Road on the west. No motors are allowed on Auburn Lake.

Forest Lake

This 51-acre lake is catch-and-release for all gamefish, although panfish may be kept. It is also a no-motor lake. Coblantz says that there are big walleye, northerns, and bass in Forest Lake because of the catch-and-release regulations. Find it just northeast of Mauthe Lake.

Butler Lake

This tiny, no-motor lake was once stocked with rainbow trout. A few of them should still be around, according to Coblantz, but the real draw is northern pike, bass, and panfish. This clear spring-fed lake is just 7 acres and is also a no-motor lake.

Long Lake

At 417 acres and 47 feet deep, Long Lake is the largest and deepest of the Kettle Moraine lakes. Big largemouth bass and respectable northerns and bluegills are the name of the game here. Its slow, no-wake rule (from 6 pm to 10 am in summer) helps keep the lake angler-friendly. Water skiing is allowed on Wednesday nights. There are three public launches off Division Road on the east side of the lake. You'll find bass, northerns, and panfish along the weedy shoreline. Take Highway 67 north out of Campbellsport to get to Long Lake.

Crooked lake

Crooked Lake tops out 32 feet deep and covers 91 acres. It is a mud-bottomed lake, as opposed to the sandy bottoms of most Kettle Moraine lakes. Northerns, bass, and panfish can be caught here. It's located just north of Highway SS, northeast of Mauthe Lake.

Lake 15 Creek

Perhaps the biggest surprise about the Northern Kettle Moraine is the brook trout stream running through it. Access to this creek is via Zilmer Trail and the Highway SS bridge. It's a brushy creek with wild and planted brook trout, according to Coblantz. Difficult to fish but pretty.

The Crawfish River

The Crawfish River rises west of Columbus in southeastern Wisconsin and snakes its way through a patchwork of farms and woodlots for some 50 miles before emptying into the larger Rock River near the town of Jefferson. Like many Wisconsin rivers, it is virtually unknown to anglers who prefer the familiar terrain of well-fished lakes and concrete launch ramps. However, for the angler willing to wade or paddle its many miles of fine fish habitat, the Crawfish offers a good mixed-bag fishery for warmwater species. Northern pike loll in the mouths of cool feeder creeks in its middle reaches, walleye frequent its deep channels, and white bass schools can be found just about anywhere in the river. If carp are your thing, try sight-casting to them in the shallows below the Milford Bridge. Smallmouth, while not a mainstay on the Crawfish, can be found in rocky bottom stretches above Mud Lake.

The only problem with the Crawfish, if it can be called a problem, is lack of access. Putting in at bridges with a small boat or canoe is one way to handle this. I like this approach because many of the best stretches of the Crawfish, as with so many Wisconsin rivers, lie hidden from view between bridges. The other approach is on foot. Since the Crawfish can be too deep and/or muddy to wade, you will likely cross private land, which means you will need landowner permission.

Between Columbus and the Highway 19 bridge in Hubbleton, a variety of micro-habitats can be found: fallen trees, springs and feeder creeks, marsh, rocky bottoms, and faster runs. Northern pike, channel catfish, and white bass are the mainstays here. Bridge crossing are at Highway TT north and south of Astico, Highway I, Highway BB, and Highway G and Highway 19 in Hubbleton. This is a good stretch for floating. Where there is structure, there will be fish. Look for springs or stream inflows, fallen trees, little riffles, and bankside eddies. A dark leech is a good fly choice. There's also a developed launch in the widespread of the Crawfish known as Mud Lake in the Mud

Lake State Wildlife Area; out of Hubbleton, follow Highway QQ along the east side of the river to the wildlife area and launch ramp.

Below Hubbleton and Mud Lake, the river takes on a decidedly wider character, going from something a good fly caster might throw a line across to a wide, deep waterway. Channel catfish and carp are common here. Unless you really like to go after rough fish on a fly rod, skip the lower reaches of the Crawfish.

Rock Lake

I've always had an affinity for marshes. Maybe that's because I love to duck hunt, and fishing gives me a way to visit marshes in the off-season. Maybe it's because they do such an important service for our environment, filtering out pollutants, acting as natural flood control structures and playing host to a wide variety of bird, plant, mammal, and amphibian life.

What does this have to do with Rock Lake? Well, Rock Lake is fine in its own right, although a little crowded with bass boats and water skiers. You can catch smallmouth and walleye on its rocky east shore and largemouth in its west shore weeds. But the good news about 1,100-acre Rock Lake is little Marsh Lake, which is attached to it. Separated from the main lake by an abandoned railroad trestle, Marsh Lake's shallow weedy waters are a haven for big bluegill and largemouth bass. Things are also a lot quieter than on Rock Lake. Bluegill can be found over the lake's abundant weedbeds, as can some dandy largemouth bass; crappies can be taken among its stumps. A free launch is located south of Marsh Lake on County A in the Lake Mills Wildlife Area. Or launch for a small fee off Sandy Beach Road and save yourself the paddle.

A nice smallmouth comes to the net.

HUB CITY: MILWAUKEE

Milwaukee is Wisconsin's largest city, with a population of over 600,000. Immigrants from all over the globe have called Milwaukee home for 150 years, and the city's ethnic diversity is reflected in its diverse eateries. (Ballisteri's for Italian, Conejito's for Mexican, King and I for Thai, and Three Brothers for Serbian, as listed below, are a few well-known establishments.) Also, the Milwaukee Public Museum is famous for its natural history dioramas.

Strangely enough, some of Wisconsin's best tributary fishing for trout and salmon can be found within easy driving distance of Milwaukee—and in the Milwaukee River itself, where dam removal and habitat improvement have opened up some 20 miles of the river to trout and salmon. The Menomonee River and Oak Creek, as well as Root and Pike Rivers to the south, offer fishing for anadromous trout and salmon. Rock Lake and the Crawfish River are probably a touch closer to Madison than Milwaukee.

Accommodations

Pfister Hotel, 424 E. Wisconsin, Milwaukee; 800-558-8222; Milwaukee's oldest hotel, known for fine accommodations; /$$$

Best Western, 710 N. Old World Third Street, Milwaukee; 866-597-9330; centrally located near many attractions; $$

Super 8 Motel–Airport, 5253 S. Howell Avenue; 800-800-8000

Campgrounds

Kohler Andre State Park, 1520 Beach Park Lane, Sheboygan; 920-451-4080; 30 miles north of Milwaukee and on Lake Michigan

Kettle Moraine State Forest–Northern Unit, Box 410, Campbellsport; 262-626-2116; excellent hiking, camping, warmwater lake fishing in unique glacial scenery 40 miles northwest of Milwaukee

Kettle Moraine State Forest–Southern Unit, Highway 59, Eagle; 262-594-6200; camping, hiking and glacial scenery 30 miles southwest of Milwaukee; Paradise Springs open to trout fishing from January to September 30

Restaurants

Conejito's Place, 539 W. Virginia Street, Milwaukee; 414-278-9106; popular Milwaukee Mexican restaurant

King and I Thai Restaurant, 823 N. 2nd Street; 414-276-4181; Milwaukee's first Thai restaurant, downtown location

Three Brother's Serbian Restaurant, 2414 S. Saint Clair, Milwaukee; 414-481-7530; unmatched Old World cooking served in southside neighborhood restaurant, reservations suggested; don't miss the roast goose and the Serbian salad

Ballisteri's, 812 N. 68th Street, Milwaukee; 414-475-1414; Milwaukee's best-known casual Italian restaurant

Brew City Brew Pub, 1114 N. Water Street, Milwaukee; 414-278-7033; good micro-brewery that serves BBQ, located near dozens of other watering holes

Fly Shops, Outfitters, Sporting Goods

The Fly Fishers, 9617 W. Greenfield Avenue, Milwaukee; 414-259-8100; guides and fly fishing service near Milwaukee

Laacke and Joy's, 1433 N. Water Street, Milwaukee; 414-271-7878; sporting goods store with good fly fishing section

Bob's Silver Doctor Fly Fishing, P.O. Box 105, Viroqua; 608-637-3417; Guides on spring creeks and Lake Michigan steelhead.

Cabela's, One Cabela Way (Richfield 53076) / 262-628-5700 / www.cabelas.com

Veterinarians

State Street Dog and Cat Hospital, 4634 State Street, Milwaukee; 414-258-3090

Medical

Froedert Memorial Hospital, 9200 W. Wisconsin, Milwaukee; 414-259-1811

Auto Rental

Enterprise (414-294-5880), **National** (414-483-9800) and others located at General Mitchell International Airport

Automobile Repair

Car-X Muffler and Brakes, 1141 N. 3rd Street, Milwaukee; 414-289-0400

Air Service

General Mitchell International Airport, 5300 Howell Avenue; 414-582-5000

For More Information

Milwaukee Visitor Information
510 W. Kilbourn
Milwaukee, WI
414-273-7222

A flyfisher works the waters of Port Washington Harbor, a hotspot for trout and salmon in spring and autumn.

PORT WASHINGTON HARBOR

If you find Lake Michigan's tributaries too low or crowded, try fishing inside the breakwater at Port Washington Harbor. Spring and fall find these shallow waters in the preferred range for trout and salmon—40 to 50 degrees. Warmwater discharges from the Port Washington Power Plant help draw in baitfish and salmonoids.

In good weather, harbor waters (from boat launches and north along the inside arm of the breakwater) can be waded or fished from a float tube. Craig Amacker of Planet Trout Guide Service in Madison likes to fish here with a sink-tip line. He fishes Zonkers and Clousers. At times rainbow trout can be seen taking flies from the surface. In these cases, try fishing a big visible dry fly like a White Wulff. (Quad-tips, made by both Cortland and Scientific Anglers, allow you to switch leader heads without changing fly lines. Simply select the leader head that best fits conditions.) All species of trout cruise these shallows. You might also tie into a coho or chinook salmon. Northern pike and smallmouth bass are present in modest numbers. Use an 8- or 9-weight rod and a reel with plenty of backing.

Sauk Creek, which flows into Port Washington Harbor, also sees a modest run of fall salmon and steelhead and spring and summer runs of Ganaraska- and Skamania-strain steelhead. It is accessible via Highway 32 and Highway KK (Moore Road).

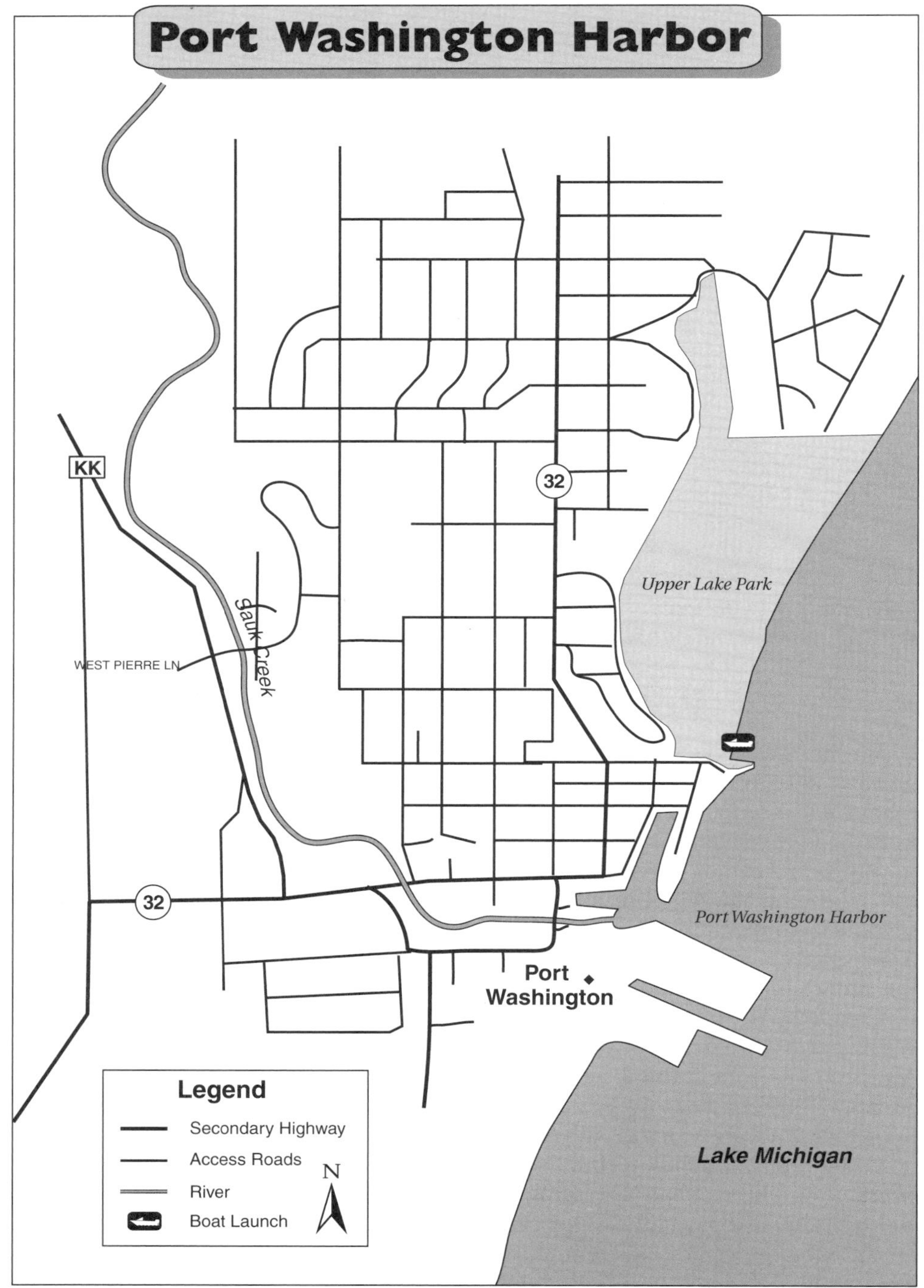
Port Washington Harbor
KK
32
32
Upper Lake Park
Sauk Creek
WEST PIERRE LN
Port Washington Harbor
Port Washington
Lake Michigan
Legend
Secondary Highway
Access Roads
River
Boat Launch
N

Pigeon River

The Pigeon River just north of Sheboygan is a pretty steelhead stream rated as class two by the DNR. This means it lacks the conditions (predictable flow and over-winter habitat) to support fall-run and over-wintering salmonoids. Thus, the DNR stocks 6,500 Ganaraska-strain steelhead, a spring-run fish, in the Pigeon each year. These fish return to the Pigeon except in the driest of springs. While you also might find trout and salmon here in a rainy autumn, you are best served fishing the Pigeon in spring, from ice-out to early May.

The Pigeon is a small tributary, similar to a trout stream in appearance, with good cover and clear water. It receives less fishing pressure than the Sheboygan, Manitowoc, and Twin Rivers, making it a pleasant place to spend a spring afternoon.

The Pigeon River flows into Lake Michigan just north of Sheboygan and begins above the Sheboygan/Manitowoc County line east of the town of Kiel. It is roughly paralleled by Highway 42 for most of its length. Access to the Pigeon is mainly at road crossings (listed from the mouth upstream): Highway LS, Highway AB, Highway 42, Highway 43, Highway Y, Highway J, Rangeline Road, Playbird Road, Highway JJ, and Highway 42, which follows the Pigeon up to the county line. Concentrate your efforts from Highway 43 down to the river mouth, as the upstream reaches get kind of tight.

Given the clarity and small size of the Pigeon, you will need to tone down your approach. Use finer leader (3X with 8-pound tippet), smaller flies (size 6 or 8 Woolly Buggers, size 10 egg patterns), and wade carefully.

The author with a Pigeon River steelhead destined for the smoker.

A trophy from the Sheboygan. (Craig Amacker)

Sheboygan River

The Sheboygan River, about 30 miles north of Milwaukee, is another Lake Michigan tributary. The Sheboygan is a large river with dependable runs of steelhead and salmon. Plenty of water flows through the Sheboygan River and into Sheboygan Harbor, triggering runs of these migratory fish. It's a favorite tributary stream of mine, and also of Craig Amacker of Planet Trout Guide Service. I've fished it about a half-dozen times and either caught fish or had hook-ups on black Marabou Leeches and Polar Shrimp. Amacker favors purple flies for the definitive shadow they cast in the Sheboygan's tinted water.

The lower portion of steelhead water runs through land with public access at highway bridges (at and along Highway PP and Highway TA/Taylor Drive); the upper 7 miles run through the Kohler River Wildlife Area and end at the Kohler Dam, which is private land. Membership fees, which come with access to surrounding land and other privileges, run about $200 per person per year. Under Wisconsin law, however, all navigable waters (rivers and streams and some lakes) are open to public use. Thus, a wading angler who legally enters and exits a stream (at a public right-of-way such as a bridge or with landowner permission) is legal to fish as long as his feet are wet.

From Sheboygan Harbor to Taylor Drive, the river is basically flat water without much structure. It is popular with anglers who fish spawn sacks, and it does hold fish; however, opportunities for wading and reaching fish with fly tackle are limited.

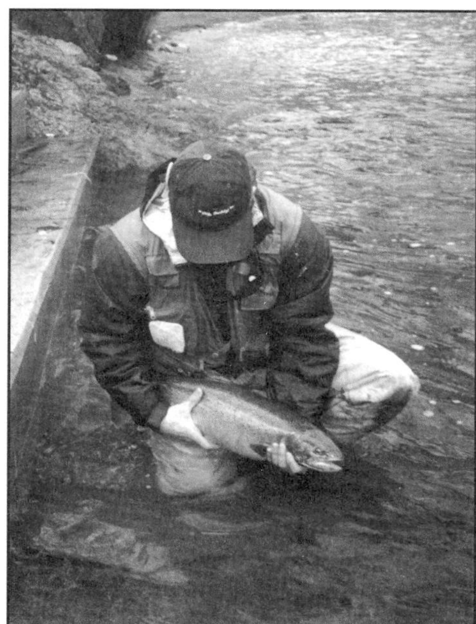

The Sheboygan produces a variety of trophy fish. (Craig Amacker photos)

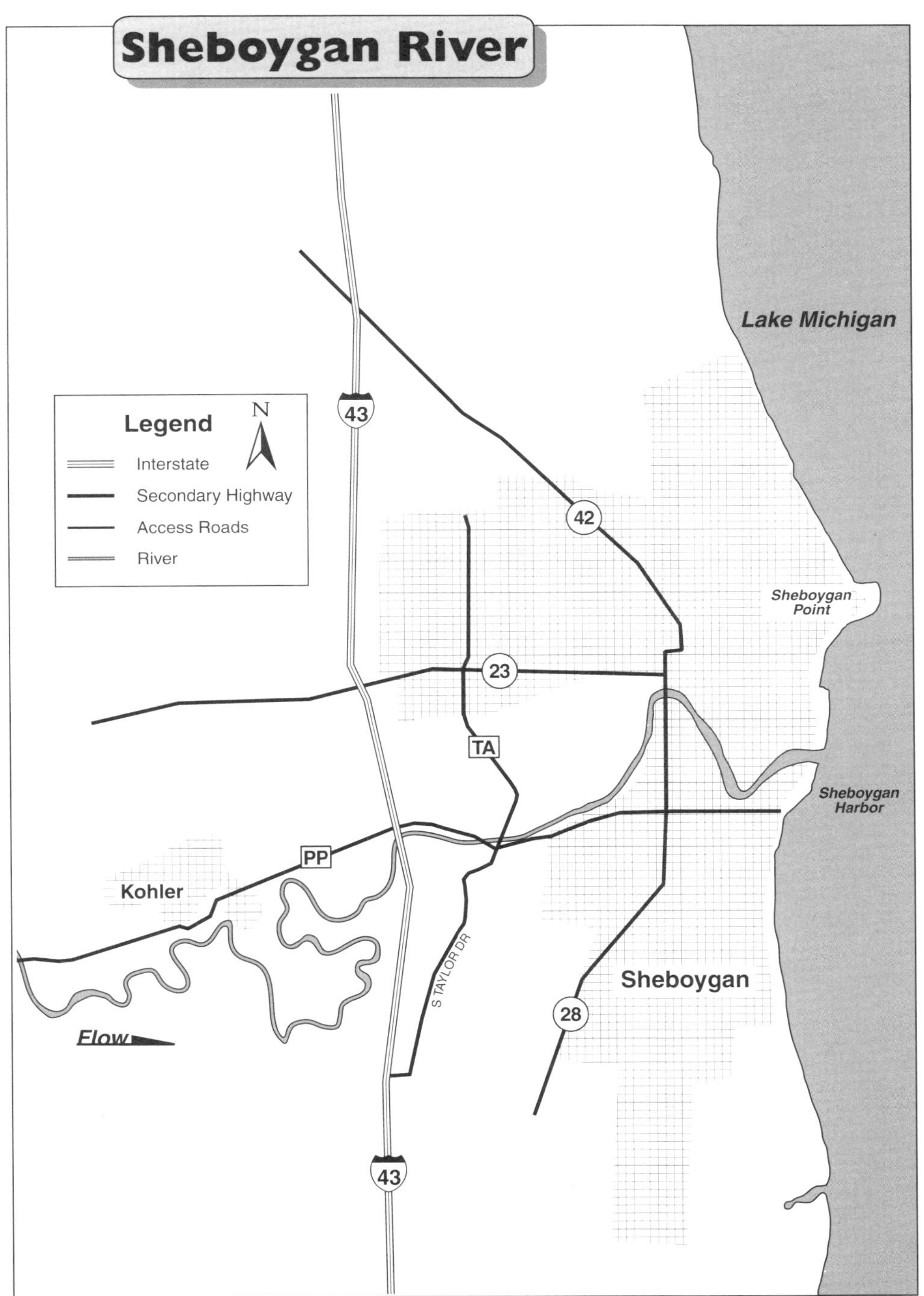
Sheboygan River
Lake Michigan
Legend
N
Interstate
Secondary Highway
Access Roads
River
43
42
23
TA
PP
Kohler
Sheboygan Point
Sheboygan Harbor
S TAYLOR DR
Sheboygan
28
Flow
43

The stretch at the Taylor Drive bridge and along Highway PP has a nice mix of riffles and deep holes. Even in a low-water year, there are pockets between 3 and 4 feet deep. In fact, right around the Taylor Drive bridge is one of my favorite stretches of the river. The bridge embankments provide good holding and resting cover. There are also a number of deep bends and gravel runs.

You'll want a sink-tip line or poly leader with 10-pound tippet. Marabou Leeches in purple and black are good bets; size 6 is about right. Egg patterns in size 8 to 10 are effective. I've also taken fish here on a Polar Shrimp, tied with a pink chenille body and white wing.

The river is at least 50 yards wide in this stretch, and there's plenty of room to throw a cast or fight fish. October and November are good months to fish the Sheboygan; by mid-December the river is generally frozen and its fish very sluggish. You'll find a mix of Skamania and Chambers Creek steelhead, plus cohos, chinooks, and brown and brook trout. Come spring, runs of Ganaraska steelhead move into the river. Lake-run fish can be taken from September to May on the Sheboygan.

The Kohler property line begins upstream from Highway 43. Kohler is a municipality built around the Kohler Corporation, manufacturers of toilets and plumbing fixtures. If you plan to be on Kohler land, you will need to purchase a membership for the River Wildlife Center from the Kohler Company. Call them for details at 800-344-2838. Seven miles of the Sheboygan River flow through Kohler land. The $200 membership fee does cut down on fishing pressure, but you'll still see other anglers. Expect to be checked for a membership pass if you fish in Kohler.

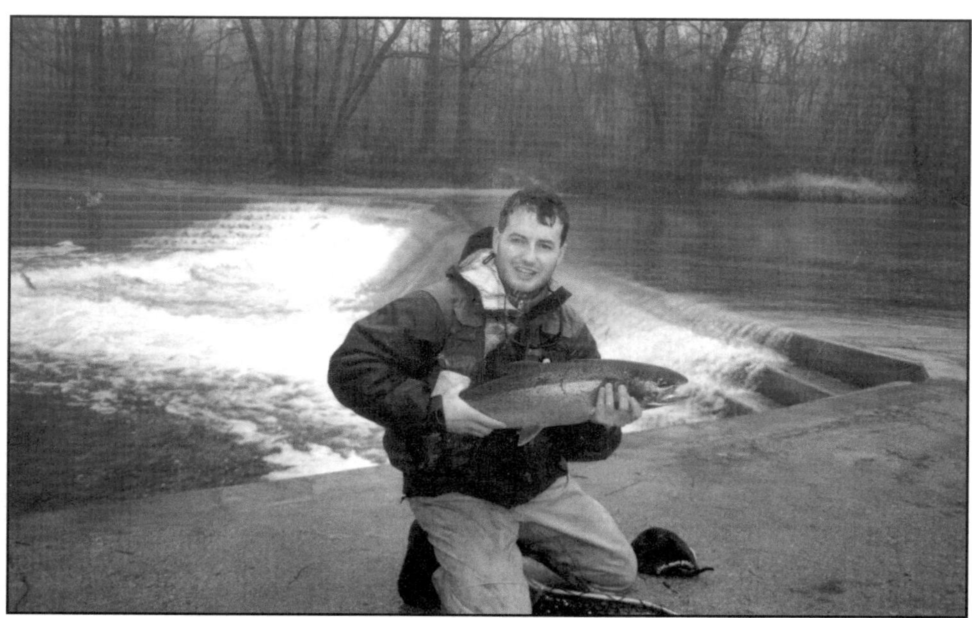

Another nice fish will be released back into the Sheboygan. (Craig Amacker)

Stream Facts: Sheboygan River

Season

- All year

Regulations

- Daily bag limit 5 trout and salmon in total, only 2 may be lake trout; size limit 10 inches; from September 15 to May 1, fishing is prohibited a half-hour after sunset to a half-hour before sunrise.

Species

- In fall, coho and chinook salmon, lake-run brook and brown trout; Skamania and Chambers Creek steelhead; spring, Ganaraska steelhead.

Miles of fly fishing water

- 15 miles

Stream Characteristics

- Flows through urban setting with some park land; upper portion runs through Kohler Village, where membership pass is required.

Access

- Public access along Highway PP and Taylor Drive; membership available from Kohler Village for $200/year for the upper river.

Fly Shops

- The Fly Fishers (Milwaukee); Laacke & Joy (Milwaukee); Midwest Fly Fishing (Kohler); and Gander Mountain (Sheboygan)

Maps

- *Wisconsin Atlas and Gazetteer*, page 47

Hub City: Sheboygan

A Lake Michigan community of 50,000, Sheboygan makes a convenient base for exploring the Sheboygan and Pigeon Rivers to the south or the Manitowoc River and Twin Rivers to the north. It is also home to a booming offshore charter-boat fishery for trout and salmon. Some excellent warmwater fishing (as well as hiking and camping) can be had in the quiet lakes of the Northern Unit of the Kettle Moraine State Forest 20 miles to the west. Kohler Andre State Park and Point Beach State Park to the north offer camping and the chance for the brave-hearted to swim in Lake Michigan. The adjacent village of Kohler offers private water (available for a $200 membership fee) and a number of exclusive dining and lodging options.

Accommodations

Super 8 Motel, 3402 Wilgus Road, Sheboygan; 800-800-8000; $
AmericInn, 3664 Taylor Drive, Sheboygan; 800-634-3444; $$
The American Club, 419 Highland Drive, Kohler; 800-344-2838; AAA 5-star rated resort; also contact for private access to Sheboygan River

Campgrounds

Kohler Andre State Park, 1520 Beach Park Lane, Sheboygan; 920-451-4080
Kettle Moraine State Forest, Box 410, Campbellsport; 920-626-2116; excellent hiking, camping, warmwater lake fishing in unique glacial scenery 20 miles west of Sheboygan
Point Beach State Forest, 9400 County O, Two Rivers; 920-794-7480; lakeside camping and hiking 30 miles north of Sheboygan

Restaurants

Culvers Frozen Custard and Hamburgers, 641 Taylor Drive, Sheboygan; 920-451-7150; quality Midwest hamburger and frozen custard chain located near Sheboygan River
Applebee's Neighborhood Bar and Grill, 526 Taylor Drive; 920-208-8253; chain restaurant located near Sheboygan River
Schwarz's Fish Market, 828 Riverfront Drive; 920-452-0576; good carryout fish dinners right along the lake
Trattoria Stefano, 522 8th Street, Sheboygan; 920 452 8453
Fountain Park Family Restaurant, 922 N. 8th Street; 920-452-3009; downtown family restaurant that serves breakfast starting at 6 every day

Fly Shops, Outfitters, Sporting Goods

Gander Mountain, 4308 County J, Sheboygan, 920-208-0800
Midwest Fly Fishing, Inc., 725 Woodlake Road, Kohler; 920-453-9722
Tight Lines Fly Fishing Company, De Pere; 920-336-4106; www.tightlineflyshop.com; good source of information on area streams and hatches located about 1.5 hour north of most streams in this region

The Fly Fishers, West Allis; 414-259-8100; guiding and fly fishing service near Milwaukee

Bob's Silver Doctor Fly Fishing, P.O. Box 105, Viroqua; 608-637-3417; Guides on spring creeks and Lake Michigan steelhead.

Veterinarians

Sheboygan Animal Hospital, 1839 Erie Avenue, Sheboygan; 920-452-2882

Medical

Sheboygan Memorial Medical Center, 2629 N. 7th Street; 920-451-5555

Auto Rental

Enterprise Automobile Rental, 3035 S. Business Drive, Sheboygan; 920-458-1414; or rent at Mitchell Field International Airport if flying into Milwaukee

Automobile Repair

J&R Automotive, Highway 42, Sheboygan; 920-918-6769; full-service garage

Pomp's Tire Service, Highway 42; 920-457-4814; tires, shocks, brakes

Air Service

Sheboygan Memorial Airport (for small private planes); 920-467-2978

Mitchell Field in Milwaukee

For More Information

Sheboygan County Chamber of Commerce
712 Riverfront Drive
Suite 101
Sheboygan, WI 53081
920-457-9491
www.sheboygan.org

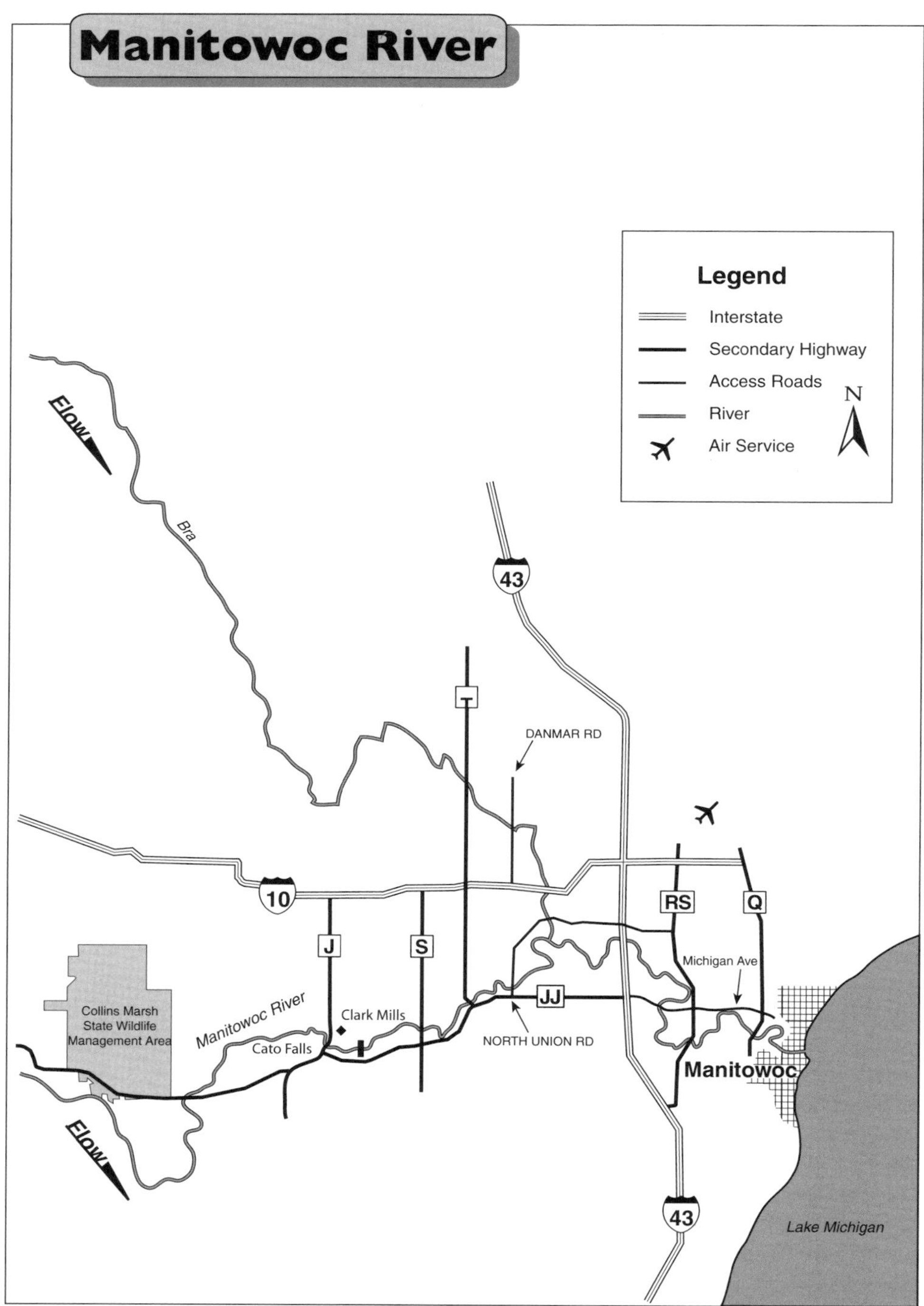
Manitowoc River
Legend
Interstate
Secondary Highway
Access Roads
River
Air Service
N
Flow
Bra
43
T
DANMAR RD
10
RS
Q
J
S
Michigan Ave
JJ
Collins Marsh
State Wildlife
Management Area
Manitowoc River
Clark Mills
Cato Falls
NORTH UNION RD
Manitowoc
Flow
43
Lake Michigan
© 2006 Wilderness Adventures Press, Inc.

THE MANITOWOC RIVER

With a number of county parks in its 15 miles of salmon and steelhead water, the Manitowoc River provides anglers with good opportunities to fish for lake-run salmonoids from the dam at Clarks Mills to the mouth at Manitowoc Harbor. It receives generous plantings of coho and chinook salmon, as well as three strains of steelhead. Stray brook and brown trout also find their way into the river from the lake. The Manitowoc, being a good-sized river, offers a dependable fall-to-spring fishery. It drains a big enough watershed to encourage fish runs even in dry years.

The shallows of Manitowoc Harbor, off Maritime Drive and Manitowoc Marina, can be productive for wading and float-tube anglers working streamers on sink-tip lines. South of Manitowoc, the water-treatment plant east of Highway 10 releases 50-degree water into the lake year-round. Even in the dead of winter, hardy souls can be found here plying the shallows for trout and salmon. Flyfishers should use streamers that imitate Lake Michigan's ubiquitous baitfish.

Most of the action sought by flyrodders takes place on the Manitowoc River itself. Four parks along the river provide the best habitat and access. The flat deep water upstream from the harbor is of limited interest; it holds fish but lacks structure and is difficult to wade. Access to this flat stretch is at Highway 10, Highway Q, and the boat launch on Michigan Avenue.

Highway R in the village of Manitowoc Rapids is the site of a county park with good access. The park on the north side of County S is another spot frequented by salmon and steelhead anglers, and it offers good river access. Cato Falls County Park upstream from here, off Highway JJ, is a scenic area with good access. Rocky bottom with deep runs characterizes this stretch. Clarks Mills on Highway J is as far upstream as trout and salmon go. There is access to the river via Clarks Mills Dam, where trout and salmon often congregate. Above the dam and upstream to Collins Marsh you will find a mix of rough fish and northern pike.

The Branch River, a tributary of the Manitowoc, is scenic and clear, according to DNR fisheries biologist Steve Hogler. Road crossings are at North Union Road, Highway 10, Danmar Road, and County T. Since this stream runs through private land you will need to ask permission from the landowner or keep your feet wet. There are no dams on the Branch River, but salmon and steelhead don't get much above Highway T, where the riverbed changes from rock to silt. Wade carefully on the Branch, use a 3X leader, and fish small egg patterns or Woolly Buggers.

On the larger Manitowoc, fish the standard 1X or 2X leader and larger flies. On either river, you might consider fishing a nymph on a dropper 18 inches behind the main fly. Smallmouth and northerns are present in both the Manitowoc and Branch. You'll find northerns around Cato Falls and smallmouth scattered throughout, according to Hogler.

Stream Facts: Manitowoc River

Season

- All year

Regulations

- Daily bag limit 5 trout and salmon in total, only 2 may be lake trout; size limit 10 inches; from September 15 to May 1, fishing is prohibited a half-hour after sunset to a half-hour before sunrise.

Access

- Manitowoc Rapids, Cato, Clarks Mills

Miles of Trout Water

- 15 miles

Stream Characteristics

- Fast and rocky-bottomed; trout and salmon go upstream as far as Clarks Mills.

Fly Shops

- The Fly Fishers (Milwaukee); Laacke & Joy (Milwaukee); Midwest Fly Fishing (Kohler); Gander Mountain (Sheboygan); Tight Lines Fly Shop (De Pere)

Maps

- *Wisconsin Atlas and Gazetteer*, page 46

Fish on! (Craig Amacker)

EAST TWIN RIVER AND WEST TWIN RIVER

The East and West Twin Rivers flow into Two Rivers Harbor north of Manitowoc. Access on these rivers is at road crossings and dams. They are heavily planted with chinook salmon and steelhead and can be fished productively from September to May, when the fish return as mature trout and salmon in search of the place where they were planted.

Both streams offer good water quality and contain inland strains of trout in their upper reaches. Smallmouth bass are also present in both rivers, particularly the West Twin. Shoreline and harbor fishing on Lake Michigan can be good in fall and spring for those willing to wade, float-tube, or fish from north and south piers. You'll want to get down to these fish with a sinking or sink-tip line and large streamers. There is also the chance of picking up a big smallmouth while fishing for trout and salmon.

Six miles of the West Twin River offer salmon and steelhead fishing, from the mouth to Shoto Dam. In low-water years, focus your efforts on the West Twin, as it is a wider, larger river than the East Twin. The East Twin, however, is more scenic and offers better fish habitat.

Just upstream from the mouth, Highway 42 crosses the West Twin. From here, it's roughly 4 miles to the next access point on Woodland Drive. Just above Woodland Drive is the dam at Shoto on Highway B (and the county park there). Shoto Dam serves as a congregation point for trout and salmon. If you find fresh-run fish here

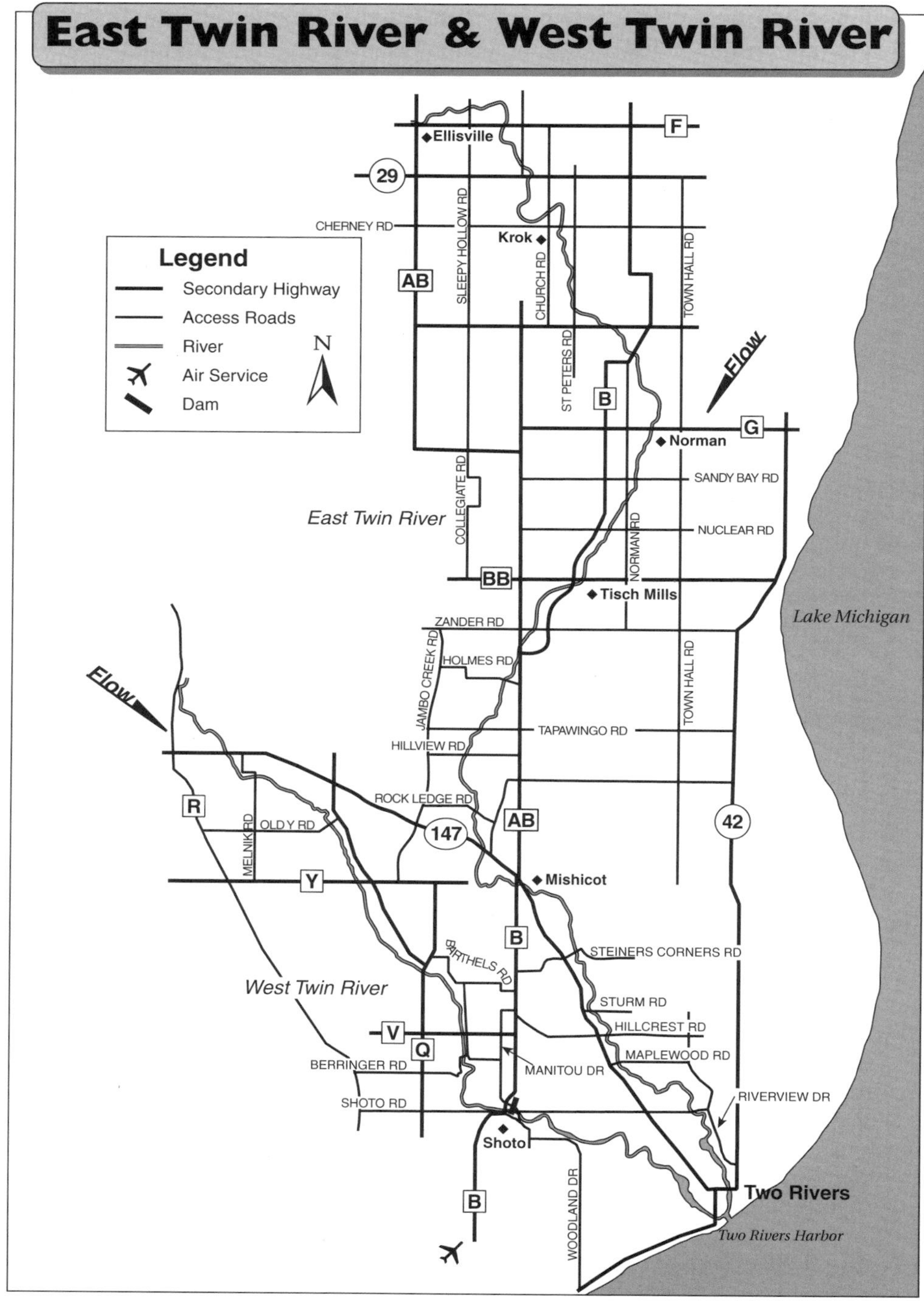
East Twin River & West Twin River
Legend
Secondary Highway
Access Roads
River
Air Service
Dam
N
Ellisville
Krok
Norman
Tisch Mills
Mishicot
Shoto
Two Rivers
Two Rivers Harbor
Lake Michigan
East Twin River
West Twin River
Flow
Flow
CHERNEY RD
SLEEPY HOLLOW RD
CHURCH RD
ST PETERS RD
TOWN HALL RD
SANDY BAY RD
NUCLEAR RD
NORMAN RD
COLLEGIATE RD
ZANDER RD
JAMBO CREEK RD
HOLMES RD
TAPAWINGO RD
HILLVIEW RD
ROCK LEDGE RD
OLD Y RD
MELNIK RD
BARTHELS RD
STEINERS CORNERS RD
STURM RD
HILLCREST RD
MAPLEWOOD RD
MANITOU DR
RIVERVIEW DR
BERRINGER RD
SHOTO RD
WOODLAND DR
F
29
AB
B
G
BB
R
147
42
Y
V
Q
© 2006 Wilderness Adventures Press, Inc.

you might have luck taking them. However, fish that have been below this dam for some time grow increasingly selective, having seen everything from spawn sacks to Rapala plugs thrown at them.

The upper reaches of the West Twin are planted with brown trout from the headwaters to the County Y bridge. Between County Y and Shoto Dam, anglers will find a mixed bag of smallmouth bass, northern pike, and rough fish.

On the East Twin River, steelhead and salmon make it as far up as the Michicot Dam, 10 miles from Two Rivers Harbor. Access is at road crossings: Riverview Drive, Maplewood Road, Hillcrest Road, Steiners Corners, and the dam found at Highway 147.

The East Twin offers a plethora of good resting cover for salmon and steelhead—lots of downed timber, boulders, bends, and even bridge embankments. Once in the stream and wading, you'll find no shortage of places to cast. Of particular interest on the East Twin is the chinook fishery. About 45,000 were stocked during the late 1990s and 2000. Some of these fish will return in the 20-pound class. Those who have never battled a mature chinook on an 8-weight rod are in for a fight they will not soon forget.

The upper reaches of the East Twin River begin in the northern swampland of Kewaunee County near the Bohemian hamlets of Pilsen and Krok. It's planted with brook and brown trout down to Tisch Mills on the Manitowoc County line and can be reached via Highway B. The water between B and Mishicot, along Highway AB, holds good numbers of smallmouths.

Stream Facts: East Twin & West Twin Rivers

Season

- All year

Regulations

- Daily bag limit 5 trout and salmon in total, only 2 may be lake trout; size limit 10 inches; from September 15 to May 1, fishing is prohibited a half-hour after sunset to a half-hour before sunrise.

Species

- Lake-run trout and salmon in lower reaches; smallmouth and stream trout in upper reaches.

Miles of Trout Water

- 6 miles on West Twin; 10 on the East Twin.

Stream Characteristics

- Rocky-bottomed stream planted heavily with trout and salmon; fish make it up to dams in Shoto and Mishicot.

Access

- Dams and road crossings

Fly Shops

- The Fly Fishers (Milwaukee); Laacke & Joy (Milwaukee); Midwest Fly Fishing (Kohler); Gander Mountain (Sheboygan); Tight Lines Fly Shop (De Pere)

Maps

- *Wisconsin Atlas and Gazetteer,* pages 46, 68

Hub City: Two Rivers

Two Rivers is a Lake Michigan community of 13,000 in Manitowoc County. It's convenient to Point Beach State Forest, a state forest that has a variety of habitats (including dunes and wetlands) and is located on Lake Michigan. The East and West Twin Rivers, noted salmon and steelhead streams, flow into Two Rivers Harbor.

Two Rivers is unofficially known as Cool City. While the rest of Wisconsin swelters in July and August, any wind but a west wind draws cool air from Lake Michigan and reduces air temperatures as much as 20 degrees compared to inland locations.

The Manitowoc River is just to the south. And the noted Kewaunee and Ahnapee Rivers are just to the north in Kewaunee County, which was settled by Czech immigrants in the late 19th century.

Accommodations

Cool City Motel, 3009 Lincoln Avenue, Two Rivers; 920-793-2244; $

Lighthouse Inn, 1515 Memorial Drive; 920-793-4524; $$$

Campgrounds

Point Beach State Forest, 9400 County O, Two Rivers; 920-794-7480

Kohler Andre State Park, 1520 Beach Park Lane, Sheboygan; 920-451-4080; located about 30 miles south of Two Rivers

Potawatomi State Park, 3740 Park Drive, Sturgeon Bay; 920-743-8869; located about 25 miles north of Two Rivers on the western edge of Door County; convenient to Kewaunee and Ahnapee Rivers

Restaurants

M&M Lunch, 1210 Washington Street, Two Rivers; 920-794-7616; dependable family restaurant open for breakfast and lunch, waterfront setting

Kurtz's Pub and Deli, 1410 Washington Street, Two River; 920-793-1222; German-style pub located in Main Street setting with stick-to-the-ribs sandwiches and just about any beer you can think of

Machut's Supper Club, 3911 Lincoln Avenue, Two Rivers; 920-793-9432; good fish and ribs and steak

Subway, 1200 Washington Street, Two Rivers; 920-794-8111; sandwich chain

Fly Shops, Outfitters, Sporting Goods

Suettinger Hardware, Washington and 17th Street, Two Rivers; 920-793-4584; for licenses and local conditions

Seagull Marina, 1400 Lake Street, Two Rivers; 920-794-7533; fishing licenses

Gander Mountain, 4308 County J, Sheboygan, 920-208-0800

Midwest Fly Fishing, Inc., 725 Woodlake Road, Kohler; 920-453-9722

Tight Lines Fly Fishing Company, De Pere; 920-336-4106; www.tightlineflyshop.com; good source of info on Lake Michigan streams

Bob's Silver Doctor Fly Fishing, P.O. Box 105, Viroqua; 608-637-3417; Guides on spring creeks and Lake Michigan steelhead.

The Fly Fishers, Milwaukee; 414-259-8100; guiding and fly fishing supplies for Great Lakes and elsewhere

Veterinarians

Two Rivers Veterinary Hospital, 2329 Roosevelt Avenue, Two Rivers; 920-793-1187

Medical

Two Rivers Community Hospital, 2500 Garfield Street, Two Rivers; 920-793-1178

Auto Rental

Enterprise Automobile Rental, 3035 S. Business Drive, Sheboygan; 920-458-1414; located about 30 miles south of Two Rivers

Cars can be rented at Mitchell International Airport if flying into Milwaukee

Automobile Repair

Auto Center, 3001 Forest Avenue, Two Rivers; 920-793-4547

Air Service

Sheboygan Memorial Airport (for small private planes); 920-467-2978, about 30 miles south

Mitchell Field in Milwaukee, 2 hours south

For More Information

Manitowoc/Two Rivers Chamber of Commerce
1515 Memorial Drive
Manitowoc, WI 54221
920-684-5575
800-627-4896

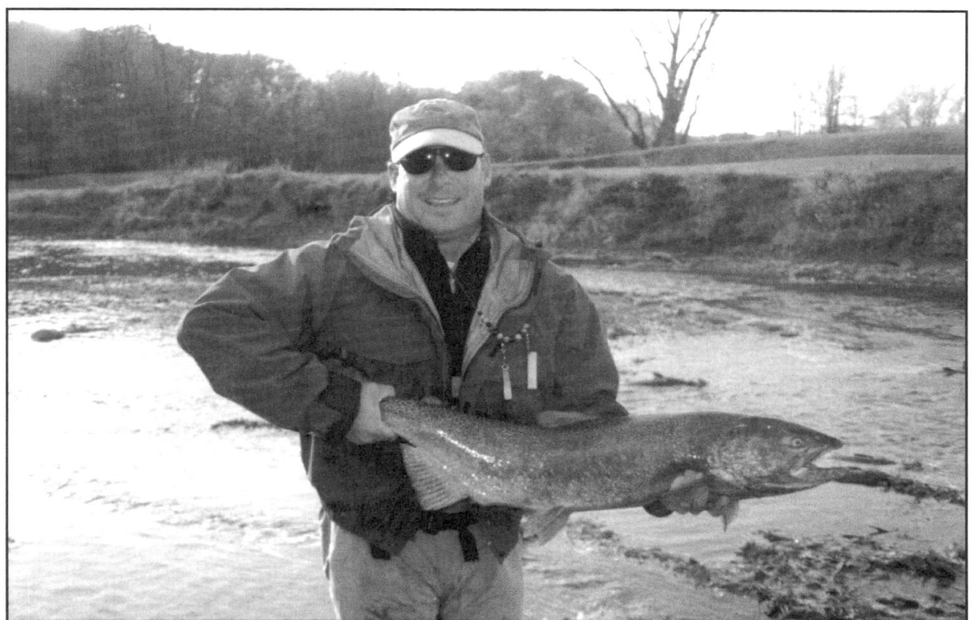

Guide Craig Amacker with a big chinook. (Craig Amacker)

Kewaunee River

Located south of Algoma in Kewaunee County, the Kewaunee River is a Lake Michigan tributary that deserves special attention. Generous stocking (over 100,000 steelhead a year, plus thousands of brown trout and chinook salmon), lots of public access, and a woods-and-marsh setting make the Kewaunee a first-class fishery for lake-run trout and salmon. Along with the Root River in far southern Wisconsin, the Kewaunee is designated by the DNR as a brood stock river. This means it offers top-quality steelhead habitat and has sufficient water levels to draw in returning fish even in low-water years. On brood stock rivers, a small portion of returning fish are stripped of eggs and milt; their young grow to yearlings in a hatchery and then are stocked in tributaries to start the cycle over.

The Kewaunee presents anglers with a full calendar of fishing. Skamania-strain steelhead enter the Kewaunee in September, followed by Chambers Creek–strain steelhead in October and November. Brown trout and chinook salmon also run up the river in fall. In late winter and early spring, these species are present in the Kewaunee, still attempting to spawn.

With spring rains and snowmelt, Ganaraska-strain steelhead move into the river from March until May. Anglers can pursue fresh-run or over-wintering fish from September to May on the Kewaunee. While water quality is good on this river, water temperatures and oxygen levels are not sufficient to support salmonoids in summer

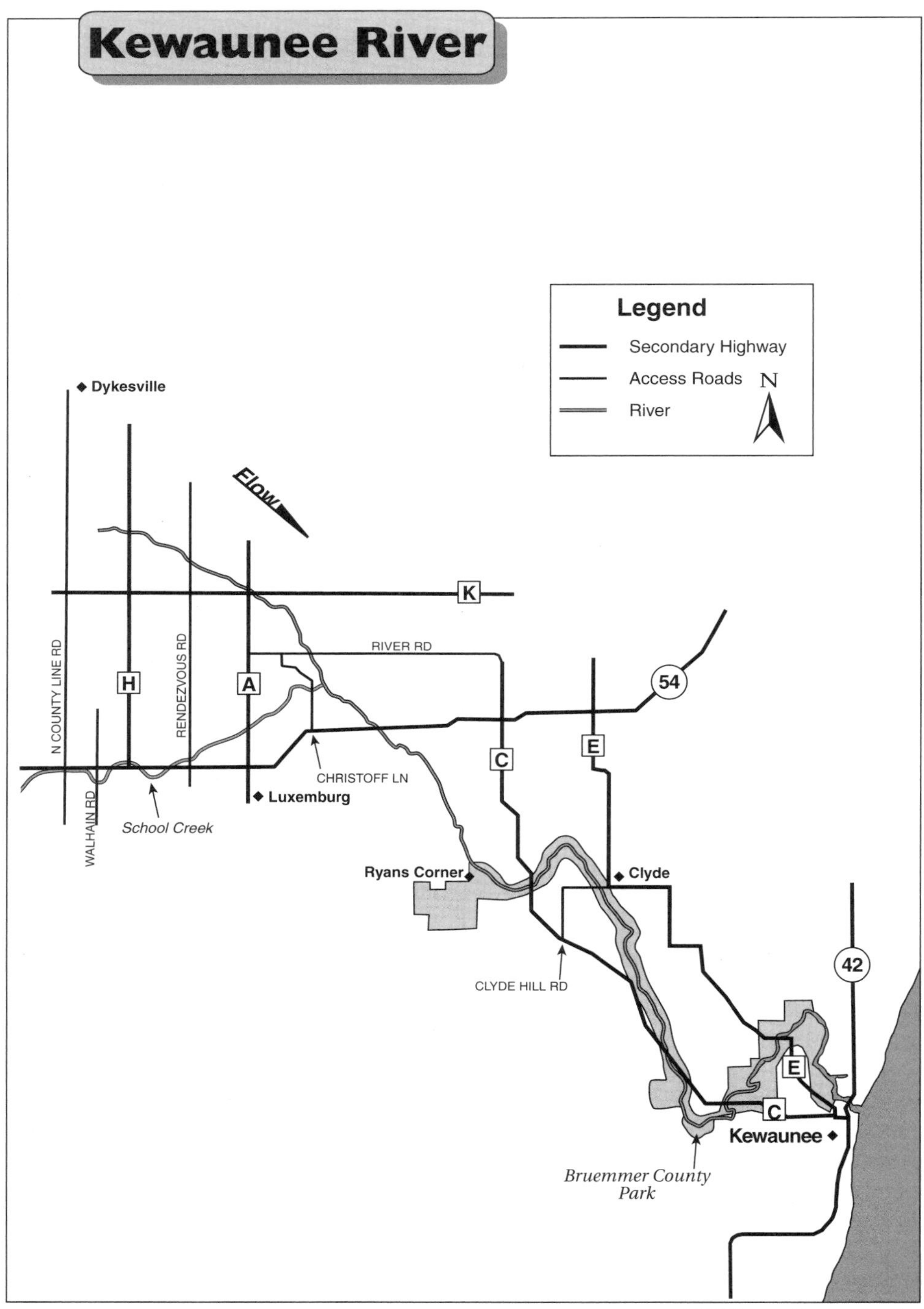
Kewaunee River
Legend
Secondary Highway
Access Roads
River
N
Dykesville
Flow
K
RIVER RD
54
N COUNTY LINE RD
H
RENDEZVOUS RD
A
E
C
CHRISTOFF LN
Luxemburg
WALHAIN RD
School Creek
Ryans Corner
Clyde
CLYDE HILL RD
42
E
C
Kewaunee
Bruemmer County Park
© 2006 Wilderness Adventures Press, Inc.

(as some streams in the state of Michigan do). Natural reproduction would make the Kewaunee a true year-round fishery.

The Kewaunee River is one of the few Lake Michigan tributaries unobstructed from its headwaters (near Dycksville) to its mouth at Kewaunee Harbor—some 30 miles. Kewaunee Harbor sees concentrations of salmon and trout in spring and fall. Fish the harbor from shore with streamers and a sink-tip line.

From its mouth upstream 3 miles to the gaging station at Bruemmer County Park, the Kewaunee might be described as flat water—deep, wide, and without much character. You can catch staging and resting fish here, to be sure, but it's not scenic. To entice these selective fish, use brightly colored flies or a dropper rig with a nymph trailing 18 inches behind an egg pattern or Woolly Bugger on 10-pound test. Access this stretch via Highway E or Highway 42 just upstream from Kewaunee Harbor.

From the gaging station to the village of Ryans Corners (about 10 miles), Highway C follows the river through northern swamp and lowland forest under DNR ownership. There is a road crossing at Clyde Hill Road near the village of Clyde downstream from Ryans Corners. The Kewaunee's thick cover and fast runs will make anglers feel as if they are fishing an inland trout stream. This is *the* stretch of the river to fish for salmon and steelhead in a wooded setting. Find them in many of the same places as their inland cousins: beneath cutbanks, holding low in deep shaded holes, or resting in the cover of fallen timber.

Upstream from Ryans Corners, the Kewaunee crosses Highway 54, River Road, Highway K, and Highway A; this stretch runs through private land and access is at road crossings. Above Highway A, the Kewaunee is small and harder to fish. School Creek joins it north of Luxemburg, and in high-water years it holds steelhead. Find School Creek along Highway 54, with road crossings at Christoff Lane, Highway A, Rendezvous Road, Highway H, Walhain Road, and North County Line Road.

While the Kewaunee does see runs of fish during low water, keep an eye on the weather forecast and fish it after a rain. Or better yet, check the flows on the river you'll be fishing on the Internet. Visit the website for the National Weather Service and click on the "River/Hydrology" section at www.crh.noaa.gov. Given the right time of year and good stream flows (after a rain in September through November and again March through May) you should find the Kewaunee River full of fish.

Stream Facts: Kewaunee River

Season
- All year

Regulations
- Daily bag limit 5 trout and salmon in total, only 2 may be lake trout; size limit 10 inches; from September 15 to May 1, fishing is prohibited a half-hour after sunset to a half-hour before sunrise.

Species
- Lake-run trout and salmon

Miles of Fly Fishing Water
- 30 miles

Stream Characteristics
- Narrow river running over sandy bottom; lots of good cover.

Access
- Flows through Kewaunee Fish and Wildlife Area; road crossings.

Fly Shops
- The Fly Fishers (Milwaukee); Laacke & Joy (Milwaukee); Midwest Fly Fishing (Kohler); Gander Mountain (Sheboygan); Tight Lines Fly Shop (De Pere)

Maps
- *Wisconsin Atlas and Gazetteer*, pages 46, 68

AHNAPEE RIVER

As Wisconsin steelhead streams go, the Ahnapee River in Kewaunee County has a lot to recommend it. It's rated as a class one steelhead stream by the DNR. This means two things for anglers: it has good steelhead habitat and holds fish from fall to spring. What's more, the Ahnapee State Trail runs along the river, protecting riverine lands from development. While steelhead rivers of the southeast—notably the Root, Pike, and Sheboygan—run through urban areas, the Ahnapee offers 15 miles of trout and salmon water against a backdrop of Door County woods and farm fields.

Runs of Skamania-strain steelhead begin in earnest during the first cold snap in late September, although a few vanguard fish will be in the river as early as August. Come October and November, Chambers Creek steelhead begin moving up the Ahnapee. As these strains are attempting to spawn in late winter and early spring, Ganaraska-strain fish move in as early as March. Brook trout, brown trout, and salmon—while not planted in the Ahnapee—do stray here from plantings in the lake. Thus, from early fall to mid-spring, the Ahnapee offers a viable fishery for a variety lake-run trout and salmon.

Egg patterns take fish, as will Woolly Buggers in a variety of colors. If your efforts are drawing a blank, try fishing a size 10 nymph off the back of one of those patterns for added enticement. Use a sink-tip line to get down to these fish.

While the Ahnapee is prettier than most Lake Michigan tributary streams, it's also tougher to read. Lacking obvious runs and riffles, the river flows through cattail marsh and has a dark cast akin to tidal rivers in southern Maine or Massachusetts.

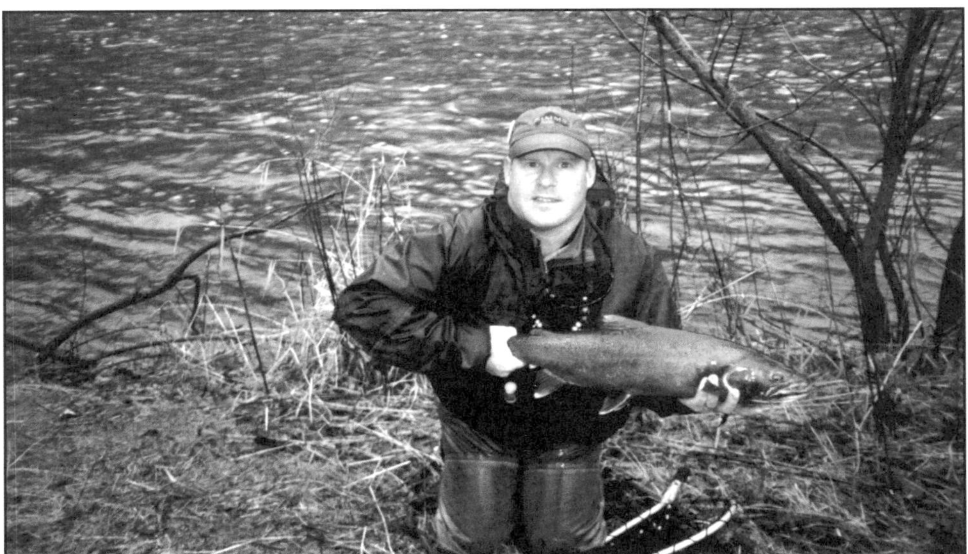

Craig Amacker with another Lake Michigan beauty. (Craig Amacker)

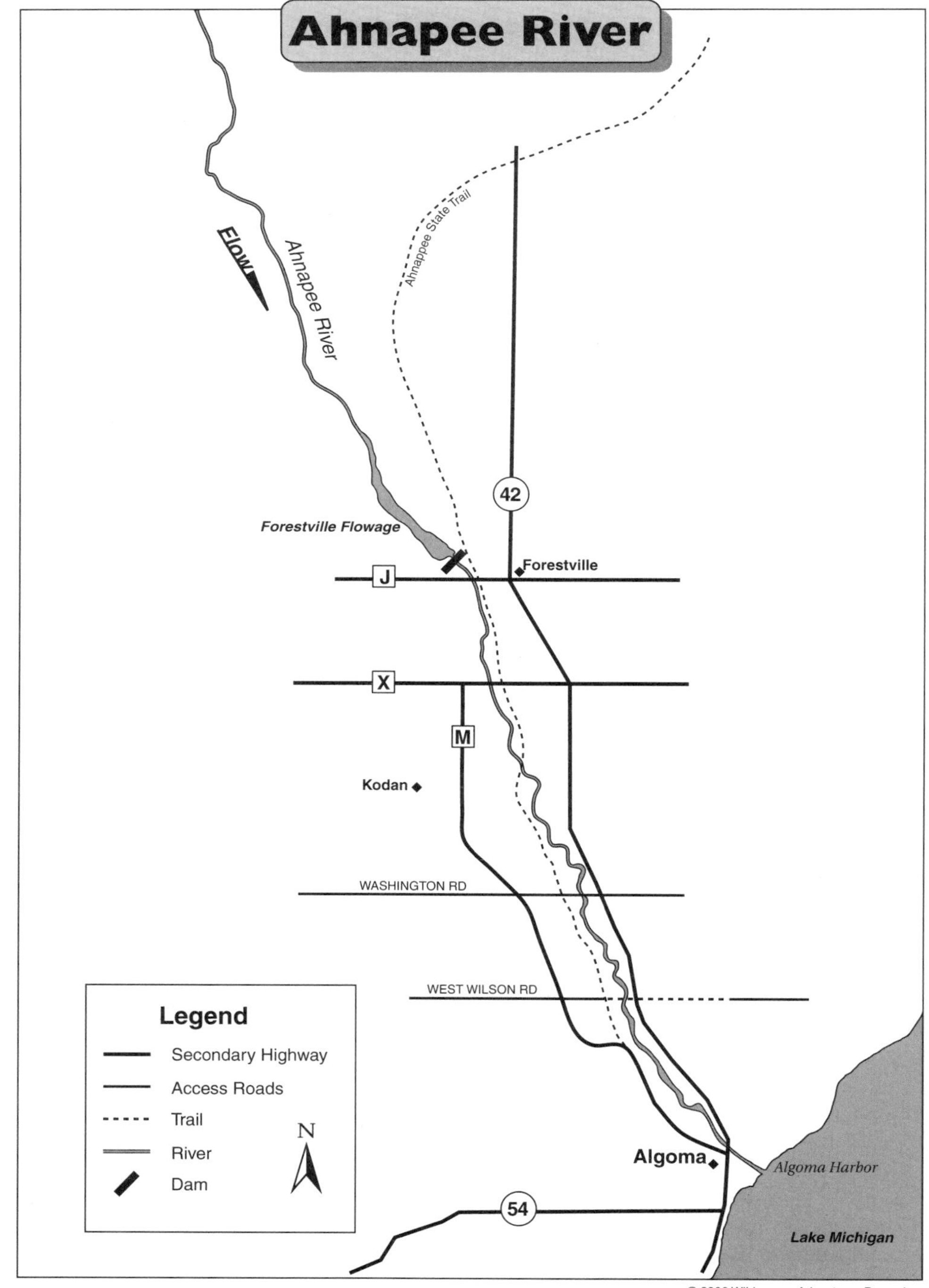
Ahnapee River
Flow
Ahnapee River
Ahnappee State Trail
42
Forestville Flowage
Forestville
J
X
M
Kodan
WASHINGTON RD
WEST WILSON RD
Legend
Secondary Highway
Access Roads
Trail
River
Dam
N
Algoma
Algoma Harbor
54
Lake Michigan
© 2006 Wilderness Adventures Press, Inc.

Thus, polarized sunglasses will be useful for spotting fish. Fish congregate in bends, at channeled stretches near bridges, and near whatever structure you can find.

Steelhead and salmon can be found in the Ahnapee from the mouth at Algoma Harbor to the Forestville Flowage 15 miles upstream. This dam blocks passage farther upstream. (See the description for the Forestville Flowage later in this section.)

To get to the Ahnapee from the south, follow Highway 42 north from Two Rivers toward Algoma. From Green Bay and points west, take Highway 54 east toward Algoma. Good public access exists on the lower 1.5 miles of the river, although the setting is more urban. A handicapped fishing platform and parking lot can be found on Highway 42 just north of Ahnapee. In the town of Ahnapee there is good access to the river all the way down to its mouth at Algoma Harbor, which provides a good shore fishery for trout and salmon in fall and spring. Highway M and the Ahnapee State Trail run along the west side of the river with road crossings at West Wilson Road, Washington Road, Highway X, and Highway J. The Ahnapee State Trail crosses the river near the village of Kodan. Highway 42 runs along the east side of the river.

To round out this entry on the Ahnapee River, I will share a family anecdote. On a hike with my wife and daughter along the river one March afternoon, our Labrador retriever, Tasha, possessed of a keen nose and desire to investigate, went down to the river. She emerged from the water proudly carrying a northern pike skull as if it were a big rooster pheasant. What's noteworthy here is not my dog's affinity for dead fish, but the size of the specimen she retrieved. Judging from other northern pike I've caught, the skull belonged to a heavy fish no smaller than 3 feet long. I can't say the Ahnapee has large populations of trophy pike, but they do exist above here in Forestville Flowage and below in Lake Michigan. Northern pike season is open year-round on the Ahnapee. Try it sometime if the trout and salmon aren't cooperating.

The Ahnapee River upstream of Algoma. (Craig Amacker)

Stream Facts: Ahnapee River

Season
- All year

Regulations
- Daily bag limit 5 trout and salmon in total, only 2 may be lake trout; size limit 10 inches; from October 1 to first Saturday in May, hook and line fishing prohibited a half- hour after sunset to a half-hour before sunrise.

Species
- Lake-run trout and salmon; northern pike.

Miles of Fly Fishing Water
- 15 miles

Stream Characteristics
- Dark, often marshy water, about 30 yards wide in most places.

Access
- In town of Algoma, road crossings, and Ahnapee State Trail.

Fly Shops
- The Fly Fishers (Milwaukee); Laacke & Joy (Milwaukee); Midwest Fly Fishing (Kohler); Gander Mountain (Sheboygan); Tight Lines Fly Shop (De Pere)

Maps
- *Wisconsin Atlas and Gazetteer*, page 69

Spring-Run Steelhead Streams

According to DNR Lake Michigan fisheries biologist Paul Peeters, some Lake Michigan tributary streams only have enough water to support runs of fish in spring; these same streams often lack sufficient flows in the fall to draw in fish. Accordingly, they are planted with spring-run strains of steelhead: Ganaraska and Chambers Creek. The situation on these small streams is aggravated by historic low-water levels on Lake Michigan (caused by dry winters, among other things).

The smaller streams discussed below can provide excellent angling during springs with sufficient rain and snowmelt. In an exceptionally rainy fall, they *may* see runs of stray trout and salmon, but these should not be counted on as reliable fall fisheries. And in dry springs, you're probably better off on bigger rivers like the Kewaunee or Ahnapee. Access to these smaller streams is generally from road crossings. From there, anglers will need to wade and keep their feet wet or secure landowner permission.

Another tip provided by Peeters is to check the gaging stations on rivers in the area you'll be fishing to make sure there is sufficient flow. You can do this by visiting www.crh.noaa.gov, the National Weather Service website.

Tone down your approach on these small waters. Lighter leaders, careful wading, and smaller flies (try a size 8 or 10 Pheasant Tail Nymph or small egg pattern) are the order of the day. Look for spawning runs to begin as early as March and to continue into late April or early May.

Fischer Creek

Located just north of Sheboygan near the village of Cleveland, Fischer Creek begins east of Interstate 43 and flows into Lake Michigan about 10 miles downstream. Above Highway X it is too narrow to accommodate lake-run trout. Access is at the following road crossings: Union Road, Fischer Creek Road, Westview Road, Highway 43, East Dairyland Road, Centreville Road, and Lakeshore Drive.

Silver Creek

Just south of Manitowoc, Silver Creek's water supports spring runs of steelhead as far upstream as Silver Lake Dam. Below the dam, road crossings are at Highway 42, Hecker Road, Highway 43, Highway CR, S. 26th Road, S. 19th Road, Silver Creek Road, and Highway LS.

Stony Creek

Located at the southern tip of Door County, Stony Creek flows some 12 miles from the town of Maplewood before emptying into Lake Michigan north of Algoma. If you find the nearby Ahnapee crowded on a weekday, make the short jaunt up to Stony Creek. Steelhead can be found as far upstream as the swampy reaches in Forestville. Road crossings are at Gier Road, Carnot Road, S. Carnot Road, Highway J, Rosewood Road, County S, and Kennedy Road/County U.

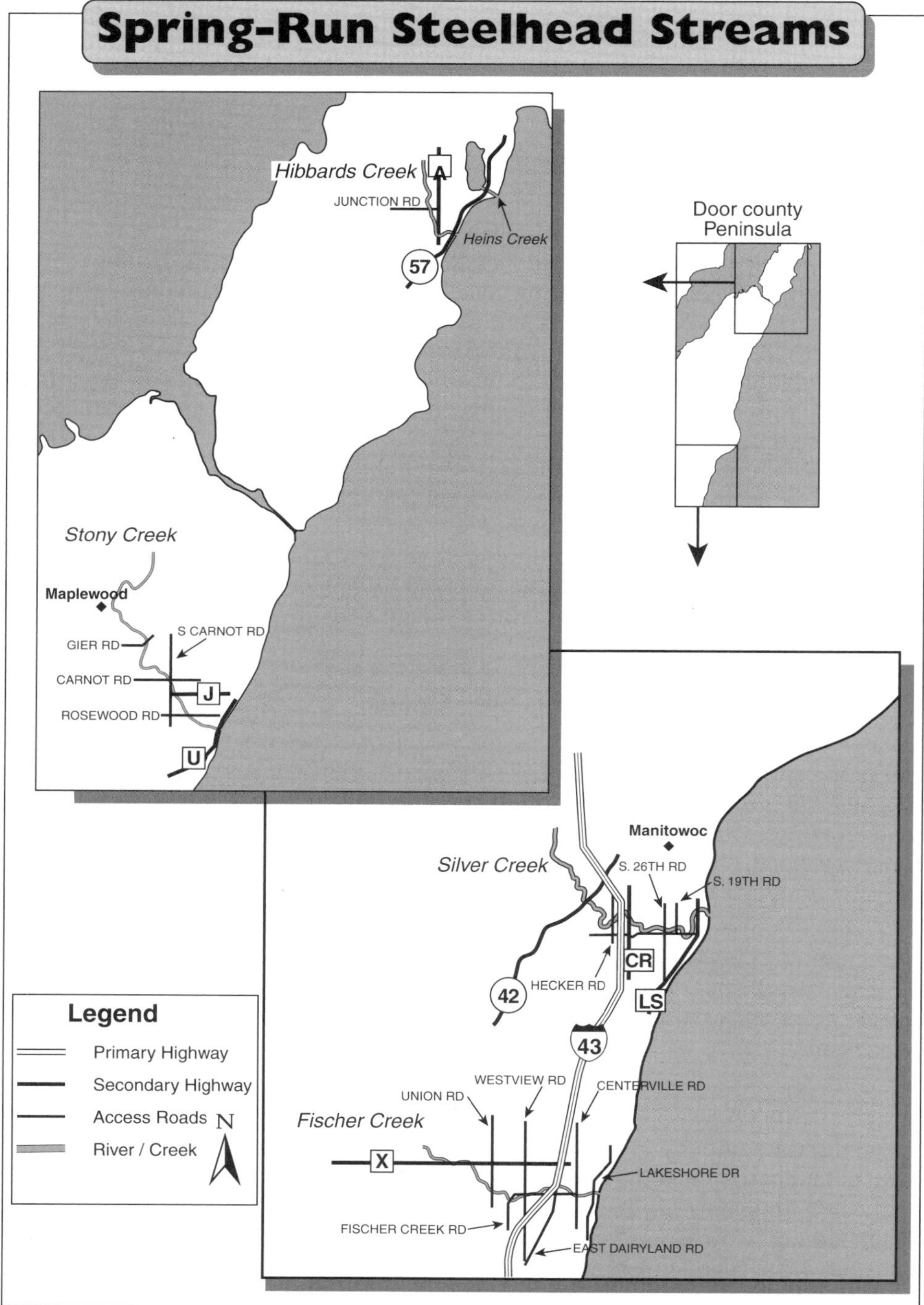
Spring-Run Steelhead Streams
Hibbards Creek
A
JUNCTION RD
Heins Creek
57
Door county Peninsula
Stony Creek
Maplewood
S CARNOT RD
GIER RD
CARNOT RD
J
ROSEWOOD RD
U
Manitowoc
Silver Creek
S. 26TH RD
S. 19TH RD
CR
HECKER RD
42
LS
43
Legend
Primary Highway
Secondary Highway
Access Roads
River / Creek
N
WESTVIEW RD
UNION RD
CENTERVILLE RD
Fischer Creek
X
LAKESHORE DR
FISCHER CREEK RD
EAST DAIRYLAND RD

Stony Creek is a pretty stream, clear in its lower reaches, darkened by tannin farther upstream. Its bends, fallen trees, and gravel runs will make those accustomed to fishing small trout streams feel at home. The disadvantage to this intimate setting is that in dry years few fish come up Stony Creek.

Hibbards Creek

Hibbards Creek was known as a brook trout stream in years past. These days, it's better known for spring-run steelhead. Still, the structure that made for good trout habitat (root tangles and fallen trees) also affords resting places and cover for steelhead. It empties into Lake Michigan north of Jacksonport. Road crossings are at Highway 57, Highway A, and Junction Road. Good, deep holes can be found at all three road crossings where the stream has been channelized. While just about the size of an average Wisconsin trout stream, it's one of the larger Door County spring-run streams—worth trying even in a dry spring.

Heins Creek

The outlet of Kangaroo Lake is known as Heins Creek. It crosses Highway 57 before joining Lake Michigan. Warmed by the outflow of Kangaroo Lake, its water temperature is higher than surrounding streams and it sees an earlier run of steelhead. Between the Kangaroo Lake outlet and its mouth, small clear Heins Creek offers a little over half a mile of steelhead water.

The sun lightens the waters of Hibbards Creek in Door County.

Hub City: Algoma

The small Lake Michigan community of Algoma offers flyfishers a good base from which to explore the Ahnapee and Kewaunee Rivers and associated harbors. Bearcat's Fish Market offers some of the best smoked and fresh fish on Lake Michigan. The Von Stiehl Winery sells wines vinted from local cherries and grapes. And there are no shortage of taverns.

The Ahnapee River Trail, a railroad bed converted to a biking and snowmobile trail, runs along the west side of the Ahnapee and makes for a nice day-hike or bike outing. While geared toward spin fishermen, the Algoma Fishing Hotline provides information on the movement of trout and salmon that will also be of interest to fly fishermen; call 800-626-3090. Algoma's just a short drive from Sturgeon Bay and the smallmouth fishery there.

Accommodations

River Hills Motel, Highway 42, Algoma; 800-236-3451; pets OK, freezer service; $$

Barbie Ann Motel, downtown Algoma; 920-487-5561; affordable lodging, near Ahnapee River; $

Harbor Lights Lodge, 211 Milwaukee Street, Algoma; 800-736-3700; $$

Campgrounds

Timber Trail Campground, N8326 County M, Algoma; 920-487-3707; located on the Ahnapee Trail with access to the river; bike and canoe rentals; 2-bedroom rental also available

Ahnapee River Trails Campground, Wilson Road, Algoma; 920-487-5777

Potawatomi State Park, 3740 Park Drive, Sturgeon Bay; 920-743-8869; 20 miles north of Algoma

Point Beach State Forest, 9400 County O, Two Rivers; 920-794-7480; 30 miles south of Algoma

Restaurants

Portside Restaurant, 709 N. Water Street, Algoma; 920-487-9704; home cooking, open 7 am to 8 p.m. daily, located a stone's throw from Ahnapee River

Hudson's Restaurant and Bar, 205 Navarino Street, Algoma; 920-487-5493; overlooks Algoma Harbor

Subway, 2217 Lake Street, Algoma; 920-487-3637

Bearcat's Fish House, Highway 42, Algoma; 920-487-2372; the best in smoked and fresh fish

Outfitters/Sporting Goods

Billy Goat's Bait and Tackle, 4th and Navarino Streets, Algoma; 920-487-9710; fishing licenses

Bob's Silver Doctor Fly Fishing, P.O. Box 105, Viroqua; 608-637-3417; Guides on spring creeks and Lake Michigan steelhead.

Gary Nault, smallmouth bass guide who operates out of Sturgeon Bay; 920-743-1100

Veterinarians

Moede Manor Pet Clinic, N6785 Moede Lane, Algoma; 920-837-2511

Medical

Door County Memorial Hospital, 323 South 18th Avenue, Sturgeon Bay; 920-743-5566

Auto Rental

Enterprise Rental Cars, 260 Main Street, Green Bay; 920-469-5262

Automobile Repair

Grosbeier Auto and Towing, N9043 Ash Lane, Algoma; 920-487-2786

Air Service

Facilities at Sturgeon Bay and Green Bay

For More Information

Algoma Area Chamber of Commerce
1226 Lake Street
Algoma WI 54201
920-487-2041
www.algoma.org

Fox River

De Pere to Green Bay

From De Pere Dam 7 miles downstream to Green Bay, the lower Fox River offers phenomenal opportunities for the fly-rod angler, according to Chris Christensen (a.k.a. Big Chris) of former sporting goods store, Bob's Bait and Tackle in Green Bay. Gizzard shad provide a forage base for the river's smallmouth, northern pike, and walleye, which migrate between Green Bay and the De Pere Dam. Riprap, piers, moorings, boulders, and just about everything else invented by man since the voyageurs traveled here 300 years ago adorn the banks of the Fox—and provide spawning habitat and cover for fish. The open season for largemouth and smallmouth bass is the first Saturday in May to March. Walleye and northern pike may be fished year-round. While water quality has improved in recent years, you will not want to eat your catch due to elevated levels of PCB and mercury content. While fly-fishing opportunities abound, the lower Fox, it should be noted, is an urban waterway.

Boating down the Fox is the way to cash in on this fishery. (Christensen says you can fish the river in a belly boat as long as you are mindful of boat traffic.) You'll need a dependable outboard to get you up and downriver. Arm yourself with a sink-tip line and 7-weight rod; then motor up and down the river until you find cover that looks appealing. Again, bass are not choosy when it comes to cover. An old sunken bicycle or lawn chair, although not aesthetically pleasing, works as well as a boulder deposited by the glaciers 10,000 years ago. Once you've found structure, chances are you'll start hitting fish. Smallmouth are a mainstay here, and fish that top the 5-pound mark aren't uncommon. Walleye, while basically bottom feeders, are occasionally taken below dams on minnow and leech patterns. Northern pike are also present in this stretch of river.

Launches on the west side of the river are at Highway 172, Highway H, and off Fort Howard Road. On the east shore, there are launches at the Fox River mouth at Green Bay north of Highway 43 and in downtown Green Bay off Highway 57.

Give Bob's Bait and Tackle a call for information on the Fox (800-447-2312). They are eager to help flyfishers discover local resources.

Neenah to De Pere

The Fox River between Neenah and De Pere offers smallmouth, walleye, pike, and white bass. The character of the river between Kaukauna and De Pere is still rural, with agricultural land and bluffs lining the water. Between Kaukauna and Neenah (just above Lake Winnebago), the scenery is decidedly urban, with more frequent locks and dams and papermills (and their odor).

Launches can be found in De Pere, Wrightstown, Kimberly, and at Highway 96 in Appleton. Highway D, Highway 96, and Highway 41 follow the west side of the river. Highway 32/57, Highway ZZ, Highway Z, and Highway 441 follow the east side of the river. From the De Pere dam downstream to Lake Winnebago, the Fox River is governed by Wisconsin inland fishing regulations for the Southern Zone.

Door County Smallmouth Bass

The rock-hewn peninsula known as Door County, bounded by Green Bay on the west and Lake Michigan on the east, is perfectly suited for smallmouth bass. Abundant crawfish, alewife, and sculpins provide food, and the many rockpiles and ledges along both sides of the peninsula offer nesting sites and cover. According to DNR fisheries biologist Paul Peeters, Door County hosts a word-class smallmouth fishery. And smallmouth tournaments in May and June confirm this.

From Little Sturgeon Bay all the way north to Gills Rock on the Green Bay side of the peninsula there is prime smallmouth fishing. On the Lake Michigan side, the larger bays also harbor dense populations of bronzebacks. While a jonboat or V-hull with a dependable outboard is needed to venture forth on open water, any of the hundreds of miles of rocky harbors and shoreline (including Newport State Park and Peninsula State Park) offer the wading or belly-boat angler a good shot at Door County smallmouths.

According to DNR fisheries biologist Tim Kroeff, the opening of gamefish season on the first Saturday in May often coincides with a push of large fish into the shallows. This push is prompted by the first flush of 60- to 70-degree weather. Warming water activates their metabolism, and they move in to feed on crawfish and minnows. These fish will run between 2 and 5 pounds, and a 5-pound smallmouth gives new meaning to the term bulldog.

Smaller bass can be taken near their nests from mid-May to mid-June. June often signals a movement of alewife and big bass into the shallows. There's also a good bite in September and October when smallmouths are bulking up for winter. Bass are keyed in on forage fish this time of year. This pre-winter bite is another good time to take trophy smallmouths.

Fishing Door County smallmouth is like hunting North Dakota ducks. Find marsh in North Dakota and you'll find ducks. Find rocks off Door County and you'll find smallmouth. On the bay side of the peninsula, good smallmouth fishing can be had as far south as Little Sturgeon Bay and Riley Bay. Sturgeon Bay, particularly Sawyer Harbor and the area known as the Flats, is perhaps the best-known spot in all of Door County to nail big bronzebacks. Continuing north, the harbor rocks at Egg Harbor, Fish Creek, Sister Bay, and Ellison Bay also hold fish. Rocky Peninsula State Park offers several miles of access to quality smallmouth habitat that is fishable from shore—either for float-tube or wading anglers.

On the lake side, try Bailey's Harbor, North Bay, and Rowley Bay. Whether fishing from a boat or from shore, you'll want to target the same kind of habitat: rockpiles, dropoffs and troughs, and stands of bulrush. Launches can be found in Bailey's Harbor, off Cana Island Road on Moonlight Bay, off North Bay Road on North Bay, and at the Wagon Wheel Resort ($9 charge) on Rowley's Bay. Washington Island and Rock Island, accessible via ferry from Gills Rock, offer good smallmouth habitat, too. You might consider hiring a guide to fish Door County smallmouth, especially if your time is limited. Gary Nault (920-743-1100) guides out of Sturgeon Bay.

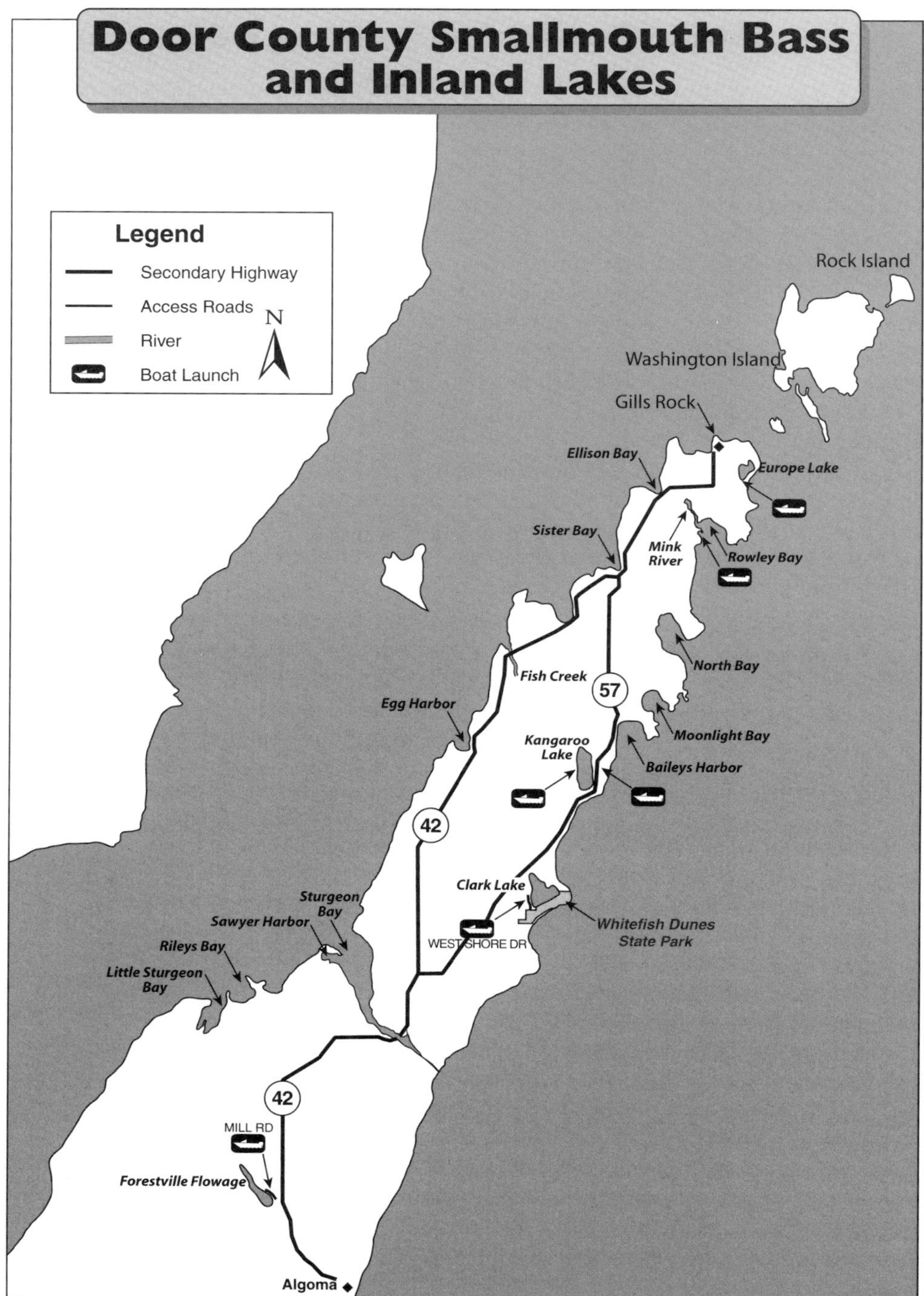
Door County Smallmouth Bass and Inland Lakes
Legend
Secondary Highway
Access Roads
River
Boat Launch
N
Rock Island
Washington Island
Gills Rock
Ellison Bay
Europe Lake
Sister Bay
Mink River
Rowley Bay
North Bay
Fish Creek
57
Egg Harbor
Moonlight Bay
Kangaroo Lake
Baileys Harbor
42
Clark Lake
Sturgeon Bay
Sawyer Harbor
Whitefish Dunes State Park
Rileys Bay
WEST SHORE DR
Little Sturgeon Bay
42
MILL RD
Forestville Flowage
Algoma

Muddler Minnows and Marabou Leeches (black and olive) are good fly choices. Crawfish are a mainstay of the smallmouth's diet, and their imitations are an excellent bet. When fish are keyed in on alewife or shiners, try a streamer pattern with some tinsel in it. Fish flies that are size 2 or 4.

A 7-weight rod of about 9 feet will give you enough power to handle a hard-running bass and make the long casts necessary to reach them. A poly leader or sink-tip line will help get your fly down to the fish. During the summer surface bite, you'll be able to use a floating line.

Fishing Facts:

Door County Smallmouth Bass

Season

- First Saturday in May to first Saturday in March for Green Bay and Lake Michigan; July 1 to first Saturday in March within a half-mile of all islands around Washington Island.

Size

- 14-inch minimum on Green Bay and Lake Michigan; 12-inch minimum within ¼ mile of all islands around Washington Island.

Daily Limit

- 5

Access

- Boat launches, state parks (Potawatomi, Peninsula, Newport, Rock Island), harbors.

Comments

- While smallmouth populations are doing well off Door County, catch-and-release is particularly important with smallmouth bass because they are so slow to reach maturity (3 to 5 years).

Door County Inland Lakes

Door County's few inland lakes absorb a fair amount of boat traffic. No surprise, as they are shallower and warm much faster than does big, cold Lake Michigan. However, during evenings and early mornings in summer and just about anytime during spring and fall, you'll find solitude on these pretty lakes. The following lakes are given in relation to their location on the Door County Peninsula from south to north.

Forestville Flowage

While the dam at Forestville on the Ahnapee River blocks the passage of trout and salmon upstream, it also creates fine largemouth bass habitat in the widening of the river known as the Forestville Flowage. Door County fisheries biologist Steve Hogler recommends it as an inland water that sees minimal boat traffic and has a population of sizeable largemouth bass. There is a launch just above the dam on Mill Road. Fish the weeds with a deerhair bass bug. A 6-weight rod will do nicely. Forestville can be reached from the south via Highway 42, just north of the town of Algoma.

Clark's Lake

Twenty miles north of Forestville, Clark's Lake is about half the size of Kangaroo Lake just to the north. It has good gamefish and panfish populations and is surrounded by cottages and resorts dating back to the 1930s. However, public access to the lake is limited. A public launch ramp can be found on the west side off West Shore Drive. There is room for a few boat trailers here, but it's pretty tight quarters.

While public access to the lake shoreline is limited, some of Whitefish Dunes State Park fronts Clark's Lake off the Green Trail. Anglers without a boat wishing to gain access to the lake could buy a park sticker and hike in through the state park and wade or fish from a belly boat. Clark's Lake is located off Highway 57 near the town of Jacksonport.

Kangaroo Lake

Kangaroo is really two lakes in one—a 50-acre, no-motor marsh north of County E and a 1,600-acre, rocky-bottom lake that sees more boat traffic.

The northern portion of Kangaroo Lake offers something few Wisconsin lakes can claim: a population of trophy rock bass. Even at 6 or 7 inches, these fellows give a good tussle on a fly rod. Steve Hogler, inland fisheries biologist for Door County, says there is a healthy population of 10- to 12-inch rock bass in the northern section of Kangaroo Lake. Rock bass are opportunistic feeders and will take just about any nymph or streamer you offer. They're also tasty when you fry them up, and since they're numerous you can keep a few for the pan without hurting populations.

You'll also find bluegills and northerns in this small weedy portion of the lake off County E. You can launch a small boat or float tube right off County E. Naturalists will note the Nature Conservancy holdings along the northern edge of Kangaroo Lake. Rare bog-loving plant communities thrive here.

The rest of the lake, some 1,600 acres, offers good angling for bass, panfish, northern pike, and small walleye. Good areas to concentrate your efforts are around the rocky dropoff in the lower-middle part of the lake and around the island in the northern part. According to Dave Listieri of Sunset Shores Resort on Kangaroo Lake, the DNR and Kangaroo Lake Association are planning to sink new fish cribs. This will provide cover for panfish and gamefish frye that fall victim to the lake's numerous northern pike. (From an ecological viewpoint you are helping other fish populations by keeping a few northerns for the pan.)

There are two pay-for-use launches, one on the eastern side off Kangaroo Lake Drive and one the western side of the lake off Beach Road. There is no fee for launching cartop boats off County E. Kangaroo Lake is just west of Highway 57 near Bailey's Harbor. While it sees some boat and water-ski traffic during the summer, Kangaroo Lake offers enough quiet nooks and crannies to make it worth your while.

Europe Lake

Europe Lake is located at the far northern tip of the Door County Peninsula, with its eastern edge in Newport State Park. It's a striking blue lake with a rocky shoreline and a bit of bulrush cover. While it is not overly fertile, DNR surveys show modest populations of smallmouth bass, northern pike, and panfish.

Craig Amacker explores the fishing on a Lake Michigan tributary. (Craig Amacker)

An angler plays a steelhead in eastern Wisconsin. (Craig Amacker)

There's a launch off Europe Bay Road. If you feel like prospecting with a streamer and sinking line as you paddle along, you might pick up a pike or a bass. The real payoff is being on Europe Lake, Door County's prettiest lake hands-down.

Mink River

Thankfully, the Nature Conservancy owns a good chunk of the upper reaches of the Mink River in northern Door County just south of Gills Rock. It is a rare ecosystem on a peninsula with sometimes rampant development that caters to vacationers. The unique thing about the Mink River is that it's one of the few estuaries on the Great Lakes, because, believe it or not, it has tides. These tides are essentially wind-dependent. When the wind blows from the west, the river appears to be flowing toward Lake Michigan and Rowley Bay. When it blows from the east or southeast, the Mink appears to run toward the Green Bay side of the peninsula. The result is a tidal ecosystem. The upper reaches of this estuary are striking, flanked by tamarack and birch trees with tannin-dark water.

The Mink River is of interest to the angler because of the smallmouth and northern pike populations it harbors. According to Steve Hogler, inland fisheries biologist for Door County, shocking surveys have turned up good numbers of both species. Smallmouth prefer the rockier habitat of Rowley Bay, which is the outlet of the Mink River. Fish them in May and June with a sinking line and an assortment of leeches and streamers; crawfish flies and any silvery minnow imitation will take fish. You'll want a 2X leader and 10-pound tippet.

For pike, fish during April and May using wire or heavy monofilament leaders and Clouser Minnows. You'll find pike all the way up the river. Cast to the channels or stands of bulrush. Fishing for pike is open year-round with no minimum size limit and a daily bag of 5 fish. Smallmouth bass are open to fishing the first Saturday in May to March 1 with a daily bag of 5 and a minimum size of 14 inches.

Launch at Highway Z near the Wagon Wheel Resort (launch fee $9). Canoes and kayaks are also available for rental. A strong wind from the northwest or southeast will make boating on Rowley Bay unsafe, so be careful.

Hub City: Bailey's Harbor

Centrally located on the Door County Peninsula, Bailey's Harbor makes a good base for exploring the area's fishing opportunities. The waters of Bailey's Harbor itself provide good near-shore fishing in spring and fall for brown trout, brook trout, steelhead, and salmon. Nearby Kangaroo Lake provides good fishing for rock bass and northern pike and offers a small, no-motor bay ideal for fly fishing. Hibbards Creek and Heins Creek see spring runs of steelhead beginning in late March, and the reedy Mink River holds northern pike. Several charter boats specializing in trout and salmon operate out of Bailey's Harbor, making for good family outings.

Door County's real draw for flyfishers is smallmouth bass, which grow fat on crawfish and forage fish in Lake Michigan's clear, rocky waters. Bailey's Harbor, Moonlight Bay, North Bay, and Rowley Bay can be fished either from a boat or by wading or float-tubing. The rocky shoreline on the Green Bay side of the peninsula offers even better smallmouth fishing.

If you're not hooking fish, you'll likely be eating them. Perch fries and fish boils are Door County trademarks. Sister Bay Bowl in nearby Sister Bay offers Door County's best perch fry. The Scandinavian tradition of fish boils—whitefish, carrots, and potatoes cooked in large kettles over an open fire—can be found anywhere that serves fish.

Door County is a favorite vacation spot for folks from throughout Wisconsin and Illinois, so book accommodations early if you plan to visit in summer. In general, Jacksonport and Bailey's Harbor on the Lake Michigan side of Door County are quieter than Egg Harbor, Fish Creek, Ephraim, and Sister Bay on the Green Bay side. Sturgeon Bay, on the southern end of the peninsula, also offers dining and lodging options in a more urban setting.

Accommodations

Ridges Resort and Guest House, 8252 Highway 57, Bailey's Harbor; 920-839-2127; established resort with old-time charm; $$$

Wagon Trail Resort and Conference Center, 1041 County ZZ, Ephraim; 920-854-2385; established resort located on mouth of Mink River and Rowley Bay

Rowley's Bay Cabins, County ZZ, Ephraim; 920-854-5580; old-time cabins located next to Wagon Trail Resort

Campgrounds

Potawatomi State Park, 3740 Park Drive, Sturgeon Bay; 920-743-8869; 30 miles southwest of Bailey's Harbor

Whitefish Dunes State Park, 3701 Clark Lake Road, Sturgeon Bay; 920-823-2400

Peninsula State Park, P.O. Box 218, Fish Creek; 920-868-3258; 10 miles west of Bailey's Harbor

Newport State Park, 415 County NP, Ellison Bay; 920-854-2500

Rock Island State Park, Washington Island; 920-847-2235; accessible via ferry from Gills Rock; all walk-in sites; no supplies on island

Restaurants

Coyote Roadhouse Tavern, County E, Bailey's Harbor; 920-839-9192; tavern located on Kangaroo Lake with good ribs, tap beer, fish, and sandwiches

Blue Ox Tavern, Highway 57, Bailey's Harbor; try the chili and the Blue Ox Burger at this low-key Wisconsin tavern

Weisgerber's Cornerstone, Highway 57, Bailey's Harbor; 920-839-2290; old fashioned corner tavern with good perch, burgers, and dinners

Harbor Fish Market and Grille, Highway 57, Bailey's Harbor; 920-839-9999; gourmet seafood with international flare

Sister Bay Bowl, Highway 42, Sister Bay; 920-bowling alley with separate dining room; the best lake perch in Door County hands-down

Fly Shops, Outfitters, Sporting Goods

Bailey's Harbor Fast Stop, Highway 57, Bailey's Harbor; 920-839-2114; groceries, licenses, gas, beer

Gary Nault, smallmouth bass guide who operates out of Sturgeon Bay; 920-743-1100

Tight Lines Fly Fishing Company., 1534 Mid Valley Dr, De Pere, WI 54115; 920-336-4106

Veterinarians

Northern Door Pet Clinic, Highway 57, Sister Bay; 920-854-4979; located a half-mile south of Sister Bay on Highway 57

Medical

Door County Memorial Hospital, 323 South 18th Avenue, Sturgeon Bay; 920-743-5566

Auto Rental

Avis Rent-a-Car, 8150 Ridges Drive, Bailey's Harbor; 920-839-2973

Automobile Repair

Kiehnau's Service Station, P.O. Box 2, Bailey's Harbor; 920-839-2070

Air Service

Facilities at Sturgeon Bay and Green Bay.

For More Information

Door County Chamber of Commerce
Box 406
Sturgeon Bay, WI 54235
920-743-4456
www.doorcountyvacation.com

Northeast Iowa

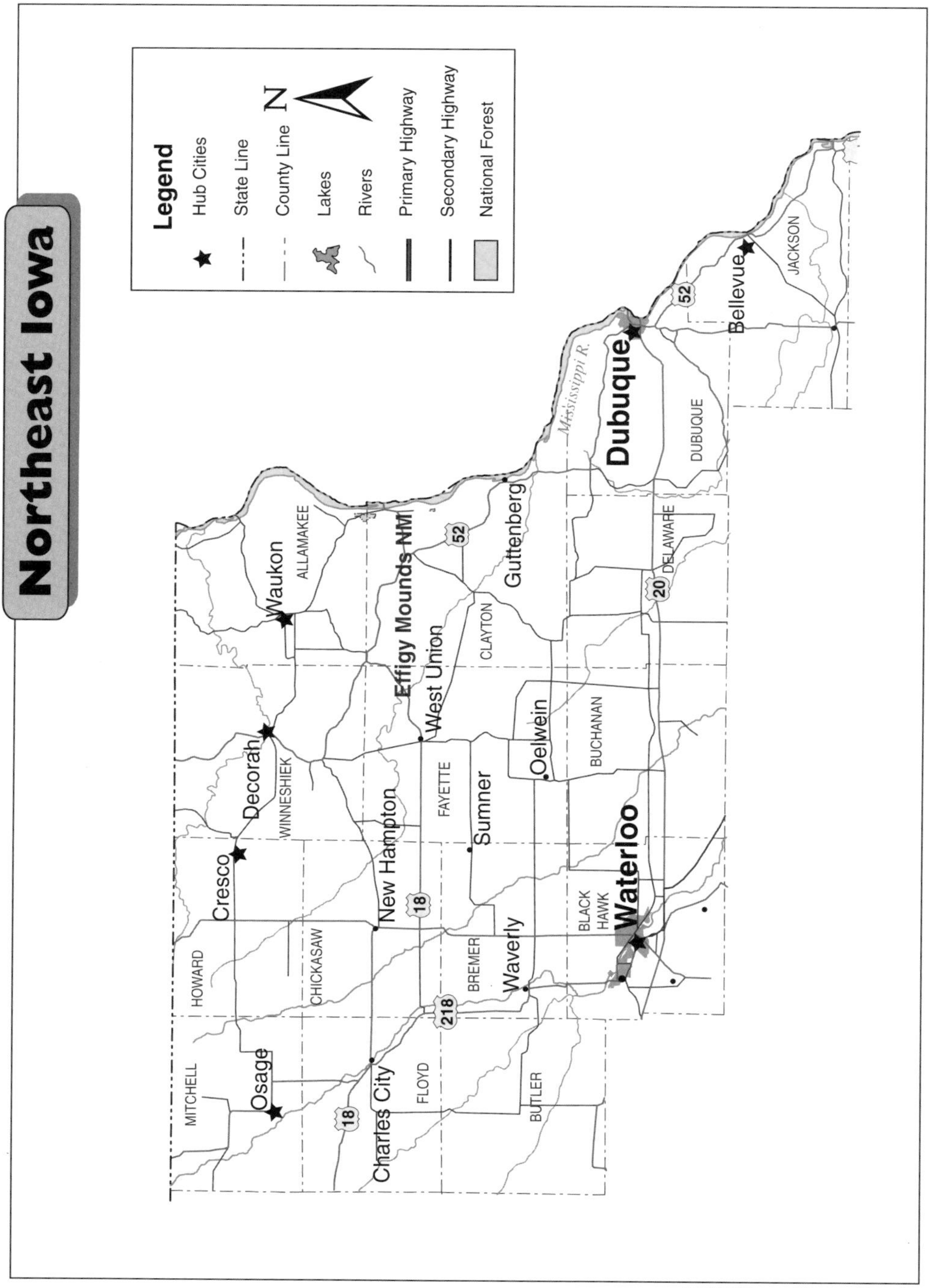

Northeast Iowa

Legend

- Hub Cities
- State Line
- County Line
- Lakes
- Rivers
- Primary Highway
- Secondary Highway
- National Forest

Northeast Iowa: Trout on the Edge of the Prairie

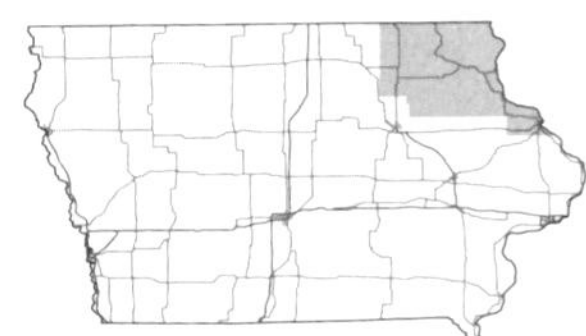

Think of Iowa, and flatland images come to mind: pheasants, prairie, and grain silos. As with many stereotypes, this contains a good bit of truth. There are roughly a hundred thousand farms in Iowa. It is, as a rule, flat; and much of the land is devoted to food production.

On a closer look, however, one realizes this high and dry prairie is bound by great rivers—Missouri in the west, Mississippi in the east—and carved up by a host of smaller ones like the Skunk, Raccoon, and Turkey. These hold a mix of bass, pike, walleye, and rough fish. But the Hawkeye State really shines for the long-rod angler in its northeast corner, with some eighty trout streams. That, plus a handful of quality warmwater venues located in this corner of Iowa, makes a true (if under fished) destination for flyfishers.

Like neighboring southeast Minnesota and southwest Wisconsin, northeast Iowa is part of the Driftless Area: a belt of land about twice the size of New Jersey that was not subject to glacial drift or flattening. Wooded bluffs and a high water table seeping up through limestone characterize this region. Iowa's spring-fed, limestone streams are highly fertile and maintain a fairly constant temperature throughout the year. What these conditions mean for the trout angler are top-quality streams that grow trout and forage like scuds, crawfish, and sculpins year-round.

While Wisconsin and Minnesota trout streams are closed to fishing from fall to spring, Iowa trout streams are open to fishing year round! Ever spent a cool fall day wishing you could be on a spring creek fishing the Blue-winged Olive hatch, or prospecting with a streamer on a mild winter day? Thanks to a full-year season, you can do this in Iowa. When most Iowans are chasing ducks, deer, or pheasant, angler pressure is light, streamside brush is minimal, and mosquitoes and horseflies are nonexistent during these off-times. An angler's paradise awaits, for the cost of an Iowa license and trout stamp. The ridge and valley scenery and welcoming small towns like Decorah and Marquette/McGregor are a bonus.

Things are only getting better for these streams. Following a general land-use trend in the Driftless Area, more land is going into set-aside and forest-crop; meaning less erosion and better water quality. Farming right down to the creek line is becoming a thing of the past. An increasingly global food economy makes farming hilly, rocky land unprofitable. In this odd and uncharacteristic twist, the free-market has actually helped environmental conditions here.

The Iowa DNR has been working hard to establish a sustainable trout program. In 1980, Iowa had only five streams with naturally reproducing trout populations. Now there are twenty-six streams with consistent natural reproduction and another twenty streams with sporadic reproduction, according to Iowa Fisheries Manager, Bill Kalishek. The Iowa DNR has also been on an aggressive campaign to acquire easements and purchase streamside land. Bank stabilization and in-stream, fish-holding structures are being worked on. Stocking is done from wild strain fish reared in Iowa streams. In spring 2005, Trout Unlimited launched TUDARE (Trout Unlimited Driftless Area Restoration), an effort to coordinate conservation efforts and preserve coldwater resources in southwest Wisconsin, northeast Iowa, and southeast Minnesota.

Iowa's best trout streams are located in its northern-tier counties. Bear, French, and Waterloo top the list in Winneshiek and Allamakee counties. Secluded Sny Magill and fertile Bloody Run are good bets in Clayton County. Small, cold Grannis Creek in Fayette County holds wild rainbows.

The Law

In neighboring Wisconsin, one can fish (or hunt, camp, swim or otherwise enjoy) a river or stream by keeping one's feet wet. No permission needed because landowners don't own the streambed in Wisconsin. This is a throwback to the Navigable Waterway clause of the Northwest Ordinance of 1787, where rivers are thought to be open to public use. Not so in Iowa. The landowner does, in fact, own the streambed and controls access to it. The Iowa DNR owns or leases land on 53 streams. Fishing-access points on these streams are marked by fence stiles, fence walk-throughs, and Public Fishing signs. A smaller class of streams, called Put and Grow by the DNR, are on private land. On these streams, permission must be gained from the landowner each time you fish. These streams are listed in a table showing the Township, Range, and Section numbers at the end of the Northeast Iowa section of this book.

Access on rivers where floating in a canoe is possible, as opposed to streams, is different. Iowa law allows access to rivers at bridges via some kind of watercraft: canoe, jonboat, belly boat. The landowner owns the riverbed; however, floating down the river to fish or hunt or otherwise recreate is permitted, as long as you stay in the boat. This opens up fishing on quality venues like the Turkey, Upper Iowa, Yellow, and Cedar Rivers. These rivers hold both warmwater species such as smallmouth bass, walleye, and channel catfish, as well as trout, which come in via streams. The Mississippi's backwaters from Lansing to Dubuque offer plenty of elbowroom, and a variety of species: bass, panfish, northern pike, and walleye. Unless posted otherwise, these waters are open to public use because they fall within the Upper Mississippi River National Wildlife Refuge.

While camping is not generally allowed on fishing and hunting grounds in neighboring Wisconsin and Minnesota, primitive streamside camping is an option on many DNR lands and county parks adjoining streams in Iowa. Some quality streams that offer this are French and Pine creeks in Allamakee County, Coon Creek in Winneshiek County, North Cedar in Clayton County, and Little Turkey in Delaware County. Paint Creek and Little Paint Creek run through Iowa's hilly 8,000-acre Yellow River State Forest, with campgrounds located right on these streams. Established campgrounds can be found along Bloody Run, Buck, Sny Magill, and Turkey River in Clayton County; Trout Run, Bear Creek, and Twin Springs in Winneshiek County; Fountain Springs, Richmond Springs, and Bailey's Ford in Delaware County; and Bankston and Swiss Valley in Dubuque County.

HOT, COLD, AND DUSTY

We began this section talking about trout on the edge of the prairie. There is something really neat, but also incongruous, about this notion. You are driving along a belt of hard-farmed land and you see a brown sign directing you to a trout stream. The corn and switch grass give way to elms and mossy canyons and soon you hear the rattle of water on rock, the harbinger of trout. How can you be up there high and dry one minute and down here in a cool green valley the next? This is one of the wonders of Iowa trout fishing.

But there's a downside to doing anything on the edge; there's a price to be paid. And here that price comes in the form of miles of dirt roads and a real prairie (read: landlocked) climate. In Wisconsin and Minnesota, where trout streams are more abundant and access laws more permissive, you can bop around from one place to another without too much distance or difficulty. In Iowa, where landowners do actually own the streambed, you must fish DNR lands or secure permission. This means a lot of windshield time driving between streams. Kind of like driving the gravel roads of the Dakotas looking for potholes. My advice: Don't try to fish too many streams in one day. Pick one or two and fish them thoroughly.

Did I mention the weather? Cold northwest winds sweeping over the prairies can be intemperate and brutal here in Iowa. And on a summer morning, nine o'clock in Iowa can feel like noon in Oklahoma. Iowa's not infrequent weather extremes take their toll on the trout; and neither one makes them more cooperative. In warm, low water conditions, I fish lots of micro nymphs because the fish are picky. In cold conditions, I work a large streamer slowly over the bottom to provoke strikes.

Keep food and water in the car to help keep you perky during long car rides. Pick one or two streams to fish in a day. And avoid fishing in extreme heat and cold if possible. With these caveats, Iowa trout fishing is fun and productive, especially when the season's closed elsewhere.

SEASON AND REGULATIONS

Iowa fishing season runs year round.

On the vast majority of Iowa streams, 5 trout may be kept daily, with a possession limit of 10. There is no minimum size limit. Special regulations, if any, appear in the text for each water and will be posted at the stream.

Consult Iowa's Fishing Regulations for a full summary of its fishing rules. While exceptions are noted in the text for individual entries, Iowa's general bag and size limits are as follows: walleye and sauger, 5 with no minimum length; northern pike, 3 with no minimum length; largemouth and smallmouth bass, 3 with a minimum length of 12 inches; channel catfish and flathead catfish, lakes 8 and rivers 15 with no minimum size in either; white bass, no minimum size or bag limit. For bluegill and crappie, there is no minimum size or possession limit; daily bag limit is 25.

Two biologists work to manage Iowa's trout program: one out of Decorah on northern-tier streams and one out of Manchester on southern-tier streams. For more information, contact:

Bill Kalishek
Fisheries Biologist for Northern Streams
Decorah Rearing Station
2321 Siewers Springs Road
Decorah, Iowa 52101
563-382-8324

Dan King
Fisheries Biologist Southern Streams
Manchester Trout Hatchery
22693 205th Avenue
Manchester, Iowa 52057
563-927-3276

General Information regarding Iowa fisheries can be obtained from the state DNR:

Iowa Department of Natural Resources
Wallace State Office Building
Des Moines, Iowa 50319-0034
515-281-FISH (3474)
www.state.ia.us/fish

Fishing Licenses

Iowa fishing license can be purchased via the Iowa DNR website at iowadnr.gov

Resident License Fees

License Type	Cost
Fishing (16+ years)	$17.50
Fishing, 7-day	$12.00
Fishing, 24-hour	$8.00
Trout Fee	$11.00
Lifetime Fishing (65+ years)	$51.00
Lifetime Combined (disabled military veteran or POW)	$31.00

Nonresident License Fees

License Type	Cost
Fishing (16+ years)	$39.50
Fishing, 7-day	$30.50
Fishing, 3-day	$16.00
Fishing, 24-hour	$9.00
Trout Fee	$13.50

A Bloody Run brown goes free.

Bloody Run

Aristotle said that first impressions are likely to describe later relationships. My first Iowa trout fishing proves this, because it has augured many happy returns. I began below a railroad bridge on Bloody Run on a late April morning with elm trees just beginning to leaf out, waters running bank-full, and trout—big trout—ready to grab my Woolly Bugger. By the time I had covered a hundred yards of stream, I'd already caught and released a 17-inch, hook-jawed brown, a pretty brook, a rainbow, and a brace of fat, 14-inchers from a tangle of fallen hackberry trees. Granted, trout are hungry and aggressive after winter. And a Marquette hardware store owner had tipped me off that the lower reaches of Bloody Run hold big trout. But, Bloody Run in particular, and a host of other northeast Iowa trout streams in general, are full of wild and planted trout and can be fished productively year-round.

Bloody Run begins near Spook Cave and runs parallel to Highway 18 for 10 miles before emptying into the Mississippi River at the village of Marquette. It is larger than most Iowa trout streams, approaching 30 to 40 feet across in its lower reaches. Numerous springs pump in cold water to keep it running in the low 60s, even in the heat of summer. You'll find naturally reproducing browns as well as stocked rainbows and brookies here.

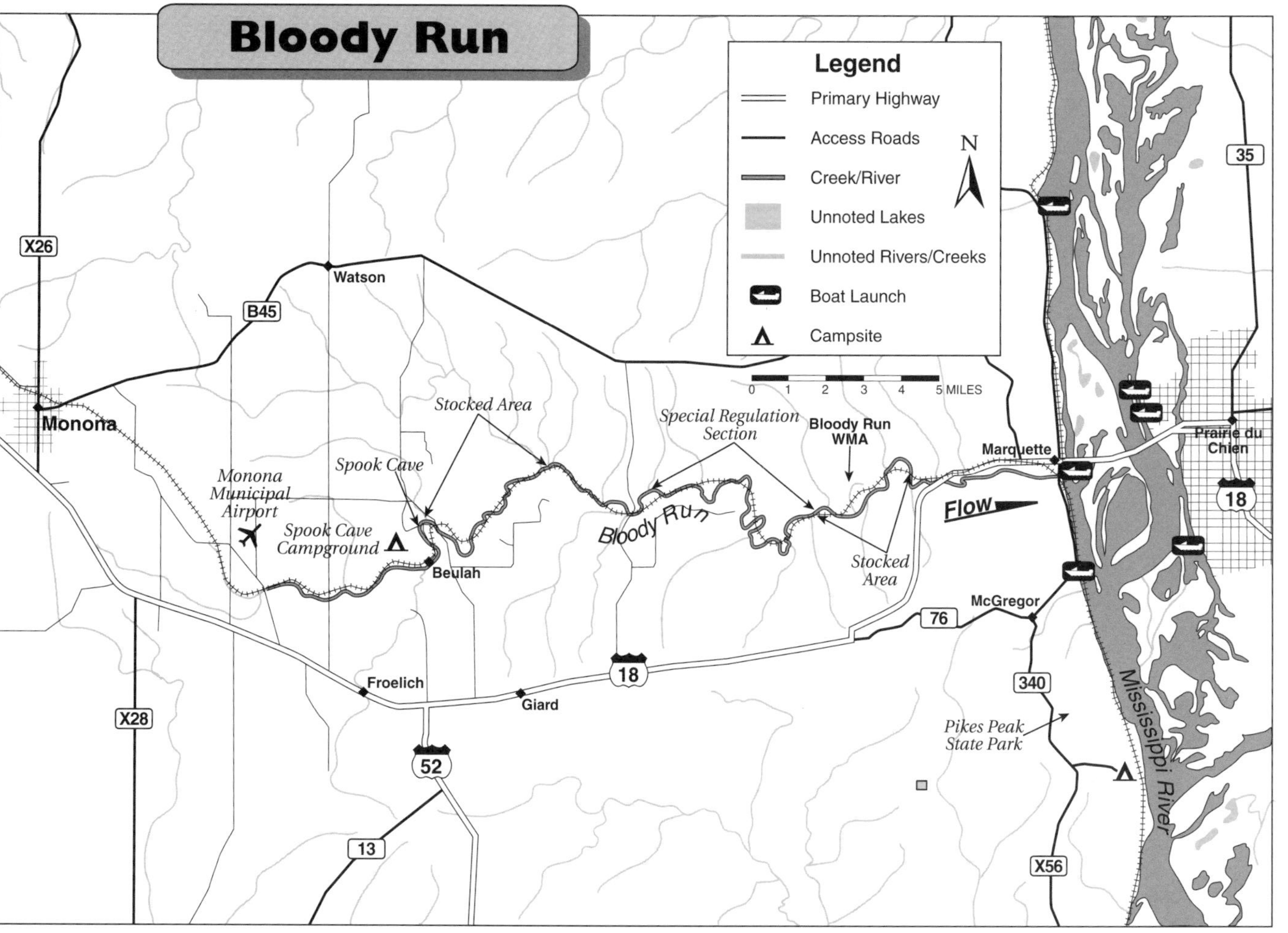

© 2006 Wilderness Adventures Press, Inc.

Blue-winged Olives are present all year, especially in October and March. Black Caddis patterns are productive in March. Hendricksons are on for most of April, and look for Gray Fox and March Brown hatches from late May through June. The dead of summer means Trico hatches in the early morning, and White Mayfly later in the day. Terrestrials such as crickets, hoppers, and beetles, work well from July through September. Midges and of course other aquatic invertebrates like scuds and crawfish are present on Bloody Run all year. An Adams in size 18 or 20 is an excellent all-around dry on any Iowa spring creek.

About half of Bloody Run's water is open to public fishing. The uppermost public fishing begins at Spook Cave Road and continues downstream for roughly a mile and a half. The stream is narrow and clear here; hit it during low light or after a rain. Iowa's 5-trout limit applies in this stretch.

Continuing downstream, Bloody Run is under private ownership for about the next 2 miles. Public access is available again at the Iris Avenue Bridge and then again along Inkwell Road. Here, deep holes and streamside bluffs are the rule; only artificials may be fished and only trout over 14 inches may be kept. Special regulations end at the county campground, and regular Iowa trout regulations are in place for the remainder of the public access, about another mile of stream. Access to this last stretch is via a dirt road, marked with a sign for Bloody Run Campground, that intersects Highway 18, about 2 miles west of the town of Marquette, and runs along the east bank of the stream. A 600-acre timbered area owned by the Iowa DNR adjoins this stretch of Bloody Run; in areas not under DNR control, there is some littering, abandoned cars, and the like. Though not stocked, the lower reaches of Bloody Run, in the vicinity of the Highway 18 Bridge are productive for big browns.

Stream Facts: Bloody Run

Regulations

- Posted area from Iris Road Bridge to Bloody Run County Park. Bloody Run County Park Campground: artificials only; 14-inch minimum

Species

- Large brown trout, stocked rainbow, and brook trout

Miles of Public Water

- 5 miles

Access

- Spook Cave Road, Iris Road, Inkwell Road; dirt road leading to Bloody Run County Park Campground

Nearest towns

- Marquette/McGregor; Farmersburg

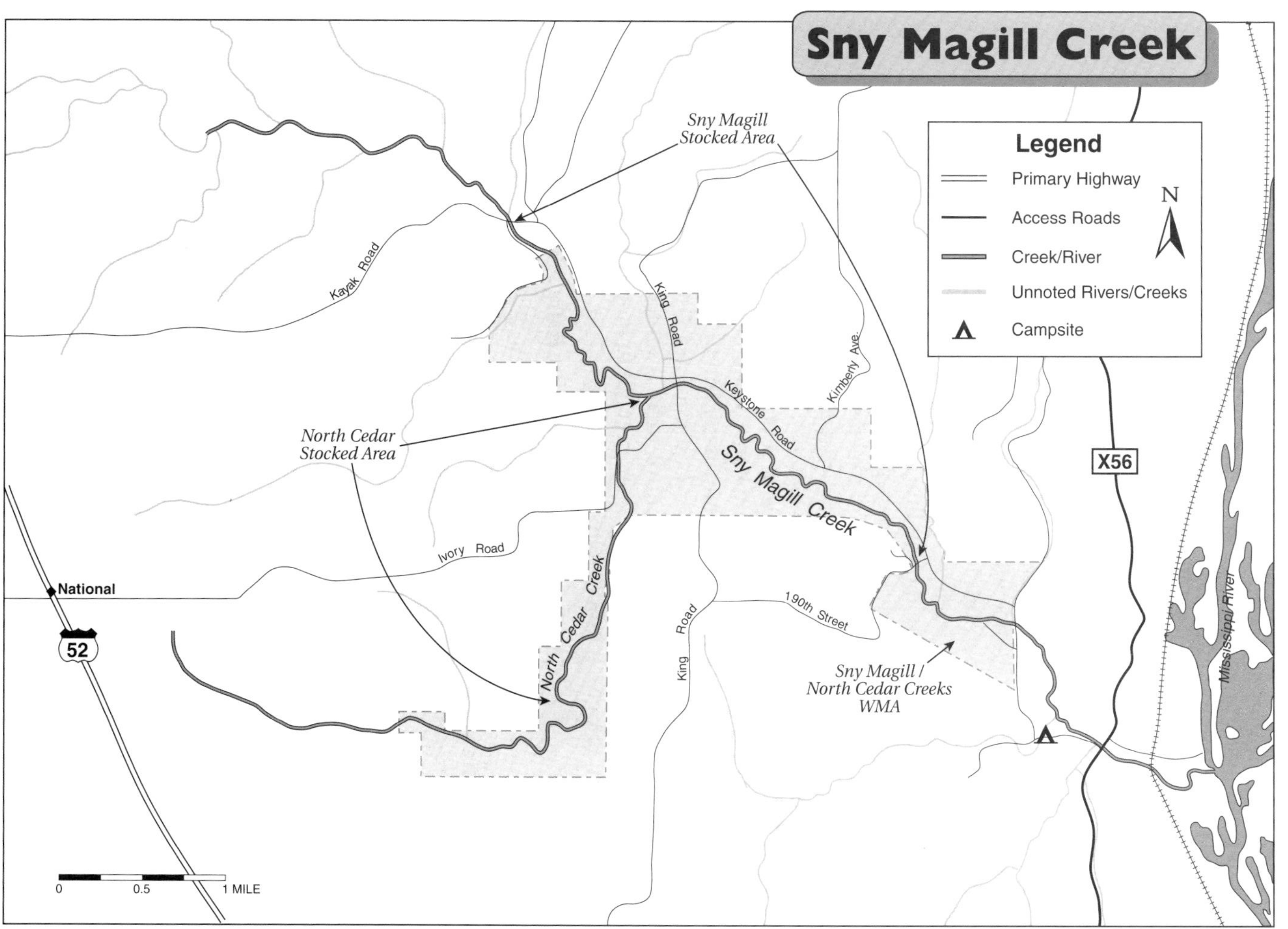
Sny Magill Creek
Legend
Primary Highway
Access Roads
Creek/River
Unnoted Rivers/Creeks
Campsite
N
Sny Magill Stocked Area
Kayak Road
King Road
Kimberly Ave.
Keystone Road
North Cedar Stocked Area
Sny Magill Creek
X56
Ivory Road
National
North Cedar Creek
190th Street
King Road
52
Sny Magill / North Cedar Creeks WMA
Mississippi River
0
0.5
1 MILE

A deep pool on Sny Magill.

Sny Magill

This scenic, wooded creek just south of Marquette/McGregor and just east of Farmersburg runs through 1,600 acres of valley land owned by the Iowa DNR. While you are only a few miles from a number of bustling river towns, you feel as if you are in a remote valley; shady and verdant, and carved by a cool green stream which bears, appropriately enough, a Welsh name. A brown Iowa DNR sign, with a picture of a duck and trout, points the way from Highway 18 just outside McGregor, down Keystone Road; follow Keystone for about 3 miles before hitting Sny Magill. Kayak, Keystone, King, and Kimberley Roads cross the stream and provide access via stiles and parking lots.

Sny Magill's valley is a wooded, gnarly place. Had I encountered a gnome or sprite, I would have only been slightly surprised. Those willing to fish in fall, winter, or early spring and tolerant of brushy banks, will be able to tangle with wary brown trout fingerlings that have grown up in the stream and behave for all practical purposes like wild fish. I found downstream nymphing and streamer fishing very productive here, letting my fly undulate in the green depths. Rainbows and a handful of brook trout are planted here from April through October, and are not nearly as wary as the stream's browns. The upper reaches of Sny Magill are narrow and clear; fish them after a rain or during low light. The lower reaches along Keystone Road, especially below the mouth of North Cedar Creek, are deeper with lots of cover. North Cedar is a small, stocked stream accessible via Ivory Road. Sny Magill's lower reaches abound in pools my angling companions and I like to call "Blue Lagoons", unfathomably deep holes where big trout wait for prey while finning over their pebbly lairs.

In March and October, Blue-winged Olive hatch, and Little Black Caddis come off in March. Hendrickson's follow in April. March Browns and Gray Foxes are on in late May and June. Summer is a good time for terrestrial patterns here, especially crickets. Midges hatch here all year.

Stream Facts: Sny Magill

Regulations
- Standard

Species
- Stream-reared brown trout; stocked rainbow and brook trout

Miles of Public Water
- 5 miles

Access
- Kayak, Keystone, Kimberly Roads

Nearest towns
- Marquette/McGregor, Farmersburg

A good day on Paint Creek.

Paint Creek

The nice thing about Paint Creek is that, for six continuous miles, there is public stream access, a rarity among Iowa streams. It is a scenic stream with the lower half running through the 8,500-acre Yellow River State Forest, which provides hiking, camping, fishing, and hunting aplenty. While Paint Creek does not have the cold temperatures and spate of aquatic life of Bloody Run to the south, it does offer easy access, clear banks, lots of stocked fish, and plenty of elbowroom. You might view it as a good warm-up, a place to take a fledging angler. The forest's hardwoods, turning yellow, gold, and red in October and leafing out into emerald green in May, provide a pretty backdrop for going after trout.

Access begins near the town of Waterville between Waukon and Harpers Ferry; X32 takes you to Waterville from either Highway 76 to the south or Highway A52 to the north. From Waterville, one can fish upstream, following Paint Creek Road, or downstream, following White Pine Road. Upstream there is a very easy access and easy fishing at the juncture of X32 and Paint Creek Drive. A deep run at the bridge here and a deep flat-water run above the bridge lend themselves to slow-water nymphing or stripping a streamer back toward you. Rainbow trout are stocked heavily

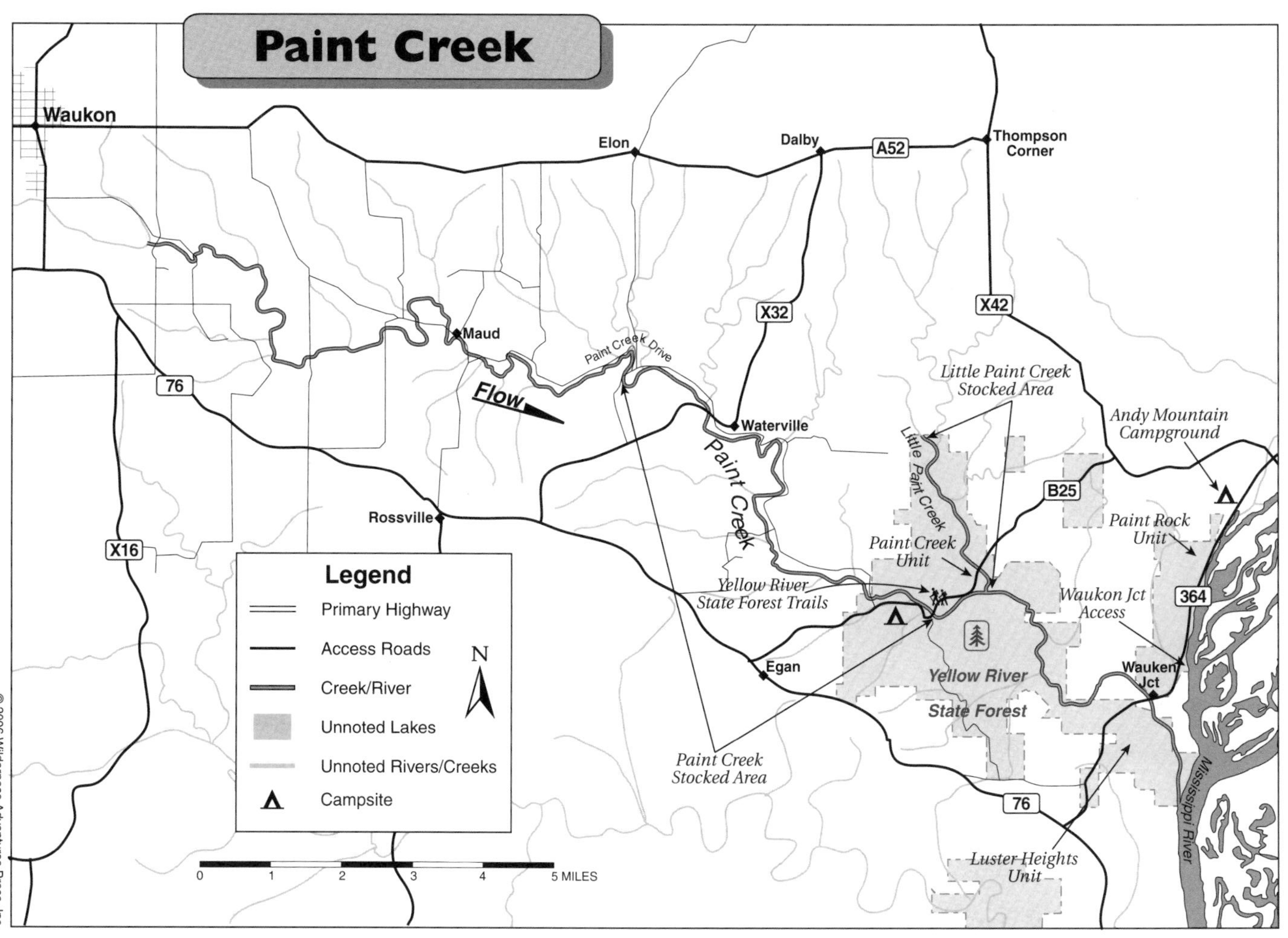
Paint Creek
Waukon
Elon
Dalby
A52
Thompson Corner
X32
X42
Maud
Paint Creek Drive
76
Flow
Waterville
Paint Creek
Little Paint Creek Stocked Area
Little Paint Creek
Andy Mountain Campground
B25
Rossville
X16
Paint Creek Unit
Paint Rock Unit
Yellow River State Forest Trails
Waukon Jct Access
364
Egan
Yellow River
State Forest
Wauken Jct
Paint Creek Stocked Area
Mississippi River
Luster Heights Unit
Legend
Primary Highway
Access Roads
Creek/River
Unnoted Lakes
Unnoted Rivers/Creeks
Campsite
N
0
1
2
3
4
5 MILES

throughout Paint along with the occasional brook trout. Below Waterville, along White Pine Drive, the State Forest begins. One can simply drive along and pull over when a good run strikes. Paint Creek warms up to marginal levels in summer but fishes well in winter, spring, and fall. Paint does not abound with structure so, if you can find a big boulder or fallen tree, chances are you will find fish, even some holdover rainbows that may reach 3 pounds or more.

Paint is not particularly known for hatches, though an Adams is a good all-around dry fly here as well as on other Iowa spring creeks. Jeff Skeate, an avid fly angler from Decorah, fishes a home-tied, Beadhead Streamer of yellow chenille, grizzly hackle, and a tinsel tail with deadly results on Iowa rainbows. Rainbows like flash, so any streamer with a bit of tinsel or yellow will take fish here.

An interesting quality of Paint Creek is the curious yellow tint shared by the nearby Yellow River. A comparison here would be central Pennsylvania's Yellow Breeches. The reason, in both cases, is the particular variety of limestone through which the surrounding springs seep.

Stream Facts: Paint Creek

Regulations

- 5 trout, no minimum length

Species

- Stocked rainbow and brook trout

Miles of Public Water

- 6 miles

Access

- Paint Creek Drive, X32, White Pine Drive

Nearest towns

- Waterville; Waukon; Harpers Ferry

Little Paint Creek

Entirely within Yellow River State Forest, Little Paint Creek is a tributary of Paint Creek and is smaller and colder than Paint Creek. It joins Paint Creek after crossing Highway B25 near the forest's equestrian campground; Donahue Road parallels Little Paint. Follow Donahue Road upstream, or just hike along the stream. The pretty rock-and-hardwood setting is bonus. Bring your 2-weight and fish Little Paint's pocket water with small nymphs. Spring and fall weekdays are especially pleasant here.

Hickory Creek

Small and narrow, Hickory Creek flows through a secluded valley north of the town of Monona, which is 15 miles west of Marquette/McGregor on Highway 18. Take Highway X26 north out of Monona and turn left (west) onto Hickory Creek Road, which parallels the stream and from which it can be accessed via numerous fence-stiles. In total, about a mile and half of Hickory Creek is open to public fishing. Bank stabilizers and lunker structures are being installed as part of a habitat restoration project by the DNR. Brown and brook trout are stocked in this clear, cold stream where there has been some natural reproduction among browns. Caddis patterns work well here in late spring; hoppers are good in late summer and early fall. Scuds are a fallback. Hickory Creek is not the place for lunker trout; try Bloody Run, Bear Creek, or Waterloo Creek for big fish. Expect trout in the 8- to 12-inch range with a few topping out at 14 inches. Hickory Creek feeds into the Yellow River near Volney, where its infusion of cold water brings with it the possibility of trout for anglers floating this larger river.

HUB CITY: MARQUETTE/MCGREGOR, IA & PRAIRIE DU CHIEN, WI

The largest hub between Dubuque and La Crosse, the tri-cities offer a good base to anglers with Cabela's (the area's largest fly fishing retailer) and some of Iowa's finest trout streams nearby, like Bloody Run, Paint Creek, and Sny Magill. Like Lansing but more centrally located, they offer river city charm with a bit more to do and look at: 2,000-acre Effigy Mounds National Monument with 200 Woodland Indian ceremonial mounds, excellent mid-nineteenth century brick buildings, good eateries, even the Isle of Capri Casino for those so disposed. Good birding and duck hunting can be enjoyed on the Mississippi River in October and November.

Accommodations

Frontier Motel, Marquette, Business Highway 18, 888-681-0144; located next to Isle of Capri Casino and Mississippi River

Hickory Ridge Bed and Breakfast, 17156 Great River Road, 563-873-1758; log home overlooking Mississippi River and popular with horse and outdoor enthusiasts

Grumpsters Log Cabins, 535 Ash Street, McGregor, 563-873-3767; cabins in wooded setting near Mississippi River

Country Inn and Suites, 1801 Cabelas Drive; 800 456 4000; located next to Cabela's with indoor waterpark and attached restaurant

Campgrounds

Bloody Run Campground, off Highway 18, 2 miles west of Marquette, 563-245-1516; good base camp for fishing this productive stream; follow dirt road that parallels east bank of creek

Spook Cave Campground, 13299 Spook Cave Rd., McGregor, 563-873-2144; private campground located on upper reaches of Bloody Run and near much-visited cave; cabins also for rent

Pike's Peak State Park, Highway 340, 6 miles south of McGregor, 563-873-2341; good view of the river on Iowa side

Wyalusing State Park, 5 miles south of Prairie du Chien, WI off Highway 35, 608-996-2261; 3,000-acre Wisconsin park with great trails, canoe rental, and flora and fauna

Restaurants

Kaber's Supper Club, 225 W. Blackhawk Avenue, Prairie du Chien, 608-326-6216; old-time Prairie du Chien institution with great steak, fish, and blockbuster cocktails

Old Man River Restaurant and Brewing, 123 A Street, McGregor; 563 873 1999; www.oldmanriverbrewery.com

Pete's Hamburger Stand, Blackhawk Avenue, Prairie du Chien; century-old outdoor stand serving the area's biggest and best; open May through October

Hungry House, Highway 35, Prairie du Chien, 608-326-4346; good buffet and comfort food, open early and late, just south of Cabela's

Valley Fish and Decoys, 304 S. Prairie Street, Prairie du Chien; 608-326-4719; local carver of fish and duck decoys and commercial fisherman, who serves outdoor fish fry, May through October

Sporting Goods

Marquette Hardware, 1301 North Street, Marquette, 563 873 3521; good source of Iowa trout information, vendor of Iowa licenses, does not sell fly-fishing equipment

Cabela's, Highway 35, Prairie du Chien, 608-326-7163; area's best supply of fly fishing gear

The Hatchery, 406 W. Water Street, Decorah, 800-944-6503; fly shop with selection of regional goods

Medical

Memorial Hospital, 705 E. Taylor Street, Prairie du Chien, 608-357-2000

Veterinarian

Tender Care Animal Hospital, 1420 Lessard Street, Prairie du Chien, 608-326-7101

Automobile Repair

Twin City Auto Repair, 127 Main Street, McGregor, 563-873-3317

Air Service

Prairie du Chien Airport, 37735 Highway 18, 608-326-2118

For More Information:

Prairie du Chien Chamber of Commerce
211 S. Main Street
Prairie du Chien, WI 53821
800-732-1673
www.prairieduchien.org

Marquette/McGregor Chamber of Commerce
146 Main Street
McGregor, IA 52157
563-873-2186

YELLOW RIVER

Iowa DNR Fisheries Manager, Bill Kalishek, calls the Yellow River a two-tier fishery. Springs and feeder creeks make it cold enough, especially at these confluences, to hold trout. About 75,000 fingerlings are planted in the Yellow's upper reaches every year, according to Kalishek. In addition, coolwater denizens like smallmouth bass, walleye, and the occasional northern pike cruise its 40 miles. And when you see this river up close, you will notice a yellow tint, the result of water seeping up through sulphur-colored limestone. As with many rivers like this (the upper Kickapoo, Trempealeau, and Black River among them in Wisconsin), not all water on the Yellow is productive. Much of it is sandy without anything to hold fish. You need to look for structure and then fish it: fallen trees, creek inlets, springs, rock runs, deep incised bends. If you are looking for a river to float while in Iowa, the Yellow is a good candidate. There is a canoe livery at the crossroads town of Volney. With a 5- or 6-weight rod, or light spinning equipment, you can paddle your way through some pretty bluff country and work at catching a variety of fish. Too often, anglers (trouters chief among them) stick to the well-known haunts and know little of the surrounding country. Float trips can help you make friends with these off-the-radar places and their denizens: tanagers,

Start them young.

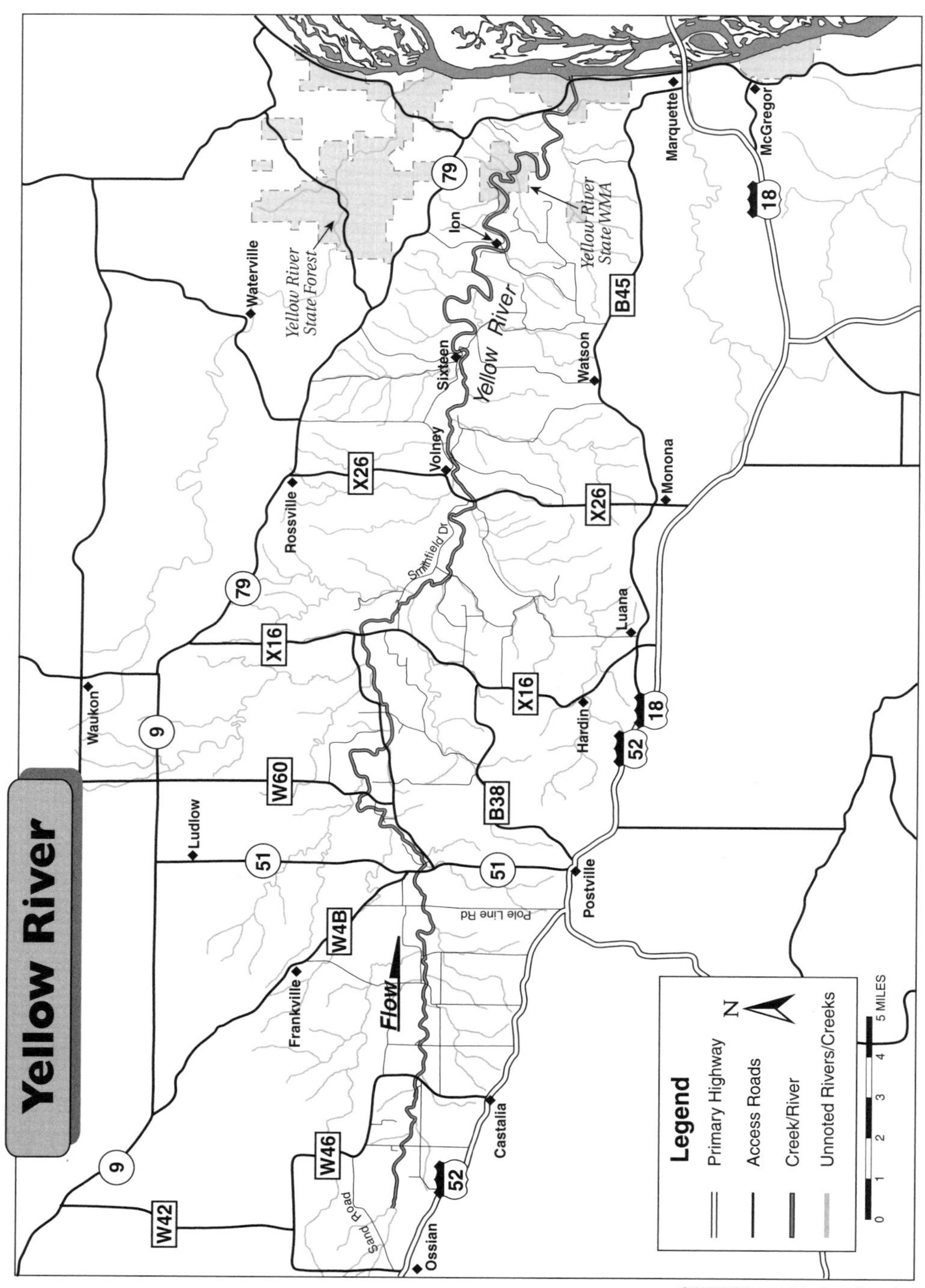

Yellow River
Waterville
Yellow River State Forest
Ion
Yellow River State WMA
Marquette
McGregor
Sixteen
Yellow River
Watson
Volney
Monona
Rossville
Smithfield Dr
Luana
Waukon
Hardin
Ludlow
Postville
Pole Line Rd
Frankville
Flow
Castalia
Sand Road
Ossian
79
18
B45
X26
X16
9
W60
B38
52
51
W4B
W46
W42
Legend
Primary Highway
Access Roads
Creek/River
Unnoted Rivers/Creeks
N
0 1 2 3 4 5 MILES

wood ducks, otters, eagles, and foxes. The stretches of river between roads are getting to be our last wilderness. Get to know them or miss out on a good thing.

Beginning near the town of Ossian, north of Highway 52, the Yellow River flows west for some 40 miles before joining the Mississippi north of Marquette/McGregor. By Iowa law, you can launch a canoe or boat at road crossings, although you cannot wade-fish unless you have permission from the landowner. Crossings on the Yellow River can be found on W46 north of Castalia, Highway 51 Postville, and X26 Monona/Volney. A popular float is from the X26 Bridge at Volney to Highway 76 just north of Marquette; some 18 miles. The last few miles of this trip pass through backwater habitat, where Mississippi River species such as catfish and largemouth bass predominate.

Stream Facts: Yellow River

Regulations

- 5 trout, no minimum size; 3 bass, at least 12 inches; 5 walleye, no minimum size; 3 northern pike, no minimum size.

Species

- Brown trout, brook trout, rainbow trout, walleye, northern pike, and rough fish

Miles of water

- 40 miles

Access

- Highway 42 in Castalia, Highway 18/52 in Postville, Highway X26 in Volney, and Yellow River State Forest. Iowa law restricts access to bridges, with boat where river flows through private land. Public access in Yellow River State Forest.

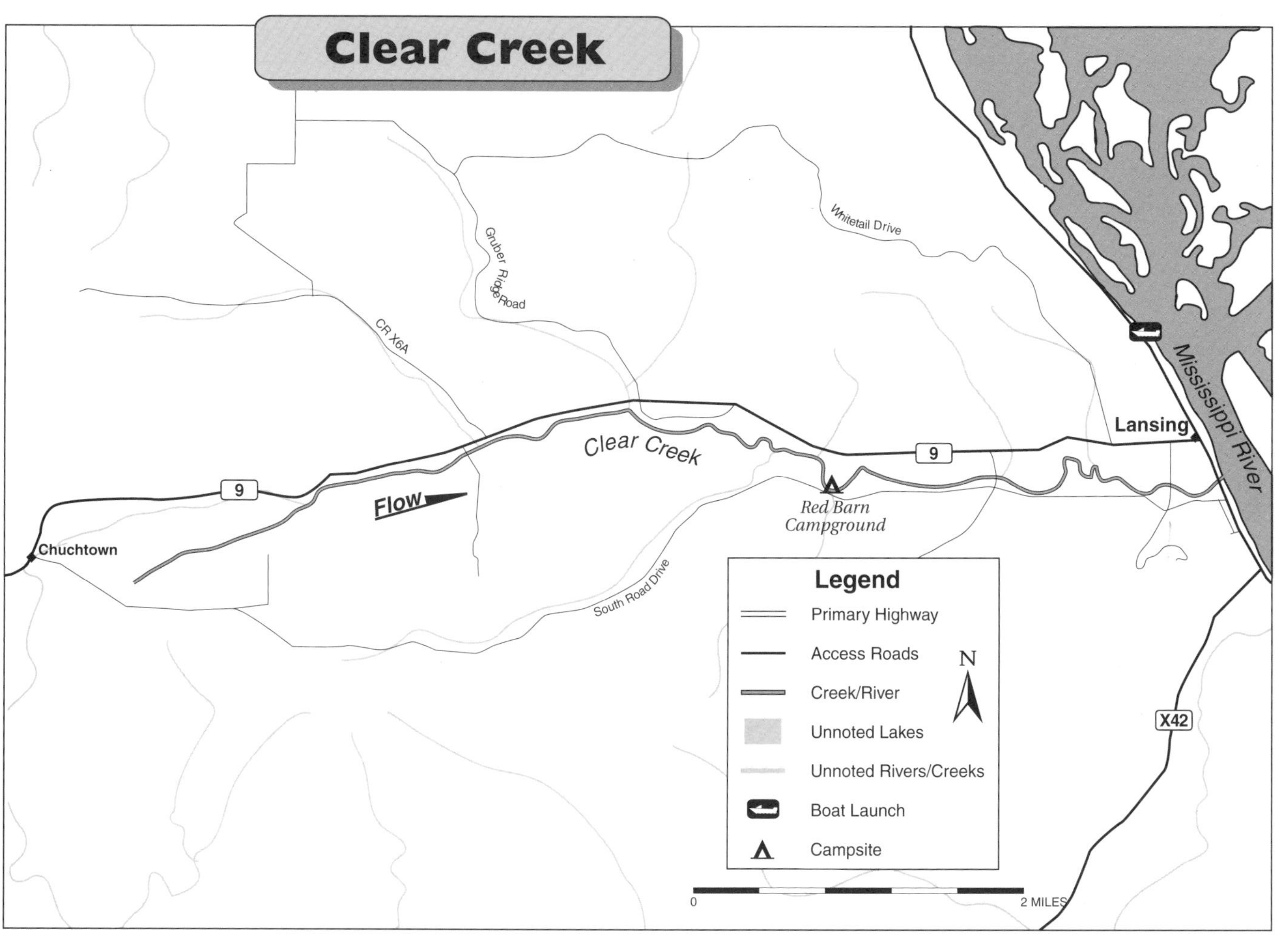
Clear Creek
Whitetail Drive
Gruber Ridge Road
CR X6A
Mississippi River
Lansing
9
Clear Creek
9
Flow
Chuchtown
Red Barn Campground
South Road Drive
Legend
Primary Highway
Access Roads
Creek/River
Unnoted Lakes
Unnoted Rivers/Creeks
Boat Launch
Campsite
N
X42
0
2 MILES

Clear Creek

Beginning west of the Mississippi River town of Lansing, Clear Creek is true to its name. Gin-clear waters roll along over a bottom of pebbles, sand, and watercress. The stream parallels Route 9 and about a mile and a half of the creek, between Driftwood Lane and Oak Hill Road, is stocked and has public access. Access is at pull-offs on the south side of Route 9 and at the Allamakee County Conservation Board Park on Oak Hill Road. There are about a half-dozen primitive campsites at this park.

The stream is loaded with scuds and caddis, making it a good bet for nymphing on a long, thin leader. It fishes well after or during cloudy weather. The deep bends and riffles immediately upstream from the Oak Hill Road parking lot provide some of the stream's best cover and fishing. Fingerling browns and catchable sizes of rainbow trout are planted here. Natural reproduction of brown trout has been documented on the upper reaches of Clear Creek.

One final note about Clear Creek: The creek itself and its lush banks are quite beautiful. However, like Bloody Run to the south, it is surrounded by a junkyard and some run-down trailer homes; and finding trash on the stream is not uncommon. If you come across some trash, help the environment and please pick it up. Clear Creek still merits fishing; anglers should just bear in mind that its surroundings are not always pristine.

A nice run on Clear Creek.

Silver Creek

All in all, about a mile of Silver Creek is open to public fishing. But that mile of water has many good attributes. It runs through pastureland, which makes for good hopper fishing. Near the end of Silver's public water, just upstream from the dirt road that crosses it, is an unfathomably deep hole that backswirls against a shady bluff and always holds decent fish. Finally, the surrounding lands are managed for upland game by the Iowa DNR. The sound of pheasant crowing or turkey gobbling is common.

To reach Silver Creek, take Highway 9 about 15 miles west out of Lansing to Lycurgus, where you will see a very prominent church steeple. Turn right on County Road X20 and watch for the brown Iowa DNR sign with the fish/duck emblem. Follow that road to Silver Creek. The public area is clearly marked by black and white signs.

Midge and Blue-winged Olive patterns are good to have on hand at Silver, as are hopper patterns for early fall. A Muddler Minnow is a good bet for prospecting the deep bluff-hole near the end of the public water. If you find too many anglers on nearby French, Silver is worth a try.

French Creek

French Creek is one of the crown jewels of Iowa's trout program. It is managed for wild trout, with brook trout predominating in the upper reaches and browns being the rule in the lower watershed. Much of it runs through the French Creek Wildlife Management Area and all water upstream from Hartley Drive is public access, about 6 miles of stream. Fish densities approach 2,500 per mile in the vicinity of French Creek Drive, making the creek second only to Waterloo Creek in its ability to grow trout. French is a low-gradient stream that runs gin clear except after heavy rains. Only artificials are permitted here and all brown trout must be released immediately. The reason for this is that eggs and milt from French Creek browns are incubated to provide the stock for all of Iowa's stocked brown trout. The theory being, if this strain thrives in French Creek, it will do well in other similar Iowa waters. Access from upstream to downstream is at French Creek Road, along Mays Prairie Road, and at Hartley Drive.

Decorah fly angler, Jeff Skeate, describes fishing French Creek as "woolly." What he means is that, especially in its upper reaches, you will be fishing in tight, wooded conditions. While this makes casting a challenge, it shades the creek, keeps water temperatures down, and cuts down on angler pressure. According to Todd Roesch, who manages the fly-fishing department at Cabela's in Prairie du Chien, a calendar of hatches here is similar to southeast Minnesota and southwest Wisconsin streams. Stoneflies are active in late February, followed by Black Caddis in March and April. A Mother's Day Caddis, named for its mid-May emergence, follows. Blue-winged Olives and midges are present and hatch all year, especially March and October. Hendricksons are on during April; Gray Fox and March Browns follow in late May and June. Good terrestrial fishing can be had here in summer and early fall, up until the first hard freeze. Scuds are present year-round as are crawfish and sculpins. A size 18

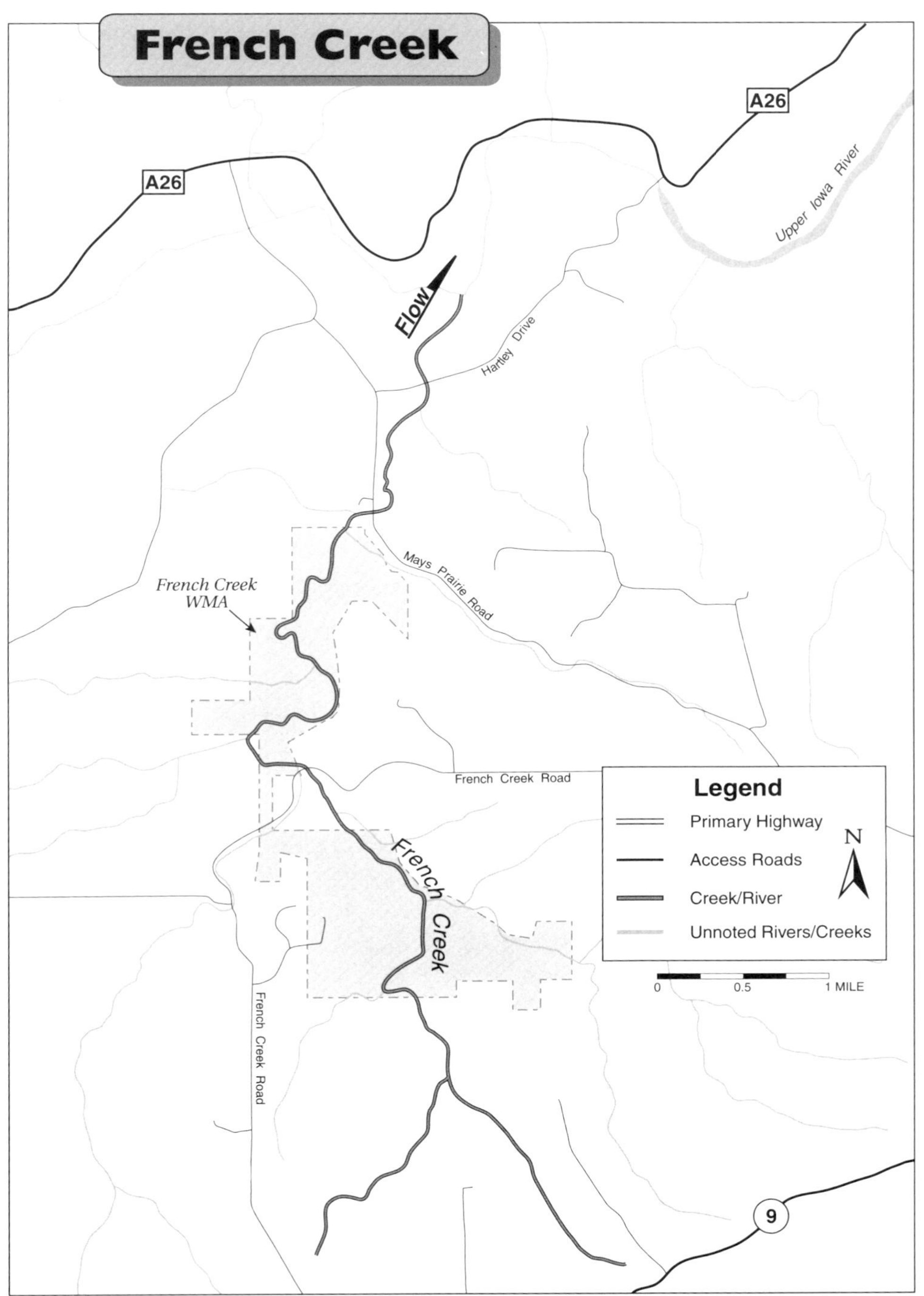
French Creek
A26
A26
Upper Iowa River
Flow
Hartley Drive
Mays Prairie Road
French Creek WMA
French Creek Road
French Creek
French Creek Road
Legend
Primary Highway
Access Roads
Creek/River
Unnoted Rivers/Creeks
N
0
0.5
1 MILE
9

Adams is a great dry on French; a size 16 Olive Scud with a bead is also a productive nymph.

I have observed an interesting phenomenon on Iowa streams during fall, winter, and spring cold fronts, which I find less pronounced on Wisconsin streams. That is the tendency of fish to really hole up and develop a serious case of lockjaw, especially for surface feeding. Perhaps, being further west, cold fronts hit Iowa a bit harder. Or, perhaps there is a subtle but important difference in the genetic makeup of Iowa trout versus Wisconsin trout; just as native brook trout in the Pine Creek watershed are genetically distinct from Wisconsin and Minnesota brook trout. Whatever the cause, it is best to be prepared for it, because these frontal systems sweeping out of Canada are a regular and defining occurrence in Iowa. It's good to have a few special arrows in the quiver for this purpose.

First, I fish out a pair of fingerless gloves and a hand warmer. Then for fly selection, I go really small or really large; or do both by means of a dropper rig. So, if you feel the temperature begins to plummet while you're on French or any other Iowa stream, reach for a Muddler or a Leech or Crawfish and try swimming it painfully slow over the bottom. If this doesn't produce, try a micro nymph. And if this fails, go with the dropper.

The lower French.

Pheasant and turkey abound in the adjacent uplands. At evening, you might glimpse a fox hunting along an old hedgerow. During spring green-up, keep your eyes peeled for the pageant of bright songbirds that love to frequent these creek valleys: scarlet tanagers, goldfinches, and orioles. If fungus is your thing, have a look around the DNR land in May; the surrounding oak and elm woods are prime morel mushroom habitat. And as fall comes on, a whole host of migrant visitors passes by, honking, quacking, rattling, croaking, and navigating by means of that avian superhighway just to the east, the Mississippi River.

Stream Facts: French Creek

Regulations

- Artificials only; all brown trout must be released.

Species

- Wild brown and brook trout

Miles of Public Water

- 6 miles

Access

- French Creek Drive, Mays Prairie Road, Hartley Drive

Nearest towns

- Lansing, Waukon

Hub City: Lansing

Call it well worn, call it River Rat Central, or call it homey. You won't find the usual outskirts chain stores, purveying everything from dog food to electronics all hours of the day and night in this Mississippi River town. What you will get is direct access to the great river as well as to some good streams like French and Clear Creeks. If you plan to do a little duck hunting, Lansing sits on a widening of the Mississippi River known as Lake Winneshiek. On the right November morning, you will find it black and white with the backs of diving ducks. The Upper Mississippi River Canoe Trail runs between Lansing and Marquette/McGregor, providing access to thousands of acres of backwaters for paddling and fishing.

Accommodations

Scenic Valley Motel, 1608 Main Street, 563-538-4245; lodging on the western edge of town, near Clear Creek

Uncle Charlie's Cabin, 221 Walnut Street, 563-538-9276; historic property on the Mississippi River that has been updated

River's Edge Retreat, 1381 N. Second Street, 608-386-9721; modern 2-bedroom apartment located on the Mississippi River

Paint Creek Cottage, 113 Main Street, Waterville, 563-535-7361; 20 miles south in small town of Waterville, near Paint Creek

Campgrounds

Yellow River State Forest, Highway 76, 364, B25, Harpers Ferry; 563-586-2254; 8,500-acre state forest containing the trout streams Paint Creek and Little Paint Creek

French Creek Wildlife Area, north of Highway 9

Lansing Wildlife Area, 5 miles north of Lansing, Highway 26

Upper Iowa River Access, New Albin

Restaurants

River's Edge, 10 Front Street, 563-538-4497; standard supper club fare with good river view

TJ Hunter's Pub and Grill, 377 Main Street, 563-538-4544; burgers and sandwiches

Veterinarians

Prairie Veterinary Services, S7414 Fortney Road, Desoto WI, 608-648-3450; located 5 miles away, across the Mississippi River, in Wisconsin

Medical

Gunderson Lutheran Clinic, 50 N. Fourth Street, 563-538-2254

Outfitters/Sporting Goods/Licenses

Farm and Home, 330 Main Street, 563-538-4884; Iowa fishing licenses and terminal tackle

Cabela's, Prairie du Chien, WI, 608-326-7163; full fly-fishing selections and Iowa licenses, though located in Wisconsin

The Hatchery, 406 W. Water Street, Decorah, 800-944-6503; fly shop with selection of regional goods

Automobile Repair

Severson's Service Center, 61 Second Street, 563-538-4828

Air Service

La Crosse Municipal Airport, 2850 Airport Road, La Crosse, WI 608-789-7464

For More Information:

Lansing Area Chamber of Commerce
PO Box 156
Lansing, Iowa 52151
563-538-9290
info@lansingiowa.com
www.lansingiowa.com

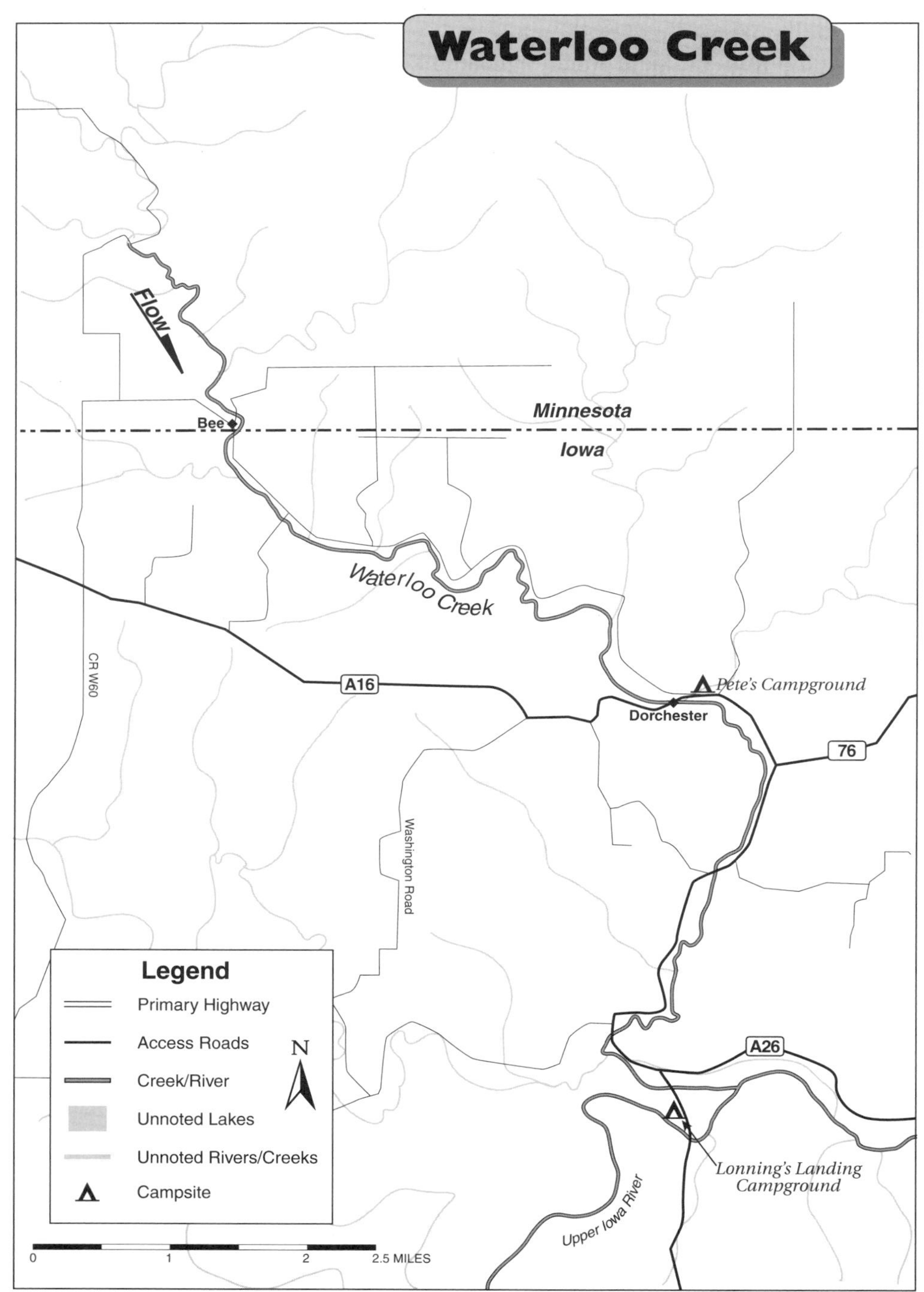
Waterloo Creek
Flow
Bee
Minnesota
Iowa
Waterloo Creek
CR W60
A16
Pete's Campground
Dorchester
76
Washington Road
A26
Lonning's Landing Campground
Upper Iowa River
Legend
Primary Highway
Access Roads
Creek/River
Unnoted Lakes
Unnoted Rivers/Creeks
Campsite
N
0
1
2
2.5 MILES

A pretty Waterloo brown.

WATERLOO CREEK

Waterloo Creek lies in a scenic valley along the Minnesota-Iowa border. The sparsely populated hill country surrounding it is at once rough, primitive, and beautiful, providing a scenic backdrop against which to cast a fly for wary, native brown trout. Larger, colder, and less brushy than most Iowa streams, Waterloo (especially in its mid and lower reaches) is an ideal fly-fishing venue and holds up to 4,000 trout per mile in some stretches. Waterloo has received national attention in publications like the *New York Times* and *Midwest Fly Fishing*. Its dramatic valley-bound setting and dense fish populations make it a true destination stream, on par with Black Earth Creek, Timber Coulee, and Minnesota's Root River.

Waterloo Creek is full of bugs. Midges and Blue-winged Olives are present all year, with March and October being excellent times to fish the latter. April sees a dependable Hendrickson hatch. Little Black Caddis come off in March. And Waterloo is perhaps best known for its Mother's Day Caddis. Look for Gray Fox and March Browns from late May through June. Things slow down a bit in summer, but mornings see trico hatches. Waterloo's grassy banks are rife with hoppers in late summer and early fall; cricket and beetle patterns work well too. And once fall cool-down comes on, the browns key in on big-game flies like muddlers, leeches, and crawfish patterns.

Waterloo Creek can be broken down into three sections, proceeding from upstream to downstream. First there are the clear and narrow upper reaches, running along Waterloo Creek Road (which intersects Highway 76) upstream of Dorchester and into Bee, Minnesota. In Minnesota, Waterloo Creek is called Bee Creek and some old-timers still use this moniker for Waterloo's upper reaches in Iowa. This area is stocked weekly from April through October with rainbow, brook, and brown trout and also holds wild browns. Access the stream at pull-offs and fence-stiles marked Public Fishing along Waterloo Creek Road. However, a portion of this stream is posted and under private control. As with any headwaters, fishing here can be tough. Narrow and clear are the rule. The best way to handle this is to scale down your gear, using a 2-weight rod with a very light leader and careful approaches or to fish during cloudy or rainy weather. Small Black Caddis imitations work well here. General Iowa trout regulations apply on this stretch.

The next section can be accessed along Highway 76 downstream from Dorchester. While fishing Waterloo's upstream portion feels tight, this is more open. The trout are not stocked here but they are larger, with many 14-inch-plus browns cruising the deep bends and grottoes. Hopper fishing is good on this stretch as is nymph and streamer fishing. There is room to throw a cast. I had fun catching thick-backed browns here on a cool late-April afternoon. They took a Beadhead Nymph, a go-to fly for limestone waters, and sported yellow bellies with deep red spots. General Iowa trout regulations are in place on this stretch of Waterloo.

The 2 miles below the Highway 76 bridge is accessible from pullouts and stiles along the road and is an artificials-only, catch-and-release water. Again, there is plenty of deep water, rocks, bank structures, and trees. Rock piles will show you where the DNR has reinforced the banks. These bank-hides are good spots to slowly drift a nymph or streamer. Some holes top out at well over 5 feet deep, making great big-fish habitat. The hopper winds of late summer can make for some very good fishing in this stretch. Few browns can resist a swirl-trapped, inch-long delicacy drifting above their nose. The intersection of A-26 and Highway 76 marks the end of public water on Waterloo. Below this, it feeds into the Upper Iowa River, a spot you might want to fish if you happen to be floating this latter waterway.

Stream Facts: Waterloo Creek

Regulations
- Catch-and-release, artificials-only in posted area downstream from Dorchester and Highway 76 bridge; otherwise, otherwise standard Iowa trout regulations apply

Species
- Wild brown trout

Miles of Public Water
- 6 miles

Access
- Highway 76; town of Dorchester

Nearest town
- Dorchester

Trout Unlimited Efforts in the Driftless Area

Museums have it easy. With cash flowing in from wealthy donors, they buy what they want and keep it behind glass. In guarded conditions, staffed with armed security personnel, viewers can come in to see it. There's not as much cash floating around conservation circles, and then there's the problem of putting good land and water under glass. Such logistical concerns notwithstanding, Trout Unlimited has undertaken one of its most ambitious projects to date: coordinating landowners and conservations agencies in a unique area, to protect and restore coldwater resources in its 24,000 square miles that spans parts of Wisconsin, Minnesota, Iowa, and Illinois. The project is known as TUDARE (Trout Unlimited Driftless Area Restoration Effort).

During an executive meeting in Galena, Illinois in June 2004, TU staff and volunteers realized the time was right for such an effort. They announced the plan at the Great Waters Fly Fishing Show in Minnesota in March 2005, and published their plans in an attractive 20-page booklet called *The Driftless Area: A Landscape of Opportunities.* Some fourteen chapters of Trout Unlimited participated. John "Duke" Welter of Eau Claire, Wisconsin, a TU Board of Trustees member, is coordinating volunteer efforts. TU's Watershed Management Director, Jeff Hastings, is coordinating staff efforts. The scope of the project is no less than 3,000 miles of tributaries, 600 streams, and six major watersheds.

Always something of shadow fishery compared to better-known Eastern and Western waters, Driftless streams and surrounding communities stand to benefit immensely from this large-scale restoration. Iowa trout streams such as Waterloo, French, Bear, and Pine would be among those included in the restoration. If sufficient funds are raised, good things stand to happen as a result of this, including:

- Better stewardship and increased landowner cooperation through strategic alliances;
- Improved water quality in drinking water, less sediment, and better upland habitat and farmland;
- Higher populations of trout and aquatic invertebrates;
- Economic benefits to surrounding communities through increased angler tourism;
- An influx of targeted state and federal grants to improve waterways.

To view the full version of the document, go to TU's Conservation Library at www.tu.org/library and click on the link for *The Driftless Area: A Landscape of Opportunities* under "Recent Reports." To aid TUDARE efforts, contact Jeff Hastings, Watershed Programs Director, 608-606-4158.

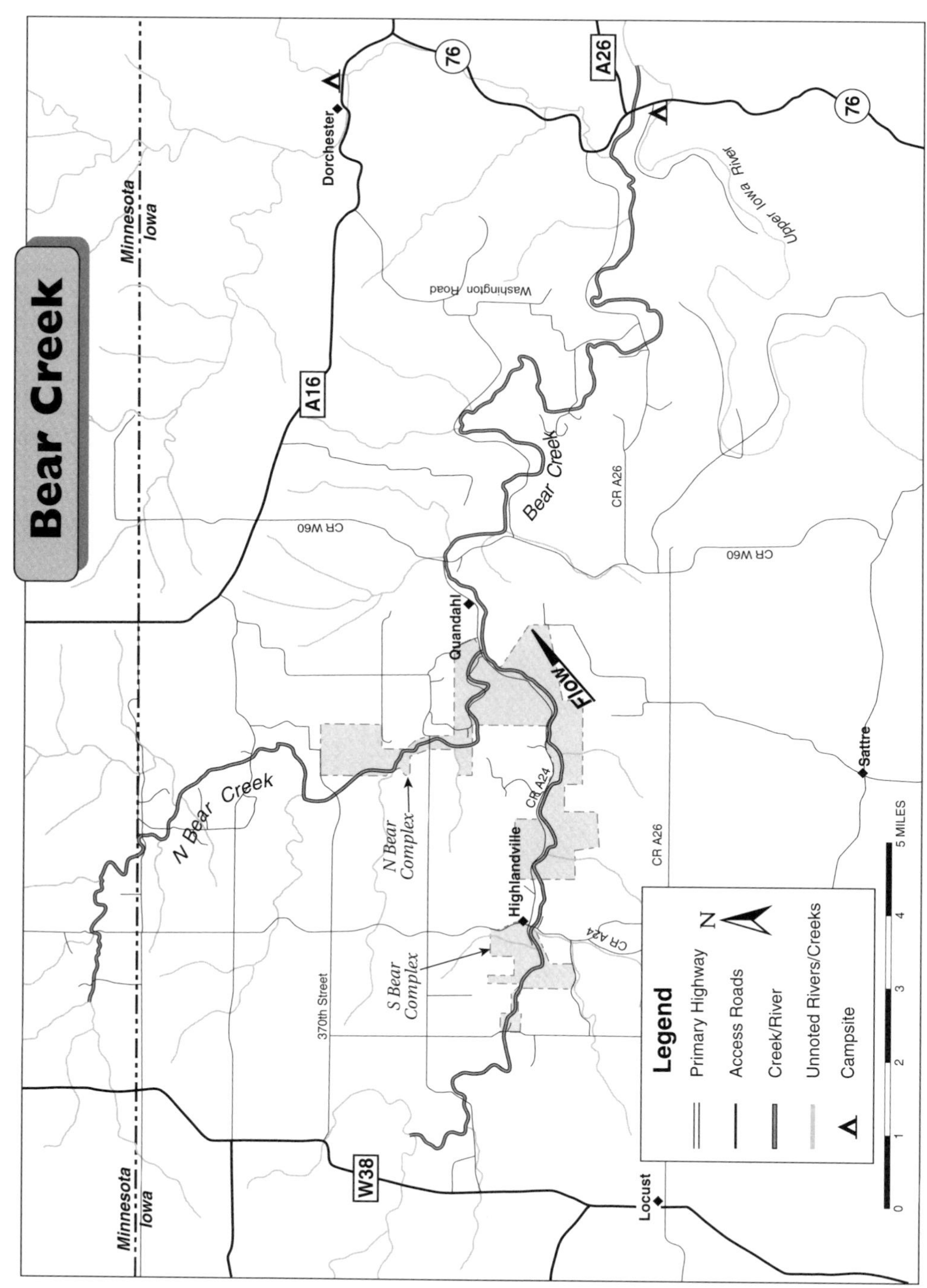
Bear Creek
Minnesota
Iowa
Dorchester
76
A26
A16
Upper Iowa River
Washington Road
Bear Creek
CR A26
CR W60
Quandahl
Flow
N Bear Creek
N Bear Complex
CR A24
Highlandville
S Bear Complex
370th Street
Sattre
W38
Locust
Legend
Primary Highway
Access Roads
Creek/River
Unnoted Rivers/Creeks
Campsite
N
0
1
2
3
4
5 MILES

Springs keep North Bear cool.

BEAR CREEK

Occurring just to the west of Waterloo Creek and just south of the Minnesota-Iowa border, Bear Creek is another high-quality trout stream that is large in size and known for hefty browns. The 15 miles of stream on the Bear Creek system, split between North Bear and South Bear, see a good portion of Iowa trout anglers. However, these two branches are almost entirely under public ownership and finding a place to fish should not be much of an issue, though you may see other anglers. The best way to attack North Bear Creek, the more productive of the two branches, is to approach from Highway W 38 and take any of the following roads east: 380th Street (a continuation of A 14), North Bear Road, or 360th Street. From 360th Street, you can take Highlandville Road to Quandahl Road to access South Bear. Fence-stiles and pullouts marked with Public Fishing signs will get you to the stream.

Alternating stretches of bluff-woods and pasture are the rule on the Bear system. While it is stocked with rainbow trout, there is also a healthy population of wild browns. Bear Creek has some exceedingly deep scooped-out holes for which you may want to bring a sinking-tip line or, at least, a few micro shot. Skitter something big and hairy, slowly and methodically, along the pebbly bottom to fool the Bear's big browns.

Decorah angler, Jeff Skeate, sees the Bear as a stream with excellent hatches. While hatches come off about the same time here as they do on other area streams, Bear Creek features a wider diversity of mayflies. Stoneflies come off as early as late February. Blue-winged Olives are heavy here in both March and September/October. If you see what you think are really big Blue-winged Olives, look again. Skeate notes an Iron Drake hatch that happens at the same time as the spring Blue-winged hatch. In addition to Hendricksons, there are Sulphurs here in April. Both March and Mother's Day Caddis are here. Look for Gray Fox and March Brown hatches here in late May and June. Trico hatches take place early during summer mornings; terrestrials are on in July, August, and September. Midges, scuds, and the usual array of high-protein offerings (sculpins, crawfish, chubs) are here year-round. If conditions are bright and fish finicky, try a micro nymph or a midge larvae.

The Bear Creek watershed is extremely rich in Native American history. The Klauke family farm, downstream from the Bear's marked trout water, was the site of an extensive excavation in the 1980s by Bear Creek Archeology. Among other things, a solar calendar, remains of longhouses, and effigy mounds were found here, near the town of Highlandville. One of the most striking finds was the turkey foot symbol, which has been found as far east as South Carolina, as far west as New Mexico, and as far north as Canada, and seems to have its origin in this region where the Upper Iowa River, Bear Creek, French Creek, and Waterloo Creek come together. It is clear from a map that the juncture of these waters does, indeed, resemble the track of a turkey. What is curious is how, and from what vantage point, our Native forbearers could have seen this. Driving through this area when the leaves are down gives one a feeling of a time past but not yet erased.

Stream Facts: Bear Creek

Regulations

- Regular Iowa trout regulations

Species

- Wild browns, stocked rainbows, and brook trout

Miles of Public Water

- 10 miles

Access

- 380th Street, North Bear Road, 360th Street, Highlandville Road, Quandahl Road

Nearest town

- Dorchester, Highlandville

SOUTH PINE CREEK

Pine Creek makes a truly impressive claim: it is Iowa's only stream to currently support a thriving population of native brook trout. What's more, as Iowa marks the western extreme of *Salvelinus fontinalis* original range, these fish are genetically distinct from Minnesota and Wisconsin brook trout. Eggs and milt from these fish are taken in the fall by the DNR, and these are incubated to produce fingerlings. These fish, genetically coded for this particular area, are then stocked in Iowa streams. You will have to make a hike of about 1 mile from the parking lot on Spring Creek Road to get in to this gem of a stream, but the chance of seeing such a natural relic makes it worthwhile. Also, consider pinching the barb down on your hook to minimize damage to these fragile fish.

Easiest access is from the small village of Locust on W38, about 10 miles north of Decorah. Take Sattree Ridge Road to the even smaller village of Sattree. Follow Sattree Ridge Road to Spring Creek Road heading east and you will see the parking lot for South Pine Creek. From, here follow the trail over some rough country, for approximately 1 mile to the creek. If you see other cars in the lot, consider hitting

A South Pine brookie.

one of the bigger streams nearby like Bear or the main branch of Pine, which accommodate more anglers. Fine leaders and careful approaches are the rule here. A small Royal Coachman wet fly is a good bet.

Stream Facts: South Pine Creek

Regulations

- Artificials only, catch and release

Species

- Iowa's last strain of wild brook trout

Miles of Public Water

- 1 mile

Access

- Walk-in from parking lot

Nearest town

- Decorah, Highlandville

PINE CREEK

Straddling the Winneshiek-Allamakee County line north of Decorah, the main branch of Pine Creek provides a chance to fish for stream-reared brown and brook trout. From A26, which runs east-west between Locust and Highway 76, take County Road W60 south and cross the stream. All public water on Pine is upstream from the W60 Bridge. Pine Creek runs through a 625-acre DNR holding that is open to hunting and primitive camping, in case anglers want to trade their long rods for long arms and take to the woods in search of grouse, squirrel, or woodcock. Yes, fantasy and reality do occasionally intersect, especially in Indian summer.

TROUT RIVER

In twenty-five years of trouting on two continents and two dozen states, I've only encountered a handful of waters as pretty as the upper reaches of Trout River. A few short miles east of Decorah, elm trees enclose the stream bank in a dark embrace, leaving the water dappled most of the day. Cool glassy runs slip into deep corners.

Wooded banks of Trout River.

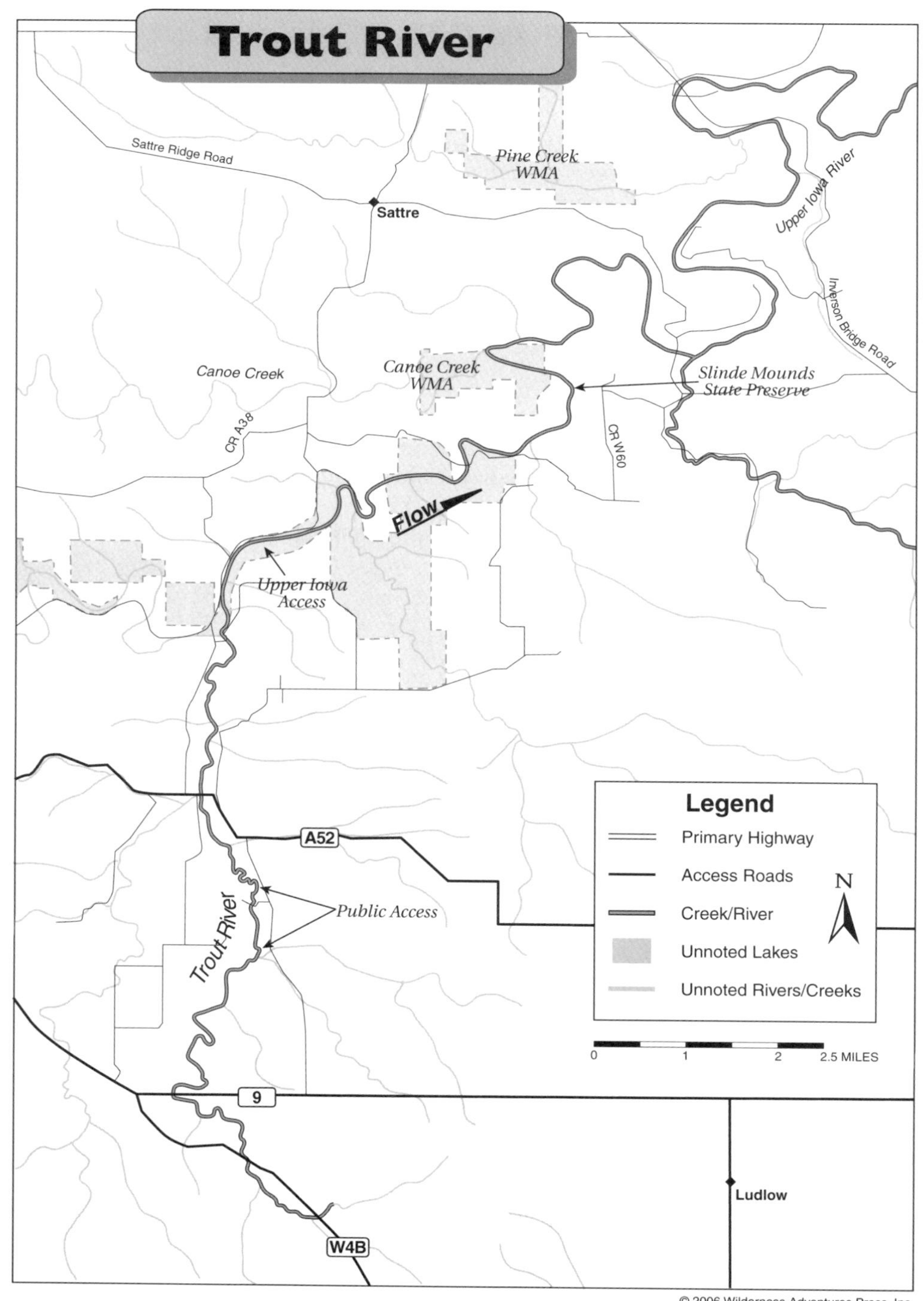
Trout River
Sattre Ridge Road
Pine Creek WMA
Sattre
Upper Iowa River
Iverson Bridge Road
Canoe Creek
Canoe Creek WMA
Slinde Mounds State Preserve
CR A38
CR W60
Flow
Upper Iowa Access
A52
Trout River
Public Access
Legend
Primary Highway
Access Roads
Creek/River
Unnoted Lakes
Unnoted Rivers/Creeks
N
0
1
2
2.5 MILES
9
Ludlow
W4B

And the water itself is a luminous green-blue. Shelves of shale poke down into the bottom and, if you sit and watch, scores of trout taking bugs can be seen at all levels of the water column.

Trout River trenches deeply into the stream. And there's also a lot of rock buttressing done by the DNR. It is 5 to 6 feet deep at its deepest parts. Fish a Beadhead Nymph unless you see something happening on top: stoneflies in late winter, caddis in spring, hoppers in summer, and midges and Blue-winged Olives all year. Crawfish and scuds are also thick here.

From Highway 9 just south of Decorah, take Highway A52/Old Stage Road to the east. Turn right (south) on 133rd Avenue and you will see stiles and pull-off parking lots with trails marked with Public Fishing signs. There are about 3 miles of stream to fish here. Mature brook and rainbow trout are planted in Trout River, as well as brook trout fingerlings. In addition, brook trout have begun to reproduce here naturally.

Trout Run

Heavily stocked, close to the town of Decorah, and offering easy access, Trout Run is a good confidence-booster and not a bad place to introduce a newcomer to the basics of fly casting, hook setting, and stream etiquette. Siewers Springs, which also feeds the Decorah Trout Hatchery, feeds Trout Run. East of the juncture of Highway 9 and Highway 52, look for Highway W38 and follow it to the south. Trout Run Road comes up on your left in about a mile and provides access to the stream. Siewers Spring State Park and the hatchery make this a good stream for a family outing. All three species of trout are stocked here.

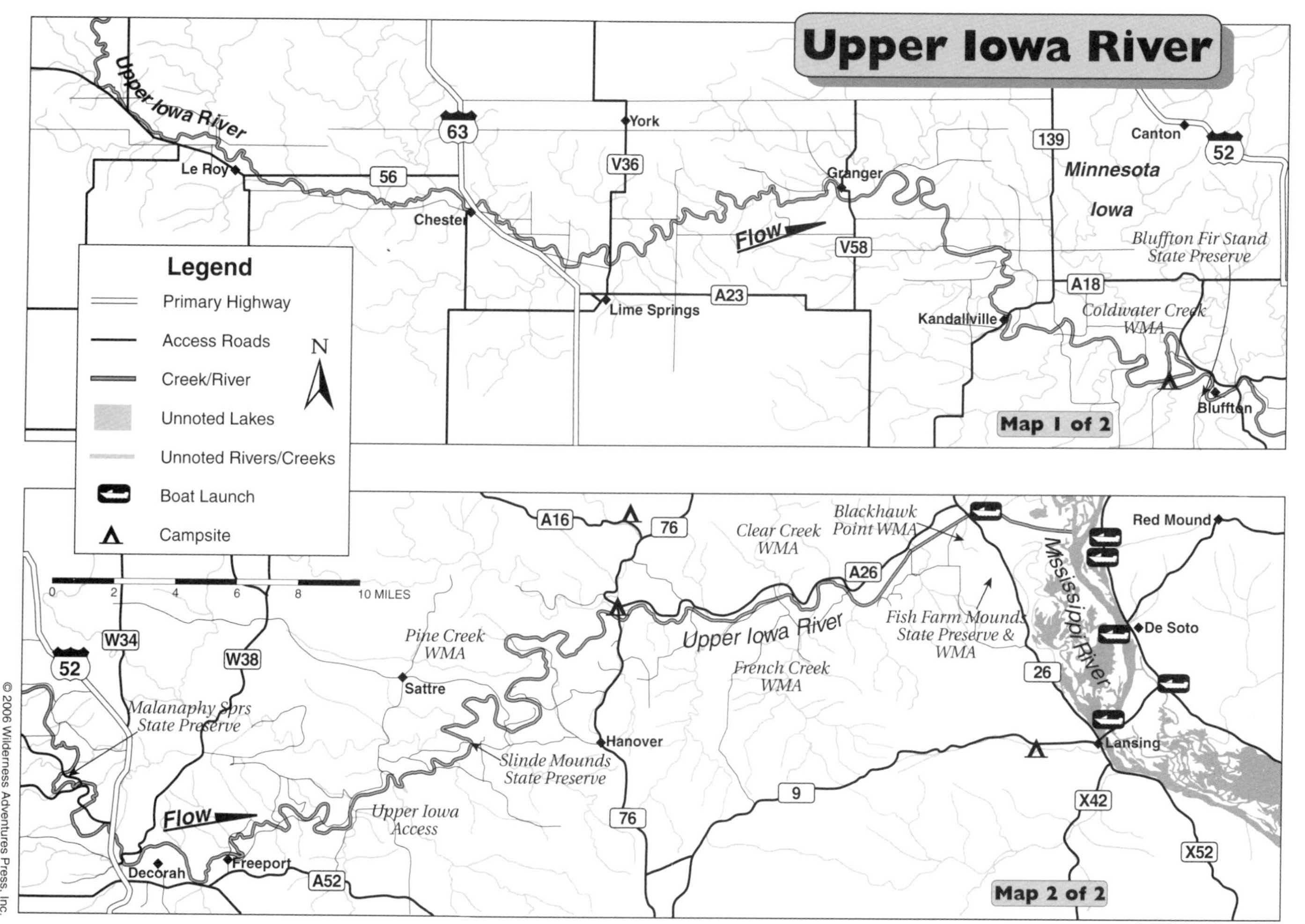
Upper Iowa River
Upper Iowa River
Le Roy
63
56
York
V36
Chester
Granger
Flow
V58
Lime Springs
A23
139
Canton
52
Minnesota
Iowa
Bluffton Fir Stand State Preserve
A18
Kandallville
Coldwater Creek WMA
Bluffton
Map 1 of 2
Legend
Primary Highway
Access Roads
Creek/River
Unnoted Lakes
Unnoted Rivers/Creeks
Boat Launch
Campsite
N
0 2 4 6 8 10 MILES
A16
76
Clear Creek WMA
Blackhawk Point WMA
A26
Red Mound
W34
52
W38
Pine Creek WMA
Sattre
Upper Iowa River
Fish Farm Mounds State Preserve & WMA
De Soto
Mississippi River
26
French Creek WMA
Malanaphy Sprs State Preserve
Hanover
Slinde Mounds State Preserve
Lansing
9
X42
Flow
Upper Iowa Access
76
Decorah
Freeport
A52
X52
Map 2 of 2

Upper Iowa River

Like the Turkey and Yellow Rivers, the bluff-lined Upper Iowa is a two-story fishery. Nineteen coldwater tributaries, including French and Waterloo Creeks, keep water temperatures cool enough to support trout that wander in. Smallmouth bass and walleye are also present throughout, with a smattering of channel catfish, pike, sauger, and white bass hanging around the dam in Decorah. The Upper Iowa winds its way for over 100 miles, from the western edge of the Driftless Area near Cresco to the Mississippi River near New Albin, Minnesota. During summer, the Upper Iowa, with its cool waters and shady bluffs, is a popular canoe venue. In spring and fall, however, it's primarily the domain of hunters and anglers.

The Old Town Dam in Lime Springs is a popular put-in. Highway V58 north of Cresco, Highway 139 near Kendalville, and W20 in the vicinity of Decorah, County Road A6W and A26 near French Creek provide access to this stretch of river, that's roughly 100 miles long. While coolwater species like occasional trout, walleye, and smallmouth bass are common above Decorah, the Mississippi River mix of catfish, white bass, and pike call the river home up to the Decorah dam. Throughout, look for structure and fish it. Stream and spring inlets are likely lies, as are fallen trees and bends that sweep along rock bluffs. A yellow Woolly Bugger or Clouser, either weighted with micro shot or on a sinking line, will do you right. If you find smallmouth taking on top, try a popper. Prairie scenery predominates from Cresco to Decorah; scenic bluffs enclose the river east of Decorah.

On the Upper Iowa, fishing for black bass (largemouth, smallmouth, and spotted) is catch-and-release between the Fifth Street Bridge and Upper Dam in Decorah; otherwise, general Iowa Inland Fishing regulations apply.

Hub City: Decorah

No doubt the classiest place to bed down in northeast Iowa, Decorah is an upper Midwest college town of 8,000 that is home to Luther College. The town is small enough to feel cozy and large enough to have things like a bistro specializing in locally-grown food, a restored opera house-turned hotel/pub, good Chinese and Mexican fare, plus enough taverns to slake the thirst of anglers suffering from dry mouth from telling too many lies. Nearby Spillville, a Bohemian crossroads, was visited by none other than Antonin Dvořák in the summer of 1893.

Accommodations

Hotel Winneshiek, 104 E. Water Street, 800-998-4164; restored opera house on National Register of Historic Places with two restaurants in downstairs; luxury and regular rooms available

Super 8 Motel, 810 Highway 9, 800-800-8000/563-382-8771; chain motel on outskirts of Decorah

Country Inn, 1202 Highway 9, 563-382-9646; affordable lodging on outskirts of town

Chase the Adventure Hunt Club, 1997 Middle Calmar Rd., 563-382-8012; private hunting and fishing club on 800 acres of land

Bear Creek Cabins, 3497 Highlandville Rd., Highlandville, 563-546-7722; access to private water on Bear Creek

Pine Creek Cabins, 206 Ellington Bridge Drive, 563-546-7912; access to private water on Pine Creek

Campgrounds

Decorah City Park, 563-382-4158

South Bear Park, 1 mile east of Highlandville on South Bear Creek

Bear Creek Park, Quandahl Road near Highlandville

Lake Meyer Park and Campground, west of Highway 24 between Calmar and Fort Atkinson, 563-534-7145; located on quality warmwater fishery 15 miles west of trout streams

Kendallville Park and Campground, 563-547-4566; off Highway 139, Kendallville

Restaurants

La Rana, 120 Washington St, 563-382-3067; continental bistro specializing in local products

Alberts, 104 Water Street, 800-998-4164; try the ribs at this pub in Hotel Winneshiek

Mabe's, 110 E. Water Street, 563-382-4297; good pizza

Family Table, 817 Mechanic Street, 563-382-2964; home cooking, open 6 to 8 daily

T-Bocks Sports Bar, 206 W. Water Street, 563-382-5970; don't miss the peanut butter cheeseburger

Nob Hill Supper Club, 2955 Highway 52, 563-382-3958; steak, fish, prime rib, and cocktails

Old World Inn, 330 S. Main, Spillville, 563-562-3767; hearty food with a nod toward Eastern Europe, located 10 miles from Decorah

Medical

Winneshiek County Memorial Hospital, 563-382-2911

Veterinary

Decorah Veterinary Clinic, 604 Montgomery Street, 888-327-7493, 563-382-3806

Outfitters/Sporting Goods/Licenses

The Hatchery Fly Shop, 406 W. Water Street, 800-944-6503; part-time fly shop, part-time chicken hatchery, plus selection of regional goods

Ozzie's Outdoors, 2349 172nd Avenue, 563 382 1211; family-owned small sporting goods store where you can buy a fishing license and waders

Cabela's, Highway 35, 608-326-7163; located 40 miles southeast in Prairie du Chien, Wisconsin

Auto Rental

Decorah Rental, 1814 Highway 9, 563-382-2351; a rent-all store that also rents cars by the day or week

Automobile Repair

Bob's Standard, 208 College Drive, 563-382-4652

Air Service

La Crosse Municipal Airport, 2850 Airport Road, La Crosse, WI 608-789-7464

For More Information:

Winneshiek County Office of Tourism
300 Water Street
Decorah IA 52101
800-382-3378
563-382-3990
www.decoraharea.com

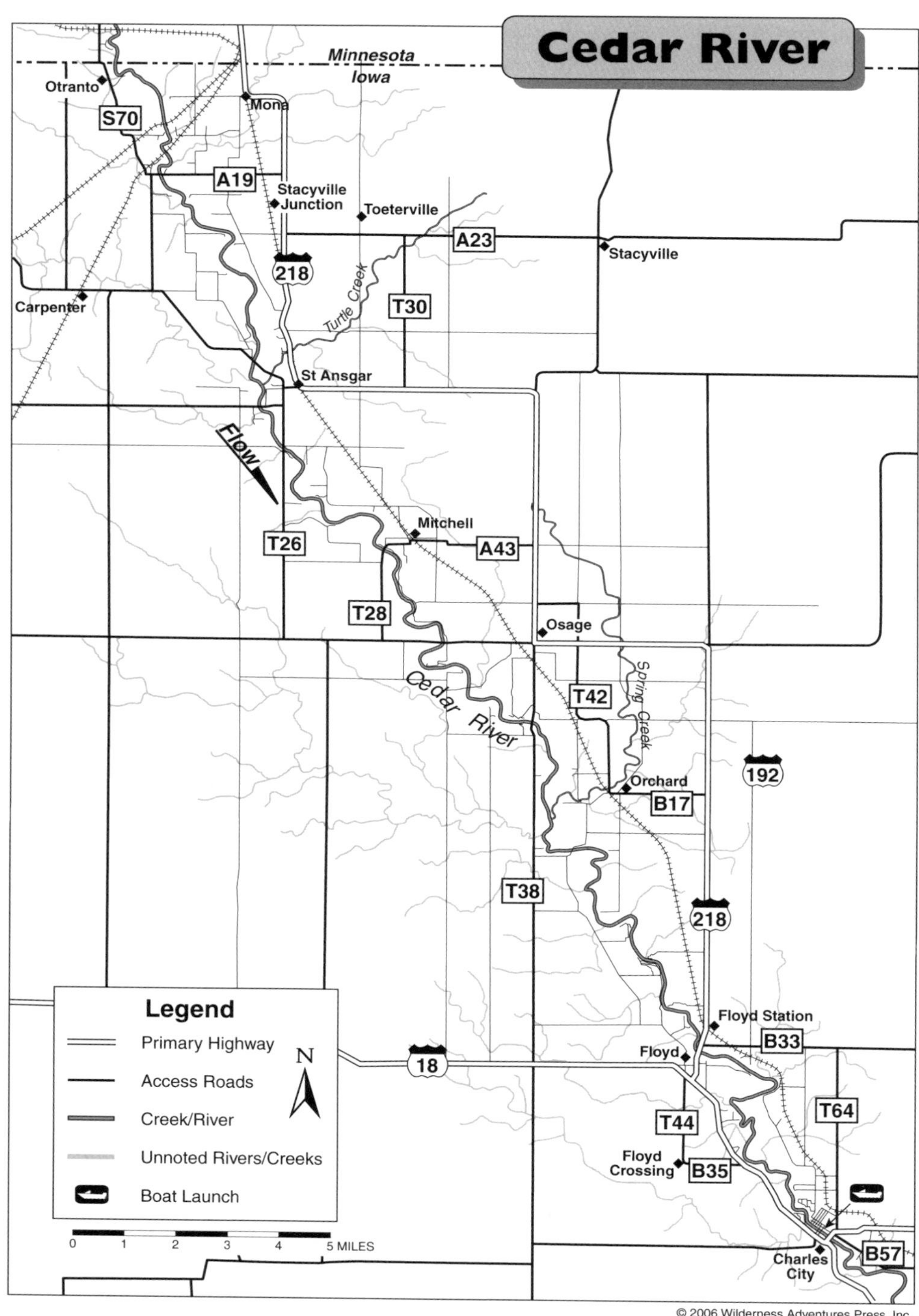

Cedar River
Minnesota
Iowa
Otranto
S70
Mona
A19
Stacyville Junction
Toeterville
A23
Stacyville
218
Turtle Creek
T30
Carpenter
St Ansgar
Flow
Mitchell
T26
A43
T28
Osage
Cedar River
T42
Spring Creek
Orchard
B17
192
T38
218
Floyd Station
B33
Floyd
18
T64
T44
Floyd Crossing
B35
Charles City
B57
Legend
Primary Highway
Access Roads
Creek/River
Unnoted Rivers/Creeks
Boat Launch
N
0
1
2
3
4
5 MILES

Bohemian Creek

Occurring just east of the hamlet of Protivin, Bohemian Creek is named for the Czech immigrants who settled here on the western edge of the Driftless Area in the middle of the nineteenth century. Fisheries Manager Bill Kalishek describes it as a "good coldwater creek with naturally reproducing rainbow trout." From Protivin, take Highway B16 east toward Decorah; in about 2 miles you will see Bohemian Creek running next to the highway. Turn north on 337th Street for access to the creek.

Turtle Creek, Spring Creek, and Cedar River

In Mitchell County, 70 miles west of Decorah, lies a pair of tributaries to the Cedar River that provide anglers with put-and-take trout fishing. While not on par with standouts like French Creek or Waterloo Creek, they add to the fishing mix for folks in north central Iowa. The creeks become too warm for trout in the summer, so they are not stocked during that season. The best time to fish them is in spring and fall.

Turtle Creek begins north of Highway A23 near Toeterville and flows into the Cedar River at St. Ansgar. Public trout water is between 440th Street and Highway 105 upstream from the town of St. Ansgar. You can also access the stream at Highway 218.

Spring Creek begins south of Highway 9, just west of Osage, and joins the Cedar River near the town of Orchard. Public trout water is between March Road and 319th Street downstream from the town of Orchard.

The Cedar River provides excellent angling for smallmouth bass, especially from the Minnesota line to Charles City, 40 miles south. Highway 218 parallels this stretch of the river. Popular put-in and take-out spots are Otranto Park, St. Ansgar, Mitchell, Highway 9 near Osage, Highway 218 in Floyd, and downtown Charles City.

Fish gravel-bottom runs and sandbar drop offs and any other obvious structure on the Cedar. It passes through pretty prairie scenery and makes a nice float in a canoe or belly boat, though you may need to drag the canoe through shallow riffles in low-water summers. Between Otranto, just below the Minnesota line, and the Highway T26 Bridge near St. Ansgar, fishing for smallmouth bass is on a catch-and-release basis. A yellow Woolly Bugger in a size 6 is a great smallmouth bass fly. Walleye and channel catfish are also present.

The bluffs on Otter Creek.

Otter Creek

The streams of Fayette County are getting near the west edge of Iowa's hill country. If you find yourself skeptical about the possibility of trout fishing around all these dusty crop fields, don't give up hope; there are trout streams here. And, as if by some twist of irony, their character is extraordinarily lush and wooded, leaving you to scratch your head and wonder if you've stepped off the map into a dream. Dusty roads and surprises are part of the fun of fishing trout on the edge of the prairie.

Otter Creek is stocked in both its upper area, near West Union and in its lower reaches near Elgin. The lower portion is marginal, heavily farmed and not worth your time. The upper reaches are scenic and run through a small canyon, which has four streamside campsites and is part of Glover Conservation Area. It has lots of rock here and, not surprisingly, good caddis hatches. It's also full of chubs so, don't neglect streamer patterns. It fishes well in April and May and then again in September and October. From West Union, take Highway B64 east and look for Echo Valley Road on your left, about 2 miles out of town. Follow this to the campground and stream.

Glovers Creek

Glovers Creek is a small tributary that feeds Otter Creek and runs through a narrow rock cleft. Keep following the dirt track that runs along Otter to the gate that says Glover Fish and Wildlife Area. Take your time on the road down to the creek because it's in bad repair. Once you see the creek you may, like me, be puzzled. I found myself unsure of whether to fish or simply admire it. And truly there was something hypnotic: the burble of water over rock, the woodland cool, patches of wild strawberry, and the groves of birch. Just a few miles from irrigation ditches and dusty fields, this did not seem possible. What must the first European or for that matter, generations of Native Americans, have thought of this place? The Jesuits talk about the Unmoved Mover. Glover Creek was designed by a Moving Mover, an aesthete of the highest order.

To get back down to earth, I did fish Glovers. Casting was absolutely out of the question. I did what an old fishing friend calls "dapping": pulling a Royal Coachman, on a very light leader, and snapping it into likely pockets. The result was several colorful brook trout about 8 inches, and a slightly bigger brown trout. Fingerlings of all three species are planted here and grow slowly, so catch-and-release seems wise to spread the resource.

You may not decide to fish Glovers Creek. But if you do, clip your barbs and tread lightly.

Grannis Creek

It was a blindingly hot, late June day when I visited Grannis Creek. An old dusty Dodge station wagon was in the lot. Through horseflies and gorse, moving way too fast, I plowed along this small stream until something told me to sit still and calm down. "Calm your body," the teachers at my daughter's Montessori school tell the students. I mopped my forehead with a handkerchief and sat down in the shade. Downstream a spring gushed from a limestone hillside. Where I sat, there was a deep swirl that pushed back against a fallen tree. I squatted, looking at the thin layer of surface film, trying to see what kind of emergers were kicking around in it, when I noticed the smell of burnt cherry. After that, I noticed a cloud of smoke swirling among the willow trees. Puffing away on a pipe was an octogenarian sitting in a green folding chair. Had he not been wearing a red seed company hat, I probably would have missed him. I began to babble about being sorry to disturb him. "Had I known," I began. I went into a litany about how hot it was, how clear the streams were, how poor my luck was.

The man did not say anything. In fact, I thought he was ignoring me, which was his right if not his duty. Some minutes later, he flicked at a stringer with his boot-tip. I cannot tell you what species they were, but they were certainly of the family salmonidae. As to size, each member of the troika was bigger than 16 inches, perhaps 20. The fish settled down and he resumed fishing, holding his cane pole right over the filmy surface. I can tell you how silly I felt at crashing up on him, but this would miss the point. As my Russian grandfather, a furrier and machinist who emigrated from the

Urals in 1920, used to say, "The quieter you go, the further you."

You can reach Grannis Creek by taking Highway C24 southeast out of Fayette and picking up Grannis Creek Road, which parallels the creek. As trout streams go, it is small; perhaps 20 feet at its widest. There are numerous springs, keeping the creek about 60 degrees even in the warmest weather; and a forest of oak, elm, and basswood flanks it for most of its length. About 2 miles of creek are open to public access and are stocked with catchable-size brook trout as well as brown trout fingerlings. Natural reproduction among rainbows has been documented here by the DNR, a rarity among Iowa creeks. Consider putting any red-stripes back in if you catch them.

Shady Grannis Creek.

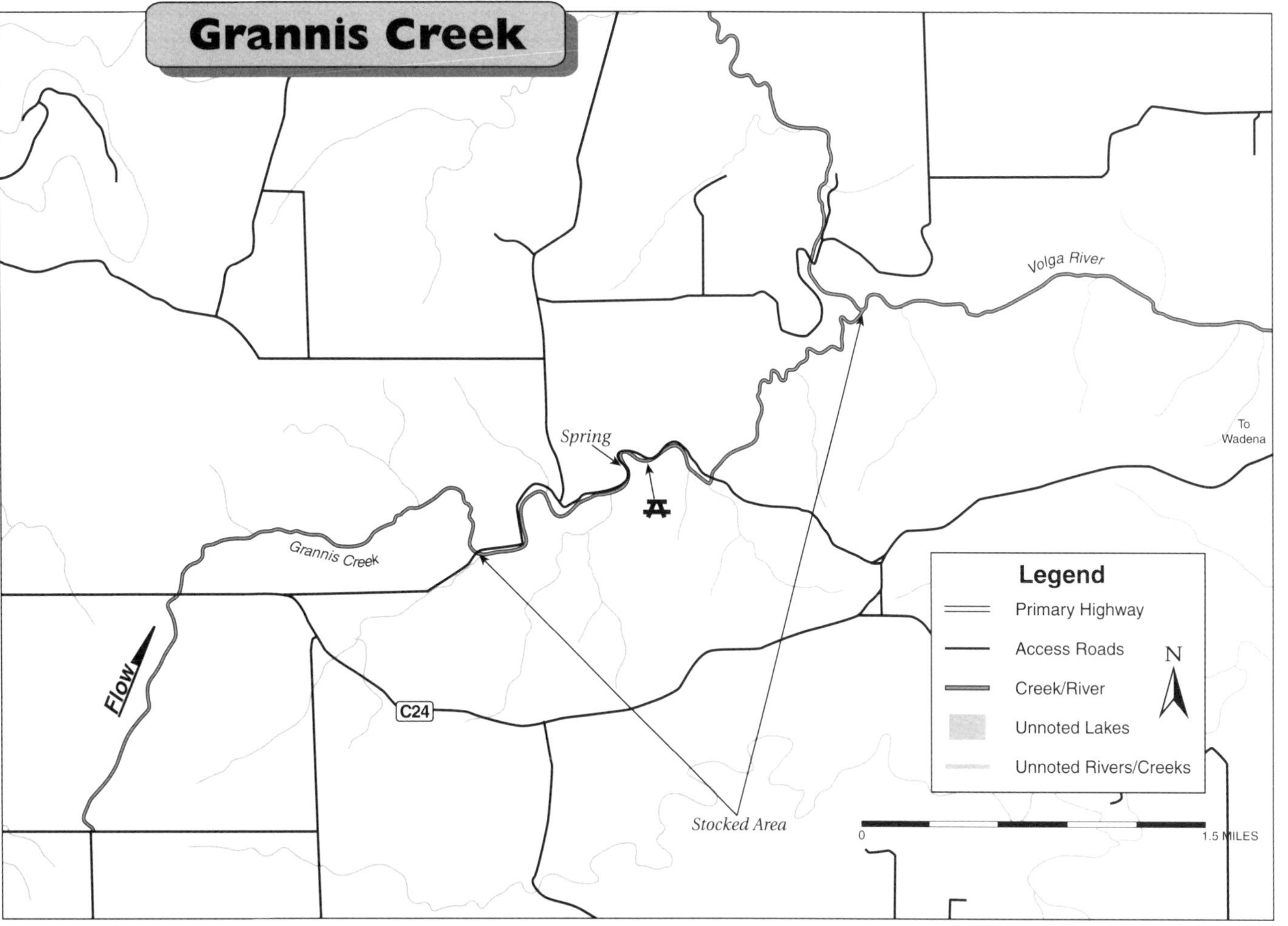
Grannis Creek
Volga River
To Wadena
Spring
Grannis Creek
Flow
C24
Stocked Area
Legend
Primary Highway
Access Roads
Creek/River
Unnoted Lakes
Unnoted Rivers/Creeks
N
0
1.5 MILES

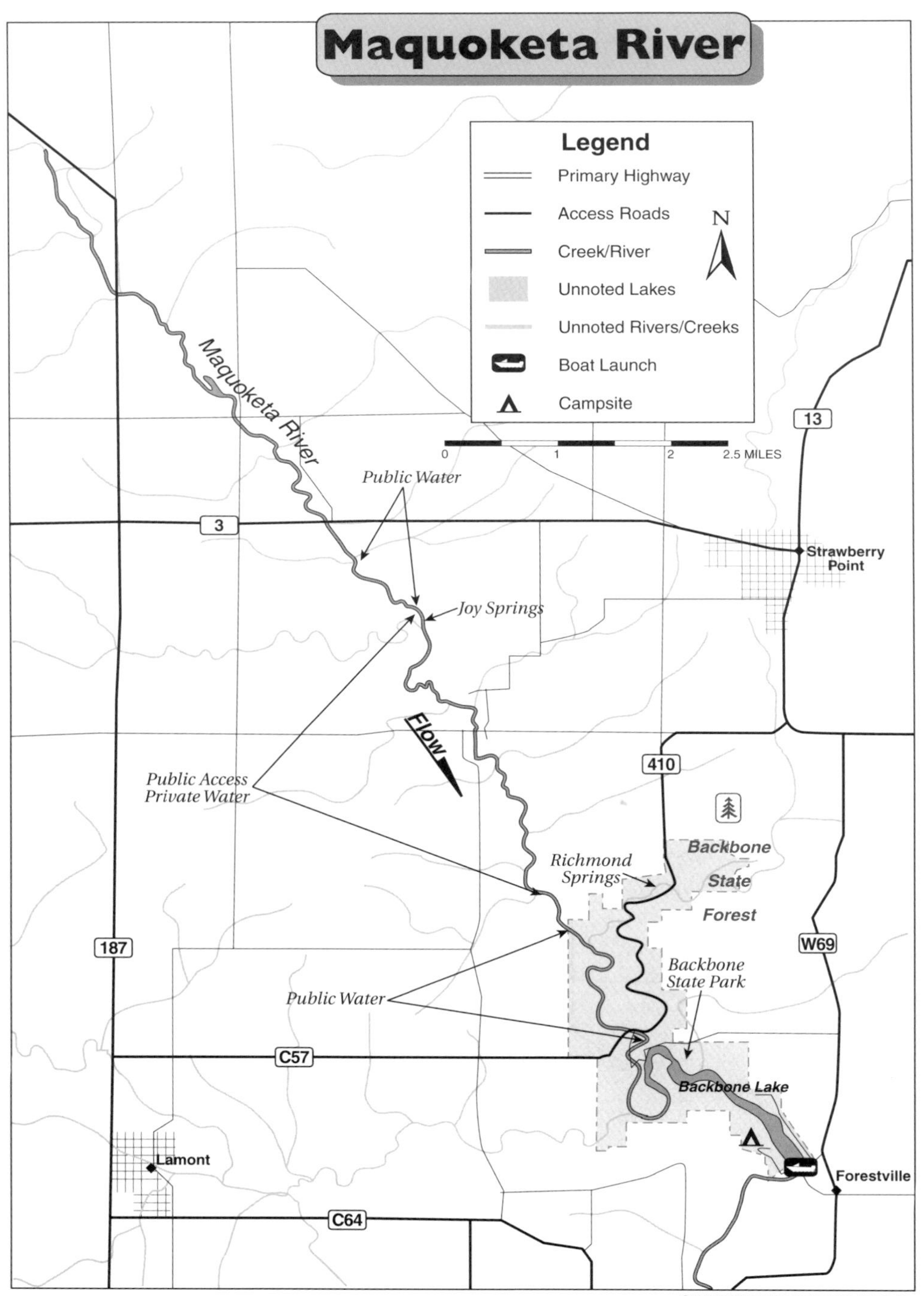
Maquoketa River
Legend
Primary Highway
Access Roads
Creek/River
Unnoted Lakes
Unnoted Rivers/Creeks
Boat Launch
Campsite
N
0
1
2
2.5 MILES
Maquoketa River
Public Water
Joy Springs
Flow
Public Access
Private Water
Richmond
Springs
Backbone
State
Forest
Backbone
State Park
Backbone Lake
Public Water
Strawberry
Point
Lamont
Forestville
3
13
410
187
W69
C57
C64
© 2006 Wilderness Adventures Press, Inc.

Richmond Springs

This coldwater tributary to the Maquoketa River, contained entirely within the north end of the 2,000-acre Backbone State Park, provides fishing for wild brown trout and stocked rainbow and brook trout. Located 4 miles from the town of Strawberry Point, Richmond Springs and Backbone State Park are best accessed from Highway 410, which joins Highway 13 south of Strawberry Point. Half a mile after entering the park, Richmond Springs crosses Highway 410. This deep pool at the road crossing, and immediately downstream where the creek turns away from the road, provides the best habitat on the stream. Richmond is heavily fished on weekends, but the fish see a lot of salmon eggs and spinners that are not always well presented. Fish small patterns (micro nymphs, midges) on fine leaders and you should do well on stockers and the occasional wild fish. Richmond flows through rocky but open country and there's enough room for casting a fly. While the stream remains cold through the park, habitat falls off as it approaches the Maquoketa River. Concentrate your efforts on Richmond's upper reaches.

Joy Spring

Joy Spring is a tributary that joins the Maquoketa River west of Strawberry Point. Contained within Joy Spring County Park, this 1.8-mile fishery provides easy access and is stocked regularly with brook, rainbow, and brown trout. Recent bank hides and lunker structures have been installed, according to Iowa DNR Fisheries Manager, Bill Kalishek. Joy Spring receives a bit less pressure than nearby Backbone State Park. Go 3 miles west of Strawberry Point on Highway 3, and turn on Alpha Lane, which gives access to the park and the stream. Camping is permitted at Joy Springs.

Maquoketa River

After receiving cold water from Joy Spring, the otherwise warmwater Maquoketa River supports trout from Joy Spring all the way downstream to its impoundment at Backbone Lake, some 4 miles of water. The only catch here is that much of the Maquoketa is clear and sandy without much habitat, so you may have to do a bit of prospecting to find fish. Look for springs, deep holes, and fallen trees, and concentrate your efforts in these areas. There are more forage fish than insect life; trout in the 20-inch range have been taken here, according to Kalishek. Minnow or crawfish patterns are the way to go.

To get to the Maquoketa, pick up Highway 410 just south of Strawberry Point on Highway 3/13; go west briefly on 410 and then follow 20th Street west until crossing the Maquoketa. Then turn left on April Avenue, which follows the south bank of the river. Access is on private land leased for fishing and marked with green and white signs. Use stiles to get to the stream and make sure to respect the land. Smallmouth bass are also present on this and other stretches of the Maquoketa, making it a popular float stream. Highway 38 provides good access to the middle stretch of this river. Backbone Lake, an impoundment of the river in Backbone Park, offers a warmwater fishery for bass, bluegills, and pike.

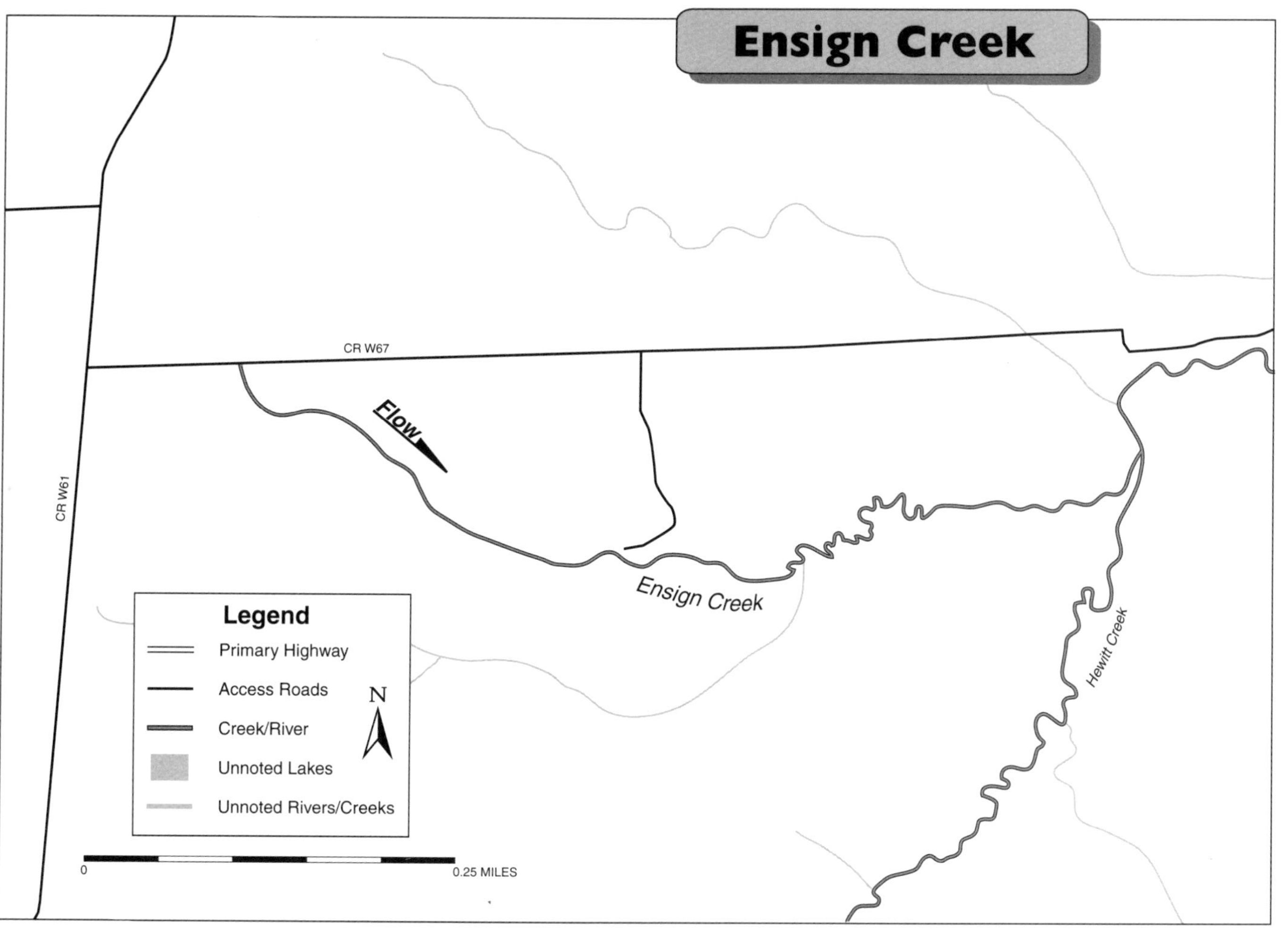
Ensign Creek
CR W67
Flow
CR W61
Ensign Creek
Hewitt Creek
Legend
Primary Highway
Access Roads
Creek/River
Unnoted Lakes
Unnoted Rivers/Creeks
N
0
0.25 MILES

Ensign Creek

Occurring between the towns of Volga and Strawberry Point, this small but productive stream holds some very large trout. It is a tributary of larger Hewitt Creek, which becomes too warm for trout shortly after the two join. Brown trout are common in the 10- to 14-inch range, and fish in the 24-inch range have been detected during electro shocking. Ensign Creek is managed as a catch-and-release, artificials-only fishery. Bryan Hayes, fisheries biologist with the Iowa DNR, says that a lot of habitat work has been done here including installing bank hides and cutting back some of the streamside willow. Even with this debrushing, Ensign is tough to fish in summer because its banks get very thick with vegetation. Better to hit it in spring, fall, or winter. From Highway C2W just west of Volga, follow Bixby Road until it runs into 322nd Street. Turn right on 322nd and access the stream via fence-stiles.

Stream Facts: Ensign Creek

Regulations

- Artificials only; catch and release.

Species

- Wild and planted brown trout

Miles of Public Water

- 1 mile

Access

- 322nd Street

Nearest town

- Volga, Strawberry Point

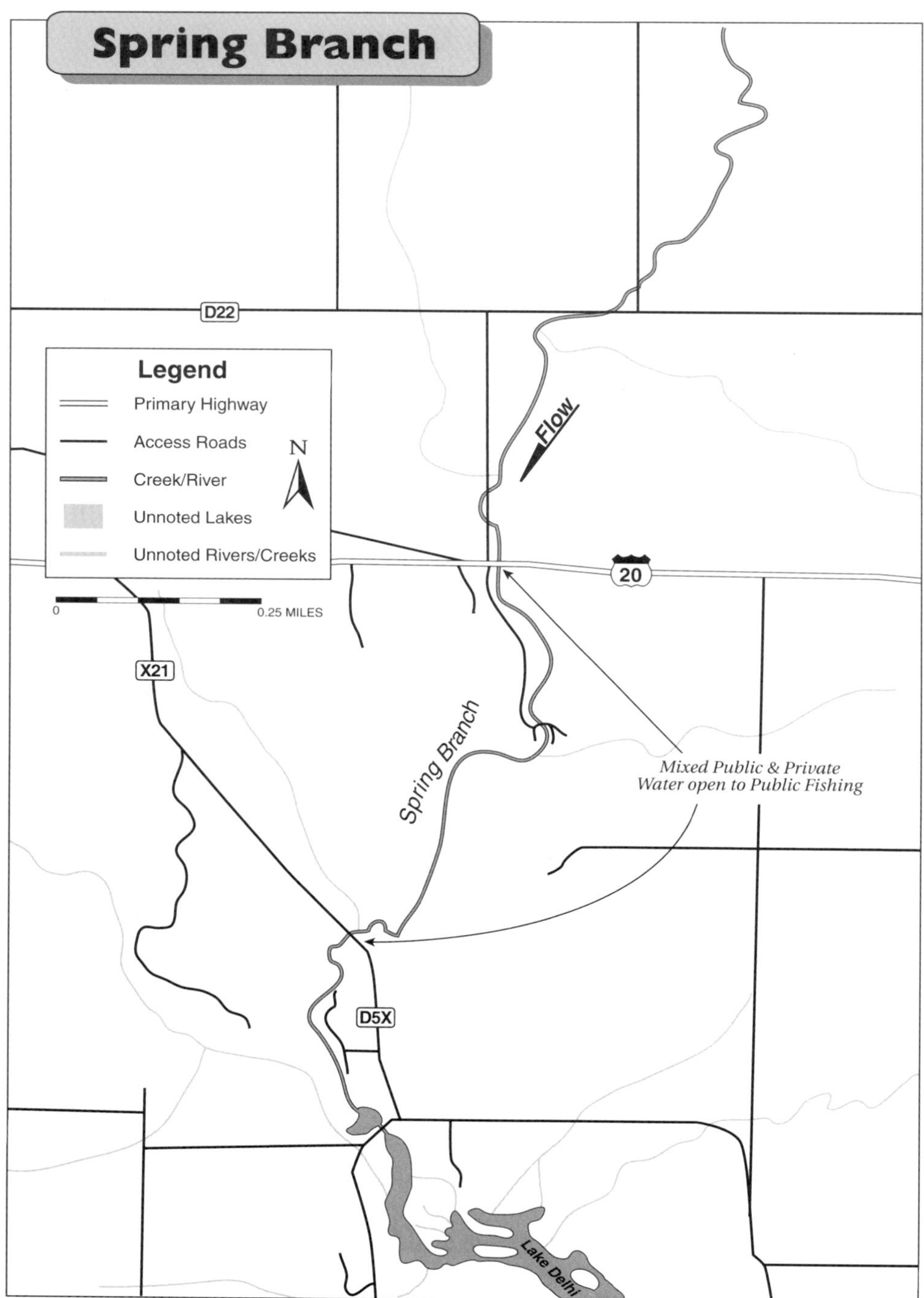
Spring Branch
D22
Legend
Primary Highway
Access Roads
Creek/River
Unnoted Lakes
Unnoted Rivers/Creeks
N
0
0.25 MILES
Flow
20
X21
Spring Branch
Mixed Public & Private
Water open to Public Fishing
D5X
Lake Delhi

Clear water, wary trout.

Spring Branch

This is one of the most productive streams in the southern tier of Iowa's trout range. It is easily accessed, lying just south of Manchester in Delaware County, and running through the grounds of the Manchester State Fish Hatchery. The fishable, public-access portion of the creek runs between Highway 20 and County Road DX5; access is at these points and via the fish hatchery. In total, about 3 miles of stream, which are clearly posted, are open to public fishing. Special regulations govern Spring Branch. Fishing is artificials-only with a minimum length of 14 inches for all trout from the source to County Road DX5.

Spring Branch is known for excellent hatches, according to Bryan Hayes, fisheries biologist with the Iowa DNR, and is popular with flyfishers. Good caddis hatches take place from late March through early May. Blue-winged Olives, handily imitated by an Adams, come off on Spring Branch most of the year with early spring and fall being the most predictable. Hendricksons follow in April, and Gray Fox and March Brown follow in late May and June. Cricket and hopper patterns work well in summer. Midges and scuds are present year round. There are also crawfish shuffling around on Spring Branch's rocky bottom, so don't neglect the hairy and scary flies.

Anglers are reaping the benefits of the extensive habitat work done here in the late 1990s. Fingerlings of all three species are stocked and grow as wary as native fish after just a short while in the stream.

The Manchester hatchery, adjacent to Spring Branch, is where Iowa's brood stock brown and brook trout are raised. The eggs and milt from these fish supply Iowa with some 400,000 trout a year. Catchable-size rainbow trout are also raised here. Originally a Department of the Interior property dating back to the 1890s, the Iowa DNR purchased the hatchery in the 1950s. All this testifies to the quality of the area's water table.

Stream Facts: Spring Branch

Regulations

- Artificials only, 14 inch minimum

Species

- Stocked brown, rainbow, brook trout; excellent hatches

Miles of Public Water

- 3 miles

Access

- Manchester State Fish Hatchery

Nearest town

- Manchester

Bailey's Ford

Occurring on the lower end of Spring Branch, below Highway D5X, Bailey's Ford is more heavily fished than the special-regulation section of Spring Branch near the Manchester hatchery. Standard Iowa trout regulations (5 fish, no minimum length) and stocking occurs twice a week from April through October. Access is easy from the County Park, off D5X. This is a fine place to bring a youngster on a weekday to introduce him or her to fly fishing in a high-success environment. A Beadhead Nymph fished below a strike indicator is a good way to go.

Fountain Spring

Between the towns of Edgewood and Colesburg northeast of Manchester, Fountain Spring runs through Fountain Spring County Park and offers easy access to a mile of stream. Take Highway 3 west from Colesburg (or east from Edgewood) for approximately 5 miles and look for the sign for Fountain Springs and County Road X 35; follow X35 south for a mile and you will come to the stream and the county park.

Brush is kept down on Fountain Spring's banks by the DNR and there is enough room to cast a fly without much of a problem here. Brown trout, stocked both as fingerlings and in catchable size, are present in good numbers. The trick on Fountain Spring is finding cover, that's the upside to those brush-choked creeks that cause us so much anguish. Find cover and you will find fish.

Fountain Spring is a tributary to Elk Creek, which in pre-settlement times was a brook trout stream. Now, it is largely a muddy agricultural waterway. However its middle reaches, at Highway 3 just west of Colesburg (known as Twin Bridges), are stocked with brown trout in spring and fall. Stocking is not done in summer due to high water temperatures. Why mention Twin Bridges? Because brown trout can survive in marginal habitat, especially when there are coldwater tributaries present, as there are on Elk Creek. Twin Bridges, with its deep, slow pools, has a good base of forage fish and crawfish. A few big browns do lurk here, especially in cool weather. Try it with a Muddler Minnow if you are passing through in spring or fall.

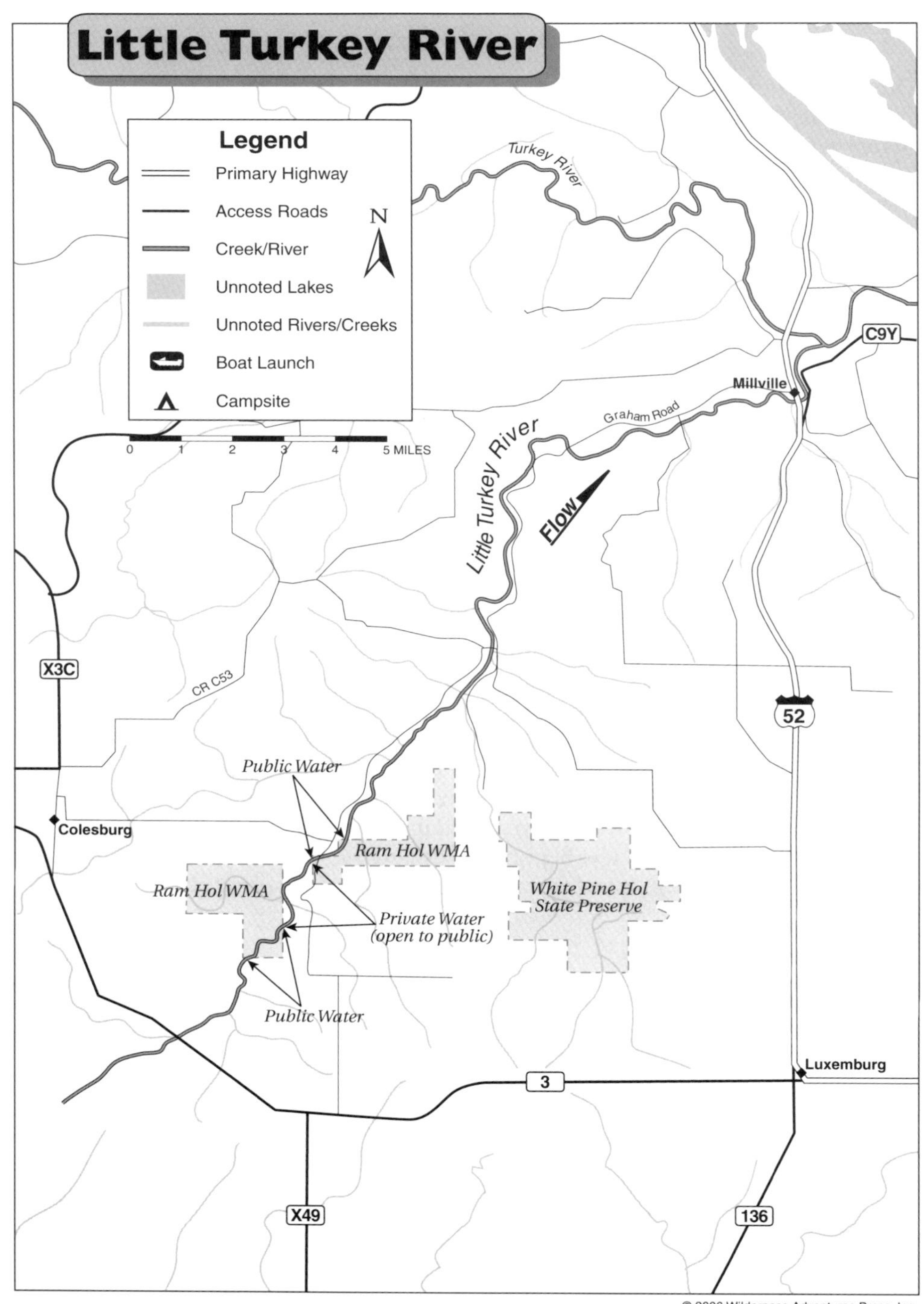

Little Turkey River
Legend
Primary Highway
Access Roads
Creek/River
Unnoted Lakes
Unnoted Rivers/Creeks
Boat Launch
Campsite
N
0 1 2 3 4 5 MILES
Turkey River
Millville
C9Y
Graham Road
Little Turkey River
Flow
X3C
CR C53
52
Public Water
Colesburg
Ram Hol WMA
Ram Hol WMA
White Pine Hol State Preserve
Private Water (open to public)
Public Water
Luxemburg
3
X49
136

Little Turkey River

The Little Turkey River is a medium-sized stream that is up to 40 feet wide in places. It runs through a 480-acre wildlife known as Hoffmann Addition. It receives little fishing pressure, according to Bryan Hayes of the Iowa DNR, and is a good place to take in some solitude in this hilly part of Iowa. From the town of Colesburg, take Voyager Road to the east for approximately 3 miles, until it comes to a T. Here, you can go north or south to access the stocked, public portions of the Little Turkey River. Catchable-size and fingerling browns are planted here. Natural reproduction has been documented on the upper stretches of Little Turkey. Large pools are the rule here, and they fish well with big flies like leeches and crawfish patterns. Midges, caddis, and Blue-winged Olives are also present. The Little Turkey's isolation and big pools notwithstanding, the browns in this river are wary. Approach with care!

Turkey River

Some 80 miles of good fish habitat exists on Turkey River between its headwaters near Cresco and Cardinal Marsh in Howard County and the scenic town of Elkader, with its prominent keystone bridge, in Clayton County. From Elkader to its confluence with the Mississippi River at Millville and Turkey River Mounds State Preserve, is another 40 miles of water, but the river is muddier and of less interest to the flyfisher. Anglers will find a two tier-fishery between Cresco and Elkader. Trout are present, especially where springs dump in, as well as a variety of coolwater species such as northern pike, walleye, smallmouth bass, and channel catfish. Riffles, long glides, fallen timber, and a rocky bottom characterize the upper Turkey; and sculpins, crawfish, and a variety of aquatic insects anchor the base of the Turkey's food chain. A Muddler Minnow or yellow Woolly Bugger fished on a 7-weight will serve you well.

There are a host of access points to the Turkey River: the town of Eldorado at Highway 150, the towns of Clermont and Elgin along Highway 51, Big Spring Road near Big Spring Hatchery, and above and below the dam in Elkader. Canoes can be rented from Turkey River Canoe Trips on 117 S. Main Street in Elkader, 800-250-2466. The 55-degree outflow of Big Spring (Iowa's largest natural spring and the water source for Big Spring Hatchery) makes for a brief stretch of stocked, cold trout water. If you are floating the Turkey and cover this stretch, try something with a bit of flash like a Beadhead Nymph. A word to the wise: crowds can grow thick in the vicinity of Big Spring, especially on summer weekends.

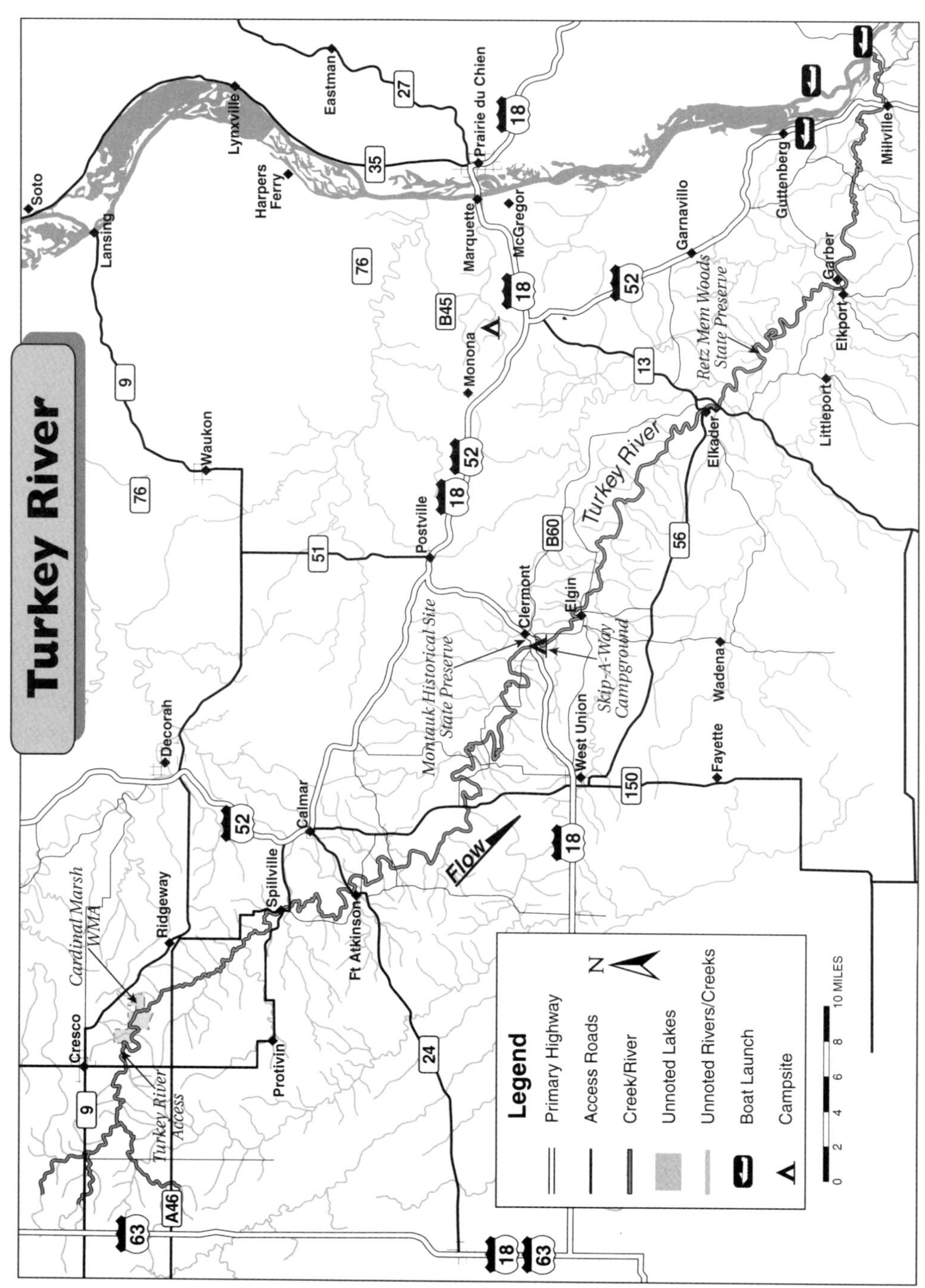
Turkey River
Soto
Lansing
Lynxville
Eastman
Harpers Ferry
Prairie du Chien
Marquette
McGregor
Garnavillo
Guttenberg
Millville
Garber
Elkport
Littleport
Elkader
Retz Mem Woods State Preserve
Monona
Waukon
Postville
Clermont
Elgin
Wadena
West Union
Fayette
Decorah
Calmar
Spillville
Ridgeway
Ft Atkinson
Cresco
Protivin
Turkey River
Montauk Historical Site State Preserve
Skip-A-Way Campground
Flow
Cardinal Marsh WMA
Turkey River Access
9
76
27
35
18
52
B45
13
51
B60
56
150
24
A46
63
Legend
Primary Highway
Access Roads
Creek/River
Unnoted Lakes
Unnoted Rivers/Creeks
Boat Launch
Campsite
N
0 2 4 6 8 10 MILES

Hub City: Elkader

The Turkey River runs through Elkader's downtown and a number of good trout creeks, such as Grannis Creek and Richmond Springs, are nearby as is Backbone State Park. Elkader was designated a Main Street Community in 1991 and has some pretty nineteenth-century brick architecture. It's a fun place to stay with a good sense of history and lots of antiques to be enjoyed. Elkader's Two Mit Burger Stand is a throwback to the 1950s.

Accommodations

Elkader Inn, 24886 Highway 13, 563-245-2020; clean motel catering to sportsmen located on the outskirts of town

Johnson's Guest House, 916 High Street, 563-245-2371; newer home located next to restaurant, for rent to larger parties

Elkader Bed and Breakfast, 401 First Street, 800-944-4860; 22-room remodeled Victorian home near downtown

Campgrounds

Elkader City Park, 563-245-2098; downtown on river in grassy area

Joy Springs, off Highway 3 west of Strawberry Point, 563-245-1516

Backbone State Park, 15 miles south of Elkader off Highway 13, 563-924-2527; ridge top setting containing Richmond Springs, Maquoketa River, and Backbone Lake

Volga River State Recreation Area, north of Fayette off Highway 150, 563-425-4161; 5,500 acres of public land offering hunting, hiking, and access to Frog Hollow Lake and Volga River

Restaurants

Johnson's, 916 High Street, 563-245-2709; breakfast all day with good lunch and dinner buffet

Burger Barn, Highway 13, 563-245-3074; open 10:00am to 8:00pm (closed Tuesdays) April-October, good for a quick meal going to or coming from the stream

Two Mit Burger Stand, Junction Highways 15/56, outdoor burger stand open April-October with very juicy hamburgers and brats

Schera's Restaurant and Bar, 107 Main Street, 563 245 1992; Algerian and American specialties

Veterinarians

Elkader Veterinary Clinic, Highway 13, 563-245-1633

Medical

Central Community Hospital, 563-245-7000

Outfitters/Sporting Goods/Licenses

Coast-to-Coast Hardware, 201 N. Main, 563-245-2521; sells licenses and terminal tackle

Turkey River Canoe Rental, 117 S. Main, 800-250-2466; will shuttle canoes and passengers on Turkey River

Cabela's, Prairie du Chien, WI, 608-326-7163; full fly fishing selections and Iowa licenses though located in Wisconsin, 30 miles to the east of Elkader

The Hatchery Fly Shop, 406 W. Water Street, Decorah, 800-944-6503; fly shop with selection of regional goods, 50 miles north of Elkader

Automobile Repair

Everett's KM Service, 307 High Street, 563-245-2231; towing and repair

Air Service

Elkader Airport, 21193 Grape Road, 563-245-2899

For More Information:

Elkader Chamber of Commerce
303 High Street
866-334-2857
www.elkader-iowa.com

A nice run on Upper Swiss Valley.

Bankston Creek

Located 20 minutes from Dubuque, wide and deep Bankston Creek offers anglers a chance to go after brown, brook, and rainbow trout within Bankston Park. While Bankston is popular with spinfishers and receives fairly heavy pressure, winter, spring and fall weekdays will give the flyfisher a bit more elbow room. Bankston lies just south of Highway 3 near the town of Rickardsville. Follow Bankston Park Road from Highway 3 to the park and the stream. Above the park, Bankston Creek flows through private land and contains some holdover and wild fish. Landowner permission is required on Bankston outside the park.

Upper Swiss Valley and Lower Swiss Valley of Catfish Creek

Located between Highway 20 and Highway 51 near the town of Cascade, and just 10 miles west of Dubuque, is Catfish Creek. Catfish Creek runs through Swiss Valley County Park and is stocked with rainbow and brown trout. The stocked areas are called Upper Swiss Valley and Lower Swiss Valley by the DNR to reflect the area's ethnic heritage.

In Upper Swiss Valley, the creek is small and colder, fed by a pair of tributaries (Monastery Creek and French Creek) that support wild brown trout. Upper Swiss

Valley has about a mile and half of stream and provides a pretty, timbered setting against which to fish. A subtle offering, like a small nymph or scud, will do well here.

Catfish Creek picks up more water at Lower Swiss Valley, where it's stocked with catchable-size rainbows. Experience has taught me that stocked rainbows like a bit of flash. Try a size 10 Muddler Minnow with a good amount of tinsel tied into it.

Water temperatures on Catfish Creek warm up to the mid 70s in summer and no stocking is done between June and August. Fall, winter, and spring are better times to fish here.

Big Mill Creek and Little Mill Creek

The Mill Creek system feeds into the Mississippi River near the town of Bellevue, south of Dubuque. Both Mill Creek and Little Mill Creek have trout-stocked portions and public access.

County Road D57, going northwest out of Bellevue, will take you to the Big Mill Stocked Area on Mill Creek; this is part of the 740-acre Big Mill Wildlife Management Area. Mill's banks in this stretch have recently been stabilized by the DNR, which provides habitat and helps water quality. Stocked rainbows do well here and continue to grow at a good rate. Wild brown trout exist in modest numbers upstream from the WMA, but landowner permission is required to fish outside the public area.

Tangles can hold good trout.

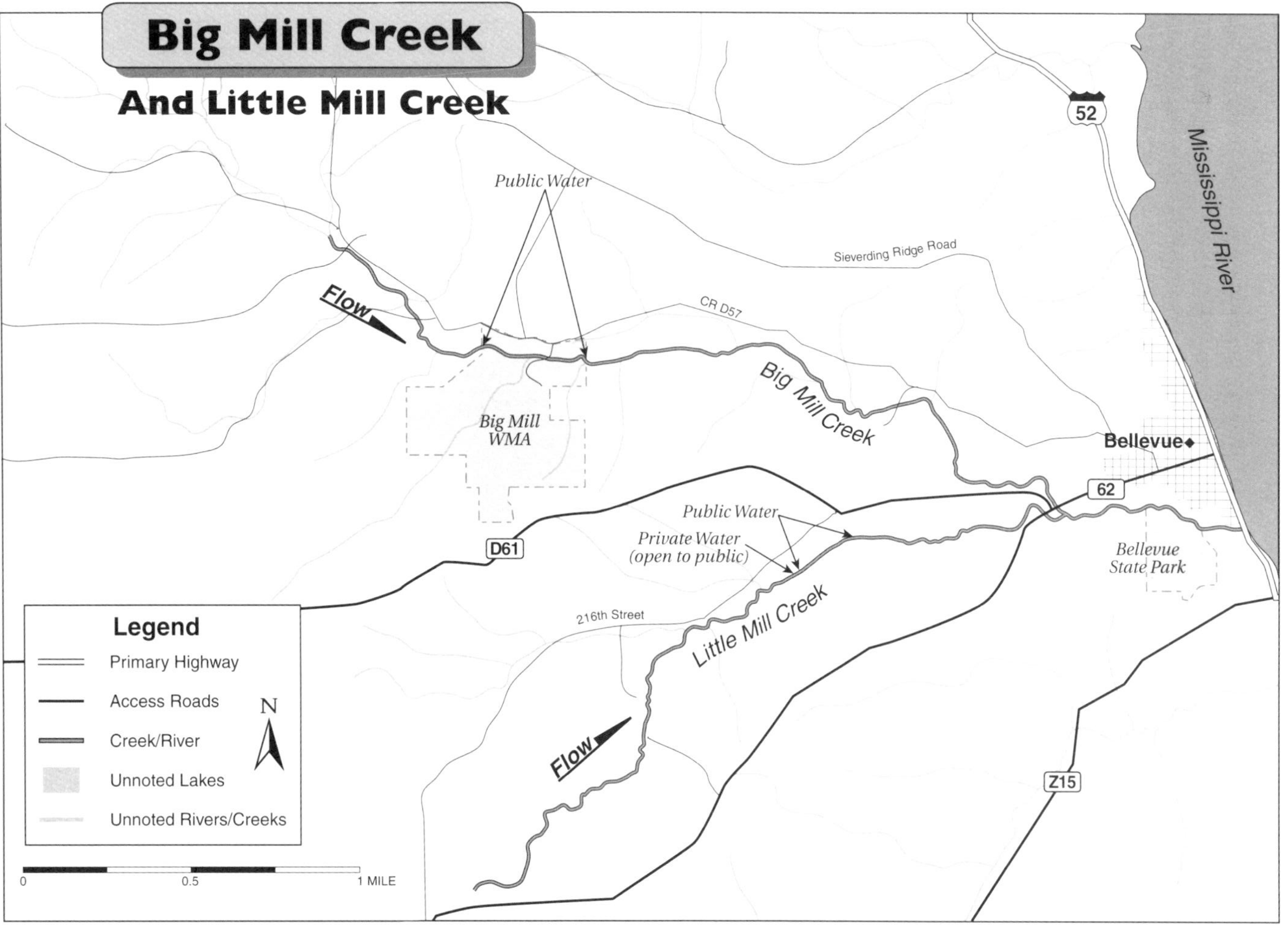
Big Mill Creek
And Little Mill Creek
52
Mississippi River
Public Water
Sieverding Ridge Road
Flow
CR D57
Big Mill Creek
Big Mill WMA
Bellevue
62
Public Water
Private Water (open to public)
D61
Bellevue State Park
216th Street
Little Mill Creek
Flow
Z15
Legend
Primary Highway
Access Roads
Creek/River
Unnoted Lakes
Unnoted Rivers/Creeks
N
0
0.5
1 MILE

From Bellevue follow County Road D61, which leads toward the Little Mill Stocked Area. A quick left turn will take you to the parking area. Iowa DNR's Bryan Hayes says Little Mill is known for big brown trout; there are plenty of big, deep pools on this stretch of stream. Bank stabilizing and lunker structures are helping to hold trout here, according to Hayes. I like to work a Beadhead Stonefly slow and deep in Little Mill's pools. If the fish are fussy, I tie on a dropper with a micro nymph.

LAKES OF NORTHEAST IOWA

Since most of Northeast Iowa occurs within the unglaciated Driftless Area, there are very few natural lakes. However, a number of impoundments here are worth mentioning for the warmwater fisheries they offer.

Lake Hendricks

Approximately 30 miles west of Cresco, just north of the town of Riceville, is 40-acre Lake Hendricks. From Riceville, take County Road T68 north and turn at the sign for the boat ramp, about a mile north of town. Due to its small size only trolling motors are allowed. This is a good fishery for largemouth bass, bluegills, crappies, and channel catfish. Given a good year-class, Lake Hendricks can sometimes produce bluegills in the 8-inch range, according Fisheries Biologist Bill Kalishek. A canoe or belly boat will make things easier here. There is a 16-inch minimum size limit on largemouth bass in Lake Hendricks.

Lake Meyer

Located just southeast of Spillville in Winneshiek County, 35-acre Lake Meyer is another good warmwater fishery, according to Kalishek. A belly boat or canoe would work well here. Bluegills run a bit small, but are plentiful. The lake also has some nice largemouth bass. It lies off Highway 24, between Calmar and Fort Atkinson.

Frog Hollow Lake

Located in 5,500-acre Volga River State Forest near Fayette, Frog Hollow Lake is known for producing good-sized bass and bluegills. The 135-acre lake lies at the northern edge of the forest. Follow signs to the lake from Highway 56 or from Highway 150. Bring the canoe or belly boat. The Volga River, a pleasant float, flows through the park and provides good fishing for smallmouth bass and channel catfish.

Lake Delhi

This 8-mile long impoundment of the Maquoketa River, located just south of the Manchester State Trout Hatchery and Highway 20 in Delaware County, provides a fishery for walleye, northern pike, panfish, and bass. It is best fished from a canoe or small boat; the launch is on County Road X15 accessible from County Road X21 running south out of Manchester. Work the bends and fallen timber with poppers or a yellow Woolly Bugger.

Iowa's Urban Trout Ponds

The Iowa DNR stocks certain urban ponds with trout in cool weather and cold-weather months. While these ponds and lakes don't support natural reproduction of trout, they do offer anglers some close-to-town fun. Following is a listing of the city and name of water. Stockings take place in fall, winter, and spring.

Ames: North Ada and Hayden lakes
Burlington/Fort Madison: Wilson Lake
Cedar Falls: North Prairie Lake
Cedar Rapids: Prairie Lake
Council Bluffs: West Lake
Davenport: Lake of the Hills
Des Moines: Banner Lake South/DMACC Pond
Dubuque: Heritage Pond
Mason City: Blue Pit
Muscatine: Discovery Park
Sioux City: Bacon Creek Lake
Spencer: Schamberg Pond

Put and Grow Streams

The twenty-eight streams listed here have good habitat and coldwater temperatures. Fingerling fish are stocked in them and soon attain average, and sometimes, trophy size. Some of these streams support natural reproducing trout. However, in contrast to Catchable Streams, where the Iowa DNR either owns the land or has negotiated easements with landowners, these Put and Grow Streams are located primarily on private property. The Iowa DNR has agreed not to release landowner names, so pressure is kept minimal, and so that the fishery stays intact.

However, using the Township (T), Range (R), and Section (S) system, with the aid of a county plat book, landowners can be located. If permission is granted, it is generally on a one-time basis, and the angler must contact the landowner each time he fishes there. The T numbers are located on the north-south vertical margins of the map; the R numbers are on the east-west horizontal margin; and the S numbers (1 through 36) are located in the center of each 1-mile square on the map.

It is absolutely crucial that landowner property is respected: gates locked or left open, as they have specified, no littering, no uninvited guests, etc. Without courtesy to the landowner, these fisheries will not continue in the future.

Stream	County	Nearest Town/ Township	Public(PU)/ Private(PR)	Location
Clear	Allamakee	Dorchester/Union City	PU/PR	T100N-R5W-S14, 15, 22, 27
Trout Run	Allamakee	Lansing/Center	PR	T98N-R4W-S9. 16
Teeple	Allamakee	Waukon/Ludlow	PR	T97N-R6W-S11, 14, 24
Williams Creek	Allamakee	Luana/Franklin	PR	T96N-R5W-S8, 9, 17
Yellow River	Allamakee	Luana/Franklin, Post, Linton	PR	T96N-R6W-S3 to T96N-R4W-S24
Bear	Clayton	Edgewood/Lodomillo	PU/PR	T91N-R5W-S23, 24, 25, 26
Dry Mill	Clayton	Elkader/Read	PR	T93N-R4W-S8, 9, 16, 17, 19, 20
Miners	Clayton	Guttenberg/Jefferson	PR	T92N-R2W-S7, 18, 20 & T92N-R3W-S12
Mossey Glen	Clayton	Strawberry Point/ Lodomillo	PU/PR	T91N-R5W-S4, 9, 10
West Fork Sny Magill	Clayton	McGregor/Clayton	PU/PR	T94N-R3W-S7
Grimes Hollow	Delaware	Colesburg/Colony	PR	T90N-R3W-S2, 3
Little Turkey River	Delaware	Colesburg/Colony	PR	T90N-R3W-S11
Ram Hollow	Delaware	Colesburg/Colony	PU/PR	T90N-R3W-S11

Spring Falls	Delaware	Colesburg/Elk	PR	T90N-R4W-S1, 2, 12
Little Maquoketa River	Dubuque	Epworth/Taylor	PR	T88N-R1W-S3, 4, 5
White Pine Hollow	Dubuque	Luxemburg/Liberty	PU/PR	T-90N-R2W-S6
Turner	Fayette	St. Lucas/Auburn	PR	T95N-R9W-S3, 4
Tete des Morts	Jackson	St. Donatus/Prairie Springs	PR	T87N-R3E-S4
Tributary to Tete des Morts	Jackson	St. Dontaus/Prairie Springs	PR	T87N-R3E-S16, 17
Burr Oak	Mitchell	Brownsville/Burr Oak	PR	T98N-R16W-S4, 5, 9, 10
Rock	Mitchell	Osage/Rock	PR	T97N-R18W-S1, 12 & T98-R18-S26, 35, 36
East Pine	Winneshiek	Locust/Canoe	PR	T100N-R9W-S21, 27, 28
Middle Bear	Winneshiek	Highlandville/Highland	PR	T100N-R7W-S14, 15, 16
North Canoe	Winneshiek		PR	T99N-R8W-S1, 2, 11, 14, 15
Pine	Winneshiek	Bluffton/Burr Oak	PR	T99-R9w-S3,4, 10 &
Casey Spring	Winneshiek	Decorah/Bluffton	PR	T99N-R9W-S25, 26
Pine	Winneshiek	Bluffton/Bluffton, Bur Oak	PR	T99-R9W-S3, 4, 10 & T100N-R9W-S20, 28, 29, 33, 34
Ten Mile	Winneshiek	Decorah/Madison	PR	T98N-R9W-S1, 2, 3

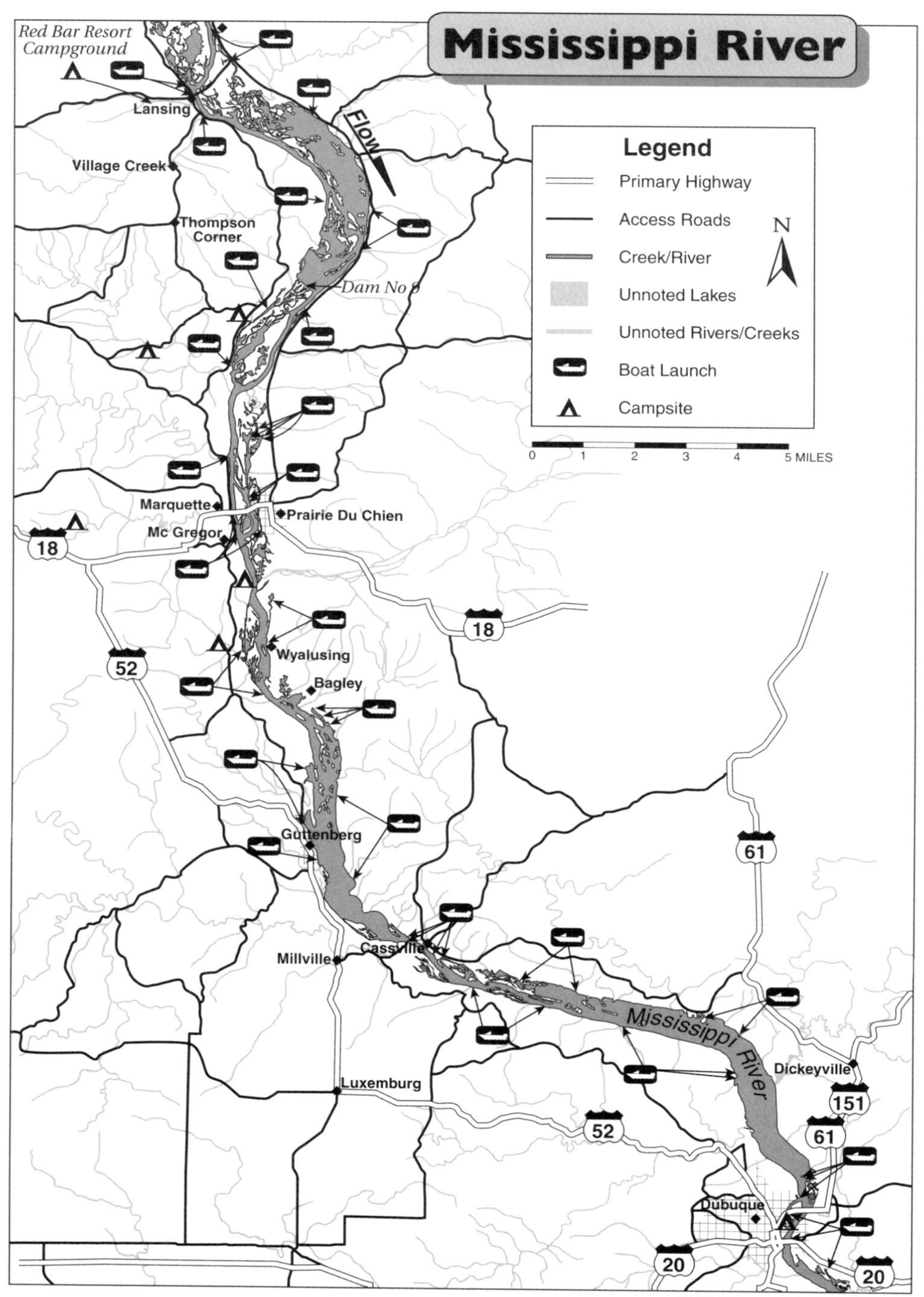
Mississippi River
Legend
Primary Highway
Access Roads
Creek/River
Unnoted Lakes
Unnoted Rivers/Creeks
Boat Launch
Campsite
N
0 1 2 3 4 5 MILES
Flow
Red Bar Resort Campground
Lansing
Village Creek
Thompson Corner
Dam No 9
Marquette
Prairie Du Chien
Mc Gregor
18
52
Wyalusing
Bagley
Guttenberg
61
Cassville
Millville
Mississippi River
Dickeyville
151
Luxemburg
52
61
Dubuque
20
20
© 2006 Wilderness Adventures Press, Inc.

Mississippi River: Lansing to Dubuque

For any writer, there ought to be a bit of trepidation in covering a gargantuan waterway whose banks have hosted such literary giants as Mark Twain, Ernest Hemingway, and T.S. Eliot. However, through classifying their writing as literary and mine as mere guidebook material, I can duck the punch and move on. Iowa's east coast on the Mississippi River runs about 300 miles north to south. For purposes of this guidebook, I will be looking at the upper third of this chunk; between Lansing, just south of the Minnesota line, and Dubuque. Within this stretch, the waters encompassed by the marked 30-mile-long trail, known as the Mississippi River Canoe Trail, running between Lansing and Marquette/McGregor are especially good. They have varied and productive habitat as well as easy access, making them a good choice for the fly rod angler.

"You can catch just about anything on the river, from mooneyes to walleyes," says Todd Roesch, fly-fishing manager of the Prairie du Chien Cabela's. Indeed, it's nice sometimes to step away from the narrow bounds of trout fishing and move to a broader canvas. Despite the river's large size, certain predictable habitat-species patterns do emerge: largemouth bass, northern pike, and panfish frequent the stump- and island-thick backwaters. Walleye, channel catfish, and smallmouth bass are taken in the deeper main channel, off rock points, near wing dams, and in faster areas. Excellent backwater fishing can be had on the upper part of Lake Winneshiek near Lansing, in the braided back channels near Harpers Ferry, and around Island 176 north of Clayton. Below the dam at Lynxville is a popular walleye haunt in spring and fall. The mouths of trout creeks like Wexford south of Lansing, Paint Creek near Harpers Ferry, and Sny Magill south of McGregor are good places to find northern pike in summer.

Roesch likes to use poppers for surface-feeding bass and bluegills. He likes a yellow Marabou Leech or a Clouser for deeper water. During what's locally known as the Shad Fly (Hexagenia elsewhere) hatch, Roesch recommends a big, spent-wing mayfly pattern in a size 4 or 6. This hatch generally occurs a week on either side of the Fourth of July. As far as gear, a 7-weight works well, unless you will be specifically targeting panfish; in which case, go down to a 5- or 4-weight. Sinking or sinking-tip line will help you get down to walleye and channel catfish in the lower water column.

There are plenty of access points along the Iowa side of the river. A canoe would be the smallest craft to use here for backwater fishing; and with that, be wary of bad weather and barge traffic. A jonboat is a good river rig because it allows you to fish both the main channel and the backwaters; a dependable motor helps you get around and find fish. In Lansing, boat landings can be found immediately above and below the Highway 82 Bridge and at the juncture of Highways X42 and 26. About 6 miles south of Lansing, off Heytman Drive, is what's locally known as Heytman's Landing. Landings can also be found at Harper's Ferry, Waukon Junction, Marquette, McGregor, Clayton, Guttenberg, Turkey River, North Buena Vista, Waupeton, and Dubuque. If you have boat or motor trouble, good marine services can be found in McGregor, Guttenberg, and Dubuque.

A Wisconsin or Iowa license suffices in this stretch of the river. Daily bag limits are as follows: 5 northern pike , 6 walleye and sauger (in aggregate), 5 largemouth bass and smallmouth bass (in aggregate), 25 panfish (crappie, sunfish, rockbass, white bass), and 25 yellow perch. The possession limit is twice the daily bag limit.

Hub City: Dubuque

Located on the banks of the Mississippi River, Dubuque offers anglers access to both that body of water and to a half dozen Iowa trout streams located within a half hour of the city, such as Big and Little Mill, the Little Turkey River, and Swiss Valley. Being an urban center with close to 100,000 people, Dubuque offers amenities and a bit more culture than do Iowa's smaller towns. The Mississippi River Aquarium is a must-see for any naturalist, young or old.

Accommodations

Holiday Inn, 450 Main Street, 563-556-2000, 888-800-3043; good downtown lodging
Richards House, 1492 Locust Street, 563-557-1492; 1883 restored Victorian home rated as one of the 25 best inns in the US
Super 8 Motel, 2730 Dodge Street, 563-582-8898, 800-800-8000, budget lodging near a cluster of other motels on commerce strip west of town

Attractions

National Mississippi River Museum and Aquarium, 350 East Third Street, 563-557-9545; a must-visit for any naturalist; dioramas and exhibits for novice and expert

Restaurants

Sugar Ray's BBQ, 1106 University Avenue, 563-583-9590; Dubuque's favorite 'cue
Yen Ching, 926 Main Street, 563-556-2574; serving Mandarin and Szechwan to eastern Iowa since 1983
Los Aztecas Mexican Restaurant, Dodge Street, 563-584-0212; real Mexican food, located near motels
Culvers, 4800 Asbury Road, 563-588-3898; dependable Midwest burger chain
Vinny Vanucchi's, 201 S. Main, Galena , WI, 815-777-8100; stand-up Italian food worth the half hour drive to historic Galena

Veterinarians

Central Animal Hospital, 1865 Central Avenue, 563-557-1515

Medical

Mercy Medical Center, 250 Mercy Drive, 563-589-8000 www.mercydubuque.com

Outfitters/Sporting Goods/Licenses

The Bait Shack, 2095 Kerper Blvd. 563-582-9395; some fly fishing gear and good information source for northeast Iowa streams

Automobile Repair

McCann's Service, Inc., 690 West Locust St., 563-557-8383

Automobile Rental

Avis, 11000 Airport Road, 563-556-0656; car rental located at Dubuque Regional Airport

Enterprise, 3250 Dodge Street, 563-583-8000; car rental located near hotels on the edge of town

Air Service

Dubuque Regional Airport, 1100 Airport Road, 563-589-4128

For More Information:

Dubuque Area Chamber of Commerce
300 Main Street
Suite 200
Dubuque Iowa 52004
800-798-8844
www.dubuquechamber.com

Color Fly Plates

1. Craig's Spring Creek Leech

2. Craig's Bass Buster

3. Fish-Stress

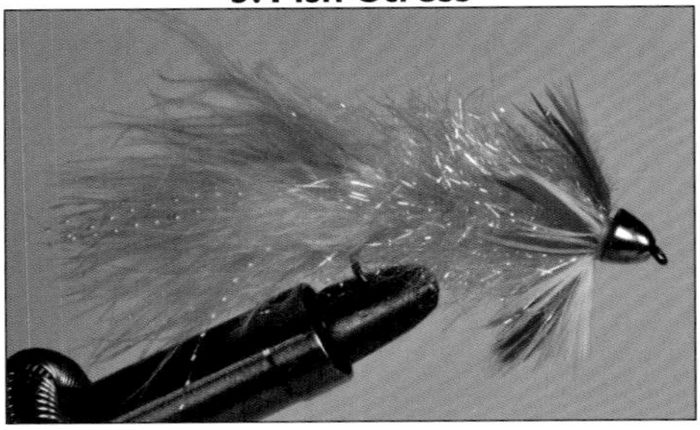

4. Sheboygan Bunny Leech

5. Egg Sucking Leech

6. Craig's Bluegill Buster

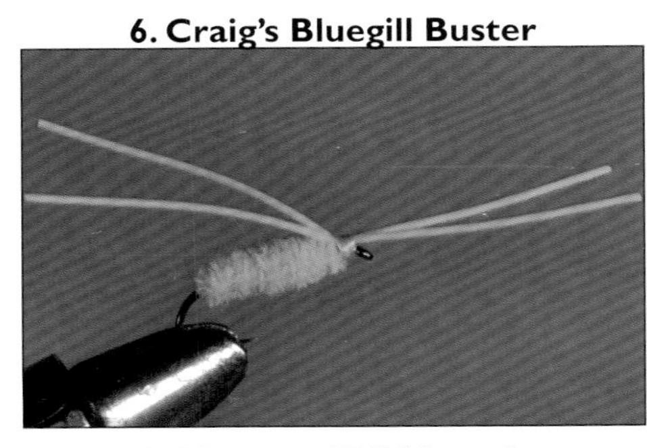

7. Pink Glo-Bug

8. Pheasant Tail Nymph

Recipes on pages 563-565

Recipes on pages 563-565

Top Wisconsin Flies

1. Craig's Spring Creek Leech

HOOK: Streamer hook with bead, #8
THREAD: Olive 6/0 (140 denier)
BODY: Olive Chenille
FLASH: MFC High Voltage, Red
HACKLE: Olive/brown rooster hackle
RIB: Red copper wire
TAIL: Olive Marabou
WEIGHT: Wire to cover hook shank

2. Craig's Bass Buster

HOOK: Streamer hook with bead, #8
THREAD: Yellow 6/0 (140 denier)
BODY: Yellow Chenille
HACKLE: Yellow rooster hackle
RIB: Red copper wire
TAIL: Yellow Marabou
WEIGHT: Wire to cover hook shank

3. Fish-Stress

HOOK: Tiemco 5260, #4, conehead
BODY: Loop-dubbed pearl Wing and Flash
HACKLE: One red saddle hackle with one white saddle hackle tied over it
TAIL: White marabou and pearl Crystal Flash, 1 ½ times hook shank
WEIGHT: 6 wraps .025 lead wire

4. Sheboygan Bunny Leech

HOOK: 2 hooks, Tiemco 5260 #4, back tied to front with 30 pound Dacron backing
EYES: Small lead eyes tied to top of front hook figure 8 style
BODY: Purple bunny strip tied into back hook palmered forward; tied down pearl crystal tied in two turns; pink rabbit fur around on front hook; point and barb cut off

5. Egg Sucking Leech

HOOK: Streamer hook, #6
THREAD: Nymo Thread, Flourescent Fire Orange
BODY: Black chenille
EGG: Fuschia chenille
FLASH: MFC High Voltage, Red
HACKLE: Black rooster hackle
RIB: Red copper wire
TAIL: Black Marabou
WEIGHT: Wire to cover hook shank

6. Craig's Bluegill Buster #10

HOOK: Tiemco 5260 #12
BODY: Chartreuse ultra chenille
LEGS: Chartreuse rubber, medium
WEIGHT: 4 wraps .020 lead wire

7. Pink Glo-Bug #10

HOOK: Egg hook, #10
THREAD: Wapsi 140 fluorescent pink
BODY: Glo Bug yarn, pink

8. Pheasant Tail Nymph

HOOK: Wet fly/nymph hook #16
THREAD: Brown 6/0 (140 denier)
TAIL: 6 to 8 pheasant tail feather barbs
RIB: Copper wire, small
ABDOMEN: Butt ends of tail fibers, twisted into a rope
LEGS: 6 to 8 pheasant tail feather barbs
THORAX: 2 to 3 strands peacock herl
WING CASE: Butt ends of leg fibers, pulled over thorax

9. Copper John

HOOK: Tiemco 5262, #16
BEAD: Gold
THREAD: 70 denier ultra thread black
TAIL: Brown goose biots
WEIGHT: Lead wire .015 inch diameter
ABDOMEN: Copper ultra wire
THORAX: Peacock herl
LEGS: Mottled brown hen neck
WING CASE: Olive and pearl flashabou covered with epoxy

10. Olive Scud

HOOK: Nymph hook, #12
WEIGHT: Nontoxic wire, size 0.020 diameter
THREAD: 6/0 (140 denier) olive
RIB: Copper wire, medium
SHELLBACK: 1/8" inch Mylar strip or latex scud back
BODY: olive nymph dubbing

11. Pink Squirrel

HOOK AND BEAD: Heavy wire hook, #14, with 1/8" gold bead
THREAD: Gray 6/0 (140 denier)
WEIGHT: Nontoxic wire, 0.20" diameter
TAIL: 6 strands of Crystal Flash
RIB: Red copper wire, small
ABDOMEN: Hare's mask fur mixed with ice dubbing
THORAX: Bright pink nymph/scud dubbing

12. Red Midge Larvae

HOOK: Light wire curved hook, #20
THREAD: Red 8/0 (70 denier)
BODY: Red tying thread

13. Foam Beetle

HOOK: dry fly, #16
THREAD: Black, 6/0 (140 denier)
BODY: Peacock herl, twisted with a piece of tying thread
OVERBODY: Black foam, 2mm (5/64") thick width equal to hook gap
LEGS: Black round rubber legs, medium
TOPPING: Brightly colored poly yarn or craft foam

14. X-Caddis

HOOK: Dry Fly, #18
THREAD: 8/0 (70 denier) brown
BODY: Dry fly dubbing, brown
TAIL: Ginger Z-lon (sparkly nylon) fibers, length equal to hook shank
WING: Elk or deer hair, length to hook bend

15. BWO Sparkle Dun

HOOK: Dry Fly, #18
THREAD: Olive 6/0 (140 denier)
BODY: Olive dry fly dubbing
TAIL: Light brown Z-lon/Antron (sparkly nylon) fibers
WING: Deer Hair

16. Deer Body Hex

HOOK: Tiemco 5262, Size 6
BODY: Yellow deer hair reverse tied on shank
HACKLE: Ginger hackle; ginger hackle around body
TAIL: Moose body hair
WING: Calf-tail Crystal Flash tied upright and divided

Fish of Wisconsin and Northeast Iowa

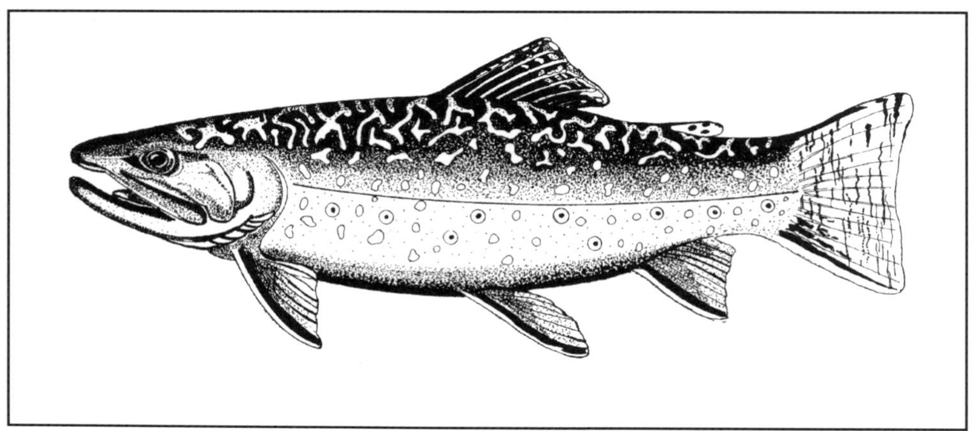

Brook Trout

Native to Wisconsin, brook trout are found in cold, clean, high-oxygen waters. Water temperatures above 70 degrees for extended periods of time are lethal to brook trout; their preferred range being water temperatures in the mid-50s to low 60s. Headwater spring creeks in western Wisconsin, gin-clear rivers in the Sand Counties, spring ponds in Nicolet National Forest, and the far north's cold, tannin-dark rivers and swamps are all home to *Salvelinus fontinalis.* Pine Creek near Highlandville and French Creek west of Lansing are good Iowa brook trout streams.

As the Latin name implies (Salvelinus meaning char), brook trout are char, and not taxonomically trout. Other North American char include lake trout, Dolly Varden trout, and Arctic char; they're distinguished from trout by light spots against a dark background. The brook trout's background is olive, black, blue, or purple; wormlike markings in yellow or white and red dots contrast this. Belly and lower fins are pink or white, orange on spawning males.

Most brook trout caught in Wisconsin waters are between 6 and 10 inches. A fish over 12 inches is a fine specimen, and anything over 14 inches is a trophy. Brook trout are opportunistic feeders. Insect larvae and nymphs make up a good portion of their diet. They'll also grab worms, crickets, grasshoppers, crawfish, and minnows. A particularly large brook trout I observed one day darted out from a shaded bank to seize a 4-inch brown trout.

Brook trout have an undeserved reputation for being dumb. The same is said of wood ducks. Curious and quickly educated would be closer to the truth. Of an opening day, the outdoorsman might enjoy easy sport with these natives, but as the season progresses they become skittish and often move into small, cold feeder streams with the advent of hot weather. Fish them with a 2- or 4-weight fly rod and fine leader. Something short—6 to 7 feet—will be easier to work in the tight canopy that often accompanies brook trout streams, where roll casts and daps are the order of the day.

Brook trout will readily take a dry fly. Pass Lakes and Royal Coachmen are classic brook trout dries. Any mayfly or stonefly nymph will take fish, with Prince Nymphs and Pheasant Tails being old reliables. In the high alkaline streams of western Wisconsin, pink and olive scuds work well on brook trout. Wet-wading a cold Sand County stream during the grasshopper hatch is a sensory experience of the first order. Finally, don't neglect minnow and crawfish patterns. It's no accident that bait fishermen often catch the biggest brookies.

Brook trout are vulnerable both to overharvest by anglers and to predation by otters and wading birds. I've caught a dozen brook trout over the years marked with the dime-sized brand of a heron or egret bill. Cover is of the utmost importance for brook trout. Try logjams, below waterfalls, small pockets behind rocks, beneath undercut banks.

In Florence and Langlade County spring ponds, where there is little cover, fishing can be frustrating. Fish are visible in the clear water and spook at the slightest vibration. Low light or rain are good times to fish spring ponds.

A restoration of coaster brook trout in Lake Superior and its tributaries in the Bayfield Peninsula is underway in Wisconsin. This, and harbor fishing for planted brook trout in Lake Michigan, present anglers with the best chance of catching a brook trout of substantial size. The record for brook trout on Wisconsin's inland streams (9 pounds, 15 ounces, caught on the Prairie River in 1944) appears to be in no immediate danger of falling.

Some noted Wisconsin brook trout streams are Lawrence Creek, Tomorrow River, Flume Creek, and Comet Creek in the Sand Counties; Elk Creek near Eau Claire in the west; the Pine, Popple, and Deerskin Rivers in the northeast; and the upper reaches of the Namekagon and Brule in the northwest. As water quality improves, wild brook trout are beginning to reproduce in Timber Coulee and other streams of southwest Wisconsin.

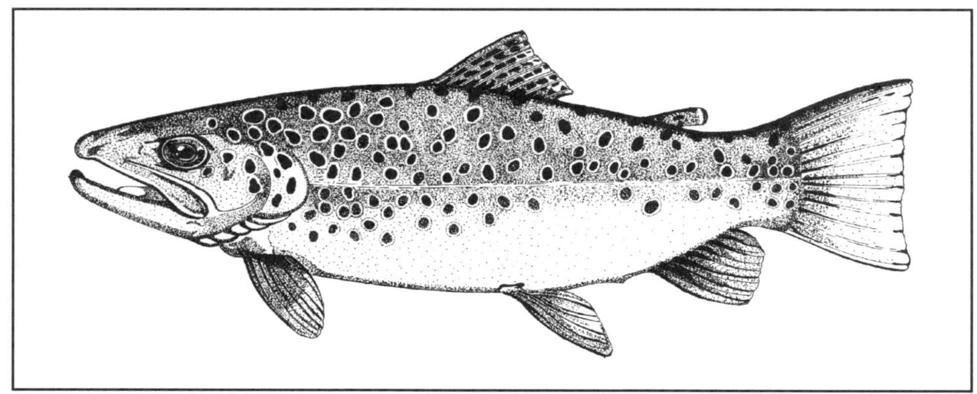

Brown Trout

In Wisconsin and Iowa taverns around the state, one hears locals wax poetic about trout fishing. How grandpa once a year took them down to the creek behind the farm after milking cows. How they caught a few German brown trout on worms. And how good the trout were fried up for breakfast with homegrown potatoes. "Wait a minute," protests our scientific angler and devotee of brown trout, "you actually kept and ate trout? Besides, Loch Leven and von Behr browns were crossed in New York hatcheries in the 1880s and we can't tell the difference anymore." Assuming our educated friend could speak these words without having his hinder booted out the door, we'd have to concede that his facts are correct. Von Behr and Loch Leven brown trout strains were, in all likelihood, crossbred, or at the very least not kept separate, in the fish culturing mania that swept over the United States in the late 19th century.

To be fair, we also need to point out a few errors on the part of our angler. It's bad manners to hold court, especially when you're on someone else's ground. And there is nothing wrong, biologically speaking, with keeping a few trout for the pan now and again. However, his greatest error—and one that echoes back to Plato's dialogues between the philosopher and the poet—is a rigidly scientific worldview.

Think for a moment of a wooded stream (Tagatz, Salzwedel, or Klatwitter) flowing behind the farm of German-speaking immigrants. Imagine the joy of this family, in a strange and hard land, beholding and eating something from the Old World—beautiful spotted fish reminiscent of those swimming in their homeland Swabian rivers. What could be more German?

When I hear Wisconsin locals refer to German brown trout, I smile. Brown trout have been in this heavily German state almost as long as sauerkraut, bratwurst, and beer. To me, they're *German* brown trout. And they're as much a part of the Midwest as pheasants taken from the Far East and now roaming the Great Plains.

Our scientific friend—if we can forgive his distaste for poetry—may be helpful in providing facts. He will tell you, quite correctly, that brown trout are the most widely distributed trout in Wisconsin. From Black Earth Creek and Timber Coulee in southwest Wisconsin to the Mecan in the Sand Counties and from the Wolf in the northeast to the Rush and Kinnickinnic in the west, brown trout, brought to Wisconsin in 1887, are here to stay.

He will also take pains to point out, if he is true to science, that they displaced the native brook trout by out-competing them for food. On the other hand, he argues, being more tolerant they can live in waters made warmer and more turbid by the inevitable agriculture and development of this state, opening scores of streams to trout fishing that otherwise would not hold trout. Temperatures in the 50s and 60s are preferred by brown trout. Temperatures in the low 70s can be tolerated; upper 70s for an extended period of time are stressful if not lethal to brown trout.

Being a student of entomology, our angler will tell you that young brown trout (up to 12 inches) are greatly found of aquatic invertebrates (mayflies, caddisflies, stoneflies, and scuds). Being a dry-fly fisherman, it pains him to point out the ungenteel eating habits of brown trout larger than 15 inches: 90 percent forage fish with a rag-tag mix of crawfish and frogs (and occasionally a small rodent) making up the balance. But dry-fly anglers needn't despair, he counsels. These big fellows can be taken on *Hexagenia* dry flies on June and July nights. He intones: "Let me tell you about this night on the Mecan River, June 21 according to my log. A warm day, and a still windless night ..."

"Exceedingly wary," he describes his beloved *Salmo trutta,* "with dark spots against a cream, olive, or bronze body." He will tell you that in farm country anglers have gone so far as to approach the stream on all fours dressed to look like a cow, but being a fashionable man he eschews the cow suit for drab clothing and a careful approach. He's never without Blue-Winged Olives or midges in his Wheatley fly box; Tricos in summer; Hendricksons and Sulphurs in spring.

A 5-weight rod is his weapon of choice, though he'll work a 4-weight on brushy water. Our angler knows to fish around cover—fallen trees and behind boulders in big freestone water like the Wolf and Prairie. On streams that have received DNR improvement he likes to dance a dry along the riprapped banks. And when all else fails, especially in flat water, he skitters his dry back toward him. And when this does not work, and none of his esteemed colleagues are looking, he will occasionally tie on a Woolly Bugger, under cover of darkness, and take phenomenally large fish.

He categorically will not fish for them, but science and thoroughness compel him to describe browns that are stocked and grow to prodigious sizes in Lake Michigan. He's even seen pictures in fly-fishing magazines of anglers hoisting 10-pounders from Lake Michigan harbors and tributaries.

His favorite Iowa waters are Waterloo Creek, French Creek, Clear Creek, and Bloody.

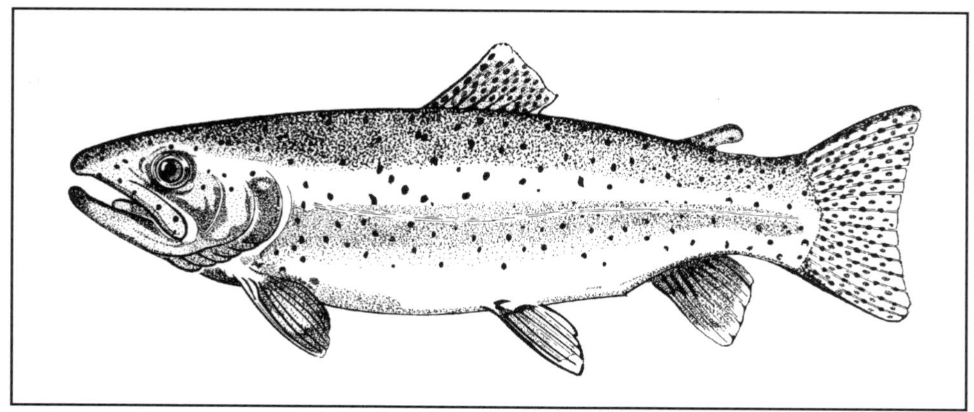

Rainbow Trout

Introduced to from the West Coast in the late 19th century, rainbow trout are widely stocked in Wisconsin's lakes and streams. Fast growth rates and the ability to withstand temperatures up to 80 degrees make them suited for a put-and-take fishery in many Iowa streams. With some notable exceptions like the West Branch of the White River near Wautoma and the Brule River in northwest Wisconsin, rainbow trout do not reproduce well in inland streams.

However, *Salmo gairdneri* is a handsome specimen, usually between 9 and 14 inches, with a steely or green background, dark spots, and a red lateral stripe. It is quick to take to the air when hooked. Fast-water habitats such as waterfalls and riffles are good areas to fish for rainbows; they are less apt to seek out in-stream cover such as trees and cutbanks and are also vulnerable to heron predation. When stocked in inland lakes they seek the cold, oxygenated substrate of the lake, thus inland lake rainbows are often taken by spin fishermen or flyfishers deliberately fishing sink-tip lines and nymphs or leech patterns.

Vilas County in northeast Wisconsin has a concentration of lakes containing rainbow trout. They're also present in northeast Wisconsin spring ponds. Predominantly insect eaters, rainbows trout are taken on any number of fly patterns. Fish any pattern that mimics the insect life of the stream and you're likely to catch rainbow trout, which are less wary than browns.

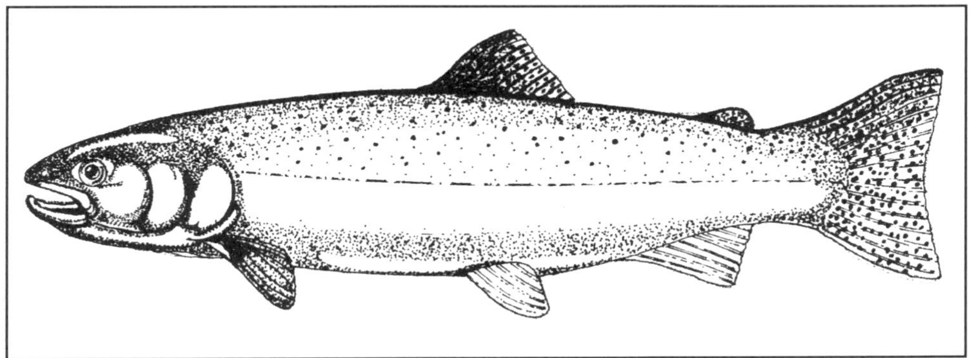

Steelhead

Three strains of steelhead (a variety of rainbow trout selected for its tendency to return to home waters) are stocked in Lake Michigan and Lake Superior tributaries—Skamania and Chambers Creek, which are fall-run fish, and the spring-run Ganaraska strain. Lake Michigan steelhead populations are supported by culturing stripped eggs and milt and planting yearling fish back in streams. Natural reproduction takes places on some Lake Superior tributaries, including the Brule River. Steelhead dwarf their inland cousins because they feed on high-protein forage fish like alewife. An average steelhead weighs 5 pounds and fish up to 10 pounds are not uncommon. Fish in the 15-pound range are considered trophies.

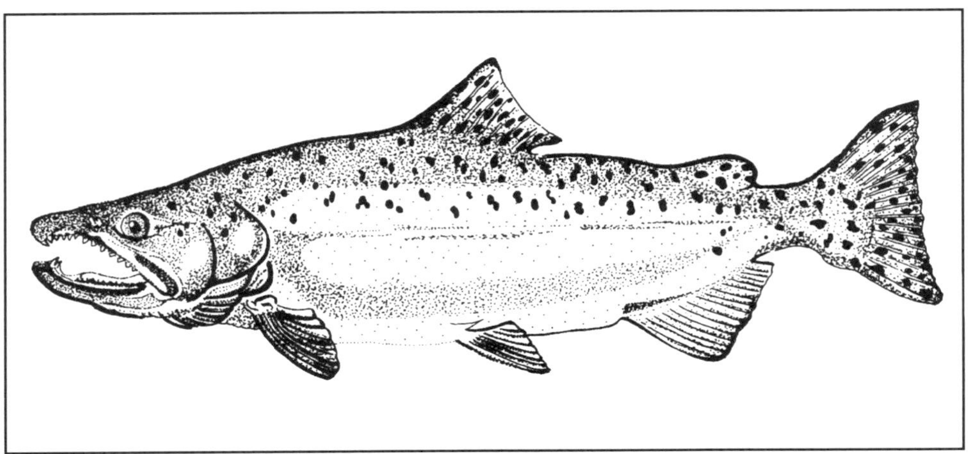

Salmon

Introduced to Lake Michigan in the late 1960s to help curb a burgeoning alewife population and a sagging sport fishery, coho (*Oncorhynchus kisutch*) and chinook

(*Oncorhynchus tshawytscha*) salmon have been wildly successful on both accounts. They were later introduced to Lake Superior and added to its sport fishery. In regard to natural reproduction, however, success has been poor. These Pacific salmon do not reproduce in Lake Michigan, and successful spawning in Lake Superior tributaries is limited at best.

What these fish do offer the fly-rod angler is the chance to battle big West Coast salmonoids without traveling across the country. Both species enter tributary streams in fall, at which time they are the target of anglers. Since neither species is actually feeding—but trying to find the specific stretch of stream where they were planted—they must be goaded into striking, often by drifting a fly over the same run numerous times. Woolly Buggers, egg flies, and even nymphs fished on 18-inch droppers will get their attention.

Use an 8-weight rod with sink-tip line and a 1X leader (lighter leaders in clear water). October and November are the best times to fish, especially after a good rain when home-scented water enters the harbors and cues the fish to move upstream. Fly casters also take salmon, particularly cohos, from harbors and river mouths along Lake Michigan.

Salmon mature in the Great Lakes and return to streams where they were planted to spawn and ultimately die after their spawning attempt. Coho salmon return to home waters in 3 years; chinooks in 4 years. Since spawning is largely unsuccessful, populations are maintained by fish culture—stripping egg and milt, growing fish to fingerling size, and stocking them in tributary streams.

On Lake Michigan, the Root, Pike, Twin, Manitowoc, Kewaunee, and Ahnapee Rivers see runs of salmon. On Lake Superior, salmon run up the Brule and larger streams like the Cranberry River on the Bayfield Peninsula. Chinook generally run between 10 and 20 pounds; cohos between 3 and 12. Breeding chinooks take on a dark, purple to brown cast, while breeding cohos are blue-green with a red lateral stripe. If you plan on keeping fish from Lake Michigan tributaries, visit http://www.dnr.state.wi.us/org/water/fhp/fish/advisories or call the DNR and ask for a hard copy of fish consumption advisories at 608-267-7498. Mercury and PCB contaminants are a problem in some waters.

The diminutive pink salmon *(Oncorhynchus gorbuscha)* is native to the West Coast. In 1955, 20,000 fingerlings were discarded into a Lake Superior tributary in Ontario, and by the 1970s the pink salmon, to everyone's surprise, had established naturally reproducing populations in Lake Superior and northern Lakes Huron and Michigan.

Pink salmon spawn in odd numbered years in tributary streams, having matured in the lakes to a size of about 15 inches and 1.5 pounds. Pink salmon make up an insignificant portion of salmon caught by Wisconsin flyfishers. They can be caught in Lake Superior tributaries on the Bayfield Peninsula in September and October. Prespawn adults are silvery-blue with large dark spots on back. Spawning males darken in color and develop a hooked jaw and a pronounced hump between the dorsal fin and head, giving them the nickname humpie or humpbacked salmon.

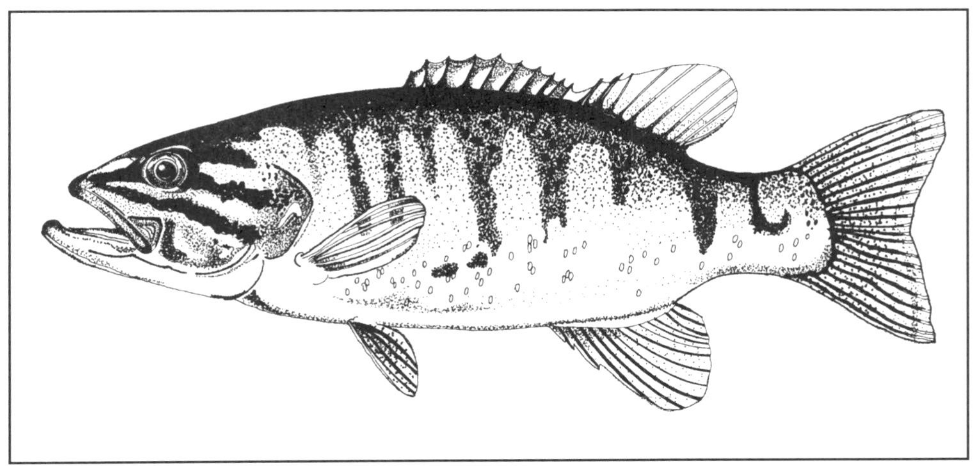

Smallmouth Bass

There is good and bad news about smallmouth bass *(Micropterus dolomieui)* populations. The bad news is that the streams of far southwest Wisconsin, just above the Illinois border, have seen dramatic decreases in smallmouth populations over the last 20 years. It's a shame because these small rocky streams, often the lower ends of trout streams, had been prolific bass producers in a unique part of the state. Whether it's floods, agricultural runoff, or some other factor not known to biologists, this fishery is now in a tailspin.

In years past anglers could count on excellent wade fishing for scrappy bronzebacks in rivers like the Grant, Galena, and Fever. On the plus side, smallmouths are appearing in rivers and lakes that formerly had marginal smallmouth populations. New and emerging smallmouth fisheries are found along the riprapped shorelines of Castle Rock and Petenwell Flowages in central Wisconsin. Improving water quality on the lower Fox River, between Green Bay and De Pere, has meant an explosion of smallmouths, with fish up to 5 pounds caught regularly. Bays along Door County and Chequamegon Bay on Lake Superior have developed into world-class smallmouth fisheries.

On these waters and major Wisconsin rivers (notably the Mississippi, Chippewa, Flambeau, Wisconsin) fly-fishing guides operate out of Western-style driftboats. But the best news is that you don't need a boat or guide to tangle with these fish. Rocky Door County, Madison's Lake Mendota, Castle Rock and Petenwell Flowages provide topnotch shore fisheries; wade fishing for smallmouths is great sport on the lower Eau Claire, lower Wisconsin and Red Cedar Rivers in the west, and the Milwaukee and East Twin in the east.

On the Iowa side, try the Mississippi, Turkey, Upper Iowa, Yellow and Cedar Rivers. Drop a clouser minnow in a deep, rocky run and hold on. On small streams and rivers, a 5- or 6-weight rod and a floating line will do the trick; just weight your flies with a bit of split shot. On big water, up the gauge. Wind and bigger water and bigger fish call for an 8- or 9-weight rod with a sink-tip line.

Smallmouth eat crawfish as voraciously as ducks forage wild rice. Baitfish also make up a crucial part of the smallmouth's diet, especially in big water systems like the Great Lakes. Dahlberg Divers, crawfish imitations, deerhair bass bugs, Muddler Minnows, and Clouser Minnows will all catch fish. In small streams, fish size 8 to 10. In big water, anything from size 2 to 6 works. Stream smallmouths generally run below 14 inches, with anything over 18 inches considered a trophy. Smallmouths inhabiting large water systems such as the Mississippi and Wisconsin Rivers and Great Lakes will easily grow to 2 or 3 pounds if allowed to mature, with specimens 5 pounds and upward taken each year.

Smallmouth bass can be distinguished from largemouth bass by the length of their jaw, which never extends beyond the posterior edge of the eye (the jaw on largemouth bass always extends beyond the eye). Dark vertical stripes extend down the fish's body, ranging in color from green to brown against a sandy background.

Spawning occurs in early summer, and big prespawn bass scouting for nests can often be taken in early May. They are slow to mature, three to five years, and prefer a coolwater habitat to warm or cold water. In hot weather they seek relief in the lower ends of trout streams, near wing dams, and in deep rocky areas of lakes.

In most Wisconsin waters, smallmouth may be fished from the first Saturday in May to March 1. Smallmouth bass fishing in Iowa is open year-round. Given that any smallmouth with enough meat to make a meal will probably be 5 years old, practicing catch-and-release is crucial.

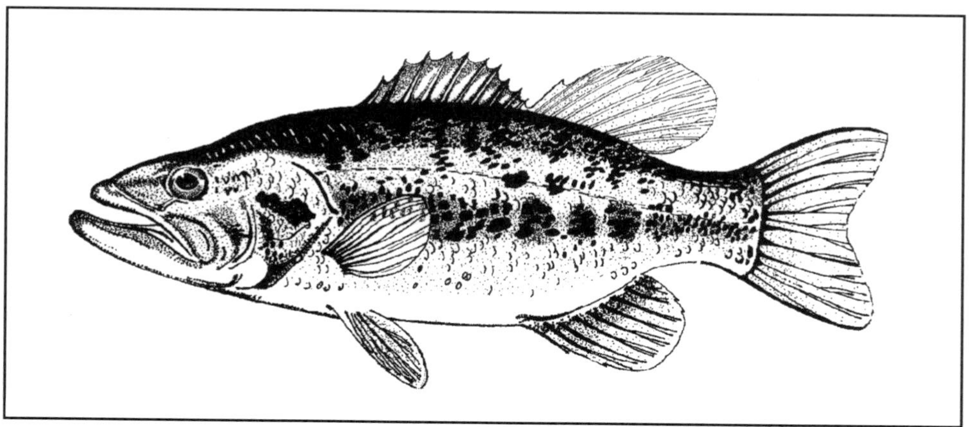

Largemouth Bass

The lifecycles of many warmwater gamefish in are strongly associated with aquatic vegetation. Northern pike and a variety of panfish spawn in weedbeds and return to them in fall. However, nowhere is the association as strong as with largemouth bass. They seek out nest sites once water temperatures hit 60 degrees and deposit eggs when waters warm to the mid-60s, never straying far from these habitats throughout the year.

Largemouth bass thrive in water temperatures well into the 80s, as evidenced by their successful introduction to Mexico, Cuba, and Puerto Rico. While northern Wisconsin marks the limit of largemouth range, they do survive in its shallow lakes. Central Wisconsin has much prime largemouth habitat. Narrow Buffalo and Puckaway Lakes near Montello and tiny Jordan and Parker Lakes near Oxford are good bets. Many cranberry flowages near Black River Falls hold trophy bigmouths. The Madison Lakes and Kettle Moraine Lakes are not to be overlooked. Sloughs and backwaters of major rivers such as the Mississippi, Wisconsin, Rock, and Black Rivers hold largemouths.

Zooplankton and insect larvae make up the bulk of a young largemouth's diet; mature bass feed on baitfish, panfish, crawfish, frogs and an occasionally unlucky mouse.

Fish largemouth with a 6-weight rod and poppers, streamers, leech patterns, or deerhair bass bugs on a floating line. Fish them near their spawning beds in late spring and early summer. As summer progresses, they are still in weedy habitats but more scattered and wary. Unlike pike, which are exclusively daytime feeders, largemouth bass feed early and late in the day and during low-light conditions.

A favorite way of fishing largemouth bass in Wisconsin is to cast toward shoreline cover from a belly boat or canoe either early or late in the day. Lily pads, dead trees, stumps, even shoreline piers are all good cover to work. A scuba-diving friend of mine has seen big solitary largemouths sulking, alone, in the depths of quarry and glacial lakes. Rowing and trolling dropoffs with a large dark streamer fished on a sinking line will take some of these big bass. The Upper Mississippi River backwaters near Lansing and Northeast Iowa lakes—Hendricks, Meyer, Frog Hollow, and Dehli—hold good largemouth populations

Sunfish

While both largemouth and smallmouth bass belong to the Centrarchidae, or sunfish, family, more commonly known Wisconsin sunfish are the bluegill *(Lepomis macrochirus),* pumpkinseed *(Lepomis gibbosus),* and rock bass *(Ambloplites rupestris).* These latter Centrarchidae all frequent weedy shorelines, will readily take a fly (aquatic insects comprise a large part of their diet), are open to fishing year-round in most Wisconsin waters with a bag limit of 25, and make fine eating.

Fish for sunfish with small nymphs or poppers. Fishing is good on and near spawning beds. I've seen sunfish on their beds as early as late April in southern Wisconsin; spawning may be as late as June or early July in lakes of the far north. Noted sunfish lakes are Lake Mendota and Monona in Madison, and Lake Pepin along the Mississippi River. Mason Lake and the small lakes near Oxford afford fine panfishing, and panfish lakes are numerous throughout the north, with the Chetek Chain being a standout. Kangaroo Lake in Door County is known for a population of hefty rock bass. The Upper Mississippi River backwaters near Lansing and Lake Hendricks hold good, eating-size bluegills.

Bluegills and pumpkinseeds both have dark vertical stripes against an orange background; pumpkinseeds have a bright orange-red spot just beyond the gill plate. Rock bass have red eyes, a sandy background, and brown to olive lateral stripes. A ½-pound sunfish is of good size and will give a lively fight on a light fly rod. Fish larger than ¾ pound are trophies. If you see dimples in the water around spawning beds, the fish are feeding on the surface and will readily take a dry.

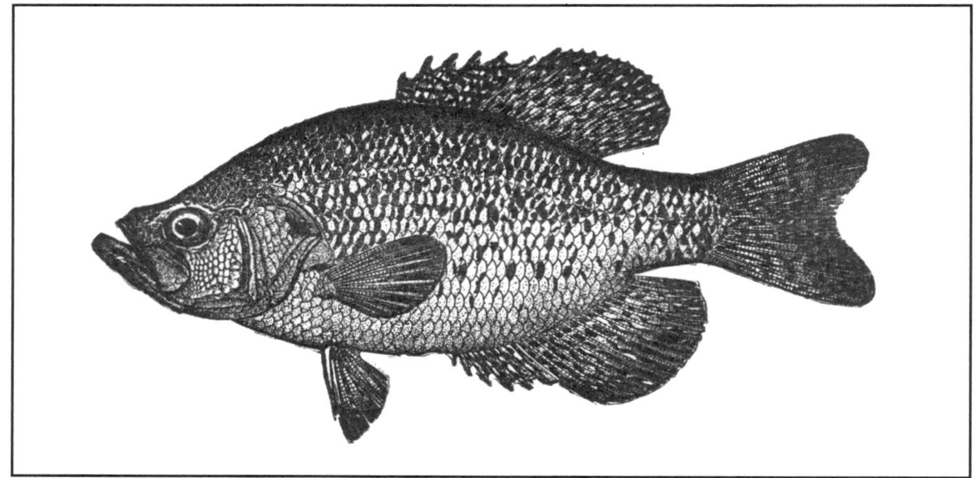

Crappie

Black and white crappie are both present in Wisconsin, with black crappie vastly outnumbering white crappie. Darker markings and the lack of vertical side bands distinguish them from white crappies. An average Wisconsin crappie is between 6 and 10 inches long and weighs less than half a pound. Some central Wisconsin flowages produce 1- and 2-pound fish as do the stump fields of the upper Mississippi along the Wisconsin Iowa border.

Habitat and food preferences of mature crappie are closer to largemouth bass than to other panfish. Forage fish make up a significant part of their diet, and they associate with largemouths in flooded stumpfields, dead timber, lily pads, and riparian vegetation, especially in spring. As waters warm, look for crappies suspended off sandbars in 5 to 10 feet of water. Crappies feed most heavily just before sundown, and also around dawn. Fish them on the lightest of fly rods using minnow-style streamers in size 10. In flowages and cranberry bogs where forage fish are scarce, fish them with nymphs, as crappies are highly adaptive feeders. Crappies have tender, papery mouths and can wriggle from the hook easily. They are prolific spawners and make unequaled table fare when batter-dipped and fried. Black crappie often survive in shallow lakes where winterkill decimates other fish populations.

White Bass

Often overlooked by flyfishers, the white bass is abundant in Wisconsin and Iowa lakes and rivers, is a scrappy fighter that can weigh in at 2 pounds or more, can produce phenomenal year classes, and, when cooled immediately on ice, provides fine eating with no guilt feelings. What's more, white bass fishing during spring spawning runs or summer school-ups can be fast and furious—the freshwater equivalent of a bluefish school. Minnows rise to the surface in a frenzied hail, birds swoop down to eat the minnows, and white bass gorge themselves, ready to savage any silvery minnow imitation thrown at them.

The lower Wolf River between Fremont and Lake Poygan, Lake Winnebago, Green Bay, the Madison Lakes, Petenwell and Castle Rock Flowages, and just about any river system of size provides a white bass run. On the Mississippi River, white bass school up throughout the year by focusing in the schools of minnoes.

White bass resemble their saltwater cousins the striped bass and, in fact, are often called stripers, though they are genetically distinct. A pronounced spiny dorsal fin, silver to white background, and black horizontal stripes characterize this handsome fish. Most white bass caught are about a foot long and under a pound; fish up to 2 pounds aren't uncommon, especially where a good base of forage fish exists.

Fishing for white bass is open year-round in most Wisconsin waterways with no minimum size and no bag limit. Given that they are predators fairly high up the food chain, you should consult DNR fish advisories when fishing industrialized waterways such as the Upper Mississippi downstream from the Twin Cities and eastern and central waterways downstream from papermills. Consult either the DNR publication *Important Health Information for People Eating Fish from Wisconsin Waters* or visit http://www.dnr.state.wi.us/org/water/fhp/fish/advisories.

Walleye

Given its preference for deep water and bottom feeding, walleye *(Stitzostedion vitreum)* and its close cousin the sauger *(Stitzostedion canadense)* are not prime targets for Wisconsin and Iowa flyfishers. Walleye spawn just after ice-out in April and May. Most inland Wisconsin lakes are closed to walleye fishing during this period, but a number of major river systems are open to year-round fishing, including the Wolf River, Fox River, Mississippi River, Chippewa River, and the St. Croix River. The Cedar Turkey and Iowa systems offer year-round walleye fishng in Iowa. During the spawn, walleye often congregate below dams in swift deep water and are heavily fished in crowded conditions that do not auger well for flyfishers.

After the spawn, walleye and sauger disperse. Chances improve for taking them on flies, though they are still taken incidentally for the most part. Smallmouth bass anglers working streamers around rockpiles and deep channels might catch an occasional walleye. And as walleye are nocturnal feeders, it's not out of the question to take them as they cruise the rocky shoreline in search of an evening meal.

Generally, a sink-tip line is best for reaching these deep-water feeders. On small waters, you can get away with a 5-weight rod. In big water, especially where current and wind are factors, graduate to a 7-weight. Crawfish and leech patterns will take walleye.

A typical walleye is between 1 and 2 pounds. Ten-pound fish are taken every year from Green Bay and the Mississippi River. Walleye are bronze to brown mottled with pale bellies and pronounced, spiny dorsal fins. Sauger are smaller and more dusky in color with a less pronounced dorsal fin. The flaky white flesh of walleye and sauger is excellent fried or baked with almonds. Adult walleye consume large quantities of baitfish and thus accumulate mercury and PCBs in waterways such as Lake Pepin, the lower Fox River system, and the Wisconsin River above the Prairie du Sac dam. Visit http://www.dnr.state.wi.us/org/water/fhp/fish/advisories or call the DNR and ask for a hard copy of fish consumption advisories at 608-267-7498.

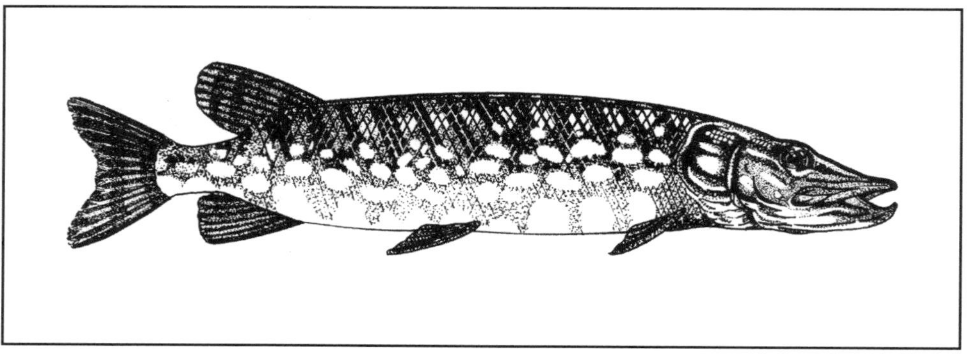

Northern Pike

Northern pike are widely distributed in Wisconsin, but they are most numerous in central and northern parts of the state where weedy shoreline spawning habitat is most abundant. These shallow grassy habitats are fine egg depositories and provide cover and food (principally zooplankton) for developing frye. Spawning occurs in these areas just after ice-out. Any river system with marshy backwaters will hold pike as will any lake with significant weeds. In southern Wisconsin, Lake Mendota is noted for large pike. Sloughs along the upper Mississippi are consistent northern producers as are lower parts of the Yellow, Turkey and Upper Iowa River in Iowa. Central Wisconsin flowages and cranberry bogs are thick with pike, which can endure the low oxygen conditions common on these shallow impoundments.

Shallow, weedy Puckaway and Buffalo Lakes are fine northern lakes. That there is no minimum size limit for northern pike in Wisconsin's Northern Zone (above Highway 10) and in Iowa speaks to their abundance. It is no sin to keep a few northern pike, especially in the Northern Zone. They prey on anything from muskies to minnows and seem to have a particular taste for young trout. Pickling gets rid of the bones in small northern pike; steaking is a good way to go for big fish. The meat on a northern is sweet, white, and succulent.

Pike remain in these grassy shoals until water temperatures warm beyond the upper 70s. They tolerate low oxygen but not excessive water temperatures. During the dog days of summer, find spring holes and you will find pike. If you are fishing a larger river or flowage, try at the mouth of cool feeder creeks. More often than not, I catch (or spook) northerns from these shallow feeders, especially if there is cover nearby. It seems to me they are lying in wait for prey. If there are no springs on a particular lake, try fishing 15 to 20 feet deep using a weighted line. As water temperatures cool in fall, pike return to marshy habitats.

While an angler can work the shoreline for bass and panfish using the same 4-weight rod, fly fishing for northerns requires special equipment. They are tenacious fighters, can grow to more than 20 pounds, and are toothy. Let me put that another way: they have teeth that can do violence to your hand. A sturdy pair of longhandled pliers or forceps is a must. Use an 8- or 9-weight rod with a steel or braided nylon leader. Pike are not wary fish—their brains are a fraction of the size of those of other gamefish—so you won't spook them with heavy leaders. Besides saving flies and landing fish, you will be cutting down unnecessary suffering, as pike can bite through 10-pound test with ease.

Use Dahlberg Divers, big gaudy streamers, and large crawfish flies in rocky areas. Big poppers will also work. As pike do not feed at night they are a good lazy man's fish. Take a break from the trout stream during the middle of the day and the pike will be waiting. On the vast majority of Wisconsin waters, northern pike can be fished from the first Saturday in May to March 1. In Iowa, they can be fished year-round with no minimum size and a bag limit of 3. They are good quarry to pursue when the trout season closes. Northern pike are open to fishing on the Mississippi and St. Croix Rivers and Green Bay year round.

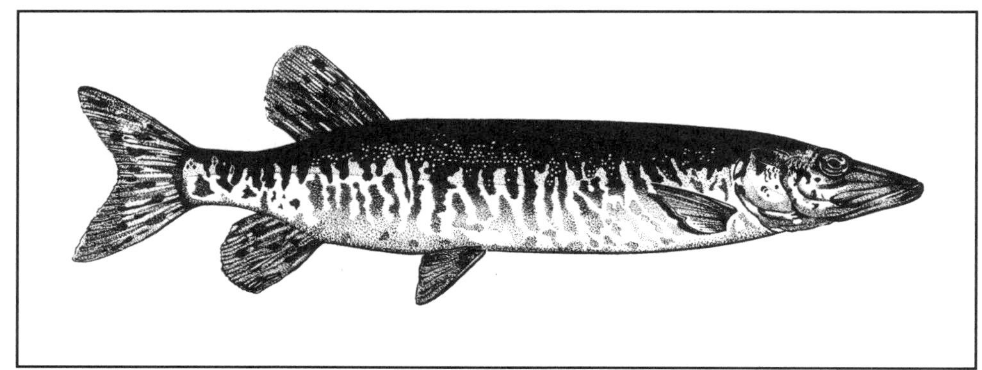

Muskellunge

The muskellunge *(Esox masquinongy)* was designated Wisconsin state fish by the State Legislature in 1955. Given Iowa's depth of lakes, muskies are not a major gamefish there. With the state record weighing in at almost 70 pounds and the muskellunge occupying the undisputed top of the food chain, it's no wonder the state chose this fish to represent itself. It's also no mystery why these giants of the pike family ignite the passion of both spinfishing and flycasting anglers. As with shark and marlin fishing in saltwater, there's something to be said for going after predator fish at the top of the chain. And muskellunge provide unrivalled sport once they are hooked, with a combination of violent shaking, deep bulldogging, and aerial acrobatics.

Much of what applies to fly fishing for pike can be extended to fly fishing for muskellunge: steel leaders, 9-weight rods, and flies drawn from the hairy and scary category. However, while pike are well distributed throughout the state, muskellunge are concentrated in northern Wisconsin. The Chippewa Flowage, Lake Wissota, and Lake DuBay are classic muskie destinations of the north. Lake Wingra in Madison, especially before and after weed-up, is the muskie hotspot of southern Wisconsin.

Fishing is best for muskellunge while they are still in the shallows in May and June and then again when lakes turn over in October or November. Dusk or night fishing with large streamers over a combination of weed and rock is a good strategy for big muskies. The diet of mature muskellunge consists almost entirely of other fish, with suckers and ciscoes being favorites.

Given their slow growth rate and low population density, muskellunge should be caught, photographed, and released. The tiger muskellunge, a naturally occurring and stocked hybrid between a muskellunge and a northern pike, is found in many of the same waters as the muskellunge and can be fished with the same techniques.

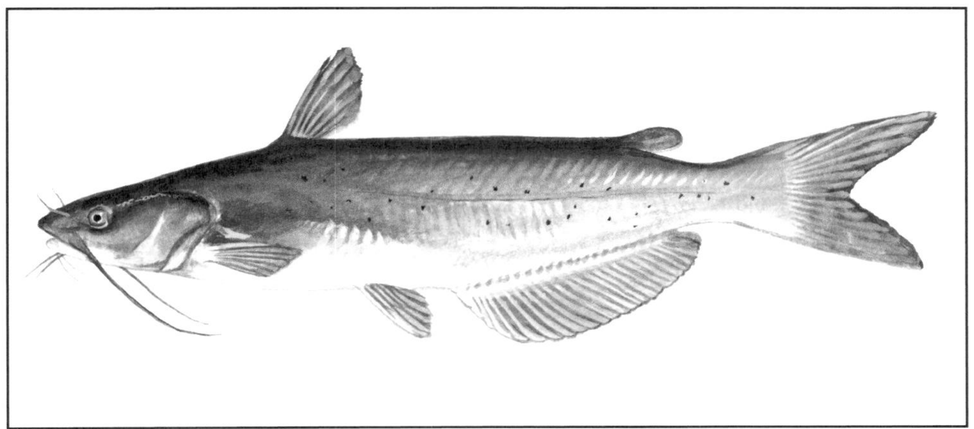

Channel Catfish

Commonly regarded as scavengers, channel catfish *(Ictalarus punctatus)* actually consume large amounts of forage fish, insects, and crustaceans. They also a frequent a variety of water not thought of as catfish habitat—including river channels and fast water below dams. A productive and enjoyable way to fish channel catfish on a fly is in small rivers like the Kickapoo, Yahara, La Crosse, Crawfish in Wisconsin or Yellow, Turkey, Turtle and Cedar in Iowa. Cast leech patterns on a 6-weight fly rod and sink-tip line. Wade or paddle along and think like a fish. Where could you capture lots of food while exerting little effort? Let your fly sweep beneath undercut banks, along fallen timber, even along the bottom of fast runs. You'll be surprised how often a channel catfish picks it up—and how much, dare I say, like trout fishing this is. Once hooked, they are tenacious fighters, making deep, bulldogging runs.

Most channel catfish are between 12 and 20 inches and weigh 1 to 3 pounds. Their body is silver-blue to gray with black spots, with a deeply forked tail. Channel catfish feed most actively during periods of rising water and during low-light conditions. To clean a catfish, make a shallow incision that goes around the gill plate, grab hold of the skin with pliers or vice-grips, pulling toward the tail. The skin should peel off like a sock, in one piece. Steak them, fillet them, or cook them whole. Fry them, grill them, or blacken them. Channel catfish, especially from clear water, are as sweet and tender as anything that swims.

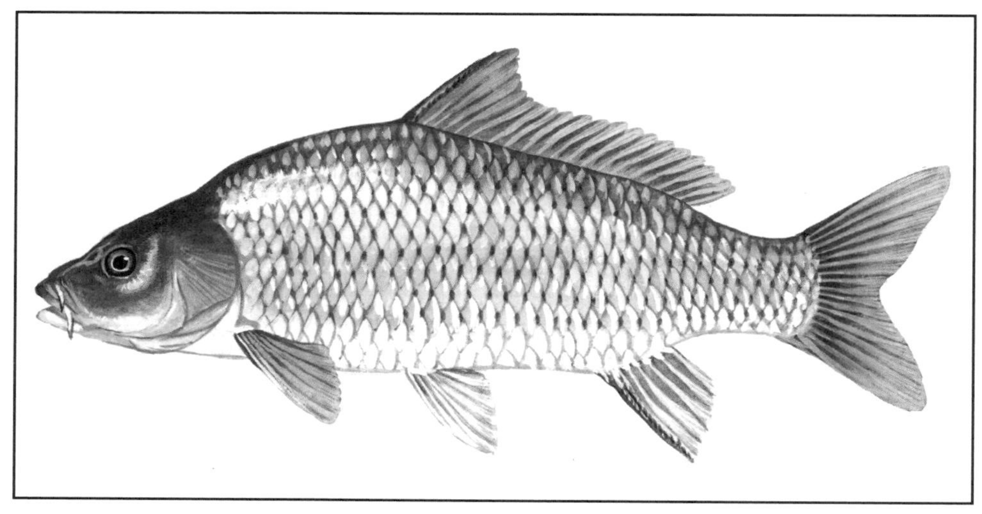

Carp

An Old World exotic introduced to America in the late 19th century, the story of the common carp *(Cyprinus carpio)* is like that of past, present, and hopefully not future invasive exotics: native species are displaced and crucial habitat lost because of the introduction or foreign species (either by accident or design). Eurasian milfoil, purple loosestrife, starlings, Norway rats, zebra mussels, and Eurasian gobes—the list goes on.

Carp have wrought havoc on the weedy waters into which they were introduced. They uproot quality vegetation in search of food and cause increased turbidity, robbing waterfowl and fish of spawning and feeding areas and sullying water quality. Like it or not, and despite the best efforts of the Iowa and Wisconsin DNR, carp are here to stay. Might as well, to jumble an old saw, make chicken salad out of chicken you-know-what. If nothing else, carp are common to the point of being a nuisance.

They can be sight-fished with nymphs as you would fish for steelhead. Occasionally they can be seen feeding on the surface or on emerging insects, in which case they can be taken on dry flies. Just about any Wisconsin lake with shallow weedy flats has carp. Their porpoising behavior makes them easy to spot. As they can grow upwards of 10 pounds, you will want sufficient backbone in your equipment: at least a 7- or 8-weight rod with a 2X leader. They are strong, if not acrobatic, fighters.

As table fare, they do not, rate highly, unless smoked. As garden fertilizer, however, they do nicely. Large scales, an orange-to-brown color, and two barbels protruding from the lower lip characterize the common carp.

FISHERIES MANAGEMENT AND CATCH-AND-RELEASE

Catch-and-release represents an important evolution in the way we think about fishing. Instead of assuming that fish are to be kept, flyfishers generally release their quarry nowadays. This is a good thing, especially with growing numbers of anglers and limited numbers of fish. Follow the tips below, from *The Wisconsin Trout Fishing Guide and Regulations,* if you decide to release your quarry. Catch-and-release is an important management tool.

How you release a fish is as important as whether you release it. If done improperly, catch-and-release is simply a mantra that makes anglers feel better while their released quarry (particularly trout) die a slow, painful death.

Don't play fish to exhaustion. Use a landing net made of cotton or some other soft netting and avoid leaders lighter than 6X. The landing net helps you gain control over fish, shortens the fight, and keeps it from flopping onto dry land.

Using ultra-fine leaders has two harmful consequences on trout. They break on large trout, leaving the fly painfully behind. And light leaders mean you have to fight fish more slowly and carefully, thus tiring them and increasing chances for mortality. A quick fight is particularly important during summer doldrums when water temperatures may climb into the 70s, or during early trout season when air temperatures may be in the teens or 20s. (You might consider switching to heartier warmwater gamefish during prolonged heat spells.)

Turn fish belly up while removing hooks. This disorients them and allows you to work with a more docile fish.

Don't keep fish out of the water more than 10 or 15 seconds. Snap a photo if you like, grasping the fish behind the head, but avoid extended shoots or spectator shows. Avoid touching the eyes and mouth, which are extremely sensitive. Wet your hands when handling trout, as dry hands can cause skin rot. Hold the fish into the current, allowing water to circulate through its gills as you release it. If all goes well, your quarry will dart back to its underwater lair.

Earlier, I said that catch-and-release is an important management tool. Just as with any toolbox, you select from it. Among the tools in the trout management box, catch-and-release is but one, albeit a crucial one. Regulations, stream improvement, season dates, and harvest are also in the box. In these days of no-kill fishing, speaking of fish harvest may sound strange. But there are situations where harvest unquestionably helps the fishery.

Carp are an obvious example. I don't think there's a fish manager around who wants carp in his or her bailiwick. Panfish, while not a nuisance, have a tendency to overpopulate. Predator fish help keep this in check. Man does his part by making sure there aren't too many, and thus stunted, bluegills (or crappie or perch or rock bass). Ditto for prolific school fish like white bass. If you want quality panfishing, have an occasional fish fry. Northern Wisconsin is also blessed with a healthy population (some might say overpopulation) of northern pike. You aren't hurting the population any by taking a few northerns to pickle with onions and peppercorns.

Trout are a different case. Fisheries biologist Gene Van Dike is credited with introducing the idea of catch-and-release fishing to southern Wisconsin on Castle Rock Creek in the 1970s. It proved a smashing success. Brown trout in the 25-inch range are taken there each year. Returned to the stream, these fish can attain maximum size and be enjoyed by many anglers. Certainly, success stories like Timber Coulee (which was barely suitable for even stocked fish in the 1950s) and the Kinnickinnic River are success stories in which the catch-and-release ethic played a crucial role.

If we apply the moral maxim of 18th-century philosopher Immanuel Kant to trout fishing—act as if your actions were simultaneous with those of all of humanity—we quickly see why it's important to practice catch-and-release. These streams wouldn't support thousands of trout per mile, as they do today, if anglers generally kept what they caught. However, like most philosophical issues, this one gets murky under closer scrutiny. Flyfishers talk of 20- or 30-fish days. We've all had them and we're all proud of them. Since most flyfishers do not keep trout, we can assume they release fish on banner days and do so promptly and correctly. Did all 20 or 30 fish survive the day? The week?

For trout that swallow a hook and have it snipped, one DNR study shows a survival rate of 80 percent. The rate for trout released by flyfishers is likely higher (since flies as a rule aren't swallowed). Let's say 90 to 95 percent of trout caught by flyfishers survive given the broad range of anglers and conditions. (This allows for hot and cold weather, which are tough on trout, and for long fights.) That translates to between one and three trout dying on a 20- or 30-fish day.

Am I saying that we should go back to creeling all fish because some will die as a result of being hooked? No. Catch-and-release is still the correct de facto course of action. And there is certainly weight to the argument that nothing is 100 percent effective and that some good is still worth doing even if it's not an absolute good. Fly fishing is a relatively low-impact sport, and a released trout has a good chance of survival while a creeled trout has none. What I'm getting at is that we need to be honest with ourselves. On a good day of trout fishing, we are likely hurting fish, and possibly killing a fish or two. And even if they do survive, trout certainly do not enjoy having any hook in their mouth—whether it is a single-hook spinner, fly, or bait hook.

Putting aside style, there appears to be little difference between the fisherman soaking a night crawler or chub on the bottom of a pool with the express purpose of taking home a few trout for the pan and the evolved flyfisher who catches large numbers of trout but releases them. Both fishermen are, ultimately, killing fish. One simply does it more overtly. From a biological point of view, keeping a few trout or having them die as a result of your actions is the same thing. We all impact this fragile resource and need to be mindful about how much we do so, whether we keep or release fish.

Keep a ceremonial trout to enjoy with a nice meal and glass of wine. It helps ground you in what you're doing (and what you're not doing). The health of streams depends not exclusively on catch-and-release fishing but on a broad picture of land-use, habitat, ground water conservation, and responsible development. Take care of the resource and remember that the fellow next to you fishing a spinner or worm may care as much for the stream as you do.

EQUIPMENT CHECKLIST

___ rods (4- or 5-piece travel rods are handy for airline travel; bring a spare if possible)

___ reels

___ extra spool with sinking line and/or poly leaders

___ fly boxes

___ portable fly-tying kit

___ nail clippers

___ small pliers or hemostats (for pinching down barbs and disgorging hooks)

___ retractable tape measure

___ stream thermometer

___ vest

___ strike indicators

___ floatant

___ tippet

___ leaders

___ Micro shot

___ landing net (one that clips to the eye-ring on the back of your vest is nice)

___ waders (tennis shoes and old blue jeans will do in a pinch during summer)

___ wader repair kit

___ bug spray and/or headnet

___ space blanket and matches

___ first-aid kit

___ flashlight

___ Hide-a-Key and/or extra set of keys

___ canteen with drinking water

___ Gore-Tex raingear

___ spare wool socks

___ wool sweater, especially in the north

___ hat

___ Polarized sunglasses

___ sunscreen

___ disposable camera (carry on-stream with no worries)

___ mini flashlight

___ mobile phone (for emergencies, not for talking while on trout streams)

___ *Flyfisher's Guide to Wisconsin & Iowa*

Resources

Wisconsin Division of Natural Resources
101 S. Webster Street
Madison, WI 53707
608-266-2621; www.dnr.state.wi.us

Wisconsin Department of Tourism
201 W. Washington Avenue
P.O. Box 7976
Madison, WI 53707-7976
800-432-8784

Reservations for campgrounds in state parks and forests: 888-947-2757

For road conditions in Wisconsin: 800-762-3974; www.travelwisconsin.com

For information on river flows and weather, visit National Weather Service at www.crh.noaa.gov

To purchase topographical maps of Wisconsin, from USGS: 608-263-7389

To purchase maps of Wisconsin lakes from Fishing Hotspots: 800-338-5957

Internet Resources

Wisconsin Fly Fishing Page
http://www.wisflyfishing.com/

FlyfishingWis.com
http://www.flyfishingwis.com/

Fish Wisconsin (by-county information on state's fisheries)
http://www.fishwis.com/

Wisconsin Trout Unlimited
http://www.wisconsintu.org/

Wisconsin Fly Fisher
http://www.wiflyfisher.com/

The Stream of Time: Angler Len Harris' Blog
http://lenharris.blogspot.com/

Conservation Organizations

Trout Unlimited
T.U. National
1500 Wilson Boulevard
Suite 310
Arlington, VA 22209
703-522-0200

Southern Wisconsin T.U.
8045 Crystal Lake Road
Lodi, WI 53555
608-592-4718

Coulee Region T.U.
2302 Onalaska Avenue
La Crosse, WI 54603
608-792-8044

Sand Counties T.U.
5006 Dorothy Street
Stevens Point, WI 54481
715-341-4503

Antigo Area T.U.
213 Mary Street
Antigo WI 54409-2536
715-623-3867
Western Wisconsin T.U.
2104 Chestnut Drive
Hudson, WI 54016
715-386-7568

Northwest Wisconsin T.U.
66625 Highland Drive
Ashland, WI 54806
715-682-4705

Federation of Fly Fishers
National Office
P.O. Box 1595
S. 19th Avenue
Bozeman, MT 59771
301-548-0150

Badger Fly Fishers (local FFF chapter)
2020 Harley Drive
Madison, WI 53711

A Rainbow from the Prairie River. (Chris Halla)

Fly Shops & Sporting Goods Stores

Wisconsin			
Ace Hardware of Apple-ton	500 E. Northland	Appleton 54911	414-731-0500
Madison Orvis	1700 Deming Road, Gre-enway Station	Madison	608 831 3181
Dick's Sporting Goods	4350 Greenville Dr.	Appleton 54915	920-954-9266
Gander Mountain	535 N Westhill Blvd.	Appleton 4914	920-731-9400
Scheels All Sports	4301 W Wisconsin Ave.	Appleton, 54913	920-830-2977
Anglers All	2803 E Lakeshore Dr.	Ashland 54806	715-682-5754
Bill Sherer's We Tie It Fly Shop	P.O. Box 516	Boulder Junct. 54512	800-948-9384
Gander Mountain	19555 W. Bluemound Rd.	Brookfield 53045	262-785-4500
Laacke & Joys	19233 W. Bluemound Rd.	Brookfield 53045	262-782-2960
Spring Creek Anglers	4132 Oak Drive Ave	Cashton 54619	608-452-3430
Mouldy's Archery & Tackle	12127 Highway OO	Chippewa Falls	715-723-3617
Steiner's Northwoods	Hwy 141 & B	Coleman 54112	920-897-2621
Rockin' K Fly Shop	PO Box 6	Coon Valley 54623	608-452-9678
Spring Creek Angler	219 Central Ave.	Coon Valley 54623	608-452-3430
R & R Sporting Goods	3115 E. Layton Ave.	Cudahy 53110	414-481-6888
Gander Mountain	6199 Metro Drive	De Forest 53532	608-242-9532
Dick Smith's Live Bait	2420 Milwaukee St.	Delafield 53018	262-646-2218
Tightlines Flyfishing Co	1534 Mid Valley Drive	De Pere 54115	920-336-4106
Eagle Sports Center	702 East Wall Street	Eagle River 54521	715-479-8804

Gander Mountain	6440 Sculy Drive	Eau Claire 54701	715-834-4594
Scheels All Sports	4710 Golf Rd.	Eau Claire 54701	715-833-1886
Fox Point Anglers Ltd	333 W. Deer Brown Rd.	Fox Point	414-352-3664
Gander Mountain	6939 South 27th St.	Franklin 3132	414-761-1500
Wolf River Outfitters	306 North Street	Fremont	920-446-3116
Buttrums Sporting Goods	5464 W Port Wash Rd.	Milwaukee 3209	414-969-1980
Bertrand's Sport Shop	419 N Broadway	Green Bay 54303	920-432-1296
Bob's Bait & Tackle	1512 Velp Ave.	Green Bay	414-499-4737
Dick's Sporting Goods	811 Pilgrim Way, Suite A	Green Bay 54304	920-490-8488
Gander Mountain	2323 Woodman Dr.	Green Bay 54303	920-491-9110
Latitude North Outfitters	2450 Velp Ave.	Green Bay 54303	920-434-7240
Nickolai's Archery	969 North Military Ave.	Green Bay 54313	920-497-0275
The Fly Shop at Bob's Bait & Tackle	1512 Velp Ave.	Green Bay 54303	920-499-4737
Happy Hooker	12272 N. Upper A Road	Hayward 54843	715-462-3984
Boulder Lodge	7296 W. Highway 77	Hayward	888-462-3002
Hayward Super Sports	16096 W U.S .Highway 63	Hayward 54843	715-634-4800
Pastika's Sport Shop	10472 State Rd. 27	Hayward 54843	800-844-2159
Gander Mountain	2900 Deerfield Dr.	Janesville 53546	608-757-2010
Monsoor's Sport Shop	517 Copeland Ave.	La Crosse 54603	608-784-0482
Arrowsmiths	2566 Hwy. 120	Lake Geneva 53147	262-249-9933
The Tackle Box	4267 County Rd. B	Land O'Lakes 54540	715-547-3434

Aurora Borealis Outfitters	6541 East Duck Lake Road	Land O' Lakes 54540	715-547-6677
Dorn True Value	127 North Broom St.	Madison 53703	608-256-0530
Dorn True Value	1348 S. Midvale Blvd.	Madison 53711	608-274-2511
Dorn True Value	1151 N Sherman Ave.	Madison 53704	608-244-5403
Fontana Sports Specialties	231 Junction Road	Madison 53703	608-833-9191
Fontana Sports Specialties	216 Henry Street	Madison	608-257-5043
Gander Mountain	7349 West Towne Way	Madison 53719	608-827-5996
D&S Bait & Tackle	1411 Northport Dr.	Madison 53704	608-241-4225
Jay's Sports	N 88 W 15263 Main St.	Menomonee Falls 53051	414-251-0550
Laacke & Joys	1515 W. Mequon Road	Mequon 53092	262-241-4500
Flambeau Flowage Sports	5228 Highway 51 N.	Mercer 54547	715-476-2526
Backwater Sports	N2460 County Rd. K	Merrill 54452	715-536-9056
The Fly Fishers Fly Shop	9617 West Greenfield	Milwaukee 53214	414-259-8100
Laacke & Joys	1433 N Water St.	Milwaukee 53202	414-271-7878
Rollie & Helen's Musky Shop	7542 US Highway 51 S.	Minocqua 54548	715-356-6011
Lunde's Flyfishing Chalet	2491 Highway 92	Mt. Horeb 53572	608-437-5465
Gander Mountain	9519 State Hwy. 16	Onalaska 54650	608-783-2820
Dorn True Value	131 W. Richards Road	Oregon	608-835-5737
Coddington's True Value	Hwy 82	Oxford 53952	608-586-4361
Cabela's	33901 St. Hwy. 35	Prairie du Chien 53821	608-326-5600
Stark's Sport Shop	119 W. Blackhawk Ave.	Prairie du Chien 53821	608-326-2478

Dick's Sporting Goods	2710B South Green Bay Rd.	Racine 53406	262-554-8117
National Sports Supply	233 Carroll St.	Random Lake 53075	920-994-9218
Mel's Trading Post	105 S Brown St.	Rhinelander 54501	715-362-5800
J.C. Bear Paw Company	824 Bear Paw Ave.	Rice Lake 54868	715-236-7300
Cabela's	One Cabela Way	Richfield, WI 53076	262-628-5700
Jaquish Hollow Angler	32491 Jacquish So. Rd.	Richland Center 53581	608-585-2239
Lund's Hardware Fly Shop	201 South Main St.	River Falls 54022	715-425-2415
Ace Sauk Prairie	500 Water St.	Sauk City 53583	608-643-2433
Gander Mountain	4308 County Rd. J	Sheboygan 53083	920-208-0800
Pigeon River Bait & Tackle	2322 N 15th St.	Sheboygan 53083	920-457-2092
Ecology Sports #2	10904 Hwy. 42	Sister Bay 54234	920-854-5724
One Stop Sport Shop	1024 Main St.	Stevens Point 54481	715-334-4540
Dorn True Value	926 Windsor Street	Sun Prairie 53590	608-837-2110
Superior Fly Angler	310 Belknap St. #A	Superior 54880	715-395-9520
Silver Doctor Fly Fishing	P.O. Box 105	Viroqua 54665	608-637-3417
Gander Mountain	2440 E. Moreland Blvd	Waukesha 53186	262-798-0424
Skupe's Corner Store	609 S Cambridge Ave.	Wautoma 54982	920-787-3816
Wolf River Fly Shop	N4216 Ricky Rips Rd.	White Lake 54491	715-882-5941
Critter's Wolf River Sports	700 W. Main Street	Winneconne 54986	920-582-0471

Iowa			
Bass Pro Shops	1000 Bass Pro Drive NW	Altoona	515-957-5500
Sportsman's Warehouse	921 SE Oralabor Road	Ankeny 50021	515-963-3500
Bass Pro Shops	2901 Bass Pro Drive	Council Bluffs	712-325-6000
The Hatchery	406 W. Water Street	Decorah	800-944-6503
River & Trail Outfitters	212 Pulpit Rock Road	Decorah	563-382-6552
The Bait Shack	2095 Kerper Blvd.#4	Dubuque	563-582-9395
Coast-to-Coast Hardware	201 N. Main	Elkader	563-245-2521
Turkey River Canoe Rental	117 S. Main	Elkader	800-250-2466
Fin and Feather	125 Highway 1 W.	Iowa City	319-354-2200
Farm and Home	330 Main Street	Lansing	563-538-4884

Minnesota			
Christopherson's Inc	309 3rd Ave East	Alexandria 56308	320-763-3255
Little Jim's Sports	900 Elm St. East	Annandale 55302	320-274-5297
Gander Mountain	14275 Edgewood Dr. #100	Baxter 56425	218-828-1736
Gander Mountain	1313 Paul Bunyan Drive	Bemidji 56601	218-755-6150
Capra's Sporting Goods	8565 Central Avenue NE	Blaine 55434	763-780-4557
The Fly Angler	10091 Central Ave. NE	Blaine 55434	763-572-0717
Gander Mountain	10650 Baltimore St. NE	Blaine 55434	763-783-7200
Thorne Brothers	10091 Central Ave NE	Blaine 55434	763-572-3782
Lakes Sport Shop	930 Washington Ave.	Detroit Lakes 56501	218-847-2645
Great Lakes Fly Shop	4426 Regent Street	Duluth 55804	218-740-3040
Gander Mountain	4275 Haines Road	Duluth (Hermantown)	218-786-9800
Fisherman's Corner	5675 Miller Trunk Hwy.	Duluth 55811	218-729-5369
Marine General Supply	1501 London Rd.	Duluth 55812	218-724-8833
Gander Mountain	12160 Technology Drive	Eden Prairie 55344	952-944-5422
Scheel's Sports	8251 Flying Cloud Drive	Eden Prairie 55344	952-826-0067
Mike's Bait & Tackle	169 Meeker Ave. E.	Eden Valley 55329	320-453-2248
John's Bait & Tackle	19826 Roberds Lake Blvd	Faribault 55021	507-332-6787
Gander Mountain	14640 W. Freeway Drive	Forest Lake 55025	651-464-0707
Bear Track Outfitting Co.	2011 W Highway 61	Grand Marais 55604	218-387-1162
Stone Harbor Wilderness Supply	20 E 1st St.	Grand Marais 55604	218-387-3136
The Outdoorsman's Headquarters	1130 3rd Ave.	International Falls 56649	218-283-9337

Bob Mitchell Fly Shop	3394 Lake Elmo Ave.	Lake Elmo 55042	651-770-5854
Gander Mountain	16861 Kenyon Avenue	Lakeville 55044	952-435-3805
The Fly Fishing Cabin	27 E Little Canada Rd.	Little Canada 55117	612-490-7901
Bobber Shop	1630 N Riverfront Dr.	Mankato 56001	507-625-8228
Gander Mountain	1940 Adams Store	Mankato 56001	507-345-3600
Scheels All Sports	River Hills Mall	Mankato 56001	507-386-7767
Gander Mountain	8030 Wedgewood Lane	Maple Grove 55369	763-420-9800
Gander Mountain	1747 Beam Avenue East	Maplewood 55109	651-770-4880
Frontier Sports	48919 State Highway 38	Marcell 56657	218-832-3901
Scheels	505 Center Ave.	Moorhead 56560	218-233-2751
Headwaters Fly Fishing Company	16920 56th Court NE	Otsego 55374	763-493-5800
Dave's Sportland Bait & Tackle	5029 City Road 13	Nisswa 56468	218-963-2401
Gene's Sport Shop	150 E Main St.	Perham 55673	218-346-3355
Gander Mountain	3470 55th Street NW	Rochester 55901	507-252-2033
Tyrol Ski and Sport	1923 Second St. SW	Rochester 55902	507-288-1683
Joe's Sporting Goods	935 Dale St. North	St. Paul 55703	651-488-5511
Cabin Fever Sporting Goods	1550 Arboretum Blvd.	Victoria 55386	952-443-2022
Gander Mountain	40 N. Waite Avenue	Waite Park 56387	320-654-6600
Reed's Sporting Goods	Main St.	Walker 56484	218-547-1505
Gander Mountain	10470 Hudson Road	Woodbury 55125	651-735-6101

Illinois			
Sports Authority	301 South Route 59	Aurora 60504	630-820-2009
The Rod Shop	224 Mistwood Lane	Aurora 60504	630-897-2897
Sports Authority	160 South Gary Ave.	Bloomingdale 60153	630-582-3995
Bass Pro Shops	709 Janes Avenue	Bolingbrook	630-296-2700
Sports Authority	257 N. Weber Road	Bolingbrook	630-378-0226
Sports Authority	400 Broadview Village Square	Broadview 60153	708-345-7040
Sports Authority	7720 South Cicero Ave.	Burbank 60459	708-499-9660
Sports Authority	1510 Torrence Avenue	Calumet City	708-895-0901
Kolar Bait & Tackle	1400 W. Army Trail Rd	Carol Stream 60188	630-372-0125
Dick's Sporting Goods	2113 N. Prospect Ave.	Champaign 61822	217-352-4173
Bass Pro Shops	6112 W. Grand Ave.	Chicago (Gurney) 60031	847-856-1229
Sports Authority	1801 West Fullerton Ave.	Chicago 60614	773-935-7729
Sports Authority	3134 N. Clark Street	Chicago 60657	773-871-8501
Sports Authority	6420 West Fullerton Ave	Chicago 60707	773-804-0044
Sports Authority	620 N. La Salle Street	Chicago 60654	312-337-6151
Chicago Flyfishing Outfitters	1729 North Clybourn #4	Chicago 60614	312-944-FISH
Coren's Rod & Reel	6001 N Nina Ave.	Chicago 60631	773-631-5202
Dan's Tackle Service	2237 W McLean Ave.	Chicago 60647	773-276-5562
Henry's Sports Bait	3130 S Canal St.	Chicago 60616	312-225-8538
Orvis	142 E Ontario St.	Chicago 60611	312-440-0662
Rods & Rackets	2237 W McLean Ave.	Chicago 60647	773-276-5562

Ed Shirley & Sons	5404 La Grange Road	Countryside 60525	708-966-5900
One More Cast	1416 W 55th	Countryside 60525	708-482-4990
Dave's Bait & Tackle	4419 Illinois Rte. 176	Crystal Lake 60014	815-455-2040
Sports Authority	4804 Cog Cir	Crystal Lake 60014	815-788-1071
Sports Authority	6000 E Northwest Hwy.	Crystal Lake 60039	815-459-5009
Sports Authority	67 Ludwig Dr.	Fairview Heights 62208	618-397-5964
Sports Authority	11185 W. Lincoln Hwy	Frankfort 60423	815-806-0285
Gander Mountain	2100 S. Randall Road	Geneva 60134	630-845-0505
Sports Authority	1777 South Randall Rd.	Geneva 60134	630-208-4998
Riverside Sports	26 N. Bennett St.	Geneva 60134	630-232-7047
Sports Authority	125 Army Trail Road	Glendale Heights	630-894-7500
Bass Pro Shops	6112 W Grand Ave.	Gurnee 60031	847-856-1229
Sports Authority	6170 West Grand Ave.	Gurnee 60031	947-855-8070
Sports Authority	4700 Hoffman Blvd	Hoffman Estates 60192	847-645-9241
Gander Mountain	3301 Essington Road	Joliet 60435	815-254-2264
GR Young Outfitters	33 N. Waukegan Rd. #3	Lake Bluff 60044	847-615-5400
Orvis	306 Yorktown Center	Lombard 60148	630-932-6573
Sports Authority	173 Yorktown Ctr	Lombard 60148	630-620-6310
Curve Fishing & Marine	4640 N 2nd St.	Loves Park 61111	815-877-0637
Dunn's Sporting Goods	1904 Rendleman	Marion 62959	618-997-3626
Sports Authority	4832 211th Street	Matteson 60443	708-748-0896
Bedford Sales	879 Bedford Rd.	Morris 60450	815-942-1333
Ed Shirley & Sons Sports	5802 Dempster St.	Morton Grove 60053	847-966-5900

Sports Authority	1033 N. Elmhurst Road	Mount Prospect 60056	847-253-0989
Sports Authority	7233 W. Dempster Street	Niles 60714	847-967-7601
Dick's Sporting Goods	200 North Greenbriar Dr.	Normal 61761	309-454-1602
Sports Authority	1800 Harlem Avenue	North Riverside 60546	708-366-6600
Trout & Grouse	840 Willow Road, Ste P	Northbrook 60062	847-501-3111
Sports Authority	9633 S. Cicero Avenue	Oak Lawn 60453	708-636-0501
Sports Authority	1385 Orland Park Place	Orland Park 60462	708-460-0900
Gander Mountain	5114 Holiday Dr.	Peoria 61615	309-692-4110
Gander Mountain	3068 McFarland Rd.	Rockford 61114	815-637-9600
Dick's Sporting Goods	6380 East State St.	Rockford 61108	815-397-7115
Stringers Tackle Shop	1841 W Golf Rd.	Schaumberg 60194	847-884-7921
Sports Authority	1015 E. Golf Rd.	Schaumberg 60173	847-517-7701
Galyan's	601 N. Martingale	Schaumburg 60173	847-995-0200
Gander Mountain	2371 Chuckwagon Drive	Springfield 62711	217-726-8219
Fly Fisher's Outfit	300 W Allen St.	Springfield 62704	217-544-7218
Sports Authority	155 E. Townline Road	Vernon Hills 60061	847-549-9700
Sports Authority	7370 Woodward Ave.	Woodridge 60517	630-852-9006

Index

A

Ahnapee River 461
  Stream Facts 464
Allen Creek 36
Allequash Springs 383
Alpine Road 34
Altoona Lake 174
Andre Govrik 162
Angelo Pond 194
Anne Lake 382
Anvil Lake 370
Archibald Lake 375
Atwood Avenue 39
Auburn Lake 432

B

Bailey's Ford 541
Bakkens Pond 99
Balsam Lake 328
Bankston Creek 547
Dave Barron 74
Basswood Creek. *See also* Pine River: West Branch
Basswood Lakes 281
Bayfield Peninsula 291
Bayfield Peninsula, Streams 271
  Cranberry River 273
  Flag River 273
  Pikes Creek 273
  Sioux River 273
Bean Lake 328
Bear Creek 71–73, 517
  Stream Facts 73, 518
Bear Lake 329
Beaver Creek 184, 185, 375
Beaver Lake 280
Bellbrook Road 33
Bibon Marsh 270, 281, 283
Big Brook 302, 304
Big Devil Lake 326
Big Falls 174, 262
Big Green River 93–94
  Stream Facts 94
Big Guide, Little Water 116–117
Big Lake 293
Big Mill Creek 548
Big Roche a Cri Creek 215
  Stream Facts 217
Big Spring Branch 65. *See* Big Spring Creek
Big Spring Creek 65
Billings Creek 108
Birch, Bearskin, and Little Bearskin Lakes 407
Bird Creeks 241
Bishops Branch 113
Black Earth 153
Black Earth Creek 25–28
  Stream Facts 28
Blackhawk Lake 51
Black River 177, 189, 193–194
Black River Falls 184, 193
Black River State Forest 193, 196
Blake Hanson 23, 71
Bloody Run 487
  Stream Facts 489
Blueberry Creek 295
Blue River 57–59
  Stream Facts 59
Bluff Creek 430
Bob Blumreich 113, 116–117
Bohemian Creek 529
Bohemian Valley 124
Bohemian Valley Creek 129–130
  Stream Facts 130
Bois Brule River 289–294
  Stream Facts 294
Boot Lake 375
Borah Creek 89
  Stream Facts 91
Boulder Lake 375
Boulder Lodge 303
Boundary Brule River 396
Brooklyn State Wildlife Area 33, 35
Brook Trout 566
Brown Trout 568
Brule County 267
Brule River 267, 295
Brule River State Forest 289, 292
Brunet Island State Park 171
Buffalo Lake 225
Buffalo River 177–179
  Stream Facts 179

Buffalo River Trail 178
Burnett County 325
Butler Lake 432
Butternut Lake 392
BWO Sparkle Dun 562

C

Cable Lake 328
Capital City Bluegills 42
Carol and Madeleine Lakes 385
Carp 582
Casey Lake 328
Castle Rock Creek 61–63
  Stream Facts 63
Castle Rock Dam 251
Castle Rock Flowage 248–250
Catfish Creek 547
Caves Creek 201, 209
Cedar River 529
Central Wisconsin 201
Chaffee Creek 214, 242
Channel Catfish 581
Chequamegon Bay 271, 275–278, 281, 306
Chequamegon National Forest 279
  Trout Lakes of 279
    Beaver Lake 280
    Patterson Lake 280
    Perch Lake 279, 280
    Pole Lake 280
    Twin Lake 280
    Wanoka Lake 279
Chernobyl Ant 561
Cherokee Marsh 37, 43
Chetek Chain of Lakes 329
Chippewa Falls 167, 171
Chippewa Falls Dam 174
Chippewa Flowage 270, 309, 312
  Making of the Flowage 309
Chippewa River 171–175, 309, 315
  East and West Forks 313
  Eau Claire to the Juncture with the Mississippi River 174–175
  Flambeau River to Chippewa Falls 171
  Main Branch 313
Chris Halla 25, 51, 61, 93, 113, 206, 333, 339, 404, 587
Civilian Conservation Corps 124
Clark's Lake 474
Clear Creek 503
Columbia Lake 226, 251
Columbia Lake Power Plant 226
Comet Creek 337
Conners Lake 326
Conservation Organizations 587
Coon Creek 124, 129
Coon Valley 124, 129
Copper John 562
Copper Range Campground 293
Coulee Country 177
County X 34
Craig Amacker xv, 29, 95, 250, 267, 306, 388, 406, 418, 421, 423, 424, 425, 436, 437, 441, 442, 444, 447, 451, 455, 457, 461, 463, 468, 475, 476
Craig's Bass Buster 561
Craig's Bluegill Buster 561
Craig's Spring Creek Leech 561
Cranberry Flowages 195
Cranberry River 273
Crane Lake 312
Crappie 576
Crawfish River 433
Crooked Creek 87
Crooked Lake 224
Crooked lake 433
Crystal Lake 382
Crystal River 259

D

Deer Body Hex 562
Double Bunny 561
Double Humpy 561
D&S Bait and Tackle 39
Dane County 43
Dan Hatleli 184
Dave Vetrano 123
Deep Lake 224
Deerskin River 393
  Stream Facts 395
Dell Creek 218
Dell Creek Wildlife Area 218
Dells 251
Dells Pond 174
Department of Natural Resources. *See* DNR Offices
Devil's Lake 219

Devil's Lake State Park 219
Devils Lake 325
DNR Offices 11
Don Bush 36
Don Schroeder vii, 243, 245
Door County Inland Lakes 474
Door County Smallmouth Bass 471, 473
  Fishing Facts 473
Driftless Country Streams 19
Derrick Duchesneau 167
Duncan Creek 169
Dunkirk Dam 47
Dunn Lake 328
Dutch Creek 195

E

Earl Loyster 95
East Twin River and West Twin River 451
  Stream Facts 454
Eau Claire/Chippewa Falls Area Brook Trout Streams 167
  Duncan Creek 169
  Elk Creek 167
  McCann Creek 169
Eau Claire River 174, 351
  East Branch 351
Eau Galle River 161, 259
Egg Sucking Leech 561
Eighteen Mile Creek 157
Elk Creek 167
Elk Creek Lake 167
Ellsworth Rod and Gun Club 144
Elward Engle 209, 241
Ensign Creek 537
  Stream Facts 537
Enterprise Lake 354
Equipment Checklist 585
Erik Seeman 74
Escanaba and Nebish Lakes 383
ESPN 25
Europe Lake 475
Evansville Wildlife Area 36

F

Fallison Lake 383
Fancy Creek 83-84
Federal Power Act 309
Firefly Lake 382
Fischer Creek 465
Fisheries Management and Catch-and-Release 583
Fishing Licenses 10
  Fees 10
Fish of Wisconsin and Iowa 566
Fish-Stress 561
Flag River 273
Flambeau River 309, 313, 316
  South Fork 320
Flambeau River to Confluence with Chippewa River 320
Flume Creek 262
Fly Patterns 17
Fly Shops & Sporting GoodsStores of Wisconsin 588
Foam Beetle 562
Forest Lake 432
Forestville Flowage 474
Fort McCoy 194
Fountain Spring 541
Fox River 251, 427, 470
  De Pere to Green Bay 470
  Neenah to De Pere 470
Fox River Valley 236
Frank Lake 384
Frank Pratt 299
French Creek 504
  Stream Facts 507
Frog Hollow Lake 551
Frye Creek 29

G

Galena River 65
Gardner Withrow 104
Gays Mills 104
Gays Mills Dam 109
General Inland Waters 248
Gene Van Dyk 55, 65, 89
Germania Marsh 212
Ghost, Teal, and Lost Land Lakes 315
Ghost Lake 315
Glen Park 156
Glovers Creek 531
Goodland 39
Gordon MacQuarrie 299
Governor Dodge State Park 68
Grannis Creek 531

Grant County 61
Grant River 67, 89
Great Lakes 275, 292
Green County 36
Grindstone Lake 316

H
Half Back 561
Hanson Creek 281
Harmony Grove 251
Harris Pond 206, 214
Hay Creek 157
Hayward Dam 304
Hayward Lake 299, 303
Heins Creek 467
Helena Marsh 99
Hey, There's a Mouse in My Trout! 137
Hibbards Creek 467
Hickory Creek 496
Holcombe Flowage 171
Horseshoe Lake 194
Hub City
  Algoma 468
  Antigo 378
  Ashland 286
  Bailey's Harbor 478
  Bayfield 285
  Black River Falls 198
  Boscobel 100
  Boulder Junction 408
  Brule 307
  Coon Valley 133
  Decorah 526
  Dodgeville 69–70
  Dubuque 558
  Eau Claire 180
  Elkader 545
  Hayward 330
  Hudson 163
  La Crosse 135
  La Farge 119
  Lansing 508
  Madison 48–50
  Marquette 497
  McGregor 497
  Milwaukee 435
  Onalaska 135
  Prairie du Chien 497
  Richland Center 85
  River Falls 165
  Sheboygan 446
  Trempealeau 191
  Two Rivers 455
  Waupaca 263
  Wausau 348
  Westby 133
  Westfield 231
  Wild Rose 254

I
Indian and Jennie Weber Lakes 407
Indian Creek 108
Indianhead Country. *See also* Wisconsin: Northwest
Internet Resources 586
Iron River 279, 291, 297

J
Jacklin's Stonefly 561
JJ Special 561
John Koch 161
John Nolan Drive 39
Johnson Creek 281
Joy Spring 535
Jug Creek 108
Julia Lake 371

K
Kakagon Slough 275, 277
Kangaroo Lake 474
Kettle Moraine State Forest-Southern Unit 428
Kewaunee River 457
  Stream Facts 460
Keyes Lake 370
Kickapoo County 104
Kickapoo Reserve 108
Kickapoo Restoration Project 103
Kickapoo River 103–111
  Headwaters to Gays Mills 104
  Main Stem 103–111
  Middle Stretch 109–110
  Primitive Bottomlands 109
  Stream Facts 111
  West Fork 113
    Stream Facts 115

Kickapoo River Water Trail 103
Kinni. *See* Kinnickinnic River
Kinnickinnic River 153–156
 Stream Facts 156
Knapp Creek 162

L

L.L. Bean 25
Lac Courte Oreilles 316
Lac du Lune 385
La Crosse River 194–195
La Crosse River State Fishery Area 195
Lafayette County 67
Lake 15 Creek 433
Lake Agassiz 185
Lake Arbutus 194
Lake Chippewa 309
Lake Delhi 551
Lake Farm Park 39
Lake George 161, 259
Lake Hendricks 551
Lake Henry 183
Lake Kegonsa 47
Lake Leota 36
Lake Lucerne 371
Lake Maria 25
Lake Mendota 37, 38, 42. *See also* Madison Chain of Lakes
Lake Menomin 157
Lake Meyer 551
Lake Michigan 209, 271
Lake Michigan Coast. *See also* Wisconsin: Eastern
Lake Monona 39, 42. *See also* Madison Chain of Lakes
Lake Namekagon 299
Lake Neshonoc 194
Lake Noquebay 377
Lake Onalaska 189
Lake Owen 306
Lake Pepin 185–188, 189
Lake Poygan 233
Lake Puckaway 213, 225
Lakes and Streams of the Nicolet National Forest Area 369
 Spectacle Lake 369
Lakes of Burnett County 325
 Conners Lake 326
 Devils Lake 325
 Mud Hen Lake 325
 Round Lake 325
 Spirit Lake 325
 Webb Lake 326
 Wood Lake 325
Lakes of Langlade County 352
 Enterprise Lake 354
 McGee Lake 352
 Moccasin Lake 354
 Rollingstone Lake 352
 Upper Post Lake and Lower Post Lake 354
LAKES OF NORTHEAST IOWA 551
Lakes of the Northern Highlands American Legion State Forest 381
Lakes of Washburn County 326
 Balsam Lake 328
 Bean Lake 328
 Bear Lake 329
 Cable Lake 328
 Casey Lake 328
 Dunn Lake 328
 Little Devil Lake and Big Devil Lake 326
 Pavlas Lake 326
 Potato Lake 326
 Red Cedar Lake 328
 Ripley Lake 326
Lake Superior 271, 275, 281, 289, 297
Lake Waubesa 39, 42. *See also* Madison Chain of Lakes
Lake Wingra 39. *See also* Madison Chain of Lakes
Lake Winnebago 309
Lake Wisconsin 251
Lake Wissota 171, 174
Bart Landwehr 71, 201, 265
Largemouth Bass 574
Larger Area Lakes 386
Lawrence Creek 204–207, 242
 Stream Facts 207
Lawrence Creek Wildlife Area 204
Legler Road 34
Little Devil Lake 326
Little Lac Courte 316
Little Mill Creek 548
Little Paint Creek 496
Little Rice Lake 371
Little Turkey River 543

Little Wolf River 262, 345
Stream Facts 347
Lonetree Lake 384
Long Lake 432
Lost Lake 370
Lost Land Lakes 315
Lower Clam Lake 313
Lower Oconto River 365
Lower Post Lake 354
Lower Rock River Basin 36
Lower Swiss Valley 547
Lucius Lake 293

M

Madison's Beltline 43
Madison Chain of Lakes 37–41
Lake Mendota 38
Governor's Island 38
Picnic Point 38
Tenney Park Breakwater 38
University Bay 38
Lake Monona 39
Lake Waubesa 39
Lake Wingra 39
Madison lakes 37
Merlin Magnuson 142
Maiden Rock 144
Mainstem Oconto River 364
Manitowish River 386
Manitowoc River 449
Stream Facts 450
Maquoketa River 535
Marietta Valley 89
Marshall Park 38
Mason Lake 221
Mauthe Lake 432
McCann Creek 169
McGee Lake 352
Mecan River 201, 209, 242
Stream Facts 213
Mecan River State Wildlife Area 212
Mecan Springs 209
Menominee River 397
Menomonee River 427
Merrick State Park 189
Michigan's Upper Peninsula 257
Middle Inlet Creek 375
Mill Creek
West Branch 79
Stream Facts 81
Milwaukee River 423
Stream Facts 425
Mink River 476
Mississippi River 289
La Crosse to Dubuque 131
Lansing to Dubuque 557
Trempealeau to Lake Pepin 189
Mississippi River Valley 185
Moccasin Lake 354
Moon Lake 297
Moon Lakes 297
Mosquito Creek 304
Mount Vernon 29
Mount Vernon Creek 29–31
Stream Facts 31
Mud Hen Lake 325
Mud Lake Public Hunting Ground 226
Murphy's Creek 38
Muskellunge 580
Muskellunge and Snipe Lakes 383

N

Namekagon River 299
Cable to Hayward 302
Hayward to St. Croix River 304
Lake Namekagon 299
Stream Facts 305
Nebagamon Creek 295
Necedah Dam 250
Neenah Creek 208
Nevin Fish Hatchery 123
Nixon Lake 384
North Branch of the Pemebonwon 400
Northeast Iowa 481
Hot, Cold, and Dusty 485
Season and Regulations 485
The Law 484
Trout on the Edge of the Prairie 483
Northern Pike 578
Northern States Power 309

O

Oak Creek 422
Oconto River 361
North and South Branches of the Oconto River 361

Ojibwa State Park 313
Okee Grove 251
Olbrich Gardens 39
Olin Park 39
Olive Scud 562
Oneida County Lakes 407
Orienta dam 297
Orienta Flowage 297
Ottawa Lake 430
Otter Creek 51, 530
  Stream Facts 53

P

Pacawong Dam 303
Paint Creek 174, 493
  Stream Facts 495
Pallette Lake 384
Paradise Springs 428
Parker Lake 222
Partridge Lake 385
Patterson Lake 280
Pavlas Lake 326
Pecatonica River 67
Perch, Squash, Crescent, and Emma Lakes 407
Perch Lake 194, 279, 280
Perot State Park 189
Peshtigo River 405
Petenwell Flowage 247, 309
Pheasant Tail Nymph 561
Phipps Flowage 302
Pierce County Islands State Wildlife Area 185
Pigeon River 439
Pike River 367, 421
  Stream Facts 368
Pikes Creek 273
Pine Creek 521
Pine Lake 371
Pine River 233–235, 404
  Stream Facts 234
  West Branch 77–78
    Stream Facts 78
Pink Glo-Bug 561
Pink Squirrel 562
Plover River 337
  Stream Facts 340
Plum and West Plum Lakes 383
Plum Run 109
Pole Lake 280
Poncho Creek 257
Ponds, Urban Trout 552
Popple, Pine, and Peshtigo Rivers 403
Popple River 403
Port Washington Harbor 437
Potato Lake 326
Potters Flowage 178, 196–197
Poygan Marsh 233
Prairie du Sac Dam 251
Prairie River 341
  Stream Facts 344
Presque Isle Lake 386
Profile of Wisconsin Rod Maker 243
Put and Grow Streams 553

Q

Quiet Lakes 315
Quiet Lakes Resort Association 315

R

Rainbow Trout 570
Razorback Lake 384
Red Cedar Lake 328
Red Cedar River 157–159
Red Midge Larvae 562
Resources 586
Rice Lake 430
Richardson Lake 371
Richland County 77
Richland Creek 89
Richmond Springs 535
Ripley Lake 326
River Falls 142
River Falls Rod and Gun Club 153
Roberts Lake 375
Roche a Cri 242
Rock Lake 434
Rocky Run Creek 226
Rollingstone Lake 352
Root River 415
  Stream Facts 419
Round Lake 325
Rowan Creek 228
  Stream Facts 230
Rullands Coulee 127–128
  Stream Facts 128–129
Rullands Coulee Creek. *See* Rullands Coulee

Rullands Creeks 124
Rush River 142–145
  Stream Facts 145

S

Salmon 571
Sand County 257
Sand County Almanac 201
Sand Creek 157
Sand Lake 316, 370
Sauk County 71
Schultz Springs 302
Sea Lion Lake 370
Seas Branch 113
Seven Pines Lodge 162
Shannon Lake 383
Shawano Lake 376
Sheboygan Bunny Leech 561
Sheboygan River 441
  Stream Facts 445
Silver Creek 465, 504
Sioux River 273
Small Lakes of Washburn County 326
Smallmouth Bass 573
Sny Magill 491
  Stream Facts 492
Soules Creek 241
South Branch of the Pemebonwon River 400
South Branch of the Scuppernong River 430
South Pine Creek 519
  Stream Facts 520
Southwest Wisconsin 19
Spectacle Lake 369
Spirit Lake 325
Spread Eagle Chain of Lakes 393
Spring-Run Steelhead Streams 465
Spring Branch 539
  Stream Facts 540
Spring Coulee 129
Spring Creek 529
Spring Green Bridge 99
Spring Ponds of Langlade County 352
Spring Valley 161
Squaw Bay 312
St. Croix 270
St. Croix National Scenic Riverway 299
St. Croix River 289, 299, 321
Starrett Lake 384
Stebbinsville Dam 43
Steelhead 571
Steve Miller xv, 31, 95, 169, 184
Stevens Lake 370
Stock Farm Bridge Campground 313
Stony Creek 465
Stormy Lake 385
Story Creek 33–35
  Stream Facts 35
Sugar River 34, 68
Sunfish 575

T

Tagatz Creek 214
Tainter Creek 119
Tainter Lake 157
Teal Lake 315
Teal River 315
Ten Mile Creek 242
Tenney Park 46
The Little Platte 67
The Northern Highland. *See also* Wisconsin: Northeast
The Western Upland. *See* Wisconsin: West-Central
The Yahara River 43–47
Timber Coulee 123–125, 129, 153, 185
  Stream Facts 125
Tim Landwehr 14, 19, 22, 33, 34, 103, 139, 183, 187, 201, 211, 236, 241, 257, 259, 260, 262, 343, 355, 397
Todd Polacek 114
Token Creek 36–37
Token Creek County Park 37
Tomorrow River 257
  Lower 259
  Middle 258
  Stream Facts 261
  Upper 257
Townsend Flowage 375
Trempealeau County 183
Trempealeau National Wildlife Refuge 183
Trempealeau River 183–184
Trimbelle River 147
Trout Creek 55
  Stream Facts 56
Trout River 521
Trout Run 523

Trout Unlimited Efforts in the Driftless Area 514
Turck's Tarantula 561
Turkey River 543
Turtle-Flambeau Flowage 317
  North Fork 317
Turtle-Flambeau Flowage Dam 317
Turtle Creek 529
Twin Lake 251, 280
Twin River 451
Twin Valley 68
Twin Valley Lake 68

U

Urban Trout Ponds 552
U.S. Army Corps of Engineers 161
Union Creek 262
Upper Chippewa River System 309
Upper Iowa River 525
Upper Mississippi River National Wildlife and Fish Refuge 131
Upper Mud Lake 39
Upper Post Lake 354
Upper St. Croix 292
Upper Swiss Valley 547

V

Van Loon State Wildlife Area 193, 194
Dave Vetrano 194
Viking County Park 47

W

Walleye 577
Wanoka Lake 279
Warner Creek 108
Waterloo Creek 511
  Stream Facts 513
Waupaca River. *See* Tomorrow River: Lower
Wausaukee River 376
Waushara. *See* Willow Creek
Webb Lake 326
Weister Creek 108
West-Central Wisconsin 139
Westfork Sportsman's Club 113
Whitcomb Creek 262
White Bass 577
White River 281, 281–284, 303
  Main Branch 241
  Stream Facts 284
  West Branch 238
    Stream Facts 239
White River Flowage 281
White River State Wildlife Area 241
Whitman Dam State Wildlife Area 189
Wildcat Lake 385
Wildcat Mountain State Park 108
Wild Rose 236, 251
Wild Rose Millpond 233
Wildwood Lake 382
Willow Creek 71, 74–75, 236–237
  Stream Facts 75, 237
Willow River 148–152
  Stream Facts 152
Willow River State Park 150
Windigo Lake 316
Winter Dam 312, 313
Wisconsin 7–16
  Central Wisconsin 201
    The Sand Counties 201
  Eastern 411
  Northeast 333
  Northwest 267
  West-Central 139
Wisconsin's Sand Counties 201
Wisconsin-Minnesota Power and Light Company 309
Wisconsin Dells 251
Wisconsin Rapids Area 242
Wisconsin Rapids Area Ditches 242
Wisconsin River 389
  Castle Rock Lake Dam to Prairie du Sac Dam 251
  Prairie du Sac to Prairie du Chien 95–100
Wisconsin River Power Company 247
Wolf Lake 222
Wolf River 355
  Stream Facts 360
Wood Lake 325

X

X-Caddis 562

Y

Yahara Place Park 46
Yahara River 37, 38
Yellow River 174, 499
  Stream Facts 501